ISBN 978-0-266-89613-5
PIBN 10906120

VE RI
TAS

PENNSYLVANIA ARCHIVES

Fifth Series

VOLUME VII.

EDITED BY
THOMAS LYNCH MONTGOMERY

UNDER THE DIRECTION OF THE
HON. FRANK M. FULLER,
SECRETARY OF THE COMMONWEALTH.

HARRISBURG, PA.:
HARRISBURG PUBLISHING COMPANY, STATE PRINTER,
1906.

HARVARD COLLEGE LIBRARY
DEC 17 1906
CAMBRIDGE, MASS.

Muster Rolls

RELATING TO THE

ASSOCIATORS AND MILITIA

OF THE

COUNTY OF LANCASTER. (a)

(2)

LANCASTER COUNTY LIEUTENANTS.

Bartram Galbraith, June 3, 1777.
Samuel John Atlee, Mch. 31, 1780.
Adam Hubley, Feb. 14, 1781.
James Ross, Nov. 17, 1783.

LANCASTER COUNTY SUB-LIEUTENANTS.

James Crawford, March 12, 1777.
Adam Orth, March 12, 1777.
Robert Thompson, March 12, 1777.
Joshua Elder, March 12, 1777.
Christopher Crawford, March 12, 1777.
Curtis Grubb, Oct. 23, 1777.
William Ross, Oct. 25, 1777.
Simon Snyder, Oct. 25, 1777.
Christian Wirtz, Oct. 31, 1777.
James Cunningham, Apr. 1, 1780.
Christopher Kucher, Apr. 1, 1780.
Abraham Dehuff, Apr. 1, 1780.
John Hopkins, Apr. 1, 1780.
John Huber, Apr. 1, 1780.
Wm. Steel, Apr. 1, 1780.
Maxwell Chambers, Apr. 1, 1780.
Jacob Carpenter, Apr. 1, 1780.
James Barber, Apr. 1, 1780.
Robert Clark, Apr. 1, 1780.
Robert Good, June 21, 1780.
William Kelley, Feb. 14, 1781.
Willam Smith, June 29, 1781.
Philip Gloninger, May 2, 1781.
Adam Orth, Nov. 13, 1782.

ASSOCIATORS AND MILITIA.

LANCASTER COUNTY COMMISSIONERS.

Richard Ferree.

LANCASTER COUNTY COMMISSIONERS OF PURCHASE.

John Miller, June 1 to 20, 1781. Chris Wirtz.

LANCASTER COUNTY ASST. COMMISSIONERS OF PURCHASE.

Timothy Oreen. Christopher Kucher.

LANCASTER COUNTY COMISSARY OF CLOATHING.

Lewis Farmer.

LANCASTER COUNTY D. Q. M. GENERAL.

George Ross.

LANCASTER COUNTY D. C. G. OF MUSTERS.

Will A. Atlee, Mar. 25, 1777.

MUSTER ROLLS OF ASSOCIATORS. (a.)

THE LIBERTY COMPANY OF LONDONDERRY.

The Association of the Liberty Company in Lancaster County.

In order to make ourselves perfect in the art of Military, &c., We, the subscribers, have associated, and severally Agree, Promise, and Resolve as follows, viz:

1st. That Jacob Cook be the Captain, William Hay the first Lieutenant, Robert McQueen the second Lieutenant, and David McQueen the Ensign of the Company in London Derry called the Liberty company, which said Officers, according to their respective stations, to have Command of said Company whilst under Arms, Mustering, or in actual Service, and that the said Officers shall remain till altered by a Majority of the Officers and two-thirds of the Company.

2d. That none of the Subscribers or Company shall disobey

the Orders of either of the said Officers whilst under Arms or Mustering, or in actual Service, under the Penalty of paying a sum not exceeding Twenty Shillings for every disobedience, to be inflicted and judged of by a Majority of the Officers.

3d. That each Person of the Company shall (if not already done) as soon as possible, provide, himself with a good Gun or Musket, in good order and repair, with a Cartouch-Box or Shot-Bag, and Powder-Horn, a half a Pound of Powder and two Pounds of Lead.

4th. That each of the said Company shall attend weekly on Saturday, and on such other Times as the officers or a majority of them shall appoint, in the Town of Lancaster, or in the county of Lancaster, at such places as the said officers shall deem necessary, under the Penalty of forfeiting and paying the sum of One Shilling, for every absence, Sickness of the person or Business out of the Town or Townships to excuse. This is to be judged of by a majority of the Officers; but in case of absence at any Meeting, the Party so absenting to show Cause to the Officers against the next succeeding Meeting, or the Fine to be absolute; every Person is to appear at such Meeting with his Arms and Ammunition as aforesaid under the Penalty of forfeiting the said Sum of One Shilling, for every default, unless a Majority of the Officers shall remit such Fine.

5th. That no Person of the said Company shall appear drunk, or curse or swear whilst under Arms Mustering, or in actual service, under the Penalty of paying Three Shillings for the first offence; Five Shillings for the second offence, and for the third offence to be expelled the Company, a Majority of the Officers are also to judge of these offences.

6th. That should any of the Soldiers, by their conduct render themselves unworthy of being a Member of said Company, a Majority of the Officers and Company may expel him; and in such case the Party expelled shall yet be obliged to pay off all arrearages of Fines.

7th. All Fines to be paid or exacted in consequence of the Resolutions or Regulations of this Company, are to be paid to the Captain for the time being, or the Person appointed by him for that purpose, and are to be laid out for use of the said Company.

8th. That the said Company shall be increased to any number, not exceeding One Hundred Men.

9th. That the said Company shall not be obliged to march out of this Province, without the Direction of a Majority of the officers, with the consent of a Majority of the soldiers.

10th. That in case it be thought expedient the Companies of this County should form themselves into Battalions or Regiments, we do hereby impower the Officers aforesaid, to join with the other officers of the County, in choosing Field Officers to command such Battalion or Regiment.

11th. That this Association to continue for the space of Eight Months next following, unless the time be enlarged by a Majority of the subscribers, or the Association dissolved by two-thirds of the Subscribers.

12th. That this Company and every member thereof shall also comply with any other Resolutions that shall be entered into by a majority of the officers and a majority of the Company for the Regulation, Government or Support of this Company.

13th. That a majority of the officers shall appoint the Sergeants, Corporals, and Drum for the Company.

14th. That the officers are to be fined for offences equal with ye privates.

In testimony whereof we have hereunto set our Hands, the seventeenth day of May, 1775.

Privates.

Alleman, John.
Bratton, John.
Bishop, Stophel.
Black, James.
Boyd, Samuel.
Bream, Peter.
Brown, James.
Buck, Robert.
Buck, Thomas.
Campble, John.
Campble, William.
Carnahan, Robert.
Chambers, Robert.
Cook, Jacob.
Creed, James.
Davis, John.
Dixon, John.
Donaldson, James.
Dougherty, Hugh.
Duncan, John.
Elliot, Archibald.
Falkner, Joseph.
Farmer, John.
Farmer, William.
Flack, James.
Foster, Andrew.
Foster, David.
Foster, James.
Fulton, Alexander.
Fureman, Daniel.
Grimm, Dewalt.
Hall, William.
Hamilton, Charles.
Hay, James.
Hay, John.
Hay, Matthew.
Hay, William.
Henry, Adam.
Hoover, John.
Hostater, John.
Hunter, Robert.
Hunter, William.

COUNTY OF LANCASTER.

Johnson, John.
Johnson, William.
Kelley, James.
Kelley, Patrick.
Kelley, Thomas.
Kenady, John.
Keyner, Adam.
Lawser, Michael.
Logan, John.
Lynch, Patrick.
McCleary, Robert.
McClintock, Alexander.
McClintock, Joseph.
McDougal, Duncan.
McQueen, David.
McQueen, Jonas.
McQueen, Robert.
Moore, William.
Moore, Edward.
Morrison, James.
Morrison, Alexander.
Notemurr, James.
Null, Christopher.
Null, George.
Pooreman, Peter.
Rheas, Robert.
Roan, John.
Shank, Stophel.
Shelly, Michael.
Shier, Jacob.
Stauffer, Christian.
Stauffer, Jacob.
Steel, Dennis.
Stevick, John.
Thompson, John.
Walker, Archibald.
Weir, John.
Wolf, Michael.

A true Copy, Certified by

JACOB COOK,
Chairman of Committee.

JAMES SULLIVAN,
Clerk.

FIRST COMPANY OF HEMPFIELD TOWNSHIP—1775. (a.)

The Association of the First Company in Hempfield township. Lancaster County.

Captain.

James Barber.

First Lieutenant.

Robert Barber.

Second Lieutenant.

Samuel Barber.

Ensign.

James Patten.

(Sergeants' names obliterated.)

Christopher Baylor.	John Marband.
Philip Snyder.	Patrick Hardy.
John Barber.	William Henry.
John Tayler.	Solomon Patten.
Joseph Houghentobler.	Adam Stonhing.
Stephen Cohick.	Nicholas Houghentobler.
Joseph May.	Isaac Houghentobler.
Joseph R———.	Thomas Locker.
John Cross.	Christopher Locker.
John Mc———.	John Neal.
Henry Meldram.	Samuel Carler.
John Cohick.	Peter Smith.
Samuel Kraght.	Joseph Aldridge.
Robert Patterson.	John Houghentobler.
Patrick Reily.	Samuel Wright.

I certify and attest the foregoing to be a true copy of the original.

JAMES BARBER,
Captain.

September 1, 1775.

WARWICK TOWNSHIP ASSOCIATION—1775. (a.)

Captain.

Peter Grubb.

Peter Grubb.	George Whitcraft.
William Old.	Isaiah Rogers.
Samuel Jones.	John Russell.
Charles Fausset.	William Coulter.
John Ashton.	Nich's Shroff.
Edward Goheen.	James Anderson.
Martin Hagy.	John Winters.
Hinriech Süss.	James Huslor.
John Jones.	H. Harrigan.

Michael Shoff.
John Douglas.
John Huber.
Samuel Bussell.
Daniel Holleger.
Jacob Walter.
Conrad Ingle.
Marks Naugle.
George Little.
Mathias Weidman.
John Royer.
Niklaus Keim.
Edward Agnew.
Jacob Batnes.
Christian Hollinger.
Conrad Merk.
David Fortney.
Christian Schmitt.
Casper Seyor.
Isaac Coby.
Jonathan Gingrick.

THE HEIDLEBERG COMPANY—1775. (a.)

Captain.
Hudson, George.

First Lieutenant.

More, John.

Second Lieutenant.

Miller, George.

Privates.

Antis Frederick.
Beaker, George.
Boab, Stofel.
Boyer, Stofel.
Brosius, Henry.
Brown, Philip.
Bulman, Adam (1).
Bulman, Adam (2).
Bulman, John.
Cap, Frederick.
Cline, Stofel.
Coppy, Israel.
Ellck, Leonard.
Foster, Jacob.
France, John.
Graford, John.
Holstone, George.
Harbeson, George.
Hartman, Samuel.
Hean, Jacob.
Hoffman, Conrad.
Hoffman, George.
Keller, Henry.
Levestone, David.
Micer, Dewalt.
Micer, George.
Micer, Henry (1).
Micer, Henry (2).
Micer, John.
Moyer, Henry.
Moyer, John.
Moyer, Michael.

Neaf, Abraham.
Neaf, George.
Noll, George.
Noll, John.
Noll, Philip.
Newman, George.
Newman, John.
Newman, Peter (1).
Newman, Peter (2).
Newman, Walter.
Peehtle, Nicholas.
Petree, Peter.
Petree, Philip.
Raup, Frederick.
Rightanour, George.
Roofe, Jacob.
Saltsgwer, Henry.
Saltsgwer, John.
Seller, Frederick.
Seller, Henry.
Seller, John.
Seller, Michael (1).
Seller, Michael (2).
Seller, Peter.
Shadewear, Henry.
Shank, Wentle.
Shefer, Michael.
Shenkle, Philip.
Shenkle, Jacob.
Shenkle, Chris.
Sholl, Adam.
Simmerman, George.
Strickler, Andrew.
Strickler, George.
Strickler, Leonard.
Stump, Leonard.
Swert, Chris.
Treeone, George.
Weiser, Martin.
Weiser, Stofel.
Wike, Chris.
Yencht, William.
Young, Jacob.

FIRST BATTALION
LANCASTER COUNTY MILITIA.

STANDING GUARD AT LANCASTER—1776. (a.)

Captain-Lieutenant Christopher Crawford's detachment of the First battalion, under his command, at Lancaster, 1776.

Captain-Lieutenant.

Christopher Crawford.

Lieutenant.

William Graham.

Ensign.

John Torbitt.

Light Infantry.

James Hand.
George Caytor.
Christian Curtz.
Solomon Manacha.
John Graff.
Jacob Graff.
Henry Small.
Philip Recam.

Capt. Samuel Boyd's company.

Christian Smith.
Michael Hoak.
Jacob Youtz.
Levy Andrew Levy.
Wage Lyon.
Andrew Specke.
Simon Hannon.
John Ripple.
Melchoir Rudysill.
Christopher Reidenhart.
Nicholas Miller.

Capt. Andrew Graff's company.

Henry Rehr.
Michael Shindle.
Lewis Latta.
Stephen Switzer.
John Shrye.
Frederick Hitzley.
Benjamin Rigart.
Frauts Shover.
Michael Shatzer.
Cornelius Curtz.
Peter Gontes.
Philip Williams.
George O'Donald.
Jacob Martin.
James Reed.
John Jontes.
Elijah Hardy.
Abraham Brown.
Christopher Rigart.

Capt. John Henry's company.

Jacob Woolrick.
Rudolph Carpenter.
John Otley.
John Conn.
Nicholas Boeke.
Dewalt Smith.
Joseph Long.
Solam Curtie.
Henry Roan.
Nicholas Martin.
William Fahnestock, one of the drafts.

Capt. Peter Hofnagle's company.

Joseph Vanhorn.
Uichael Lightner.
Leonard Benedict.
John Woltz.
Christian Widle.
John Lightner.
George Wein.
John Lecron.
John Miller.
Adam Reisinger.

Regimental Orders.

Lieutenant Crawford is ordered to take the detachment of the First battalion, ordered for the guard of the borough of Lancaster, under his command, to have the roll called morning and evening, and consult with the committee for mounting proper guard, and pay proper attention to their requisitions.

GEORGE ROSS.
Colonel.

July 1st, 1776.

ACCOUNT OF MONIES EXPENDED BY MICHAEL DIEFFENDERFER FOR THE SUPPORT OF THE WIVES & CHILDREN OF SUCH MILITIA MEN BELONGING TO CAPT. GEO. MUSSER'S CO. IN COL. GEORGE ROSS BATTALION OF LANCASTER CO. AS WERE IN THE ACTUAL SERVICE OF THE UNITED STATES OF AMERICA IN THE YEAR 1776, TO WIT. (c.)

1776.			
Aug. 14,	Cash pd. Margaret, the wife of Hugh McElroy Rech,	No. 1,...	0 7 6
	Cash pd. Johanna, the wife of Adam Rupert,.	No. 2,...	7 6
	Cash pd. Ann, the wife of Henry Hains, ...	No. 3,...	5 0
	Cash pd. Margaret, the wife of Henry Lyeinger,	No. 4,...	7 6
	Cash paid Christina, the wife of John Plattenberger,	No. 5,...	7 6
16,	Cash pd. Ann, the wife of Robt. Campbell,....	No. 6,...	7 6
	Cash pd. Margaret, the wife of Sottlich Nowman,	No. 7,...	7 6
	Cash pd. Margaret, the wife of Isaac Bartgis,	No. 8,...	7 6
	Cash pd. Margaret, the wife of Gehrart Utenstine,	No. 9,...	5 0
	Cash pd. Elisebeth, the wife of John Walker,	No. 10,...	7 6
	Cash pd. (This line torn).		
	Cash pd. Sarah, the wife of Casper Greble,....	No. 12,...	7 6
	Cash pd. Margaret, the wife of John Lutman,	No. 13,...	7 6
	Cash pd. Catharine, the wife of Christ. Illiger,	No. 14,...	7 6
	Cash pd. Mary, the wife of John Wydle, ...	No. 15,...	7 6
Oct. 10,	Cash pd. Christine, the wife of Mich. Huber,..	No. 16,...	4 0
	Cash pd. the wife of Hugh McElory, ...	No. 17,...	15 0
	Recd. at times from W. A. Attlle, ...	....	6 6 6
	Bal. due to the state, ...	....	5 13 6
	Exd. & Settled, ...	....	12 0 0

JNO. NICHOLSON,
Comp. Gen. Office,
March 31, 1787.

IN THE JERSEY CAMPAIGN, 1776—7. (a.)

List of Captains whose companies of Militia went to Jersey in August, 1776, Were Absent till Jan. and Feb., 1777. Indorsed "Muster Rolls of Lancaster County Militia, 1776."

Adams, Isaac.
Boyd, John.

Boyd, Samuel.
Brown, William.
Campbell, Robert.
Cowden, James.
Crawford, Christopher.
Doebler, Albright.
Evans, Joshua.
McCallen, Robert.
McQuown, Richard.
McKee, Robert.
Morgan, David.
Murray, James.
Morrison, James.
Martin, Alex.
Musser, George.
Peden, Hugh.
Reed, John.
Ross, James.
Sherer, Joseph.
Steele, William.
Page, Nathaniel.
Parry, William.
Fridley, Jacob.
Graff, Andrew.
Hollinger, Christian.
Hoofnagle, Peter.
Johnston, ———.
Jones, John.
King, Jacob.
Koppenheffer, Thomas.
Manning, Richard.
Rutherford, John.
Tweed, John, Lieut. Comdt.
Watson, James, company Comd. by Lieut. John Patton.
Weaver, Henry.
Whiteside, Thomas.
Wilson, Dorrington. Commanded by Lieut. John Eckman.
Withers, John.
Wright, Joseph.
Yeates, Jasper.
Zantzinger, Paul.
Ziegler, Frederick.
Zimmerman, Bernard.

"THE FLYING CAMP."—1776. (a.)

[Although Pennsylvania furnished apart from the three State Regiments, four thousand five hundred troops for the so-called "Flying Camp," it has been impossible up to the present time to find the names of more than five hundred officers and men. It is hoped, however, that with the increased interest recently taken in hunting up the records of a patriotic ancestry, much may be discovered and preserved. It is greatly to be regretted that the information herewith given is so meagre.]

First Battalion of the Flying Camp of Lancaster county, Pennsylvania—1776.

Colonel.

James Cunningham.

Lieutenant Colonel.

William Hay.

Major.

Thomas Edwards.

Adjutant.

John Davis.

Surgeon.

William Smith.

Quartermaster.

James Porter, p. t.

First Company.

Captain.—Robert Clark.
First Lieutenant.—William Steel, promoted captain.
Second Lieutenant.—James Turner.
Third Lieutenant.— William Nelson.

Second Company.

Captain.—James Watson.
First Lieutenant.—Thomas Lindsay.
Second Lieutenant.—Robert Coleman.
Third Lieutenant.—Matthew Swan.

Third Company.

Captain.—Jacob Klotz, promoted.
First Lieutenant.—Thomas Robinson, promoted.
Second Lieutenant.—John Campbell.
Third Lieutenant.—Andrew Boggs, discharged on account of wounds received at Long Island.
Third Lieutenant.—Thomas Whitmore, promoted from sergeant.

Fourth Company.

Captain.—George Graeff.
First Lieutenant.—Conrad Connor.
Second Lieutenant.—Dorrington Wilson.
Third Lieutenant.—William Calhoun.

Fifth Company.

Captain.—John Reed.
First Lieutenant.—James Collier.
Second Lieutenant.—John Gilchrist, discharged August 14, 1776, on account of wound in right arm.
Third Lieutenant.—Thomas Johnston, promoted second lieutenant.
Third Lieutenant.—John Cochran, from sergeant.

Sixth Company.

Captain.—Daniel Oldenbruck.
First Lieutenant.—Ludwig Meyer, promoted to Klotz's company.
Second Lieutenant.—William McCullough.
Third Lieutenant.—Benjamin Fickle, discharged on account of wound.
Third Lieutenant.—John Rohrer, from sergeant.

Seventh Company.

Captain.—Joseph Work.
First Lieutenant.—Patrick Hays, discharged for disability.

Second Lieutenant.—William Patterson, reported killed or taken prisoner at Long Island.
Third Lieutenant.—Richard Keys, discharged for disability.
Third Lieutenant.—James Barker, from sergeant.

Eighth Company.

Captain.—Timothy Green.
First Lieutenant.—William Allen, wounded at Long Island.
Second Lieutenant.— ——— Weiser.
Third Lieutenant.—John Barnett.

Ninth Company.

Captain.—John McKown.
Second Lieutenant.—John Bishop.
Third Lieutenant.—Henry Buehler.

Sergeants.

——— Davis.
James Barber, promoted third lieutenant.
——— Kerr.
Andrew Boggs, promoted third lieutenant.
William Hunter.
James Harkness.
John Smille.
Mark McCord.
——— Scott.
John Driver.
John Ellison.
George Princely.
Frederick Charles.
Lawrence Dowling.
Charles Connor.

Corporals.

Peter Cipher.
Patrick Donnelly.
Christopher Ketley.

Privates.

Christopher Taylor.
Samuel Boude.
John Barber.

Detachment of Captain Watson's Company.

William Steel.
Alexander Scott.
William Walker.
John McKnight.
John Polk.
John Steel.
William Robb.
James Calhoon.
Andrew Cummings.
John Pegan.
John Thompson.
Daniel Carmichael.
John Miller.
Robert Black.
Samuel Ankrim.
John Clark.
Hugh Caldwell.
Pettis Hanlin.
John Post.
William McGriger.

OFFICERS FIRST BATTALION—1777. (a.)

Colonel.

Philip Greenawalt.

Lieutenant Colonel.

Philip Marsteller.

Major.

Samuel Jones.

Adjutant.

Adam Fisher.

Quarter Master.

Peter Miller.

First Company.

Captain.—Casper Stoever.
First Lieutenant.—Andrew Fickes.
Second Lieutenant.—Sebastian Wolf.
Ensign.—Charles Rebrick.

Second Company.

Captain.—William Paine.
First Lieutenant.—Anthony Kelker.
Second Lieutenant.—Jacob Matter.

Third Company.

Captain.—Philip Weiser.
First Lieutenant.—Ludwig Shott.
Second Lieutenant.—John Stone.
Third Lieutenant.—John Thomas.

Fourth Company.

Captain.—George Null.
First Lieutenant.—James Mortersteel.
Second Lieutenant.—Michael Minigh.
Ensign.—George Meiser.

Fifth Company.

Captain.—Michael Holderbaum.
First Lieutenant.—George Nagle.
Second Lieutenant.—Lucas Shally.
Ensign.—Alexander Martin.

Sixth Company.

Captain.—Leonard Immel.
First Lieutenant.—Michael Diffenbaugh.
Second Lieutenant.—Peter Berry.
Ensign.—Michael Spengler.

Seventh Company.

Captain.—Valentine Shouffler.
First Lieutenant.—Matthew Henning.
Second Lieutenant.—John Gossert.
Ensign.—Peter Basehore.

Eighth Company.

Captain.—Henry Sheaffer.
First Lieutenant.—Philip Wolfersberger.
Second Lieutenant.—Nicholas Zollinger.
Ensign.—George Frank.

Ninth Company.

Captain.—Daniel Oldenbruck.
First Lieutenant.—Abraham Smith.
Second Lieutenant.—John Rewalt.
Ensign.—Peter Heckert.

A REPORT OF THE FIRST BATTALION, LANCASTER COUNTY MILITIA COMMANDED BY COLONEL PHILIP GREENAWALT.

Field Officers.

Philip Greenawalt, Col.
Philip Marstteller, Lieut. Col.
Sam'l Jones, Maj'r.

Staff Officers.

Adam Fisher, Adjut.
Peter Miller, Quarter Master.

1ST COMPANY.

Captain.
Casper Stever.

1st. Lieut.
And. Fricker.

2nd Lieut.
Seb't Wolf.

Ensign.
Cha'ls Rerich.

Court Mart. Men.
John Eisenhover.
Michael Herner.

South West District of Lebanon Township
May 7th. 1777.

Meeting of a Number of the Inhabitants of the South West District or Sub division of Lebanon Towns[illegible] for choosing Officers &c.a for the Company of Militia to be found in said District, it appears, that the following Persons, were by a Majority of Votes [illegible] to the several Offices mentioned agreeable to the Directions of an Act of General Assembly of this State of Pennsylvania —— viz.t

William Paine, Captain
Anthony Kelcher, first Lieut.t
Jacob Maller [illegible] Lieut.t
Frederick Stiser Ensign &
Curtis Grubb & Balser Orth, Court Martial Men

Testimony whereof we have hereunto set our Hands the Day and Time above written ——

Curtis Grubb
Balser Orth
} Judges of y.e Election

inal of above in possession of Mr. Rudolph F. Kelker, Harrisburg, Pa.

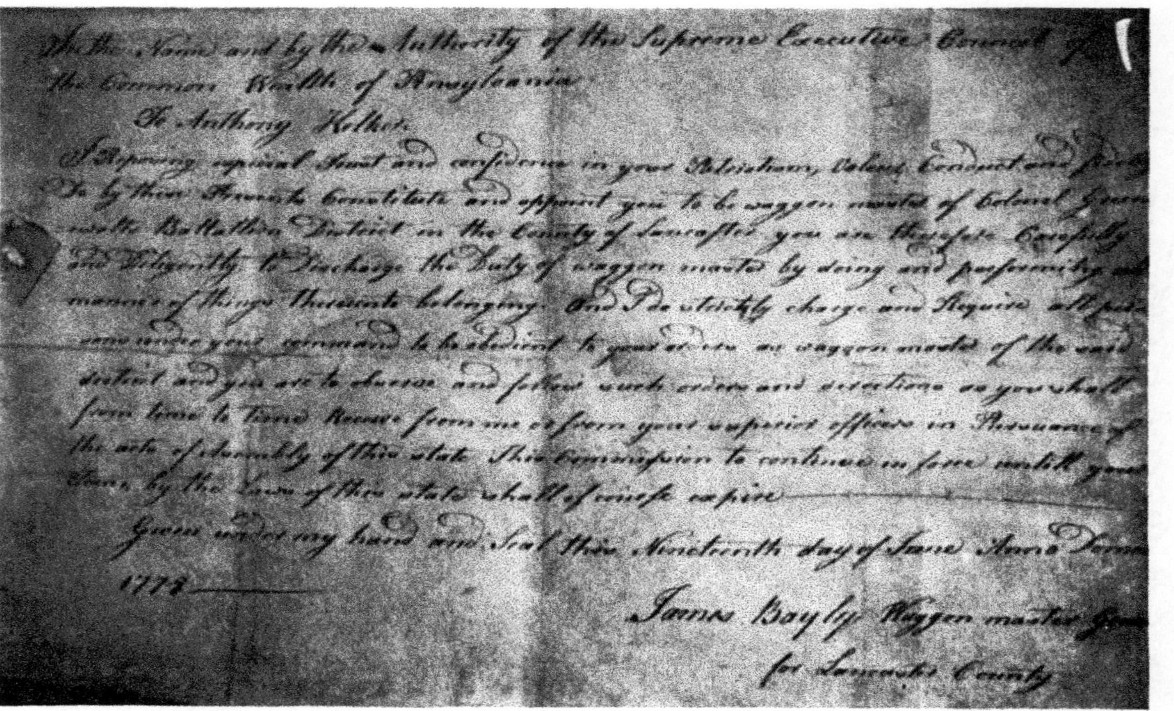

In the Name and by the Authority of the Supreme Executive Council of
the Common Wealth of Pennsylvania

To Anthony Kelker

I Reposing especial Trust and confidence in your Patriotism, Valour, Conduct and Fidelity
Do by these Presents Constitute and appoint you to be waggon master of Colonel Green-
walts Battallion District in the County of Lancaster you are therefore Carefully
and Diligently to Discharge the Duty of waggon master by doing and performing all
manner of things thereunto belonging. And I do strictly charge and Require all persons under your command to be obedient to your orders as waggon master of the said
district and you are to observe and follow such orders and directions as you shall
from time to time Receive from me or from your superior officers in Pursuance of
the acts of Assembly of this state This Commission to continue in force untill your
time by the Laws of this state shall of course expire

Given under my hand and Seal this Nineteenth day of June Anno Domini
1777

James Boyle Waggon master General
for Lancaster County

Rank & File.
108 Men.

2ND COMPANY.

Captain.
Wm. Paine.

1st. Lieut.
An. Keiker.

2nd Lieut.
Jacob Matter.

Ensign.

Court Mart. Men.
Curtis Grubb.
Balzer Orth.

Rank & File.
160.

3D COMPANY.

Captain.
Philip Weiser.

1st. Lieut.
Lod. Shot.

2nd Lieut.
John Stone.

---

*Some misguided person erased the name of the Ensign on the original roll and substituted that of Martin Thomas.

Ensign.

Jno. Thomas.

Serjts.

4.

Corpl.

4.

Court Mart. Men.

Nich'l Shawk.
Christian Brand.

Rank & File.

137.

4TH COMPANY.

Captain.

Geo. Null.

1st. Lieut.

Jno. Morterstcck.

2nd Lieut.

Mich'l Minigh.

Ensign.

Geo. Meiser.

Serjts.

4.

Corpl.

4.

Court Mart. Men.

Mich'l Treon.
Fred'k Capp.

Rank & File.

70.

5TH COMPANY.

Captain.

Michl. Holterbaum.

1st. Lieut.

Geo. Nagle.

2nd Lieut.

Lucas Shalley.

Ensign.

Allex'r Martin.

6TH COMPANY.

Captain.

Leonard Immel.

1st. Lieut.

M'l Defenbough.

2nd Lieut.

Peter Berry.

Ensign.

Mich'l Spengler.

Serjts.
4.

Corpl.
4.

Rank & File.
119.

7TH COMPANY.

Captain.
Val. Shoufler.

1st. Lieut.
Mat. Hening.

2nd Lieut.
John Gosser.

Ensign.
Peter Bashore.

Serjts.
4.

Corpl.
4.

Court Mart. Men.
John Bright.
Michael Creal.

Rank & File.
108.

8TH COMPANY.

Captain.
Henry Sheaffer.

1st. Lieut.
P. Wolfelsberger.

2nd Lieut.
N. Zollinger.

Ensign.
George Frank.

Serjts.
4.

Corpl.
4.

Court Mart. Men.
Michael Egolf.
Philip Erbs.

Rank & File.
117.

9TH COMPANY.

Captain.
Daniel Oldenbreck.

1st. Lieut.
Abr. Smith.

2nd Lieut.
Jno. Rewalt.

Ensign.
Peter Hecter.

Serjts.
4.

Corpl.
4.

Court Mart. Men.
Robert Patton.
Peter Miller.

Rank & File.
128.

Commissions Dated first July, 1777.

Rec'd 25th. August, 1777, of Colonel Timothy Matlack the Commissions for the Officers of the within return.

JACOB COOK.

OFFICERS OF FIRST BATTALION. (a.)

Returned August 26, 1780.

Lieutenant Colonel.
George Stewart.

Major.
William McCausland.

First Company.

Captain—John Slater.
Lieutenant—James Henry.
Ensign—Nicholas Shreiner.

Second Company.

Captain—Enoch Hastings.
Lieutenant—William McCulloch.
Ensign—[Vacant.]

Third Company.

Captain—Alex. White.
Lieutenant—Matthias Slaymaker.
Ensign—William Slaymaker.

Fourth Company.

Captain—William Skyles.
Lieutenant—Abraham Henry.
Ensign—William McCausland.

Fifth Company.

Captain—William Smith.
Lieutenant—Samuel Hawthorn.
Ensign—Edward Lintner.

Sixth Company.

Captain—[Vacant.]
Lieutenant—[Vacant.]
Ensign—[Vacant.]

Seventh Company.

Captain—[Vacant.]
Lieutenant—[Vacant.]
Ensign—[Vacant.]

Eighth Company.

Captain—William Brisben.
Lieutenant—William Willson.
Ensign—George Whitehill.

GENERAL RETURN OF THE OFFICERS OF THE MILITIA OF THE COUNTY OF LANCASTER IN THE STATE OF PENNSYLVANIA, AUG. 26TH, 1780. (c.)

First Battalion.

Field Officers.

Lieut. Col.
George Stewart.

Maj.
Willm. McCausland.

Captains.

1. John Slater.
2. Enock Hastings.
3. Alexander White.
4. William Skyles.
5. William Smith.
6.
7.
8. William Brisban.

Lieutenants.

1. James Henry.
2. William McCulloch.
3. Matthias Slaymaker.
4. Abraham Henry.
5. Samuel Hawthorn.
6.
7.
8. William Willson.

Ensigns.

1. Nichl. Shreiner.
2.
3. Willm. Slaymaker.
4. Willm. McCausland.
5. Edmd. Lintner.
6.
7.
8. George Whitehill.

Second Battalion.

The commissions for the 2d have been sent to W. Kucher, S. Lieutenant.

A MUSTER ROLE OF THE FIRST SALISBURY COMPANY AND THE EIGHT CLASS OF THE FIRST BATTALION OF LANCASTER COUNTY MILITIA COMANDED BY LIEUT. COL. GEO. STEWART, NOVR. 20TH, 1780. &C. (c.)

Comissioned Officers.

Captain.
William Brisben.

Lieutenant.
William Wilson.

Ensign.
George Whitehill.

Sargent.
Colen Marten.

1st Class.

Archibald McCurdy.
David Cowan.
Thomas McNeall.
Jacob Kizer.
Daniel Fleming.
James Cowan.
Joseph Wike.
Dinnis Harkens.
Joseph Shannon.
Charles Jacobs.

2d Class.

Michel Grahm.
James Mayers.
James Douglass.
Michel McCloskey.
Charles Murrey.
James Gault.
Samuel Siemons.
James Wilson.
Owen Thomas.
Robert Moore.
James Ross.
Charles Jacobs.

3d Class.

James Johnston.
Hugh Forgey.
John Beggs.
John Gorden.
James Cullen.
Andrew Lytle.
Jacob Curtz.
Michel Jack.
Robt. Potts.
Daniel Harkens.
Thomas Boyd.

4th Class.

John Douglass.
William Armstrong.
Christen Curtz.
William Patton.
Thomas Siemons, Sr.
John Coop.
John Armor.
John McKinnly.
Jacob Bleasor.
Robert Auld.
Harmon Skiles.
Samuel Holaday.
Archibald McNeall.
Garret Cowan.

5th Class.

Joseph Belford.
Adam Gault.
James Hughes.
Robert Huston.
Robert Crosbey, in Capt. White's Company.
John Crosbey.
William Lee.
John Plank.
George Rutter.
George Boyd.
Mathew Henderson.
James Lytle.
George Kizer.
James Borland.
James Armo·
Jonathan Green.
Samuel Coop.

6th Class.

Joseph Welch.
Edward Runshaw.
James Watson.
William Beggs.
Thomas Siemons, Jr.
Alexr. Brown.
Robert Huey.
James Anerson.
Archibald McAfee.
Andrew Smith.
Nethaniel Rutter.
Jacob Pee.
James Whitehill.
George Stover.

7th Class.

James McFadden.
William Richardson.
Jacob Hains.
William Holaday.
John Whitehill.
William Cowan.
John Holey.
James McCamont.
Michel Kenneday.
William Jones.
Leonard Euroch.
Samuel Hughes.
Moses Wilson.
John Boyd.
George McIntier.
Joseph Gilles.
Joseph Hains.

8th Class.

William Boyd.
Samuel Armor.
John McComb.
Thomas Henderson.
Robert Cowan.
James Dunlap.

John Murphey.
John McGown.
Samuel Young.
James McCafferty.
David Harris.
Joseph Garver.
James Hamilton.
Isaac McCamont.

THE CLASSES OF MEN BELONGING TO CAPT. WILLIAM SMYTH'S COMPANY DESTINGUISHED. 1780. (c.)

Privates.

1st Class.

John Eckman.
John Verner.
Abram Bowman.
Simon Haynold.
Peter Hole.
Peter Rush.
Henry Beam.
John Hare, Junr.
Henry Eckman.
Jacob Miller, Carpenr.
John White.
Philip Cassler.
George Richman.
George Smith.
John Rosor.
Jacob Miller, Junr.
James Molston.
Henry Isaberger.
John Martly.
Saml. Bear.
David Shaver.

2d Class.

Thomas Leckey.
Martin Eckman.
Henry Miller.
George Fisher.
Peter Musser.
John Brua.
John Howrey.
Jonas Cafman.
Jacob Bear.
Christian Huber.

3d Class.

Jacob Frits.
John Rush.
William Logan.
Jacob Rush.
Christian Byars.
Christian Shap.
Henry Hare.
Nicholas Sorrowes.
John Foundersmith.
Everard Gruber.
William Hugans.
Saml. Hugans.
Andrew Hikis.
John Cremer.
Jacob Drum.

4th Class.

John Shitlenhelm.
Balser Peterman.
Martin Kendrick.
John Brubeker.
Joseph Oterbough.
Jacob Sides.
Jacob Huber.
Nicholas Hart.
Daniel Miller.
Christian Martin.

Jacob Eckman.
Daniel Daniel.
Christian Eternaught.
William Davis.
Alexander Hunter.
Simeon Miller.
David Brown.
Christian Stoner.
Jacob Fouls, Junr.
Henry Bear.

5th Class.

Conrad Heak.
Robert Charleton.
John Free.
Christian Beaker.
Henry Huber.
Andrew Spitser.
John Cremer, coopr.
John Simpson.
Aram Hare.
John Brackbill.
Michael Fouls.

John Small, Junr.
Torrence Duffy.
John Road.
Isaac Widdows.
John Kendrick.
William Bowslick.
John Humphreys.
Nicholas Walters.
James Brown.
Saml. McComsey.

6th Class.

Jacob Kendrick.
Barnet Houser.
Jacob Frelick.
Jacob Neff.
Henry Rush.
Jacob Miller.
Saml. Miller.
John Moore.

Charles Philips.
Noah Hagey.
Philip Bear.
John Fronk.
Jacob Brubeker.
Lodwick Rinhart.
Thomas Law.
Windle Troutt.

7th Class.

John Withers.
Valentine Fondersmith.
Jacob Huber, Senr.
John Millar.
George Martly.
Henry Bowman.
John Bear.

Jacob Eckman.
Daniel Bowman.
Henry Bushman.
Nicholas Macky.
Peter Shofstall.
Martin Hare.
Henry Kendrick.

Frederick Smith.
Joseph Ross.
George Mires.
John Grahams.
Fredrick Bowan.
John Cremerhick.
John McNaught.
Andrew Kell.

8th Class.

John Stoutsaberger.
Matthias Miller.
Jacob Miller.
Michael Withers.
Christian Sholts.
Martin Still.
George Bright.
Jacob Kendrick.
Henry Stoner.
Jacob Foutts.
Henry Road.
Daniel Mowra.
William Kenney.
Michael Mires.
Aram Brubeker.
George May.
John McMullan.

Certifyed by,

WILLIAM SMYTH,
Capt.

MUSTER ROLL OF THE 2ND CLASS, 1ST BATALION LANCR. COUNTY MILITIA COMMD. BY CAPT. ENOCH HASTINGS. (c.)

Names of Persons Who Performed the Tour.	Names of Persons Who Furnished Substitutes.	When duty commd.	When duty ended.
Captain.		1781.	1781.
Enoch Hastings,		May 2,	June 30.
Lieut.			
James Henry,		do.	do.
Ensn.			
Wm. Brandor,		do.	do.
Sergt.			
Fredk. Doersh,	Michl. Widler,	do.	do.
Geo. Mathiot,	Jno. Slaymaker,	do.	do.
Jno. Gramer,	Joseph White,	do.	do.
Corpl.			
Chris. Odswalt,	Geo. McCullouch,	do.	do.
Michl. Eley,	Jacob Swope,	do.	do.
Peter Messersmith,	Jno. McConoughey,	do.	do.

MUSTER ROLL OF THE 2ND CLASS, 1ST BATALION LANCR. COUNTY MILITIA—Continued.

Names of Persons Who Performed the Tour.	Names of Persons Who Furnished Substitutes.	When duty commd.	When duty ended.
Drum.		1781.	1781.
Geo. Thomas, ...	Peter Musser, ...	do.	do.
Fifer.			
Fredk. Melinger, ...	Nicholas Weaver, ...	do.	do.
Privates.			
Jacob Marks, ...	Jacob Hoffman, ...	do.	do.
Jno. Libely, ...	Jno. Lerue, ...	do.	do.
Casper Treeple, ...	Joseph Buckwalter, ...	do.	do.
Jacob Balmer, ...	David Brown, ...	do.	do.
Henry Eger, ...	Peter Ebey, ...	do.	do.
Wm. Dyer, ...	Jno. Bander, ...	do.	do.
Geo. Brecht, ...	Henry Swope, ...	do.	do.
Jno. Libely, Junr., ...	Jacob Sharrer, ...	do.	do.
Jno. Seely, ...	Peter Klyne, ...	do.	do.
Chris. Apple, ...	Jno. Fowler, ...	do.	do.
Wm. Sebrile, ...	Jno. Hamerman, ...	do.	do.
Jno. Gerloch, ...	Wm. Fasson, ...	do.	do.
Jno. Stormbach, ...	Jno. Ebright, ...	do.	do.
Jno. Marquart, ...	Jacob Pickle, ...	do.	do.
Willm. Hamilton, ...	....	do.	do.
Jacob Shuler, ...	Jno. Hamell, ...	do.	do.
James Goete, Jun., ...	James Goete, Junr., ...	do.	do.
Geo. Kistler, ...	Charles Caldwell, ...	do.	do.
Wm. Farrell, ...	Joseph Rutter, ...	do.	do.
Philip Mosher, ...	Joseph Allison, ...	do.	do.
Wm. Codey, ...	David Sterret, ...	do.	do.
Jno. Switzer, ...	*Peter Shoemaker, ...	do.	do.
Jacob Shindle, ...	Wm. Whitehill, ...	do.	do.
Jno. Davis, ...	Benjn. Whitmore, ...	do.	do.
Jno. Lucey, ...	James Willson, ...	do.	do.
Jno. Hamilton, ...	....	7th, ...	do.
George Baker, ...	Robert Crosby, ...	13th, ...	do.
Casper Ehrmar, ...	Jno. Scott, ...	15th.	do.
Thomas Carmichael, ...	Michl. Graham, ...	2d, ...	do.
Jno. Ucome, ...	Joseph Evett, ...	do.	do.
Dennis Harkins, ...	James Douglass, ...	do.	do.
Michl. McCloskey, ...	....	do.	dc.
Charles Murray, ...	....	do.	do.
Patrick Malholm, ...	....	do.	do.
James McPike, ...	....	do.	do.

True company.

Lancr. May 8th, 1781. Then mustered within company as within specified.

ADM. HUBLEY,
S. L. Lr. Cy.

A RETURN OF CAPT. WILLIAM SKILESES COMPY. OF THE FIRS BATTN. OF LANCASTER COUNTY MELITA COMMANDED BY COLO. JAMES MERCER, ESQR., MAY THE 28D, 1781. (c.)

Abraham Gibbons.
John Rush.
Henry Musser.
John Musser.
Jacob Sensnick.
Abram Sensnick.
Christian Sharp.
Baltzer Bashore.
Daniel Bashore.
John Shaver.
Stophel Cling.
William Billomy.
George Alexander.
Charles McGowan.
Henry Hartman.
William Randles.
Caleb Harpman.
John Ebby.
William Crow.
Jacob Myers.
James Robison.

WILLIAM SKILES,
Capt. 7th Copy.

MUSTER ROLL OF 3RD CLASS, 1ST BATT. LANCR. COUNTY MILA. COMD. BY CAPT. MATHIAS SLAYMAKER NOW ON DUTY AT LANCR. (c.)

Names of Persons Who Served.	Names of Persons who Furnished Substitutes.	Time when duty commd.	Time when duty ended.
Capt.		1781.	1781.
Mathias Slaymaker, ...	....	June 28,....	July 30.
Lieut.			
Abram. Henry.			
Ensign.			
James Patterson.			
Serjts.			
Robt. Willson, ...	Andw. Caldwell, ...	....	Aug. 23.
Fredk. Doent, ...	Michl. Jack,		
Clerk.			
Joseph Renshaw.			

MUSTER ROLL OF 3RD CLASS, 1ST BATT. LANCR. COUNTY MILA.—Continued.

Names of Persons Who Served.	Names of Persons who Furnished Substitutes.	Time when duty commd.	Time when duty ended.
Corpl.			
Daniel Peler,	Jno. Draber.		
Michl. House,	Jas. Smith.		
Peter Messersmith,	Thos. Fullerton.		
Drum.			
George Thomas,	Jos. Whitehill,	July 2.	
Fifer.			
Fredk. Mellinger,	Henry Sherrick,	July 3.	
Privates.			
Daniel Hustin,		June 30,	July 21.
Jacobs Marks,	Andw. Bear,		Aug. 23.
Maths. Shipe,	Fredk. Baker.		
Jno. Thompson,	Robert Simpson.		
Benjn. Crawford,			July 29.
Conrad Shitz,			Aug. 23.
Henry Winger,	Saml. McElhatton.		
Fredk. Dochterman,	Saml. Young.		
Joseph Jacobs,	John Johns,	July 2.	
Michl. Buch,	Jacob Stotsaberger.		
Jacob Britzius,	Daniel Peck.		
James Winter,	Robert Potts.		
Jno. Verner,	George Wither,	July 2,	Aug. 23.
Jno. Maddiss,	James Cooper,	July 3,	July 28.
Danl. Graner,	James Knox,	June 30,	Aug. 23.
John Seger,		July 2,	July 28.
Wm. Wise,	John Boggs,	July 4,	Aug. 23.
Hugh Forgey,		4,	July 29.
John Gerdon,		4.	
Alexr. Brown,		4.	
George Reese,	Michl. Surrerous,	4,	Aug. 23.
James Carr,	John Fondersmith,	4,	do.
Cornelius Wier,	Robert Byers,		5. Inlisted.
Andw. Little,		4.	

Lancr. July 6th, 1781. Then mustered Capt. Slaymaker's Company as above specified.

ADM. HUBLEY,
S. L. Lr. Cy.

MUSTER ROLL OF THE 4TH CLASS OF THE 1ST BATTALION, LANR. COUNTY MILITIA ON A TOWER OF DUTY AT LANCASTER GUARDING BRITISH PRISONERS OF WAR. 1781. (c.)

Names of Persons who perform a touer of duty.	What Class.	Names of Persons who furnished substitutes.	Time when Duty Commenced.	Time when Duty Ended.
Capt.			1781.	1781.
William Skiles, ...	4th,	....	Augt. 20th.	Oct. 20th.
Lieut.				
Thomas Buffington, ...	4th,	....	Augt. 20th.	Oct. 20th.
Ensgn.				
Nicholas Shreiner, ...	4th,	....	Augt. 20th,	Oct. 20th.
Clk.				
Frederick Doersh, ...	4th,	William Fullerton,	Augt. 20th,	Oct. 20th.
Sergt. Majr.				
Adam Keller, ...	4th,	Abraham Wittemore,	Augt. 20th,	Oct. 20th.
Qu. Mar. Serjt.				
Robert Wilson, ...	4th,	John Christey, ...	Augt. 20th,	Oct. 20th.
Serjt.				
Samuel Davis, ...	4th,	Henry Winger, ...	Augt. 20th,	Oct. 20th.
James McPike, ...	4th,	Daniel Huston, ...	Augt. 20th,	Oct. 20th.
Archd. Craig, ...	4th,	....	Augt. 20th,	Oct. 20th.
Corpl.				
Robert Grounsel, ...	4th,	Henrey Divenbough	Augt. 20th,	Oct. 20th.
John Lightner, ...	4th,	Dewald Spring, ...	Augt. 20th,	Oct. 20th.
George Leonhere, ...	4th,	John Bingley, ...	Augt. 20th,	Oct. 20th.
Drum.				
David Lindon, ...	4th,	Emanuel Ferrey,..	Augt. 20th,	Oct. 20th.
Fife.				
William Halleday, ...	4th,	Samuel Holleday,.	Augt. 20th,	Oct. 20th.
Privates.				
James Kelley, ...	4th,	John Miller, ...	Augt. 20th,	Oct. 20th.
David Harris, ...	4th,	John Harris, ...	Augt. 20th,	Oct. 20th.
Henry Doblins, ...	4th,	John Turbert, ...	Augt. 20th,	Oct. 20th.
John Skiles, ...	4th,	Thomas Skiles, ...	Augt. 20th,	Oct. 20th.
James Kean, ...	4th,	Price Clarck, ...	Augt. 20th,	Oct. 20th.
Isaac Ferrey, ...	4th,	William Welce, ...	Augt. 20th,	Oct. 20th.
Joseph Lefever, ...	4th,	Neal Kenney, ...	Augt. 20th,	Oct. 20th.
John Glass, ...	4th,	Daniel Miller, ...	Augt. 20th,	Oct. 20th.

MUSTER ROLL OF THE 4TH CLASS OF THE 1ST BATTALION LANR. COUNTY—Continued

Names of Persons who perform a tour of duty.	Wha tClass.	Names of Persons who furnished substitutes.	Time when Duty Commenced.	Time when Duty Ended.
Bastian Marquart, ...	4th,	Christian Eyman,.	Augt. 20th,	Oct. 20th.
Casper Treeple, ...	4th,	Henry Riece, ...	Augt. 20th,	Oct. 20th.
Joseph Burcele, ...	4th,	David Baar, ...	Augt. 20th,	Oct. 20th.
Peter Long, ...	4th,	Leonhard Dihler, .	Augt. 20th,	Oct. 20th.
James Bourland, ...	4th,	William Patton, ..	Augt. 20th,	Oct. 20th.
Lorentz Borst, ...	4th,	John Shiten Helm, say clippertohr.	Augt. 20th,	Oct. 20th.
Peter Mearow, ...	4th,	Thomas Sleamens,	Augt. 20th,	Oct. 20th.
Frederick Byroth, ...	4th,	John Watt, ...	Augt. 20th,	Oct. 20th.
Michael Sauder, ...	4th,	John Buckwalter,.	Augt. 20th,	Oct. 20th.
Joseph Hamphill, ...	4th,	James Alleson, ...	Augt. 20th,	Oct. 20th.
Abm. Hare, ...	4th,	Thos. Man, ...	Augt. 20th,	Oct. 20th.
Joseph Brown, ...	4th,	Robert Caldwell,..	Augt. 20th,	Oct. 20th.
Frederick Mellinger, ...	4th,	Martin Mixell, ...	Augt. 20th,	Oct. 20th.
Isaac Farlow, ...	4th,	Daniel Wittmore,..	Augt. 20th,	Oct. 20th.
Michael Reinhart, ...	4th,	James Cooper, ...	Augt. 20th,	Oct. 20th.
Martin Eyler, ...	4th,	Samuel Harris, ...	Augt. 20th,	Oct. 20th.
Mathew McClung, ...	.....	....	Augt. 20th,	Oct. 20th.
Samuel Watt, ...	.....	....	Augt. 20th,	Oct. 20th.
George Kurtz, ...	.....	....	Augt. 20th,	Oct. 20th.
John Guise, ...	.....	....	Augt. 20th,	Oct. 20th.
William Henrey, ...	.....	....	Augt. 20th,	Oct. 20th.
John McComsey, ...	.....	....	Augt. 20th,	Oct. 20th.
John Handerson, ...	.....	....	Augt. 20th,	Oct. 20th.
John Armor, ...	.....	John Gordon, ...	Augt. 20th,	Oct. 20th.
John McKinley, ...	.....	....	Augt. 20th,	Oct. 20th.
Robert Auld, ...	.....	....	Augt. 20th,	Oct. 20th.
Arhd. McNeal, ...	.....	....	Augt. 20th,	Oct. 20th.
Garret Cowen, ...	.....	....	Augt. 20th,	Oct. 20th.
Patrick McVay, ...	.....	....	Augt. 20th,	Oct. 20th.
Thomas Skiles, ...	.....	say James, ...	Augt. 20th,	Oct. 20th.
Jacob Keller, ...	.....	....	Augt. 20th,	Oct. 20th.
John Simpson, ...	.....	Chrisn. Echternacht	Augt. 20th,	Oct. 20th.
Jacob Heckman, ...	.....	....	Augt. 20th,	Oct. 20th.

A LIST OF THE CLASSES OF CAPT. JOHN SLETER'S COMPANY OF THE 1ST BATTALION OF LANCASTER COUNTY, NOVR. 10TH, 1781. (c.)

1st Class.

Martin Grove.
Daniel Keepots.
Henry Landis.
Wm. Hains.
Jacob Rorer.
Andrew Hellar.
David Rorer.
Christian Rorer.
Henry Buckwalter.
George Kesbler.
Christian Hartman.
John Burkholder.
George Bard.
George Young.
Henry Tetrick.
Henry Peck.
Philip Bard.

2d Class.

Peter Mosser.
Jacob Pickel.
Benjamin Whitmore.
Jacob Hofman.
John Fowler.
Jacob Stopher.
Christian Trybot.
John Ebright.
John Scott.
Jacob Keithler.
Benjamin Overstake.

3d Class.

Isaac Rorer.
Jacob Crider.
John Seager.
Martin Mosser.
Conrad Shits.
Abram Buckwalter.
Ben. Landis.
Saml. Young.
Christian Low.

4th Class.

Jacob Stopher.
Robert Rudick.
Daniel Whitmore.
John Millar.
Abram Downer.
John Binkley.
Samuel Watt.
John Christy.
Dewalt Spring.
George Curts.
Abram Whitmore.
Benjamin Carpenter.
John Gice.

5th Class.

John Crider.
John Kirk.
Joseph Bowman.
Henry Hartman.
John Landis, Sr.
John Landis, Junr.

Christian Ford.
John Rodacre.
Isaac Farlow.
Jonas Roup.
Christian Hartman, Jr.
Andrew Shanike.
Abram Buckwalter.
Wm. Finley.
John Busham.
Jno. Moore.

6th Class.

John Stopher.
Leonard Bender.
Jacob Landis.
George Shingle.
Tobias Wanner.
Daniel Millar.
Henry Whitmore.
Jacob Kirk.
Martin Mellinger.
John Roatney.
Henry Shoot.
Henry Locker.
Jacob Roop.
Fredk. Hersh.

7th Class.

George Kendrick.
David Grove.
John Buckwalter.
Tobias Crider.
Jeremiah Kirk.
Nicholass Hess.
John Craig.
Jacob Shumake.
Henry Amens.
Henry Gall.
Conrad Nishwender.
Henry Smith.
James Dotty.
John Sheets.

8th Class.

John Jonce.
Daniel Server.
Adam Lefever.
Christian Yorty.
Abram Landis.
Ulrick Huber.
Philip Busham.
John Gibbony.
John Lonce.
Charles Rynhart.
John Brown.
Adam Clemens.

I Do Certify that the above Class Role is Just and true.

JOHN SLETER,
Capt.

LIST OF THE CLASSES IN CAPTAIN ENOCH HASTINGS COMPANY, NOV. 10TH, 1781. (c.)

1st Class.

William Chamberlain.
James Douglass.
Joseph Dickenson.
Samuel Johnston.
James Sterrat.
Wm. Cambell.
Samuel White.

2d Class.

Joseph Hall.
John Millar.
David Sterrat.
Charles Colwell.
Stewart Monteith.

3d Class.

Joseph Whitehill.
Robert Byars.
Frederick Baker.
Joseph Moore.
Josiah Brodley.
John Leviston.
John Whitehill, Light Horse.
George McDill.

4th Class.

James Henderson.
James Allison.
John Harris.
John Anderson.
William Fullerton.
Robert Colwell.
William Hervey.
John Watt.
James Gibb.
John Henderson.
Ellis Teter.

5th Class.

James Boyd.
William Wallace.
Joseph Warner.
Isaac Taylor.
John Clemson.
John Hannan.
Thomas Johnston.
Amos Slaymaker.
Wm. Boone.
John Hopper.

6th Class.

William Linvill.
John Allison.
James Allison.
John Hastings.
Christey Bower.
James Auld.
William Clera.
Isaac Linvill.

7th Class.

Josiah Ensin.
Moses Auld.
Jonathan Hore.
William Goudy.
Thomas Clemson.
Andrew Attleman.
Thomas Craig.

8th Class.

Archibald Henderson.
Thomas Henderson.
William Liviston.
Leonard Elmaker.
John Middleton.
Paul McGown.
Barnard Laferty.
Christopher Griffith.
David Whitehill.
Christian.

I do Certify the above is a just and true state of my company.

ENOCH HASTINGS,
Capt.

8TH COMPANY, 1ST BATT. LANC. CO. MILITIA, 1781. WM. BRISBEN, CAPT. (c.)

Comisoned Officers.

Captain.

William Brisben.

Lieutenant.

William Wilson.

Ensign.

George Whitehill.

Sergeants.

Colen Marten.
James McPike.

1st Class.

Archibald McCurdy.
David Cowan.
Thomas McNeall.
Jacob Kizer, Jur.
Joseph Wike.
Daniel Fleming.
James Cowan.
Dinnies Harkens.
John Cowan.
Alexr. McFadden.
Edward Rachford.
Jacob Euroch.

2d Class.

Michel Grahm.
James Douglass.
Michel McCloskey.
Charles Murrey.
James Gault.
James Wilson.
Charles Jacobs.
Patrick Milholem.

3d Class.

James Johnston.
Hugh Forgey.
John Beggs.
John Gorden.
Andrew Lytle.
Jacob Kurtz.
Michel Jack.
Robert Potts.
Daniel Harkens.
William Andrew.
Robert Mathers.
John Sharraden.
James Shannon.
Alexr. Brown.

4th Class.

John Douglass.
Wm. Armstrong.
Christen Kurtz.
William Patton.
Thomas Siemons, Senr.
John Coop.
John Armor.
John McKinnley.
Jacob Bleazur.
Robert Auld.
Samuel Holaday.
Archd. McNeall.
Garret Cowan.
Patrick McVea.
Thomas Clark.
James Watters.

5th Class.

Joseph Belford.
Adam Gault.
James Hughs.
Robert Houston.
John Crosbey.
William Lee.
John Plank, Jur.
George Rutter.
Andw. Cullen.
George Boyd.
Mathew Henderson.
James Lytle.
George Kiser.
James Borland.
James Armor.
Samuel Coop.
Patrick King.
Wilm. Slemons.

6th Class.

Joseph Welch.
Edward Runshaw.
James Watson.
Alexr. Brown, stiller.
Robert Huey.
James Anderson.
Archd. McAfee.
Andw. Smith.
Nethaniel Rutter.
Jacob Pee.

George Stever.
James Whitehill.
John Hemphill.
Joseph Beggs.

7th Class.

James McFadden.
William Richardson.
Jacob Hains.
Wilm. Holaday.
Wilm. Cowan.
Lenord Euroch.
Samuel Hughs.
Moses Wilson.
George McIntier.
Joseph Hains.
Wilm. Coday.
Charles McIlhenney.

8th Class.

William Boyd.
Samuel Armor.
John McComb.
Thomas Henderson.
Robert Cowan.
James Dunlap.
John Murphey.
John McGown.
James McCafferty.
David Harris.
James Hamilton.
William Burchill.
John Wrigert.
Terrance Falls.
Samson Wilson.

Certified by

WM. BRISBEN,
Capt.

A RETURN OF THE 5, 6, 7, & 8 CLASES OF MY COMPANY TO MARCH BY IN YEAR 178?. JOHN GRAHAM, CAPT. (c.)

5th Class.

James Beverland.
James Lusk.
Michael Graham.
James Buchanan.
Jaret Graham.
Mathew Buchanon.
Elice Chapman.
Samuel Lacy.
Robert Lusk.
Israel Irwin.

6th Class.

James Hanah.
Samuel Christy.
John Gatt.
Ezekel Irwin.
Isaac Tregor.
Abraham Graham.
James Gatt.
Samuel Gardner.

7th Class.

John Henock.	Robert Hineman.
William Hunter.	William Willson.
Mathew Marten.	James Cambel.
John Soock.	Jacob Matsibachr.
Jacob parker.	Jame Sceen.

8th Class.

Jacob Lacy.	James kerr.
Daniel Graham.	Ezekel Thomas.
Jacob Milison.	Nathaniel Porter.
Christian Fisher.	Owen Thomas.
William Logan.	William Cloud.

MUSTER ROLL OF THE 5, 6 & 7 OF THE FIRST BATALION LANR. COUNTY MILITIA ON A TOUER OF DUTY TO BUCK'S COUNTY. (c.)

Names of Persons who perform a tour of duty.	What Class.	Names of Persons who furnished substitutes.	Time when Duty Commenced.	Time when Duty Ended.
Capt. Martin Huey.			1781.	1781.
Lieut. William Wilson.				
Ensgn. Jacob Bear.				
Adjud.				
——— Armor.				
Qr. Mar. Alex.				
Ensgn. George Whitehill.				
Adjud.				
——— Armor.				

ROLL OF THE 5, 6 & 7 CLASS OF THE 1ST BATALION —Continued.

Names of Persons who perform a tour of duty.	What Class.	Names of Persons who furnished substitutes.	Time when Duty Commenced.	Time when Duty Ended.
Qr. Mar.			1781.	1781.
Alexr. Brown,.				
Privates.				
Henrey Shute.				
James Boyd, ...	......	Hugh Mc euing.		
Isaac Ferrey.				
Thomas Love.				
Charles McGowen.				
John McCoye,				
James Moore,				
Jacob Meyer, ...	......	Robert Brinsler.		
John Underwood.				
James Bowd.				
Oliver Montgomery.				
Conrad Nesents Winter.				
Christopher ford.				
William Ramsey.				
Samuel McComsey.				
Martin Heller, ...	......	John Hamilton.		
Bastian Shenck,				
Joseph Belford.				
Adam Gault.				
Robert Huston.				
Robert Potts, ...	......	George Boyd.		
Patrick King.				
William Armstrong.				
James Ould.				
Alexr. Ligget.				
John Johnston.				
Robert McCurday.				
Jacob Fralley, ...	......	William Logar		
John McCollistor, ...				
Robert Crab.				
Edward Runshaw.				
James Smith, ...	......	Abraham Kurtz.		
James Wattson.				
James Anderson.	......	William Burckard.		
Adam Ekels.				
Archd. McOffett.				
Andrew Smith.				
John Hamphill.				
Joseph Baggs.				
Josia Ervin, ...	......	Barnard Dimsey.		
Joseph Alles.				
Moses Awl.				

ROLL OF THE 5, 6 & 7 CLASS OF THE 1ST BATALION —Continued.

Names of Persons who perform a tour of duty.	What Class.	Names of Persons who furnished substitutes.	Time when Duty Commenced.	Time when Duty Ended.
			1781.	1781.
Thomas Creed.				
Cornilis Tree.				
James Huse,	.....	James Winter.		
Andrew Collin.				
Thomas Lekey.				
John Williams.				
Henrey Smith.				
Samuel McClitey.				
Joseph Shanck.				
William Willson.				
John Mallor,	.....	Jacob Drum.		
John Boyd,	.....	Daniel Harkings.		
Henrey Bushman,	.....	John Andrew.		
Thomas Clarck,	.....	James Scot.		
Samuel McChley, Jr.				
Jacob Hart,	.....	——— Simons.		
William Holleday,	.....	Dennis Harckens.		
William Carvrey,	.....	Hugh McBrid		
William Cowdey.				
David Wittmore.				
Christian Hearbmond,	.....	John Segar.		
John Moore.				
George McOher.				
Jacob Miller.				
John Pursley,	.....	Jacob Line.		
John Lind,	.....	Michael Garner.		
Peter Horse.				
James Henrey,	.....	David Line.		
Edward Harkey.				
Henrey Lokert.				
John Mcfadeen.				
Joseph Wellsh.				
Owin Thomas.				
John Potts.				
John Ellison,	.....	Jacob Hains.		
Robert Hughy.				
John Cramer.				
Moses Willson.				
William Hunter,	.....	Robt. Charlonton.		
James Shannon.				
George Stuart.				
Neal Kenney.				
George Thomas,	.....	Leonard Bender.		
William Cody,	.....	Mathew Henderson.		

A RETURN OF THE 8 COMPANY AND FIRST BATTALION L. C. M. FROM OCTR. 7TH, 1782. (c.)

WM. BRISBEN,
Capt.

1st Class.

Joseph Wike.

2d Class.

James Douglass.

3d Class.

Jacob Curtz.

4th Class.

Christen Curtz.

5th Class.

John Plank.
Mathew Henderson.
Samuel Coop.

7th Class.

Jacob Hains.
Joseph Hains.

MUSTER ROLL OF CAPT. WM. BRISBEN'S COMPANY 1ST BATTALION, LANCASTER CO. 1782. (c.)

Captain.
William Brisben.

Lieutenant.
William Wilson.

Ensign.
George Whitehill.

1st Class.

Daniel Fleming.
Thomas McNeall.
Jacob Kiser, Jur.
Joseph Wike.
Daniel Harkens.
Alexr. Mcfadden.
James Gault, Jur.
James Warren.
John Dunlap.
John Kizeer.

2d Class.

Michel Grahem. Patrick Melholem.
James Douglass. John Thompson.
Charles Murrey. John Skiles.
James Gault, Jur. Charles Caldwell.
James Wilson. James Mcpike.
Charles Jacobs. Mathew Marten.

3d Class.

James Johnston. Robert Mathers.
Hugh Forgey. John Sharreden.
John Beggs. Alexr. Brown.
John Gorden. George Landers.
Andw. Lytle. Daniel McDonnel.
Jacob Kurtz. David Cowan, Jur.
Daniel Harkens. James Shannon.
William Andrew. Robert potts.

4th Class.

John Douglass, Surgen. Archd. McNeall.
William Armstrong. Garret Cowan.
Christen Curtz. James Watters.
William patton. Isaac Ricnardson.
Thomas Siemens, Jur. Robert McNeall.
John Armor. John Watt.
John McKinnley. Thomas Skiles.

5th Class.

Joseph Belford. Mathew hendeison.
Adam Gault. George Kizer.
James Hughs. Samuel Coop.
John Crosbey. Patrick king.
John plank, Jur. John McCartey.
George Rutter. Arch'd Henderson.
Andw. Cullen. John Kettle.
George Boyd.

6th Class.

Joseph Welch. Nethaniel Rutter.
Edwd: Runshaw. James Whitehill.
Alexr. Brown, Stilr. Joseph Boggs.
Robert Huey. Peter Rapp.
James Anderson. Isaac Gilkeson.
Archd. McAfee. Christen Bower.
Andw. Smith. Thomas Siemens, Jur.

7th Class.

James Mcfadden.	Charles McIlhenney.
William Richardson.	Charles Rowan.
Jacob Hains.	John purrel.
William Holaday.	William Boyd, Jur.
William Cowan.	Patrick Shealds.
Lenord Enroch.	Owen Thomas.
Moses Wilson.	Ludwick kyle.
George McIntier.	Samuel Armor.
Joseph Hains.	Robert Hineman.

8th Class.

William Boyd, Stllr.	James Hamilton.
Samuel Armor.	William Burchell.
Thomas Henderson.	John Wright.
Robert Cowan.	James Robeson.
James Dunlap.	Abraham Bower.
John Murphey.	Robert Wright.
John McGowan.	John Wisharts.

Muster Role, 1782.

A TRUE AND EXACT LIST OF THE NAMES, OF EACH AND EVERY MALE WHITE PERSON, INHABITING OR RESIDING WITHIN MY DISTRICT, IN THE FIRST COMPANY, OF THE FIRST BATTALION OF LANCASTER COUNTY MILITIA BETWEEN THE AGE OF EIGHTEEN AND FIFTY-THREE YEARS. TAKEN FOR THE YEAR 1782. (c.)

Captain.
John Sleter.

Lieutenant.
James Henry.

Ensign.
Nicholus Shriner.

Almonar.
Philip Busham, Sr.

1st Class.

Mart Grove.	George Bard.
Daniel Keeports.	Henry Tetrick.
Henry Landis.	Philip Bard.
Jacob Rorer.	John Hersh.
Andrew Heller.	Fredrick Seigmiller.
David Rorer.	Jacob Miller.
Christ. Rorer.	Henry Peachley.
Peter Busham.	Jos. Hepple.
Henry Buckwalter.	Abrm. Downer, Jr.
Baltzer Thumb.	George Young.
Christ Hartman, Jr.	James Reaken.
Jno. Burkholder.	William Evans.

2d Class.

Peter Moser.	John Highsey.
Jacob Pickle.	John Gasner.
Benj. Whitmore.	William Russel.
John Fowler.	Philip Meck.
Jacob Stofer, Jr.	John Shaffer.
John Ebright.	Benj. Brown.
John Scott.	Peter Sipe.
Benj. Overstake.	Barnard Turner.
Jos. Highsey.	

3d Class.

John Sayger.	Samuel Young.
Conrod Shitz.	Christ. Low.
Isaac Rorer.	Stephen Atkinson.
Jacob Crider.	Isaac Leafavor.
Mart Moser.	Adam Alow.
Abrm. Buckwalter.	Stophel Bard.
Benj. Landis.	

4th Class.

Jacob Stofer, Sr.	John Christy, Jr.
Robert Rudick.	George Curtz.
John Miller.	Christ. Miller.
Abraham Downer, Sr.	Luke Rhenmer.
John Binkley.	George Garnieghen.
Saml. Watt.	Philip Hoffman.

5th Class.

John Crider.
John Busham.
Jos. Bowman.
Henry Hartman.
John Landis, Sr.
John Landis, Jr.
Christefer Fordd.
John Roadaker.
Isaac Farlow.
Christ. Hartman, Sr.
Abrm. Buckwalter.
John Moor, Jr.
Henry Wander Baugh.

6th Class.

John Stofer.
Leonard Bender.
Jacob Landis.
George Shingle.
Tobias Wanner.
Daniel Miller.
Henry Whitmore.
Jacob Kirk.
Mart Melinger.
John Reakey.
Henry Loker.
Jacob Roop.
Frederick Hersh.
John Melinger.
Henry Busham.
Christ. Jonce.
Robert Parker.
John Meck.
Samuel Moore.
Henry Kendrick.

7th Class.

George Kendrick.
David Grove.
John Buckwalter.
Tobias Crider, Jr.
Jeremiah Kirk.
Nichos. Hess.
John Craig.
Henry Amens.
Henry Gail.
Henry Smith.
Jacob Meck.
Conrad Fry.
Micheal Bard.
Henry Rorer.
Tobias Beam.
Benj. Buckwalter.

8th Class.

John Shonce.
Daniel Suver.
Adam Leafavor.
Christ. Yorty.
Abrm. Landis.
Philip Busham.
John Giboney.
John Lonce.
Charls Rinehart.
Adam Cleamens.
John Rorer.
John Walmer, Jr.
John Lutz.
Christ. Lonce.
Valentine Fritz.
John Neaff.
Henry Christy.
William at Stofer.

I do Swear, on the Holy Evengilest of Almighty God: That the above list is a just and true state of the Male White

Inhabitants, residing in my District, agreeable to Law, and without any fraud to the State, to the best of my knowledge.

JOHN SLETER.

Sworn before me this Eighth Day of May, 1782.

JOHN HOPKINS, Sub-Lt.

The above names Bloted before Return made.

JOHN SLETER.

A TRUE AND EXACT LIST OF THE NAMES, OF EACH AND EVERY MALE WHITE PERSON, INHABITING OR RESIDING, WITHIN MY DISTRICT, IN THE SECOND COMPANY, OF THE FIRST BATTALION OF LANCASTER COUNTY, MILITIA, BETWEEN THE AGE OF EIGHTEEN AND FIFTY-THREE YEARS. TAKEN FOR THE YEAR 1782. (c.)

Capt.
Enoch Hastings.

Lieut.
William McCulauh.

Ens.
Thomas Henderson.

Almonar.
William Hamilton.

Adjutant.
Thomas Boyd.

Privates.

1st Class.

Wilum Chemberlin.
James Duglass.
Joseph Dickeson.
Samuel Johnson.
James Staret.
Samuel Whyt.
Robart Bakim.
James O'Dare.
Robart Hite.

2nd Class.

Joseph Hall.
John Millir.
Daved Staret.
Stuard Menteeth.

John Allison.
John Richeson.
Gorg Burger.
Daved Hore.

3rd Class.

Joseph Whithil.
Robart Byars.
Fredrick Baker.
Joseph More.

John Leveston.
John Whithil.
Mikel Gake.
Robart Dill.

4th Class.

James Alleson.
John Hares.
Willum fullerton.
Robart Coldwell.
Willum Henery.
James Gib.

John Hendeson.
Elles Tater.
Grify Hendeson.
John Hoite.
James Waters.

5th Class.

James Boyd.
John Clemson.
Thomas Johnson.

Amas Slamaker.
Danul Buckley.
Willum Wallis.

6th Class.

Willum Linvil.
John Alleson.
James Alleson.
John Hastings.
Willum Armstrong.
Isak Linvil.

Jacob pee.
Georg Stevers.
Jacop McDill.
Thomas Linvil.
James McFadden.

7th Class.

Josiah Erwain.
Johnnathen Hore.
Thomas Clemson.
John Dunlap.
John Boyd.

John Hoper.
John Carson.
John king.
Henery Smith.
James Shannon.

8th Class.

Archeble Henderson.
Willum Leveston.
Lenard Elmaker.

John Midelton.
Willum Watson.
Barney Laforty.

Christyfor Grify.
Daved Whithill.
Chrisly Humble.
James Leveston.
Thomas Hares.
James McCafferty.

I Do Swear, on the Holy Evengilest of Almighty God: That the above list is a just and true state, of the Male White Inhabitants, residing in my District, agreeable to Law, and without any fraud to the State, to the best of my knowledge.

ENOCH HASTINGS,
Capt.

Sworn before me this Eleventh Day of May, 1782.

JOHN HOPKINS.

A TRUE AND EXACT LIST OF THE NAMES, OF EACH AND EVERY MALE WHITE PERSON, INHABITING OR RESIDING, WITHIN MY DISTRICT IN THE THIRD COMPANY OF THE FIRST BATTALION OF LANCASTER COUNTY MILITIA, BETWEEN THE AGE OF EIGHTEEN AND FIFTY-THREE YEARS. TAKEN FOR THE YEAR 1782. (c.)

Capt.
Mathias Slaymaker.

Lieu.
Thomas Buffington.

Ens.
Adam Drauker.

Privates.
1st Class.

Thomas White.
Peter Tayler.
Conrad Gram.
John Miller.
Samuel Lefever, Junr.
Henry Slaymaker, Senr.
Balser Barkman.
Abraham Carpenter.
Balser Peterman.
Frank Rowe.
John Barr.
Samuel Messer.
John Brackbill.
George Pursley.

2nd Class.

George Carpenter. Peter Shomaker.
George McCullough. Peter Carpenter.
Alixr. White. Henry Slaymaker, Junr.
John Slaymaker, Junr. George Irigh.
John Tenlinger. Joseph Allison.
Constantine Winagh. Robt. Crosbey.

3rd Class.

Jacob Esleman. Jacob Stambaugh.
Thomas Renney. Nicholas Walter.
Jacob Stotsaberger. Abraham Lefever.
Daniel Peek. Henry Peterman.
David Foster. Benjamin Bower.
John Ferree.

4th Class.

John Tayler. Daniel Hustan.
Daniel Ferree. Adam Birly.
Peter Steman. Joseph Lefever.
Frederick Derr. Michael Myer.
Jacob Barkman. Isaack Widows.
Paul Trout. Robt. Buchamen.
Peter Lefever.

5th Class.

Isaac Ferree. Robt. Ligit.
Charles McGowen. Henry Stoufer.
Wm. Tayler. Wm. Foster.
Jacob Ludwick, Junr. John Harkins.
John Williams. Wm. Ramsey.
James Kelley.

6th Class.

Henry Stambaugh. Wm. Gram.
Hieranimous Bireley. Soloman Hema.
John Graft. Torrance Duffye.
Michael Hass. Henry Bertholomew.
David Whitmore. George McIlwaine.
Valentine Myer.

7th Class.

Jacob Bower. Conrad Coon.
Cornelious Ferree. Thomas Ferree.
Thomas Lackey. John Carpenter.
John Barkman. John Lesher.

Jacob Ferree.
Thomas Kraig.
Jacob Brumbacker.
Joseph Bower.
Wm. Mash.

8th Class.

George Sando.
Nicholas Hull.
Danl. Slaymaker.
Wm. Ferree.
James Kenney, Junr.
John Foster.
Michael Bower.
James Quigley.
Andw. Ferree.
James Rodgers.
Robt. Neal.
Wm. Slaymaker, Junr.
Wm. Slaymaker, Senr.
John Sheepstable.
George Ruchart.

I Do Swear, on the Holy Evengilest of Almighty God: That tne above list is a just and true state, of the Male White Inhabitants, residing in my District, agreeable to Law, and without any fraud to the State, to the best of my knowledge.

THOMAS BUFFINGTON,
Lieut.

Sworn before me this twentieth Day of May, 1782.

JOHN HOPKINS.

A TRUE AND EXACT LIST OF THE NAMES, OF EACH AND EVERY MALE WHITE PERSON, INHABITING OR RESIDING, WITHIN MY DISTRICT, IN THE FOURTH COMPANY, OF THE FIRST BATTALION OF LANCASTER COUNTY, MILITIA, BETWEEN THE AGE OF EIGHTEEN AND FIFTY-THREE YEARS. TAKEN FOR THE YEAR 1782. (c.)

Captain.
William Skiles.

Lieutenant.
Abram Henry.

Ensign.
David Glen.

First Class.

Robert Stewart.
Daniel Basor.
Alexdr. Millar.
John Eby.
James Abram.
Wm. Mathers.
Henry Hartman.
Abram Sensnich.
peter Lemon.
Mick Stever.
James Hamilton, Jr.

Second Class.

Joseph Evits.
William Whitehill.
Joseph Rutter, Jr.
Benjamin Hern.
Wm. Hamilton.
John Hamilton, Jr.
George Alexander.
Wm. porter.
John Leru.
John Crawford.

Third Class.

Jacob Sensnich.
Ben. Crawford.
James McNeal.
Benjamin Vernon.
Joseph Rutter, Sr.
Andrew Caldwell.
Robt. Simpson.
Danl. Huston.
Thomas Fullerton.
James Knox.
Wm. McCanless.
John Musser.
Adam Millar.
George Stewart, Sr.
Archibald Montgomery.
Wm. Borton.

Fourth Class.

Matthew McClung.
James Skiles.
Isaac Ferree.
John Rush.
Archbd. Gormley.
Harmon Skiles.
Emanuel Ferree.
Brice Clark.
John Twebit.

Fifth Class.

John Abram.
John McCoy.
James Moore.
Jacob Myers.
John Underwood.
James Boyle.
Oliver Montgomery.
Robert Young.
Robert Knox.
Christian Sharp.
John Shaver.
John Rutter, Jr.

Sixth Class.

George Seldomridge.
Alexdr. Liggot.
David Watson.
John Johnston.
George Leru.
Peter Millar.
Robt. McCurdy.
Thomas Harris.
James McA. Naul.
Hugh McClung.
Andrew Oliver.

Seventh Class.

Wm. Montgomery.
Abram Gibbons.
Balsor Basor.
Wm. Rutter.
John McFadden.
Danl. McCallister.
Wm. Lightner.
Adam Lightner.
John Henry.
Saml. McAllilly.
James peel.
Stophel Kling.
Joseph Shank.
Joseph Trimble.
Joseph Ellis.
Wm. Wilson.
Isaac Lemon.
George Stewart, Jr.
Wm. Skiles, Jr.
Danl. Lemon.
John Wilson.
John Rutter.

Eighth Class.

William Hamilton.
Hervey Biggart.
Ephraim McCollom.
Thomas Lyon.
John Teply.
Hugh Hamilton.
Nathaniel Lightner.
Daniel Herbert.
Wm. Huston.
John McComb.
Wm. Wa.son.
Wm. Crow.
Wm. Randles.
Wm. McCausland, Sr.
David Ault.

I Do Swear, on the Holy Evengilest of Almighty God: That the above list is a just and true state, of the Male White Inhabitants, residing in my District, agreeable to Law, and without any fraud to the State, to the best of my knowledge.

WM. SKILES.

Sworn before me this 19th day of Augt., 1782.

JOHN HOPKINS,
Sub-Lt.

A TRUE AND EXACT LIST OF THE NAMES, OF EACH AND EVERY MALE WHITE PERSON, INHABITING AND RESIDING, WITHIN MY DISTRICT, IN THE FIFTH COMPANY, OF THE FIRST BATTALION OF LANCASTER COUNTY, MILITIA, BETWEEN THE AGE OF EIGHTEEN, AND FIFTY-THREE YEARS. TAKEN FOR THE YEAR 1782. (c.)

Capt.

Edmond Lintner.

Lieu.

Samuel Hawthorn.

Privates.

First Class.

John Eckman.
John Verner.
Simon Hynold.
Peter hole.
Peter Rush.
John Hare, J'r.
Henry Eckman.
Jacob Millar, Carpt'r.
John White.
philip Casler.
John Rasor.
Jacob Millar, Jun'r.
Henry Isaberger.
John Markley.
Jerry Rae.
Conrad Shaver.
John Hawry.
Andrew Rush.
Wm. Fegan.

Second Class.

Peter ———.
John Brewar.
Peter Kline.
Jacob Fight.
John Terriflinger.
George Swartsley.
James Williams.

Third Class.

Jacob Frits.
Wm. Logan.
Jacob Rush.
Christian Shap.
Henry Hare.
Nicholas Sorreras.
John Foundersmith.
Wm. Huggins.
John Cremer.
Jacob Drum.
George Rine.
Nicholas Nebely.
Balser Ramberger.
Michal Rine.
Cutlip Hartman.

Fourth Class.

John Shittenhelm.
Martin Kendrick.
John Brubaker.
Joseph Otterbough.
Jacob Sides.
Daniel Millar.
Christian Martin.
Jacob Eckman.
Christian Eternaught.
Simon Millar.
Jacob Fouts, Jr.
peter Shot.
Jacob Roup.
Dan'l Young.
Martin Bear.

Fifth Class.

Conrad Haak.
Robert Charlton.
Henry huber.
John Cremer Cooper.
Abram Hare.
Michal Fouts.
John Small, Jr.
John Road.
John Kendrick.
James Brown.
Georg Haak.
peter Good.
Alexd'r Work.
Rob't McComsy.

Sixth Class.

Jacob Frelich.
Jacob Neff.
Henry Rush.
Jacob Millar.
Samuel Millar.
John Moore.
Charles philips.
philip Bear.
Felty Fronk.
Ludwick Rinhart.
John McComsy.
Dan'l Shultz.
John Kendrick.
Abram Calliday.

Seventh Class.

John Withers.
Valentine Fundersmith.
Henry Bowman.
John Bear.
Jacob Eckman.
Daniel Bowman.
Henry Buchman.
Nicholas Macky.
peter Shofstall.
Martin Hare.
Henry Kendrick.
Fred Smyth.
George Myers.
Wm. Calliday.
Dan'l Carron.
Fred. Turner.
Rob't McClelland.

Eighth Class.

John Stoutsberger.
Mathias Millar.
Christian Sholts.
Martin Stoll.
Jacob Kendrick.
Henry Stoner.
Henry Road.
Daniel Mowra.

Michal Mires.
Abram Brubaker.
George May.
John Hare.
John Morrison.
Joseph Wahob.
Henry Dickhoover.

I Do swear on the Holy Evengilest of Almighty God; That the above list is a just and true state of the Male white Inhabitants residing in my District, agreeable to Law and without any fraud to the State, to the best of my knowledge.

EDMOND LINTNER, Capt.

Sworn before me this 23d Day of September, 1782.

JOHN HOPKINS.

A TRUE AND EXACT LIST OF THE NAMES, OF EACH AND EVERY MALE WHITE PERSON, INHABITING OR RESIDING, WITHIN MY DISTRICT, IN THE SIXTH COMPANY, OF THE FIRST BATTALION OF LANCASTER COUNTY MILITIA, BETWEEN THE AGES OF EIGHTEEN AND FIFTY-THREE YEARS. TAKEN FOR THE YEAR 1782. (c.)

Captain.

Samuel Henry.

Lieutenant.

John Brisband.

Ensign.

Henry Diffenbough.

Almonar.

Daniel Leamon, Senr.

First Class.

James Smith, Senr.
Andraw Allison.
Jacob Dinglinger.
Abraham Leamon.
Robert Smith.
William Meloney.
Joseph Norton.
Martin Kendrick.
John Driver.

Second Class.

Joseph Smith.
John Hamble.
David Miller.
Frances Hare.
Christian Hemerly.
William Feagan.
Joseph Buckwalter.
Benjaman Bowman.
Jacob Rees.
Dewolt Spring.
Martin Kitch.
Henry hoover.
John Harnish.
John Lerew.

Third Class.

James Smith, Junr.
George Leamon.
Peter Miller.
John Whitmoor.
George Withers.
Frances Smith.
Isack Kendrick.
Steven Goff.
Jonas Cofman.
Jacob Joner.
Christian Leamon.

Fourth Class.

Allixr. Leamon.
John Hare.
Samuel Hanes.
Christian Miller.
Daniel Meloney.
Abraham Hare.
Abraham Dinlinger.
Christian Eyman.
Felty Stoner.
Daniel Kendrick.
Jonas Roup.

Fifth Class.

Jacob Hartmon.
Jacob Leamon.
John Furee.
Isack Hanes.
Conrod Spiteer.
Christian Miller.
Daniel Hanes.
Joseph Snider.
John Miller.
Melcher milinger.

Sixth Class.

John Neal.
Fredrick Pouts.
Henry Spiteer.
John Nestlrot.
Jacob Weavor.
David Swisher.
David Hare.
Henry Eyman.
Daniel Norton.
Martin Miley.
Christian Rora.
John Inery, Junr.
Jacob Miller.
Robert McCullquin.
Peter Thomas.
Calip Branan.

Seventh Class.

Henry Fults.
Abraham Longnaker.
Henry Speelman.
Benjaman 'Williams.
Daniel Lefavour.
Windle Bowman.
John Devenboch.
George Devenboch.
Christian Hare.
Phillip Barnet.
John Longnaker.
John Snebly.
John Milley.
William Allixsander.
Henry Gaul.
Bornet Howser.
Peter Ekman.

Eighth Class.

Petter Bresler.
Benjaman Sowder.
John Fults.
Christian Denglinger.
Thomas Evans.
Thomas Williams.
Abraham Snebly.
John Weavour.
Samuel Meloney.
Benjaman Hare.
Nickalas Bresler.
Henry Rees.
Henry Martin.
Fredrick Smith.
John Smith.
John Funk.
John Fury, Senr.
John Graham.
Henry Shoop.
Mical Shurts.
Henry Kendrick.

I Do swear on the Holy Evengilest of Almighty God: That the above list is a just and true state of the Male white Inhabitants, residing in my District, agreeable to Law and without any fraud to the State, to the best of my knowledge.

Sworn before me this Eight Day of May, 1782.

JOHN HOPKINS, Sub. Lt.

The above names Blotted before Return made.

SAMUEL HENRY.

A TRUE AND EXACT LIST OF THE NAMES OF EACH AND EVERY MALE WHITE PERSON INHABITING OR RESIDING WITHIN MY DISTRICT, IN THE SEVENTH COMPANY OF THE FIRST BATTALION OF LANCASTER COUNTY MILITIA, BETWEEN THE AGE OF EIGHTEEN AND FIFTY-THREE YEARS. TAKEN FOR THE YEAR 1782. (c.)

Captain.
Martin Huey.

Lieut.
John Rose.

Ensign.
Jacob Bear.

1st Class.

John Roland, Junr.
Jacob Johnsten.
Henery Bare.
William Shelan.
Henery Shively.
Samuel Eaby.
John Kilheifer.
John Hiler.
George Fransuques.
Stophel Shower.
William Wagonman.
Adam Winger.
Lodwick Tetrah.
Samuel Bigart.

2nd Class.

Jacob Swobe.
Petter Eaby, Junr.
John Painter.
Peter Eahler.
Henery Swobe.
Michall Wielan.
George Eahler.
Jacob Shevan.
John Garver.
Moses Johnston.
Hanikel Weaver.

3rd Class.

William Care.
Adam Millar, Ju'r.
Andrew Bare, Ju'r.
John Johnsten.
Joseph Brinten.
Jacob Garver.
Fredrick Doubler.
John Hamilton.
John Garver.
John Care.
Moses Edwards.
Michall Grossman.
Peter Fenefroch.

4th Class.

Abraham Garver.
John Curts.
David Bare.
Isack Garver.
John Buchwalter.
Martin Maxwel.
Abraham Eaby.
Lenard Tiler.
Jacob Deher.
Joseph Eaby.
Henry Winger.

5th Class.

Petter Smith.
John Eaby.
Martin Hiller.
Hugh Caboone.
Daniel Swobe.
Jacob Bine.
Michall Garver.
Isack Rife.
Sebaston Shirk.
John Willson, Ju'r.
Henery Chelllain.
William Abram.

6th Class.

John Molister.
Petter Kilheifer.
Petter, Eaby, Shoemaker.
Henery Peck.
David Line.
Jaco Maxwel.
Michall Vencanen.
Abraham Curts.
Moses Brinten.
Henery Eager.
Adam Ekel.
John Eaby, Jun'r.
Lodwick Wise.

7th Class.

John Maxwel.
George Bard.
Michall Shalabarger.
William Brinten.
Abraham Johnsten.
Samuel McLilley.
James Scott.
John Garver.
Michall Hest.
Michall Bare.
Henery Taig.
Peter Miller.

8th Class.

Jonathen Oans, Ju'r.
David Rife.
Adam Swobe.
Jacob Snevely.
Jacob Shively.
Crisley Myres.
Andrew Maxwel.
David Painter.
Bengaman Oans.
Daniel Eaby.
John Myrs.
John Pots.
Henery Herr.
Alexander Mcleary.

I do swear on the Holy Evenglless of Almighty God: That the above list is a just and true state of the male white Inhabitants residing in my District, agreeable to Law, and without any fraud to the State to the best of my knowledge.

Sworn before me this 13th Day of June, 1782.

JOHN HOPKINS.

MARTIN HUEY.

A TRUE AND EXACT LIST OF THE NAMES OF EACH AND EVERY MALE WHITE PERSON INHABITING OR RESIDING WITHIN MY DISTRICT IN THE EIGHT COMPANY OF THE FIRST BATTALION OF LANCASTER COUNTY MILITIA, BETWEEN THE AGE OF EIGHTEEN AND FIFTY-THREE YEARS. TAKEN FOR THE YEAR 1782. (c.)

Capt.

William Brisben.

Lieut.

William Wilson.

Ens.

George Whitehill.

Almonar.

John Wilson.

First Class.

Daniel Fleming.
Thomas McNeall.
Jacob Kizer, Jun.
Joseph Wike.
Dennis Harrkens.
Alex. McFadden.
James Gault, Ju'r.
James Warren.
John Dunlap.
John Kizer.
Rapp, Sn'r.

Second Class.

Michel Graham.
James Douglass.
Charles Murrey.
James Gault, Sen'r.
James Wilson.
Charles Jacobs.
Patrick Milholem.
John Thompson.
John Skiles.
Charles Caldwell.
James McPike.
Mathew Marten.

Third Class.

James Johnston.
Hugh Forgey.
John Beggs.
John Gorden.
Andrew Lytle.
Jacob Kurtz.
William Andrew.
Robert Mathers.
John Sharraden.
Alex. Brown.
George Landers.
Daniel McDonel.
David Cowan, Ju'r.
James Hopkins.

Fourth Class.

John Douglass, Surgeon.
William Armstrong.
Christen Curtz.
William Patton.
Thomas Siemons, Ju'r.
John Armor.
John McKinley.
Archibald McNeall.
Garret Cowan.
Isaac Richardson.
Robert McNeall.
John Watt.
Thomas Skiles.

Fifth Class.

Joseph Belford.
Adam Gault.
James Hughs.
John Crosbey.
John Plank.
George Rutter.
Andrew Cullen.
George Boyd.
Matthew Henderson.
George Kizer.
James Armor.
Samuel Coap.
Patrick King.
John McCartey.
Arch'd Henderson.
John Kettle.

Sixth Class.

Joseph Weich.
Edward Runshaw.
Alex'r Brown, Stil'r.
Robert Huey.
James Anderson.
Arch'd McAfee.
Nethaniel Rutter.
James Whitehill.
Joseph Beggs.
Petter Rapp.
Isaac Gilkeson.
Christen Bower.
Thomas Siemens, Ju'r.
Henry Kinzer.

Seventh Class.

William Richardson.
Jacob Haines.
William Holadey.
William Cowan.
Lenard Euroch.
Moses Wilson.
George McIntier.
Joseph Haines.
Charles McIlhenney.
Charles Rowan.

John Purrel.
William Boyd, Jur.
Patrick Sheids.
Owen Thomas.
Ludwick Kyle.
Robert Hineman.

Eighth Class.

William Boyd, Stil'r.
Samuel Armor.
Thomas Henderson.
Robert Cowan.
James Dunlap.
John Murphey.
John McGowen.
James Hamilton.
William Burchell.
John Wright.
Abrahm Bower.
Robert Wright.
James Robeson.
John Wishert.

I do swear, on the Holy Evengileat of Almighty God: That the above is a just and true state of the male white Inhabitants residing in my District, agreeable to Law, and without any fraud to the State, to the best of my knowledge.

Sworn before me this thirty first Day of May, 1783.

JOHN HOPKINS.

The above names Bloted before return made.

WM. BRISBEN, Capt.

RETURN OF OFFICERS, ELECTED IN THE FIRST BATTALION OF LANCASTER COUNTY MILITIA, AGREEABLE TO ORDERS PUBLISHED FOR THAT PURPOSE, ON THE 15TH DAY OF APRIL, 1783. (c.)

Field Officers.

Lieu. Colonel.

John Rogers.

Major.

Abraham Latcha.

Captains.

1. James Willison.
2. James McCreight.
3. Ambrose Crane.
4. Michael Brown, Ju'r.
5. William Allan.
6. George Lower.
7. Daniel Bradley.
8. Robert McCollen.

Lieutenants.

James Rogers.
John Robeson.
James Stuart.
John Stone.
John Barnett.
John McFarland.
Jacob Latcha.
Samuel Weir.

Ensigns.

James Wallace.
Robert Greenlee.
Henry Grahams.
John Weaver.
James Willson.
Philip Blissly.
Jacob Stone.
George Killinger.

I certify the above to be a just state agreeable to returns made to me of the officers elected in 1st Batal. Lan. Co's Mil'a.

AD'M HUBLEY, JR., S. Lt. L'r C'o.

A RETURN OF CAPT. M'CALLEN'S COMPANY OF 1ST BATT. LANCASTER COUNTY MILITIA, COL. RODGER'S BATTALION. (c.)

Robert Clark.
Patt. Hays.
Wm. Sawyer.
Arch'd McCallister.
Thos. Mitchel.
David Mitchel.
Jno. Sawyer.
Jas. Sawyer.
Sam. Broadley.
Benj. Sawyer.
Joseph Sawyer.
Wm. Sawyer, Jun.
Wm. Shaw.
David McDonald.
Jas. Donaldson.
David Hays.
Robert Hays.
Jas. McFaddin.
Jno. Hays.
Jas. Willson, Jun.
Robert Wray.
Peter Linawever.
Nicholas Mussar.
Mich'l Nowlen.
Emanuel Kingright.
Anth. Dunlevi.
Thos. McCallen.
Christopr. Erwin.
Robert Crocket.
John Sheakle.
Walter Clark.
And'w Wallace.
Jno. Over, dead.
Peter Over.
Jas. Low.
Jno. Gibb.
Jas. Carningham.
Wm. McAuley.
Jno. Weir.
France Taylor.
Jno. Farley.
Thos. Espey.
John Fleegar.
Christoly Tanner.

Christoly Weyland.
Ludwick Bail.
Jno. Landis.
Vendil Henry.
George Henry.
Feltey Keatrine.
Jas. Johnson.
Jno. Clark.
Benj. Boyd.
Wm. Hunter.
David Haynes.
Abrim Mitchel.
Sam. Jonston.
Geo. Foulk.
Jas. Hays.
Jas. Willson, Sen.
Wm. Maffet.
Joseph Poke.
Lambert Vandite.
Geo. Bell.
Edw. Stridle.
Wm. Watt.
Jas. Queen.
Jno. Mayers.
Jas. Kirkswell.
Ulrick Weltmore.
Abram Waltmore.
Jas. Swartzel.
Christoly Stoner.
Stoph. Shank.
Jas. Sullivan.
Jno. Minsker.
Jas. Minsker.
Jno. Earley.
Jno. Shuster.
Henry Garret.
Anthony Fearor.
Christoly Shuelts.
Jno. Balam.
Wm. Balam.
Nicholas Balam.
Jacob Balam.
Peter Balam.
Adam Dinigar.
Mich. Dinigar.
Jacob Kinsley.
Mich. Eley.
Wm. Earley.
Henry Shell.
Martin Pinogle.
Christoly Forney.
Jno. Forney.
Peter Cashnets.
Jacob Boman, Jun.
Jacob Boman, Sen.
Henry Boman.
Joseph Nafscar.
Wm. Nay.
John Nay.
Peter Nay.
Martin Long.
Jacob Hoover.
Martin Hoover.
Fredrick Swarts.
Henry Wray.
Abraham Earley.
Peter Baker.
Christoly Beem.
Abraham Ramsey.
Smith Poke.
Peter Ball.
Jno. Switsler.
Christoly Cooper.
Christoly Nafscar.
Abra. Petlion.
Jacob Willhelm.
Michal Nay.
Jacob Stouver.
Jacob Hethler.
Mich. Tillman.
Fred. Hetsler.
Feltey Starger.
Jno. Praght.
Peter Forney.
Archd. Boyd.
Christo. Wisebaugh.
Christly Beam.
John White.

Devalt Henry. John Hachbarger.
Jacob Lenon. Andrew Boyers.
Jacob Stover. Benjam Harshey.

The abov is a true State of the Company this 15th of May, 1783, By me.

ROB'T McCALLEN, Capt.

Sworn before me.

JOHN RODGERS.

A LIST OF THE CLASSES OF CAPT. WM. BRISBAN'S COMPANY OF THE 1ST BATTALION OF LANCASTER COUNTY MILITIA. (c.)

1st Class.

Archibald McCordy. Joseph Walke.
David Cowan. Daniel Fleming.
Thomas McNeal. Dennis Harkens.
Jacob Keisor, Jr. Alexd'r Mcfadden.

2nd Class.

Michal Graham. James Galt.
James Douglass, S'r. James Wilson.
Michal McClosky. Patrick Melholm.
Charles Murray. James McPike.

3rd Class.

Daniel Harkins. Michal Jack.
James Johnston. Robert Potts.
Hugh Forgey. John Sharadan.
John Beggs. Peter Rapp.
John Gordon. Robert Greer.
Andrew Lytle. Alexd'r Brown.
Jacob Curts. Wm. Andrew.

4th Class.

Wm. Armstrong. Robert Auld.
Christian Curts. Samuel Holliday.
Wm. Patton. Archibald McNeal.
Thomas Siemons. Jared Cowan.
John Cope. Patrick McNea.
John McKinly. Thomas Clark.
Jacob Bleaser. James Waters.

5th Class.

Joseph Belford.
Adam Galt.
James Hughs.
Robert Huston.
John Crosby.
William Lee.
John Plank, Jr.
George Rutter.
Andrew Cullen.
George Boyd.
Matthew Henderson.
James Lytle.
George Kisor.
James Borland.
James Armor, Adjt.
Samuel Cope.
Patrick King.
Wm. Siemons.

6th Class.

Joseph Welch.
Edward Runshaw.
Alexd'r Brown.
Robert Huey.
James Anderson.
Archib'd McAfee.
Andrew Smith.
Nathaniel Rutter.
Jacob Pee.
George Stever.
John Hemphill.
Joseph Beggs.
James Watson.

7th Class.

James McFadden.
Wm. Richardson, Light Horseman.
Jacob Hains.
Wm. Holliday.
Wm. Cowan.
Leonard Euroch.
Samuel Hughs.
Moses Wilson.
George McIntire.
Joseph Hains.
Wm. Cody.
Charles McIlhenny.
Owen Thomas.

8th Class.

Wm. Boyd.
Samuel Armor.
John McComb.
Thomas Henderson.
Robert Cowan.
James Dunlap.
John Murphy.
James McCafferty.
David Harris.
John Magoun.
Joseph Garver.
James Hamilton.
Wm. Burchell.
Tarrence Fills.
John Wright.

I certify the above Role is a just & true state of my Company.

WM. BRISBEN, Capt.

MUSTER ROLL OF CAPT. WM. BRIZBEN'S CO. OF 1ST BATTALION, LANCASTER COUNTY. (c.)

Captain.

Wm. Brizben.

Lieutenant.

Wm. Willson.

Ensign.

George Whitehill.

Privates.

Archd. McCurdy.
David Cowan.
Thomas McNeal.
Jacob Kizer, Junr.
Michel Tryer.
John Scott.
Michel Graham.
James Majers.
James Douglass, Senr.
Charles Murrey.
Michel McCloskey.
James Gault.
Samuel Siemons.
James Wilson.
Colen Marten.
Owen Thomas.
John Carmichel.
James Cullen.
James Johnston.
George Wike.
Andw. Lytle.
Hugh Forgey.
Jacob Curtz.
John Richardson.
Michl. Jack.
George Stever.
Robert Potts.
John Beggs.
John Gorden.
John Douglass.
Wm. Armstrong.
Christen Curtz.
Wm. Patton.
Thomas Slimons, Snr.
John Coop.
John Armor.
John McKinley.
Andrew Cullen.
Jacob Blazer.
Robert Aullt.
James Roach.
John Plank.
Joseph Bellford.
George Rutter.
Adam Gault.
George Boyd.
Matthew Henderson.
James Lytle.
George Kizer.
Robert houston.
John Crosbey.
James Hughs.
Joseph Welch.
James Watson.
William Beggs.
Thomas Slemons, Jur.
Alexr. Brown.
Robert Huey.

James Anderson.
Archibald McAfee.
John Hopkens.
Andrew Smith.
James McCafferty.
James Mcfadden.
William Richardson.
Jacob Hains.
William Holaday.
John Whitehill.
William Cowan.
John Holey.
James McCamont.
Micheal Kenneday.
William Jones.
William Boyd.
Thomas henderson.
Robert Cowan.
John McComb.
James Dunlap.
John Murphey.
Samuel Armor.
James Runshaw.
James Hamilton.
James Watters.
Joseph Shannon.
David Harris.
Samuel Holaday.
Moses Willson.
Thomas Boyd.
Daniel Fleming.
James Cowan.
Joseph Wike.
Samuel Young.
Archibald McNeail.
Charles Jacobs.
Petter Melholem.
Daniel harkens.
Leonard Earuch.
Joseph Gettes.
Harmen Skills.
John McGown.
Daniel Dimon.
Nathaniel Rutter.
James Armor.
Jonathan Green.

CAPTAIN HASTINGS CLASS ROLE. (c.)

1st Class.

Willum Chemberlin.
Jas. Duglass.
Jos. Dickeson.
Samuel Jonson.
Jas. Starret.
Nail keny.
Willum Camel.

2nd Class.

Jos. Hall.
John Miller.
Daved Staret.
Henery Smith.
Charls Colwel.
Stuart Menteeth.

3rd Class.

Jos. Whithil.
Robart Byars.
Fredrick Bakir.
Jos. More.
Josiah Bradly.
John Leveson.
John Whithil.

4th Class.

Jas. Hendeson.
Jas. Alleson, Shum'r.
John Harris.
John Anderson.
Willum fulerton.
Robart Colwel.

Willum Henry.
John Wat.
James Gib.
John Hendeson.
Eiles Tater.

5th Class.

James Boyd.
Willum Walis.
Jos. Wardnor.
Isake Tallir.
John Clemson.
John Hannah.

Thos. Johnston.
Ames Slameker.
Willum Boun.
Danuel Baely.
John Hopor.

6th Class.

Willum Linvil.
John Alleson.
Jas. Alleson.
John Hastings.

Chrisly Boun.
James All.
Willum Clark.

7th Class.

Josiah Erwain.
Moses (illegible).
Johnnathen Hore.
Jacop Millir.

Willum Goudy.
Thos. Clemenson.
Andrals Attelmen.
Craig Thomas.

8th Class.

Archebele Hendeson.
Thos. Hendeson.
Willum Leveston.
Lennard Elmaker.
John Midelton.

Paul Megouen.
Barny Laferty.
Christy Grify.
Daved Whithil.

Cert,ued by

ENOCH HASTINGS, Capt.

A LIST OF CAPTAIN SAMUEL HENRY CLASSES OF THE FIRST BATTALION OF LANCASTER COUNTY MILITIA. (c.)

1st Class.

James Smith.
Andrew Allison.

Jacob Dinlinger.
Thomas Beham.

James Regan.
Abraham Leamon.
John Millar.
Rob't Smith.
W'm Melony.
Henry Kendrich.

Henry Norton.
Jacob Hoar.
John Sneavely.
Jeremiah Stilwell.
John Parker.

2nd Class.

Joseph Smith.
John Leru.
John Hamil.
Francis Hare.
Christian Hammerly.
W'm Fegan.

Joseph Buckwalter.
John Harnish.
David Brown.
Peter Hersh.
David Millar.

3rd Class.

James Smith.
George Lemon.
Peter Millar.
George Withers.
Francis Smith.

Stephen Goff.
Robert Parker.
Isaac Kendrick.
W'm Thompson.

4th Class.

Alexd'r Lemon.
John Hare.
Samuel Hains.
Christian Millar.
George Oirich.
Christian Eyeman.

George Bright.
Daniel Melony.
Abram Hare.
Henry Diffebough.
Henry Reese.
Abram Beaty.

5th Class.

Jacob Hartman.
Jacob Leamon.
John Harmon.
Conrad Spitser.
Christian Millar.
John Millar.
Misick Erb.

Joseph Lemon.
James Kelly.
Henry Eyeman.
John McKee.
Isaac Hains.
Philip Hartman.
David Hoover.

6th Class.

John Nial.
Frederick Powts.
W'm Alley.
John Asselrote.
Daniel norton.

Martin Miley.
Christian Rora.
Daniel Brammar.
John Furrey.

7th Class.

Daniel Lemon.
Henry Fults.
Abram Longaker.
Henry Speelman.
Windle Bowman.
Jonas Kellar.
John Diffebough.
Philip Barnet.
John Longanekar.
John Miley.
Jeremiah Eany.
Benjamin Williams.
George Diffebough.

8th Class.

Benjamin Souders.
Christian Dinlinger.
John Potts.
Thomas Evans.
John Weaver.
Samuel Melony.
Thomas Williams.
Jacob Hains.
Frederick Smith.
John Furrey, S'r.
Ebraim Sneavely.
John Funk.
Joseph Sneider.
Nicholas Breslar.
John Brisband, Jr.
Peter Bretlar.

I Do Certify that the above Class Role is Just and true.

SAMUEL HENRY.

CLASS ROLL OF CAPT. MARTIN HUEY'S CO. OF THE 1ST BATT. LANCASTER COUNTY. (c.)

1st Class.

John Roland.
Jacob Johnes.
Henery Bare.
Adam Rumbarger.
William Shelar.
Henery Shively.
Philip Shower.
Samuel Eaby.
Abraham Myer.
John Kilheser.
John Hiller.
Stophel Shour.
William Waganman.
Adam Winger.
Lodwick Tetrech.

2nd Class.

Jacob Swobe.
Samuel Smith.
Petter Eaby, Jun.
John Painter.
Petter Eaken.
Henery Swobe.

Micall Widler.
George Eaken.
Jacob Shever.
John Garven.
John Snoots.
Moses Jonsten.
David Walker.
Henery Eagen.
John McConahy.

3rd Class.

Samuel McKatten.
Andrew Bare, Jun.
Mathias Ault.
John Johns.
Joseph Brinten.
Henery Eaby.
George Pricker.
Abram Sheneman.
Jacob Garver.
Cullip Hemple.
Henery Shirk.
Isack Bare.
Jacob Hammer.

4th Class.

Elis Nealor.
Abraham Garver.
John Rose.
John Curts.
John Stalter.
David Bare.
Isack Garver.
John Buckwalter.
Martin Maxwel.
Abraham Eaby.
James Rees.
Samuel Hemple.
Lenard Tiller.
Jacob Pecher.
Joseph Eaby.
Henery Winger.

5th Class.

John Eaby, Jun.
Martin Hiller.
William Guinn.
Daniel Swobe.
Jacob Lyne.
Andrew Bare.
Micall Garver.
Stophel Weaver.
Petter Garver.
Nicles Clasen.
Isack Rife.
Bosten Shirk.
John Wilsen, Jun.
Peter Smith.

6th Class.

John McAlister.
Petter Kilhefer.
Petter Eaby, shoemaker.
Robert Crabb.
David Lyne.
Jacob Garver.
Martin Bare.
Jacob Maxwel.
Mical Vancanen.
Abram Curts.
Adam Miller, Jun.
Moses Brinten.
Daniel Smith.

7th Class.

John Maxwel.
Georg Bare.
Mical Shalabarger.
William Brinten.
Abram Johns.
Samuel McLilly.
James Scott.
John Garver.
John Pots.
Francis Buckwalter.
Petter Eaby.
Mical Hess.
Mical Bare.
Henery Taig.
Jonathen Dauble.

8th Class.

James McNaule.
Jonathan Owens, Jun.
David Rife.
Adam Swoby.
Jacob Snevely.
Jacob Shively.
Crisley Myer.
Andrew Maxwel.
David Painter.
Benjamen Owens.
John Shirk.
Isack Garver.
Daniel Eaby.

Certified by

MARTIN HUEY, Capt'n.

A LIST OF THE CLASSES OF CAPT. MARTIN HUEY COMPANY. (c.)

Privates.

1st Class.

John Roland.
Jacob Johns.
Henry Bear.
Adam Rumberger.
William Shelar.
Henry Shively.
Philip Shower.
Samuel Eby.
Abram Myer.
John Kilheifer.
John Hillar.
Stophel Shower.
William Waggoner.
Adam Winger.
Ludwick Tetrick.

2nd Class.

Jacob Swobe.
Peter Eby, Junr.
John Painter.
Peter Eaker.
Henry Swobe.
Michal Widler.
George Eaker.
Jacob Sharer.

John Garver.
Moses Johnston.
John McConohy.

Samuel McElhatton.
Andrew Bare.
John Johns.
Joseph Brinton.
Henry Eby.

John Curts.
John Buckwalter.
Abram Garver.
David Bear.
Isaac Garver.

Peter Smith.
John Eby.
Martin Hillar.
Hugh Cahoon.
Daniel Swobe.
Andrew Bear.
Michal Garver.

John McCallister.
Peter Kilhiefer.
Peter Eby.
David Line.
Jacob Garver.
Jacob Maxwell.
Michal Vencanon.

John Maxwell.
George Bard.
Michal Shalaberger.
William Brinton.
Abram Johns.
Samuel McAllibe.
James Scott.
John Garver.

Hannikle Weaver.
Adam Hostitter.

3rd Class.

Abram Sheneman.
Henry Shirk.
Jacob Hammer.
Frederick Doubler.

4th Class.

Martin Maxwell.
Ebram Eby.
Leonard Tillar.
Joseph Eby.
Henry Winger.

5th Class.

Stophel Weaver.
Peter Garver.
Nicholas Claser.
Isaac Rife.
Sebastian Shirk.
John Wilson, Jr.
Jacob Hatto.

6th Class.

Abram Curts.
Moses Brinton.
Daniel Smith.
Henry Eager.
Adam Eagle.
John Eby, Jr.

7th Class.

John Potts.
Michal Hess.
Michal Bard.
Henry Tague.
Jonathan Double.
Peter Millar.
Robert Crabb.

8th Class.

James McAnawl.
Jonathan Owens.
David Rife.
Adam Swobe.
Jacob Sneavely.
Jacob Shively.
Christian Mayrs.
Andrew Maxwell.
David Painter.
Benjamin Owens.
John Shirk.
Daniel Eby.
John Myars.
John Hatvole.
Jacob Peker.

I do Certify the Above is a just & true state of my Company.

MARTIN HUEY, Capt.

A CLASS ROLE OF CAPT. WILLIAM SKILE'S COMPANY.
(c.)

1st Class.

Rob't Stuart.
Denis Kane.
Dan'l Bashore.
Alex'r Miller.
William Wallace.
John Ebby.
James Ebraim.
William Mathers.
Henry Hartman.
Abram Sensnick.
Patrick McGoughy.

2nd Class.

Honical Weaver.
Joseph Evans.
Henry Musser.
William Whithill.
David Glen.
Peter Kline.
Jos. Ruter, J'r.
John Skiles.
Benj'n Haw.
Will'm Hamilton, J'r.
John Hamilton.

3rd Class.

Jacob Sensnick.
Benj'n Crawford.
James McNeal.
Benj'n Vernon.
Jos. Ruter, S'r.
James Cooper.
And'w Caldwell.
Robt. Simpson.
Daniel Huston.
William Morgan.
Thomas Fullerton.
James Knox.
William McCandles.
John Musser.

4th Class.

Henry Ruter, S'r.	Thos. Skiles.
Mathew McClung, J'r.	Emanuel Ferree.
James Skiles.	Archibald Craig.
Isaac Feeree.	James Cooper, J'r.
John Russh.	Brice Clark.
Arch'd Gormly.	Thos. Hamil.
John Twibett.	James Climpson.

5th Class.

John Abram.	Oliver McGomery.
John McCoy.	Robert Young.
Thos. Woods.	William Huston.
James Moore.	Rob't Knox.
John Tarbett, Smith.	Christian Sharp.
Joseph McMulland.	Andrew Thompson.
Jacob Myers.	Sam'l Crawford.
John Underwood.	William Ramsy.
Sam'l Bigert, Ju'r.	William Skiles.
James Bole.	

6th Class.

George Sildomridg.	Petter Miller.
Ab'r Liget.	Robt. McCurdy.
David Watson.	William McNabb.
John Johnston.	James Crawford.
George Lerue.	

7th Class.

James-Mongomery.	James Peel.
Abram Gibbons.	Joseph Ash.
Palser Basshore.	Stephen Kling.
Wm. Ruter.	Joseph Shank.
John Ruter, S'r.	Joseph Trunal.
John McFaden.	Joseph Ells.
Dan'l McCalester.	William Wilson.
Henry Smith.	Isaac Lemon.
Wm. Lightner.	Henry Bigert.
John Henry.	George Stuart, Jr.
Sam'l McAlille.	Adam Lightner.

8th Class.

Ephraim McColem.
Thos. Lyon.
John Tepley.
Hugh Hamilton.
Will'm Hamilton, J'r.
Nath'l Lightner.
Alex'r McCoy.
Daniel Herbert.
Charles McClung.
Robt. Bresler.
John Pursell.

Certified by

WM. SKILES, Capt.

A LIST OF THE CLASSES IN CAPT. WM. SKILES COMPANY. (c.)

1st Class.

Robert Stewart.
Dennis Kane.
Daniel Basor.
Alex'r Millar.
William Wallace.
John Eby.
James Abram.
Wm. Mathers.
Abram Bear.
Henry Hartman.
Abram Sensinick.
Patrick McGaughey.

2nd Class.

Joseph Evets.
Henery Musser.
William Whitehill.
Peter Cline.
Joseph Rutter, Jr.
John Skiles.
William Hamilton, Jr.
John Hamilton.
Benjamin Haw.

3rd Class.

Jacob Sensinich.
Benjamin Crawford.
James McNeal.
Benjamin Vernor.
Joseph Rutter, S'r.
James Cooper.
Andrew Caldwell.
Robert Simpson.
Daniel Huston.
Thomas Fullerton.
James Knox.
Wm. McCandless.
John Musser.

4th Class.

Henry Rutter, S'r.
Matthew McClung.
James Skiles.
Isac Ferree.
John Rush.
Archibald Gormley.
John Torbet.
Thomas Skiles.
Emanuel Ferree.
Archibald Craig.
James Cooper, J'r.
Brice Clark.

5th Class.

John Abram.
John McCoy.
James Moore.
Joseph McMollon.
Jacob Myers.
John Underwood.
Samuel Biggart.
James Boyle.
Oliver Montgomery.
Robert Young.
Robert Knox.
Christian Sharp.
Andrew Thompson.
Samuel Crawford.
Wm. Ramsey.

6th Class.

George Seldomridge.
Alexd'r Liggot.
David Watson.
John Johnston.
George Leru.
Peter Millar.
Robert McCordy.
Samuel Biggart, Weaver.

7th Class.

James Montgomery.
Abram Gibbons.
Balser Basor.
William Rutter.
John Rutter, S'r.
John McFadden.
Dan'l McCollister.
Henry Smith.
Wm. Lightner.
John Henry.
Samuel McAllille.
Joseph Ash.
Joseph Shank.
Joseph Ellis.
William Wilson.
Isaac Leamon.
George Stewart.
Adam Lightner.
Stophel Cling.
Joseph Trimble.
James Peel.

8th Class.

Ephraim McCollum.
William Huston.
Henry Biggart.
Thomas Lyon.
John Teply.
Hugh Hamilton, 2nd Class.
Wm. Hamilton, 2nd Class.
Nathaniel Lightner.

Alexd'r McCoy.
Daniel Herbert.
Charles McClung.
Robert Breslen.
John Pursill.

I do certify the above role is a just & true state of my Company.

WM. SKILES, Capt.

A LIST OF THE CLASSES OF CAPT. WILLIAM SMITHS COMPANY OF THE FIRST BATTALION OF LANCASTER COUNTY MILITIA. (c.)

Privates.

1st Class.

John Eckman.
John Verner.
Abram Bowman.
Simon Hynold.
Peter Hole.
Peter Rush.
Henry Beam.
John Hare, Junr.
Henry Eckman.
Jacob Millar, Carp.
John White.
Philip Kesbler.
George Richmond.
George Smith.
John Royor.
Jacob Millar, Jr.
James Molston.
Henry Isaberger.
John Martley.
David Shaver.

2d.

Martin Eckman.
Peter Musser.
John Brua.
John Howry.
Jonas Caufman.
Jacob Bear.

3rd Class.

John Rush.
Wm. Logan.
Jacob Rush.
Christian Byers.
Christian Shapp.
Henry Hare.
Nicholas Sorrer.
John Foundersmith.
Evard Gruber.
Wm. Huggins.
Andrew Hyeas.
John Cremer.
Jacob Drum.
John Cashady.

4th Class.

John Clipenholn.
Martin Kendrick.
Joseph Otterbough.
Jacob Sides, Jr.
Jacob Huber.
Daniel Millar.
Christian Martin.
Jacob Hickman.
Christian Eternought.
Simon Millar.
David Brown.
Jacob Fouts, Jr.
Henry Bear.

5th Class.

Conrad Hoak.
Robert Charlton.
John Ferree.
Henry Hoover.
Andrew Spitser.
Michal Fouts.
John Small, Jr.
Torrence Duffy.
Isaac Widdows.
John Kendrick.
Wm. Bowstick.
James Brown.
John Cremer.
Samuel McComsey.

6th Class.

Barnet Houser.
Jacob Freliegh.
Jacob Neal.
Henry Rush.
Samuel Millar.
John Moore.
Charles Philips.
Philip Bear.
Felty Fronk.
Ludwick Rinhart.
Jacob Millar.

7th Class.

Jacob Hickman.
John Withers.
Valentine Foundersmith.
Jacob Hoover, Sr.
John Millar.
George Martley.
Henry Bowman.
John Bear, not at home nor warned, but to serve in the Eighth.
Nicholas Macky.
Peter Shofstall.
Martin Hare.
Henry Kendrick.
George Myars.
Solomon Hemer.
Henry Bushman.

8th Class.

John Stotsaberger.
Mathias Millar.
Jacob Millar.
Michal Wither.
Christian Shults.
Martin Stoll.
Jacob Kendrick.
Henry Stoner.
Jacob Fouts.
Henry Road.
Daniel Mowra.
Michal Mires.
Abram Brubaker.
George May.
John McMollon.

I do Certify that the above Class Role is Just and true.

WILLIAM SMYTH, Capt.

A LIST OF YE COMMISS'D AND NON COMMISS'D OFFICERS & PRIVATES ENROLLED IN CAPT. SAMUEL HENRY'S COMP. OF YE FIRST BATT. OF LANCAST. COUNTY MELITIA COMMANDED BY COLL. GEORGE STEWART. (c.)

Commissioned.

Capt.

Sam'l Henry.

Lieut.

Joseph Gourney.

1st Class.

John Parker.
Jas. Smith.
An'd Allison.
Jacob Denlinger.
Thos. Behom.
Jas. Regan.
Abr'm Leamon.
John Miller.
Robt. Smith.
Wm. McLoney.
Henry Kendrick.
Henry Norton.
Jacob Hoar.
John Snevely.
Jeremiah Stillwell.

2nd Class.

Joseph Smith.
John Lerue.
John Hamil.
David Miller.
Peter Free.
George Nailer.
Frances Hair.

Christian Hemmerly.
Wm. Fegan.
Jos. Buckwalter.
Jno. Harnish.
Benjamin Bowman.
David Brown.

3rd Class.

Jas. Smith.
Geo'r Leamon.
Jno. Shofstall.
Peter Miller.
Geo'r Withers.
Francis Smith.
Stephen Gaff.

Peter Miller.
Robt. Parker.
Nicholas Miller.
Martain Kendrick.
Jacob Kendrick.
Jno. Brown.
Wm. Thompson.

4th Class.

And'w Morland.
Alx'r Leamon.
Ab'm Beaty.
Geo'r Hart.
Jno. Hair.
Sam'l Hains.
Christ'n Miller.
Dan'l McLoney.

Henry Devenbough.
Abr'm Hair.
Martain Miley.
Geor. Oyrich.
Geo'r Bright.
Christian Eyman.
Christian Denlinger.

5th Class.

Jacob Hartman.
Jacob Leamon.
Jno. Souders.
Isaac Evans.
Jno. Harman.

Conrad Spiteer.
Mercer Erb.
Jos. Leamon.
Henry Eyeman.
Jno. McKee.

6th Class.

Jno. Neal.
Frederick Pouts.
Wm. Thompson.
Wm. Alley.
Henry Spiteer.
Jno. Asselrote.
Jacob Weaver.
David Swisher.

David Hair.
Henry Eyeman.
Dan'l Norton.
Martain Milly.
Christian Rora.
And'w Sides.
Gorg. Breslan.

7th Class.

Dan'l Leamon.	Jno. Defanbough.
Jacob Druckamiller.	Christian Hair.
Henry Fultz.	Philip Barnet.
Abr'm Longnaker.	Jno. Longnaker.
Henry Speelman.	Jno. Miley.
Dan'l Lefever.	Jeramiah Eany.
Windle Bowman.	Adam Hoar.
Jonas Kelar.	Benjamin Williams.

8th Class.

Peter Bressler.	Sam'l McLoney.
Jno. Pots.	Benj. Hair.
Benj. Souders.	Nicholass Bressler.
Thomas Eavans.	Barnabass Fegan.
Thos. Williams.	Henry Martain.
Abr'm Snevly.	Peter Laurance.
Jno. Weaver.	Jas. Ramsey.

Certified by

SAMUEL HENRY, Capt.

A LIST OF CLASSES OF CAPT. MATHIAS SLAYMAKER'S COMPANY OF THE 1ST BATTALION OF LANCASTER COUNTY MILITIA. (c.)

Privates.

1st Class.

Thomas White.	Richard Copeland.
Peter Taylor.	Balser Barkman.
Conrad Gram.	Abram Carpenter.
John Millar.	George Pusley.
Samuel Lefever.	Balser Peterman.
Henry Slaymaker.	Frank Rowe.

2nd Class.

George Carpenter.
George McColough.
John Slaymaker, Jr.
Frederick White.
John Richardson.
Joseph White.
George Wallick.
Robert Crosby.
Joseph Allison.
John Waggoner.
Peter Shumaker.

3rd Class.

Jacob Esleman.
Henry Bragoner.
Thomas Kenny.
Jacob Stotsaberger.
Daniel Peck.
David Foster.
John Ferree.
Jacob Stambach.
John Andrew.
John Driber.
Nicholas Walter.
John McComsy, served in the 4th Class, not being at home when the 3d served.

4th Class.

Nicholas Neasor.
John Taylor.
Benjamin Brackbill.
Daniel Ferree.
Peter Stayman.
Frederick Derr.
Jacob Barkman.
Paul Trout.
Peter Lefever.
Daniel Huston.
Michal Myer.
John Shaver.
Joseph Lefever.

5th Class.

Jacob Shirts.
John Shirt.
Isaac Ferree.
David Bower.
Thomas Love.
Charles McGoun.
Wm. Taylor.
Jacob Ludwick.
John Williams.
John Slaymaker, Sr.

6th Class.

Jacob Millar.
Hervey Stambach.
Hieronomus Birley.
George Swartsley.
John Graft.
John Lefever.
Moses Baird.
Michal Hess.
David Whitmore.
Valentine Myar.
George McElvaine.

7th Class.

Jacob Bower.
Cornelius Ferree.
John Hare.
Michal Buch.
Neal Kenny.
Jacob Brewa, Jr.
John Barkman.
Peter Horse.
Conrad Kuntz.
Thomas Ferree.
Thomas Lecky.
John Carpenter (found Soldier during the war).

8th Class.

John Bower.
Abram Bower.
Benjamin Graft.
Nicholas Hull.
Daniel Slaymaker.
Wm. Slaymaker, Sr.
Wm. Ferree.
James Kenny, Jr.
John Foster.
Michal Bower.
James Quigley.
Andrew Ferree.
Wm. Slaymaker, Jr.
James Rodgers.
Robert Neal.

I do certify the above Role is a just & true State of my Company.

MATHIAS SLAYMAKER, JR., Capt.

A LIST OF THE CLASSES OF THE FIST COMPANY OF THE FIRST BATALION OF LANCASTER COUNTY MILITIA. (c).

Captain.

John Sleter.

Lieutenant.

James Hennery.

Ensign.

Nichs. Shriner.

1st Class.

Martin Grove.
Daniel Keepots, Junr.
Henry Landis.
William Hains.
Jacob Rorer.
Andrew Heller.

David Rorer.
Henry Buckwalter.
George Keseler.
Christin Harkman.
John Birkholder.
George Bard.
George Young.
Henry Tetrick.
Henry Pech.
Philip Bard.
Christian Rorer.

2d Class.

John Kennedy.
Jacob Yorty.
Joseph Buckwalter.
Frd. Wendel.
Peter Mooser.
Jacob Pikle.
Benj. Whitmore.
Jacob Hoofman.
John Fowler.
Jacob Stofer.
Christ. Frebort.
John Ebright.
John Scot.
Balser Thumb.
Jacob Keechler.
John Seager.
Benjam. Orenstake.
George Swizer.

3d Class.

Isac Rorer.
Daniel Hawer.
Isac Crider.
John Seager.
Jacob Grove.
John Yonce, Sr.
Martin Moser.
Conrod Shitz.
Isac Leafover.
Abraham Buckwalter.
Abraham Buckwalter.
Benj. Landis.
Blchr. Burk.
Samuel Yong.
John Moor.

4th Class.

Philip Meek.
Henry Lyeman.
Jacob Sthofer.
Robert Rudick.
Danl. Whitmore.
John Miller, smith.
Abrahm. Downer.
John Bingley.
Saml. Watt.
John Christy, Junr.
Nicls. Spring.
Cunrod Shitz.
Solomon Denler.
William Fagon.
Dewalt Spring.
George Curtz.
Abrahm. Whitmor.

5th Class.

Nicholas Meek.
George Trukebroad.
John Crider.
John Busham.
John Kirk.
Joseph Bowman.
Henry Horkman.
John Landis, Sr.
John Landis, Jr.
Christian Fordat.
John Rodaker.
Conrad Fry.
Isac Forlow.

6th Class.

John Hofer.
Leander Bender.
Jacob Landis.
George Shingle.
Tobias Wanner.
Daniel Miller.
Henry Whitmore.
Jacob Kirk.
Martin Milinger.
John Regy, at Harkens.
Henry Shoot.
Henry Locker.
Jacob Roop.

7th Class.

George Kendrick.
David Grove.
Henry Grove.
John Buckwalter.
Tobias Crider.
Jeremiah Kirk.
Nichos. Hess.
John Craig.
Adam Mow.
Stephon Atkeson.
Jacob Shewmaker.
John Higsey.
Henry Amons.
Henry Gall.
Conrad Ashwendor.

8th Class.

John Yonce.
Daniel Suver.
Adam Lefever.
Christon Yorty.
Abrm. Landis.
Ulrick Huver.
George Kimbirlin.
Philip Busham.
John Jonston.
John Gibney.
John Lance.
John Harsh, shoemaker.
Charles Reynhart.
Patrick Harkns.
John Gasnor.
John Brown.

Certified by,

JOHN SLETER,
Capt.

A RETURN OF CAPT. ALLEXANDER WHITE'S COMPANY OF THE FIRST BATTALLION OF LANCASTER COUNTY COMMANDED BY COL. GEORGE STEWART. (c.)

1st Class.

John Buckley.
Peter Holl.
Thomas White.
Peter Taylor.
Andrew Bird.
Conrad Gram.
John Miller.
Samuel Lefever.

Henry Slaymaker.
Richard Copland.
Balser Barkman.
Abraham Carpenter.
George Pursley.
John White.
Frank Rowe.

2d Class.

George Carpenter.
Robert Crosbey.
George McCullouch.
John Slaymaker, Jr.
George Wallick.
Frederick White.
John Richardson.
David Feree.
Joseph White.
Ludwick Road.
Joseph Ellison.
John Waggoner.
Peter Shomaker.
Michael Frank.

3rd Class.

Jacob Esleman.
Henry Bragooner.
Thomas Kenney.
Jacob Stoutsaberger.
Daniel Peck.
Wm. McCandles.
David Foster.
John Feree.
Jacob Stambouch.
John McCumsey.
John Andrew.
Nicholas Walter.
John McFerson.

4th Class.

Nicholas Neasor.
John Taylor.
Benjamin Bracbill.
Daniel Feree.
Mertin Esleman.
Peter Steaman.
Frederick Derr.
Jacob Barkman.
Paul Trout.
Peter Lefever.
John Myer.
James Rodgers.
Bolser Peterman.
John Longanecker.
James Messer.

5th Class.

Jacob Shirts.
John Shirts.
Isaac Feree.
Thomas Love.
Charles Megown.
Jacob Hill.
Wm. Watson.
Stewart Menteeth.
John Tinglinger.
Wm. Taylor.
Wm. Slaymaker.
George McElvain.

6th Class.

Joseph Lefever.
Jacob Miller.
John Clerk.
Windle Trout.
George Hart.
Christian Bower.
Thomas Buffington.
Henry Stamback.

Hironomous Birley.
George Swartsley.
John Graft.
Moses Baird.
Michael Hass.
Michael Myer.
Wm. Clark.
Robert McQuilken.

7th Class.

Jacob Bower.
Cornelious Feree.
John Carpenter.
Robert Mertin.
Michael Buch.
Nale Kenney.
Thomas Lackey.
John Hare.
Adam Frauker.
Jacob Bruah, Junr.
Mertin Cochenberger.
John Cashaday.
John Borkman.
Peter Hass.
Conrad Contz.
John Driber.
Daniel Huston.

8th Class.

John Bower.
Wm. Randles.
Abraham Bower.
Benjamin Graft.
Nicholas Holl.
Daniel Slaymaker.
Wm. Feree.
James Kenney, Jr.
John Taylor.
Michael Bower.
James Quigley.
Andrew Feree.
Jacob Ludwick.
David Whitmore.
John Barr.

ALEXR. WHITE,
Capt.

FIRST BATTALION, LANCASTER COUNTY. (c.)

Peter Eakert.
Adam Miller.
John Shaver.
Isack Rife.
David Rife.
Mathias Ault.
John Painter.
William Waganer.
Alexander M (illegible)y.
Moses Jonsten.
John Joseph Eby.
Peter Eaby.
Daniel Eby.
Joseph Branten.
William Brinten.
Moses Brinton.
Cristen Myer.
Abraham Eaby.
John Eby.
Samuel Eaby.
Henry Eaby.
Peter Eaby.

Henry Bare.
John Hiller.
Frances Buckwalter.
John Buckwalter.
James Reese.
Cristen Pricker.
Micail Garver.
Stophel Shower.
Jacob Shower.
Jacob Line.
Jacob Garver.
Jonathen Owens.
Bengeman Owens.
David Bare.
Daniel Smith.
Samuel Smith.
John Garver.
Abraham Garver.
Peter Garver.
Henry Garver.
Henry Shively.
Jacob Shively.
Jacob Jonshus.
John Johnsten.
Abraham Johnsten.
Abraham Curts.
John Curts.
Peter Hiltabran.
Michael Shalabarger.
John Stolter.
George Beiser.
John Wilson.

SECOND BATTALION
LANCASTER COUNTY MILITIA.

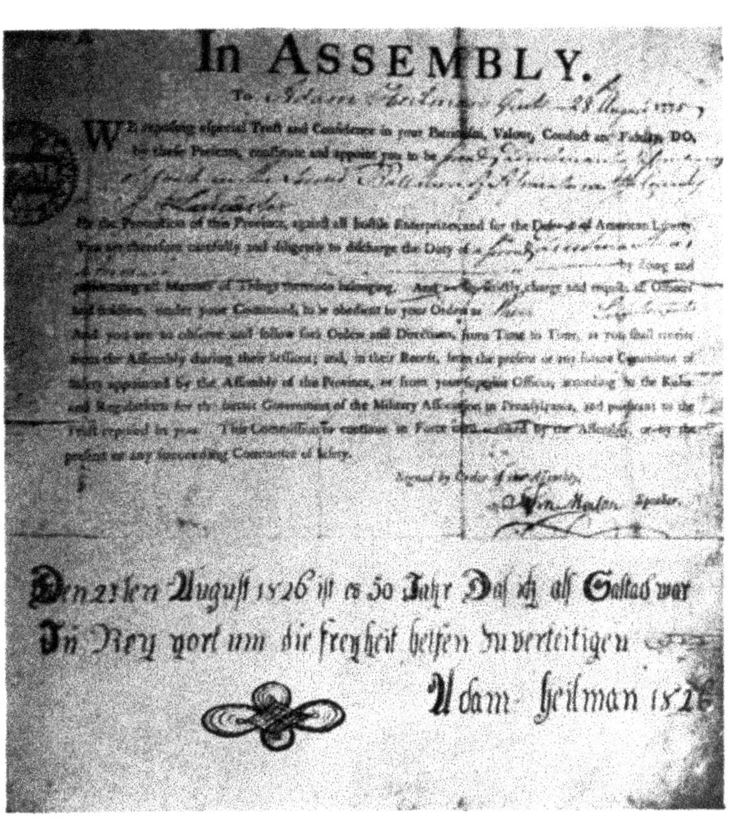

In ASSEMBLY.

To

WE reposing especial Trust and Confidence in your Patriotism, Valour, Conduct and Fidelity, DO, by these Presents, constitute and appoint you to be

For the Protection of this Province, against all hostile Enterprizes, and for the Defence of American Liberty. You are therefore carefully and diligently to discharge the Duty of by doing and performing all Manner of Things thereunto belonging. And we do strictly charge and require all Officers and Soldiers, under your Command, to be obedient to your Orders as And you are to observe and follow such Orders and Directions, from Time to Time, as you shall receive from the Assembly during their Sessions; and, in their Recess, from the present or any future Committee of Safety appointed by the Assembly of this Province, or from your superior Officers, according to the Rules and Regulations for the better Government of the Military Association in Pennsylvania, and pursuant to the Trust reposed in you. This Commission to continue in Force until revoked by the Assembly, or by the present or any succeeding Committee of Safety.

Signed by Order of the Assembly,

Speaker.

Den 23ten August 1826 ist es 50 Jahr Das ich als Soldat war In New york um die freyheit helfen zu vertaitigen

Adam Heilman 1826

Original of above in possession of Mr. George G. Heilman, Heilmandale, Lebanon Co.

And

your Orders as

and follow such

Original of above in possession of Mr. Rudolph F. Kelker, Harrisburg, Penna.

OFFICERS SECOND BATTALION. '77 (a.)

Colonel.
James Watson.

Lieutenant Colonel.
James Porter.

Major.
Dorrington Wilson.

Fife Major.
Alexander Russell.

First company.

Captain—John Scott.
First Lieutenant—John Cunningham.
Second Lieutenant—John Duncan.
Ensign—Daniel Carmichael.

Second company.

Captain—Joshua Anderson.
First Lieutenant—Robert Miller.
Second Lieutenant—Alexander Hason.
Ensign—John Andrews.

Third company.

Captain—John Johnston.
First Lieutenant—Joshua (sic) Joseph Walker.
Second Lieutenant—Joshua (sic) Joseph Tweed.
Ensign—William Herd.

Fourth company.

Captain—Thomas White.
First Lieutenant—Thomas Clark.
Second Lieutenant—John Reed.
Ensign—Peter Simpson.

Fifth company.

Captain—James Morrison.
First Lieutenant—Robert King.
Second Lieutenant—Thomas Neil.
Ensign—William Nelson.

Sixth company.

Captain—Joshua (sic) Joseph Allison.
First Lieutenant—James Patterson.
Second Lieutenant—Samuel Jamison.
Ensign—Robert Johnston.

Seventh company.

Captain—Patrick Marshall.
First Lieutenant—John Caldwell.
Second Lieutenant—William Calhoun.
Ensign—William Bigham.

Eighth company.

Captain—John Paxton.
First Lieutenant—William Ramsey.
Second Lieutenant—John Shannon.
Ensign—William Brown.

SECOND BATTALION OF MILITIA OF LANCASTER COUNTY, COMMANDED BY COLONEL JAMES WATSON, JUNE 20, 1777. (b.)

Lieutenant Colonel.

James Porter.

Major.

Dorrington Willson.

Quarter Master.

John Anderson.

Fife Major.

Alexander Russell.

Captains.

John Scott.
Joshua Anderson.
John Johnston.
Thomas White.
James Morrison.
Joseph Ellison.
Patrick Marshall.
John Paxton.

Lieutenants.

John Cunningham.	Robert King.
John Duncan.	Thomas Neil.
Robert Miller.	James Patterson.
Alexander Hasson.	Samuel Jameson.
Joseph Walker.	John Caldwell.
Joseph Tweed.	William Calhoon.
Thomas Clark.	William Ramsey.
John Reed.	John Shannon.

Ensigns.

Daniel Carmichael.	Wm. Nelson.
Jn'o Andrews.	Robert Johnston.
William Herd.	William Bigham.
Peter Simpson.	William Brown.

Court Martial Men.

William King.	James Bigham.
William Arbuckle.	James Ramsey.
Daniel McConnel.	David McCombe.
Richard Ferree.	Joseph Lorimer.
John Stephson.	Andrew Caldwell.
Thomas Cully.	Andrew Work.
James Buchanan.	Nath'l Coulter.

A GENERAL REPORT OF THE STATE OF THE SECOND BATTALION OF MALITIA OF LANCASTER COUNTY COMMANDED BY COLLONEL JAMES WATSON, JUNE THE 20TH, 1777. (c.)

Field Officers.

Colonel.

James Watson.

Lieutenant Colonel.

James Porter.

Major.

Dorrington Willson.

Quarter Master.

John Anderson.

Fife Major.

Alexander Russel.

First company.

Capt'n—John Scott.
1st Lieut.—John Cunningham.
2nd Lieut.—John Duncan.
Ensign—Daniel Carmichall.

Court Martial Men.

William King.
William Arbuckle.
Serjeants, 4.
Corperals, 4.
Drum & Fife, 2.
Rank & File, 90.
Total of non commissd. officers & privates, 100.

Second Company.

Capt'n—Joshua Anderson.
1st Lieut.—Robert Miller.
2nd Lieut.—Alexander Hason.
Ensign—Jno. Andrews.

Court Martial Men.

Daniel McConnel.
Richd. Ferree.
Serjeants, 4.
Corperals, 4.
Drum & Fife, 2.
Rank & File, 80.
Total of non commissd. officers & privates, 90.

Third Company.

Capt'n—John Johnston.
1st Lieut.—Joseph Walker.
2nd Lieut.—Joseph Tweed.
Ensign—William Hird.
Serjeants, 4.
Corperals, 4.
Drum & Fife, 2.
Rank & File, 90.
Total of non commissd. officers & privates, 100.

Fourth Company.

Cap't—Thomas White.
1st Lieut.—Thomas Clark.
2nd Lieut.—John Reed.
Ensign—Peter Simpson.

Court Martial Men.

John Stephson.
Thomas Cully.
Serjeants, 4.
Corperals, 4.
Drum & Fife, 2.
Rank & File, 160.
Total of non commisd. officers & privates, 170.

Fifth Company.

Capt'n—James Morrison.
1st Lieut.—Robert King.
2d Lieut.—Thomas Nell.
Ensign—William Nelson.

Court Martial Men.

James Buchanan.
James Bigham.
Serjeants, 4.
Corperals, 4.
Drum & Fife, 2.
Rank & File, 76.
Total of non commissd. officers & privates, 86.

Sixth Company.

Capt'n—Joseph Ellison.
1st Lieut.—James Patterson.
2d Lieut.—Samuel Jameson.
Ensign—Robert Johnston.

Court Martial Men.

James Ramsey.
David McCombe.
Serjeants, 4.
Corperals, 4.
Drum & Fife, 2.
Rank & File, 67.
Total of non commissd. officers & privates, 77.

Seventh Company.

Capt'n—Patrick Marshal.
1st Lieut.—John Caldwell.
2d Lieut.—William Calhoon.
Ensign—William Bigham.

Court Martial Men.

Joseph Lowrimor.
Andrew Caldwell.
Serjeants, 4.
Corperals, 4.
Drum & Fife, 2.
Rank & File, 64.
Total of non commissd. officers & privates, 74.

Eighth Company.

Capt'n—John Paxton.
1st Lieut.—William Ramsey.
2nd Lieut.—John Shannon.
Ensign—William Brown.

Court Martial Men.

Andrew Work.
Nattl. Coulter.
Serjeants, 4.
Corperals, 4.
Drum & Fife, 2.
Rank & File, 98.
Total of non commissd. officers & privates, 108.

Total.

Serjeants, 32.
Corporals, 32.
Drum & Fife, 16.
Rank & File, 725.
Total of non commissd. officers & privates, 805.

A Just Return of the Above Battalion Certified By

JAMES WATSON,
Col.

Commissions dated first of July, 1777.

RETURN OF THE SECOND CLASS OF MILITIA LANCASTER CO., COMMANDED BY COLL. JAMES WATSON. (c.)

Companies	Officers Present.										
	Commissioned.						Staff.				
	Colonel.	Lieut. Col.	Major.	Captains.	Lieutenants.	Ensigns.	Chaplain.	Adjutant.	Quarter-Mas.	Surgeon.	Mate.
Capts.											
James Collier,				1	2	1					
Thomas Robeson,				1	2	1					
(Mu tla ed),				1	2	1					
(Mu tla ed),				1	2	1			1		
(Mu tlated),					2						
	1		1	5	10	4			1		
David Whitehill,				1		1					
	1		1	6	10	5			1		

Companies.	Officers Present.									Alterations since last Return.			Total.	
	Non-Com.			Rank and File.										
	Serjeants.	Drummers.	Fifers.	Fit for Duty.	Sick Present.	Sick Absent.	On Command.	On Furlough.	Total.	Dead.	Discharged.	Deserted.	Substitutes.	Non-Substitutes.
Capts.														
James Collier,	4	1	......	29	2	......	4	2	37	......	......	......	......	......
Thomas Robeson,	4	......	......	37	......	......	10	1	48	......	......	......	......	......
(Mutilated),	4	1	......	33	......	......	4	......	37	......	......	......	......	......
(Mutilated),	3	1	1	34	......	......	......	......	34	......	......	1	......	......
(Mutilated),	3	1	1	37	......	......	1	......	38	......	......	......	......	......
	18	4	2	170	2	......	19	3	194	......	......	3	......	......
David Whitehill,	4	......	......	22	......	......	......	......	22	......	......	1	......	......
	22	4	2	192	2	......	19	3	216	......	......	3	......	......

(Mutilated) Chester, Augst. 28, 1777.
LODK. SPROGELL, M. M. G. of P.

A RETURN OF PART OF THE SEVENTH CLASS OF THE SECOND BATTALION LANCASTER COUNTY MILITIA COMMAND. BY COL. PORTER UNDER MARCHING ORDERS FOR NORTHUMBERLAND COUNTY, AUGUST 11TH, 1779. (c.)

1st Company.

Capt. William Arbuckle Co.
None.

2nd Company.

Capt. Robert Miller Co.
James Orsburn, 7th.
John Beard, 7th.

3rd Company.

Capt. Joseph Walker Co.
None.

4th Company.

Capt. Thomas Clerk Co.
Jno. Rodgers, 7th.

5th Company.

Capt. Robert King's Co.
Wm. McGlaughlin, 6th class.

6th Company.

Capt. Josep Allison Co.
Jno. Tannehill, 7th.
Francis Henry, 6th.
Jno. Patterson, 6th.

7th Company.

Capt. John Caldwell Co.
John Heckman, 6th.
John Turner, 7th.
Wm. Taylor, 7th.

8th Company.

Capt. John Paxton Co.
None.

7 The above return certifyd to be just by me.

JOHN CALDWELL,
Capt.

N. B.—None of the Officers belong to the seventh class proposed marching.

JOHN CALDWELL,
Capt.

A ROAL OF THE MARCHING TROOPS OF THE EIGHT CLASS OF THE 2D BATTN. LANCASTER COUNTY MILITIA COMMANDED BY COL. JAMES PORTOR UNDER MARCHING ORDERS FOR SUNBURRY IN THE COUNTY OF NORTHUMBERLAND 23RD AUG. 1779 AT STEELS TAVERN. (c.)

1st Company.

Capt. Arbuckle, 8th class.
None.

2nd Company.

Capt. Anderson, 8th class.
None.

3rd Company.

Capt. Walker, 8th class.
None.

4th Company.

Capt. Clerk, 8th class.
None.

5th Company.

Capt. King, 8th class.
James Reed.

6th Company.

Capt. Allison, 8th class.
Thomas Campbel.

7th Company.

Capt. Caldwell, 8th class.
William Cummins.
James Grierr.
John Williamsón.

8th Company.

Capt. Paxton, 8th class, ready to march.
Nathaniel Coalter.

I do certify the above roal to the state of the eight class of the 2d Battn. & the troops now under my command on their march.

WM. CALHOON,
1st Lieut.

Danegale, Aug. 27, 1779.

PAY ROLE OF SUCH A PART OF CAP'T CALDWELL'S COMPANY OF THE 2ND BATT. OF LANCASTER COUNTY MILITIA EMPLOYED ON DUTY IN NORTHUMBERLAND COUNTY IN THE MONTHS OF AUGUST, SEPTEMBER & OCTOBER, 1779 AS WERE PAID IN SPECIE IN THE YEAR 1782 & 1783 BY PHILIP MARSTELLERS PAY MASTER. (c.)

Benj. Mills, Lieut., served 2 mo. 6 days
John Tumbletee, Private.
Richd. Allison, Private, served 2 mo. 6 days.
Robt. McCleary, Private, served 2 mo. 6 days.
Andrew Foster, Private, served 2 mo. 6 days.
Saml. Thompson Private, served 2 mo. 6 days.
James Cooke, Private, served 2 mo. 6 days.
Anthony Snyder, Private, served 2 mo. 6 days.
Patrick Bryan, Private, served 2 mo. 6 days.
John Dukemanles, Private, served 2 mo. 6 days.
John Johnson, Private, served 2 mo. 6 days.
John Alexander, Private, served 2 mo. 6 days.
Robt. Duglas, Private, served 2 mo. 3 days.
David Caldwell, Private, served 2 mo. 3 days.
Jonathan Woodside, Private, served 2 mo. 3 days.
John Wirtz, Private, served 2 mo. 2 days.
Adam Wirtz, Private, served 2 mo. 3 days.
Henry Bitner, Private, served 1 mo. 26 days.

		Specie.
The Lieut. pay Bounty & Liquor in Cont.,		£45 11 6
11 men their pay, Bounty & Liquor in Cont.,		316 16 0
5 men their pay, Bounty & Liquor in Cont.,		142 0 0
1 man his pay, Bounty & Liquor in Cont.,		27 6 0
		531 13 6
30 for one		17 14 5
May 21, 1782, pd. 2 militia men for service in specie,	£10 0 6	95 17 9
Their pay by the Scale of Depriciation,	3 4 0	
Overpaid,	£6 16 0	6 16 0
		£102 13 9

The above one hundred and two pounds thirteen shillings and nine pence were not allowed to Philip Marsteller, Esq., at settlement altho the voucher for pay must have been rendered.

JNO. NICHOLSON,
Compt. Genl. Office,
May 14, 1790.

Sundry Persons Overpaid by P. Marsteller for Militia Service to wit——

		Specie.
Order to Compt.		
	Maj. Tuml. Jones,	£10 8 0
	Maj. Thouffler for QMr. John Crener, State,	10 18 9
	Capt. Holderbaum his Co., State,	8 12 6
	Capt. Holderbaum, his Co., Specie,	6 1 0
Order to Compt.		
	Col. Hubley for the Staff Col. Ross Bat.,	7 17 6
	Col. Hubley for the Staff of Col. Carpenter,	7 15 10
		£51 13 1

Certified by,
JNO. NICHOLSON,
Compt. Genl. Office,
May 14th, 1790.

PAY ROLE OF SUCH OF CAPT. CALDWELL'S COMPANY OF THE 2D BATTALION OF LANCASTER COUNTY MILITIA EMPLOYED ON DUTY IN NORTHUMBERLAND COUNTY IN THE MONTH OF AUGUST, SEPTEMBER & OCTOBER, 1779 AS WERE PAID IN SPECIE IN THE YEAR 1782 & 1783 BY P. MARCHELLER PAY MASTER. (c.)

Benj. Mills, Lieut. servd,	2 mo. 6 days.
John Tumbletee, priv.,	2 mo. 6 days.
Richd. Allison,	2 mo. 6 days.
Robt. McCleary,	2 mo. 6 days.
Andrew Faster,	2 mo. 6 days.
Saml. Thompson,	2 mo. 6 days.
James Cooke,	2 mo. 6 days.
Anthony Sneider,	2 mo. 6 days.
Patrick Bryans,	2 mo. 6 days.
John Dickmanier,	2 mo. 6 days.
John Johnson,	2 mo. 6 days.
John Alexander,	2 mo. 6 days.
Robt. Duglas,	2 mo. 3 days.
David Caldwell,	2 mo. 3 days.
Jonathan Woodside,	2 mo. 3 days.
John Wirtz,	2 mo. 3 days.
Adam Wirtz,	2 mo. 3 days.
Henry Bitner,	1 mo. 25 days.

The Lieuts. pay Bounty & liqr. acct. in cont.	£ 46 11 6
11 men their pay do. do.,	316 16 0
5 men their pay do do.,	142 0 0
1 man his pay do. do.	27 6 0
old continental,	£531 13 6
ca 30 for one,	17 14 5
	£ 96 17 9

PAY ROLE CAPT. CALDWELL'S COMPANY OF THE 2D BATTALION OF LANCASTER COUNTY—Continued.

2 militia men say Kleinfelder & Vangundey pd. them their touer of duty on the 21st May, 1782,	£10	0	0	specie.
Their pay by the scale of depreciation,	3	4	0	loss.
	£ 6	16	0	
	£95	17	9	
	6	16	0	
	£102	13	9	

ROLL OF THE OFFICERS OF THE SECOND BATTALION OF LANCASTER COUNTY MILITIA COMMANDED BY LIEUTENANT COLONEL THOMAS EDWARDS. 1780. (c.)

Field Officers.

Date When Appointed.

Lt. Colo.

Thomas Edwards, April 29th.

Major.

Vallentine Shouffler, May 16th.

Staff.

Chaplain.

Rev. Conrad Bucher, May 16th.

Quarter Mr.

Robert Patton, May 9th.

Surgeon.

Daniel Oldenbruck, May 17th.

Adjutant.

Mathias Primer, May 15th.

Serjt. Major.

John Geoninger, May 15th.

Quarter Mr. Serjt.

Jacob Shaffner, May 15th.

1st Company.

Captain—Baltzer Orth, May 6th.
Lieutenant—John Orth, May 6th.
Ensign—Daniel Stouffer, May 6th.

2nd Company.

Captain—Michael Holderbaum, May 6th.
Lieutenant—Alexander Martin, May 6th.
Ensign—Henry Fogt, May 6th.

3rd Company.

Captain—Casper Steover, May 15th.
Lieutenant—Michael Hernner, May 15th.
Ensign—Nicholas Conrad, May 15th.

4th Company.

Captain—David Krause, May 6th.
Lieutenant—Philip Greenawalt, May 6th.
Ensign—Jacob Embigh, May 6th.

5th Company.

Captain—John Moore, May 6th.
Lieutenant—Jacob Zollinger, May 6th.
Ensign—Michael Mease, May 6th.

6th Company.

Captain—John Stone, May 9th.
Lieutenant—George Bowman, May 9th.
Ensign—Michael Tice, May 9th.

7th Company.

Captain—Wendel Wever, May 20th.
Lieutenant—Michael Teeffenbagh, May 20th.
Ensign—Michael Haag, May 20th.

8th Company.

Captain—John Gassert, May 17th.
Lieutenant—John Field, May 6th.
Ensign—Jacob Lehman, May 6th.

A MUSTER ROLL OF CAPT. BALTZER ORTH'S COMPANY OF THE SECOND BATTALION OF LANCASTER COUNTY MILITIA COMMANDED BY MAJOR SHOUFFLER ON SERVICE AT NORT'N COUNTY, 1780. (c.)

COMMISSIONED OFFICERS.

Captain.	
Baltzer Orth,	Entered 17 Oct.
Lieutenant.	
Alexander Martin,	Entered 17 Oct.
Ensign.	
Jacob Embigh,	Entered 17 Oct.

NON-COMMISSIONED OFFICERS.

Sergeants.	
1. George Strow,	Entered 17 Oct.
2. Peter Berry,	Entered 17 Oct.
3. John Smith,	Entered 17 Oct.
Corporal.	
1. Christian Smith,	Entered 17 Oct.
2. Michael Krebs,	Entered 17 Oct.
3. Rudy Miller,	Entered 17 Oct.
Drummer.	
Martin Weitsel,	Entered 17 Oct.

PRIVATES.

1. Jacob Keilinger,	Entered 17 Oct.
2. Abraham Raiguel,	Entered 17 Oct.
3. John Righard,	Entered 17 Oct.
4. Frederick Weyman,	Entered 17 Oct.
5. John Imboden,	Entered 17 Oct.
6. George Matter,	Entered 17 Oct.
7. Adam Orth,	Entered 17 Oct.
8. Christian Stouffer,	Entered 17 Oct.
9. Henry Emrich,	Entered 17 Oct.
10. Adam Sheffer,	Entered 17 Oct.
11. Vencins Brown,	Entered 17 Oct.
12. John Loutermilch,	Entered 17 Oct.
13. Michael Groh,	Entered 17 Oct.
14. Michael Steckbeck,	Entered 17 Oct.
15. John Umberger,	Entered 17 Oct.
16. George Hess,	Entered 17 Oct.
17. John Rewalt,	Entered 17 Oct.; discharged 23 Oct at Boafler.

PRIVATES—Continued.

18. Christian Embigh, ...	Entered 17 Oct.
19. Jacob Steep, ...	Entered 17 Oct.
20. Rudy Kelker, ...	Entered 17 Oct.
21. John Sholl, ...	Entered 17 Oct.
22. Henry Ekolf, ...	Entered 17 Oct.
23. George Troutman, ...	Entered 17 Oct.
24. Anthony Kapp, ...	Entered 17 Oct.
25. Peter Shitz, ...	Entered 17 Oct.
26. John Bawsler, ...	Entered 17 Oct.
27. Ulrey Beckly, ...	Entered 17 Oct.
28. George Spengler, ...	Entered 17 Oct.
29. Henry Bowman, ...	Entered 17 Oct.
30. Adam German, ...	Entered 17 Oct. at Boafler.
31. Michael Miller, Geo Son,..	Entered 17 Oct.
32. John Dusing, ...	Entered 17 Oct.
33. Michael Miller, ...	Entered 17 Oct.
34. Baltzer Shaaly, ...	Entered 17 Oct.
35. Peter Fisher, ...	Entered 17 Oct.
36. Jacob Neff, ...	Entered 17 Oct.
37. Henry Yeakel, ...	Entered 17 Oct.
38. Daniel Miller, ...	Entered 17 Oct, 4 Batt.
39. John Hay, ...	Entered 26 Oct, 7 Batt.
40. George Mehs, ...	Entered 19 Oct.
41. Thomas McClanaghan, ...	Entered 17 Oct., 4 Batt.
42. John Smith, ...	Entered 17 Oct., 4 Batt.
43. Christian Kremmer, ...	Entered 17 Oct.; Disch 23 Oct.
44. Peter Conrad, ...	Entered 21 Oct.
45. Christopher Slosser, ...	Entered 23 Oct.
46. Jacob Hower, ...	Entered 31 Oct.
47. George Shok, ...	Entered 31 Oct.
48. John Line, ...	Entered 31 Oct.
49. William Yeengst, ...	Entered 31 Oct.
50. Christian Greenawalt, ...	Entered 31 Oct.
51. Henry Zeller, ...	Entered 17 Oct.
52. Michael Grove, ...	Entered 17 Oct.

I do Certify to have Mustered Capt. Orth's Company as Specified in the above Roll.

Decr. 16th, 1780.

SAML. HUNTER,
Lt. Nd.

PROOF OF THE EFFECTIVES.

	Capt.	Lieut.	Ensign.	Serj.	Corp.	Drum.	Private.
Present, ...	1	1	1	3	2	1	47
Absent, ...	....	....	....	....	1	....	4
Total, .	1	1	1	3	3	1	51

I do hereby Certify that the within Muster Roll is a True State to my Company without Fraud to the United States or to any individual according to the best of my knowledge.

BALTZER ORTH,
Capt.

Affirmed to before me Decr. 16th, 1780.

SAM'L. HUNTER.
Lt. N. C.

RETURN OF THE FIRST CLASS OF CAPT. BALTZER ORTH'S COMPANY OF THE 2D BATTALION LANCASTER COUNTY MILITIA. (c.)

Jacob Killinger, marched.
Rudolph Miller, marched.
Abraham Raignel, marched.
John Reighart, marched.
Frederick Weyman, marched.
John Imboden, marched.
George Matter, marched.
Adam Orth, marched.
Christian Stoufer, marched.
Christian Smith, L1275.
Michael Brechtbiel, L675.
John Sweigart Imboden, acquitted.

I do hereby Certify that the above return is a true State of my Company taken from the Company Role, Octr., 1780.

BALTZER ORTH,
Capt.

RETURN OF THE FIRST CLASS OF CAPT. GASSERT'S COMPANY OF THE 2D BATTALLION OF LANCASTER COUNTY MILLITIA. (c.)

Henry Fux, L 720.
Wendel Fisher, L 720.
Christian Kaufman, L 975.
Peter Kenny, L 675.
Ulrey Kneagy, Jun., L 675.

Henry Yeakle, marched.
Henry Merk, acquitted.
Daniel Miller, marched.

I do certify that the above is a true state taken from my company role. Dec. 1, 1780.

JOHANNES GASSERT,
Capt.

RETURN OF THE FIRST CLASS OF CAPT. HOLDERBAUM'S COMPANY OF THE 2D BATTALION LANCASTER COUNTY MILITIA. (c.)

John Loutermilk, marched.
Jacob Ellenberger, fined.
David Steel, fined.
Michael Steckbeck, marched.
Jacob Wilhelm, fined.
John Oyer, fined.
John Umberger, marched.
Henry Humberger, acquitted.

I do hereby Certify that the above is a true State taken from my Company return the 1st Day of December, 1780.

MICHAEL HOLDERBAUM,
Capt.

RETURN OF THE FIRST CLASS OF CAPT. STONE'S COMPANY OF THE 2D BATTALLION LANCASTER COUNTY MILITIA. (c.)

Christian Smith, marched.
Martin Weitzel, marched.
Henry Bowman, marched.
John Kleber, L 675.
Henry Rudy, L 875.
Adam Garman, marched.
Peter Meyer, L 975.
Michael Miller, Geo. son, marched.
John Dusing, marched.
George Strohm, L 715.
Abraham Meyer, L 955.

Michael Miller, marched.
John Strohm, L 715.
Baltzer Shaally, marched.
Peter Fisher, marched.
John Shott, L 675.
Jacob Becker, L 675.
Christopher Slosser, marched.
Peter Spyker, acquitted.

I do certify that the above is a true state taken from my company roll the 1st day of December, 1780.

JOHN STONE,
Capt.

RETURN OF THE FIRST CLASS OF CAPT. MOORE'S COMPANY OF THE 2D BATTALION LANCASTER COUNTY MILITIA. (c.)

John Smith, marched.
John Sholl, marched.
Henry Eckolf, marched.
George Troutman, marched.
Jacob Loutermilk, acquitted.
Anthony Kaap, marched.
Peter Shitz, marched.
Jacob Neff, marched.
Michael Neff, acquitted.
George Mehs, marched.
Jacob Zartman, acquitted.
George Shock, marched.
Henry Zeller, marched.

I do Certify that the above is a true State taken from my Company Role.
Dec. 1780.

JOHN MOOR,
Capt.

RETURN OF THE FIRST CLASS OF CAPT. STEEVER'S COMPANY OF THE 2D BATTALION OF LAN. COTY. MILITIA. (c.)

Henry Emrich, marched.
John Kunckle, fined.
Jacob Fedderhauf, fined.
David Peffly, fined.
Adam Sheffer, marched.
Vincins Brown, marched.

Michael Grob, marched.
Martin Shuey, fined.
Peter Conrad, marched.
Jacob Houer, marched.
Michael Hoffman, fined.

I do Certify that the foregoing of the first class is a true Copy, taken from my Company Return the 1st Day of Dec. 1780.

CASPER STEOVER,
Capt.

RETURN OF THE FIRST CLASS OF CAPT. WEAVER'S COMPANY OF THE 2D BATTALLION OF LANCASTER COUNTY MILLITIA. (c.)

Peter Berry, marched.
John Bawsler, marched.
George Spangler, marched.
John Lantz, L 675.
Uhlrey Beckly, marched.
John Line, marched.
William Yeengst, acquitted.
Martin Bartturff, acquitted.

I do certify that the above is a true state taken from my company roll.

Dec. 1780.

WENDELL WEAVER,
Capt.

MUSTER ROLL OF THE 2ND CLASS 2ND BATALION LANCR. COUNTY MILITIA COMMANDED BY CAPT. MICHL. HOLDEBAUM ON A TOUR OF DUTY AT LANCASTER. (c.)

Names of Persons Who Performed the Tour.	Names of Persons Who Furnished Substitutes.	When duty Commd.	When duty ended.
Capt.		1781.	1781.
Michl. Holdebarn,		May 1,	June 30.
Lieut.			
John Ordt,		May 1,	June 30.
Ens.			
Nicholas Conrad,		May 1,	June 30.
Serjt.			
Jno. Calonen,	George Walburn,	May 1,	June 30.
Peter Harter,	Charles Orndt,	May 1,	June 30.
Jno Cryner,	Geo. Miley,	May 1,	June 30.
Corpl.			
Fredk. Koutz,	Jacob Hartman,	May 1,	June 30.
Conrad Rynehill,	Francis Baylor,	May 1,	June 30.
Fred'k Doughtermar,	Peter Lane,	May 1,	June 30.
Fifer.			
Peter Shindle,	Abraham Saybol,	May 1,	June 30.
Geo. Foltz,	Jno. Cossard,	May 1,	June 30.
Danl. Riblet,	Nicholas Tingess,	May 1,	June 30.
Tobias Hess,	Jno. Saltzgeber,	May 1,	June 30.
Henry Yenghst,	Harman Potdorf,	May 1,	June 30.
Peter Lyne,		May 1,	June 30.
Jno. Young,	Martin Myer,	May 1,	June 30.
Jno. Clerk,	Henry Myer,	May 1,	June 30.
Peter Stayer,	Jno. Stayer,	May 1,	June 30.
Henry George,	Danl. Fitzberger,	May 1,	June 30.
James Mosher,	Jno. Stalssmith,	May 1,	June 30.
Wm. Hydler,	Conrad Klyne,	May 1,	June 30.
Valentine Knopp,	Laurence Segrist,	May 1,	June 30.
Michl. Sowder,	Henry Feisler,	May 1,	June 30.
Adm. Stieger,	Francis Geeman,	May 1,	June 30.
Jno. Brown,		May 1,	June 30.
Melcher Abmyer,		May 1,	June 30.
Peter Ruth,	Philip Urleh,	May 1,	June 30.
Jno. Petree,	Adam Hyeman,	May 1,	June 30.
Chris'r Rynold,	Geo. Reynold,	May 1,	June 30.
Adm. Frocklick,	Martin Ulrich,	May 1,	June 30.
Jacob Hains,	Michl. Stump,	May 1,	June 30.
Jno. Gentzner,	Jno. Webner,	May 1,	June 30.
Joseph Stephenson,	Philip Peters,	May 1,	June 30.
Henry Fitzer,	Fredk. Fernsler,	May 1,	June 30.
Jacob Grove,	Jno. Snely,	May 1,	June 30.
Jno. Rohrer,	Peter Woissberger,	May 1,	June 30.

MUSTER ROLL OF THE 2ND CLASS 2ND BATALION, LANC. COUNTY MILITIA.—Continued.

Performed the Tour. Names of Persons Who	Names of Persons Who Furnished Substitutes.	When duty Commd.	When duty ended.
		1781.	1781.
Barnet Embich,		May 1,	June 30.
Philip Embich,	Geo. Evinger,	May 1,	June 30.
Jacob Goltman,	Daniel Diel,	May 1,	June 30.
Laurence Bout,	Henry Wyand,	May 1,	June 30.
Geo. Trump,	Geo. (say Jno.) Corman,	May 1,	June 30.
Martin Jordan,	Thos. Copenhaver,	May 1,	June 30.
Chris. Wiedley,	Andw. Crause,	May 1,	June 30.
Daniel Wiale,	Nichl. Waggoner,	May 1,	June 30.
Geo. German,	say for Geo. Myer,	May 1,	June 30.
Adam Detrich,	Jno. Steer,	May 1,	June 30.
Chris'n Reed,	Jacob Chamberlin,	May 1,	June 30.
Geo. Shaffer,	Harmar Spies,	May 1,	June 30.
Willm. Steel,	Adm. Freed,	May 1,	June 30.
Fredk. Steger,	Michl. Laintz,	May 1,	June 30.
Casper Shitz,	Chris'n Reese,	May 1,	June 30.
Jacob Lindey,	Jno. Wilhelm,	May 1,	June 30.
Jno. Landie,	Michl. Rambler,	May 1,	June 30.
Felix Young (wounded).		May 1,	June 30.
Jno. Hener.			
Chris'. Hildebrand.			
Ant. Steekle.			
Wm. Etchberger.			
Chris. Myer.			
Michl. Brydenback.			

Lancr. May 8th, 1781. Then mustered above compy. as above specified.

ADM. HUBLEY,
S. L. Lr. Cy.

MUSTER ROLL OF 3D CLASS OF 2ND BATALL. LANCR. COUNTY MILA ON A TOUR OF DUTY AT LANCASTER. (c.)

Names of Persons Who Served.	Names of Persons Who Furnished Substitutes.	Time when duty Commd.	Time when duty ended.
Capt.		1781.	1781.
Andw. Ream,		June 22,	July 30.
Clk.			
Jacob Swartzell,			
Serjt.			
Gotlib Younkman,	George Zeller,		Aug. 21.
David Ream,			July 28.
Corpl.			
Joseph Brandle,	Philip Brandle,		Aug. 21.
Gotlib Mock,			July 28.
Drumr.			
Joseph Allis,			Aug. 21.
Fifer.			
Fredk. Millinger.			
Privates.			
George Trout,			July 28.
Jno. Buch,	John Haker,		Aug. 21.
Peter Steffy,			July 28.
Fredk. Ream.			
Chrisn. Dilleman,	Leonard Krouse,		Aug. 21.
Caspar Tripple.			

MUSTER ROLL OF 3D CLASS 2ND BATALL. LANCASTER CO'Y MILITA ON A TOUR OF DUTY AT LANCASTER. (c.)

Names of Persons Who Served.	Names of Persons Who Furnished Substitutes.	Time when duty Commd.	Time when duty ended.
Capt.		1781.	1781.
Caspar Stoever, ...	....	July 1.	
Lieut.			
Philip Greenawalt.			
Serjt.			
Peter Hasten, ...	John Gushwa, ...	July 2.	
Simon Lough, ...	Mathew Grow, ...	July 2.	
Danl. Henning, ...	Peter Carsnids.	July 1.	
Jacob Snevely (clerk),...	Jacob Pfeiffer,		
Corpl.			
Jacob Mellinger, ...	Abraham Grow.		
Philip Embich, ...	George Fieser, ...	July 2.	
Henry Brosius, ...	Adam Schole.		
Drumer.			
Christophr. Rinehill, ...	John Bealer, ...	July 2.	
Privates.			
Archd. Hays, ...	John Dubs, ...	1st.	Inlis. 8 July
George Teerwachter, ...	....	....	July 29.
Christr. Zebold, Jr., ...	Chris. Zebold, Sen'r.,..	July 2. Zebold, Jr., did not m own class pears he Qur.	July 29. appear arch in his and ap- was in this
George Gilbert, ...	....	July 1.	July 29.
Michl. Streher, ...	Jacob Gettle, ...		
Walter Newman, (say Peter.	Jacob Lehn, ...		
John Greenwalt, ...	Jacob Gryder, ...	July 2.	
Henry Kelker, ...	Antho'y Kelker, ...		
Christ'r Beck, ...	Peter Smith, ...		
Chrisn. Ambroit, ...	....	July 1.	July 29.
Wm. Ward, ...	....	....	July 29.
George Ellinger,..........	George Gisseman,.		
Peter Yengst, ...	John Zimmerman.		
John Mickle, ...	John Knap.		
Henry Kehly, ...	....	July 1.	July 29.
Henry Yingst, ...	Michl. Zimmerman.		
James Jones, ...	Peter Stiner.		
Fredk. Kritzer, ...	Nicholas Hawk, ...		
John Fisher, ...	Chrisn. Seibert, ...		
Adam Specht, ...	Chris'n, Toce,		
Henry Dum, ...	Michl. Mawlfer, ...		
John German, ...	Saml. Moyley, ...	July 2.	
John Lemy, ...	Adam Balmer, ...	July 1.	

MUSTER ROLL OF 3D CLASS 2ND BATALL. LANCASTER CO'Y MILITIA ON A TOUR OF DUTY AT LANCASTER. —Continued.

Names of Persons Who Served.	Names of Persons Who Furnished Substitutes.	Time when duty Commd.	Time when duty ended.
		1781.	1781.
Michl. Swanger, ...		....	July 29.
Henry Meisser.			
Wm. Hughin.			
Jno. Henning.			
John Holl.			
George Weber.			
Jacob Feel, ...	Chrisn. Seltzer.		
Adam Henning, ...	John Neff.		
Peter Shaffer, ...	Henry Shaffner.		
Jno. Derredinger, ...	George Weaber.		
Michl. Radmacher, ...	Peter Spingler, ...	July 2.	
Wm. Dyer, ...	Micheor Loudermilch, .	Inlis	ted July 3
Jacob Newman, ...	Benjn. Miller.		
Chrisn. Reed, ...	Nichs. Meas, ...	July 4.	
Ludwig Ornbeim, ...	Jno. Sharff.		
Peter Rood, ...	....	July 5.	July 29.
Michl. Boltz, ...	....	July 2.	
Jno. Yeager, ...	Fredk. Stiner, ...	July 4.	
Maths. Bocher, ...	....	July 4.	July 29.
Peter Stephen, ...	Valentine Bocher, ...	July 4.	

July 6th, '81. Then mustered above company as above specified.

ADM. HUBLEY,
S. L. Lr. Cy.

MUSTER ROLL OF THE 4TH CLASS OF THE 2D BATALION LANR. COUNTY MILITIA ON A TOUER OF DUTY AT LANCASTER GUARDING BRITISH PRISONERS OF WAR. (c.)

Names of Persons who Perform a Touer of Duty.	What class.	Names of Persons who Furnished Substitutes.	Time when duty commenced.	Time when duty discharged.
Cap't.			1781.	1781.
David Kraus,			Aug't 20th,	Oct'r 20th.
Lieu't.				
Michael Herner,			Aug't 20th,	Oct'r 20th.
Ensg'n.				
Daniel S ouffer,			Aug't 20th,	Oct'r 20th.
Cl'k.				
Philip Empigh,			Aug't 20th,	Oct'r 20th.
Serj't.				
Jacob Matter,			Aug't 20th,	Oct'r 20th.
George Welsh,		Ludwick Wirtenberg,	Aug't 20th,	Oct'r 20th.
Corp'l.				
John Rohrer,		Henry Hileman,	Aug't 20th,	Oct'r 20th.

Jacob Groff,		Martin Cramer,	Aug't 20th,	Oct'r 20th.
Peter Jingst,			Aug't 20th,	Oct'r 20th.
Drum.				
Christ'n Reinehl,		Mich'l Uhrich,	Aug't 20th,	Oct'r 20th.
Fife.				
Frederick Mellinger,			Aug't 20th,	Oct'r 20th.
Privates.				
Peter Steffy,			Aug't 20th,	Oct'r 20th.
John Matter,			Aug't 20th,	Oct'r 20th.
John Greenewald,		Jacob Cryder,	Aug't 20th,	Oct'r 20th.
Michael Crawford,			Aug't 20th,	Oct'r 20th.
George Hess,		Adam Louderwick,	Aug't 20th,	Oct'r 20th.
Frederick Leonhard,		Jacob Kitzmiller,	Aug't 20th,	Oct'r 20th.
Francis Reinhard,		John Strayer,	Aug't 20th,	Oct'r 20th.
Mathias Harter,		Thomas Morgan,	Aug't 20th,	Oct'r 20th.
Henrey Swartz,			Aug't 20th,	Oct'r 20th.
Hugh Black,			Aug't 20th,	Oct'r 20th.
Mathias Shipe,		James Long,	Aug't 20th,	Oct'r 20th.
Bernhart Empigh,		John Fireavent,	Aug't 20th,	Oct'r 20th.
George Weirich,			Aug't 20th,	Oct'r 20th.
George North,		Peter Fizer,	Aug't 20th,	Oct'r 20th.
Jacob Weaver,			Aug't 20th,	Oct'r 20th.
Henrey Shell,			Aug't 20th,	Oct'r 20th.
John German,			Aug't 20th,	Oct'r 20th.
William Cuningham,			Aug't 20th,	Oct'r 20th.
Adam Diedrich,		Thos. Clark,	Aug't 20th,	Oct'r 20th.
Christopher Reed,		John George Smith,	Aug't 20th,	Oct'r 20th.
Simon Newman,		George Miller,	Aug't 20th,	Oct'r 20th.
George Shram,			Aug't 20th,	Oct'r 20th.
George Kochenderfer,			Aug't 20th,	Oct'r 20th.

ROLL OF THE 4TH CLASS OF THE 2D BATALION.—Continued.

Names of Persons who Perform a Touer of Duty.	What class.	Names of Persons who Furnished Substitutes.	Time when duty commenced.	Time when duty discharged.
			1781.	1781.
[illegible]ob [illegible]an,		And'w Cap,	Aug't 20th.	Oct'r [illegible]h.
Alexad'r Shoupe,			Aug't 20th.	Oct'r 20th.
[illegible]n Crawford,			Aug't 20th.	Oct'r 20th.
Christian Berringer,		John Frantz,	[illegible]'t [illegible].	Oct'r 20th.
Nicholas Groch,		George [illegible]er,	Ag't [illegible].	Oct'r 20th.
William Hains,		Henry Herchelbroad,	Aug't 20th.	Oct'r 20th.
George Null,	4th,		[illegible]g't [illegible].	[illegible]'r 20th
John [illegible]e,	4th,	George Smisser,	Aug't [illegible].	Oct'r [illegible]h.
Christian Miller,	4th,		Aug't [illegible].	Oct'r 20th.
Peter Wentz,	4th,	Fred'k Wolferberger,	Aug't [illegible].	[illegible]t'r 20th.
Frederick Kopp,	4th,		[illegible]'t [illegible].	[illegible]t'r 20th.
Leonhard Newman,	4th,	Ludwig Peffer,	[illegible]g't [illegible].	Oct'r 20th.
Henrey Shram,	4th,		Aug't [illegible].	Oct'r 20th.
Henrey [illegible]y,	4th,		Aug't [illegible].	Oct'r 20th.
John Loeb,	4th,	George Holtzstine,	Aug't 20th.	Oct'r 20th.
[illegible]ob Wentz,	4th,		Aug't [illegible].	[illegible]'r 20th.
John Shroyer,	4th,	Math's Bronewile,	Aug't [illegible].	[illegible]t'r 20th.
Adam Jacobey,	[illegible]th,		[illegible]g't [illegible].	Oct'r 20th.

Christian Goldman,	4th,		Aug't 20th,	Oct'r 20th.
Adam Garman,	4th,	Jacob Sicks,	[illegible] 20th,	[illegible] 20th.
Jacob Hartman,	4th,	Baltzer Laber,	Aug't 20th,	Oct'r 20th.
John Gassert, Jun'r,	4th,	Isaac Brandt,	Aug't [illegible]	Oct'r 20th.
Casper Deemer,	4th,		Aug't [illegible]	Oct'r 20th.
Christian Brost,	4th,	Martin Spengler,	Aug't [illegible]	Oct'r 20th.
Jacob Lentz,	4th,		Aug't 20th,	Oct'r 20th.
Francis Stalsmith,	4th,		Aug't 20th,	Oct'r 20th.
John Heffelfinger,	4th,		Aug't [illegible]	Oct'r 20th.
Henry Kelker,	4th,	Jacob Spengler,	Aug't [illegible]	Oct'r 30th.
[illegible]y Dearwachter,	4th,		Aug't 20th,	[illegible] 20th.
[illegible] Swartz,	4th,		Aug't 20th,	Oct'r 20th.
Ulrich Felty,	4th,		Aug't 20th,	Oct'r 20th.
Casper Seidelmyer,	4th,	George Leidelmeyer,	Aug't 20th,	Oct'r 20th.
Jacob Goldman,	4th,	George Gebhart,	Aug't 20th,	Oct'r 20th.
John Barr,	4th,		Aug't 20th,	Oct'r 20th.
Philip Deboy,	4th,	John Breght,	Aug't [illegible]	[illegible] 20th.
Peter Seyler,		John Seyler,	Aug't [illegible]	Oct'r 20th.
George Folmer,	4th,		Aug't [illegible]	Oct'r 20th.
Peter Ruth,	4th,		Aug't 20th,	Oct'r 20th.
Israel Gremer,	4th,	John McClintick,	Aug't [illegible]	Oct'r 20th.
Jacob Sneveley,	4th,	Isaac Snevely,	Aug't 20th,	Oct'r 20th.
John [illegible]y,	4th,	Jacob German,	Aug't 20th,	Oct'r 20th.
[illegible] Strayer,	4th,	John Tise,	Aug't 20th,	Oct'r 20th.
William Rutford,	4th,			
Henry Gilwart,	4,			
Caspar Yost,	4,			
Sam'l Hartman,	4,			
Jno. Fehler,	4,			
John Reed,	4,			
Jacob Geissert,	4,			

MUSTER ROLL OF THE 5TH, 6TH & 7TH CLASS OF THE 2D BATALION LANCASTER COUNTY MILITIA ON A TOUER OF DUTY TO BUCK'S COUNTY. (c.)

Names of Persons Who Perform a Touer of Duty.	What class.	Names of Persons Who Furnished Substitutes.	Time when duty commenced.	Time when duty ended.
Cap't.			[illegible]	1781.
John Moore,	5th,		Sep't 25d,	
Lieu't.				
George Bowman,	5th,		Sep't 25d,	
Ensg'n.				
Jacob [illegible],	5th,		Sep't 2d,	
Clerck.				
John Miller,	5th,		Sep't 25d,	
Serj'ts.				
Peter Swanger,	5th,		Sep't 2d,	
Casper Leop,	5th,		Sep't 25d,	

Corp'l.				
Jacob Hoff,	5th,		Sep't 25d,	
Balzer Mies,	5th,	George Zinn,	Sep't 25d,	
Privates.				
Leonard Stump,	5th,		Sep't 25d,	
Frances Seybritt,	5th,	Michael Swanger,	Sep't 25d,	
George Strickler,	5th,		Sep't 25d,	
Jacob Umbehand,	5th,		Sep't 25d,	
George Hoffman,	5th,	John Smith,	Sep't 25d,	
Frederick Miller,	5th,		Sep't 25d,	
Ludwick Miller,	5th,		Sep't 25d,	
Christopher Meyer,	5th,		Sep't 25d,	
John Sheffer,	5th,		Sep't 25d,	
Henrey Fortney,	5th,		Sep't 25d,	
John Kuster,	5th,	Abraham Sebolt,	Sep't 25d,	
Mathias Fogt,	5th,		Sep't 25d,	
Simon Diemer,	5th,		Sep't 25d,	
Henrey Miller,	5th,		Sep't 25d,	
Nicholas [illegible]e,	5th,		Sep't 25d,	
[illegible]in Benner,	5th,		Sep't 25d,	
[illegible]drew [illegible]e,	5th,	John Dietrick Ourhand,	Sep't 25d,	
Martin Walburn,	5th,		Sep't 25d,	
Charles Shoak,	5th,		Sep't 25d,	
Abraham Brand,	5th,		Sep't 25d,	
Adam Shouer,	5th,		Sep't 25d,	
John [illegible]r,	5th,	Ludwick Dorman,	Sep't 25d,	
Henrey Mieley,	5th,	Edward Bryans,	Sep't 25d,	
Christopher Esterlein,	5th,		Sep't 25d,	
Peter Feetzler,	5th,	[illegible]e Peffer,	Sep't 25d,	
Jacob Conrad,	5th,		Sep't 25d,	
Martin [illegible]e,	5th,		[illegible]t 25d,	
Adam Bard,	5th,	Henry Redigh,	Sep't 25d,	
John Snog,	5th,	Adam Hening,	Sep't 25d,	

MUSTER ROLL OF THE 5TH, 6TH & 7TH CLASS OF THE 2D BATALION LANCASTER COUNTY MILITIA ON A TOUER OF DUTY TO BUCK'S COUNTY.—Continued.

Names of Persons Who Perform a Touer of Duty.	What class.	Names of Persons Who Furnished Substitutes.	Time when duty commenced.	Time when duty ended.
			1781.	1781.
[illegible],	5th,		Sep't 25d,	
John Yager,	5th,		Sep't 25d,	
Peter Kalp,	5th,		Sep't 25d,	
John Butturff,	5th,		Sep't 25d,	
Michael Sheffer,	5th,		Sep't 25d,	
Henrey German,	5th,		Sep't 25d,	
Thomas Harveson,	5th,		Sep't 25d,	
Casper Mies,	5th,		Sep't 25d,	
Nicholas Greenawald,	5th,		Sep't 25d,	
Frederick [illegible]ne,	5th,		Sep't 25d,	
Henry Shell,	5th,		Sep't 25d,	

MUSTER ROLL OF THE 5TH, 6TH & 7TH CLASS OF THE 2D BATALION LANCASTER COUNTY MILITIA ON A TOUER OF DUTY TO BUCK'S COUNTY. (c.)

Names of Persons Who Perform a Touer of Duty.	What class.	Names of Persons Who Furnished Substitutes.	Time when duty commenced.	Time when duty ended.
			781.	1781.
Cap't.				
John Stone,	6th,		Sep't 23d,	
Lif't.				
Jacob Zollinger,	6th,		Sep't 23d,	
Ensg'n.				
Michael Hawke,	6h,		Sep't 23d,	
Clark.				
John Iago,	6th,		Sep't 23d,	
Serj'ts.				
Christian Greenawald,	6th,		Sep't 23d,	
George Shell,	6th,		Sep't 23d.	
Adam Spangler,	6th,		Sep't 23d,	

MUSTER ROLL OF THE 5TH, 6TH & 7TH CLASS OF THE 2D BATALION LANCASTER COUNTY MILITIA ON A TOUER OF DUTY TO BUCK'S COUNTY.—Continued.

Names of Persons Who Perform a Touer of Duty.	What class.	Names of Persons Who Furnished Substitutes.	Time when duty commenced.	Time when duty ended.
Privates.			1781.	1781.
Mtin Miller,	6th,		Sep't 25d,	
[illegible]ab Penter,	6th,		Sep't 25d,	
C[illegible] [illegible]r,	6th,		Sep't 25d,	
George Featherhoof,	6th,		Sep't 25d,	
[illegible]id Miller,	6th,		Sep't 25d,	"
Christian Coore,	6th,		Sep't 25d,	"
Emunuel Henner,	6th,		Sep't 25d,	"
John Strow,	6th,		Sep't 25d,	"
Henrey Campbell,	6th,	Mich'l Uhler,	Sep't 25d,	
Christian Stantel,	6th,	Thomas Atkinson,	Sep't 25d,	"
Frederick Dupple,	6th,	Conrad Mark,	Sep't 25d,	"
Michael Stoke,	6th,	John Melser,	Sep't 25d,	"
Jacob Kitzmiller,	6th,		Sep't 25d,	
Francis Fols,	6th,		Sep't 25d,	"
Adam Shitz,	6th,		Sep't 25d,	"
Jacob [illegible]s,	6th,		Sep't 25d,	"

William Neyman,	6th,		Sept. 25d,	
Michael Crytzer,	6th,		Sep't 25d,	
Barnhart Reinhart,	6th,	Christian Brand,	Sep't 25d,	
Jacob Shoop,	6th,	Henrey Shupp,	Sep't 25d,	
John Zollinger,	6th,		Sep't 25d,	
Peter Campbell,	6th,	Daniel Miller,	Sep't 25d,	
Christian Yeager,	6th,		Sep't 25d,	
Adam Cryst,	6th,		Sep't 25d,	
Jacob Ressley,	6th,	John Ressley,	Sep't 25d,	
John Bashore,	6th,		Sep't 25d,	
Jacob Terkis,	6th,	John Terkis,	Sep't 25d,	
Henrey Linnenweaver,	6th,		Sep't 25d,	
Henrey Tumn,	6th,	Daniel Tice,	Sep't 25d,	
Henrey Yingst,	6th,		Sep't 25d,	
William Yewen,	6th,	Henry Gring,	Sep't 25d,	

MUSTER ROLL OF THE 5TH, 6TH & 7TH CLASS OF THE 2D BATALION LANCASTER COUNTY MILITIA ON A TOUER OF DUTY TO BUCK'S COUNTY. (c.)

Names of Persons Who Perform a Touer of Duty.	What class.	Names of Persons Who Furnished Substitutes.	Time when duty commenced.	Time when duty ended.
Cap't.			1781.	18 1.
Wendel Weaver,	7th,		Sept. 25d,	
Lieu't.				
John Fiel,	7th,		Sept. 25d,	
Ensg'n.				
Michael Tice,	7th,		Sept. 25d,	
			Sept. 25d,	
Serj'ts.			Sept. 25d,	
Christian Ley,	7th,		Sept. 25d,	
John McCrearey,	7th,			
Nicholas Eshway,	7th,			
Jacob Tice,	7th,		Sept. 25d,	
Drum.				
Jacob Gassent,	7th,		Sept. 25d,	

Fifer.				
Philip Heffelfinger,	7th,		Sept. 2[illegible]d,	
Privates.				
Michael Killinger,	7th,	George Teedrick,	Sept. 25d,	
Godfreid [illegible],	7th,		Sept. 25d,	
John [illegible]er,	7th,		Sept. 25d,	
[illegible] [illegible]in,	7th,		Sept. 25d,	
William Long,	7th,		Sept. 25d,	
Frederick Beyer,	7th,		Sept. 25d,	
John Diel Klein,	7th,		Sept. 25d,	
Lucas Shoaly,	7th,	Henrey Snotterly,	Sept. 25d,	
Martin Uller,	7th,	Michael Deker,	Sept. 25d,	
John Wetzler,	7th,		Sept. 25d,	
Frederick Gundrum,	7th,	John Makel,	Sept. 25d,	
John Greenawald,	7th,		Sept. 25d,	
John Groff,	7th,		Sept. 25d,	
Thomas McElrath,	7th,		Sept. 25d,	
Peter [illegible]r,	7th,		Sept. 25d,	
Peter Sheffer,	7th,		Sept. 25d,	
[illegible] Eichelberner,	7th,	William Heins,	Sept. 25d,	
Michael Kap,	7th,	Jonathan Klingel,	Sept. 25d,	
Andrew Streikler,	7th,	Conrad Strikler,	Sept. 25d,	
Henrey Zimmerman,	7th,		Sept. 25d,	
[illegible] Leresser,	7th,		Sept. 25d,	
George Tryon,	7th,	Christopher Reed,	Sept. 25d,	
Vallentine Miller,	7th,		Sept. 25d,	
Michael Zeller,	7th,		Sept. 25d,	
George Beyer,	7th,		Sept. 25d,	
Christian Werk,	7th,		Sept. 25d,	
Walter Newman,	7th,		Sept. 25d,	
George [illegible]ht,	7th,		Sept. 25d,	
Christopher [illegible]le,	7th,	Christian Lutz,	Sept. 25d,	
Thomas [illegible]r,	7th,	Michael Miller,	Sept. 25d,	

MUSTER ROLL OF THE 5TH, 6TH & 7TH CLASS OF THE 2D BATALION LANCASTER COUNTY MILITIA ON A TOUER OF DUTY TO BUCK'S COUNTY.—**Continued.**

Names of Persons Who Perform a Touer of Duty.	What class.	Names of Persons Who Furnished Substitutes.	Time when duty commenced.	Time when duty ended.
			1781.	1781.
[illegible]an Necker,	7th,	Jacob Lehn,	Sept. 25d,	
[illegible]ge Roth,	7th,		Sept. 25d,	
[illegible]hael Frantz,	7th,		Sept. 25d,	
Jacob Elghold,	7th,		Sept. 25d,	
Christian Kantz,	7th,	Michael Altigh,	Sept. 25d,	
Frederick Steger,	7th,		Sept. 25d,	
James Fiel,	7th,		Sept. 25d,	
John [illegible]y,	7th,		Sept. 25d,	
[illegible]el Strehr,	7th,	David Tice,	Sept. 25d,	
Henry Dubs Sadler,	7th,	John Winter,	Sept. 25d,	
Henrey Dum,	7th,	Joseph Gundy,	Sept. 25d,	
Rudey Yackel,	7th,		Sept. 25d,	
Philip Fernsler,	7th,		Sept. 25d,	
Adam Henning,	7th,		Sept. 25d,	

Henrey Beeckle,	7th,		Sept. 25d,	
Mich'l Boyer,	7th,		Sept. 25d,	
George Urland,	7th,		Sept. 25d,	
Henrey Dum,	7th,			

(c.) This is to Certify that Thomas McCannaughan and John Smith having Served in the first Class of Lancaster County Militia and was discharged on the sixteenth Day of December in the Year one thousand seven Hundred and Eighty the have served in my Company in Northumberland County for the space of sixty seven Days the Pay is 30 Dol. per Day on the exchange in state Money at 75 for one—The said Smith J. McClanarhan have received 100 Dollars each on account of their Pay Witness my Hand the 24 Day of November, 1781—

To Jas. Barber, Esq., S. Lel.

BALTZER ORTH,
Capt.

ROLL OF THE FIELD AND OTHER OFFICERS OF THE 2D BATTALION OF LANCASTER COUNTY MILITIA. DEC. 25TH, 1781. (c.)

Leut. Colo.

Thomas Edwards.

Major.

Vallentine Shouffler.

Captains.

Balthasor Orth.
Michael Holderbam.
Casper Steover.
David Krause.
John Moore.
John Stone.
Wendel Weaver.
Mathias Hening (sic) John Gassert.

Lieutenants.

John Orth.
Alexander Martin.
Michael Herner.
Philip Greenawalt.
Jacob Zollinger.
George Bowman.
Michl. Dieffenbach.
John Fiel.

Ensigns.

Daniel Stouffer.
Vallentine Knop.
Nicholas Conrad.
Jacob Embigh.
John Mehs.
Michael Teis.
Michael Haag.
Jacob Lehmy.

Staff.

Surgeon.

Daniel Oldenbruck.

Qr. Master.

Robt. Patton.

Adjd.

Mathias Primer.

Serjt. Majr.

Philip Huber.

Qr. Mr. Serjs.

Jacob Shaffner.

Drum Majr.

Alexander Benjamin.

CAPTAIN BALTZER ORTHS COMPANY OF MILITIA DEVIDED INTO EIGHT CLASSES, IT BEING THE FIRST COMPANY OF THE 2D BATTALION. (c.)

Captain.

Balser Orth.

First Lieutenant.

John Orth.

Ensign.

Daniel Stouffer.

First Class.

John Imboden.
Christian Stouffer.
Christian Smith.
John Sweigand Imboden.
George Marter.
Abraham Raigue (above age).
John Righard.
Nicholas Brechbeil.
Rudolph Miller.
George Shambach.
Jacob Kuntz.

Second Class.

George Melly.	John Webner.
Christian Long.	Michael Brydenbach.
Christopher Meyer.	Christian Cryder, Jun'r.
Felix Young.	Philip Uhrick.
John Dohner.	Conrad Klein.
Henry Reinoel.	Melchior Abmeyer.
Michael Gingrih.	Jacob Siegrist.
Jacob Greitter (Tobias Son).	John Burkholder (Ch'r Con).
Lorentz Siegrist.	John Reish, Jun'r.

Third Class.

Michael Stouffer.	Christian Borkholder.
Jacob Greiter.	Peter Ensminger.
Ulrich Burkholder, Jr.	John Zimmerman.
Jacob Behm.	George Gieseman.
George Snevely.	Jacob Steohr.
Abraham Bowman.	Henry Yorty.
Michael Young.	Henry Worst.
Henry Long.	John Eshelman.
Peter Aderhold.	Thomas McDeMovia.

Fourth Class.

Jacob Bachman.	Robert Hander.
Tobias Cryder.	Christian Helsey.
Michael Black.	Peter Ebersold.
Daniel Bryans.	Peter Stephy.
John Steover.	Henry Shell.
Herman Long.	Peter Johnson.
Peter Heisy.	John Matter.
George Cryder, Senr.	John Smith, Weaver.
Hugh Black.	Jacob Matter.
George Cryder, Jr.	Martin Kremer.
Jacob Cryder, Senr.	

Fifth Class.

John Seyler.	Michael Kleber.
Henry Meily.	Augustine Gerst.
Paul Sieg.	Abraham Huber.
Peter Reish (above age).	Adam Steover.
Peter Faurneh.	John Baghman (above age).
Peter Yorty.	John Karmany, Junr.

Christian Behm.
Christian Burkholder (John Son).
John Wampler.
Ludwick Zehring.
Christopher Esterlein.
John Dohner, Junr.

Sixth Class.

Christian Stouffer (near Zinns)
Peter Miller.
George Holtz.
John Steohr.
Jacob Ebersold.
Michael Killinger, in 7th Class.
David Short.
Caspar Geiger.
Jacob Saunder.
Tobias Steover.
Jacob Holtz.
Abraham Ebersold.
John Cryder.
Jacob Bender.
Thomas Williams.
Martin Miller.
Ludwick Casier.

Seventh Class.

John Heisy, Sen'r, (above age).
John Peter, Junr.
Peter Karmany.
John Cample (moved away).
Mathias Righard.
Martin Cryder.
John Heisy, Junr.
Daniel Ensminger.
Jacob Dohner.
John Yorty.
Godfried Saunder.
Jacob Rohland.
Christian Ober.
Neal Lehman.
Uhrey Borkholder (Weaver's son) (dead).

Eighth Class.

John Ebersold, Jr.
Peter Snevely.
George Wampler.
Frederick Williams.
John Miller, stump nose.
James McClain.
Christian Gingrich.
Christian Bachman.
Peter Reish, Junr.
Peter Wittmer.
John Bornholder.
Henry Johnston.
John Meyer.
Henry Bell.
Henry Geiseman.
Henry Lind.
John Lehman.
Adam Zimmerman.
Michael Gingrich, Junr. (Michael son).

I do Certify that the foregoing is a true State of my Company.

BALTZER ORTH, Capt.

CAPTAIN MICHAEL HOLDERBAUMS COMPANY IT BEING THE SECOND COMPANY OF THE 2D BATTLION OF LANCASTER COUNTY MILITIA. (c.)

Captain.

Michael Holderbaum.

First Lieutenant.

Alex. Martin.

Ensign.

Vallentine Knop.

First Class.

John Umberger.
Jacob Fernsler.
Samuel Etter.
Jacob Ellenberger.
David Stiel.
Mathias Strehr.
Henry Humborger.
John Loattermilch.
Jacob Wilhelm.
John Henner.
Christian Wilhelm.
Michael Steckbeck.
Jacob Oyer.
Benjamin Cernith.

Second Class.

Frederick Fernsler.
Martin Ulrich.
Adam Heilman.
George Kemmerling.
John Wilhelm.
George Meyer.
Henry Weyand.
Peter Becker.
Abraham Blough.
Christian Walter.
Herman Spies.
Philip Peter.
Henry Felger.

Third Class.

Christian Neff.
Vallentine Boger.
Mathias Boger, Junr.
Michael Kreitter.
Mathias Harder.
Henry Gingrich.
Michael Boltz, Sen'r.
Martin Waggner.
Michael Breneisen.
Peter Grehbiel.
Ansted Heilman.
Michael Mouhlfehr.
John Knop.

Fourth Class.

John McClindigh.
Peter Ney.
George Wolff.
Henry Hellman.
John Fireabend.
Jacob Kitzmiller.
John Strehr.
Jacob Sieghly.
Thomas Morgan.
Adam Louttermilch.
James Long.

Fifth Class.

John Heilman.
Jacob Eshelman (not to be found).
Henry Knoll.
Michael Boltz, Junr., to march in 8th Class.
Michael Ney.
Christian Eshelman (moved away).
Peter Frank.
John Meyer.
Andreas Kremmer.
Martin Funk.
Martin Meyer.
Adam Bard, Jun'r.
Christian Ellenberger.
Christian Meyer.
Christopher Ulrich.
John Ulrey (above age)

Sixth Class.

Michael Uller.
Christian Huber, Jun'r, not to be found.
David Klein.
Jacob Laubsher.
John Walter, Jun'r.
John Snog, alias Strok.
John Nafsker.
John Eber Bender.
John Huber, under age by Certi.
James Norris, to mar. in 8th Class.
Sigmond Shoner.
John Snevely.
Emanuel Henner.

Seventh Class.

John Ellenberger.
Frederick Gundrum.
John Shallenberger.
Abraham Kauffman.

John Blough.
William Long.
Henry Peter.
Martin Uller.
John Gingrich, at Swattara.
John Diebrick Klein.
John Raser.
Frederick Beyer.
Lucas Shaaly.

Eighth Class.

Peter Hellman.
Henry Neff.
Adam Helm.
Anthony Long.
John Wolff.
John Miller, Son of Jno., at Swatara.
Daniel Biely.
Jacob Boltz, Jun'r.
Jacob Keller.
Adam Bare, Sen'r.

I do Certify that the foregoing is a true state of my Company.

MICHAEL HOLDERBAUM, Capt.

CAPTAIN CASPAR STEOVERS COMPANY, BEING THE THIRD COMPANY OF THE 2D BATTALION OF LANCASTER COUNTY MILITIA. (c.)

Captain.

Casper Stoever.

First Lieutenant.

Michael Herner.

Ensign.

Nicholas Conrad.

First Class.

John Kunkel.
Jacob Fedderhawf.
Michael Groh.
David Peffly.
Christian Walburn.
Martin Shuy.
Michael Hoffman.
Vencins Brown.
Jacob Honer.
Adam Sheffer.
Henry Emrich.

Second Class.

Henry Stettler.
Jacob Heckman.
Bernard Honer.
Henry Tiddel.
Martin Rudy.
Ludwick Shuy.
George Walburn.
Adam Brecht.
Henry Meyer.
Michael Groh, Jun'r.
Jacob Keller.
Abraham Sheffer.
George Lentz.
Henry Light.

Third Class.

Abraham Strohm.
Peter Smith.
John Emmerich.
John Gushwah.
George C. Armengost.
John Groh.
Jacob Goldman, Jun'r.
Baltzer Fedderhawf.
George Feeser.
Christian Brecht.
Philip Eisenhower.
Philip Weller (above age).

Fourth Class.

Jacob Newcomer.
Frederick Buchmer.
Christian Lentz.
Jacob Oberholtzer.
Christian Zehring.
John Benbacher.
Mathias Fedderhawf.
Martin Stehly.
Peter Shower.
Nicholas Soutter.
Jacob Fester.
Peter Feeser.
William Redford.

Fifth Class.

Joseph Bicksler.
Jacob Leittner, mar'd in 8th Class.
Jacob Conrad.
Christian Wolff.
Daniel Redford (not to be found).
Martin Yeorg.
Nicholas Shnee.
Henry Meily.
Henry Beckel.
Peter Dietzler.
Abraham Sherk.
Andreas Walburn.

Sixth Class.

David Miller.
Christian Kohr.
Jacob Dahny.
Peter Teisinger.

Christian Brechbiel.
Albert Kleinfelder.
Daniel Breshoar.
Peter Bucher.
George Houtz.
John Lentz.
George Fedderhawff.

Seventh Class.

Samuel Hunsricker.
John Dietzler.
Jacob Fawber.
Christian Hunsricker.
Daniel Mattern.
Melchior Behny.
Nicholas Wolff.
Christian Stetler.
Michael Conrad, Removed.
Nicholas Gerst.
Jacob Groff.
John Kitzmiller.

Eighth Class.

Henry Houtz.
Jonas Rudy.
John Light.
Frederick Gamper.
Frederick Gerst.
Martin Walburn.
John Holdman.
Philip Stertzer.
Dielman Doub.
John Kohr.
John German.
Sebastian Wolff.
Charles Rehrich.
George Sheffer, Junr.
Hyranomus Rudy.

I do Certify that the foregoing return is a true state of my Company.

CAPTAIN CASPAR STEOVER.

CAPTAIN DAVID KRAUSE COMPANY BEING THE FOURTH COMPANY OF THE 2D BATTALION OF LANCASTER COUNTY MILITIA. (c.)

Captain.

David Krause.

First Lieutenant.

Philip Greenawalt.

Ensign.

Jacob Embigh.

First Class.

Michael Krebs.
George Strow.
Christian Kremmer.
Jacob Stiep.
Rudolph Kelker.
Christopher Embigh, Jun'r.
George Hess.
John Rewalt.
Christian Greenawalt.

Second Class.

John Shne.
Charles Arnd.
Francis Baylor.
George Reinoel.
Leonard Kepler.
Daniel Fetzberger.
Conrad Reinoll.
Henry Meyer.
Francis Zehrman.
Peter Shindel.
Bernard Embigh.
George Kornman.
John McElrath.
John Steohr.
Michael Waggner.
Andrew Krause, Jun'r.

Third Class.

Jacob Folmer.
Jacob Peiffer.
Vallentine Kornman.
Samuel Melly.
John Dups.
George Gilbert.
Christopher Ambrosius.
Peter Smith.
Henry Baylor.
William Ward.
Anthony Kelker.
Henry Shaffner.
David Sherick.
Henry Kehly.
John Callolin.

Fourth Class.

Peter Richard.
Henry Gilbert.
Nicholas Gebhard.
Michael Ulrick.
Anthony Doebler.
Caspar Yost.
George Folmer.
George Folk.
Philip Embigh.
John German.
Conrad Fasnacht.
Thomas Clark.
William Cunningham.
Christopher Beistel.
Peter Yeengst.
Philip Mathias.

Fifth Class.

John Bittner.
John Yeager.
Michael Ensminger.
Caspar Leop.
Caspar Mies.
Doc'r John Greff.
John Finkel, mar'd 8th Class.
Jacob Merk.
Jacob Geigel.
Jacob Stohler.
Jacob Mellinger.
William Heidler.

Sixth Class.

Martin Yensel.	John Thorne.
Jacob Weirick.	John Jago.
Daniel Hening.	George Welsh.
John Philip Beck.	Conrad Merk.
Henry Yeengst.	Jacob Miller.
Ludwick Kornman.	Frederick Nagel.
Thomas Atkinson.	Hugh McEnallen.

Seventh Class.

Adam Mathias.	Thomas McEbrath.
Christopher Uhler.	Peter Harder.
Philip Fernsler.	George Leop.
Peter Miller.	John McCreary.
Philip Depoy.	John Groff.
Godfried Eighelberger.	Peter Sheffer.
David Dishong.	Nicholas Greenawalt.
Christian Beck, Jun'r.	John Meyer.
John Hop.	George Gloninger.
Simon Lough.	John Greenawalt.

Eighth Class.

John Eighelberger.	Caspar Youngblood.
Henry Rewalt.	Jacob Eighelberger.
Joseph Sturgins.	Adam Reise.
Benjamin Spyker.	Frederick Steover.
Philip Mies.	George Trump.
James Reed.	Michael Kock.
Christopher Leop.	Bernard Reinhard.
Michael Leop.	Bartholomew Wigard.
George Stone.	Jacob Snevely.
John Rohrer, Jun'r.	Jacob Soutter.

I do Certify that the foregoing return is a true State of my Company.

DAVID KRAUSE, Capt.

CAPTAIN JOHN MOORES COMPANY, BEING THE FIFTH COMPANY OF THE SECOND BATTALION OF LANCASTER COUNTY MILITIA. (c.)

Captain.

John Moore.

First Lieut.

Jacob Zollinger.

Ensign.

John Mehs.

First Class.

Jacob Zartman.
Peter Shitz.
Anthony Kapp.
George Mehs.
George Shock.
Michael Neff, Jun'r.
John Sholl.
Henry Zeller.
Henry Ekolf.
John Smith.
Jacob Louttermilch.
Adam Specht.
John Jacob Newman.
Christopher Hainly.

Second Class.

Michael Grebbiel.
Jacob Kemberling.
Anthony Stickel.
Christopher Raap.
Adam Fried.
John Shenk.
John Dickman.
John Henmigh.
Michael Stump.
John Saltzgeber.
Peter Wolffersperger.
Adam Feehman.
Crawft Achenbach.

Third Class.

Peter Spengler.
Henry Shram.
George Weaver.
John Eberly.
Nicholas Mehs.
George Emmert.
George Deerwechter.
Leonard Strickler.
Benjamin Miller.
Peter Newman.
Adam Sholl.
Peter Stein.
Peter Young.
Melchior Loutermilch.
Henry Meiser.
Andrew Wey.

Fourth Class.

Frederick Wolffersperger.
Jacob Philipy.
George Kockenderffer.
Henry Meyer.
Henry Hechelroad.
George Shram.
Andrew Kapp.
George Miller.
Frederick Kapp.
Samuel Hartman.
George Holstein.
John Frantz.
George Meiser.
Ludwick Peffer.
George Layer.
George Noll.
Mathias Stock.
Christian Miller.
John George Smith.
Henry Dierwechter.

Fifth Class.

George Kapp.
Christopher Seyler.
Rudy Meyer.
Thomas Durst.
George Hoffman, Jacob Son.
Henry Achy.
Peter Riem.
John Smith.
Francis Seybert.
John Meyer.
George Strickler.
Peter Swanger.
Frantz Ulrick.
Michael Zeller.
Henry Meyer.
John Noll.
Leonard Stump.
Ludwick Miller.
John George Brown.
Frederick Miller.
Jacob Umbehend.
Peter Kolp.
Jacob Hoff.
Christopher Meyer.
Frederick Stump.

Sixth Class.

Henry Lineweber.
George Klein.
Jacob Kitzmiller.
Joseph Kratzer, Tanner.
Martin Keller.
John Neip.
Christian Weise.
Henry Brunner.
Michael Miller.
Henry Saltzgeber.
John Bollman.
John Meiser.
Philip Wolffersperger.
Christopher Weiser.
Henry Kring.
John Becker, Jun'r.
John Young.
Michael Minigh.
Henry Hubshman.
Conrad Spielman.
Jacob Miller.
John Jacob Hoffman.
Peter Gally.
Nicholas Zollinger.
Anthony Wilson.

Seventh Class.

George Albrech.
John Balsly.
Jacob Hain.
George Stohler, Jun'r.
Michael Kapp.
Abraham Neff.
George Beyer.
Peter Newman.
Christian Weik.
Andrew Strickler.
Michael Meyer.
Vallentin Miller.
Walter Newman.
Henry Zimmerman.
Michael Zeller.
John Grum.
Vallentine Selller.
Jacob Loaser.
Christian Shenkel.

Eighth Class.

Christian Swanger.
George Hoffman.
David Levenstein.
Henry Peffer.
Henry Krall.
Martin Hess.
Philip Null.
Henry Borky.
Frederick Dupler.
Joseph Kratzer.
Philip Brown.
Frederick Heberling.
Henry Sheffer, Esq'r.
Henry Brosius.
Henry Klinger.
George Neff.
John Klingel.
Peter Houser.
Jacob Engelhard.
Jacob Houser.
Jacob Brosius.
Conrad Strickler.
Henry Newman.
Jno. George Newman.
Henry Weise.

December 25, 1781.

I do Certify that the foregoing return is a true State of my Company.

JOHN MOOR, Captain.

CAPTAIN JOHN STONES COMPANY, BEING THE SIXTH COMPANY OF THE SECOND BATTALION OF LANCASTER COUNTY MILITIA. (c.)

Captain.
John Stone.

First Lieut.
George Bowman.

Ensign.
Michael Teis.

First Class.

Adam German.
Henry Rudy.
Peter Gingrich.
Henry Bowman.
John Kleber.
Paul Shoemacher.
Peter Meyer.
George Strohm.
Martin Weitzel.
Abraham Meyer.
Jacob Becker.
Christian Smith.
Michael Miller.
Peter Spyker.
John Strohm.
John Dusing.
John Shott.
Michael Miller, Geo. Son.
Christopher Slosser.
Peter Fisher.
Andreas Shaak.
Christian Smutz.
George Gish.
Peter Burgner.

Second Class.

Abraham Sebolt.
Abraham Smutz.
Jacob Hartman.
Nicholas Dinges.
Peter Glassbrenner.
John Brown.
John Light, Jacob Son.
John Steger.
Peter Wentz.
Michael Lentz.
Lorentz Orndorff.
Jacob Garty.

Third Class.

Abraham Groh.
Michael Heisy.
John Smith.
Adam Ballmer.
George Eby.
Christian Gish, Sen'r.
Christopher Zibolt.
John Baylor.
William Hughen.
Mathias Groh.
Michael Zimmerman.
Henry Kuntz.

Fourth Class.

Martin Getz.
Jacob Sigs.
George Glassbrenner.
Balser Lauber.
Jacob Wentz.
Mathias Brownewell.
John Miller.
Isaac Brand.
Daniel Kenigh, belongs to 8th Class.
Christian Goldman.
Isaac Sheffer.
Adam Jacoby.
Jacob Sheffer.

Fifth Class.

Adam Huber.
Abraham Diel.
George Baylor.
Caspar Ellinger.
George Zinn.
Henry Strohm.

Christian Frankhouser.
Henry Light, S'r.
Abraham Smutz, Son of Math.
Abraham Brand.
George Miller.
Thomas Miller.
Charles Shaak.
Henry Riddel.
Henry Shell.
George Ellinger.
Abraham Huber.

Sixth Class.

Joseph Horst.
Michael Beyer.
Christian Brand.
David Miller.
John Ressly.
Daniel Heisy.
Charles Beener.
Jacob Light.
Henry Werner.
Adam Jacoby.
Henry Shop.
Mathias Smutz, Jr. (not to be found).
John Shaaly.
Christopher Zibolt, Jun'r.
Michael Keller, belongs to 8th Class.
Christian Riesser (not to be found).
Henry Wild.
Christian Yeager.
Michael Meyer.

Seventh Class.

John Backenstose.
Joseph Bamberger.
Christian Gingrich.
Michael Gingrich (above age).
Christian Kantz.
Jacob Tice.
John Mehs.
John Smith, Jun'r.
Jacob Shaak.
Peter Ginter.
George Willand.
Frederick Steger.
Jacob Light, Jno. Son.

Eighth Class.

George Ressly.
Henry Eby.
Peter Becker.
Vallentine Reifwein.
Mathias Smutz.
Nicholas Seholt.
Abraham Krall.
Andreas Ley.
Martin Thomas.
Edward Bryans.
Jacob Kuntz.
John Behring.
Peter Arnold.
Lorentz Houtz.

I do Certifyy that the foregoing return is a true State of my Company.

JOHN STONE, Capt.

CAPTAIN WENDEL WEAVERS COMPANY, BEING THE 7TH COMPANY OF THE SECOND BATTALION. (c.)

Captain.

Wendel Weaver.

First Lieut.

Michael Dieffenbach.

Ensign.

Michael Haag.

First Class.

Peter Berry, Jr.
Peter Conrad.
Uhrich Beckly.
George Spengler.
John Line.
Martin Batturff.
John Lantz.
John Bawsler.
Ludwick Rehl.
William Yeengst.
George German.
Christian Ley.

Second Class.

Peter Lehn.
Henry Stahlsmith.
George Ewinger.
Nicholas Noll.
Martin Meyer.
Christopher Ries.
Michael Ramler.
Peter Line.
William Etshberger.
John Gasser.
Thomas Koppenhever.
Daniel Diel.

Third Class.

Frederick Steiner.
Peter Neidigh.
John Sharff.
Michael Wolff.
William Neyman.
Herman Walburn.
Nicholas Haak.
Francis Stahlsmith.
Jacob Lehn.
Baltzer Oberkwish.
Christian Seyber.
George Teerwechter.
Peter Stein.
Christian Beyler.
Christian Tice.

Fourth Class.

John Roth.
Martin Spengler.
John Teis.
Jacob German.
George Swartz.
John Fehler.
Jacob Spengler.
Henry Deerwechter.
Jacob Lontz.
John Ried.
John Heffelfinger.
Caspar Dieemer.

Fifth Class.

Jacob Armbreester.
Henry Miller.
Henry Fortney.
Peter Shell.
Martin Walbwin.
Henry Koppenhever (above age).
Mathias Fogt.
Peter Battweff, to march 8th class.
Christian Shnell.
John Batturff.
Jacob Stough.
Andreas Graff.
Michael Wolfard.
Marlin Benner.
Henry German.
William Gies.
John Sheffer.
Leonard Batturff.
Frederick Stein.
John Kuster.
Simon Diemer.

Sixth Class.

Leonard Immel.
Adam Shitz.
John Heffley.
Jacob Meyer.
Adam Christ.
John Haak.
Christian Lutz.
Jacob George, not to be found.
Adam Spengler.
William Blecher.
Vallentine Uhrich.
Michael Ley.
Michael Kreitzer.
Christian Noecker.
Simon Bawsler.
Nicholas Kreitzer.
Jacob Behney, march 8th class.
Frantz Foltz.
Nicholas Fehler.
Jacob Lutz.

Seventh Class.

Henry Bawsler.
Frederick Noecker.
Martin Weiser.
Christop. V. Leiss.
Michael Frantz.
Thomas Bawsler.
Michael Spengler.
Christopher Amlong.
John Teis.
George Roth.
Jacob Heighold.
Nicholas Eshwey.
Jacob Gasser.
Philip Heffelfinger, Fifer.

Eighth Class.

Christopher Koppenheffer.	Leonard Swartz.
Rudy Kinsley.	Jacob Wolff.
Christian Lehman.	Samuel Lantz.
George Gehrhard.	Nicholas Berry.
Adam Sharm.	Peter Behney.
George Simon.	Frederick Kreitzer.
George Michl. Grof.	Frederick Foltz.
Christian Walburn.	George Shiffler.

A true State of my Company.

WENDEL WEAVER, Captain.

CAPTAIN JOHN GASSERTS COMPANY, BEING THE EIGHTH OF THE 2D BATT. (c.)

Captain.

John Gassert.

First Lieut.

John Fiel.

Ensign.

Jacob Lehmy.

First Class.

Henry Yeakley.	Dewalt Gerst.
Henry Merk.	Wendel Fisher.
Martin Walburn.	Henry Fux.
Philip Gasser.	Ulrich Kneagy.
Christian Kauffman.	

Second Class.

George Meyer.	Jacob Blank.
Dietrick Heikman.	Henry Brubacher,
John Mies.	Peter Long.
Jacob Fisher.	

Third Class.

Christian Seltzer.	John Heil.
John Long.	John Hening.
George Beshoar.	Jacob Gettle.
Peter Hershberger.	John Cample.
John Neff.	Daniel Waggner.

Fourth Class.

Christian Goldman.	George Gebhard.
John Been (not to be found).	Isaac Snevely.
Jacob Gasser.	John Breght.
Henry Meese.	John Kornman.
William Rough.	Ubrey Felty.
John Fawber.	Peter Roop.
Ludwick Wirttenberg.	John Seyler.
Adam Brand, Jr.	Abraham Wenger.
George Seidelmeyer.	Jacob Walburn.

Fifth Class.

Henry Been (not to be found).	John Beshoar, Jun'r.
Conard Folty (not to be found).	Philip Zehring.
Henry Dingis.	Killian Long, Jr.
Adam Shower.	Christian Walburn (in Capt. Stever's Co.
Yose Kneagy.	Andrew Heckman.
Henry Snotterly.	

Sixth Class.

Caspar Prinuncover.	Conrad Waggner.
John Darges.	Richard Foset.
Christopher Kapp.	Daniel Stroh.
John Beshoar, at Holdsman.	John Winger, Jr.
David Teis.	Jacob Wilhelm (not to be found).
Jacob Stehly.	

Seventh Class.

John Lehmgn.	Henry Dups.
Henry Dumm.	Christian Shouffler.
Peter Sadelzaum.	Jacob Brand.
Rudy Yeakley.	John Dups.
Henry Dups, Sadlar.	Henry Brecht.
Jacob Sneably.	James Field.

Martin Winger, not to be found.
Conrad Krowel.
Michael Strehr.
David Young.
Henry Yeorgan.

Eighth Class.

Abraham Depoey.
John Spittlar.
Thomas Mees.
Philip Fawber.
Honsly Winger.
Henry Miller.
Isaac Krall.
Leonard Wingelbleck.
Henry Minick.
Peter Beshoar.
John Kapp.
Christian Brand.
Martin Meily.
Jacob Melly.
John Mark.
Abraham Stone.
John Sneavly.
Michael Breght.
Henry Neas.
Henry Cample.
John Gasser.
Henry Zehring, Jr.
Christian Long.

A true state of the Company.

To JOHN GASSERT, Capt.

Lebanon, March 4th, 1782.

(c.) S'r:—

Be pleased to pay unto Alex'a Benjamin late Drum Major in my Battalion of Militia the Sum of Twenty Dollars in Specia, It being a Reasonable Compensation allowed him for his Services in the Battaliin and for Instructing and learning the Drummars of the Battalion, from April, 1777, to April, 1780. I am S'r.

Your Hum. Serv't

PHILIP GREENAWALT,
late Col. 2d B't'l L. C. M.

To
COL. ADAM ORTH,
Lt. of Militia.

A JUST AND EXACT RETURN OF THE NAMES OF EACH AND EVERY MALE WHITE PERSON INHABITING OR RESIDING WITHIN MY DISTRICT IN THE FRST COMPANY OF THE SECOND BATTALION OF LANCASTER COUNTY MILITIA BETWEEN THE AGE OF EIGHTEEN & FIFTY THREE YEARS. TAKEN FOR THE YEAR 1782. (c.)

Captain.

Baltzer Orth.

Lieutenant.

John Orth.

Ensign.

Daniel Stouffer.

First Class.

John Imboden, Jun'r.
Christian Stouffer.
Christian Smith.
John Imboden, Sen'r.
George Matter.
John Righert.
Rudy Miller.
George Shambagh.
Adam Orth.
John Hoghstetter.
Peter Farneh, by Overs.
Jacob Over, by Overs.
John Righter.
Hugh Roberts.

Second Class.

George Meiley.
Christian Long.
Christopher Meyer.
Felix Young.
Henry Reinoel.
Michael Breittenbagh.
Michael Gingrich, Yost Son.
Lorentz Siegrist.
John Wehner.
Christian Greitter, Jun'r.
Philip Urich.
Conrad Klein.
Melchior Abmeyer.
Jacob Siegrist.
John Burckholder, Christ'r Son.
John Reish.
Christopher Herbster.
Henry Felger.
John Brown.
Jacob Heisey.
Jacob Yorty.
Israel Rembigh.

Third Class.

Jacob Cryder, Jun'r.
Ubrey Burckholder.
George Snevely.
Abraham Bowman.
Michael Young.
Peter Adderhold.
Henry Long.
Christian Burckholder.
John Zimmerman
Jacob Steohr.
Peter Ensminger.
Michael Holtz.
Henry Yorty.
Henry Worst.
Jacob Behm, Jun'r.
John Eshelman.
Thomas McDeMovia.
Christian Mosser.

Fourth Class.

Jacob Baghman.
Michael Black.
Daniel Bryans.
John Steover.
Herman Long.
George Cryder, Sen'r.
Jacob Cryder, Sen'r.
Robert Hunder.
Jacob Matter.
Peter Ebersold.
John Smith, Weaver.
John Matter.
Peter Johnston.
Martin Kremmer.
Henry Heisey.

Fifth Class.

John Seyler.
Henry Meiley.
Paul Sieg.
Peter Farneb.
Peter Yorty.
Michael Gleber.
Augustine Gerst.
Christopher Esterlein.
Adam Steover.
John Karmany.
Rudy Behm.
John Linsey.
John Wampler.
Ludwick Zehring.
John Dohner.
Martin Heisey.
Emanuel Saunder.
Christian Ensminger.
Philip Shambagh.
Abraham Landis.

Sixth Class.

Christian Stouffer, near Zinn.
Peter Miller.
George Holtz.
John Steohr.
Jacob Ebersold.
Michael Killinger.
David Short.
Jacob Saunder.
Christian Baghman, Jun., Mich'l Son.
Tobias Steover.
Jacob Holtz.
Thomas Williams.
John Greitter.
Jacob Bender.
Martin Miller.
Peter Grubb.
Ludwick Cassel.

Seventh Class.

John Peter, Jun'r.
Philip Karmeny.
Christian Over.
Daniel Ensminger.
Jacob Dohner.
John Yorty.
Godfried Saunder.
Jacob Ruland.
Neal Lehman.
Adam Zimmerman.
Ulrey Burckholder, Weaver Son.
Martin Cryder.
John Smith, Jun'r.
Peter Smith.
Godliep Orth.
Daniel Wunderligh.
Franck Johnston.

Eighth Class.

John Ebersold.
Peter Snevely.
George Wampler.
Frederick Williams.
John Miller.
John Meyer, Sen'r.
Christian Gingrich.
James McClain.
Christian Baghman.
Peter Reish, Jun'r.
Michael Gingrich, Jr.
Henry Gieseman.
Peter Wittmer, Jun'r.
John Burkholder, Weaver Son.
Henry Johnston.
Henry Lind.
Abraham Ebersold, Shoe Maker.
Jacob Righert.
Jacob Grey.
William Ervine.

I do Swear that the above list is a Just and true State of the Male White Inhabitants residing in my district, agreeable to Law, and without Fraud to the State to the best of my knowledge. Sworn and Subscribed before me the 8th Day of July 1782.

JOHN GLOMNGER, Sub. Lieut. Lanc. Co'y

JOHN ORTH, Lieut. Comm'd 1st Comp., pro Temp'r.

A RETURN OF THE NAMES OF EACH AND EVERY MALE WHITE PERSON INHABITING OR RESIDING WITHIN MY DISTRICT IN THE SECOND COMPANY OF THE SECOND BATTALION OF LANCASTER COUNTY MILITIA BETWEEN THE AGE OF 18 AND 53 YEARS. TAKEN FOR THE YEAR 1782. (c.)

Captain.

Michael Holderbaum.

Lieutenant.

Alexander Martin.

Ensign.

Valentine Knop.

1st Class.

John Umberger.
Jacob Fernsler.
Samuel Etter.
Jacob Ellenberger.
David Stiel.
Henry Hamburger.
John Louttermilch.
John Henner.
Christian Wilhelm.
Jacob Oyer.
Adam Weber.
Christian Wirth.
John Knoll.
Thomas Folkan.
Peter Wolff.
Jacob Kilinger.
John Albreght.
Christopher Slosser.

2nd Class.

Frederick Fernsler.
Martin Ullerich.
Adam Heilman.
George Kemmerling.
John Wilhelm.
George Meyer.
Michael Steckbeck.
Peter Miller.
Peter Becker.
Abraham Blough.
Christian Walter.
John Hicks.
Henry Redigh.
Philip Peter.
Peter Walter.

3rd Class.

Christian Neff.
Vallentine Boger.
Mathias Boger, Junr.
George Keller.
Michael Kreitter.
Mathias Harder.
Henry Gingrich.
Martin Waggner.
Peter Grehbiel.
Ansted Heilman.
Michael Mouefehr.
John Knop.
John Umberger, Junr.
Philip Aghenbach.
Andrew Shitterly.
Henry Ensminger.

4th Class.

John McClintock.
Peter Ney.
George Wolff.
Henry Heilman.
John Fireabend.
Jacob Kitzmiller.
John Strebr.
Jacob Sieghly.

Thomas Morgan.	John Miller.
Adam Louttermilch.	John Karman.
Charles Reighard.	Christian Oyer.
James Long.	John Seyler.

5th Class.

John Heilman.	Adam Bard, Junr.
Henry Knoll.	Christian Ellenberger.
Michael Baltz, Junr.	Christian Meyer.
Peter Frank.	Christian Ullerich.
John Meyer.	John Snog.
Andrew Kremer.	Philip Dietz.
Martin Funck.	Jacob Franck.

6th Class.

Michael Uller.	Sigmond Shoaer.
Christian Huber, Junr.	John Snevely.
David Klein.	John Stroh, Junr.
Jacob Laubsher.	George Helm.
John Stroh.	Frederick Leonard.
John Nafsker.	John Boltz.
Jno. Eber Bender.	John Becker.
John Huber.	John Garlin.
James Norris.	John Walter, Jr.

7th Class.

John Ellenberger.	Jacob Waggner.
Frederick Gundrum.	Lucas Shally.
John Shallenberger.	John Bender.
Abraham Kauffman.	Henry Fernsler.
John Blough.	John Wetzler.
Godliep Zimmerman.	Michael Meyer.
William Long.	John Miller, Junr.
Henry Peter.	Jacob Boltz.
Martin Uller.	Nicholas Ney.
John Gingrich.	John Klein.
John Dietter Klein.	Michael Miller.
Frederick Beyer.	

8th Class.

Peter Hellman.	Adam Helm.
Henry Neff.	Anthony Long.

Jacob Keller.
Adam Bard, Senr.
John Mackel.
Henry Eshelman.
Philip Ney.
Jacob Ellenberger.

I do Swear that the above List is a Just and true State of the Male White Inhabitants, residing in my district, agreeable to Law and without Fraud to the State to the best of my Knowledge.

Sworn & subscribed before me the 10th Day of July 1782.

JNO. GLONINGER, Sub. Lt. G. Co.
MICHAEL HOLDERBAUM, Capt.

A JUST AND EXACT RETURN OF EACH AND EVERY MALE WHITE PERSON INHABITING OR RESIDING WITHIN MY DISTRICT OF THE THIRD COMPANY OF THE SECOND BATTALION OF LANCASTER COUNTY MILITIA BETWEEN THE AGE OF 18 AND 53 YEARS. TAKEN FOR THE YEAR 1782. (c.)

Captain.

Casper Steover.

Lieutenant.

Michael Harner.

Ensign.

Nicholas Conrad.

1st Class.

John Kunkle.
Jacob Fodderhawf.
David Peffly.
Christian Walburn.
Martin Shuey.
Michael Hoffman.
Jacob Houer.
Adam Sheffer.
Henry Emrich.
Michael Miller.

2nd Class.

Henry Light.
Henry Stetler.
Jacob Heckman.
Henry Tidel.
Martin Reedy.
Ludwick Shuey.
George Walburn.
Henry Meyer.
Christian Shuey.
Jacob Keller.
Mathias Neytigh.
Christian Dietzler.

3rd Class.

Abraham Strohm.
George Arbogast.
Peter Smith.
John Emrigh.
John Gushwa.
George Bawtz, Junr.
John Groh.
Jacob Goldman.
Baltzer Federhawf.
George Fieser.
Philip Eisenhouer.
Peter Neycommer.
Christian Groh.
George North.
Henry German.
Michael Federhawf.
John Eisenhouer, Junr.

4th Class.

Jacob Neycomer.
Christian Lentz.
Jacob Overholtzer.
Christian Zehring.
Martin Stehly.
Peter Shouer.
Nicholas Soutter.
Jacob Dester.
Peter Fieser.
William Redford.
Adam Bender.
Jacob Kuntz.
George Dester.
Jacob Groff.
John German.

5th Class.

Jacob Leightner.
Joseph Bicksler.
Abraham Sherick.
Andrew Walburn.
Peter Tietzler.
Jacob Conrad.
Martin Yoarg.
Christian Wolff.
Henry Melly.
Henry Snevely.
Jacob Walburn.
Nicholas Sheffer.
Jacob Meyer, Junr.

6th Class.

David Miller.
Christian Kohr.
Jacob Dahny.
Peter Teisinger.
Christian Broghbiel.
Albert Kleinfelder.
Daniel Beshoar.
Peter Bugher.
John Lentz.
George Federhawff.
William Kriegbaum.
Henry Wild.
Philip Kunselman.
Joseph Gundy.

7th Class.

Samuel Hunsricker.
John Dietzler.
Jacob Fowber.
Christian Hunsricker.
Daniel Mattern.
Melihior Bebny.
Christian Stettler.
John Kitzmiller.
Christian Gantzer.
John Campble.
Michael Horn.
Jacob Wolff.

8th Class.

Henry Cample
Henry Houtz.
Jonas Rudy.
John Light.
Martin Walburn.
John Holdeman.
Philip Stertzer.
Dielman Doub.
John Kohr.
Sebastian Wolff.
George Sheffer.
John German.
Ludwick Lehman.
David Peffly, Junr.

I do Swear that the above List is a Just and true State of the Male White Persons residing in my district agreeable to Law without Fraud to the State to the best of my Knowledge.
Sworn & subscribed before me
the 9th Day of July 1782.

JOHN GLONINGER, Sub. Lt. L. Co.

A JUST AND EXACT RETURN OF EACH AND EVERY MALE WHITE PERSON INHABITING OR RESIDING WITHIN MY DISTRICT IN THE FOURTH COMPANY OF THE SECOND BATTALION OF LANCASTER COUNTY MILITIA BETWEEN THE AGE OF 18 AND 53 YEARS. TAKEN FOR THE YEAR 1782. (c.)

Captain.

David Krause.

Lieutenant.

Philip Greenawalt, Jun'r.

Ensign.

Jacob Embigh.

Almoner.

John Rohrer.

1st Class.

John Cowan.
George Strok.
Leonard Grumbein.
Jacob Stiep.
Rudolph Kelker.
Christopher Embigh.
George Hess.
Christian Greenawalt.
Jacob Eppreght.
Mathues Berntheisel.
Frederick Dups.
George Freligh.

2nd Class.

John Sneh.
Charles Arndt.
Francis Baylor.
George Reinoel.
Leonard Keohler.
Daniel Fetzberger.
Conrad Reineel.
Henry Meyer.
Francis Zerman.
Peter Shindel.
John McElrath.
Philip Gloninger.
John Steohr.
Michael Waggner.
George Kornman.
Andrew Krause, Junr.
Ludwick Dornman.
John Huber.
Bernard Embigh.

3rd Class.

Jacob Folmer.
Jacob Peiffer.
Vallentine Harnman.
Samuel Melly.
John Dupe.
George Gilbert.
Benjamin Moore.
Peter Smith.
Henry Baylor.
William Ward.
Anthony Kelker.
Henry Shaffner.
David Sherick.
Adam Dietrick.
Jacob Bugher.
Charles Shaffner.
Peter Ruth.
Philip Weiser, serj.

4th Class.

Henry Gilbert.
Nicholas Gebhard.
Michael Urich.
Anthony Deobler.
Caspar Yost.
George Folmer.
George Folk.
Philip Embigh.

Conrad Fasnaght.
Peter Yeengst.
Thomas Clark.
Samuel Grimes.
Henry Dups.
Leonard Riese.
Jacob Groff.
William Dornman.
Christopher Reinvel, Drum.

5th Class.

John Bittner.
John Yeager.
Michael Ensminger.
Caspar Leop.
Caspar Mies.
John Greffy.
John Finkel.
Jacob Merk.
Jacob Geigel.
Jacob Mellinger.
William Heidler.
George Young.
Joseph Lisly.
Jacob Weirigh.

6th Class.

Martin Yensel.
Jacob Weirich.
John Beck.
Henry Yeengst.
Ludwick Cornman.
Thomas Atkinson.
John Thome, Esq.
John Jago.
George Wilsh.
Conrad Merk.
Jacob Miller.
Hugh MEnally.
Frederick Nagel.
John Keher.
——— Mouse.

7th Class.

Christopher Uller.
Adam Mathias.
Philip Fernier.
Peter Miller.
Philip Depoey.
Godfried Eighelberger.
David Dishong.
Christian Beck.
Simon Lough, Sergt.
Thomas McElrath.
Henry Kelker.
John Greenawalt.
John Groff.
Peter Sheffer.
Nicholas Greenawalt.
David Young.
Peter Harder, Sergt.
Adam Rees.

8th Class.

John Eighelberner.
Henry Rewalt.
Joseph Sturgius.
Benjamin Spyker.
Philip Mies.
James Reed.
Christopher Leop.
Michael Leop.
George Stone.
John Rohrer, Junr.
Caspar Youngblood.
Jacob Souter.
Bernhard Reinhard.
Bartholomew Wigard.

Jacob Eigheberner.
Adam Reise.
Frederick Steover.
Michael Koch.
Jacob Beegher.
Jacob Ressly.
Jacob Freligh.
John Slotterbeck.
Daniel Kenigh.
George Trump.
Jacob Ensminger.

I do Affirm that the above List is a Just and true State of the Male White Persons residing in my district agreeable to Law without Fraud to the State to the best of my Knowledge.

DAVID KRAUSE, Capt.

Aff'd and Subscribed before me
the 8th day of July 1782.

JNO. GLONINGER, Sub. Lt. of L. Co.

A JUST AND EXACT RETURN OF EACH AND EVERY MALE WHITE PERSON INHABITING OR RESIDING WITHIN MY DISTRICT OF THE FIFTH COMPANY OF THE 3RD BATT. OF LAN. COUNTY MILITIA BETWEEN THE AGE OF 18 AND 53 YEARS. TAKEN FOR THE YEAR 1782. (c.)

Captain.

John Moore.

Lieutenant.

Jacob Zollinger.

Ensign.

Michael Mehs.

First Class.

Jacob Zartman.
Peter Shitz.
Anthony Kap.
Peter Neff.
George Mehs.
George Shock.
Michael Neff, Junr.
John Sholl.
Henry Zeller.
Henry Ekoff.
John Smith.
Adam Speght.
Christopher Hehnly.
Jacob Neff.
Tobias Zeller.

Second Class.

Michael Grehbiel.	John Saltzgeber.
Jacob Kemberling.	Frederick Rap.
Anthony Stiegel.	Peter Wolffersperger.
Christopher Roap.	Adam Feehman.
Adam Fried.	John Dickman.
John Shenk, Senr.	Adam Shneiber.
John Hemigh.	Nicholas Swanger.
John Beeker.	Alexr. Shoup.
Michael Stump.	Simon Newman.

Third Class.

Peter Spengler.	Adam Sholl.
Henry Shram.	George Zimmerman.
George Weaver.	Peter Young.
John Eberly.	Melchior Louttermilch.
Nicholas Mehs.	Andrew Wey.
George Emmert.	Henry Aghy, Junr.
Leonard Strickler.	Michael Swanger.
Benjamin Miller.	John Shenk.
Peter Newman, Junr.	Adam Moore.

Fourth Class.

Alexander Kissinger.	Samuel Hartman.
Frederick Wolffersperger.	George Holstein.
Jacob Philipy.	John Frantz.
George Kogherderffer.	George Meiser.
Henry Meyer.	George Lemen.
Henry Herghebroad.	George Noll.
George Shram.	Mathias Stock.
Andrew Kaap.	George Smith.
George Miler.	Simon Sholl.
Freaerik Kap.	

Fifth Class.

George Kaap.	Francis Seybert.
Christopher Seiller.	John Meyer.
Rudy Meyer.	George Strickler.
George Hoffman.	Francis Ulrey.
Henry Aghy, Senr.	Henry Meyer (Joiner).
Peter Ream.	John Noll.
John Smith.	Leonard Stump.

Christopher Meyer.	Jacob Unbehend.
Frederick Stump.	Peter Kolp.
Ludwick Miller.	Peter Swanger.
George Brown.	Jacob Hoff.
Frederick Miller.	Jacob Reidebagh.

Sixth Class.

George Klein.	Philip Wolffsperger.
Jacob Kitzmiler.	Henry Kring.
Martin Albreght.	Henry Heebshman.
Joseph Kratzer Taner.	Jacob Miller.
Martin Keller.	Jacob Hoffman.
John Neip.	Nicholas Zollinger.
Christian Weise.	Anthy. Wilson.
Henry Bruner.	Michael Zeller, Peter Son.
Michael Miller.	George Fleisher.
Henry Saltzgeber.	Henry Beyer.
John Bollman.	Christian Yeager.
John Meiser.	

Seventh Class.

George Albreght.	Vallentine Miller.
John Baltzly.	Walter Newman.
Jacob Hehn.	Henry Weise.
Michael Kaap.	Henry Zimmerman.
Abraham Neff.	Michael Zeller.
George Beyer.	John Krum.
Peter Newman.	Jacob Louser.
Christian Weik.	Christian Shenkel.
Andrew Strickler.	Philip Brown, Taylor.
Michael Meyer.	John Weiser.

Eighth Class.

Jacob Sheffer.	Joseph Kratzer.
Martin Heisey.	Philip Brown.
George Hoffmer.	Frederick Heberling.
David Levenstein.	William Sheffer.
Henry Peffer.	Henry Brosius.
Henry Grall.	Henry Klinger.
Philip Noll.	George Neff.
Henry Borkey.	Peter Hollser.
Frederick Dubler.	Jacob Engelhard.

Jacob Houser.
Conrad Strickler.
Henry Newman.
John George Newman.
Henry Sheffer.
Peter Metz.
George Dissinger.

I do Swear that the above List is a Just and true State of the Male White Persons Inhabiting or residing in my district agreeable to law and without Fraud to the State to the best of my knowledge.

Sworn before me
the 8th Day of July 1782.

JOHN GLONINGER, Sub. Lieut. Lanc. Co.
JOHN MOOR, Capt.

A JUST & EXACT RETURN OF EACH AND EVERY MALE WHITE PERSON INHABITING OR RESIDING WITHIN MY DISTRICT IN THE SIXTH COMPANY OF THE SECOND BATTALION OF LANCASTER COUNTY MILITIA BETWEEN THE AGE OF 18 AND 53 YEARS. TAKEN FOR THE YEAR 1782. (c.)

Captain.
John Stone.

Lieutenant.
George Bowman.

Ensign.
Michael Tice.

Almoner.
Peter Fisher.

Privates.

First Class.

Adam German.
Henry Rudy.
Peter Gingrich.
John Gleber.
Paul Shoemaker.
Peter Meyer.
George Strohm.
Martain Weitzel.
Jacob Becker.
John Strohm.

John Dusing.
John Shott.
Peter Fisher.
Andrew Shaak.
Christian Smutz.
Peter Burgner.
Christ'n Zibolt.
Christian Baylor.
John Light, Hen'y Son.

Second Class.

Abraham Smutz.
Nicholas Dingis.
Peter Glassbrenner.
John Light.
Abraham Hell.
John Steger.
Larentz Orndorff.
Peter Wentz.
Jacob Heisey.
Michael Lentz.
Jacob Garty.
Michael Hell.
George Fenghel.

Third Class.

Abraham Groh.
Michael Heisey.
John Smith.
George Ebey.
Christopher Zibolt, Senr.
John Baylor.
Henry Kuntz.
Michael Zimmerman.
Christian Ornderff.
William Hughen.
George Geiseman.

Fourth Class.

Martin Getz.
Jacob Sigs.
George Glassbrenner.
Baltzer Lauber.
Jacob Wentz.
Mathias Brownewell.
Isaac Brand.
Samuel Strohm.
Christian Goldman.
Isaac Sheffer.
Jacob Sheffer.

Fifth Class.

Adam Huber.
Abraham Diel.
George Baylor.
Caspar Ellinger.
Henry Strohm.
Christian Frankhouser.
Henry Light, Senr.
Abraham Smutz, Math's Son.
Abraham Brand.
George Miller.
Abraham Becker.
Thomas Miller.
Charles Shaak.
Jacob Riddel.
Henry Shell.
Jacob Light, John Son.
George Ellinger.
Abraham Huber.
John Heisey.
Edward Long.
John Becker.
Andrew Huber.
John Benner.

Sixth Class.

Joseph Horst.
Christian Brand.
David Miller.
Daniel Heisey.
Charles Beener.
Jacob Light, Senr.
Henry Werner.
Adam Jacoby.
Mathias Smutz, Junr.
John Shaally.
Michael Keller.
Christian Yeager.
Michael Meyer.
John Zollinger, Fifer.
Jacob Shop.

Seventh Class.

Mathias Groh.
Joseph Bamberger.
Christian Gingrich.
John Backenstose.
Jacob Teise.
John Mehs.
Nicholas Shaak.
Jacob Shaak, Junr.
Peter Ginter.
George Williand.
Frederick Steger.
Jacob Light, Martin Son.
Abraham Smith.
Jacob Houtz.

Eighth Class.

George Ressly.
Vallentine Reifwein.
Mathias Smutz.
Nicholas Sehbold.
Abraham Krall.
Henry Ebey.
Andrew Ley.
Martain Thoma.
Edward Bryans.
Michael Miller.
Peter Arnold.
Lorentz Houtz.
John German.
Jacob Reifwein.

I do Swear that the above List is a Just and true State of the male white persons inhabiting or residing within my district agreeable to law & without fraud to the State to the best of my knowledge.

GEORGE BOUMAN, Leut.
Comd. 6th compy,
Pro Temp.

Sworn & subscribed before me
the 7th day of July 1782.

JOHN GLONINGER, Sub. Lt.

A TRUE AND EXACT RETURN OF EACH AND EVERY MALE WHITE PERSON INHABITING OR RESIDING WITHIN MY DISTRICT IN THE SEVENTH COMPY OF THE 2ND BATT. OF LANCASTER COUNTY MILITIA, BETWEEN THE AGE OF 18 AND 53 YEARS. TAKEN FOR THE YEAR 1782. (c.)

Captain.

Wendel Weaver.

Lieutenant.

Michael Diffenbaugh.

Ensign.

Michael Haag.

Almoner.

Peter Berry.

1st Class.

Peter Berry, Jur.
Peter Conrad.
Urich Beckley.
George Spengler.
John Line.
John Lantz.
John Bawsler.
George German.
John Smith.
Christian Ley.
Benjmain Dieffenbaugh.

2nd Class.

Peter Lehn.
Henry Stahlsmith.
George Evinger.
Nicholas Nole.
Martin Meyer.
Christopher Ries.
Michael Rammler.
Peter Line.
William Elshberger.
John Gasser.
Thomas Koppenhever.
Daniel Diel.
Christopher Kopenhever, Jr.
John Meyer.

3rd Class.

Frederick Stoner.
Peter Neitigh.
John Sharff.
William Neyman.
Nicholas Mosser.
Nicholas Haag.

Francis Stalsmith.
Jacob Lehn.
Baltzer Oberkirsh.
Christian Seybert.
Peter Stone.
Christian Beyler.
Jacob Farneh.
George Lentz.
Christian Teise.
George Huber.
Michael Woolff.

4th Class.

Martin Spengler.
John Teise.
Jacob German.
George Swartz.
John Fehler.
Jacob Spengler.
Henry Dierweghter.
Jacob Lentz.
John Reed.
John Heffelfinger.
Caspar Diemer.
Peter Benedume.
Mathias Gost.
Christian Miller.
Christian Breidenbagh.

5th Class.

Jacob Armbreester.
Henry Miller.
Henry Fortneh.
Peter Shell.
Martin Walburn.
Mathias Fogt.
Peter Batturff.
Christian Shnell.
Jacob Stough.
Andrew Groff.
Michael Wolfard.
Martin Benner.
Henry German.
John Sheffer.
Leonard Battur.I.
Frederick Stoner.
John Kuster.
Peter Miller.
Christian Smith.

6th Class.

Adam Spengler.
Vallentine Urich.
Michael Ley.
Michael Kreitzer.
Christian Noecker.
Simon Bosler.
Francis Foltz.
Nicholas Fehler.
Jacob Lutz.
Leonard Immel.
Adam Shitz.
John Heffley.
Jacob Meyer.
Adam Chreest.
Henry Lineweber.
John Haag.
Philip Breittenbagh.
Daniel Cook.

7th Class.

Nicholas Eshwey, Segt.
Jacob Gasser, Drummer.
Philip Heffelfinger, Fifer.
Frederick Noecker.
George Fogt.
Martin Weiser.
Christopher Leise.
Michael Frantz.

Thomas Bawsler.
Michael Spengler.
John Teise, Junr.
George Roth.
Jacob Heighold.
John Walburn.
Philip Seyler.
John Lininger.

8th Class.

George Shiffler, Segt.
Nicholas Berry, Corpl.
Christopher Koppenhever.
Rudolph Kinsel.
Christian Lehman.
George Gehret.
Adam Shwarn.
George Simon.
Christian Walburn.
Leonard Swartz.
Frederick Kreitzer.
Frederick Foltz.
Simon Bawsler, Junr.
Peter Batturff, Junr.
Christian King.

I do Swear that the above List is a Just and true State of the Male White Persons residing in my district agreeable to Law without Fraud to the State to the best of my Knowledge.
Sworn & subscribed before me
this 8 Day of July 1782.

JOHN GLONINGER, Sub. Lt. L. Co.

A TRUE AND EXACT LIST OF THE NAMES OF EACH AND EVERY MALE WHITE PERSON INHABITING OR RESIDING WITHIN MY DISTRICT, IN THE EIGHTH COMPANY, OF THE SECOND BATTALION OF LANCASTER COUNTY MILITIA BETWEEN THE AGE OF 18 AND 53 YEARS. TAKEN FOR THE YEAR 1782. (c.)

Captain.

Mathias Henning.

Lieutenant.

Abraham. Stone.

Ensign.

Jacob Leman.

1st Class.

Ulrich Gneagy.
Henry Fox.
Wendel Fisher.
Dewalt Garst.
Christian Kaufman.
Henry Yeakle.
Philip Gosser.
Peter Heaney.
Fredrick Keffar.
Jacob Feald.
Peter Camble.
Michael Groe.
Lorentz Kuntz.

2nd Class.

George Moyer.
Deterick Heckman.
John Mees.
Jacob Fisher.
Jacob Plank.
Henry Brubaker.
Peter Long.
Fedrick Phiffer.
Daneal Reazer.

3rd Class.

Tobias Leman.
Christian Seltzer.
John Long.
George Bashore.
Peter Hersberger.
John Neal.
John Hoyl.
John Wingleblech.
Jacob Gettle.
Daniel Wagoner.
John Henning.
John Stealey.
Michel Straw.
Adam Winglebleck.
Jacob Weaver.
Abraham Sebolt.

4th Class.

John Been.
Jacob Gosser.
Henry Mees.
William Bough.
John Faber.
Ludwick Witenbergh.
Adam Brand.
George Kephart.
Isaac Snevely.
John Bright.
Ulrich Felty.
Peter Roop.
Abraham Winger.
Henry Light.

5th Class.

Henry Been.
Henry Dergass.
Adam Shower.
Yost Gneagy.
Henry Snotterly.
John Bashore, Jur.
Philip Zehring.
Killian Long, Jur.
John Brubaker.
Sebastian Felty.
Jacob Basehore.
Robert Foster.
Abraham Weader.

6th Class.

Casper Princenhober.
John Dergass.
Christopher Cop.
John Bashore, Senr.
David Tue.
Jacob Stealy.
Henry Zehring, Senr.
Daniel Stroh.
John Winger, Jur.
Jacob Yerian.
John Bashore, sadler.
Jacob Snevely, Jur.
George Hoyhman.
Tobias Leaman, Jur.
George Kuntz.

7th Class.

John Leman.
Henry Dum.
Peter Sattazaun.
Rudy Yeakle.
Henry Dubs, Jur.
Henry Dubs, Senr.
Jacob Snevely, Senr.
Christian Shoufler.
Jacob Brand.
John Dubs.
Henry Bright.
James Field.
Martin Winger.
Conrad Kroul.
Michael Strayor.
Nicholas Krehl.
John McCreery.
Adam Henning.

8th Class.

Abraham Depoey.
John Spitlar.
Henry Snotterly, Jur.
Henry Shoub.
Philip Faber.
John Winger, Senr.
Henry Miller.
Leonard Wingleblech.
Peter Bashore.
John Cop.
Christian Brand.
John Mark.
Henry Nease.
Michael Bright.
Henry Campble.
John Gosser.
Henry Zehring, Jur.
Daniel Weidle.
George Brand.
Fredrick Gamber.
Saml. Jones.
Jacob Miley.
Martin Miley.

Total 121 men.

I do swear, on the Holy Evangiliest of Almighty God: That the above list is a just and true state, of the Male White Inhabitants, residing in my District, agreeably to Law, and without any fraud to the State, to the best of my knowledge.

Sworn before me
this 9th Day of July 1782.

JOHN GLONINGER, Sub. Lt. L. Co.
MATHIAS HENNING, Capt.

A RETURN OF OFFICERS ELECTED IN THE SECOND BATALLION OF LANCASTER COUNTY MILITIA, AGREEABLE TO ORDERS, PUBLISHED FOR THAT PURPOSE, ON THE 15TH DAY OF APRIL 1783. (c.)

Field Officers.

Lieut. Colonel—John Gloninger.
Major—Baltzer Orth.

Staff.

Daniel Oldenbruck—Surgeon.
Philip Huber—Adjutant.
John Snevely—Quarter Master.

Captains.

1. David Krause.
2. Michael Holderbaum.
3. Jacob Meily.
4. Matthias Hening.
5. Leonard Immel.
6. George Bowman.
7. John Orth.
8. Henry Sheffer.

Lieutenants.

1. Philip Greenawalt.
2. Allexander Martin.
3. George Fisser.
4. Abraham Stone.
5. Christopher Leis.
6. Allexander Montgomery.
7. Peter Ensminger.
8. George Noll.

Ensigns.

1. Jacob Emblch.
2. John Strow, Jur.
3. Henry Snevely.
4. Martin Meily.
5. Christian Ley.
6. Martin Weitzel.
7. Daniel Stouffer.
8. George Teesinger.

I certify the above to be a just state of the officers ellected in 2nd Bat. of Lancaster County Militia agreeable to returns made.

ADM. HUBLEY, JR., S. Lt. of Lr. Cy.

RETURN OF THE FIRST CLASS OF CAPT. KRAUSS'S COMPANY OF THE 2D BATTALION OF LANCASTER COUNTY MILLITIA. (c.)

George Straw, marched.
Michael Krepps, marched.
George Hess, marched.
John Rewalt, marched.
Christopher Embigh, marched.
Jacob Steel, marched.
Rudy Kelker, marched.
Christian Kreamer, marched.
Christian Greenawalt, marched.

I do Certify that the Above is a true State taken from my Company Role—the 1st Day of Dec.

DAVID KRAUSE, Capt.

THIRD BATTALION
LANCASTER COUNTY MILITIA.

OFFICERS THIRD BATTALION—1777. (a)

Colonel.

Alexander Lowrey.

Lieutenant Colonel.

James Cunningham.

Major.

Jacob Cooke.

Adjutant.

William Tate.

Quarter Master.

John Jamison.

Sergeant Major.

John Robinson.

Quarter Master Sergeant.

David Jamison.

First Company.

Captain—Robert McKee.
First Lieutenant—James Scott.
Second Lieutenant—Hugh Hall.
Ensign—James Carothers.

Second Company.

Captain—Thomas Robinson.
First Lieutenant—Robert Robinson.
Second Lieutenant—James Miller.
Ensign—Robert Boal.

Third Company.

Captain—Joseph Work.
First Lieutenant—William Wilson.
Second Lieutenant—James Cook.
Ensign—James Wilson.

Fourth Company.

Captain—David McQuown.
First Lieutenant—Robert McQuown.
Second Lieutenant—Matthew Hays.
Ensign—James Hays.

Fifth Company.

Captain—Robert Craig.
First Lieutenant—John Cook.
Second Lieutenant—Zacharias Moore.
Ensign—Walter Bell.

Sixth Company.

Captain—Andrew Boggs.
First Lieutenant—George Redsecker.
Second Lieutenant—Robert Jamison.
Ensign—William Meyers.

Seventh Company.

Captain—Abraham Scott.
First Lieutenant—Michael Peters.
Second Lieutenant—John Bishop.
Ensign—Abraham Scott, Jr.

Eighth Company.

Captain—Hugh Pedan.
First Lieutenant—Patrick Hays.
Second Lieutenant—Benjamin Mills.
Ensign—Arthur Hays.

A ROAL CALL FOR CAPT. ABRAHAM FOREY'S COMPENEY IN THE MIDDLE DISTRICKT OF RAPPO TOWNSHIP COMMANDED BY MR. ALEXANDER LOWRY COLONELL OF THE THIRD BATTALION OF MELISHEY IN LANCASTER COUNTY, MANHIME, AUGUST 16TH 1777. (c.)

Sarjents.

Christian Detter.	Jacob Coladen.
Jacob Earehart.	George Stake.

Corprels.

Benge Nowman.
Adam Wauffel.
Philip Bratz.
George Warner.

Privets.

Christen Marten.
John Fritz.
Abraham Lamon.
John Laman.
Mical Bambarger.
Solamon Langanker.
John Hetey.
Christen Meshey.
Cristen Wenger.
John Wenger.
Jonas Humer.
Joseph Humer.
Peter Humer.
Casper Lesher.
John Wetmore.
Jacob Lithey.
Peter Fuks.
Daniel Langenkr.
Henry Langenkr.
Mical Langenkr.
Daniel Laman.
Jacob Rile.
Henrich Hensy.
Henry Hamacher.
Christen Hernly.
John Hernly.
Jacob Shoal.
William Giger.
Jacob Myer.
Henry Kiens.
Christen Herkelrode.
Abraham Hestand.
Conrad Wert.
Fredrik Nowman.
Mical Gotadel.
Walrick Lambarter.
John Noaker.
Adam Matzaboch.
Henry Werley.
George Gock.
Marten Getter.
George Fishhooke.
Matties Long.
Hanukel Lebrech.
John Fooks.
Peter Fisher.
Fridrick Druckannel.
John Fisher.
George Fisher.
Matties Helton.
Corl Welker.
Fredrick Balzer.
Christen Reab.
Henry Cling.
Cristen Brand.
John Brand.
Basten Wetmore.
John Eaby.
Marten Eaby.
Henry Kefer.
John Sharer.
Mical Druckamel.
Andres Betz.
George Hatz.
Thomas William.
George Hoanstone.
Stofel Walls.
Stofel Walls, Junr.
Edward Helton.
John Bungart.
John Hagey.
John Hagey, Junr.
Marten Betz.
Peter Readabock.
Jacob Stroal.
Gotlepe Spone.

Fredrick Kercher.
John Baumgardanar.
Abraham Whitmore.
Casper Ludwick.
Philip Baker.
John Baker.
Ventel Mortzal.
Jacob Mickey.
Marten Nesley.
Mical Shfer.
Jacob Gady.
Mical Gady.
Mical Stake.
Jacob Owen.
Christen Crinar.

ABRAHAM FORRY, Capt.

RETURN OF CAPT. ABRAHAM FOREY'S COMPANY IN THE MIDLE DETREKT OF RAPPO TOWNSHIP UNDER COMMAND OF ALEXANDER LOWRY COLONEL OF THE 3D BAT'N OF MELISHEY IN LANCASTEER COUNTY, MARCH 17TH, 1778. (c.)

Capt.

Abraham Forey.

Left.

1st.—Noah Carey.
2d.—Steven Wimer.

Ensign.

John Dyer.

Sargent.

1st.—Chresten Detter.
2d.—George Ferhoake (?).
3d.—Jacob Galadèr.
4th.—Henry Hamaker.

Corp.

1st.—Bengeman Nowman.
2d.—Adam Woeffel.
3d.—Phillip Braty.
4th.—George Warner.

Privates.

1st Class.

John Noaker.
Edward Helton.
John Wetmore.
Casper Lesher.
George Hatz.
Daniel Laman.
John Merhey.
Henry Hershey.

2nd Class.

Peter Readaboh.
Christen Wenger.
Mical Gotadel.
William Giger.
Peter Foke.
Jacob Myer.
Jonas Hamer.
Basten Wetmore.

3rd Class.

Wolreek Lambaster.
Henry Hires.
Jacob Stroal.
Gotlepe Spone.
Christen Meshey.
Abraham Laman.
Mical Longanekr.
Mical Bambarger
Casper Lodawck.
Fredrek Beler.

4th Class.

Fredrek Kerages.
Philip Baker.
John Fritz.
Christer Hernly.
Danial Longanekr.
Jacob Geldeg.
Jacob Rife.
John Bomgardnr.
John Brand.
John Sharer.

5th Class.

Peter Fisher.
Solamon Longaneker.
Henry Cling.
Andrew Betz.
Charls Weeker.
Henry Warley.
Abraham Hestand.
Wendel Mortzal.
Jacob Ober.
Chrestan Herkebrod.
John Gabeg.

6th Class.

Joseph Hamer.
Conrad Wert.
Thomas Williams.
Jacob Lithey.
Marten Nisley.
Christen Marten.
Henry Longaneker.
Adam Motzabokr.
Christen Brand.
George Hourston.

7th Class.

George Fisher.
Nickles Lebrick.
George Yoake.
Mattiese Long.
Mical Yudey.
Christen Reape.
Peter Humer.
Marten Yetter.
Abraham Wetmore.
Henrey Reffer.

8th Class.

John Hernley.
Christen Chrimer.
Marten Betz.
Fredrek Newman.
John Fisher.
Mical Stoke.
John Laman.
Jacob Shoal.
Stoffel Wals.
John Beaker.
Jacob Coachart.
Fredrek Douchameter.

A MUSTER ROLL OF THE MEN IN CAPTAIN THOMAS ROBINSON'S COMPANY OF MOUNTJOY TOWNSHIP COMMENCING APRIL THE 20 ANNOQUE 1778. (c.)

Commissioned Officers.

Capt.

Thomas Robinson.

Lieutenants.

1st.—Robert Robinson. 2nd.—James Miller.

Ensign.

Ephraim Litle.

Non. Com. Officers.

Serjants.

John Allman. William Boal.

Privates.

First Class.

Stophel Misenhalter.
Abraham Wolgamout.
John Stouffer.
Matthias Plantz.
David Gish.
John Hay.
John Forry.
John Stern.
John Alison.
Henry Eatter.

Second Class.

Nathan Patton.	Henry Kinter.
Robert Moorhead.	Christian Schneider.
Fredrick Stoller, snr., over age.	James Karnanan.

Third Class.

Hugh Black.	George Gibford.
John Leoman.	Phillip Fredrick.
John Robinson.	Joseph Wolf, snr.
John Gibford.	John Young.
Christian Wolgamout.	Henry Gibford.

Fourth Class.

Henry Stouffer.	Michael Black.
Isaac Titty.	Jacob Keener.
John Holdeman, stiller.	Abraham Peesor.
John Leoman, black.	Andrew Allison.
Peter Stern.	

Fifth Class.

James Moorhead.	Jacob Shelly.
William Alison.	Christian Reesor.
John Nicky.	Peter Fredrick.
John Gish.	John Whitmore.

Sixth Class.

James Cunningham.	Thomas Weilly.
John Karnahan.	Jacob Shire.
Joseph Wolf, Jr.	John Foglesang.
Christian Herr.	Christian Whitmore.

Seventh Class.

Fredrick Stollar, Jr.	Hermon Latour.
Jacob Holdiman.	Henry Limper.
Peter Walker.	Jacob Eckhert.
Abraham Shelly.	Castle May.

Eighth Class.

Jacob Forry.
Abraham Stoller, under age 2 years.
Daniel Conrod.

John Schneider.
David Misenhalter.
John Vernor.
Robert Boal.
John Holdiman.
William McKean, jr.

I Do Certify that the Above is a true State of the Company.

THOMAS ROBINSON, Capt.

A MUSTER ROLE OF CAPT. ROBERT McKEES COMPANY OF THE FIRST CLASS OF COLL. LOWREY'S BATTALION ON GUARD AT MIDDELTOWN APRIL 24TH 1778. (c.)

Capt. McKees, first class.

Joseph Chambers.
William Jameson.
James fox.
Thomas Ramsey.
James Vanlear.
William harvey.
Philip Sellers.
Thomas Ogle.
Jos. Crathers.
Samuel Bell.
John Dean.
John Fox.
George Allison.
Daniel Eliott.
John Gingrey.
James hinman.
Henry McGee.

Capt. Robisons.

Robt. Robison.
Nathen Patten.
John Yong.

Capt. Work's.

James Cook.
Robert Currey.

Capt. M'Queen's.

Ensign.

James Hays.
Rob't Ray.
John hays.
Thomas Keneday.

Capt. Boggs.

Joseph Joans.
Henry McMullen.
Fredrick Gedy.
Robt. Mayrs.
Samuel Boyd.
John Drivenstrots.
Fredrick Strouce.

Capt. Scott.

Peter Shaver. Lenard Peters.
Jacob Shaver.

Capt. Crage.

John Conn. Jacob Shireman.
John Goener. Zarias Grimes.

Capt. Pedon.

William Campble. John Hays.

Capt. Earhart.

James Kilpatrick. Abraham Trotey.
Casper fister.

A LIST OF THE FIRST CLASS OF THE DIFRENT CAPT. COMPANYS BELONGING TO COLL. LOWREYS BATTALION, MAY THE 25TH, 1778. (c.)

Capt. McKees.

William Harvey.
George Wolf.
William Gray.
David Hansminger.
Henry Booser.
Jacob Coss, Jr.
Henry McGee.
George Allison.
Joseph Rife.
Jas. Vanlear.
John Fox.
Philip Sellers.
Abraham Strickler.
John Ritzel.
Nickles Lightey.

Capt. Robinson's.

Stophel Wizenhalter.
Abraham Wilgemood.
John Stover.
Mathies Blants.
John Chis.
John Hays.
John Farrey.
John Stern.
Henry Etter.
John Allison.

Capt. Works.

James Cook.
David Scott.
David Wiant.
Philip Wiant.
Jacob Tundover.
Fredrick Mumma.
James Clingan.
Peter Bowman.
Christian Mussleman.
William Hawk.
Alexander McNight, left the parts.

Capt. McQueens.

John Hays.
Mathew McGomrey.
Robert Allison.
Jas. Kelley.
Jacob Shank.
Peter Bream.
Micheal Brand.
John McClintock.
Michael Shank.

Capt. Craigs.

Jacob Shireman.
John Eversole.
Fredrick Yeight.
Abraham Ream.
Jacob Holtzaple.
Jas. Flin.
John Krill.
John Nicoles.

Capt. Boggs.

Robert Mayres.
John Smith.
Crisley Wiand.
Michael Laird.
Henry McMullen.
John Smith.
Samuel Boyd.
Fredrick Strouce.
John Mummaok.
Cristian Blazer.

Capt. Scotts.

John Miller.
Henry Hine.
Abr. Black.
Frances Whitmore.
Lenard Negley.
Peter Funk.
Abraham Sharer.
Abraham Strickler.
John Black.

Capt. Peden.

Gilbert Clark, gone off.
Arch. McBride.
Samuel Lockard.
Christ Huffman.
John Shank.
Edward Waterson.
John Hays.
John Lisher.
Christ Erishman.
James Cloun.
Patrick Burns.

Capt. Furrey.

John Nocker.
Edward Hilton.
John Whitmore.
Casper Lasher.
George Hotts.
Daniel Leamon.
Ben. Nowman.
John Meshe.
Henry Hersha.

Capt. Earhart.

Martan Griner.
James Sky.
Adam Cover.
Henry Eshelman.
Jacob Conrad.
Martan Shook.
Casper Fister.
Christ Eversole.
Michael Shilly.
John Peter.
Peter Caley.
Abraham Trotey.
Gorge Gants.

Capt. McKee's Guard called to Middletown the 1st Class in full.

A MUSTER ROLE OF CAPT. ROBERT McKEE COMPANY OF MELITIA OF THE THIRD BATTALION OF LANCASTER COUNTY COMMANDED BY COLL. ALEXANDER LOWREY AUGUST THE 24, 1778. (c.)

Captain.

Robert McKee.

Lieutenants.

1.—James Scott.
2.—Hugh Hall.

Privates.

1st Class.

William Harvey.
George Wolf, over age.
William Gray.
David hansminger.
Henry Booser.
Jacob Coss, Junior.
Henry McGee.
James Riden, gone away.
George Allison.
Joseph Rife.
James Vanlear.
John Fox.
Philip Sellers.
Abraham Strickler.
John Ritzel.
Nicklous Lightey.

2nd Class.

Jacob Rife.
John Fifer.
Alexander Dean.
James Kile.
George Brooks.
James Defrance.
Fredrick Shoats.
John Singer.
Woly Hansbarger, dead.
James Fox.
Stephen Felix.

3rd Class.

John Reser.
William Jamison.
Jacob Neasley.
David tatwiler.
John Shar.
Abraham Kingrey.
Jacob Fritzes.
Henry Singer.
Jacob Miszer.
Philip Righart.

4th Class.

Jacob Smith.
John Branser.
Barney Queen.
John Ridel, gone away.
James Hinman.
Thomas Ogle.
John Myers.
Patrick Lynch.
Henry Shaver.
Mathias Singer.
Petter Books.
John Cain.
James Crathers.

5th Class.

William Greap.
Samuel Clark.
Joseph Prim.
Petter Stoner.
Christopher Newver.
Jacob Long.
John Whitmer.
Michael Roads.
John Ginerey.
Henry Landis.
John Campble.
Antony Yeats.
James Noble.

6th Class.

Christopher Branser.
William Mills.
Jacob Tatwiler.
Christopher Burgholder.
Daniel Benine.
Mathias Bricker.
Petter Yeats.
John Dean.
John Foster.

7th Class.

Jacob Coss.
Daniel Elliot.
David Rose.
William Smith.
Thomas Trivey.
Samuel Finten.
Henry Eger.
Jacob Bricker.
Petter Roadrock.
Fredrick Sellers.
John Soop.
Henry Ridley.

8th Class.

David Thrum.
Samuel Bell.
Petter Perst, Junr.
Henry Newver.
Samuel Hannan.
Fredrick Shaffner.
Jacob Whitmore.
Joseph Chambers.
James Blair, gone away.
Daniel Shelley.
Jacob Strickler.
Robert Breaden.
John Long.

I Do Certify the above to be a true Return.

ROBT. McKEE, Capt.

A MUSTER ..OLL OF CAPT. THOMAS ROBISON'S COMPANY OF LOUNTJOY TOWNSHIP LANCASTER COUNTY MILITIA COMMENCING ANGUST 24TH A. D. 1778. (c.)

Commissioned Officers.

Captain.

Thomas Robison.

1st Lieut.

Robert Robison.

2nd Lieut.

James Miller.

Ensign.

Ephraim Litle.

Serjeants.

John Flack 1st.
John Alleman 2nd.
William Boal 3d.

Privates.

1st Class.

Stophel Missenhalter.	John Hay.
Abraham Wolgamout.	John Forry.
John Stouffer.	John Stern.
Matthias Plantz.	Henry Eatter.
David Gish.	John Allison.

2nd Class.

Nathan Patton.	Henry Kinter.
Robert Moorehead.	Christian Schnider.
Fredrick Stollar, Snr.	James Karnahan.

3rd Class.

Hugh Black.	Christian Wolgamout.
John Lesman.	George Gibford.
John Young.	Phillip Fredrick.
John Robison.	Joseph Wolf, Snr.
John Gibford.	Henry Gibford.

4th Class.

Henry Stouffer.	Michal Black.
Isaac Titty.	Jacob Keener.
John Holdiman, stiller.	Abraham Ressor.
John Leoman, black.	Andrew Allison.
Peter Stern.	

5th Class.

James Moorhead.	Jacob Shelly.
William Allison.	Christian Ressor.
John Nicky.	Peter Fredrick.
John Gish.	John Whitmore.

6th Class.

James Cunningham.	Thomas Weilly.
John Karnehan.	Jacob Shire.
Joseph Wolf, Jr.	John Foglesong.
Christian Herr.	Christian Whitmore.

7th Class.

Fredrick Stoller, Jr.
Herman Latour.
Henry Limper.
Jacob Holdiman.
Peter Welker.
Jacob Eckert.
Abraham Shelly.
Castle May.

8th Class.

David Missenhalter.
Jacob Forry.
Abraham Stollar.
Daniel Conrod.
Robert Boal.
John Schneider.
John Vernon.
John Holdiman.
William McKean, Jr.

A MOSTER ROALE FOR CAPT. ARLHARTS COMPENY THE FIFTH CLASS OF THE THIRD BATTALON OF MILITIA IN LANCASTER COUNTY COMMANDED BY MR. ALEXANDR LOWREY COLN AS FOLLOWS. OCTOBER THE 29TH 1778. (c.)

Captain.

Marten Arlhart.

Lieutenants.

1.—Noah Ceasey.
2.—Andras Shell.
3.—John Florey.

Sargents.

1.—Tobias Kuster.
2.—Michal Shell.
Melker Secrist.
Henry Hine.

Corprals.

Steven Misenheld.
John Keller.
Marten fare.
Benge Bonten.

Drummer and Fifer.

Marten Earchar, Junr.
John Crouse.

Privets.

Jacob Secriste.
Mickal Sheealy.
Jacob Kener.
Henry Kessner.
John Moser.
John McBride.
John McClintock.
James Kenady.
Thomas Kenady.
George Keparet.
Robert Alexandra.
John Meshon.
William Moor.
Samal Cambell.
John Caufman.
William (illegible).
Phelop Smith.
Philip Ceaser.
John Easlinger.
John Stahman.
Christefer Keatly.
John Kingry.
Joseph Woolf.
John Gray.
George Snapen.
Patrick Linzey.
Samal Clark.
Jeams Nobele.
Robart Morehead.
John Linch.
Rendel Meckgland.
Jacob Conrod.
Philip Bishope.
Alexandra McClintik.
Andra foster.
Michal Black.
John fanes.

A MUSTER ROLE OF CAPT. ROBERT McKEES COMPANY OF MELITIA OF THE THIRD BATTALION OF LANCASTER COUNTY COMMANDED BY COLL. ALEXANDER LOWREY APRIL 19TH 1779. (c.)

Captain.

Robert McKee.

1st Lieut.

James Scott.

2nd Lieut.

Hugh Hall.

1st Class.

William Harvey.
William Gray.
David Hansminger.
Henry Booser.
Jacob Coss, Junior.
Henry McGee.

Gorge Allison.
Joseph Rife.
James Vanlear.
John Fox.
Philip Sellers.
Abraham Strickler.
John Ritzel.
Nicklous Lightey.
James McKee.
James McClester.
Alexander Russel.

2nd Class.

Jacob Rife.
John Fifer.
Alexander Dean.
James Kile.
George Books.
James Defrance.
Fredrick Shoats.
John Singer.
James Fox.
Stephen Felix.

3rd Class.

John Reser.
William Jamison.
Jacob Nesely.
David totiviler.
John Sharer.
Abraham Kingrey.
Jacob Fritzes.
Henry Singer.
Jacob Mistzer.
Philip Righart.

4th Class.

Jacob Smith.
John Branser.
Barney Queen.
John Ridel (Gon away).
James Hinman.
Thomas Ogle.
John 'Myers.
Patrick Lynch.
Henry Shearer.
Mathias Singer.
Petter Books.
John Cain.
James Crathers.

5th Class.

William Greap.
Samuel Clark.
Joseph Prim.
Petter Stoner.
Christopher Newver.
Jacob Long.
John Whitmore.
Michael Roads.
John Gingrey.
Henry Landis.
John Campble.
Antony Yeats.
James Noble.

6th Class.

Christopher Branser.
William Mills.
Jacob tatwiler.
Christopher Burgholder.
Daniel Benlwe.
Mathias Bricker.
Petter Yeats.
John Dean.
John Foster.

7th Class.

Jacob Coss (I belive over age).
Daniel Elliot.
David Rose.
William Smith.
Thomas Tribey.
Samuel Finten.
Henry Eger.
Jacob Bricker.
Petter Roadrock.
Fredrick Sellers.
John Soop.
Henry Ridley.

8th Class.

David thrum.
Samuel Bell.
Petter Perst, Junior.
Henry Newver.
Samuel Hannan.
Fredrick Shaffner.
Jacob Whitmore.
Joseph Chambers.
James Blair (gon away).
Daniel Shelley.
Jacob Strickler.
Robert Breden.
John Long.

I Do Certy that the above is a true Return.

ROBERT McKEE.

A MUSTER ROLL OF THE MEN IN CAPT. THOS. ROBINSON'S COMPANY, MOUNTJOY TOWNSHIP COMMENCING APRIL 19TH A. D. 1779. (c.)

Commissioned Officers.

Captain.

Thomas Robinson.

1st Lieut.

Robert Robison.

2nd Lieut.

James Miller.

Ensign.

Ephraim Little.

Sarjeants.

1st.—John Flack.
2d.—John Alliman.
3d.—William Boal.

Privates.

1st Class.

Stophen Misenhalter.
Abraham Wolgamout.
John Stouffer.
Mathias Plantz.
David Gish.
John Hay.
John Forray.
John Stern.
Henry Eater.
John Allison.

2nd Class.

Nathan Patton.
Robert Moorehead.
Henry Kinter.
Christian Snider.
James Kernatan.

3rd Class.

Hugh Black.
John Leaman.
John Young.
John Gibford.
Christian Weigamoot.
George Gibford.
Joseph Wolf, Sr.
Philip Fredrick.
Henry Gibford.
Joseph Wolf, Sr.

4th Class.

Henry Stouffer.
Isaac Titty.
John Haldeman, miller.
John Leoman, black.
Peter Stern.
Michael Black.
Jacob Keener.
Abraham Reesor.
Andrew Allison.

5th Class.

James Moorhead.
William Allison.
John Nickey.
John Gesh.
Jacob Shelly.
Christian Reessor.
Peter Frederick.
John Whitmore.

6th Class.

James Cunningham.
John Kernahan.
Joseph Wolf, Jr.
Christian Herr.
Thomas Willey.
Jacob Shire.
John Foglesang.
Christian Whitmore.

7th Class.

Fredrick Stolar, Jr.
Hermon Latoore.
Henry Limper.
Jacob Haldemon.
Peter Welker.
Abraham Shelly.
Cotle May.

8th Class.

David Misenhalter.
Jacob Forry.
Abraham Stolar.
Daniel Conrod.
John Vernor.
John Haldeman.
William McKean, Jr.

A LIST OF THE ATTENDERS IN CAPT. JOS. WORK'S COMPANY FROM APRIL 19TH TO MAY 24TH 1779. (c.)

Commissioned Officers.

Captain.

Joseph Work.

1st Lieut.

William Wilson.

2nd Lieut.

James Cook.

Ensign.

James Wilson.

Serjeants.

William Montgomery.
William Cummins.
Robt. Curry.
Malcolm McPhatridge.

Privates.

1st Class.

Felty Steer.
David Scott.
Danl. Elliot.
John Dunlap.

2nd Class.

James Karr.
John Barber.
John Maze.
Nicholas Peck.
John Fauntz.
James Macky, jr.

3rd Class.

Phillip Bramor.
Saml. Cook.
George Clingan.

4th Class.

Hugh Caldwell.
Saml. McClung.
Thomas Weilly.

5th Class.

Joseph Kilpatrick.
Robert Heaslip.
James Anderson, Jr.
Robert Connel.
Joseph Millar.
James Bayly, Esqr.

6th Class.

Abraham Albert.
Richd. Allison.
David Cook.

7th Class.

Robert Ballance.
John McKenny.
Robert Caven.
William Clingan.
Matthias Clyne.

8th Class.

John Crookshanks.
John Dukemanear.
William McKean, Jr.

Certify'd by

WM. McKEAN, JR.,
Clerk of the Company.

A RETURN FOR CAPT. ABRAHAM FOREY'S COMPANY UNDER COMMAND OF ALEXANDER LOWNEY COLNEL OF THE THIRD BATTALON OF MILITIA IN LANCASTER COUNTY. JUNE THE 8TH 1779. (c).

Captain.
Abraham Forey.

1st Lieut.
Noah Ceasey.

2nd Lieut.
Steven Wimer.

Ensign.
John.

1st Sergt.
Christian Petter.

2nd Sergt.
George Fishhook.

3rd Sergt.
Bengeman Nowman.

4th Sergt.
Henrey Hamaker.

1st Corpl.
Phillop Bratz.

2nd Corpl.
Jacob Myar.

3rd Corpl.
Christian Griner.

4th Corpl.
Matthize Helton.

Privates.

1st Class.

John Noaker.
Edward Helton.
John Welmer.
Casper Lesher.
George Hatz.
Daniel Lame.
Henrey Hershey.
Jacob Rosel.
Albreght Miller.

2nd Class.

Peter Readobock.
Christian Wenger.
Michal Godadel.
Peter Fooks.
John Gearhart.
Christian Wengger.
Sebastian Wetmore.
John Shoumaker.
John Lesher.

3rd Class.

John Hatz.	Michal Bombarger.
Henry Hines.	Casper Lodowick.
Gotleipe Spone.	Fredrick Belger.
Christian Meshey.	Jacob Myar.
Abraham Lame.	John Heanley.
Michal Longanecker.	

4th Class.

Fredrick Kenaga.	John Bomgardner.
Phillip Beaker.	John Brand.
John Fritz.	John Sharer.
Christian Heanly.	Adam Warffel.
Daniel Longanecker.	Adam Rease.
Jacob Rife.	John Michel.

5th Class.

Peter Fisher.	Abraham Heaston.
Solomon Longanecker.	Wendel Mortzall.
Henrey Kling.	John Eabey.
Andrew Betz.	Henrey Lesher.
Charls Welker.	Gabrall Davis.
Henrey Warley.	

6th Class.

Joseph Humer.	Adam Metzaboch.
Conrad Wert.	Christian Brand.
Thomas Williamson.	George Hounston.
Jacob Lithey.	George Stager.
Marten Nisley.	Mattise Kepler.
Christian Marten.	Daniel Weller.
Henrey Longaneker.	

7th Class.

George Fisher.	Marten Getter.
Nickles Lebrey.	Abraham Wetmore.
Mattise Long.	George Snyder
Michal Gudey.	John Noaman.
Christian Reasse.	Abraham Hamer.
Peter Humer.	Wm. Smith.

8th Class.

John Hearnly.
Morten Betz.
Fredrick Nowman.
John Fisher.
Jacob Shoal.
John Beocker.
George Stake.
Jacob Earehart.
George Werner.
Joseph Rosell.
Michal Huber.
Peter Bribliuier.
Andrew Holtere.

I do hereby certify this is a true and exact Return of the within mentioned Company.

Certified by me.

NOAH CEASEY, Lut.

June 8th, 1779.

A RETURN OF THE SEVENTH CLASS OF COL'O ALEXANDER LOWREY'S BATTA., BEING THE 3D BATTA. LANCASTER COUNTY MILITIA, COM'D BY CAPT. ABR'M SCOTT. (c.)

1st Capt.—Robert McKee.

Daniel Elliott.
Thos. Tribby.
Saml. Finton.
Henry Eigar.
Jacob Bricker.
Peter Rodrock.
Fredrick Sellers.
John Soop.
Henry Ridley.

2nd Capt.—Thos. Robison.

Fredrick Stolar.
Henry Limper.
Jacob Holdiman.
Peter Wilker.
Abr'm Shelley.
Castle May.

3rd Capt.—Jos. Work.

Wm. Montgomery.
Sam'l Smith.
Jacob Hershey.
Robt. Ballance.
John Grayble.
John McKinny.

Christian Culp.	John Hoarst.
Geo. Lindemount.	Wm. Clingan.
Daniel Miley.	Mathias Cline.
Robt. Caven.	

4th Capt.—David McQueen.

Peter Poorman.	Elias Conrod.
Christ'r Dolabeck.	Robt. McCleary.
John Johnston.	John Buck.
Adam Henry.	William Kigar.
Charles Johnston.	Mich'l Felteberber.

5th Capt.—Robt. Craig.

Nichlass Crane.	Fred'r Sailer.
David Leamon.	Adam Wiant.
Sam'l Thompson.	James Hoover.
James Cook.	James Murphey.
John Yeight.	Robert Cairns.
Daniel Kingsingan.	

6th Capt.—And'w Boggs.

Peter Hilsson.	John Horst.
Sam'l Holmes.	John Drivenstoots.
Jacob Angle.	Frederick Keatty.
William Hawk.	Jos. Ream.
David Martain.	Jasper Muser.
Henry Kintick.	Sam'l Shavor.
George Snoke.	Jacob Laver.
Jacob Shimph.	

7th Capt.—Abrm. Scott.

Peter Leman.	Abrm. Kish.
John Alexander.	Jacob Shorah.
Henry Pinther.	Isaac Harnly.
Casper Shinghass, Junr.	Casper Shinghass, Senr.
Anthoney Snider.	Christian Martain.

8th Capt.—Hugh Peden.

Sam'l Brand.	James Staret, Senr.
Henry Hubley.	Neal Welsh.
Abrm. Holdiman.	John Rora.

John Millar.
Sam'l Patterson.
Olarey Strickler.
John Gray.
Peter Heston.

9th Capt.—Christ. Earhart.

Michal Humer.
John Winger.
George Nickey.
Christian Brand.
Lorance Sneeringer.
Peter Bicker.
John Himer, Junr.
John McBride.
John Bender.
Bastian Dunkle.
Milker Fortney.

6th Class of Capt. McQueen's Company.

Andrew Foster.
John Rea.

7th. Capt. Work.

Richard Allison.

A LIST OF THEIR NAMES IN THE 6 & 7TH CLASS OF COL. LOWREY BATALION WHO APEARED AT ELISABETH TOWN ON 13TH AUGUST, 1779, WILLING TO MARCH TO SUNBURY AGREEABLE TO ORDERS.

---

7 Class Capt. McKee's Company.

Hendry Egar.

The 7th of Scott's.

John Alexander. Anthony Snider.
Hendry Penther.

6th Class.

Thos. Wiley. Andrew Foster.
Richard Alison.

7th Class. Capt. Robinson's.

None.

7th Class. Capt. Works.

None.

7th. Capt. McQueen's.

John Jonstone. Rob't McCleary.

7th. Capt. Crage.

Sam'l Thompson. James Cook.

7th of Boggs.

Joseph Reams.

7th of Earhart's.

None.

A RETORN OF MY COMPANY, BEING THE EGHT COMPNEY OF THE THIRD BATALEN OF LANCASTER COUNTY MILITIA, COMMAND BY CON'L ALEXANDER LOWERY.

October ye 25, 1779. (c.)

Captain.

Hugh Peden.

Lieutenant.

Patrick Hays. Benjamen Mills.

Ensign.

John Boggs.

1 Class.

Christian Hufman. Christian Erisman.
John Shanck. Patrick Borns.
Edward Waterson. Jacob Aran.
John Hays. Phillip Gelmar.

2 Class.

John Shilhorn. Cornalus Tolen.
John Scott. Joseph Tidball.
Abraham Castle. John Gray.

3 Class.

Ludwick Mats. Samuel Robeson.
Christan Loung. Henry Strickler.
Henry Strickler. John Beard.
Balser Walter. John Ishbach.
Samuel Robeson. Petter Funck.

4 Class.

James Petterson. Jacob Penter.
Joseph Littel. James Staret, Juner.
Samuel Coran. John Some.
Joseph Flacher. Balser Shilhorn.
Robart Ales.

5 Class.

Hugh Grims.
Michal Horst.
Petter Walter.
Jacob Hostater.
Christan Loungneker.
Henry Ocker.
John Meshey.
Cherls Newcom.

6th Class.

James Hucheson.
Christan Holdeman.
Abraham Mats.
Isaac Gellmer.
John Chembers.
Thomas Minto.

7th Class.

Samuel Brand.
Henry Hubly.
Petter Hestan.
Abraham Holdeman.
James Staret.
Neal Walch.
John Rora.
John Millir.
Samuel Petterson.
Obrey Strickler.

8th Class.

Jacob Erisman, Sen'r.
Jacob Mats.
Jacob Erisman.
John Swene.
Jacob Kensler.
James Beard.
Abraham Cobert.
David Moorr.

Certifyd the Within pr. me.

HUGH PEDEN, Capt.

A RETURN OF CAPT. DAVID McQUEEN'S CO. OF THE 3D BETALLION OF LANCASTER COUNTY MELITIA COMANDED BY COL'N ALLEXANDER LOWRY. FOR THE YEAR 1779. (c.)

Officers.

Captain.

David McQueen.

Lieut.

Robt. McQueen.

Lieut.

Mat'w Hay.

Ens'n.

Jas. Hay.

Privates.

Hen'y Alleman.
Mic'l Fellebargar.
Jno. Hay.
Robt. Allen.
Jas. Kelly.
Jac'b Shank.
Mic'l Shank.
Peter Bream.
Mic'l Brand.
Wm. Hay, Ju'r.
Patk. Kelly.
Rob't Hunter.
Christ. Keatly.
Rob't Buck.
Mark Worst.
John Campel.
Abr'm Stevick.
Corn's Green.
Jos. Morrison.
John Reasor.
Dew't Grim.
Geo. Null.
Jab. Stopher.
——— Stukley.
Jno. Stevick.
Mic'l Eaby.
Jas. Kennady.
Abr'm Reamer.
Jno. Duncan.
Cht'n Null.
Stop'l Bishop.
Cht'n Snyder.
Phip. Reamer.
Denis Stall.
Da'd Foster.
Con'd Wolf.
Wm. Hay.
An'd Foster.
Sto'l Shank.
Phip. Roghman.
Jno. Thompson.
Pet'r Reasor.
Pet'r Poorman.
Cht'n Dolobogh.
Jno. Johnston.
Adam Hendry.
Chas. Johnston.
Elias Conrod.
Jacob Weglor.
Dan'l Plaugh.
Jac'b Meckley.
Thos. Cloyde.
And'w Hunter.
Met'w Wolf.
Cht'n Buch.
Anthony Buck.
Michall Shoats.
Jno. Dunlap.
Jas. Carnaughan.
Henry Rowland.
Robt. Rhea.
Jno. Rhea.
Wm. Buck.
Jno. Kenedy.
Thos. Kenedy.
Jno. McLintick.
Jas. Rockpatrick.
Andrew Foster.
John Herring.
Alexander McLintick.
Jacob Shue.
Andrew Moore.
Jno. Carnaughan.
Alex. Long.*

Jas. Noteman.	Hen'y Rowland.
Wm. Moore, Jun'r.	Robt. Hunter.
Robt. McLeary.	Jno. Delap.
Nic'ls Prats.	Abr'm Longnecker.
Mic'l Prats.	Jas. Carnaghan, Ju'r.
Wm. Crosier.	Wm. Carnaghan.
Barnet M Glahlin.	Jas. M Clintock.
Han'l Painter.	Wm. Hall.
Abr'm Evil.	Jas. Huey.
Geo. Keapford	Arch'd Ellot.
Chr'tn Brand.	Jas. Donelson.
Hen'y Keapford.	Jno. Shearer.
Sam'l McCleary.	Cht'n Wolf.
Mic'l France.	Cht'n Stevick.
Cht'n Plough.	

OFFICERS OF THIRD BATTALION. (a.)

Returned August 26, 1780.

Lieutenant Colonel.

Jacob Bower.

Major.

Wendle Hipsman.

FIRST COMPANY.

Captain—Philip Dock.
Lieutenant—John Weyman.
Ensign—John Smith.

SECOND COMPANY.

Captain—Andrew Ream.
Lieutenant—Henry Ream.
Ensign—Christian Baltzley.

THIRD COMPANY.

Captain—George Reist.
Lieutenant—George Hoke.
Ensign—Michael Gingrich.

FOURTH COMPANY.

Captain—Joseph Gehr. Ensign—George Brunner.
Lieutenant—Peter Geistwhite.

FIFTH COMPANY.

Captain—Jacob Vanderslice. Ensign—Henry Gyer.
Lieutenant—John Bechtold.

SIXTH COMPANY.

Captain—Philip Peck. Ensign—Michael Oberly.
Lieutenant—Peter Pence.

SEVENTH COMPANY.

Captain—[Vacant.] Ensign—[Vacant.]
Lieutenant—[Vacant.]

EIGHTH COMPANY.

Captain—John Smuller. Ensign—[Vacant.]
Lieutenant—[Vacant.]

A RETURN OF CAPT. JOHN ASHTON'S COMP'Y OF THE 3D BATTALION OF MILITIA OF LANCASTER COUNTY. OCTOB'R 22, 1780. (c.)

Captain.

John Ashton.

Lieutenant.

Daniel Hollingler.

Ensign.

George Hoverter.

1st Class.

Jacob Keefer. John Eby.
John Hair. Jacob Kinsey.

Daniel Hollinger.
John Fleman.
John Grove.
John Shitts.
Samuel Sinclear.
John Boyer.
Frederick Lucord.
John Curts.

2nd Class.

George Miller, stiller.
Ellexander Sortman.
Frederick Witmire.
Jacob Musselman.
Peter Sheffer.
William Keezel.
Balser Seese.
John Brubaker, Ju'r.
John Jones.
Nathaniel Spensor.
Adam Eicholse.

3rd Class.

John Rudy.
Henry Wincle.
Adam Keener.
John Crotson.
Conrod Mark.
Stophel rauber.
George Saum.
Samuel Wislor.
George Poatsor.
Christian Stover.
Francis Noland.
Samuel Cromer.

4th Class.

John Cromer.
Nicholas Bale.
Peter Crotsor.
Jacob Mire.
Nicholas Srofe.
Michael Sortman.
Henry Rudy.
Samuel Jones.
Samuel Brassington.
John Brubaker.
Christian Suck.
John Trump.

5th Class.

Martin Cromer.
Abram Stover.
Manuel Seese.
Jacob Burtner.
George Betts.
Lenard Smith.
Christian Kumerer.
George Hollinger.
James Bradford.
Thomas Hollinger.
George Miller.

6th Class.

Frederick Shitts.
Ulry Koysor.
Andrew Shover.
William McKelvey.
Methias Hoymer.
Thomas Owens.
Conrad Plastor.
David Fortney.
Michael Houghlander.
George Witcraft.
Charles Smith.
John Brubaker.

7th Class.

George Day.
Christian Hollinger.
John Cline.
Lenord Witmere.
John Porry.
Daniel Porry.
Samuel Russel.
David Smith.
Heny Mack.
Ellexander Sortman, J'r.
Michael Horning.
John Peter.

8th Class.

Peter Gaubb.
Mark Nagle.
Malcom McNeel.
Christian Smith.
Mathias Peter.
Jacob Brubaker.
William Trugo.
Adam Kerver.
William Smith.
John Harriss.
Thomas Goodfellow.
William Marshall.

A MUSTER ROLL OF CAPT. ANDREW REMS COMPANY OF THE THIRD BATT. OF LANCASTER COUNTY MILITIA, DATED REMS TOWN, DECEMBER 20TH, 1780. (c.)

Captain.

Andrew Ream.

Lieut.

Henry Ream.

Ensign.

Christian Baltzley.

Serjeants.

David Ream.
Godlieb Mack.
Abraham Killian.

Corpr.

Henry Landes.
Jacob Snyder.
Casper Keiper.

Fifer.

George Ream.

Drummer.

Andrew Ream.

Nicklaus Wolff.
Nicklous Snyder.
Christian Showalder.
Daniel Bowman.
Jacob Duck.
Jacob Leasher.
Jacob Mohler.
Jacob Deathweiler.
Peter Groff.
Henry Eberly.
George Hittebrant.
Adam Kingmaker.
Andrew Heitler.
John Kline.

The 2nd Class.

Nicklaus Duck.
Michael Sherg.
Joseph Bear.
Abraham Bixler.
David Meinser.
Leonhard Keller.
William Cram.
Samuel Bowman.
Jacob Hagy.
Peter Sheoner.
George Drout.
Jacob Bucher.
Margus Mantillius.
Jacob Shwartzwelder.

The 3rd Class.

Henry Mohler.
Abraham Kline.
Christian Knop.
David Maredy.
John Mellinger.
John Mohler.
Abraham Wolf.
Jacob Sandag.
William Mellinger.
Jacob Zentmyer.
Joseph Groff.
Jacob Landes.
James Right.
Cunrad Laub.
Jacob Ream.

The 4th Class.

Michael Reiter.
George Merkol.
Uly Sherg.
Dewalt Meder.
Jacob Showalder.
William Wheeler.
George Speath.
Friderick Leader.
John Sloth.
George Firestone.
Lazarus Levi.
Joas Miller.
Mardin Gleber.
Henry Hartman.

The 5th Class.

George Kunss.
Abraham Landes.
Adam Mosser.
Joseph Leisy.
Peter Brubacher.
Jacob Keller, Sen'r.
Samuel Groff.
John Landes.
Jacob Mishler, Jun'r.
John Ream, Jun'r.
John Gear.
Jacob Mellinger.
John Heffer.

The 6th Class.

Bernard Geiger.
Joseph Mishler.
Adam Epright.
Henry Hershberger.
Peter Snyder.
Martin Mohler.
George Hohe.
Abraham Hershberger.
Jacob Killian.
Jacob Rohland.
Abraham Groff.
Jacob Beaker.
John Hingel.
Myls Grauly.

The 7th Class.

John Martin.
Michael Bear.
Christian Cunrath.
Caper Sryt.
John Holtry.
John Bucher.
Isac Hershberger.
Henry Miller.
John Beaker.
Jacob Kunrath.
Joseph Spregel.
Daniel Ream.
Daniel Groff.
Nickloūs Wilt.
Christian Frantz.
William Showmacher.

The 8th Class.

John Sloth, se.
Peter Reyer.
David Sherg.
Abraham Ream.
Abraham Ream, Mill.
John Musselman.
Michael Wolff.
Christian Showalder.
John Mohler, Jr.
Andrew Ream, Jr.
Abraham Bear.
Jacob Groff.
Abraham Rohland.
Dames Norres.
Samuel Mether.
Jacob Frantz.
John Hart.
Christian Knysly.
Barnad Getz.
Michael Killian.
Jacob Keller.

This return Certifyed to be a True return of my Company for Fall 1780.

ANDREAS REHM, Capt.

RETURN OF THE 7TH COMPANY CAPTAIN JOHN ASHTON'S OF THE 3D BATTALION OF LANCASTER COUNTY MILITIA, 1780. (c.)

1st Class.

Jacob Keefer.
John Hair.
John Eby.
Jacob Kinsy.
Daniel Hollinger.
John Fleman.
John Groff.
John Shitz.
Samuel Sinclair.
John Boyer.
Fredrick Luckhard.
John Curtz.

2nd Class.

George Miller (Stiller).
Allexander Zortman.
Fredrick Wittmoyer.
Jacob Musselman.
Peter Shiffer.
William Gessell.
Balsor Seess.
John Brubaker, Bro. son.
John Jones.
Nathaniel Spencor
Adam Eicholtz.

3rd Class.

John Rudy.
Henry Winckle.
Adam Keener.
John Crotzer.
Conrad Marck.
Stoffel Faber.
George Saum.
Samuel Wissler.
George Potzer.
Christian Stouffer.
Francis Noland.
Samuel Cromer.

4th Class.

John Cromer.
Nickloss Bale.
Peter Crotzer.
Jacob Meyer.
Nickloss Shrofe.
Micheal Zartman.
Henry Rudy.
Samuel Jones.
Samuel Brassington.
John Brubaker, Son.
Christian Zuck, gone off.
John Trump.

5th Class.

Martin Cromer.
Abraham Stouffer.
Manuel Scess.
Jacob Bordner.
George Betz.
Lenhard Smith.
Christian Kemmerer.
George Hollinger.
James Bradford.
Thomas Hollinger.
George Miller.

6th Class.

Frederick Shitz.
Ulrick Keyser.
Andrew Shover.
William McKelvey.
Mathias Weymar.
Thomas Owings.
Conrad Plaster.
David Fortiney.
Michael Hoghlander.
George Witcraft.
Charles Smith.
John Brubaker, over age.

7th Class.

George Day.
Christian Hollinger.
John Cline.
Lenhard Wittmeier.
John Parry.
Daniel Parry.
Samuel Rusel.
David Smith.
Henry Marck.
Allexandor Zartman.
Micheal Horning.
John Peter.

8th Class.

Pater Grubb.
Marx. Nagle.
Macolm McNeel.
Christian Smith.
Mathias Peter, over age.
Jacob Brubaker.
William Trago.
Adam Kerver.
William Smith.
John Harriss.
Thomas Goodfellow.
William Marshall.

This is a True return of my Company.
Witness my Hand this 28 Dec'r, 1781.

JOHN ASHTON,
Capt. 7 Comp.

RETURN OF THE 6TH COMPY. OF THE 3D BATTALLO. LANCASTD. COUNTY MILITIA. (c.)

Captain.

Philip Beck.

Lieutenant.

Peter Bentz.

Ensign.

Michael Oberly.

Privates.

1st Class.

Jonathan Kelb.	Henry Caffroth.
Jacob Anguish.	Peter Fahnestock.
Geo. Michael Seyler.	Michael Snerely.
Jacob Feierstein.	Christoph Westeberger.
John Keller.	Michael Pitz.
Christian Weiland.	Peter Salter.
Elias Wolff.	

2nd Class.

Christian Wiland.	George Kouch.
John Fahnestock.	Adam Kelb.
Jacob Gorgas, Junr.	Henry Bear.
Christopher Mathei.	Conrad Hanshue.
Daniel Bollinger.	Christian Feig.
John Shaffer.	

3rd Class.

Dietrich Walk.	Henry Frymeyer.
Jacob Landes.	Peter Feather.
Jacob Gorgas.	Benjamin Bowman.
Bernard Feather.	Jacob Feather.
Jacob Oberly.	Daniel Neagly.
Martin Laber.	Joseph Hempfield.
John Witmer.	Peter Gerber.
Jacob Caffroth.	

4th Class.

Jacob Househalder.	Daniel Weaver.
Daniel Miller.	Dietrick Fahnestock.
Henry Eberly.	Henry Brendle.
George Illig.	Rudy Bollinger.
John Bear.	Abraham Zerfass.
Peter Bollinger.	Abraham Bollinger.
Jacob Wheitman.	

5th Class.

Nicholus Lesher.	Henry Feather.
George Walter.	Christophr Striegel.
William Stover.	William Drishong.
John Miller.	Jacob Witmer.
Peter Witmer.	David Landes.

6th Class.

John Becker.
Jacob Kimmel.
Bernard Gardner.
Christophl Weldman, jr.
Bend. Landes.
Leonard Spitznagel.
John Jones.
John Fredrick.
Jonathan Rowland.
John Snearly.
Durst Amon.
John Shimpp.
*Benjamin Bear.
Conrad Haas.
Abraham Wirtz.

7th Class.

John Ryer.
William Wecker.
John Neas.
Christian Luther.
Martin Mayer.
Conrad Meintzer.
Jacob Wolff.
Christian Trabinger, jr.
Michael Weber.
James Dick.
Henry Neuman.
Adam Dreish.
John Apple.

8th Class.

John Belsner.
John Senseman.
Christie Bowman.
John Westhoeffer.
George Wheitman.
Fredrick Hacker.
Abraham Brubacher.
Henry Miller.
Frederick Adam.
Henry Shaffer.
Samuel Harlacher.
Daniel Ryer.

RETURN OF CAPT. HENRY CUSTERS COMPY. BEING THE 3D OF THE 3D BATT'A LANCASTER CO'Y MILITIA, 1780. (c.)

Captain.

Henry Custer.

Lieutenant.

And's Erman.

Ensign.

Nicholas Unger.

1st Class.

John Ricksecker.	Jacob Hochstedler.
John Gieb.	Henry Gippel.
Bartel Hoak.	Jacob Hochstedler.
George Hoffart.	Henry Gippel.
Joseph Bucher.	Jacob Burkholder.
Joseph Gingery.	David Frye.
Abraham Reist.	

2nd Class.

John Bucher.	Jacob Eberly.
Christie Graybiel.	Henry Kinsy.
Henry Hoach.	Valentine Greiner.
John Stauffer.	Peter Erb.
Martin Gross.	Christian Musselman.
Daniel Gingerig.	Jacob Mayer, junior.

3rd Class.

Christie Ruhl.	Lorentz Kiener.
George Mayer, Jr.	Peter Huber.
Jacob Hirshy.	Jacob Young.
John Erb.	Christie Hirshy.
Abraham Gippel.	Jacob Gippel.
John Shoemacher.	Michael Gingery.
Christie Guthjahr.	

4th Class.

Andreas Eby.	Nicholas Morret.
John Duth.	Andreas Long.
John Longenecker.	Peter Armshong.
George Mayer.	John Hans.
Martin Bealer.	Christie Weaver.
Mathias Kamerer.	Michael Behm, jun'r.
Christian Reisht.	Jacob Oberholtzer.

5th Class.

John Reist, jun'r.	Fredrick Armstrong.
Henry Leib.	Henry Miller.
John Reisht.	George Ruhl.
John Fredrick.	Fredrick Mengel.
Jacob Armshong.	David Heistand.
Godfried Gudjahr.	Jacob Gingerig.
Nicholas Stroh.	

6th Class.

Michael Huber.
Adam Hollinger.
John Eby.
Christie Bomberger.
John Summy.
John Armshong.
Philip Smith.
John Spickler.
John Gippel.
Daniel Heffelbaur.
Martin Spickler.
George Alspack.

7th Class.

John Kissel.
Abraham Long.
Jacob Bomberger.
John Bomberger.
Adam Greiner.
Ludwick Goodyahr.
Jacob Longenecker.
Christian Stouffer.
Stophel Gippel.
Michael Behm.
George Mengel.
John Lauman.

8th Class.

Daniel Erb.
Henry Bender.
Jacob Haller.
Christian Zug.
Jacob Gingerig.
Jonathan Gingerig.
Hartman Morret.
George Geiger.
Michael Witmer.
George Kissel.
Adam Seitz.
John Gingerig.

This Return of my Company is to the best of my knowledge True.

HENRY CUSTER, Capt.

A RETURN OF CAPT. DUCK'S COMPANY, BEING THE 1ST COMP'Y 3D BATT'A LANCASTER COUNTY MILITIA, 1780. (c.)

Lieut.

Peter Sneider.

Ens'g.

David Smith.

1st Class.

John Alexander, jun'r.	Thomas McGomery.
John Hammer.	Christian Ryer.
John Stucky.	John Gantz.
Baltzer Gantz.	John Bowman.

2nd Class.

Peter Eberly.	Christian Willy.
Peter Bernard.	John Wonderlick.
Henry Good.	Jacob Bonder.
Bernard Grouss.	

3rd Class.

George Weiman.	Jacob Kissinger.
Adam Sheiner.	Jacob Berringer.
Christian Gesell.	Henry Long.
James Jacobs.	

4th Class.

Martin Bear, swamp.	Alexander Clagg.
Solomon Shrode.	George Ryer.
Mathias Grall.	Jacob Turk.
Jacob Sheiner.	Peter Bowman.

5th Class.

Mathias Betz.	Michael Berringer.
Ulry Crall.	John Martin.
Henry Shingler.	Durst Gander.
Christie Zwally.	

6th Class.

George Bear.	John Ruth.
Conrad Engel.	Jacob Weyman.
Joseph Tounker.	George Pflantz.
Jost Martin.	Michael Neff.
George Hammer.	

7th Class.

Joseph Mathes.	John Lents.
Robert Coleman.	Neal Layman.
George Kaucher.	John Shear.

8th Class.

David Merckly.
Jacob Becker.
George Gantz.
John Carson.
Michael Balmer.
Conrad Weaver.
John Bemesderffer.
Martin Bear.

The above is a True Return of my Comp'y for ye Spring 1780.

PHILIP DUCK, Capt.

RETURN OF CAPTAIN HENRY KUSTER'S COMPANY BEING THE THIRD COMPANY OF THE THIRD BATTALION OF LANCASTER COUNTY MILITIA COMMANDED BY COLONEL GEORGE FEATHER, 1780. (c.)

1st Class.

John Ricksacker.
John Gipe.
Bartal Hock.
George Hoffart.
Joseph Bucher.
Joseph Gingery.
Abraham Riest.
Jacob Hosteter.
Henry Giple.
Jacob Burckholder.
David Frye.

2nd Class.

John Buchér.
Christian Graybil.
Henry Hogh.
John Stouffer.
Martin Gross.
Daniel Gingery.
Jacob Eberly.
Henry Kinsy.
Valentin Griner.
Peter Erb.
Christian Musselman.
Jacob Moyer, Junr.

3rd Class.

Christian Rule.
George Moyer.
Jacob Hershy.
John Erb.
Abraham Giple.
John Shoemaker.
Christian Goodyear.
Lawrence Keener.
Peter Huber.
Christian Hershy.
Jacob Giple.
Micheal Gingery.
Nickloss Unger.

4th Class.

John Dud.
John Longnecker.
Martin Bealer.
Mathias Komerer.
Christian Riest.
Nickloss Morret.
Andrew Lontz.
Peter Armstrong.
John Hans.
Christian Weaber.
Micheal Beam, Junr.
Jacob Oberholtzer.

5th Class.

John Riest, Junr.
Henry Lieb.
John Riest (over age).
John Frederick.
Jacob Armstrong.
Godfrid Goodyear.
Nickloss Stro.
Fredrick Armstrong.
Henry Miller.
George Ruhl.
Fredrick Mengel.
David Hinstand.
Jacob Gingery (by Rudy Beam).

6th Class.

Christian Huber.
Adam Hollinger.
John Eby.
Christian Bomberger.
John Summy.
John Armstrong.
Philip Smith.
John Spickler.
John Giple.
Martin Spickler.
George Alspogh.

7th Class.

Abraham Long.
Jacob Bomberger.
John Bomberger.
Lodwick Goodyear.
Jacob Longenecker.
Christian Stouffer.
Stoffel Giple.
Micheal Behm.
George Mengel.
John Lowman.

8th Class.

Daniel Erb.
Henry Bender.
Jacob Haller.
Christian Zuck.
Jacob Gingery.
Jonathan Gingery.
Hardman Morred.
George Giger.
Micheal Wittmore.
——— Kissel.
Adam Seids.
John Gingory.

I do hereby certify that the above is a just & true return of my company.

HENRY KUSTER, Capt.

A ROLL OF CAPT. NICH'L LUTZ COMPANY OF THE THIRT BATTALION OF LANCASTER COUNTY 5TH COMPANY—1780. (c.)

Lieuts.

John Behtoll.

Ensign.

Henry Geyer.

Sergants.

David Bahrrinyer.
John Lutz.
Joseph Brendel.

Corprals.

Henry Laush.
Philip Brendel.
Michel Winehold.

Class the 1st.

George Westhaffer.
Jacob Hoober.
Adam Grill.
Nichalaus Lesher.
John Linniger.
Jacob Hershe.
Christian Hoober.

Class the 2d.

Jacob Weeber.
Petter Staffe.

Class the 3d.

Christian Weeber.
John Lesher.
Michel Hording.
Adam Leed.
George Coppes.
Ruty Miller.
George Keiler.
Henry Zimmerman.
John Geets.

Class the 4th.

Petter Feeser.
Henry Bastian.
Henry Brendel.
Richd. Adams.
John Miller.
Isaac Adams.
Phillip Bratinstone.
Adam Bower.
Petter Miller.
Petter Wise.
Martin fernsler.

Class the 5th.

George Ury.
Joseph Wengert.
John Grill.
John Rush.
Henry Lead.
Henry Shnyder.
Ector Pain.
John Sweigert.
Petter Smith.

Class the 6th.

Nicholas Shower.
Michal Young.
Jacob Gemberling.
Frederick Gerner.
Rudy Bear.
John Beckerd.
Philip Shalback.
Casper Bussart.
Henry Walter.
Henry Lutz.

Class the 7th.

Henry Eichholtz.
David Title.
Mathias Walck.
Jacob Vanneeda.
John Hoober.
Jost Spengler.
Adam Kissinger.
Michel Kachrize.
Nicholas Rup.
John Colman.
Casper Shimps.
Jacob Zinn.
Petter Ulrich.

Class the 8th.

Christian Horting.
Christ. Zimmerman.
Charles Tritch.
Sebastean Nagle.
George Rimmel.
Isaac Pettecoffer.
Andrew Rihm.
John Miller, Jur.
John Wengert.
Peter Zimmerman.
Henry Kelbert.

I Do Certifye that the above is a Just & true Return of my Company 7th December, 1780.

NICHOLUS LUTZ,
Capt. of the 5th Company.

RETURN OF THE 8TH COMPY. IN THE 3 BATT'N MIL'A OF L'R COUNTY—1780. (c.)

Capt.
Jno. Smuller.

Lieut.
David Taneberger.

Ensign.

John Spoonhawer.

Serjeants.

John Zeller. George Zeller.
Henry Feather.

Drummer.

Jacob Kittle.

Fifer.

Jacob Harbacker.

Class 1.

Herman Ernst.	Danl. Habecker.
Christ'n Balmer.	Adam Pletz.
Abraham Widder.	Philip Mickel.
Christ'n Brown.	Peter Christ.
Curad Long.	Christoph. Widder.

Class 2.

Jacob Fierling.	Dan'l Christ.
Lenhard Tulepan.	Henry Rough.
Henry Franck.	John Foutz.
Jacob Eby.	Peter Creyder.
Peter McMullin.	Greenbery Peticoats
John Sheffel.	Lenhard Krauss.

Class 3.

Abraham Snyder.	Christ'n Musselman.
Henry Netzly.	Peter Miller.
Mich'l Ballmer.	Abraham Huber.
Christ'n Leinbach.	Cunrad Westheaver.
Christ'n Blickensderfer.	John Mickel.

Class 4.

John Geyer.	Christ'n Erb.
Jacob Cassler.	Mich'l Creyder.
Christ'n Stucky.	Frederick Lehman.
Peter Eltzer.	Peter Bessinger.
Jeremias Woolf.	Casper Walter.
Christ'n Eyer.	Henry Brendle.

Class 5.

Jacob Roth.	Joseph Willis.
Henry Wanner.	Lenhard Widder.
Peter Snyder.	Christ'n Lesher.
Christ'n Hubecker.	John Stees.
Nicklauss Kleine.	John Engel.
John Erb.	George Meyr.
George Rothe.	

Class 6.

Lenhard Miller.	Geo. Mich'l Eichelberg.
Abraham Dierdorf.	Simon Dantz.
Gottfried Thomas.	Samuel Tune.
Andres Creyder.	Christ'n Becker.

Class 7.

Jacob Rudy.	Mich'l Meyer.
John Shanck.	Christ'n Huber.
Lorentz Herchelroth.	John Sensenig.
John Buch.	John Geyer, son of J. G.
Peter Ritsecker.	Christ'n Eby, Jun.
Andres Wissler.	Solomon Smuck.

Class 8.

Henry Foltz.	Jacob Snyder.
Mich'l Groffe.	Peter Creyder.
Christoph. Miller.	Jacob Spoonharver.
Jacob Stees.	Wil'm Cassler.
Martin Spenck.	Peter Bruner.
Jacob Hockman.	John Enck.
Jacob Smuck.	Jacob Geyer.
Sam'l Krauss.	John Bender.
George Geyer.	

This return certified by me to the best of my knowledge.

JOHN SMULLER, Capt.

A ROLL OF CAPT. J. VANDERSLICE COMPYNE OF THE THIRT BATTALION OF LANCASTER COUNTY, COMMENTED BY COR'N JA'B BOWER—1780. (c.)

Lieut.

1. John Bechtoll.

Ensign.

1. Henry Geyer.

Sargeant.

1. David Bahringer.
2. John Lutz.
3. Joseph Brendel.

Corporal.

1. Henry Laush.
2. Philip Brendel.
3. Michal Vinehold.

Class the 1 of Privates.

1. Geo. Westhaffer.
2. Jacob Hoober, Jr.
3. Adam Krill.
4. Nicholas Lesher.
5. John Linniger.
6. Jacob Hershe.
7. Christean Hoober.

Class the 2nd.

8. Jacob Weeber.
9. Petter Staffa.

Class the 3d.

10. Christian Weeber.
11. John Lesher.
12. Michal Horting.
13. Adam Lead.
14. Geo. Coppes.
15. Rudy Miller.
16. Geo. Keller.
17. Henry Zimmerman.
18. John Getts.

Class the 4th.

19. Petter Binkly.
20. Petter Feeser.
21. Henry Bastian.
22. Henry Brendel.
23. Richd. Adams.
24. John Miller.
25. Thomas Holms.
26. Isaac Adams.

27. Philip Broatenstone.
28. Adam Bower.
29. Peter Miller.
30. Petter Wise.
31. Martin fernsler.

Class the 5th.

32. Geo. Ury.
33. Joseph wengert.
34. John Grill.
35. John Rush.
36. Henry Lead.
37. Henry Shnyder.
38. Ector Pain.
39. John Sweigert.
40. Petter Smith.

Class the 6th.

41. Nicholaus Shower.
42. Michal Young.
43. Jacob Gemberling.
44. Fredrich Gerner.
45. Rudy Bear.
46. John Becherd.
47. Philip Shlabach.
48. Casper Bussert.
49. Henry Walter.
50. Henry Lutz.

Class the 7th.

51. Henry Eicholtz.
52. David Title.
53. Mathias Walck.
54. Jacob Vauneeda.
55. John Hoober.
56. Jost. Spengler.
57. Adam Kissinger.
58. Michal Kacherize.
59. Nicholaus Rup.
60. John Colman.
61. Casper Shimpf.
62. Jacob Zinn.
63. Peter Ulrich.

Class the 8th.

64. Christean Horting.
65. Christ'n Zimmerman.
66. Charls Tritch.
67. Sebastian Nagel.
68. George Kimmel.
69. Isaac Petteoober.
70. John Petteeober.
71. Andrew Rihm.
72. John Miller, Jun'r.
73. John Wengert.
74. Petter Zimmerman.

This is to Certify that the within is a true Return of my Compy.

J. VANDERSLICE, C'n.

RETURN OF THOSE ORDERED TO MARCH IN THE FIRST CLASS OF THE 3D BATTALLION LANC'S COUNTY MILITIA IN 1780. (c.)

Second Company—First Class.

Peter Groff, March'd.

Fourth Company—First Class.

William Snyder, Marched.
Jacob Heil, March'd by Subs't.
Peter Beinhour, belongs to the 2d Class.
Michael Huber, Prov'd himself Over Age.
Philip Hoffman, Marched.

Fifth Co.—First Class.

Jacob Huber, Jun'r, gone of.
Adam Grill, Marched by Son.
Nicholas Lesher, Marched by Subs't.
John Lininger, Marched.
Jacob Hershe, March'd by Subs't.
Christian Hoober, March'd by Subs't.

Seventh Co.—Class first.

Daniel Hollinger, gone.
John Fleman, gone, Listed.
John Shitz, over age.
Samuel Sinclair, gone.
John Boyer, gone.
Fredrick Lukard, gone, Listed.
John Curtz, gone.

These Lived at ye Iron Works.

Lancaster County, March 21st day 1781.

THIS IS TO CERTIFY THE GENTILMEN THAT THIS IS A TRU RETORN OF APART OF THA THIRT BATILLION COMMANDIT BY GEORGE FEATHER CORNALL OF THA NAMS OF EIGH OF EIGHTEEN TIEL DO FIFTY THREE IN MICHAEL OBERLYS CAPTIN DISTRICKT. (c.)

Class tha First.

Henray Koffroth.
Peter Fahnastick.
Michael Shnearer.
Christopher Westenberger.
Michael Pitz.
Peter Zeller.
Jacob Engguish.
George Michael Seiler.
George Duck.
John Killer.
Elas Wolff.
Jacob Folss.
Jonathan Kelp.
Daniel Zerfass.

Class the Second.

Christian Weland.
John Fahnastock.
Jacob Gorgas, Junr.
John Shaffer.
George Houck.
John Urich.
Adam Kelb.
Henray Bear.
Christian Fight.
John Hacker.

Class the Third.

John Seiler.
Jacob Landes.
Joseph Ellers.
Martin Sober.
John Witmer.
Jacob Koffroth.
Michael Long.
Peter Feather.
Jacob Feather.
Daniel Negley.
Peter Gerwer.
Jacob Eberley.

Class the Fourth.

George Tillig.
John Bear.
Peter Bollinger.
Jacob Widman.
Daniel Weber.
Dedirick Fanattick.
Daniel Wittman.
Benjamin Bowman.
Rudolph Bollinger.
Aberham Cervass.
Aberham Bollinger.
Daniel Miller.
Henray Eberley.
Narzeous Earnst.
Adam Bower.
George Firestone.

Class the Fifth.

George Wechter.
Christian Lutter, Jr.
William Stober.
John Miller.
Henray Feather.
Christophiel Spregel.
William Dushang.
Jacob Wittmer.
David Landis.
Nicoles Lasser.
Felix Bucker.
Wendle Trout.

Class tha Sixth.

Jacob Kimmel.
Christophel Widman, Light Horseman.
Benjamen Landes.
John Jons.
John Fridrick.
Thorst Ammen.
Benjamen Bear.
John Becker.
Samuel Fahnastick.
John Shimps.
Conrad Hass.
Christophel Hacker.
Peter Martin.
John Hirshberger.

Class the Seventh.

William Wogert.
John Arnd.
Martien Myer.
Conrad Meinzer, dead.
Jacob Wolff.
Henray Miller.
Christophel Trabinger.
Jeams Dick, British Deserter.
Adam Irisch.
John Apple.
John Lutter.
George Weber.
John Brubacker.
Jacob Beck.

Class the Eighth.

Friedrick Hacker.
Friedrick Adam.
Samuel Harlacher.
Casper Traubinger.
John Senseman.
George Widman.
John Zeger.
Henray Frimyer.
Christn. Bowman.
John Shod.
Adam France.
Conrad Henshu.
Micheal Roub.

"Scherson's" (Sarjants).

Christophel Oberly.
Jacob Fyerstone.
Jacob Houshalter.

Corpals.

Jacob Oberly.
John Westhaver.
John Snearer.

This is to Certify that the above is a True return.

MICHAE OBERLY, Capt.

Cocalico township,
Lancaster County May 23, 1781.

THIS IS A TRUE RETORN OF THA NAMES OF THA SIXTH COMPYNAY IN THA THIRD BATILLION COMMANDED BY COL. GEORGE FEATHER AND CAP. MICHAEL OBERLY. (c.)

Class tha First.

Henry Coffrad.
Peter Fahnastick.
Michael Shrerrer.
Christopher westeberger.
Michael Pitz.
Peter Zeller.
Jacob Engquish.
George Michael Syler.
John Keller.
Elias Wolff.
Jacob Folss.
Jonatan Kalp.
george dock.
danial Zerfass.

Class tha Second.

Christian Weland.
John Fanastick.
Jacob Gorgas, Junior.
John Shaffer.
George Hauck.
Adam Kalb.
Henrey Bear.
Christian Fight.
John Uhrich.
John Hacker.

Class tha Third.

Jacob Landes.
Martien Lober.
John Wittmer.
Jacob Caffrad.
Michael Long.
Peter Feather.
Jacob Feather.
daniel Neglay.
Peter gerber.
Jacob Eberlay.
John Seyler.
Benjamin Bowman.

Class tha Fourth.

George Ellig.
John Bear.
Peter Bollinger.
Jacob Widman.
Daniel Weaver.
deadarick Fanastick.
Daniel Witman.
Rudolph Bollinger.
Aberham Zerfass.
Aberham bollinger.
Daniel Miller.
Henrey Eberly.
Narceuss Ernst.
Adam bower.
george Feierstine.

Class tha Fifth.

George wichter.	William dushgong.
Christian Luter.	Jacob Witmer.
William Stober.	david Landis.
John Miller.	Nicolas Lasor.
Henrey Feather.	Wendel trout.
Christopher Streagel.	Falix Borggert.

Class tha Sixth.

Jacob Kimmel.	Samuel Fanastock.
Christophel Wideman.	John Becker.
Benjamin Landes.	John Shimpff.
John Jons.	Conrad Hass.
John Fredrick.	Christopher Hacker.
Thurst Aman.	Peter Martien.
Benjamin Bear.	John Hershberger.

Class the Seventh.

William Wugert.	Adam drish.
Johannas Arnt.	John appleal.
Martiean Myar.	John Ludear.
Conrad Menzer.	George Weber.
Jacob Wolff.	John Brubacker.
Christopher trobinger.	Henrey Miller.
Jeams dick.	Jacob Black.

Class tha Eaight.

Fradrick Hacker.	Henrey Frimler.
Fradrick Adam.	Christian Bouman.
Samuel Harlacker.	Adam Frauss.
Casper Trabinger.	John Shodt.
John Sanseman.	Conrad Handshu.
George Wightman.	Mechael Roub.
John Ziager.	

Lieut.

Peter Benss.

Ensign.

Nicolauss Fogelgesang.

Sert.

Christopher oberly.
Jacob Fierstine.
Jacob Haussbalder.

Corp.

Jacob Oberly.
John Shnearer.
Johannes Westhafer.

This Return is Certified by me.

MICH'L OBERLY, Capt.

RETURN OF THE SEVENTH COMP'Y IN THE THIRD BATTALLN. LANC. COUNTY MILITIA. 1781. (c.)

Captain.

John Ashton.

Lieutenant.

Daniel Hollinger.

Ensign.

George Hoverter.

1st Class.

Jacob Keeffer.
John Hair.
John Eby.
Jacob Kinsy.
John Boyer.

2nd Class.

George Miller.
Fredrick Witmyer.
Peter Shiffer.
Balser Sees.
John Brubacher Bro S.
Jesse Massy.

3rd Class.

Henry Wincle.
Adam Kiener.
John Crotzer.
Conrad Mark, junior.
Stophel Fabour.
George Zaame.
Samuel Wissler.
George Pfotzer.
Christian Stouffer.
Francis Knowland.
Samuel Cromer.

4th Class.

John Cromer.
Nicholas Beal.
Jaçob Myer.
Nicholas Shroff.
Michael Zartman.
Henry Rudy.
John Trump.

5th Class.

Valentine Witmyer.
Martin Cromer.
George Hollinger.
Abraham Stouffer.
Jacob Bordner.
George Betz.
Christian Kamerer.
George Miller, smith.

6th Class.

Fredrick Shitz.
Ulry Kyser.
Andreas Shober.
William McKelvy.
Mathias Weimer.
Thomas Owens.
Conrad Plesterer.
Henry Hogh.
Michael Hoghlender.
George Whitcraft.
Charles Smith.

7th Class.

John Hoyl.
John Jones.
Leonard Witmyer.
John Porry.
Samuel Russel.
Henry Mark.
Sandy Zartman.
Michael Horning.
William Gesel.
Casper Seager.
Daniel Porry.
William Davis.
Christian Crise.

8th Class.

John Peter.
Marx Nagel.
Michael Shoff.
Jacob Brubacher.
Christie Smith.
William Green.
Solomon Shrode.
Evan Evans.
Henry Getz.

This is to Certify That the Return anexd to this is a True Return of my Company.

Witness my Hand this Seventh day of June 1781.

JOHN ASHTON.

MUSTER ROLL OF 2ND CLASS 3D BATTALL. LANC'R COUNTY MIL'A ON A TOUR OF DUTY AT LANCASTER, FOR THE PURPOSE OF GUARD OF BRIT. PRISS'RS. (c.)

Names of Persons Who Served Their Tour.	Names of Persons Who Furnished Substitutes.	Time when duty commd.	Time when duty ended.
Capt.		1781.	1781.
Andw. Ream,		June 22,	July 30.
Clk.			
Jacob Swartsell,			July 28.
Serjeants.			
Gotlib Youngman,	George Zeller,		Aug. 24.
David Ream,			July 28.
Corpl.			
Joseph Brandle,	Philip Brandle,		Aug. 21.
Gotlib Mock,			July 28.
Drum.			
Joseph Allis,			Aug. 21.
Fifer.			
Fredk. Mellinger,			
Privates.			
George Trout,			July 28
Jno. Buch,	Jno. Hoker,		Aug. 21.
Peter Stiffy,			July 28.
Fredk. Ream.			
Chris Dilleman,	Leonard Kreus,		Aug. 21
Caspar Tripple,	Jacob Fourman		
George Koppas,	Stephen Bollinger.		
Chris. Everman,	Jno. Shaffer.		
Valentine Hovarter,	Peter Shaffer.		
Danl. Firestine,	Adm. Krill.		
Henry Leeder,			July 28.
Andw. Ream,	Baltzer Sleze,		Aug. 21.
Jno. Fisher,	Jno. Sheffle.		

Lanc'r Aug. 21st, 81. Then mustered above company (as also on the 26th June last) as above specified.

AD'M HUBLEY, S. L. L'r C'y.

MUSTER ROLL OF 3RD CLASS OF 3D BATALE LANC'R CO'Y MIL'A ON A TOUR OF DUTY AT. (c.)

Names of Persons Who Served.	Names of Persons Who Furnished Substitutes.	Time when duty commd.	Time when duty ended.
		1781.	1781.
Danl. Hollinger,	Conrad Mack,	July 3,	Aug. 24.
Jacob Metzgar,	Chrisr. Guthyahr.		
Andw. Heidler,	John Moller.		
John Gatz,			July 28.
Nicholas Loescher,	John Loesher.		
George Zinn,	Rudolph Miller,		Aug. 24.
Joseph Spangler,	Michl. Harding.		
Adam Leed,			July 28.
Fredk. Kissinger,			
Henry Zimmerman,			
Caspar Jordan,	Jacob Fetter,		Aug. 24.
Jno. Helsell,			July 28.
Francis Nolin.			
David Grove,	Joseph Grove.		
Joseph Grant,			Aug. 24.
Ludwig Keal.			
George Smith.			
Joseph Etters.			
Saml. Welty.			
Laurence Swartzer.			
James Ream.			

1781 Lanc'r July 5th. Then mustered above compy. as above spesified.

AD'M HUBLEY, S. L. L'r C'y.

MUSTER ROLL OF THE 4TH CLASS OF THE 3RD BATALION LAN'R. COUNTY MILITIA ON A TOUER OF DUTY AT LANCASTER. (c)

Names of Persons who perform a touer of Duty.	What class.	Names of Persons who furnished substitutes.	Time when Duty commenced.	Time when Duty ended.
Capt.			1781.	
Joseph Gehr,			Augt. 20th,	Dischd. Oct. 20, '81
Lieut.				
Andrew Ehrman,			Augt. 20th,	Dischd. Oct. 20, '81
Clk.				
Gootlob Youngman,		John Jones,	Augt. 20th,	Dischd. Oct. 20, '81
Sergt.				
Nicholas Srove,			Augt. 20th,	Dischd. Oct. 20, '81
Henry Miller,		Nathaniel Ernst,	Augt. 20th,	Dischd. Oct. 20, '81
Corpl.				
Abraham Bauer,		John Miller,	Augt. 22d,	Dischd. Oct. 20, '81
George Feuerstone,			Augt. 20th,	Dischd. Oct. 20, '81

MUSTER ROLL OF THE 4TH CLASS OF THE 3RD BATALION LAN'R. COUNTY MILITIA ON A TOUER OF DUTY AT LANCASTER—Continued.

Names of Persons who perform a touer of Duty.	What class.	Names of Persons who furnished substitutes.	Time when Duty commenced.	Time when Duty ended.
Privates.				
Michael Reinhart,		Allexr. Clagg,	Augt. 23rd,	Dischd. Oct. 20, '81
John Zeller,			Augt. [illegible],	Dischd. Oct. 20, '81
[illegible] Geyer,			Augt. 20th,	Dischd. Oct. 20, '81
[illegible] Shaffer,		Henry Bastian,	Augt. 20th,	Dischd. Oct. 20, '81
Jost Shiffer,			Augt. [illegible],	Dischd. Oct. 20, '81
Martin Fernsler,			Augt. 20th,	Dischd. Oct. 20, '81
[illegible] Zinn,		John Keller,	Augt. 20th,	Dischd. [illegible]
David Hirshberger,		Joas Miller,	Augt. [illegible],	Dischd. [illegible]
George [illegible],		Michael Zartman,	Augt. [illegible],	Dischd. Oct. 20, '81
Peter Numan,		Michael Reiter,	Augt. [illegible],	Dischd. Oct. 20, '81
John Slott,			Augt. 20th,	Dischd. Oct. 20, '81
Philip Breitenston,			Augt. [illegible],	Dischd. Oct. 20, '81
John Cromer,			Augt. 20th,	Augt. [illegible]th.
[illegible] Blattenberger,		Martin Boehler,	Augt. 21st,	
Jacob Hanshalter, Jur.,			Augt. 22d,	
John Smith,		Jacob Weidman,	Augt. [illegible],	
Thomas Rush,		George Elleck,	Augt. 20th,	
Robert Dyer,		Henry Brendle,	Augt. [illegible],	
		Mustered Aug. 26th, '81.		

Cocalico township, December 4th, 1781.

THIS IS A TRUE RETORN OF THA SIXTH COMPYNY OF CAPTIN MICHAEL OBERLIE OF THA THIRD BETILLION COMMANDIT BY CORNALL GEORGE FEATHER OF THA NAMS OF THA EIGHT BETWEEN EIGHTEEN AND FIFTY THREE. (c.)

Leitinant.

Peter Penss.

Insine.

Necalaus Fogelgesang.

Cerjon.

Christopbel Oberlie.
Jacob Feierstine.
Jacob Haushalter.

Class tha First.

Henrey Kaffrad.
Mechael Shnerrer.
Christopher Vesteberger.
Michael pitz.
Jacob Engquish.
Michael Seilar.
Elas Wolff.
Jacob Folss.
Jonatan Kalp.
George Dock.
Peter Zeller.

Class tha Second.

Christian Veland.
John Shaffer.
george Houk.
Adam Kelp.
Henrey Bear.
Christian Fith.
John Uhrich.

Class tha Third.

Jacob Landis.
Martin Laber.
John Widmer.
Jacob Kaffrad.
Michael Long.
Peter Feather.
Jacob Feather.
danial Naglay.
Peter Gerber.
Jacob Eberly.
John Seilar.
John Ebey.

Class tha Forth.

George Ellig.
John Bear.
Peter bollinger.
Jacob Widtman.
Deadarick Fahnastick.
Rudolph bollinger.
Aberham Zerfass.
Aberham bollinger.
Henrey Eberley.
Narzerus Ernst.
Adam Bower.
George Felerstine.
Johan beacker.

Class tha Fifth.

George Wechter.
Christian Luttor.
William Stober.
John Miller.
Henrey Feather.
Christopel Streagel.
Daved Lanqis.
Nicolaus Lasor.
Vendil traut.
Felix borgart.

Class tha Sixth.

Jacob Kimmel.
benjamen Landis.
John Jons.
benjamen Bear.
Samuel Fahnastick.
Conrad Hass.
Christophel Hacker.
Peter Merdin.
John Hersberger.

Class tha Seventh.

William Wugert.
John Arnent.
Jacob Wolff.
Christophel trabinger.
Henery Miller.
Adam drish.
John Appel.
John Luttor.
George Weaver.
John Brubacher.
Henrey Miller.
Jacob Beck.
William dushshang.

Class tha Eight.

Freadarick Kacker.
Freadarick Adam.
Samuel Harlacher.
John Sanseman.
George Widtman.
John Zeager.
Henrey Frimaier.
Christian bauman.
Adam Frantz.
Conrad Handshu.
John unger.

This is to Certify that the above is a True Return of my Company for the Fall 1781. Witness my Hand this 10th dec'r 1781.

MICHAEL OBERLY.

MUSTER ROLE FOR THE YEAR 1781 OF CAPT. REAM'S COMPING OF THE 2 CLASS AND 3RD BATTALION OF LANCASTER COUNTY MILLITIAN COMMANDED BY LEF. COL. GEORGE FETHER, DECEMBER 10TH, 1781. (c.)

Left.

Henry Ream.

Insingn.

Christian Balsle.

Serjint.

Casper Shrit.
Martin Mohler.
Abraham Killian.

Corprl.

Henrey Landes.
Jacob Snyder.
Caspert Kipert.

Drum.

Andoney Beltzer.

Fiffer.

George Ream.

Clark.

Jacob Shwartzwelder.

Privates.

1st Class.

Nicholas Woolf.
Daniel Bethaleme.
Nicolaus Snyder.
Frideick Rate.
John Kiln.
Daniel Bowman.
Jacob Duck.
Jacob Lasher.
Jacob Mohler.
Jacob Detwiller.
Peter Graff.
John Gartner.
Henrey Everley.
George Hiltebrand.
Adam Kingmaker.
Andrew Hitler.

2nd Class.

Niclaus Duck.
Mickel Sharck.
Joseph Bain.
Abraham Bicksler.
David Minzer.
Lannert Keller.
Samuel Bauman.
William Gram.
George Draught.
Jacob Bucher.
Abraham Landes, Milrigh.
Henrey Lieder.
Andrew Ream; Junr.
Fridrick Ream.
Gotleb Mock.

3rd Class.

Henrey Mohler.
Christian Wenger.
Abraham Klin.
Christian Nop.
David Meratey.
John Mellinger.
John Mohler.
Abraham Woolf.
Jacob Sandag.
William Mellinger.
Jacob Zentmyer.
Josaph Grof.
Jacob Landes.
Jeams Right.
Jacob Ream.
Frans Brumbach.
Vallentin Shovalter.

4th Class.

Michel Riter.
Uly Sharck.
Davalt Meder.
Jacob Shovalter.
Gorge Spate.
Fridrick Leder.
John Sloth, Jr.
Gorge Fyerston.
Teas Miller.
Martin Klever.
Henry Hartman.
Jacob Hagy.
Phillip Krigg.
Josaph Shiffer.

5th Class.

George Kuns.
Abraham Landes.
Adam Mosser.
Josaph Lysy.
Peter Brubaker.
Jacob Keller, Sinr.
Samuel Groff.
John Landes, Jonr.
Jacob Mishler.
John Ream, Jonr.
John Heaffer.

6th Class.

Barnd Gigger.
Josaph Mishler.
Henry Hershberger.
Peter Snyder.
Abraham Hershberger.
Jacob Killian.
Jacob Rohland.
Mils Kroley.
John Hinkle.
Jacob Witmore.

7th Class.

John Martin.	Jacob Conrate.
Michel Bair.	Josapsh Sprigle.
Christian Conroth.	Daniel Graff.
John Haltrey.	William Shomaker.
John Bucher.	Niclaus Wilt.
Jack Hershberger.	Christian Frans.
John Backer.	Henrey Good.

8th Class.

John Sloth, Sinr.	Samuel Meder.
Peter Ryer.	Barnd Gatz.
David Sharck.	Jacob Keller.
Abraham Ream, miller.	Jacob Frantz.
John Musselman.	Abraham Ream.
Michel Woolf.	John Mohler, Jon'r.
Christian Shovalter, Jor.	John Right.
Andrew Ream.	Phillip Siever.
Abraham Bair.	Adam Wigxel.
Jacob Grof.	George Barkert.
Abraham Rohland.	Marcus Montillius.
Dammes Warress.	Dammes Hanskippel.

I do hereby certify that the above return is a just and true return of my company of the third Battalion of Lancaster County Mila.

Pr. ANDREW REAM, Capt.

RETURN OF THE 7TH COMPANY IN THE 3D BATALION LANCASTER C'Y MILITIA. (c.)

Capt.

John Ashton.

Lt.

Daniel Hollinger.

Ens.

George Hoverter.

1st Class.

Jacob Keefer.
John Hair.
John Eby.
Jacob Kinsey.
John Boyer.
Lewes Walker.

2nd Class.

George Miller.
Fredrick Wittmoyer.
Peter Sheffer.
Jacob Musselman.
Balsor Seese.
John Brubaker, Jun.
Jessey Massey.

3rd Class.

Henry Winkle.
Adam Keaner.
John Crotsor.
Conrod Mark, Junr.
Stoffel Fauber.
George Saum.
Samuel Wislor.
George Poutson.
Christian Stover.
Francis Noland.
Samuel Cromer.

4th Class.

John Cromer.
Nicholas Bale.
Jacob Mies.
Nicholas Srope.
Michael Sortman.
Henry Rudy.
John Trump.

5th Class.

Felty Wittmier.
Martin Cromer.
George Hollinger.
Abraham Stoufer.
Jacob Bordner.
George Betts.
Christian Kemerer.
George Miller Smith.

6th Class.

Frederick Shitz.
Ulrich Koysor.
Andrew Shover.
William McKelvey.
Mathias Wimer.
Thomas Owinge.
Conrod Plasterer.
Henry Hogh.
Michael Houghlander.
George Witcraft.
Charles Smith.

7th Class.

John Hoyt.
John Jones.
Lenard Wetmore.
John Porry.
Samuel Russel.
Henry Mark.
Sandy Sortman.
Michael Horning.
William Gesell.
Casper Seager.
Daniel Porry.
William Davis.
Christian Crise.

8th Class.

John Peter.
Maxx Nagle.
Michael Shope.
Jacob Brubaker.
Christian Smith.
William Green.
Solomon Shrode.
Evans Evans.
Henry Gitts.

The above is a true return of my company, witness my hand ec.

JOHN ASHTON, Capt.

RETURN OF WHITE MALE INHABITANTS IN CAPT. JOHN ASHTON'S COMP. BEING YE 7TH OF YE 3D BATT. 1781. (c.)

John Ashton.
Daniel Hollinger.
George Hoverter.

Privates.

1st Class.

Jacob Keffer.
John Hair.
John Eby.
Jacob Kinsy.
John Boyer.

2nd Class.

George Miller.
Fredrick Witmyer.
Peter Shiffer.
Balzer Sees.
John Brubacher.
Jessey Massy.

3rd Class.

Henry Winch.
Adam Kiener.
John Crotzer.
Conrad Mark, Junr.
Stophel Fabour.•
George Zaame.
Samuel Wissler.
George Pfotzer.
Christian Stouffer.
Francis Knowland.
Samuel Cromer.

4th Class.

John Crimer.
Nicholas Beal.
Jacob Myer.
Nicholas Shoff.
Michael Zartman.
Henry Rudy.
John Trump.

5th Class.

Valentine Witmyer. Jacob Bordner.
Martin Cromer. George Betz.
George Hollinger. Christle Kamerer.
Abraham Stouffer. George Miller, Smith.

6th Class.

Fredrick Shitz. Conrad Plesterer.
Ulry Kyser. Henry Hogh.
Andrew Shober. Michael Hoghlender.
William McKelvy. George Whitecraft.
Mathias Weimer. Charles Smith.
Thomas Owens.

7th Class.

John Hoyl. Michael Horning.
John James. William Gesell.
Leonard Witmyer. Casper Seager.
John Porry. Daniel Porry.
Samuel Russel. William Davis.
Henry Mark. Christle Creis.
Sandy Zartman.

8th Class.

John Peter Marx Nagel. William Green.
Michael Shoff. Solomon Shrode.
Jacob Brubacker. Evan Evans.
Christle Smith. Henry Getz.

The above is a true return of ye best of my knowledge.
JOHN ASHTON, Capt. of Comp'y.

RETURN OF THE 7TH COMPANY OF THE 3D BATALION OF LANCASTER COUNTY MILITIA COMMANDED BY LT. COL. GEO. FEATHER 1781. (c.)

Captain.
John Ashton.

Lieut.
Daniel Hollinger.

Ensign.

George Hoverter.

1st Class.

Jacob Keefer.	Jacob Kinsey.
John Hair.	Daniel Hollinger.
John Ebey.	John Boyer.

2nd Class.

George Miller.	John Brubaker.
Peter Sheffer.	

3rd Class.

John Crotsor.	George Poutsor.
Conrod Mark.	Christian Stover.
Stophel Fauber.	Samuel Cromer.
Samuel Wislor.	

4th Class.

John Cromer.	Michael Sortman.
Nicholas Bale.	Henry Rudy.
Jacob Miac.	Leonard Seese.
Nicholas Srofe.	Fredrick Hair.
Daniel Brubaker.	

5th Class.

Felty Witoyr.	George Betts.
Thomas Hollinger.	George Miller, Smith.
George Hollinger.	James Carr.
Abraham Stoufer.	Godfry Thomas.
Abraham Day.	Peter Kemerer.
Jacob Burtner.	

6th Class.

Fredrick Shitts.	Michael Hoghlander.
Andraw Shover.	George Witcraft.

7th Class.

John Jones.	Sand Kortman.
Leonard Witmere.	Michael Horning.
John Porry.	William Gessell.
Samuel Russel.	Jacob Deal.
Stophel Horning.	Daniel Porry.
Henry Mark.	

8th Class.

John Beamisderfer.
John Peter.
Marks Nağel.
Michael Shofe.
Jacob Brubaker.
Christian Smith.
Solomon Srode.
Evan Evans.
Henry Gates.

The above is a true Return of my Company as witness my hand.

JOHN ASHTON, Capt. 7th Co.

RETURN OF THE 4TH COMPANY IN THE 3D BATT'L LANCASTER COUNTY MILITIA. 1781. (c.)

Lieutenant.

Fredrich Cerper.

Ensign.

George Brunner.

Serjeant.

1.—George Achy.
2d.—Adam Oberly.
3d.—John Bruner.

Corporals.

1st.—Phillip Hoffman.
2nd.—Fredrick Walter.
3rd.—Balthes Hoffman.

Drummer.

Conrad Snyder.

Fiffer.

Peter Sneyder.

1st Class.

George France.
Jacob France.
Christian Bricker.
William Wheeler.
Daniel Solleberger.
Jacob Blank.
Jacob Sherp.

2nd Class.

Jacob Fuhrman.
Jost Miller.
Christie Flickinger.
Stephan Bohlender.
Bastian Gackly.
Peter Beinhower.

3rd Class.

Henry Henshing, Sr.
Samuel Eby.
Mathias Bitner.
George Eby.
Jacob Eberly.
Henry Smith.

4th Class.

(Martin Klever is Charged in Capt. Ream Return).
Martin Klever.
Jacob Bear.
John Keller.
John Flickinger.
John Blank.
Christie Hornly.
Stophel Kline.;
George Mose.

5th Class.

Henry Binkly.
Daniel Riech.
Christie Harnish.
Adam Sherp.
Thomas Willson.
William Walter.
Abraham Hassler.
Christie Wiest.
Hannes Achy.
Michael Walder.
Christian Ely.
Jacob read Joseph Flickinger
John Gelir.

6th Class.

Joseph Jacob.
Peter Sneyder.
John Kuntz.
Stophel Sherp.
Andreas Gehr.
Zander Kissinger.
Jacob Heldebeutel.
George Long.
David Bricker.
Peter Geistweid.
Peter Fuhrman.

7th Class.

John Bricker.
Abraham Soffel.
Henry Burkholder.
Philip Heft.
Christie Kinsy.
Joseph Conrad.
Fredrick Reinhold.
Henry Reinhold.
Philip Kissinger.
Ludwick Porry.
Peter Shoemacher.
David Heckernell.
Jeremias Miller.

8th Class.

David Gackly.
Martin Kissinger.
Paul Fuhrman.
Philip Shenkel.
Lorentz Ludwick.
Stephy Hassler.
Jacob Dissler.

The above is a True Account of The 4th Company pr.
FREDRICH CERPER.

AN ACCOUNT OF YE MALE WHITE INHABITANTS BETWEEN YE AGES OF 18 & 53 YEAHS IN THE 3D COMPY, 3D BATT'N LANCR. COUNTY MILA. 1781. (c.)

Andreas Erman.
Nicholas Unger.

1st Class.

John Ricksecker.
John Geib.
Bartel Hoak.
George Hoffart.
Joseph Bucher.
Joseph Gingerich.
Abraham Reisht.
Jacob Hochstedter.
Henry Gippel.
Jacob Burkolder.
David Frye.
Edward Hilton.

2nd Class.

John Bucher.
Christie Graybiel.
John Stauffer.
Martin Gross.
Daniel Gingerich.
Henry Kinsy.
Valentine Greiner, Jr.
Peter Erb.
Christie Muselman.
Sylvester Gruber.
Bernard Houtzman.

3rd Class.

John Erb.
John Shoemacher.
Christian Goodyahr.
Christian Hirshe, Jr.
Michael Gingerich.
Joseph Huber.
Christian Armstrong.
George Mayer, Junior.
Jacob Hirshe.
Joseph Grant.
Ludwig Keal.

4th Class.

Christie Ruhl.	Peter Armstrong.
John Longenecker.	John Hans.
Martin Bealer.	Christie Weaver.
Mathias Kamerer.	Michael Beam, Jr.
Christie Reisht.	Jacob Oberholzer.
Nicholas Morret.	Frederick Kissel.

5th Class.

John Reisht, Junior.	John Noecker.
Henry Leib.	Henry Shembeno.
John Fredrick.	Jacob Eberly.
Godfried Goodyahr.	Jacob Kippel.
Nicholas Stroh.	Christie Huber.
Fredrick Armshong.	Adam Hollinger.
Henry Miller.	John Ely.
George Ruhl.	Christie Bambereger.
Mathias Armshong.	John Sumy.
Lorentz Kiener.	John Snyder.
Jacob Gingerich.	Jacob Armstrong.

6th Class.

John Armstrong.	Martin Spickler.
Philip Smith.	George Alspach.
John Spickler.	David Zug.
John Gippel.	

7th Class.

Peter Young.	John Lowman.
Jacob Bomberger.	Christie Spickler.
Ludwick Goodyahr.	Christie Shertzer.
Jacob Longenecker.	Peter Funk.
Christie Stouffer.	John Bomberger.
Christoph Gippel.	Daniel Miller.
Michael Beam.	Jacob Tussinger.
George Mengel.	

8th Class.

John Thomas, Serjt.	Christie Zug.
Daniel Erb.	Jacob Gingerich.
Henry Bender.	Hartman Morret.

Jonathan Gingerich.
George Geiger.
Michael Witmer.
George Kissel.
Adam Seitz.
John Gingerich.
Rudy Ream.

The above is a true return for ye year 1781.

HENRY CUSTER, Capt.

RETURN OF CAPTIN PHILIP DUCK HIS COMPENY THE FIRST COMPENY IN THE THIRD BATTALIA OF LANCASTER COUNTY MILITIA 1781. (c.)

Lieut.

John Martin.

Insin.

Christaan Willi.

Privates.

1st Class.

Davit Smith.
John Hamer.
John Slukey.
Baltis Gons.
Christaan Reyer.
George Groff.
John Gons.

2nd Class.

Peter Eberly.
Peter Barnhard.
Henry Good.
Adam Pruoh.

3rd Class.

George Winman.
Christofell Josell.
James Jacaps.
Jacob Kissingre.
Jacob Baringre.

4th Class.

Martin Beare, swamp.
Mathias Groll.
Eliksanter Klak.
Peter Bouman.

5th Class.

Christian Groll.
Ollrig Groll.
Henrey Shingler.
Christean Zolly.
Mickel Baringer.
Lutrig Long.

6th Class.

George Hammor.
George Beare.
Josseph Yonger.
Yost Martin.
Jacop Winman.
Jamas McCharty.
George Pfonth.
George Jigel.
Jacap Sander.
Conret Jigel.

7th Class.

Windel Baninger.
Joseph Mathis.
William Hotchason.
George Kouger.
John Sans.
Adam Shiner.

8th Class.

Dalrt Markell.
George Gons.
Mickel Bollmer.
John Demerderfer.
Martin Beare.
John Sander.
Jacop Detwiller.
Christofel Golt.
Conret Conete, Sharjast.

I do hearby cartifi that this iss a just and thrue return from mey compeney.

PHILIP DUCK, Capt.

RETURN OF CAPTAIN PHILEP DUK JN HIS COMPANY THE FIRST OF ELIZEBETH TOWNSHIP IN THE THIRD BATTALION LAN'R CON'Y MILI. RETURN OF THE YEAR 1781. (c.)

lit.

Joseph baginger.

insin.

Christian Willy.

Shar Jant.

Hinry Long.

Conert Conrets.

Corpel.

John Bouman.

John Conrets.

1st Class.

Davit Smith.
John nommer.
John Stuky.
Boltis Gons.

Christaan ryer.
Gorge groff.
John Gons.

2nd Class.

Peter Eberly.
Peter bernhard.
Henry Good.

peter Staly.
Adam prua.

3rd Class.

Gorge Winman.
Christofel Josell.
James Jacops.

Jacob Kissinger.
Jacob Barhinger.

4th Class.

Martain Bar Swomp.
Jacop Shinner.
Mathias Croll.

Eliksander klark.
Peter bouman.

5th Class.

Christain Croll.
Ulrick Croll.
henry Shindaler.
Christean Zolly.

Meckal barhinger.
John Martain.
Lutvig Long.

6th Class.

Gorge Bar.
Joseph yonger.
yost Martain.
George Hommer.
Jacop Winman.

Gorge plonts.
Gorge Ingel.
Jacop Sander.
Connert Ingel.

7th Class.

Windal banjinger.
Joseph Mathes.
Robert Colman.
Willim hogeson.

Gorge koger.
John Sanss.
Adam Shiner.

8th Class.

Davit Markell.
Gorge Gons.
Mickal bolmer.
John bemesderfer.
Martain Bar.
John Sander Ju.
Jacop Detwiler.
Christofel golt.

I do heorby Certefye that the above is a Just and true Return of my Company.

PHILEP DUCK, Captain.

RETURN OF THE FOURTH COMPANY IN THE 3D BATTL. LANC'R CO. MILITIA 1781. (c.)

Capt.

Joseph Gehr.

Lt.

Frederick Kerper.

Ens.

George Brunner.

Serjt.

1st.—George Achy.
2nd.—Adam Obely.
3d.—John Brunner.

Corpl.

1st.—Philip Hoffman.
2d.—Fredrick Walter.
3d.—Balther Hoffman.

Drum.

Conrad Sneider.

Fiffer.

Peter Sneider.

Privates.

1st Class.

George France.
Jacob France.
Christian Bricker.
William Wheeler.
Daniel Solleberger.
Jacob Blank.
Jacob Sherp.

2nd Class.

Jacob Fuhrman.
Jost Miller.
Christie Flickinger.
Stephan Bohlender.
Bastian Gackly.
Peter Beinhour.

3rd Class.

Henry Hendshing, Senr.
Henry Hendshing, Ju.
Samuel Ely.
Mathias Bitner.
George Eby.
Jacob Eberly.
Henry Smith.
David Gachy.

4th Class.

Martin Kleber.
Jacob Bear.
John Keller.
John Flickinger.
John Blank.
Christie Hornly.
Staphel Kline.
George Mose.
Peter Blank.

5th Class.

Henry Binkly.
Daniel Riech.
Christie Harnish.
Adam Sherp.
Garhard Walter.
Thomas Willson.
John Gerhard.
William Walter.
Abraham Hassler.
Christie Wiest.
Hans Achy.
Michael Walder.
Christian Elv.
Joseph Flickinger.
John Gehr.
John Conrad.

6th Class.

Joseph Jacob.
Peter Sneyder.
John Kuntz.
Stophel Sherp.
Andreas Gehr.
Zander Kissinger.
Jacob Haldebeutel.
John Hashower.
George Lang.
David Bricker.
Peter Geistweist.
Peter Fuhrman.
John Gackly, junr.

7th Class.

John Bricker.
Henry Burkholder.
Philip Heft.
Christie Kintzy.
Joseph Conrad.
Frederick Reinhold.
Henry Reinhold.
Philip Kissinger.
Ludwick Torry.
Peter Shoemaker.
David Heckernell.
Jeremeas Miller.

8th Class.

David Gackly.
Martin Kissinger.
Paul Fuhrman.
Philip Shinkel.
Lorentz Ludwick.
Stephy Hassler.
Jacob Dishler.
Jacob Dornbach.

This is to certify that the within is a true return of my company for ye year 1781.

RETURN OF THE 3D COMPANY IN THE 3D BATALION OF LANCASTER COUNTY MILITIA. 1781. (c.)

Captain.

Henry Kuster.

Lieut.

Andraw Earman.

Ensn.

Michael Ginrich.

1st Class.

John Ridsaker.
John Kipe.
Bartle Hoke.
George Hofford.
Joseph Bucher.
Joseph Ginarich.
Abram Risht.
Jacob Hougsteter.
Henry Gipple.
Jacob Burkholter.
David Fry.
Edverd Hilton.

2nd Class.

John Bucher.
Christian Graybill.
John Stoufer.
Martin Gross.
Daniel Ginrich.
Henry Kinsey.
Felty Griner, Junr.
Christian Musselman.
Silvester Gruber.
Barnard Coutsman.
Martin Griner, Junr.

3rd Class.

John Erb.
Christian Goodeore.
Christian Hershey.
Christian Armeshong.
George Mire (run off).
Jacob Hershey.
George Toote.

4th Class.

John Longinakre.
Martin Baylor.
Mathias Comerer.
Christian Risht.
Nicholas Morret.
Peter Armeshong.
John House.
Christian Weaver.
Michael Beam, Junr.
Jacob Overholser.
Fredrick Kessel.

5th Class.

Henry Libe.
John Frederick.
Jacob Armeshong.
Godfry Goodeore.
Nicholas Strow.
Frederick Armeshong.
Henry Miller.
George Rule.
John Noaker.
Henry Shampeno.
Mathias Armeshong.
Larance Keener.

6th Class.

John Armeshong.
John Gipple.
John Ebey.
Christie Bumbarger.
John Sume.
Martin Spegler.
David Suck.
Peter Young.
Jacob Toosinger.
Adam Hollinger.

7th Class.

Jacob Bumberger.
Ludwick Goodeore.
Christian Stoufer.
Stophel Gibble.
George Mingle.
John Lowman.
Christian Spegler.
Christian Shatser.
Peter Funk.
John Bumberger.
Daniel Weller.

8th Class.

George Hoke.
Daniel Erb.
Henry Painter.
Christian Suck.
Jacob Ginrich.
Michael Witmere.
Jonathan Ginrich.
George Keassel.

John Ginrich.	John Shomaker.
Rudy Beam.	John Ebey.
Jacob Gibble.	Isaac Mares.
Jacob Holler.	Jacob Eberly.

I Certifie this to be a just & true return of my company.

HENRY KUSTER.

MUSTER ROLL OF THE 5TH, 6TH & 7TH CLASS OF THE 3D BATALION OF LAN'R COUNTY MILITIA ON A TOUER OF DUTY TO BUCKS COUNTY. (c.)

Names of Persons who perform a touer of Duty.	What class.	Names of Persons who furnished substitutes.	Time when Duty commenced.	Time when Duty ended.
Capt.			1781.	1781.
Nicholas Lutz.				
Lieut.				
David Donnaberger.				
Privates.				
Andrew Ream,		John Ream.		
Henrey Leet.				
[illegible] Smuk.				
John Gerber.				
[illegible] Shride.				
John Gril[illegible].				
Christian [illegible]se.				
John [illegible]in.				
Michael Honnich.				
William Davis.				
David [illegible],		John Hinkle.		
John [illegible]h,		Joseph Brendel		

Adam Ziegler,		Mars Berkley.
Mathew Norris,		John Bucher.
John Ellen,		George Wachter.
George Winder,		Jacob Keller.
Danl. Groff,		

MUSTER ROLE FOR THE 1781 FOR REAMSTOWN DISTRICT. CAPT. ANDREW REAM OF THE 2D COMPANY AND 3D BATTALION OF LANCASTER COUNTY MILITIA. (c.)

Captain.

Andrew Ream.

Lieutenant.

Henry Ream.

Elnsing.

Christian Balsle.

Serjints.

David Ream.
Gotlob Mack.
Abraham Killian.

Corprl's.

Henry Landes.
Jacob Snyder.
Casper Kipert.

The 1st Class.

Niclaus Woolf.
Daniel Bethalene.
Niclaus Snyder.
Daniel Bowman.
Jacob Duck.
Jacob Lasher.
Jacob Mobler.
Jacob Batewiler.
Peter Groff.
John Gattner.
Henry Everley.
George Hiltebrand.
Adam Kingmaker.
Andrew Kitler.

The 2nd Class.

Niclauss Duck.
Michel Shiarck.
Josaph Bair.
Abraham Bicksler.
David Minser.
Lanert Keller.
Samuel Bowman.
Willian geom.
George Draught.
Jacob Bucher.
Abraham Lanelcs.
Henry Lieder.
Fridrick Ream.

The 3rd Class.

Henry Mohler.	William Mellinger.
Christian Wenger.	Jacob Zentmyer.
Abraham Kline.	Josaph Groff.
Christian Nop.	Dobles Ream.
David Mercadey.	Jacob Landes.
John Mellinger.	Jeams Right.
John Mohler.	Jacob Ream.
Abraham Woolf.	Francess Brumbach.
Jacob Sonday.	Vallentin Shovalter.

The 4th Class.

Michel Rigteter.	George fyerstone.
uly Sherck.	Joas Miller.
Davalt Meder.	Martin Klever.
Jacob Shovalter.	Lazerus Leve.
George Spaid.	Henry Hartman.
Fridrick Leeder.	Phillip Krigg.
John Sloth, Jonr.	Adam Nees.

The 5th Class.

George Kuns.	Samuel Groff.
Abraham Landes.	John Landes, Jonr.
Adam Mosser.	Jacob Mishler.
Josapsh Lysy.	John Ream, Jonr.
Peter Brubaker.	John Haffer.
Jacob Keller, Senr.	

The 6th Class.

Bafnd Giger.	Abraham Hershberger.
Josapsh Mishler.	Jacob Killian.
Henry Hershberger.	Jacob Rohland.
Peter Snyder.	Mils Kroley.
Martin Mohler.	John Hingle.
George Hogh.	Jacob witmer.

The 7th Class.

John Martin.	Jacob Conrad.
Michel Beair.	Josapsh Sprigle.
Christian Conrad.	Daniel Ream.
Casper Shritt.	Daniel Groff.
John Haltrey.	William Thomaker.
John Bucher.	Niclaus Wilt.
Isick Hershberger.	Christian frons.
Henry Miller.	Henry good.
John Backker.	

The 8th Class.

John Sloth Sinr.
Peter Ryer.
David Sharck.
Abraham Ream Miller.
John Musselman.
Michel Woolf.
Christian Shovalter, Jonr.
Andrew Ream, Jonr.
Abraham Bair.
Jacob Groff.
Abraham Roland.
Dommes Norress.
Samuel Moder.
Barned Gatz.
Jacob Keller.
Jacob Frans.
Abraham Ream.
John Mohler, Jenr.
John Right.
Phillip Seber.
Adam Wigsel.
George Borgert.
Margus Montilius.

JACOB SWARTZWELDER, Clarok.

This is to Certify That ye above is a True Return of my Company.

Witness my Hand.

ANDREAS REAM, Capt.

RETURN OF WHITE MALE INHABITANTS IN YE 2D COMPY. 3D BA. LANCS. COUNTY MILITIA, 1781. (c.)

Andreas Ream, Capt.

Henry Ream.
Christie Baisly.
David Ream.
Gotlieb Mock.
Abraham Killian.
Henry Landes.
Jacob Sneider.
Casper Kippert.

1st Class.

Nicholas Wolff.
Daniel Bartholome.
Nicholas Sneider.
Daniel Bowman.
Jacob Duck.
Jacob Lesher.
Jacob Mohler.
Jacob Detweiler.
Peter Groff.
John Gartner.
Henry Everly.
George Hildebrand.
Adam Kingmaker.
Andrew Hatler.

2nd Class.

Nicholas Duck.
Michael Sherk.
Joseph Bear.
Abraham Bixler.
David Meintzer.
Leonard Keller.
William Gram.
Samuel Bowman.
George Draught.
Jacob Bucher.
Abraham Landes.
Henry Leeder.
Fredrick Ream.

3rd Class.

Henry Mohler.
Christie Wenger.
Abraham Cline.
Christie Nop.
David Merredy.
John Mellinger.
Saml. Welty.
John Mohler.
Abraham Wolff.
Jacob Sontag.
William Mellinger.
Jacob Zentmyer.
Joseph Groff.
Tobias Ream.
Jacob Landes.
James Wright.
Francis Brombach.
Valentine Showalder.

4th Class.

Michael Richter.
Ulry Sherk.
Dewald Meder.
Jacob Showalder.
George Spade.
Fredrick Leedr.
John Slott, junr.
George Feierstine.
Joas Miller.
Martin Klever.
Lazarus Levy.
Henry Hartman.
Philip Kreek.
Adam Neas.

5th Class.

George Keins.
Abraham Landes.
Adam Mosser.
Joseph Leishy.
Peter Brubacher.
Jacob Keller, senr.
Samuel Groff.
John Landes, Junr.
Jacob Mishler.
John Ream, junr.
John Heffer.

6th Class.

Bernard Geiger.
Joseph Mishler.
Henry Hershberger.
Peter Sneider.
Martin Mohler.
George Hoke.
Abraham Hershberger.
Peter Sneider.
Jacob Killian.
Jacob Rowland.
Miles Growly.
John Hincle.
Jacob Witmer.

7th Class.

John Martin.
Michael Bear.
Christie Conrad.
Casper Shride.
John Holtry.
John Bucher.
Isaac Hershberger.
Henry Miller.
John Becker.
Jacob Conrad.
Joseph Spriegel.
Daniel Ream.
Daniel Groff.
William Shoemaker.
Nicholas Wilt.
Christie Fronce.
Henry Good.

8th Class.

John Slott, senr.
Peter Ryer.
David Sherk.
Abraham Ream, miller.
John Musselman.
Michael Wolff.
Christie Showalter, jr.
Andrew Ream, jr.
Abraham Bear.
Jacob Groff.
Abraham Rowland.
Thomas Norris.
Samuel Meder.
Bernard Getz.
Jacob Heller.
Jacob Fronce.
Abraham Ream.
John Mohler, jr.
John Wright.
Philip Seber.
Adam Wizsell.
George Borkerd.
Marcus Montelius.
Jacob Swartzwalder, Clk.

The above is a True Account.

ANDREAS REAM,
Capt. 2d Compy. y 3d Battn. Lancastr. Cy. Militia.

A PAY ROLL OF THE MEN OF THE FIRST CLASS OF THE 3D BATTL. OF LS. CY. MILT. (c.)

Captain.

John Sleter.

Lieut.

Henry Ream.

Sr.

John Lininger.

Corp'r.

Hactor Paine.

Peter Groff.
William Snyder.
Joseph Brentel.
Philip Hofman.
John Lesher.
John Krill.
Matias Laub.

JOHN SLETER, Capt.

Received of Mr. John Huber Sub. Lt. Lanc. County, the sum of eighteen thousand five hundred and sixty six dollars, for the use of the men of the 1st Class of the 3rd Battalion of Lancaster County Militia late on duty in Northumberland.

Received by me this 16th day of February, 1781.

JOHN SLETER, Capt.

A LIST OF MALE WHITE INHABITANTS BETWEEN 18 & 53 YEARS IN LIDITZ DISTRICT 8TH COMPY. 3D BATT, 1781. (c.)

Persons Names.

David Taneberger.
Jno. Spoonhawer.
John Zeller.
Henry Feather.
Jacob Habacker.
George Zeller.
Henry Feather.

1st Class.

Herman Ernst.
Christian Bailmer.
Abraham Widder.
Christian Brown.
Conrad Long.
Danl. Habecker.
Adam Pletz.
Philip Michel.
Peter Christ.

2nd Class.

Jacob Fierling.
Lenhard Tulepane.
Henry Franck.
Jacob Eby.
Peter McMullin.
Jno. Sheffel.
Daniel Christ.
Joseph Wittmer.
Henry Rough.
Jno. Foutz
Peter Creyder.
Greenberry Peticoats.
Lenhard Krauss.
Christ'n Erb.

3d Class.

Abraham Snyder.
Jacob Brown.
Henry Netzly.
Mickel Balmer.
Christ'n Leinbach.
Christ'n Blickensderf.
Christ'n Muselman.
Peter Miller.
Abraham Huber.
Cunrad Westheaver.
Lorentz Swartzer.
Jno. Heltzel.
Cunrad Meyer.

4th Class.

Jno. Geyer.
Jacob Cassler.
Christ'n Stucky.
Peter Eltzer.
Jeremias Woolff.
Christ'n Eyer.
Christ'n Erb.
Michl. Creyder.
Fredrick Lehman.
Edward Moore.
Philip Burbach
Peter Bessinger.
Henry Brendle.

5th Class.

Jacob Roth.
Henry Wanner.
Peter Snyder.
Christ'n Habecker.
Nicklass Kleine.
Jno. Erb.
George Rothe.
Joseph Willis.
Lenhard Widder.
Christ'n Lesher.
Jno. Stees.
Jno. Engle.
George Meyr.

6th Class.

Lenhard Miller.
Abraham Dierdorf.
Gottfried Thomas.
Geo. Michl. Eichelberger.
Simon Dant.
Saml. Tune.
Christn. Becker.
Henry Dierdorf.
Abraham Sensening.
Andrew Creder.

7th Class.

Jacob Rhudy.
Jno. Shanck.
Lorentz Herchelroth.
Jno. Buch.
Peter Ritsecker.
Andres Wissler.
Michl. Meyr.
Christn. Huber.
Jno. Sensening.
Jno. Geyer.
Christn. Eby, Jur.
Salomon Smuck.
Antony Ronner.
Joseph Gembold.
Geo. Geydner.

8th Class.

Henry Foltz.	Jacob Snyder.
Michl. Groff.	Peter Kreyder.
Christoph Miller.	Jacob Spoonhawer.
Jacob Stees.	Willm. Cassler.
Martin Shenck.	Peter Brunner.
Jacob Hackman.	Jno. Enck.
Jacob Smuck.	Jno. Bender.
Samel Krauss.	Jacob Geyer.
George Geyer.	

This is certified a true List of male white inhabitants to the best of my Knowledge.

JNO. SMULLER, Capt.

RETURN OF THE 8TH COMP'Y IN YE 3D BAT'N MIL'A OF LANCASTER COUNTY, 1781. (c.)

Capt. Jno. Smuller.
Lieut. Dav'd Tanneberger.
Ens. Jno. Spoonhawer.

Serjeants.

Jno. Zeller.	Geo. Zeller.
Henry Feather.	

Drum'r.

Jacob Kitel.

Fifer.

Jacob Habecker.

1st Class.

Herman Ernst.	Danl. Habecker.
Christn. Ballmer.	Adam Pletz.
Cunrad Long.	Peter Christ.

2nd Class.

Lenhard Tulepane.	Jacob Eby.
Henry Frank.	Peter McMullin.

John Sheffel.
Danl. Christ.
Joseph Wittmer.
Henry Rouch.
John Foutz.
Peter Kreiter.
Greenberry Peticoart.
Lenhard Krauss.
Peter Becker.
John Mickel.

3d Class.

Abraham Sneyder.
Henry Netzly.
Michl. Bahner.
Christ'n. Leinbach.
Christ'n. Blickensdefer.
Christ'n. Musselman.
Peter Miller.
Abraham Huber.
Cunrad Westheaver.
Jacob Geyr.
John Heltzel.
Cunrad Meyr.

4th Class.

Jacob Cassler.
Christn. Stucky.
Peter Eltzer.
Jeremiah Woolf.
Chritn. Eyr.
Chritn. Erb.
Michl. Kreiter.
Philip Burbach.
Peter Bessinger.
Fredrick Lehman.
Chritn. Hess.

5th Class.

Jacob Roth.
Henry Wanner.
Peter Snyder.
Christn. Habecker.
Nichs. Kleine.
John Erb.
Geo. Roth.
Lenhard Widder.
Christn. Lesher.
John Stees.
John Engel.
Geo. Meyr.
Jacob Erb.

6th Class.

Lenhard Miller.
Abraham Dierdorf.
Gotfried Thomas.
Simon Dantz.
Saml. Tune.
Christn. Becker.
Henry Dierdorf.

7th Class.

Jacob Ruhdy.
John Shonck.
Lorentz Herchelroth.
John Buch.
Peter Ritsecker.
Andres Wissler.
Michl. Meyer.
Christn. Huber.
Jno. Sensening.
Solomon Smuk.
John Geir.
Christn. Eby, Jur.
Antony Ronner.
Joseph Gembold.
Peter Eby.
George Geydner.

8th Class.

Henry Foltz.	Jacob Snyder.
Michl. Grof.	Peter Kreider.
Christoph Miller.	Jacob Spoonhawer.
Jacob Stees.	Wilm. Cassler.
Martin Shenck.	Peter Bruner.
Jacob Hackman.	John Enck.
Saml. Krauss.	Jacob Geyer.
George Geyer.	Christn. Eby, upper.

This Return is certified by me to the best of my knowledge.
JOHN SMULLER, Capt.

RETURN OF THE 7TH COMPANY 3D BATTALION OF LANCASTER COUNTY MILITIA, COMMANDED BY LIEUT. COLONEL GEORGE FEATHER, 1782. (c.)

Captain.

John Ashton.

Lieutenant.

Daniel Hollinger.

Ensign.

George Hoverter.

1st Class.

Jacob Keefer.	George Grove.
John Hair.	Daniel Hollinger.
Jacob Kinsey.	John Boyer.

2nd Class.

George Miller.	Balsor Seese.
Frederick Witmire.	John Brubaker.
Peter Sheffer.	

3d Class.

John Crotson.
Conrod Mark.
Thomas Hamton.
Stophel Fauber.
Samuel Westor.
George Poutsor.
Christian Stover.
Samuel Cromer.

4th Class.

John Cromer.
Nicholas Bale.
Jacob Mire.
Nicholas Srofe.
Daniel Brubaker.
Michael Sortman.
Henry Rudy.
Leonard Seese.
Frederick Hair.

5th Class.

Felty Witmire.
Thomas Hollinger.
George Hollinger.
Abraham Stoufer.
Abraham Day.
Jacob Burtner.
George Betz.
George Miller.
Godfry Thomas.

6th Class.

Frederick Shitz.
Andraw Shover.
Henry Hogh.
Conrod Plaster.
Michael Houghlander.
George Witcraft.

7th Class.

John Jones.
William Davis.
Leonard Witmire.
John Porry.
Samuel Russel.
Stophel Horning.
Henry Mark.
Sandy Sortman.
Michael Horning.
William Gesell.
Jacob Deal.
Daniel Berry.

8th Class.

John Beamisderfer.
John Peter.
Marks Nagel.
Michael Shofe.
Jacob Brubaker.
Christian Smith.
Solomon Srode.
Evan Evans.
Henry Gatts.

The above is a true Return of my Company.
Witness my Hand.

JOHN ASHTON, Capt.

A TRUE AND EXACT LIST OF NAMES OF EACH AND EVERY MALE WHITE PERSON INHABITING OR RESIDING WITHIN MY DISTRICT IN THE SEVENTH COMPANY OF THE THIRD BATTALION OF LANCASTER COUNTY MILITIA BETWEEN THE AGE OF EIGHTEEN AND FIFTY-THREE YEARS. TAKEN FOR THE YEAR 1782. (c.)

Capt.

John Ashton.

Lieut.

Daniel Hollinger.

Ens.

George Hoverter.

Privates.

1st Class.

Jacob Keefer.
John Hair.
Jacob Kinsy.
George Groff.
Daniel Hollinger.
John Boyer.

2nd Class.

George Miller.
Fredrick Wittmoyer.
Peter Sheffer.
Balser Sees.
John Brubaker.

3d Class.

John Crotzer.
Conrad Marck.
Thomas Hampton.
Stoffel Faber.
Samuel Wissler.
George Potzer.
Christian Stover.
Samuel Cromer.

4th Class.

John Cromer.
Nicholas Bale.
Jacob Mire.
Nicholas Shrove.
Daniel Brubaker.
Michael Zartman.
Henry Rudy.
Lenhard Sees.
Fredrick Hair.

5th Class.

Felty Wittmeir.
Thomas Hollinger.
George Hollinger.
Abraham Hollinger.
Abraham Stouffer.
Abraham Day.
Jacob Burtner .
George Betz.
George Miller (Smith).
Goafrid Thomas.

6th Class.

Fredrick Shitz.
Andrew Shover.
Henry Hogh.
Conrad Plaster.
Micheal Hoghlander.
George Wittcraft.

7th Class.

John Jones.
William Davis.
Lenhard Wittmire.
John Porry.
Samuel Russel.
Stoffel Horning.
Henry Marck.
Sandy Zartman.
Micheal Horning.
William Gessel.
Jacob Deal.
Casper Scager (gon of since this).
Daniel Porry.

8th Class.

John Bemesderfer.
John Peter.
Marx Nagle.
Micheal Shofe.
Jacob Brubaker.
Christian Smith.
Solomon Shrode.
Henry Gattz.
Evan Evans.

I do swear, on the Holy Evangilest of Almighty God: That the above list is just & true state, of the male white inhabitants, residing in my District, agreeable to law, and without any fraud to the state to the best of my knowledge.

JOHN ASHTON, Capt.

Sworn before me this 25th day of May, 1782.

JOHN HUBER, Sub. Lt. L'r C'y.

RETURN OF THE FIRST COMPANY OF THE THIRD BATALION OF LANCASTER COUNTY MILITIA COMMANDED BY LT. COL. GEORGE FEATHER, 1782. (c.)

Captain.
Philip Duck.

Lieutenant.
John Martin.

Ensign.
Christian Willy.

Serjeant.
Conrod Conreds.

Corp'r.
John Bowman.

Corperal.
John Conrods.

1st Class.

David Smith.
John Hammer.
John Stuckey.
Balsor Gontz.
Christian Royer.
John Gontz.
* John Sander.
Frederick Miller.

2nd Class.

Peter Eberly.
Peter Barnet.
Adam Prua.

3d Class.

George Winman.
James Jacobs.
Jacob Kesinger.
Jacob Barringer.
Frank Noland.

4th Class.

Martin Bare, swomp.
Metbias Crall.
Ellckzander Clag.
Peter Bowman.

5th Class.

Christian Crall.
William Stover.
Jacob Frans.
Henry Shingler.
Christian Swolley.
Michael Barringer.
Daniel Shiner.
Joseph Crall.
Joseph Bart.

6th Class.

George Bare.
Joseph Yonker.
Yosht Martin.
Jacob Winman.
George Plantz.
George Ingel.
Jacob Sander.
Conrod Ingel.
Martin Boyer.
George Hammer.
Thomas Butlar.
Detrick Folk.

7th Class.

Windel Beninger.
Joseph Mathews.
William Hogeson.
Nicholas Unger.
George Kougher.
Adam Shiner.
Ingel Martin.
Robert Westin.

8th Class.

George Gontz.
Martin Bare.
John Sander.
Jacob Tatwiler.
Christopher Gott.

The above is a true Return of my Company as Witness my Hand.

PHILIP DUCK, Capt.

A TRUE AND EXACT LIST OF THE NAMES OF EACH AND EVERY MALE WHITE PERSON INHABITING OR RESIDING WITHIN MY DISTRICT, IN THE FIRST COMPANY, OF THE THIRD BATTALION OF LANCASTER COUNTY, MILITIA, BETWEEN THE AGE OF EIGHTEEN, AND FIFTY-THREE YEARS. TAKEN FOR THE YEAR 1782. (c.)

Captain.
Philip Duck.

Lieutenant.
John Martin.

Ensign.

Christian Willey.

1st Class.

David Smith.
John Hamer.
John Sticky.
Balzer Gantz.
Christian Royer.
John Gantz.
John Sander.
Fredrick Miller.
Isaac Lorspack.

2nd Class.

Peter Eberly.
Peter Barnhard.
Adam Prua.
Robert Anderson.

3d Class.

George Weinman.
James Jacobs.
Jacob Kissinger.
Jacob Barringer.
Francis Knowland.
George Pitzson.

4th Class.

Martin Bear, swamp.
Mathias Groll.
Alexander Clack.
Peter Bowmon.
William James.

5th Class.

Christian Groll.
William Stover.
Jacob Frantz.
Henry Shigler.
Christian Zwolley.
Michael Berringer.
Daniel Shiner.
Joseph Groll.
Joseph Carl.

6th Class.

George Bear.
Joseph Younger.
Jost Martin.
Jacob Weinman.
George Plantz.
George Engel.
Jacob Sander.
Conrad Engel.
Martin Boyer.
George Hamer.
Thomas Butler.
G. Dietrich Folck.

7th Class.

Wendle Benninger.
Joseph Mathews.
William Hageson.
Nickloss Unger.
George Kougher.
John Sands.
Adam Shiner.
Engel Martin.
Robert Youson.
Daniel McColly.

8th Class.

David Markel.
George Gantz.
Martin Bear.
John Sander, Junr.
Jacob Dedweiler.
Christophel Gold.
Henry Boffenmeyer.

I do swear, on the Holy Evengilist of Almighty God: That the above list is a just and true state, of the Male white Inhabitants, residing in my District, agreeable to Law, and without any fraud to the States, to the best of my knowledge.

Sworn before me this twenty seventh Day of November, 1782.

JOHN HUBER, Sub. Lt.
· PHILIP DUCK, Capt.

RETURN OF CAPTAIN PHILIP DUCK HIS COMPENY THE FURST COMPENY IN THE THIRT BATTALIA OF LANCASTER COUNTY MILITIA, 1782. (c.)

Lt.

John Martin.

Insin.

Cristaen Willi.

1 Class.

Davith Smith.
John Hommer.
John Stukey.
Boltis Gons.
Christian ryer.
John Gons.
John Sander.
Fridrick Millir.
Isac Larsbach.

2 Class.

Peter Ebarleay.	Adam prua.
Peter Barnhard.	Robert Anderson.

3 Class.

George Winman.	Jacop Baringer.
James Jacops.	franck Nolin.
Jacop kissinger.	George Pitson.

4 Class.

Martin Beare, swamp.	Peter Bouman.
Mathis Groll.	William Jamas.
Eliksander klak.	

5 Class.

Christaan Groll.	Mickal Baringer.
Wihalm Stouver.	Daniel ekiner.
Jacop frans.	Joseph Groll.
Henry Shinderier.	Joseph Carl.
Christaan Zolly.	

6 Class.

George Beare.	Jacop Sander.
Joseph Yonger.	Conrad Ingel.
Yost Martin.	Martin Beyer.
Jacop Winman.	George hommer.
George plonts.	Thomas Butler.
George Ingel.	G. Dieter folk.

7 Class.

Windal Baninger.	Jonn Sans.
Joseph Mates.	Adam Shiner.
William hogeson.	Ingel Martin.
Nicolos ounger.	Roberd Yonson.
George kouker.	Daniel McColly.

8 Class.

Davit Markell.	Jacop Datwiler.
George Gons.	Christoffel Golt.
Martin Beare.	Henry Boffanmeyer.
John Sauder, Jr.	

I do hereby Certifye that the above is a just & true Return **of my Company.**

PHILIP DUCK, Capt.

RETURN OF THE FOURTH COMPANY THIRD BATTALION LANCASTER COUNTY MILITIA, 1782. (c.)

Captain.
Joseph Gehr.

Luti'n.
Fridrick Kerper.

Ins.
George Brunner.

Sher.

George Acke.
Adam Oberly.

Corp.

Phillb kofeman.
Baulser kofeman.
fridrick Wagener.

Drummer.
Conrad Shlneder.

Fifer.
Petter Shueder.

Almoner.
Petter Beenhauer.

Clerk.
Jacob Gehr.

first Clase.

Jearge frantz.
William Shider.
Danlel Sollenberger.
Jacob blanck.
Jacob Sherb.

2 Clase.

Jacob fuhrman.
Jost Miller.
Christian flickyinger.
Steffen Bollender.
Baustian gauckly.
fridrick kissinger.

3 Clase.

Saml. Eby.	Jacob Eberly.
David Guackly.	Henry Smith.
mathias bitner.	Henry Henshing Jn.

4 Clase.

Jacob Baer.	John Blanck.
John Keller.	Christian kernly.
Marttin kleber.	George Mose.
John flickginger.	Mathias fetterhafe.

5 Clase.

Henry Binkly.	Christian Wist.
Daniel Rich.	John Gehr.
Christian harnish.	Michael Walter.
John conrath.	John Gerhard.
Adam Sherb.	Christian Ely.
William Walter.	Joseph flickginger.
thomas Wilson.	John flickginger, Jr.
Abraham Hasler.	John Acke.

6 Clase.

Joseph Jacob.	David Briker.
Petter Shnieder.	John ganckly.
John Kuntz.	Petter Gistwelt.
Stoffel Sherp.	fridrick Walk.
Jacob heidebutel.	Petter fuhrman.
George longe.	

7 Clase.

John Bricker.	Petter Shumakr.
Abraham Sop.	David Ganckly.
Henry borgholder.	David becanel.
Christian kintz.	John koshower.
Joseph Conrath.	Jermias miller.
George kissinger.	michael keller.

8 Clase.

Martin kissinger.	Lorentz Ludwick.
Philib Shenkel.	Jacob Dissler.
Jacob Dorbach.	Steffen hasler.
Paul furman.	

I do hereby Certifye that the within is a just & true state **of my company. As witness** my hand.

JOSEPH GEHR.

A TRUE AND EXACT LIST OF THE NAMES OF EACH AND EVERY MALE WHITE PERSON, INHABITING OR RESIDING, WITHIN MY DISTRICT, IN THE FORTH COMPANY OF THE THIRD BATTALION OF LANCASTER COUNTY, MILITIA, BETWEEN THE AGE OF EIGHTEEN AND FIFTY THREE YEARS. TAKEN FOR THE YEAR 1782. (c.)

Captain.

Joseph Gehr.

Lieutenant.

Frederick Kerber.

Ensign.

George Bruner.

Almonar.

Peter Binehower.

Non Comitioned Officers.

Sergeants.

George Ockey.
Adam Overley.
John Bruner.

Corporals.

Philip Hoofman.
Baltzer Hoofman.
Frederick Wagoner.

Drummer.

Conrad Snider.

Fifer.

Peter Snider.

First Class.

1. George France.
2. William Snider.
3. Daniel Solbereger.
4. Jacob Blonk.
5. William Wheeler.
6. Jacob Sharp.

Second Class.

7. Jacob Foreman.
8. Yeoast Miller.
9. Chris'n Flickenger.
10. Stephen Bolander.
11. Bostian Cockley.
12. Frederick Kisenger.

Third Class.

13. Henry Henchey, Junr.
14. Saml. Ebey.
15. David Cockley.
16. Mathias Bitner.
17. Jacob Everly.
18. Henry Smith.

Fourth Class.

19. Jacob Bare.
20. John Keller.
21. Martin Cleaver.
22. Jno. Flickinger.
23. John Plonk.
24. Chris'r Hernley.
25. George Moose.
26. Mathias Feterhoffer.

Fifth Class.

27. Henry Benkley.
28. Daniel Reath.
29. Chris'r Hornish.
30. John Knopser.
31. Adam Sharp.
32. Thos. Willson.
33. William Waller.
34. John Conrad.
35. Abra. Hassler.
36. Chris'r Wuast.
37. John Gehr.
38. Mich'l Walter.
39. John Gehrhort.
40. Gerard Walter.
41. Chris'r Eley.
42. Jos. Fleckenger.
43. John Cockley.

Sixth Class.

44. Joseph Jacob.
45. John Hoonce.
46. Stophel Sharp.
47. Andrew Gehr.
48. Jacob Hilderbidle.
49. George Long.
50. David Bricker.
51. John Cockley.
52. Peter Gestwhite.
53. Peter Foreman.
54. Frederick Walk.

Seventh Class.

55. John Bricker.
56. Abraham Sophel.
57. Henry Burkholder.
58. Philip Heft.
59. Joseph Conrad.
60. Frederick Rihnhold.
61. Henry Rinehold.
62. Geo. Philip Kisinger.
63. Ludwick Barry.
64. Peter Shoemaker.
65. David Hickernal.
66. Chris'r Shewalder.
67. Jeremiah Miller.
68. Mich'l Keller.

Eighth Class.

69. David Cockley, Junr.
70. Martin Kisenger.
71. Philip Shenkle.
72. Jacob Dornboh.
73. Paul Foreman.
74. Lawrence Ludwick.
75. Jacob Fisler.
76. Stephen Hassler.

I Do swear, on the Holy Evengileet of Almighty God: That the above list is a just and true state of the Male White Inhabitants, residing in my District, agreeable to Law, and without any fraud to the State, to the best of my knowledge.

JOSEPH GEHR, Capt.

Sworn before me this first Day of November 1782.
JOHN HUBER, Sub. Lt.

A TRUE AND EXACT LIST OF THE NAMES OF EACH AND EVERY MALE WHITE PERSON INHABITING OR RESIDING WITHIN MY DISTRICT IN THE 3D COMPANY OF THE 3D BATTALION OF LANCASTER COUNTY MILITIA BETWEEN THE AGE OF EIGHTEEN & FIFTY THREE YEARS. TAKEN FOR THE YEAR 1782. (c.)

Capt.

Henry Kushter.

Lieu.

Andrew Earman.

Ens.

Michael Genrich.

Privates.

1st Class.

John Ridzaker.
Bartil Hoke.
George Hafferd.
Joseph Bucher.
Joseph Gingerich.
Abraham Risht.
Jacob Hoghsteter.
Jacob Burkhotter.
David Fry.

2nd Class.

John Bucher.	Peter Erb.
Christian Greybill.	Christian Musselman.
John Stoufer.	Silvester Gruber.
Daniel Gingerich.	Barnard Coutzman.
Felty Grimer.	Martin Griner.

3rd Class.

John Erb.	George Moyr.
Christian Goodlore.	Peter Eshelman.
Christian Hershey.	

4th Class.

Marten Balor.	Peter Armstrong.
Mathias Comerer.	John House.
Christian Risht.	Frederick Kessel.
Nicholas Morrit.	John Kissel.

5th Class.

John Frederick.	John Noaker.
Jacob Armeshong.	Mathias Armeshong.
Godfrey Goodeore.	John Snider.
Nicholass Strow.	Andrew Lantz.
Henry Miller.	John Spigler.
George Rule.	

6th Class.

John Sumey.	Peter Young.
John Armeshong.	Jacob Toosinger.
John Gipple.	Adam Hollinger .
Martin Spegler.	John Markey.

7th Class.

Jacob Bumbereger.	Peter Funk.
Ludwick Goodeore.	John Bumberger.
Christian Stoufer.	Daniel Weller.
Stophel Gipple.	Jacob Shirde.
George Mingel.	Christian Spegler.
John Lowman.	Nicholas Spegler.

8th Class.

Daniel Erb.
Christian Zuck.
Jacob Gingerich.
Jonathan Gingerich.
Michael Witmore.
George Kessel.
John Gingerich.
Rudy Beam.
Jacob Gipple.
John Shomaker.
John Ebey.
George Guyger.
Hartman Morret.
Jacob Eberly.

I do swear on the Holy Evengilest of Almy. God: That the above list is a just & true state of the male white inhabitants, residing in my district, agreeable to law & without any fraud to the State, to the best of my knowledge.

HENRY KUSHTER, Capt.

Sworn before me this first day of October 1782.
JOHN HUBER, Sub. Lt. Lr. Cy.

RETURN OF CAPT'N KUSHTER'S COMPANY BEING THE 3D OF THE 3D BATTALION OF LANCASTER COUNTY MILITIA COMMANDED BY LIEUT. COLONEL GEORGE FEATHER 1782. SPRING. (c.)

Captain.

Henry Kushter.

Lieutenant.

Andrew Earman.

Ensign.

Michael Gingirich.

1st Class.

John Ridsaker.
Bartil Hoke.
George Hofford.
Joseph Bucher.
Joseph Gingerich.
Abram Risht.
Jacob Hoghsteter.
Jacob Burkholter.
David Fry.

2nd Class.

John Bucher.	Peter Erb.
Christian Greybill.	Christian Musselman.
John Stoufer.	Silvester Gruber.
Daniel Gingerich.	Barnard Coutzman.
Filty Griner.	

3rd Class.

John Erb.	George Moyer.
Christian Goodeore.	Peter Eshelman.
Christian Hershey.	

4th Class.

Martin Baylor.	Peter Armestrong.
Mathias Commerer.	John House.
Christian Risht.	Fredrick Kissel.
Nicholas Morrit.	John Kissel.

5th Class.

John Fredrick.	John Noaker.
Jacob Armestrong.	Mithias Armestrong.
Godfrey Goodeore.	John Snider.
Nicholas Strow.	Andrew Lantz.
Henry Miller.	John Spegler.
George Rule.	

6th Class.

John Sumer.	Peter young.
John Armstrong.	Jacob Toosinegr.
John Gipple.	Adam Hollinger.
Martin Spegler.	John Markey.

7th Class.

Jacob Bumberger.	Peter Funk.
Ludwick Goodeore.	John Bumberger.
Christian Stoufer.	Daniel Miller.
Stoppel Gipple.	Jacob Shride.
George Mingel.	Christian Spegler.
John Louman.	Nicholas Spegler.

8th Class.

Daniel Erb.	Jacob Gingerick.
Christian Zuck.	Jonathan Gingerick.

Michael Witmire.	John Shomaker.
George Kessel.	John Ebey.
John Gingerich.	George Guyger.
Rudy Beam.	Hartman Morrit.
Jacob Gepple.	Jacob Eberly.

The above is a True Return of my Company as Witness my Hand.

HENRY KUSHTER, Capt.

RETURN OF THE 3D COMPANY IN THE 3D BATALION LANCASTER COUNTY MILITIA COMMANDED BY LIEUT. COLONEL GEORGE FEATHER 1782. FALL. (c.)

Captain.

Henry Kushter.

Lieutenant.

Andrew Earman.

Ensign.

Michael Gingerich.

1st Class.

John Ridsaker.	Abraham Risht.
Bartel Hoke.	Jacob Moghsteter.
George Hoffor.	Jacob Burkholder.
Joseph Bucher.	David Fry.
Joseph Gingerech.	

2nd Class.

John Bucher.	Peter Erbb.
Christian Graybill.	Christian Musselman.
John Stoyfer.	Silvester Gruber.
Daniel Gingerich.	Barney Coutzman.
Felty Griner.	Martin Griner.

3rd Class.

John Erb.	Christian Hershey.
Christian Goodeore.	Peter Esselman.

4th Class.

Martin Baylor.
Methias Commerer.
Christian Risht.
Nicholas Morrit.
Peter Armeshong.
John House.
Frederick Kissel.
John Kissel.

5th Class.

John Frederick.
Jacob Armeshong.
Godfry Goodeore.
Nicholas Strow.
George Ruhl.
John Noaker.
Methias Aremshong.
John Snider.
John Spegler.

6th Class.

John Summy.
John Armeshong.
John Gippel.
Martin Spegler.
Peter young.
Jacob Toosinger.
Adam Hollinger.
John Markey.

7th Class.

Jacob Bumberger.
Ludwick Goodore.
Christian Stoufer.
Stophel Gippel.
George Mengel.
John Lowman.
John Bumberger.
Daniel Weller.
Christian Spegler.
Nicholas Spegler.

8th Class.

Daniel Erb.
Christian Zuck.
Jacob Gingerich.
Jonathan Gingerich.
Michael Witmoyer.
George Thissel.
John Gingerich.
Rudy Beam.
Jacob Gippel.
John Shomaker.
John Ebey.
George Guyer.
Hartman Morrit.
Jacob Eberly.

The above is a True Return of my Company as Witness my Hand.

HENRY KUSHTER, Capt.

A TRUE AND EXACT LIST OF THE NAMES OF EACH AND EVERY MALE WHITE PERSON INHABITING OR RESIDING WITHIN MY DISTRICT, IN THE FIFTH COMPANY, OF THE THIRD BATTALION OF LANCASTER COUNTY MILITIA, BETWEEN THE AGE OF EIGHTEEN, AND FIFTY-THREE YEARS. TAKEN FOR THE YEAR 1782. (c.)

Capt.
Nicholas Lutz.

Lieut.
John Bechtold.

Ens.
Henry Geyer.

Almonar.
Adam Grull.

Clerk.
Philip Lutz.

Phiffer.
Jacob Zinn.

Sergents.

David Baringer.
John Lutz.
Joseph Brendel.

Corpral.

George Laush.
Mihal Winhole.

Privates.

1st Class.

George Westheffer.
Nicholas Lesher.
Jacob Hershy.
Christian Hoober.
Jacob Hyle.
Friderick Steffy.
Baltzer Stone.
Andrew Shimp.
George Gensemer.

2nd Class.

Jacob Weeber.	John Weeber.
Philip Grell.	Henry Sheffer.
George Zinn.	Henry Brauck.

3rd Class.

John Lesher.	Rudy Miller.
Michal Harding.	George Keller.
Adam Leod.	Henry Zimmerman.
George Copey.	

4th Class.

Henry Bastian.	Peter Wise.
Henry Brendel.	Martin Fernsler.
Richard Adems.	John Eigenberger.
John Miller.	Matias Holorg.
Isaac Adams.	Henry Brendel.
Philip Broutstone.	

5th Class.

John Greell.	John Shweigert.
John Ruch.	Peter Smith.
Henry Leed.	Peter Fry.

6th Class.

Nicholas Shower.	Casper Bushert.
Michal Young.	Christian Shlaugh.
Fridrick Gerner.	Marx Banckly.
Rudy Bear.	John Shoup.

7th Class.

Henry Eighold.	Nicholas Rup.
David Didlo.	John Colman.
Jacob Vaneda.	Peter Banckly.
John Hoobor.	Henry Shneider.
Jost Spengler.	George Sidebonder.
Adam Kissinger.	George Mengel.
Michal Kegerys.	John Westhefer.

8th Class.

Christian Harding.
Cherls Tritsh.
George Rimel.
Isaac Betteeoffer.
John Betteeoffer.
John Miller, Junr.
John Wengert.
Peter Zimmarman.
John Jost.
Henry Walter.
George Miller.
Christian Eiseman.
Mathias Sheffer.
Peter Ulrick.

I do swear, on the Holy Evenglilest of Almighty God: that the above is a just and true state, of the male white Inhabitants, residing in my District, agreeable to Law, and without any fraud to the State to the best of my knowledge.

Sworn before me this 21st day of July 1782.

JOHN HUBER, Sub. Lt. L'r C'y.

NICHOLAS LUTZ, Capt.

A TRUE AND EXACT LIST OF THE NAMES OF EACH AND EVERY MALE WHITE PERSON INHABITING OR RESIDING WITHIN MY DISTRICT IN THE SIXTH COMPANY, OF THE THIRD BATTALION OF LANCASTER COUNTY, MILITIA, BETWEEN THE AGE OF EIGHTEEN AND FIFTY-THREE YEARS. TAKEN FOR THE YEAR 1782. (c.)

Captain.

Micheal Oberly.

Lieutenant.

Peter Bentz.

Ensign.

Nichloss Fogelsang.

Serjants.

Christophel Oberly.
Jacob Feierstone.
Jacob Houshalter.

Corperals.

Jacob Oberly.
Micheal Pitz.
John Snearer.

Drummer.

Peter Zeller.

Fifer.

Samuel Harlacher.

First Class.

Henry Kafrode.
Micheal Snearer.
Christophel Westenberger.
Jacob Anguish.
Micheal Seller.
Elias Woolf.
Jacob Foltz.
Jonathan Kelb.

Second Class.

Christian Weeland.
John Shaffer.
George Houck.
Adam Keib.
Henry Bear.
Christian Felt.
John Urigh.
Jacob Gorgas.

Third Class.

Jacob Landis.
Martin Laber.
John Wittmer.
Jacob Kaffrod.
Micheal Long.
Peter Feather.
Jacob Feather.
Daniel Negly.
Peter Garber.
Jacob Eberly.

Fourth Class.

George Ellig.
Peter Bollinger.
Jacob Weidman.
Dedrick Fanestock.
Rudolf Bollinger.
Abraham Zerfass.
Abraham Bollinger.
Henry Eberly.
Narceus Ernst.
Adam Bower.
George Feierstone.
John Beacher.

Fifth Class.

Christian Luther.
John Miller.
Henry Feather.
Christophel Streagel.
David Landis.
Nickloss Leaser.
Wendle Traut.
Felix Burckhard.

Sixth Class.

Jacob Kimmell.	Christophel Hacker.
John Jones.	John Hershberger.
Benjamin Bear.	Henry Feather.
Samuel Fanestock.	John Gardner.
Conrad Haass.	

Seventh Class.

William Wucker.	George Weaver.
John Arnt.	John Brubaker.
Jacob Wolf.	Henry Miller.
Christophel Trabinger.	Jacob Beck.
Henry Miller.	William Dushong.
Adam Treish.	George Zeller.
John Aple.	John Royer.
John Luther.	

Eighth Class.

Fredrick Hacker.	Conrad Handshu.
Fredrick Adam.	John Unger.
John Senseman.	Micheal Roub.
John Zieger.	Christophel Miller.
Henry Freymeyer.	Jacob Groff.
Christian Bowman.	Daniel Royer.
Adam Frantz.	

I DO swear, on the Holy Evengilest of Almighty God: That the above list is a just and true state, of the Male Wnite Inhabitants, residing in my District, agreeable to Law, and without any fraud to the State, to the best of my knowledge.

MICHAEL OBERLIE, Capt.

Sworn before me this First
Day of November, 1782.
JOHN HUBER, Sub. Lt.

RETURN OF THE SIXTH COMPANY IN THE THIRD BATTALLION LANCASTER COUNTY MILETIA 1782. (c.)

Capt.
Michael Oberley.

Lt.
Peter Bentz.

Ens.

Necoleus Fogelsong.

Sergt.

1st.—Chestophel Oberley.
2d.—Jacob Feierstine.
3d.—Jacob Haushalter.

Corpl.

1st.—Jacob Oberley.
2d.—John Shneary.
3d.—Michael Pfut.

Drummer.

Peter Zeller.

Peiffer.

Samuel Harlacher.

Privates.

1st Class.

Henry Kaffrad.
Michael Shnearer.
Christophel Toestberger.
Jacob Engquish.
Michael Seiller.
Eliass Wolff.
Jacob Folss.
Jonaten Kelp.

2nd Class.

Chrestian Weallend.
John Shaffer.
George Houk.
Adam Kelp.
Henrey Bear.
Christian Fled.
John Uhrig.
Jacob Gorges.

3rd Class.

Jacob Landes.
Martin Laber.
John Wittmer.
Jacob Kafrad.
Michael Long.
Peter Feather.
Jacob Feather.
Danial Negley.
Peter Gerber.
Jacob Eberly.

4th Class.

George Ellig.
Peter Bollinger.
Jacob Weidman.
Deadarick Fasnastick.
Rudolph Bollinger.
Aberham Zearfass.
Aberham Bollinger.
Henrey Eberley.
Narditious Eernst.
Adam Bower.
George Feierstine.
John Becker.

5th Class.

Christian Luttor.
John Miller.
Henrey Feather.
Christophel Streagel.
Daved Landes.
Necolass Leasor.
Wendel Trout.
Falix Borgert.

6th Class.

Jacob Kennel.
John Jons.
Benjamen Bear.
Samuel Fahnastock.
Conrad Hass.
Christiphel Hacker.
John Hershberger.
Henrey Feather, juneor.
John Geardner.

7th Class.

William Wogert.
John Arnt.
Jacob Wolff.
Chritophel Trabenger.
Henrey Miller.
Adam Irish.
John Appel.
John Luttor.
George Weaver.
John Brubacher.
Henry Miller.
Jacob Beck.
William Dushong.
George Zeller.
John Royer.

8th Class.

Fredarick Hacker.
Fredarick Adam.
John Sensaman.
George Weidman.
John Zeager.
Henrey Frimier.
Christian Bowman.
Adam Frantz.
Conrad Handshu.
John Unger.
Michael Raub.
Christophel Millar.
Jacob Groff.
Daniel Royer.

I do hereby certify that this is a just & true return of my company.

MICHANL OBERLIE, Capt.

RETURN OF THE SIXTH COMPANY IN THE THIRD BATTALLION LANCASTER COUNTY MILITIA 1782. (c.)

Capt.

Michael Oberlin.

Lt.

Peter Bentz.

Ens.

Nicholas Fogelsong.

Sergt.

1st—Christopher Oberlin.
2nd.—Jacob Fierstein.
3d.—Jacob Haushalter.

Corpl.

1st.—Jacob Oberlin.
2d.—John Shnearer.
3d.—Michael Petz.

Drum.

Peter Zeller.

Piper.

Samuel Harlacher.

Privates.

1st Class.

Henrey Kaffrad.
Michael Schrearer.
Jacob Engquish.
Michael Sailer.
Elias Wolff.
Jacob Foltz.
Jonathan Kelp.

2nd Class.

Christian Wenland.
John Sheffer.
George Hauk.
Adam Kelp.
Henrey Bear.
Chrettian Fide.
John Uhrig.
Jacob Gorgas.

3rd Class.

Jacob Landes. | Peter Feather.
John Wittmer. | Jacob Feather.
Martian Laber. | Daneal Nagly.
Jacob Kaffrad. | Peter Gerbor.
Michael Long. | Jacob Eberly.

4th Class.

George Ellig. | Aberham Bollinger.
Peter Bollinger. | Henrey Eberly.
Jacob Witeman. | Narcious Ernst.
Deatric Fanastock. | Adam Bower.
Rudolph Bollinger. | George Feierstine.
Aberham Zerfass. | John Becker.

5th Class.

Christian Luttor. | Daved Landas.
John Miller. | Necholous Leasor.
Henrey Feather. | Wentel Trout.
Chritophel Streagel. | Fellix Borgert.

6th Class.

Jacob Kemel. | Chrestophel Hacker.
John Jons. | Peter Martien.
Benjamin Bear. | Henrey Feather, Junr
Samual Fanatock. | John Geardner.
Conrad Hass.

7th Class.

William Wogart. | George Wever.
John Arnt. | John Brubacker.
Jacob Wolff. | Henrey Miller.
Christophel Irobinger. | Jacob Bick.
Henry Miller, Junr. | William Iuschgong.
Adam Irish. | George Zeller.
John Apple. | John Royer.

8th Class.

Freaderick Hacker. | John Zeager.
Freaderick Adam. | Henrey Frimier.
John Sensaman. | Christian Bauman.

Adam Frantz.
Conrad Handschow.
John Ungoe.
Michael Raub.
Christaphel Miller.
Jacob Groff.
Daniel Royer.

I do hereby certify that the above is a just & true return of my company.

MICHAEL OBERLIN, Capt.

A TRUE AND EXACT LIST OF THE NAMES, OF EACH AND EVERY WHITE PERSON, INHABITING OR RESIDING WITHIN MY DISTRICT, IN THE SECOND COMPANY OF THE THIRD BATTALION OF LANCASTER COUNTY MILITIA, BETWEEN THE AGE OF EIGHTEEN AND FIFTY-THREE YEARS. TAKEN FOR THE YEAR 1782. JOHN WREGHT, AS CLARK. (c.)

Capt.

Andw. Ream.

Lieu.

Henery Ream.

Ens.

Christen Bolsey.

Almonar.

John Shit.

Sargent.

Casper Sroid.
Abraham Killin.
Marten Mohler.

Corplers.

Henery Landes.
Jacob Snider.
Casper Kiper.

Privates.

1st Class.

Nickles Wolf.
Danil Bartholomaw.
Danil Bowman.
Jacob Duck.
Jacob Lasher.
Jacob Mohler.
Jacob Detwiler.
Petter Groff.
Henery Everly.
George Hiltebrant.
Nickles Snider.
Adam Kingmaker.
Andrew Hotler.
Casper Pruner.

2nd Class.

Nickles Duck.
Mickel Shirk.
Joseph Bear.
Abraham Bickler.
David Manser.
Leanord Killer.
Samuel Bowman.
William Cram.
Jacob Boucher.
Abraham Landes, Mill Wright.
Henery Leder.
Fredrick Ream.
Coutlip Mock.
Andrew Ream, Junr.
David Graff.

3rd Class.

Henery Mohler.
Christin Winger.
Abraham Kline.
Christin Knop.
David Meredey.
John Mohler.
Abraham Wolf.
William Millinger.
Jacob Santmyer.
Joseph Graff.
Tobis Ream.
Jacob Landes.
James Wright.
Jacob Ream.
Franses Brumback.
Valintine Savalder.
John Millinger.
Jacob Sunday.
Detrick Walck.

4th Class.

Adam Neas.
Mickel Rider.
Uley Shirk.
Jacob Shavelder.
George Spade.
Fredrick Leder.
John Shit, Junr.
Yeast Miller.
Marten Klever.
Henery Hartman.
Jacob Hagy.
Philip Greek.
Benjamin Landes.
Samul Killer.

5th Class.

George Kones.
Abraham Landes.
Adam Musser.
Joseph Lysey.
Petter Brubaker.
Jacob Killer, Sinr.
Samuel Groff.
John Landes, Junr.
Jacob Mishler.
John Ream, Junr.
John Hafer.
Petter Eberly.
Marten Miller.
George Sprigle.

6th Class.

Barnet Giger.
Joseph Mishler.
Henery Harshbarger.
Jacob Killin.
Jacob Rohalend.
John Hinkel.
Jacob Whitmare.
David Ream.
Abraham Knysley.
John Heke.
Petter Snider.

7th Class.

John Marten.
Mickel Bear.
Christian Conrode.
John Houltory.
John Boucher.
Isaac Harshbarger.
Jacob Conrod.
Joseph Springle.
Denil Ream, Junr.
Deniel Groff.
William Shomaker.
Nickles Wilt.
Christen Frants.
Henery Good.
John Lininger.
Henery Ciper.
Daniel Firstone.
Joseph Flickner.

8th Class.

Petter Ryer.
David Shirk.
Abraham Ream, Miller.
John Musseleman.
Mickel Wolf.
Christin Shuwalder.
Andrew Ream.
Abraham Bear.
Jacob Groff.
Abraham Rohalend, junr.
Thomas Norras.
Samal Mader.
Barnet Geats.
Jacob Killer.
Jacob Frants.
Abraham Ream.
John Mohler, junr.
Adam Wisel.
Markes Mantiles.
David Harshbarger.
George Cober.

I do Affirm, on the Holy Evengilest of Almighty God: That the above is a just and true state, of the male white inhabitants residing in my District, agreeable to Law, and without any fraud to the State to the best of my knowledge.

ANDREW REEHM, Capt.

Efirmed before me this third
day of October 1782.
JOHN HUBER, Sub. Lt. L'r C'y.

A MUSTER ROWL OF CAPT. REAM'S COMPANY OF THE SECONT CLASS & THIRD BATELION OF LANCASTER COUNTY MILITIA FOR THE YEAR OF 1782. (c.)

Lieut.

Henery Ream.

Ensign.

Christin Bolsey.

Sergents.

Casper Sroide.
Abraham Killin.
Morten Mohler.

Corplers.

Henery Landes.
Jacob Snider.
Casper Kiper.

Privates.

1st Class.

Nickles Wolf.
Danil Bartholomew.
Nickles Snider.
Daniel Bowman.
Jacob Duck.
Jacob Lasher.
Jacob Detwiler.
Petter Groff.
Henery Hiltebrant.
Adam Kingmaker.
Andrew Hitler.
Jacob Moller.
Casper Pruner.

2nd Class.

Nickles Duck.
Mickel Shirk.
Joseph Bear.
Abraham Bixler.
David Menser.
Leanord Killer.

Samuel Bowman.	Fredrick Ream.
William Cram, away.	Cotlip Mock.
Jacob Boucher.	Andrew Ream, Jr.
Abraham Landes, Millwribt.	David Groff.
Henery Leader.	

3rd Class.

Henery Mohler.	Tobias Ream.
Christin Winger.	Jacob Landes.
Abraham Kline.	James Wright.
Christin Knop.	Jacob Ream.
David Meredey.	Franses Brumback.
John Mohler.	Valintine Shovalder.
Abraham Wolf.	John Millinger.
William Millinger.	Jacob Sunday.
Jacob Santmyer.	Deterick Walck.
Joseph Groff.	

4th Class.

Adam Neas.	Yeost Miller.
Mickel Rider.	Henery Hartman.
Uley Shirk.	Jacob Hagy.
Jacob Shavelder.	Philip Greek.
George Spade.	Benjamin Landes.
Fredrick Leder.	Samul Killer.
John Shit, Junr.	

5th Class.

George Kons.	John Landes, Junior.
Abraham Landes.	Jacob Mishler.
Adam Musser.	John Ream, Junr.
Joseph Lisey.	John Hafer.
Petter Brubaker.	Petter Eberly.
Jacob Killer, Siner.	Marten Moller.
Samel Groff.	George Sprigle.

6th Class.

Barnet Giger.	Jacob Rohalend.
Joseph Mishler.	John Hinkel, Deserter.
Henery Harshbarger.	Jacob Whitman.
Petter Snider.	David Ream.
Abraham Harshbarger.	Abraham Kingsley.
Jacob Killin.	John Heke.

7th Class.

John Marten.	Daniel Groff.
Mickel Bear.	William Shomaker.
Christin Conroad.	Nickles Wilt.
John Holtery.	Christin Frans.
John Bouchar.	Henery Good.
Isaac Harshbarger.	John Lininger.
Jacob Conroad.	Henery Ciper.
Joseph Sprigel.	Danil Firston, on fulriou.
Daniel Ream, Junr., away.	Joseph Flickner.

8th Class.

Petter Ryer.	Barnet Yeats.
David Shirk.	Jacob Killer.
Abraham Ream, Miller.	Jacob Frants.
John Musselman.	Abraham Ream.
Mickel Wolf.	John Mohler, Jr.
Christin Showelder.	Adam Wisel.
Andrew Ream.	Markes Mantiles.
Abraham Bear.	David Harshbarger.
Jacob Groff.	George Cober.
Abraham Rohalend, Jun'r.	John Wright.
Thomas Norres.	Henery Trosdel.
Samel Meader.	Adam How.

I do hereby sertify that the within return is just & true to the best of my knowledge.

ANDREAS REIHM, Capt.

A TRUE AND EXACT LIST OF THE NAMES, OF EACH AND EVERY MALE WHITE PERSON, INHABITING OR RESIDING, WITHIN MY DISTRICT, IN THE EIGHT COMPANY, OF THE THIRD BATTALION OF LANCASTER COUNTY, MILITIA, BETWEEN THE AGE OF EIGHTEEN AND FIFTY-THREE YEARS. TAKEN FOR THE YEAR 1782. (c.)

Capt.
John Smuller.

Lieu.
John Sponhour.

Ens.

Casper Shimp.

Serjts.

Conard Radman.
Michael Miller.
Casper Jordan.

Drummer.

Jacob Kittle.

Fifer.

John Habecker.

Privates.

1st Class.

Herman Ernst.
Christian Balmer.
Conrad Long.
Daniel Habecker.
Adam Bletz.
Abraham Musselman.
Peter Christ.
David Jones.
Jacob Musselman.

2nd Class.

Jacob Eby.
Peter McMullen.
Daniel Christ.
Peter Beaker.
John Foutz.
Peter Krider.
Greenbery Peticoart.
Christian Erb.
George Stoner.
Lenhard Krouss.
Lenhard Shenlein.

3rd Class.

Jacob Brown.
Henry Netzly.
Michael Balmer.
Christian Blickenderfer.
Christian Musselman.
Peter Miller.
John Micheal.
Abraham Huber.
Conrad Westheafer.
John Heltzel.
John Seyler.

4th Class.

Fredrick Lehman.
Jacob Castler.
Christian Stuky.
Christian Hess.
Micheal Krider.
Peter Bessinger.

5th Class.

Jacob Rode.
Jacob Erb (Brother Son).
Christian Eby, Junr.
Henry Wanner.
Peter Snider.
Christian Habecker.
Nikloss Kline.
John Erb.
George Rode.
Lenhard Widder.
Christian Lesher.
John Steess.
George Moyer.
Andrew Betz.
John Oblinger.

6th Class.

John Bletz.
Lenhard Miller.
Jacob Snider, Junr.
Abraham Dirdorf.
Andrew Krider.
Simon Dantz.
Samuel Tune.
Christian Beaker.
Daniel Kline.

7th Class.

Gorge Statler.
William Bletz.
Jacob Rudy.
Lornece Herkelrode.
John Buch.
Peter Ricksacre.
Andrew Wissler.
Michael Moyer.
Christian Huber.
Peter Eby.
John Sensenigh.
John Geyer (son of Jacob).
Christian Eby (Lower).
Solomon Smuck.
Joseph Gambold.
George Geldner.
Anthoney Runner.

8th Class.

Henry Foltz.
Jacob Stees.
Martin Shenck.
Jacob Hackman.
George Geyer.
Peter Krider.
Jacob Sponhour.
William Cassler.
Peter Brunner.
Christian Eby (uper).
John Enk.
Daniel Erb.
John Freymeyr.
Henry Vonfleck.
Zacharias Bard.
John Dirdorf.
Daniel Sheller, Junr.
Joseph Shenk.
Jacob Seyler.
George Craft.
Peter Hole.
George Firling.
Jacob Metzel.

I do swear, on the Holy Evangilest of Almighty God: That the above is a just and true state, of the male white In-

habitants, residing in my District, agreeable to Law, and without any fraud to the State, to the best of my knowledge.

JOHN SMULLER, Capt.

Sworn before me this
second day of October
1782.

JOHN HUBER, Sub. Lt.

OFFICERS OF THIRD BATTALION. (a.)

Returned April 15, 1783.

Lieutenant Colonel.

James Ross.

Major.

Stephen Chambers.

Surgeon.

Frederick Kuhn.

Adjutant.

John Snyder.

Quarter Master.

Andrew Graff.

1st Company.

Captain—John Miller.
Lieutenant—John Offner.
Ensign—George Burckhart.

2nd Company.

Captain—John Weidley.
Lieutenant—John Burke.
Ensign—Jacob Reigart.

3rd Company.

Captain—Henry Deering.
Lieutenant—Philip Hood.
Ensign—Gerhard Bubach.

4th Company.

Captain—Daniel Newman.
Lieutenant—Frederick Mann.
Ensign—Michael Grubb.

5th Company.

Captain—Philip Weitzel.
Lieutenant—William Bausman.
Ensign—[Vacant.]

6th Company.

Captain—George Tripler.
Lieutenant—George Lightner.
Ensign—Daniel Whitmore.

7th Company.

Captain—Martin Wybright.
Lieutenant—David Snyder.
Ensign—Nicholas Shreiner.

8th Company.

Captain—Daniel Bard.
Lieutenant—Barnet Cryder.
Ensign—Martin Bart.

RETURN OF OFFICERS ELECTED IN THE THIRD BATTALION OF LANCASTER COUNTY MILITIA—AGREEABLE TO ORDERS, PUBLISHED FOR THAT PURPOSE, ON THE 15TH DAY OF APRIL 1783. (c.)

Field Officers.

Lieu. Colonel.
James Ross.

Major.
Stephen Chambers.

Staff.

Frederick Kuhn .... Surgeon.
John Snyder .... Adjutant.
Andrew Graft .... Qu. Master.

Captains.

1. John Miller.	5. Philip Weitzell.
2. John Weidley.	6. George Trisler.
3. Henry Derring.	7. Martin Wybright.
4. Daniel Newman.	8. Daniel Bard.

Lieutenants.

1. John Offner.	5. William Bausman.
2. John Burke.	6. George Lightner.
3. Philip Hard.	7. David Snyder.
4. Frederick Mann.	8. Barnet Cryder.

Ensigns.

1. George Burckarts.	5.
2. Jacob Reigart.	6. Daniel Whitmiere.
3. Gerhard Bubach.	7. Nicholas Shriner.
4. Michael Grubb.	8. Martin Bart.

I do Certify the above to be a just state agreeable to returns made to me of the officers in 3d Battalion Lan. Cout'y Mil'a.

AD'M HUBLEY, JR., S. Lt. L'r C'y.

(c.) This may Certify all whom it may Concern that I was present at the Widow Howell's when the last Militia Tour was Performed as an officer in Capn. Moores Company & at the Request of Leut. Rue of Cap'n. Rolands Company Entered James Brown as a Marching man in their Compy., he Being fully Satisfyd that he ought to be Enter'd as he was then When we where Dismis'd on Furlough & did Duty in the Ranks.

JOSEPH GRIFFITH, Leut.

N. B. I being Present at the Time above Mention'd as a Serjeant in Capn. Roland's Company do Certify the above true State of the Case.

Sept. 8th, 1785.

JAMES NELLEY.

Tredyffrin Township
Chester County.

GENERAL RETURN OF OFFICERS IN LANCASTER COUNTY MILITIA APRIL 15, 1783. (c.)

THIRD BATTALION.

Field Officers.

Lieut. Col.

Jacob Bower.

Maj.

Wendle Hipsman.

Captains.

1. Philip Duck.
2. Andrew Ream.
3. George Rist.
4. Joseph Gear.
5. Jacob Vanderslice.
6. Philip Peck.
7.
8. John Smuller.

Lieutenants.

1. John Weyman.
2. Henry Ream.
3. George Hoke.
4. Peter Guistwhite.
5. John Beachtell.
6. Peter Pence.
7.
8.

Ensigns.

1. John Smith.
2. Christian Baltzley.
3. Mich'l Gingre.
4. George Brunner.
5. Henry Gyer.
6. Mich'l Oberly.

MUSTER ROLL OF CAPTIN PHILIP DUCK COMBENI THE FIRST FO ELIZEBETH TOWNSHIP IN THE THIRT BATTALION LAN. COUNTY L'T JOSEPH BAHINGER INSIN CHRISTEAN WILLE SHARJANT, HENRY LONG, SHARJANT CONRET CONOETS COR. JOHN BOUMAN COR. JOHN CONRITS. (c.)

1st Class.

Davit Shmith.
John Hommer.
John Stuky.
Boltis Gons.
Christean Ryer.
George Goff.
John Gons.

2nd Class.

Peter Ebirly.
Peter Barnhart.
Hinry Good.
Peter Staly.
Adam Prua.

3rd Class.

Gorge Winman.
Christofel Josell.
James Jacops.
Jacop Kissinger.
George Smith.
Jacob Barhinger.
James Rean.

4th Class.

Martain Bar swomp.
Mathis Croll.
Jacop Shinner.
Eliksander Clak.
Peter Bouman.

5th Class.

Christian Croll.
Ulrick Croll.
Hinry Shindeler.
Christean Zolly.
Mickal Barhinger.
John Martain.
Lutrig Long.

6th Class.

Gorge Bar.
Joseph Yonge.
Yost Martain.
Jacop Winman.
Gorge Plonts.
Gorge Ingel.
Jacop Sander.
Georg Hommer.

7th Class.

Windel Baningar.
Joseph Mathas.
Robert Colman.
William Hogeson.
Gorge Hoger.
John Sans.
Adam Skiner.

8th Class.

Davit Markal.
Gorge Gons.
Mickal Bohner.
John Bemesderler.
Martain Bar.
John Sonder Jr.
Jacop Datviler.
Chritofel Golt.
Armbrist Simmin.
James McDonly.
James McCarty.
Joseph Therombel.

A RETURN OF YE 6TH. CLASSES OF THE COMPANY; OF MILITIA OF LANCASTER COUNTY 3D. BAT. COMAND'D BY COLO. ALEX'D LOWRY. THE 6TH CLASS OF CAPT. McKEES. (c.)

1st.

Crisley France.
Wm. Mills.
Jacob Tatwiller.
Chriley Burghold.
Daniel Beniner.
Mattheas Brokar.
Philip Cugh.
Petter Yeats.
Jon. Dean.
Jon. Foster.
Jacob Marten.

2nd.

Capt. Robson.
James Cunningham.
Jon. Carnachan.
Joseph Wolf Jur.
Christan Herr.
Thom. Willey.
Jacob Shire.
Jon. Foglesoung.
Christan Whitmor.

3rd.

Capt. Work.
Rich'd O'Donald.
Chritan Veninger, a weaver at Keeseys.
Mich'l Hoofman.
Jacob Wiant.
Jacob Foutz.
Rich'd Alison.
David Cook, Jur.
Wm. Megery.
Frer. Stewart.
Wm. Cumins.

4th.

Capt. McQueen.
Andw. Foster.
Stophel Shank.
Phil. Boughman.
Climis Shire.
Peter Reasor.

Jon. Rhea.
Jossia McQueen.
Jon. Hoover.
Thom. Kelly.
Wm. Hunter.
Jon. Thomson.

5th.

Capt. Crage.
Chrily Seler.
Chrily Bruneman.
Jon. Russel.
Jon. Seller.
Barny Savage.
Barny Shutter.

Wilm. Messer, Jur.
Chrily Oxer.
Gorge Blaser.
Jon. Longnecker.
Saml. Batzner.
Hugh Moore.
Petter Root.

6th.

Capt. Boggs.
Sam. Wilson.
Andw. Gross.
Jon. Beaver.
Jon. Chank, Jur.
Jon. Grider.
Jacob Trayor.

Adam Plats.
Joseph Sink.
Jacob Oldwilor.
Samuel Woods.
Jas. Coner.
Jacob Smith.
Jacob Brubacker.

7th.

Capt. Scotts.
Phridrick Batz.
Peter Shafer.
Peter Erstin.
Thom. Philips.

Christian Black.
Hendry Snigar.
Lenard Peters.
Jacop Palmer.

8th.

Capt. Pedens.
Jas. Hutcheson.
Christan Holdeman.
Abraham Mats.
Samuel Hess.
Isack Gilman.

John Chambers.
Thom. Ments.
Gorge A Stiller.
Sal. McCrakan.
Wm. Wilson.
Jon. Vance.

Return by

AND'W. BOGGS, Capt.

6th C. L. C. M.

The within class was called to randisvouse at the sign of

the Barr this 12th April 1779 to march to Bedford town and it appears that only five Privates are willing to march as by the above roal.

B. G.

RETURN OF THE WHITE MALE INHABITANTS IN YE 5TH COMPY. 3D. BA. LANCASTER COUNTY MILITIA BY CAPT. LUTZ. (c.)

Nicholas Lutz.
John Bechtol.
Henry Geiger.
David Berringer.
John Lutz.
Joseph Brendle.
Henry Laush.
Philip Brendle.
Michael Winehold.

1st Class.

George Wesshaver.
Adam Grill.
Nicholas Lesher.
John Lininger.
Jacob Hershy.
Christler Huber.
Philip Lutz.
Jacob Heit.
Philip Fernsler.
Fredrick Steffy.

2nd Class.

Jacob Weber.
Peter Steffy.
Adam Grill.

3rd Class.

Christie Weber.
John Lesher.
Michael Harding.
Adam Leed.
George Coppes.
Rudy Miller.
George Keller.
Henry Zimerman.
John Getz.

4th Class.

Henry Bastian.
Henry Brendle.
Richard Adams.
John Miller.
Isaac Adams.
Philip Breitenstein.
Peter Wise.
Martin Fernsler.
John Eigenberger.

5th Class.

George Ury.	Henry Sneider.
Joseph Wenger.	John Sweigert.
John Grill.	Peter Sm.th.
John Reech.	Peter Frye.
Henry Leed.	Henry Laush.

6th Class.

Nicholas Shower.	Henry Walter.
Michall Young.	Henry Lutz.
Jacob Gemberling.	Christie Slough.
Frederick Gerner.	Marx Binkly.
Rudy Bear.	John Gerber.
Casper Bossert.	

7th Class.

Henry Eicholtz.	Jacob Zinn.
David Title.	Peter Ulrich.
Mathias Walk.	Peter Binkly.
Jacob Voneada.	Chrictie Harding.
John Huber.	Christie Zimerman.
Jost Spengler.	Charles Fritch.
Adam Kissinger.	George Rimel.
Michael Kerich.	Isac Petticoffer.
Nicholas Rup.	John Petticoffer.
John Coleman.	John Miller, Junr.
Casper Sh.mp.	

8th Class.

John Wengert.	John Rohrer.
Peter Zimerman.	Adam Martin.
Henry Keefer.	

The above is a True Return to ye best of my Knowledge.

NICHOLAS LUTZ, Capt.

RETURN OF THE EIGHT COMP'Y IN THE 3D. BATN. LT. C. MA. (c.)

Capt.

John Smuller.

Lieut.

David Taneberger.

Ens.

John Spoonhower.

Serjeants.

John Zeller.
George Zeller.
Henry Feather.

Fifer.

Jacob Habecker.

1st Class.

Herman Ernst.
Daniel Habecker.
Christn. Balmer.
Adam Pletz.
Abraham Widder.
Philip Michel.
Christn. Brown.
Peter Christ.
Cunrad Long.

2nd Class.

Jacob Fierling.
Joseph Witmer.
Lenhard Tulepane.
Henry Rough.
Henry Franck.
Jno. Foutz.
Jacob Eby.
Peter Creyder.
Peter McMullin.
Greenbery Peticoats.
John Sheffel.
Lenhard Krauss.
Daniel Christ.
Christie Erb, gone.

3rd Class.

Abraham Snyder.
Christn. Mussleman.
Jacob Brown.
Peter Miller.
Henry Netzly.
Abraham Huber.
Michel Balmer.
Cunrad Westheaver.
Christn. Leinbach.
John Heitzel.
Christn. Blickensderfer.
Cunrad Meyer.

4th Class.

John Geyer.
Michl. Kreider.
Jacob Cassler.
Edward Moore.
Christn. Stuchy.
Philip Burbach.
Peter Eltzer.
Peter Bessinger.
Jeremias Woolf.
Henry Brendle.
Christn. Eyar.
Fredrick Lehman.
Christn. Ero.

5th Class.

Jacob Roth.
Jacob Erb.
Henry Wanner.
Christn. Eby.
Peter Snyoder, Jur.
Christn. Habecker.
Nicklaus Kleine.
John Erb.
George Rothe.
Joseph Willis.
Lenhard Widder.
Chirstn. Lesher.
John Stees.
John Engel.
George Meyer.

6th Class.

Lenhard Miller.
Abraham Dierdorf.
Gottfried Thomas.
Geo. Michl. Eichelberger.
Simon Dantz.
Samuel Tune.
Christn. Becker.
Henry Dierdorf.
Abraham Sensening.
Andrew Krider.

7th Class.

Jacob Rhudy.
Jno. Shanck.
Lorentz Herchelroth.
Jno. Buch.
Peter Ritsecker.
Andres Wissler.
Michl. Meyer.
Christn. Huber.
John Sensening.
John Geier.
Christn. Eby, Jur.
Solomon Smuck.
Antony Ronner.
Joseph Gembold.
Geo. Geydner.

8th Class.

Henry Foltz.
Michl. Groff.
Christoph Miller.
Jacob Stees.
Martin Shenck.
Jacob Hackman.
Jacob Smuck.
Saml. Krauss.
George Geyer.
Jacob Snyder.
Peter Kreyter.
Jacob Spoonharver.
Willm. Cassler.
Peter Brunner.
Jno. Enck.
John Bender.
Jacob Geyer.

To the best of my knowledge. This is to Certify That This is a True Return of my Compy.

Witness my Hand.

JNO. SMULLER, Capt.

A RETURN OF THOSE WHO SERVED THEIR TOUR OF DUTY IN MY COMPY. OF THE 2ND, 3D, & 4TH CLASSES OF COLO. LOWRY'S BATT. FROM THE 18TH. OF JULY TO THE 22ND. OF SEPR. LAST PAST. (c.)

Sarjt. James Defrance, Cap't McKees Compy.
Barney Quinn, Cap't McKees Compy.
James Currithers, Cap't McKees Compy.
Thomas Wiley, My own Compy.
Abraham Scott for Sam. Scott, My own Compy.
James Sample, my own Compy, killed Aug. 8th.
Cornelius Green, Cap't McQuinns Co.
Mathias Wolf, Cap't McQuinns Co.
James Carney for Wm. Hay, Cap't McQuinns Co.
Sarjt. William Mercer, Cap't Craig's Co.
William MGérrey for John Ematt, Cap't Craig's Co.
William Gallaghar for Jacob Hofman, Cap't Craig's Co.
Daniel Sullivan for Jacob Shireman, Capt. Craig's Co.
Henry Hains, Cap't Craig's Co.
George Bower, Cap't Craig's Co.
John Alexander, Capt. Scott's Co.
Joseph Sink for Joseph Eakenroad, Cap't Scotts Co.
Charles Emhoff for Jacob Peters, Cap't Scotts Co.
William Hall for Sims Chambers, Cap't Scotts Co.
Henry Metzler, Cap't Scotts Co.
Gotlip Bishops. Deserted 25th July, Cap't Scotts Co.
Joseph Tytball, Cap't Pedin's Compy.
James Porter for Samuel Robinson, Cap't Pedin's Compy.
Robert Ellis, Cap't Pedin's Compy.
Daniel Cassedy for Joseph Little, Killed or Taken Aug. 8th, Capt. Pedin's Compy.
John Cook, Volunteer.

I do certify the above.

J. WORK, Capt. 3d. Batt.,
Lancaster Co.

FOURTH BATTALION

LANCASTER COUNTY MILITIA.

RETURN OF THE OFFICERS OF SEVEN COMPANIES, FOURTH BATTALION LANCASTER COUNTY ASSOCIATORS, COLONEL JAMES BURD, MARCH 13, 1776.

We the Subscribers Officers of the Fourth Battalion of Lancaster County do Certify that the Following Gentlemen agreeable to their Ranks are voted by a Majority of every Individual Private of the Battalion as officers of the said Battalion and Request the Commissioners may Issue accordingly. As Witness our hands this 13th March 1776. (e.)

James Burd, Col.
Thomas Murray, Lieut. Col.
Cornelius Cox, 1st Major.
Frederick Hummel, 2d Major.

1st.—James Croutch, Captn.
William Mackey, 1st Lieut.
Frederick Hubley, 2d Lieut.
Simon Snyder, Ensign.

2d.—James Cowden, Capt.
John Gilcrest, 1st Lieut.
William Cochrane, 2d Lieut.
Thomas McArthur, Jr., Ensign.

3d.—Joseph Sheerer, Capt.
James Collier, Jr., 1st. Lieut.
Samuel Rutherford, 2d Lieut.
Samuel Hutcheson, Ensign.

4th.—Richard Manning, Capt.
Thomas Foster, 1st Lieut.
Samuel Martin, 2d Lieut.
Elijah Buck, Ensign.

5th.—John Reed, Capt.
James Clark, 1st. Lieut.
George Clark, 2d Lieut.
Samuel Oram, Ensign.

6th.—James Murray, Capt.
Peter Sturgeon, 1st Lieu.
John Simpson, 2d Lieut.
John Ryan, Ensign.

7th.—Jacob Fridley, Capt.
John McFarland, 1st Lieut.
Mathias Howver, 2d Lieut.
Philip Blesing, Ensign.

There is two Companys more who have altered their officers on accot of Resignations; when the Returns are given in they shall be Punctually Transmitted.

Signed at the Request of the Board of Officers the original Remaining in my hands.

JAMES BURD,
Col. 4th Batt. Lan. County.

Tinian, 12th June 1776.

Sir:—

On the other side is a Return of the officers of my Battalion which I am Requested to Transmit to our County Committee & to Request of them that they will be pleased to procure the Commissions to the Officers as soon as they Conveniently can of the 7 Companys, the Return of the other 2 Companys will be sent as soon as possible in order that they may also have their Commissions. In the meantime I am with much Respect,

Gent'm,
Your most Humble Servt.,
JAMES BURD,
Col. 4th Batt.

JASPER YEATES, ESQR., Chairman, & the other Members of the Committee of Lancaster County.

COLONEL JAMES BURD'S BATTALION. (a.)

CAPTAIN JAMES COWDEN'S COMPANY.

A true return of Capt. James Cowden's company of the Fourth Battalion of Lancaster County, commanded by Col. James Burd, Esq., March 13, 1776.

Captain.

James Cowden.

First Lieutenant.

John Gilchrist

Second Lieutenant.

William Cochran.

Ensign.

Thomas McArthur.

Sergeants.

Berryhill, Andrew.
Swan, William.
James, Derrick.
Cochran, Samuel.

Court-Martial.

Bell, Thomas.
Hilton, John.

Clerk.

Montgomery, Robert.

Privates.

Allison, David.
Allison, William.
Askens, Thomas.
Barnett, John, Jr.
Barr, Samuel.
Barnett, Samuel.
Berryhill, Samuel.
Berryhill, Andrew, Jr.
Boggs, James.
Boggs, William.
Boyd, William.
Brann, John.
Brisben, William.
Cook, James.
Crabb, William.
Cummens, John.
Davis, John.
Duncan, James Jr.

Duncan, John.
Duncan, William.
Elder, John.
Farrier, Robert.
Finney, James.
Gamble, Andrew.
Gilchrist, John, Jr.
Gilchrist, Matthew.
Gilchrist, Robert.
Gilchrist, Thomas.
Glen, William.
Graham, Michael.
Hatfield, John.
Harbeson, Patrick.
Hogan, William.
Ingram, William.
Jamison, John.
Johnston, Joseph.
Jones, Benjamin.
Jones, William.
Linton, Thomas.
Lochary, William.
Marshall, Joseph.
McClanachan, William.
McClure, William.
McConnel, Matthew.
McElhenny, John.
McGaw, William.
McMath, James.
McMullen, George.
McMullen, William.
McNamara, James.
McRoberts, William.
Miller, John.
Byers, James.
Caldwell, David.
Caldwell, James.
Caddow, George, Jr.
Caddow, Thomas.
Calhoun, Matthew.
Campbell, Colin.
Carson, John.
Carson, Richard.
Cavet, Andrew.
Chambers, James.
Cochran, Andrew.
Cochran, James.
Milligan, John.
Montgomery, William.
Neel, Robert.
Patterson, James.
Patterson, Peter.
Patterson, William.
Patton, David.
Peden, John.
Peterson, Thomas.
Potts, Robert.
Ranken, William.
Richardson, Andrew.
Richey, David.
Scott, John.
Shaw, Joseph.
Smith, Andrew.
Smith, George.
Smith, Peter.
Smith, Robert.
Spence, James.
Stephen, Andrew.
Stephen, Hugh.
Stephen, Zachary.
Stuart, Elijah.
Swan, Richard.
Taggart, James.
Thompson, Samuel.
Twoey, Hugh.
Wallace, Samuel.
Warnick, Robert.
Wylie, Robert.
Wiggins, James.
Wilson, Abraham.
Wilson, Alexander.
Wilson, James.
Wilson, John.
Wilson, Joseph.
Wilson, William.

CAPTAIN JAMES MURRAY'S COMPANY. (a.)

[This company, with others, went into service in November or December, 1775, and were present at the battles of Trenton and Princeton.]

A return of Capt. James Murray's company of Associators of the Fourth Battalion of Lancaster county, commanded by James Burd, Esq., March 13, 1776.

Captain.
James Murray.

First Lieutenant.
Peter Sturgeon.

Second Lieutenant.
John Simpson.

Ensign.
John Ryan.

Privates.

Ayres, John.
Bell, George.
Bell, Isaac.
Bell, James.
Bell, John, Sr.
Bell, John, Jr.
Bell, William, Jr.
Bell, William.
Bell, William, Sr.
Boyce, John.
Boyce, William.
Brown, John.
Brown, Peter.
Christy, John.
Cochran, George.
Cochran, John, Sr.
Cochran, John, Jr.
Cochran, Samuel.
Colligan, Joseph.
Colligan, John.
Davis, David.
Dice, John.
Eyeman, Christopher.
Eyeman, Jacob (1).
Eyeman, Jacob (2).
Gallacher, Thomas.
Gartner, George Adam.
Goudey, John.
Goudey, Robert.
Hilton, William.
Hoane, Anthony.
Johnston, Richard.
Lafferty, Patrick.
Lindsey, William.
Linord, James.
Lockart, Moses.

McCloskey, Henry.
McFadden, John.
McGill, Robert.
Mooney, Abraham.
Peacock, James.
Plough, Samuel.
Richmond, John.
Smitb, Robert.
Smith, William.
Sturgeon, Samuel.
Sturgeon, Thomas.
Thomas, John.
Thompson, Thomas.
Tinturf, Jacob.
Tinturf, Philip.
Vincent, William.
Yenelet, Michael.

CAPTAIN JOHN REED'S COMPANY. (a.)

[Capt. John Reed, the commander of the following company during the Jersey campaign of 1776-77, was the son of James Reed, who located near the south of Powell's creek, Lancaster, now Dauphin county, probably as early as 1728. On maps prior to 1860, the location is marked "Reed's." John Reed had been a ranger on the frontiers during the French and Indian wars, and when the war of the Revolution came he was ready for the conflict. He organized the company of associators which is herewith given, and was in service until after the battles in and around Philadelphia. Capt. Reed died in 1789.]

A true return of Capt. John Reed's company of the Fourth Battalion, Lancaster county, commanded by Col. James Burd, Esq., March 13, 1776.

Captain.
John Reed.

First Lieutenant.
James Clark.

Second Lieutenant.
George Clark.

Ensign.
Samuel Oram.

Sergeants.

John Gilmore.
Henry Lick.
Alexander Taylor.
William Johnston.

Corporals.

Ludwick Shellman.
William Kennedy.
John Chambers.
John Black.

Privates.

Allison, Richard.
Armstrong, Andrew.
Armstrong, Robert.
Baker, Jeremiah.
Black, James, Sr.
Black, James, Jr.
Black, James.
Black, Thomas, Sr.
George Alexander.
George, Robert.
Goldenberry, John.
Holmes, George.
Jiltson, John.
Jones, Isaac.
Jones, Peter.
Keays, John.
Kennedy, Alexander.
Ketsner, Samuel.
Ketsner, John.
Kinter, Henry.
Kinter, John.
Little, Joseph.
Knees, John.
McCall, James.
McClure, George.
McClure, Patrick.
McClure, John.
McGowan, John.
Brown, Joseph.
Buchanan, John.
Butler, John.
Carpenter, John.
Chambers, Elisha.
Clements, Brice.
Colhoon, Hugh.
Fairman, James.
McElhenny, John.
McMullen, Samuel.
Meetch, John.
McIlrath, Joseph.
Mellan, John.
Mills, Mathias.
Neal, William.
Oram, Thomas.
Powell, Malachi.
Packer, Aaron.
Simmons, George.
Sweigert, John.
Sweigert, Adam.
Striker, Jacob.
Swagerley, Peter.
Taylor, George.
Taylor, Samuel.
Waggoner, George.
Waggoner, Adam.
Walker, Robert.

CAPTAIN JOHN REED'S COMPANY. (a.)

A list of Captain John Reed's company, on the march to the Jerseys, July 24th, 1776.

Privates.

Allison, David.
Bell, Andrew.
Bell, Arthur.
Bell, George.
Berryhill, Andrew.
Black, James.
Brinzen, Daniel.
Burges, Erid.
Cavet, Andrew.
Chambers, Elijah.
Chambers, James.
Chambers, Robert.
Cochran, George.
Colgan, Edward.
Johnston, William.
Jones, William.
Leard, John.
Martain, Nicholas.
Macky, William.
McClure, William.
McCoy, Charles.
McKinny, Henry.
McMullen, William.
Means, Adam.
Miller, George.
Moegy, John.
Montgomery, Hugh.
Murrey, Barney.
Crage, Aaron.
Christy, John.
Dicky, William.
Elder, John.
Fareman, James.
Forster, Thomas.
Frickaber, John.
Galcrist, Matthew.
Goldenberg, John.
Graham, Michael.
Gray, Robert.
Heater, George.
Higgins, Thomas.
Hutcheson, Samuel.
Neece, Peter.
Reed, Hugh.
Ritter, Adam.
Robertson, James.
Shearer, Samuel.
Shields, Barnard.
Steen, Andrew.
Sturgeon, Jeremiah.
Sturgeon, Peter.
Taylor, Samuel.
Toot, Conrad.
Walker, William.
Wiggins, James.

MEMORANDUM OF THE DAMAGE OF CAPT'N JOHN REED'S COMP'Y OF FLYING CAMP FROM LANCASTER COUNTY, COMMANDED BY COLO. JAS. CUNINGHAM. (a.)

Men's Names.	When lost.	Where lost.	Blankets.	Appraisement.			Guns.	Appraisement.			Horns and Pouches.	Appraisement.		
				£	s	d		£	s	d		£	s	d
Cap. John Reed,	27 Aug.	Long Island,	1	0	15	0								
Lieut. James Collier,	27 Aug.	Long Island,	1	1	2	6								
Edward Colkan,	27 Aug.	Long Island,	1	.	2	6								
Adam Riter,	27 Aug.	Long Island,	1	0	15	6								
Hugh Reed,	27 Aug.	Long Island,	1	1	2	6								
James Fairman,	27 Aug.	Long Island,	1	1	2	6								
Andrew Stephen,	27 Aug.	Long Island,	1	1	0	0								
Conrod Soot,	27 Aug.	Long Island,	1	0	12	0								
William Jones,	27 Aug.	Long Island,	1	0	13	0								
William McMullan,	27 Aug.	Long Island,	1	1	0	0								
Michael Grahmes,	27 Aug.	Long Island,	1	1	2	6								
William Johnston,	27 Aug.	Long Island,	1	1										
John Laird,	27 Aug.		1	0	15	6								
Henry McKenney,	27 Aug.		1	1	2	9								
Charles McCoy,	27 Aug.		1	1	3	6								
Andrew Bell,	27 Aug.		1	0	18	0								
James Chambers,	27 Aug.		1	1	2	6				0	1		10	[illegible]

MEMORANDUM OF THE DAMAGE OF CAPT'N JOHN REED'S COMPY.—Continued.

Men's Names.	When lost.	Where lost.	Blankets.	Appraisement. £	s	d	Guns.	Appraisement. £	s	d	Horns and Pouches.	Appraisement. £	s	d
Andrew Cavet, pd.,	27 Aug.	....	1	0	18	0		3	15	0	1	0	10	0
Thomas Higgans,	27 Aug	....	1	1	2	6		4	2	0	1	0	10	0
Daniel Brunson,	27 Aug	....	1	......	......	......		3	0	0	1	0	10	0
David Allison,	27 Aug.	....	1	0	18	0		3	0		1	0	10	0
Aaron Creag,	27 Aug.	....	1	1	2	6					1	0	10	0
John Elder,	27 Aug.	....	1	0	18	6		4	10	0	1	0	10	0
Samuel Taylor,	27 Aug	....	1	0	18	6								
James Collier,	27 Aug.	Frog's Point, ..	1	1	10	0								

Robert Gray,	18 Oct.	White Plains,				1	2	10	0					
Henry McKenny,	16 Oct.	White Plains,				1	5	0	0					
			30	15	0		43	7	0			2	10	0
			43	7	0									
			2	10	0									
			77	12	0									

N. B. The gun set down to Daniel Brunson was the property of Philip Fisher.
A True Copy taken from the Original. Certified by us the 19th October, 1778.

MAX. CHAMBERS,
JOSEPH HUTCHISON.

CAPTAIN RICHARD MANNING'S COMPANY. (a.)

[This company was raised in Upper Paxtang and Hanover.]

A true return of Capt. Richard Manning's of the Fourth Battalion of Lancaster county, commanded by James Burd, Esq., March 13, 1776.

Captain.

Richard Manning.

First Lieutenant.

Thomas Forster.

Second Lieutenant.

Samuel Martin.

Ensign.

Elijah Burke.

Privates.

Armstrong, Robert.
Ayres, John.
Ayres William.
Bonnel, John.
Cain, Charles.
Cain, Neal.
Clemens, Samuel.
Crague, Aaron.
Forster, James.
Forster, William.
Foulks, William.
Goudy, John.
Hulings, Thomas.
Higgins, John.
Jones, Hugh.
Leech, William.
Martin, Alexander.
McCord, Robert.
McCreight, James.
McMullen, John.
McMullen, William.
Reynolds, Alexander.
Parker, Moses.
Shields, Bernard.
Smith, John.
Stover, Michael.
Troster, Stephen.

CAPTAIN ALBRIGHT DEIBLER'S COMPANY. (a.)

[The company of Capt. Deibler was in active service for nearly a year, returning home in January, 1777. A portion of the command was captured at the battle of Long Island, and were not released from captivity until the year 1778. During that and the following year, the company was commanded by Capt. John Hoffman, and under him they were on the frontiers, protecting the defenceless inhabitants from the encroachments of the Indians and Tories who had their headquarters in southern New York, and against whom Gen. Sullivan's army was successfully sent in 1779.]

A true return of Capt. Albright Deibler's company of Associators of the Fourth Battalion, commanded by Col. James Burd, Esq., March 14, 1776.

Captain.
Albright Deibler.

First Lieutenant.
John Hoffman.

Second Lieutenant.
Martin Weaver.

Ensign.
Abraham Neighbour.

Privates.

Bretz, Lodwick.
Chesley, Christian.
Chesley, Jacob.
Chesley, John.
Cline, William, Sr.
Cline, William, Jr.
Clinger, Philip.
Conway, Francis.
Deibler, Matthias.
Deibler, Michael.
Fonderback, Henry.
Harman, Jacob.
Harman, Daniel.
Hoffman, John Nicholas.
Jury, Samuel.
Keadley (Keayler), Michael.
Keller, Jacob.
Kench, John.
Larue, Francis.
Lark, Stophel.

Meetz, Bastian.
Meetz, Jacob.
Meetz, Peter.
Minich, George.
Motter, John.
Neevling, Jacob.
Normier, Henry.
Reigel, George.
Rousculp, Philip.
Salladay, Michael.
Shots, Jacob.
Smith, Peter.
Snider, Leonard.
Snokes, Christly.
Steever, Leonard.
Stonebreaker, Bastian.
Work, Adam.
Wolf, Adam.
Wolf, Henry.
Yeager, Andrew.
Yeager, Matthew.

CAPTAIN JOSEPH SHERER'S COMPANY. (a.)

[The captain of the company following was Joseph Sherer, whose farm adjoined Col. Burd's, near Highspire. It was in active service during the whole of the spring and summer campaign of 1776, and a number of the men were wounded in a skirmish with a party of British cavalry near Amboy, N. J.]

A true return of Capt. Joseph Sherer's company of the Fourth Battalion of Lancaster county, commanded by Col. James Burd, Esq., March 25, 1776.

Captain.
Joseph Sherer.

First Lieutenant.
James Collier.

Second Lieutenant.
Samuel Rutherford.

Ensign.
Samuel Hutchinson.

Sergeants.

Larue, Henry.
Sherer, Samuel.
McClure, Richard.
McKinney, Henry.

Privates.

Alleman, John.
Bowl, Michael.
Bowman, John.
Brown, Benjamin.
Boyd, Samuel.
Brunson, Barefoot.
Brunson, William.
Brunson, Danile.
Carson, George.
Chambers, Maxwell.
Chambers, Robert.
Coulter, John.
Dimsey, John.
Finney, John.
McClure, Alexander.
McClure, Rowan.
McClure, William.
McCord, James.
McCoy, Charles.
McFadding, Samuel.
McKinney, James.
McKinney, John.
McKinney, Matthew.
McPhilip, Hugh.
Means, Adam.
Means, James.
Means, John.
Morrison, Roger.
Murray, William.
Reed, Hugh.
Rennick, Thomas.
Fulton, Richard.
Gilmor, John.
Gray, George.
Gray, John.
Gray, Joseph.
Gray, Robert.
Harbison, Adam.
Hutchinson, Joseph.
Kerr, William.
Larue, George.
Mayes, Thomas.
Mahon, James.
Mahon, John.
McClure, Andrew.
Roan, Stewart.
Rutherford, James.
Rutherford, John.
Sheets, Leonard.
Sherer, John.
Smith, Joseph.
Smith, William.
Sterrett, Robert.
Steel, John.
Stewart, John.
Stuart, William.
Thome, James.
Wilson, Sr., John.
Wilson, Jr., John.
Wilson, John.
Wolf, Michael.
Wylie, Samuel.

CAPTAIN JACOB FRIDLEY'S COMPANY. (a.)

[This company was raised in the neighborhood of Hummelstown, and served in the campaign of 1776, and were present at Trenton and Princeton. The minutes of this association are as follows:

"May 25, 1776. This is to certify that we, the associators of Derry township, in Lancaster county, Province of Pennsylvania, in the Fourth Battalion, commanded by James Burd, Colonel, do bind ourselves in all the rules and regulations made by the honorable Congress for the militia of this Commonwealth.

"Derry township, May 25, 1776. We, the undersigned are willing to serve in the Fourth Battalion, commanded by Col. James Burd, agreeable to order of Congress, and agree to serve until the first day of November, 1776, in the land service of the country in favor of the flag of liberty.

"FREDERICK HUMMEL,
"ALEXANDER MONTGOMERY,
"DAVID HUMMEL,
"PHILIP BLESSING,
"PHILIP FISHBURN,
"HENRY MILLER,
"NICHOLAS ZIMMERMAN,
"SAMUEL RAMSEY,
"PETER GROVE,
"MATTHIAS HOOVER,
"JOHN McFARLAND,
GEORGE LAUER,
THOMAS ROWLAND."]

A true return of Capt. Jacob Fridley's company of the Fourth Battalion of Lancaster county, commanded by Col. James Burd, Esq., May 27, 1776.

Captain.

Jacob Fridley.

First Lieutenant.

John McFarland.

Second Lieutenant.

Matthias Hoover.

Ensign.

Philip Blessing.

Privates.

Becker, Jacob.
Bell, Samuel.
Brewster, Charles.
Byers, John.
Chambers, Rowland.
Currey, James.
Derry, Jacob.
Dunbar, John.

Ernest, Stophel.
Fishburn, Peter.
Fishburn, Philip.
Fridley, Bernard.
Fridley, Peter.
Harris, Jacob.
Hummel, Frederick.
Hummel, Valentine.
Kecker, Philip.
Kisner, Jacob.
Krosklos, Peter.
Laird, John.
Laird, William.
Lauér, George.
Miller, Henry.
Montgomery, Alexander.
Rouse, Martin.
Rowland, Thomas.
Shad, Lodwick.
Spidel, Jacob.
Spidel, Michael.
Spidel, Maxwell.
Suitle, Joney.
Wetherhold, John.
Wilson, William.
Zimmerman, Nicholas.

AN APPRAISEMENT OF ARMS, BLANKETS & ACCOUTREMENTS. LOST IN ACTUAL SERVICE BELONGING TO THE FOURTH BATTALION OF LANCASTER COUNTY MILITIA, COMMANDED BY COL. JAMES BURD. BELONGING TO CAPTAIN COWDEN'S COMPANY. (a.)

	Guns.	Pouches and horns.	Blankets.	Napsacks.
	£ s d	£ s d	£ s d	£ s d
John Rutherford,	5 0 0	6	1 0	3 4
Col. James Burd,	3 15 0	12 6		
John Steel (Weaver),	4 10 0	6 6	15	
John Agheny,	2 5 0			
Zachariah Stephen,	.....	.....	1 4 0	3 6
John Arm,	2 15 0			
John Nidick,	2 5 0			
Hugh Stephen,	.....	.....	1 4 0	
William Hadden, pd.,	4 10			
Col. James Burd,	4 0 0			
Col. James Burd,	3 0 0			
Robert Elder in right of Christian Sharts,	5 10 0			
Adam Hamaker,	3 7 6			
Frederick Castle,	4 15 0			
John Stuart,	.....	3 6	1 2 6	11 6
Christian Sharts,	3 10 0			
Christian Sharts,	3 0 0			
Charles Stuart, pd.,	2 10 0	.....	1 0	
Derick Jones,	.....	7 6	.....	5
Samuel Taylor,	.....	3		
Thomas Renick,	3 10 0			
Jacob Kesinger,	.....	.....	1 2 6	
John Laird,	3 5 0			
William Gillespie,	.....	pd.	1 5 0	
Peter Smith,	4 10 0			
Christian Gross,	5 10 0	4 6	.....	11
William Kirkpatrick,	.....	9	18	4
Guns,	70 7 6	3 12 0	9 17 0	1 16 6
Pouches & horns,	3 12 0			
Blankets,	9 17 0			
Napsacks,	1 16 6			
Total,	85 13 0			

The above is a true Copy taken from the Original Appraisement Bill of Capt'n Cowden's Comp'y, is Certified by us the Appraisors.

JAMES THOM,
HUGH STEPHEN.

I Do hereby Certify that the Losses herein Mentioned were sustained on the 16th Nov'r, 1776, at the Reduction of Fort Washington. Given under my hand this 8th Day of August, 1777.

JAS. COWDEN, Capt.

BELONGING TO CAPTAIN MURRAY'S COMPANY. (a.)

	Guns.			Pouches and horns.			Blankets.			Napsacks.		
	£	s	d	£	s	d	£	s	d	£	s	d
John Kisbler,	5	0	0		7	6	1	5	0			
Samuel Orum,	2	0	0		4							
Adam Verts in right of Michael Saliday,	3	10	0		7	6	1	5	0			
John Kistner,	2	10	0									
Peter Bobb,	2	0	0									
Lieut. William Bell,	5	10	0				1	5	0		2	6
James Munteeth,	....			....			1	5	0		2	6
John Forster,	3		0									
Sebas. Stonebrecker,	5	5	0		5							
Albright Diveler,	5	5	0		7	6						
Adam Wagner,	5	10	0		10		....				6	
Lieut. William Bell,	3	10	0									
James Woodside,	2	10	0									
Ludwick Bretz,	4	15	0									
Jacob Niveling,	2	15	5	....				10			2	6
William Rither,	4	0	0		9		1	0	0		2	
Jost Stover,	5	0	0		2		....				2	4
Jacob Shots,	5	5	0									
Christian Snoak,	3	0	0		4		....				2	
Capt. James Murray,	3	0	0									
William Glover,	2	0	0									
Adam Verts,	2	0	0									
Widow Diveler, to repair of George Cooper's gun,		6	0									
Hugh Stuart,	....				2							
John Gallagher,	....				2							
Widow Shell,	....				2							
John Pottomer,	....				1	6						
John Caldwell,	....				2							
Barney Shoop,	....				1							
John Caldwell,	....				1							
James McCord,	....				1	6						
*Thomas Mayes,	....				3							
John Neil,	....				1	6						
James Cowden,	....				2	6						

*pd. J. Dickey, £3 10.

BELONGING TO CAPTAIN MURRAY'S COMPANY.—Continued. (a.)

	Guns.			Pouches and horns.			Blankets.			Napsacks.		
	£	s	d	£	s	d	£	s	d	£	s	d
John Pottomer,	.....				2							
Jacob Eyeman,	.....				1							
John Kisinger,	.....				1	6						
Samuel Rutherford,	.....				2							
William Bell,	.....				1	6						
Robert Elder,	.....				1	6						
Michael Bowles,	.....				1	6						
Samuel Rutherford,	.....				3	6						
Capt. Murray, for repairs as per order,	1	12	3									
George Wagner,	.....				12							
John Stuart,	.....			.....			0	18	0			
William Mullan,	.....			.....			1	5	0			
John Wilson, Jr., repairs,		2	9									
Jacob Poorman,	5		0									
Peter Swagert,	.....			.....			0	18	0			
Robert Elder,	.....				12	6	.....				7	6
George Fockler,	3	0	0									
Guns,	90	11	0	6	4	6	9	11	0	1	9	6
Pouches & horns,	6	4	6									
Blankets,	9	11	0									
Napsacks,	1	9	6									
Total,	107	16	0									

CAPT. REED'S COMPANY. LOSSES OMITTED IN COL. CUNINGHAM'S DRAUGHT.

	Guns.	Pouches and horns.	Blankets.	Napsacks.
Andrew Cavet, for gun repairs,	0 15 0			
Capt. Fred. Hummel, to repairs besides Moulds, Thimble & Screw,	1 2 6			
Robert Chambers,	....	....	2 10 0	
John Backestow,	....	0 12 6		
Thomas McArthur,	....	1 6		
Widow Shell,	3 5 0			
Thomas Sturgeon,	2 10 0	0 12 0	1 10 0	
Guns,	7 12 6	1 6 0	4 0 0	
Pouches & horns,	1 6 0			
Blankets,	4 0 0			
Total,	12 18 6			
Brought forward,	107 16 0			
Brought over,	85 13 0			
Sharts' acct.,	7 16 6			
	3 12 6			
	217 16 6			

I Do hereby Certify that the Losses herein mentioned were sustained during the Time I belonged to Capt'n Reed's Company at the Retreat from long Island & the white plain. Given under my hand this 8th Day of August, 1777.

JAS. COLLIER, 1st Lieut.

Aug't 25th, 1777. Then Rec'd of Joshua Elder the Counter part of this in order to Receive the Money in Philad'a.

PETER SHIELDS.

The above is a true Copy taken from the original appraisement Bill of Capt'n Reed's Comp'y is Certified by us the appraisors.

JAS. THOM,
HUGH STEPHEN.

The within Transaction were during the Time I Commanded the Fourth Battalion of Militia of Lancaster County, and the Bearer Mr. Jashua Elder will receive the Money & pay the same to the Different Persons of the Battalion to whom it is due. Witness my hand this 30th Day of May, 1777.

JAMES BURD.

A true Copy.

The Within Bills are true Copies taken from the Original. Is Certifyed the 19th Oct'r, 1778, by us.

MAX'LL CHAMBERS,
JOSEPH HUTCHISON.

CAPTAIN WILLIAM BELL'S COMPANY. (a.)

A just and true return of the Associators of Capt. William Bell's company of the Fourth Battalion of Lancaster county, commanded by Col. James Burd, 1776.

Captain.
William Bell.

First Lieutenant.
Andrew Stuart.

Second Lieutenant.
Conrad Jontz.

Ensign.
Samuel Simpson.

Privates.

Albright, George.
Bell, Andrew.
Bell, Arthur.
Berryhill,* Alexander.
Boggs, James.
Burk, James.
Carson, William.
Chambers, David.
Clark, Robert.
Cline, John.
Cogley, Robert.
Cowden, William.
Davis, Stephen.
Dickey, John.

Dickey, William.
Diffenbaugh, George.
Dunlap, John.
Elder, John.
Elder, John, Jr.
Elder, Robert.
Elder, Robert, Jr.
Elder, Joshua.
Erwin, Alexander.
Forster, John.
Garber, John.
Gillespie, John.
Gillespie, William.
Glover, William.
Golaher, John.
Harris, John.
Heany, Patrick.
Johnston, James.
Laikey, John.
McLaughlin, James.
McFadden, Alexander.
Martin, Samuel.
Matthews, John.
Miller, Thomas.
Miller, George.
Montgomery, David.
Montgomery, Hugh.
Montgomery, Hugh, Jr.
Monteith, James.
Moore, John.
Nase, Jacob.
Nicholson, Thomas.
Pingerton, James.
Porter, Alexander.
Postlewait, John.
Reneger, George.
Richards, Aquila.
Robertson, James.
Scott, Patrick.
Simon, George.
Simpson, Joseph.
Simpson, Thomas.
Simpson, Nathaniel.
Simpson, Samuel.
Smyth, Samuel.
Smyth, Joseph.
Smyth, Stophel.
Snider, Felty.
Spangler, Felty.
Stuart, Charles.
Sturgeon, Jeremiah.
Sturgeon, Jeremiah, Jr.
Wagoner, Adam.
Walker, James.
Walker, James, Jr.
Walker, William.
Wallace, James.
Whitehill, John.
Whitely, Michael.
Whitely, Michael, Jr.
Wiser, Jacob.

CAPTAIN JOHN RUTHERFORD'S COMPANY. (a.)

Return of Captain John Rutherford's company of the Fourth battalion, Colonel Robert Elder, as it stood at Middletown, August 12, 1777, on its march to Philadelphia.

Captain.
John Rutherford.

Lieutenant.
Jonathan McClure.

Ensign.

Samuel Sherer.

Sergeants.

John Graham. **Elisha Chambers.**
Benjamin Jones. **Philip Newhouse.**

Corporals.

John Swineford. **Adam Ritter.**
Jacob Weiser. **Jacob Miller.**

Drummer.

George Swineford.

Privates.

Allison, Richard.
Barnett, Samuel.
Bell, John.
Boyd, William.
Castle, Frederick.
Cochran, James.
Cochran, Samuel, Sr.
Cochran, Samuel, Jr.
Conway, Francis.
Dougherty, Dennis.
Galey, James.
Grogan, Charles.
Herron, Robert.
Hogan, William.
Kennedy, Dr. Robert.
Light, Ludwig.
Little, John.
McAllister, Tobias.
McCord, James.
McWhorter, Robert.
Miller, John.
Morrison, James.
Neighbour, Abraham.
Packer, Jesse.
Pancake, George.
Pancake, Peter.
Raredon, Simon.
Sheattel, Michael.
Steever, Michael.
Smith, John.
Woodside, John.

(Joined the company September, 1777.)

Cisler, Samuel.
Snyder, Leonard.
Swinefold, Albright.
Yeager, Andrew.

A REPORT OF THE FOURTH BATTALION OF LANCASTER COUNTY MILITIA COMMANDED BY COL. ROBERT ELDER. (c.)

Field Officers,	Robert Elder, Col., James Cowden, Lieut. Col., Stephen Forster, Major,	Sergt. Major. Q. M. Sergt.
Staff Officers,	Benjamin McKinzie, George McMillen,	Drum Maj. Fife Maj.

No.	Capt.	1st Lieut.
1st Compy,	Jas. Murray,	Go. Cochran.
2d Compy,	Jas. Collier,	Henry McKenny.
3d Compy,	Jno. Rutherford,	Thos. McArthur.
4th Compy,	Jas. Crouch,	Jonathan McClure.
5th Compy,	Jas. Clark,	M. Johnson.
6th Compy,	Martin Weavr,	Philip Newpecker.
7th Compy,	Mhl. Whitley,	Andw. Stewart.
8th Compy,	John Gilchrist,	Wm. Swan.

A REPORT OF THE FOURTH BATTALION OF LANCASTER COUNTY MILITIA COMMANDED BY COL. ROBERT ELDER—Continued.

2d Lieut.	Ensigns.	Serj.	Corp.	Court Mar. Men.	Rank & File.	No. in each class.
Geo. Bell,	Peter Sturgeon,	4	4	Saml. Cochran,	54	8
				John Bell.		
Saml. Hutchinson,	Saml. Shearer,	4	4	Alexr. McClure,	74	10
Wm. Montgomery,	Robt. Gray,	4	4	Wm. McClure,	56	8
				Thos. Bell.		
Fred. Hubly,	Danl. Dowdle,	4	4	John Steel,	99	10
				Abram Der.		
Geo. Clark,	Elisha Chambers,	4	4		52	8
Philip Rausculp,	John Scheesley,	4	4	Ludwick Brats,	48	6
				Stephen Bend.		
Jno. Dickey,	Jos. Simpson,	4	4	John Gallagher,	60	8
				John Moore.		
Mat. Gilchrist,	Andw. Berryhill,	4	4		46	7
		32	32		409	

Commissions dated first of July 1777.

ROBT. ELDER, Col.

Recd. 25th of August of Colonel Timothy Matlack the Commissions for the officers of the within return.

Commissions awanting for the fourth Battalion Lancaster County Melitia commanded by Col. Robt. Elder.

Benjamin McKinzie, Aujutant.
George McMillen, Qurtr. Mastr.
Andw. Berryhill, Ensign, 8th Compy.

Certifyd by Bartrem Galbraith, Lieut.
Lancaster County.

Lancr. 25th Oct. 1777.

1777. October 25th Recd. of Timothy Matlack Esqr. the commissions agreeable to this certificate.

ROBT. ELDER, Col.

OFFICERS FOURTH BATTALION—1777.(a.)

Colonel.
Robert Elder.

Lieutenant Colonel.
James Cowden.

Major.
Stephen Forster.

Adjutant.
Benjamin McKinzie.

Quarter Master.
George McMillen.

First Company.

Captain—James Murray.
First Lieutenant—George Cochran.
Second Lieutenant—George Bell.
Ensign—Peter Sturgeon.

Second Company.

Captain—James Collier.
First Lieutenant—Henry McKen.
Second Lieutenant—Samuel Hutchinson.
Ensign—Samuel Shearer.

Third Company.

Captain—John Rutherford.
First Lieutenant—Thomas McArthur.
Second Lieutenant—William Montgomery.
Ensign—Robert Gray.

Fourth Company.

Captain—James Crouch.
First Lieutenant—Jonathan McClure.
Second Lieutenant—Frederick Hubley.
Ensign—Daniel Dowdle.

Fifth Company.

Captain— James Clark.
First Lieutenant—William Johnson.
Second Lieutenant—George Clark.
Ensign—Elisha Chambers.

Sixth Company.

Captain—Martin Weaver.
First Lieutenant—Philip Newbecker.
Second Lieutenant—Philip Rausculp.
Ensign—John Scheesley.

Seventh Company.

Captain—Michael Whitley.
First Lieutenant—Andrew Stewart.
Second Lieutenant—John Dickey.
Ensign—Joseph Simpson.

Eighth Company.

Captain—John Gilchrist.
First Lieutenant—William Swan.
Second Lieutenant—Mat. Gilchrist.
Ensign—Andrew Berryhill.

Court-Martial Men.

First—Samuel Cochran, John Bell.
Second—Alexander McClure.
Third—William McClure, Thomas Bell.
Fourth—John Steel, Adam Der.
Sixth—Ludwick Brets, Stephen Bender.
Seventh—John Gallagher, John Moore.

(c.) February 2d 1782. These to Certify that Mathew Montgomery Belonging to the first Class of my Company Served a tower of Duty under Capt. Robert McKen in the Year 1777 the first class being Call'd the second time in the Year 1778 the Said Mathew Montgomery was then Engaged in the Boat service against the Indians in the New Purchase.

Certifyed by......................David McQueen, Capt.

(c.) I Do hereby Certify that the Bearer hereof George Wolf of the fourth Betalyon a private has mustered in the yeares 1777, 1778 under Captain Ludwick Myer and Likewise in the year 1779 under Captain Jacob Writtelinger & me James Jackson Ensign.

May the 3d 1781.

A RETURN OF THE FIRST CLASS OF THE FOURTH BATTALION THAT SERVED THEIR TOWER OF DUTY AT LANCASTER 15H APRIL 1778. (c.)

Captain.

James Murray.

Lieutenant.

Henry McKinney.

Privates of the first compy.

George Johnston. John Bell.

Second Compy.

Allexr. McClure. Joseph Hucheson for the year 77.

Third Compy.

Wm. Lochrey. Wm. Stewart.

Fourth Compy.

Adam Miller.
Christian Shertz.
Mark Snider.
Jacob Hetter for the year 1777.
George Mitsher for the year 1777.
John Parks for the year 1777.
Henry Harris.

Fifth Class.

James Black.
John Elder.
John Gillson for the year 1777.

Sixth Compy.

Daniel Conn.

Seventh Compy.

Alexr. Heatherington.

Eighth Compy.

Wm. Rowling.

A RETURN OF CAPT. JAS. CLARK COMPY. OF THE FIFTH CLASS OF THE FOURTH BATT'N LANCASTER COUNTY MILITIA COMMANDED BY ROBT. ELDER, MAY 20TH, 1778. (c.)

Captain.

James Clerk.

1st Lieut.

Wm. Johnston.

2d Lieut.

George Clark.

Ensn.

Elisha Chambers.

Serjants.

Allexr. Taylor.
Henry Leek.
George Simmons.
Robt. Kennedy.

Corporals.

John Kays.
Michael Herring.
John Goldenberry.
Herman Leek.

Clerk.

Saml. Taylor.

Court Marsl. Men.

Thomas Orom.
George Taylor.

1st Class.

Isaac Jones.
John Elder.
William Kinough.
Joseph McElwraith.
Liedwick Shellman.
Thomas Black.
John Swaigart.

2nd Class.

Robt. George.
Valentine Prough.
Joseph Little.
Isaiah Jones.
Andrew Richeson.
John Chambers.
Aaron Pecker.

3rd Class.

Jacob Neese.	Patrick Martin.
James McCall.	Archibald Murray.
Malabla Powel.	John Mellon.
Jacob Stricker.	

4th Class.

John Kinter.	John Gillson.
Jas. Buchanan.	Samuel Oram.
Allexr. George.	

5th Class.

George Wagoner.	John McElhaney.
Peter Swaigart.	James Black.
John Gillmore.	Mathew Taylor.

6th Class.

John Butler.	Allexr. George.
Allexr. Speer.	Saml. Oram.
James Speer.	John Gillsom.
Francis Connoway.	George Wagoner.
James Bohonan.	George Simmers.

7th Class.

Peter Swaigart.	George Taylor.
John Gilmore.	George Simmons.
James Black.	Michl. Herring.

A RETURN OF THE SECOND, THIRD & FOURTH CLASS OF THE FOURTH BATT'N THAT SERV'D THEIR TOWER OF DUTY AT FORT MUNCEY IN NORTHUMBERLAND COUNTY JULY 22D 1778. (c.)

Capt.

James Collier.

1st Lieut.

Geo. Cochran.

Ensign.

Robt. Gray.

Capt. Murray's Comp'y.

Philip Tinturff.	Saml. Cochran.
Henry Hone.	John Bell, Junr.
Michael Stiver.	Patrick Lafferty.

Capt. Collier's Comp'y.

George Sample.	John Little.
Joseph Fulton.	William Murray.
Abraham Brunson.	John Means.
Peter Boal.	Thos. Strahan.

Capt. Rutherford's Comp'y.

Jas. Spence.

Capt. McClure's Comp'y.

Rob't Minchell.

Capt. Clark's Comp'y.

Elisha Chambers for Jno. Chambers.
Robert George.
Isaac Jones.

Capt. Weaver's Comp'y.

Peter Mitz.

Capt. Stewarts Comp'y.

John Parker.	John Grogan for Charlie.
Nathaniel Randolph.	Andrew Bell.

Capt. Gillchrist's Comp'y.

William McMillen.	James Muray.
Rob't Smith.	John Hogan for Wm. Hogan.
James Morrison.	

A RETURN OF CAPT. JOATHAN McCLURES COMP'Y OF THE FOURTH CLASS OF THE FOURTH BATTN LANCASTER COUNTY MILITIA COMMANDED BY COL. ROB'T. ELDER AUG'T 2D, 1778. (a.)

Captain.

'Jonathan McClure.

1st Lieutenant.

Fred'k Hubley.

2d Lieutenant.

Dowdle.

1st Class.

Henry Harris.
Martin Hemberley.
Henry Caldwell.
Fred'k Overlander.
Christian Shartz.
Adam Miller.
Mark Snider.
John Barnut.
Henry Stoner.
Simon Snider.

2nd Class.

Christian Spade.
John Kisinger.
Jacob Snider.
John Snider.
John Stitt.
Valintine Walker.
Conrad Toot.
Robt. M'Whorter.
James Harris.
Jacob Bargley.
John Heflick.
Rechart Bradrick.

3d Class.

Adam Ritter.
John Mitzher.
Conrad Wolfley.
Christian King.
Jacob Miller.

4th Class.

Philip Wirrick.
Abraham Tarr.
george Frey.
Christ'r Sebough.
Samuel Parke.
George Lowman.

William Walls.	Peter Florey.
Joseph Florey.	George Miller.
William McWhorter.	David McCashland.
Robt. Minshall.	

5th Class.

George Gross.	James Currey.
Samuel Seratchey.	Lawrance Smith.
Peter Richert.	Micl. Pisinger.
Jacob King.	Edward Brison.
John Miller.	

Sixth Class.

Nicholas Castle.	Philip Atley.
Jacob Hetter.	Philip Pattomer.
Abraham Gross.	Peter Shuster.
Henry McCann.	Henry Miller.
John Backestoe.	Henry Davis.
Philip Shocking.	Willm. Widner.

Seventh Class.

Philip Graft.	John Parks.
Valintine Wirrick.	John Lennig, Docr.
Simon Snider.	Abner Wikersham.
Thos. Crabb.	John King.
Peter Miller.	Thos. Toott.
Christr. Hepeck.	

Eighth Class.

George Mitzker.	John Snider.
Lodwick Hemberly.	Jacob Bowman.
John Myers.	David Toot, Junr.
Conrod Tarr.	Albright Skerr.
Fred'k Sebernick.	John Steel.
Michal Gross.	Amanwell Bullinger.
Patrick Scott.	

A RETURN OF CAPT. JAS. MURRAY'S COMPY. OF THE FIRST CLASS OF THE FOURTH BATTN. LANCASTER COUNTY MILITIA COMMANDED COLO. ROB'T. ELDER AUGUST 13TH 1778. (c.)

Captain.

James Murray.

Lt.

George Cochran.

2 Lt.

George Bell.

Ensn.

Jno. Ryan.

First Class.

Robt. McCord.
Wm. Bell.
Daniel M'Cay.
Jno. Clindinin.
Jas. Watts.
George Johnston.
Jas. Leonard.

Second Class.

Jno. Heirs.
Jno. Bell, Senr.
Laurence Hatton.
Rob't McGill.
Wm. Smith.
Jas. Veetch.
Patk. Lafferty.
Anthy. Hoone.
Jno. Linsey.

3d Class.

Micl. Stiver.
Jno. Barnett.
Saml. Polough.
Philip Tintirf.
Wm. Forster.
Saml. Cochran.
Jacob Kisner.

4th Class.

Jno. Bell.
Jacob Eyman.
Jno. Bollan.
Wm. Foulks.
Jno. Malone.

5th Class.

Jas. Forster.	Rob't. Armstrong.
Jno. Richmond.	Peter Duffey.
Henry Keller.	Wm. Bell.
Micl. Ryan.	Philip Newbecker.

6th Class.

John Simpson.	Jno. Cochran, Junr.
Henry McCloskey.	Wm. Boyce.
John Collogan.	Jas. Burney.
Joseph Collogan.	Wm. Murray.
John Thomas.	

7th Class.

Thos. Sturgon.	Christie Eyman.
Martin Newbaker.	Thos. Gallaher.
Jas. Bell.	Robt. Smith.
Thomas Kerns.	James Reed.

8th Class.

Allexr. Randels.	Robt. Boyce.
Jno. Brown, Junr.	John Fisher.
Abraham Mooney.	George Adm. Gardner.
John Bell.	John Haggins.
Willm. Glover.	

A RETURN OF THE FIFTH CLASS OF THE FOURTH BATTALION THAT SERVED THEIR TOWER OF DUTY AT LANCASTER 7H DECEMBER 1778.(c.)

Capt.

Jonathan McClure.

1st Lieut.

Philip Rouscalp.

2nd Lieut.

John Mathews.

Capt. Murray's Compy.

William Bell.
Robt. McGill.
Sam'l Polough.
Peter Sturgon.

Capt. Collier's Comp'y.

Wm. Wright.
Arthur Chambers, went down and was sent home.
Barefoot Brunson.
John Willson.

Capt. Rutherford's Comp'y.

Elijah Stewart.
Wm. McClure.
Jacob Limes.
George Carson.
Jacob Awl.
Fred'k Castle.
Saml. Brown.
John McGearey.

Capt. McClure's Comp'y.

Christian Spade.
John Kisinger.
Jacob Snider.
John Snider.
Felty Welker.
Conrod Toot.
Jacob Bargley.
Adam Ritter.
Jno. Mitsker.
Christian King.
Jacob Miller.
George Lowman.
Joseph Florey.
George Gross.
Jacob King.
John Miller.

Capt. Clark's Comp'y.

Thos. Oram.
Allex'r Taylor.
John Elder.
James McCall.
John Kinter.
Richard Allison.

Capt. Weaver's Comp'y.

John Philips.
Henry Werfell.
Lodwick Light.
Michl. Salondine.
Abraham Neighbour.
Anthoney Yeager.
Lenhard Stiver.
John Harmon.
George Lark.
Philip Philips.
George Menick.

Capt. Stewart's Comp'y.

Paul Randolph.
Georg Devibaugh.
[illegible]xr. Porter.
John Harris.
Nathl. Simpson.
Arthur Bell.

Capt. Gillchrist's Comp'y.

John Meider.
George Shupe.
John Fleming.
Jas. Boggs.
Andw. Cochran.
Robt. Ferrier.
James Caldwell.
Zacharias Stephen.
Wm. Willson.
Wm. McRoberts.
John Boyd.
Andw. Berryhill, Jr.
Samuel Barr.

A RETURN OF CAPT. JAS. COLLIER'S COMP'Y OF THE SECOND CLASS OF THE FOURTH BATTN LANCASTER COUNTY MILITIA COMMANDED BY COLO. ROB'T. ELDER DEC. 26, 1778. (c.)

Captain.

Jas. Collier.

Lt.

Henry McKinney.

2d Lt.

Saml. Hucheson.

Ensign.

Saml. Shearer.

First Class.

Henry Alliman.
Allexr. McClure.
Nicholas Alliman.
George Lerue.
Stophel Alliman.
Jacob Brand.
Jno. Roop.
Jas. Means.
Elias Neigley.

2d Class.

Christopher Roop.
Jacob Roop.
Barefoot Brunson.
John Mumma.
Wm. Murray.
Wm. Smith.
Gustavis Grimes.
John Means.
Lodwick Dagon.

3d Class.

Stophel Earnist.
James M'Cord.
George Consor.
Jno. Little.
Jno. Brand.
Conrad Alliman.
Mathias Winagle.
Abraham Brunson.
Wm. Steel.
Arthur Brisbon.

4th Class.

Jacob Kerr.
Abraham Neidick.
Stophel Poorman.
Jacob Fisher.
Jno. Showmaker.
Andw. M'Clure.
Rob't Boyde.
John Willson.
Peter Winderley.
Jno. Rennick.
Jno. Postlewaite.

5th Class.

John Bowman.
John Consor.
Christopher Temey.
Wm. Wright.
Christopher Alliman.
Henry Alliman.
Henry Fleckiner.
Saml. Wiley.
George Newley.
Mathew McKinney.
John McKinney.
Arthur Chambers.

6th Class.

Maxl. Chambers.
James Finney.
Jas. Thom.
Peter Sheilds.
John Shearer.
George Gray.
Adam Means.
John Alliman.
Nicholas Neigh.

7th Class.

Wm. M'Clure.
Michl. Woolf.
Charles McCoy.
Richard M'Clure.
Jacob Springer.
Wm. Kerr.
Joseph Smith.
Hugh Cuningham.
Joseph Fulton.
John Steel.
Joseph Hucheson.

8th Class.

Rob't Chambers.
Joseph Gray.
Mic'l Boall.
Rowan M'Clure.
James Mahon.
James McKinney.
James Rutherford.
Mic'l Shearer.
Rowland Chambers.
John Maxwell.
Francis Lerue.

A RETURN OF CAPT. JNO. RUTHERFORD'S COMPY. OF THE THIRD CLASS OF THE FOURTH BATT. LANCASTER COUNTY MILITIA COMMANDED BY COL. ROBT. ELDER, DEC. 26TH, 1778. (c.)

Capt.

John Rutherford.

Lieut.

1st. Thos. McArthur.
2d. Wm. Montgomery.

Ensign.

Robert Gray.

Serjts.

Micl. Limes.
William Stewart.
James Spence.

Corpls.

John Dempsey.
Thos. Askin.
John Page.
John Miller.

Fifer.

George Smith.

Privates.

1st Class.

Richard Carson.
John Castle.
William Duncan.
William Lochrey.
Jacob Poorman.
John Buck.
John Miller, Sadler.
Hugh Robertson.

2d Class.

Abraham Eagley.
Peter Smith.
William McClure.

3d Class.

Martin Houser.
Jacob Miller, Junr.
Peter Pancake, Sr.
Jacob Limes.
George Sheets.
George Sample.
Jacob Snyder, Jun.
George Carson.
Joshua Elder, Esqr.

4th Class.

Jacob Awl.
Fredrick Castle.
George Dixson.
William Ingram.
Barnabas Shupe.
Michael Castle.
George Pile.
Adam Stong.

5th Class.

Valentine Baker.
Vandle Fockler.
Leonard Sheets.
Elijah Stewart.
Jacob Syder, Ser.
Adam Lampart.
John McGarey.
Saml. Brown.

6th Class.

Daniel Cooper.
John Gray.
Adam Kitsmiller.
Joseph Willson.
John Davis.
Peter Brenar.
Jacob Houser.

7th Class.

John Fritz.
George Page.
Jacob Beck.
Conrad Bobb.
David Richey.
Jacob Pile.
Stophel Shupe.
Jacob Smith.
John Donaley.
Valentine Pancake.
Gabriel Davis.

8th Class.

Joseph Shaw
Michael Shaver.
David Shaw.
Allexr. Willson.
Jno. Joy.
Jno. Sybourt.

A RETURN OF CAPT. JAMES MURRAYS COMPY. OF THE FIRST CLASS OF THE FOURTH BATTALION LANCASTER COUNTY MILITIA FOR THE YEAR 1778. (c.)

Capt.

James Murray.

Lieut.

1st. Geo. Cochran.
2d. Geo. Bell.

Ensign.

Peter Sturgeon.

Privates.

1. Willm. Ashcraft.
2. Robt. McCord.
3. Willm. Bell, Jur.
4. Dan. McCay.
5. John Clandining.
6. James Watts.
7. John Ayers.
8. John Bell, Senr.
9. Robt. McGill.
10. Laurance Hatton.
11. Willm. Smith.
12. James Veetch.
13. Patt. Lafferty.
14. Anthoney Hoone.
15. Philip Newbecker.
16. John Linsey.
17. Michl. Stiver.
18. John Barnet.
19. Saml. Plouge.
20. Philip Tintwiff.
21. Willm. forster.
22. Saml. Cochran.
23. Jacob Kesner.
24. John Bell.
25. Jacob Eyman.
26. John Bollan.
27. Willm. foulks.
28. John Malone.
29. James forster.
30. John Richmond.
31. Henry Kellar.
32. Michal Ryan.
33. Robt. Armstrong.
34. Peter Duffey.
35. Willm. Bell.
36. John Simpson.
37. Henry McCloskey.
38. John Colligan.
39. Joseph Colligan.
40. John Thomas.
41. John Cochran, Jur.
42. Willm. Boyce.
43. James Birney.
44. Willm. Murray.
45. Thos. Sturgeon.
46. Martin Newbecker.
47. James Bell.
48. Thos. Kerns.
49. Cristley Eyman.
50. Thos. Galachor.
51. Robt. Smith.
52. James Reed.
53. Alexdr. Randels.
54. John Brown, Jur.
55. Abraham Mooney.
56. John Bell, Jur.
57. John Ryan.
58. Willm. Glover.
59. Robt. Boyce.
60. John fisher.
61. Geo. Adam Gartner.
62. John Haggins.

Court Martial Men.

John Bell, Junr.

Saml. Cochran.

A RETURN OF CAPT. JAMES COLLIER'S COMP'Y OF THE SECOND CLASS OF THE FORTH BATTALION LANCASTER COUNTY MILITIA FOR THE YEAR 1778. (c.)

Captain.

Jam's Collier.

Lieutenants.

1st henry Mckenney. 2d Samul. Huchison.

Ensign.

Samul Serer.

1st Class.

Heney Aleman.
Alexander McCluer.
Nicoles Alleman.
George Lerue.
Stophel Alleman.
Jacob Brand.
John Roop.
Eleab Negly.

2d Class.

John Noop.
John Windrly.
Christopher Roop.
Berefoot Brunson.
John Mumma.
Will'm Murrey.
Will'm Smyth.
Gustoves Grahams.
John Means.
Ludeack Dagon.
Jacob Roop.

3d Class.

Stoppel Ernest.
James McCord.
Geoarge Consor.
John Little.
John Brand.
Conrad Allemon.
Mathies Winagel.
Abraham Brunson.
Will'm Stell.
Arthur Brysben.

4th Class.

Jacob Kerr.
Abraham Nedeck.
Stophel Poorman.
Jackob fisher.
John Shoumaker.
Anrew McCluer.
Robt. Boyd.
John Wilson.
Peetter Wondrly.
John Renweck.
John Boldright.

5th Class.

John Boman.	John Flacknor.
John Consor.	Samu'l Wyle.
Christopher Temey.	Geoorge Nevely.
Will'm Right.	Mathew Mckinney.
Christopher Alleman.	John Mckinney.
Henry Alleman.	Arthur Chembers.

6th Class.

Maxwell Chambers.	Geoorge Gray.
James Finny.	Adam Means.
James Thorn? (Thom)?.	John Alleman.
Petter Shecks.	Nicoles Nigh.
John Sherre.	

7th Class.

Will'm McClure.	Joseph Smyth.
Michel Woolf.	hugh Cunningham.
Charles McCoy.	Joseph Fulton.
Richard McClurr.	John Stell.
Jacob Springer.	Hugh Crocket.
Will'm Kerr.	Joseph huchison.

8th Class.

Robt. Chambers.	James Maglon.
Joseph Gray.	James McKenne.
Mechel Bool.	James Rutherford.
Petter Bool.	Rowland Chambrs.
John Means.	John Maxwell.
Rowan McCluwer.	Francis Lerue.

JAMES COLLIER, Capt.

A RETURN OF CAPT. JOHN RUTHERFORD'S COMP'Y OF THE THIRD CLASS OF THE FOURTH BATTALION LANCASTER COUNTY MILITIA FOR THE YEAR 1778. (c.)

Captain.

John Rutherford.

Lieut.

Thos. McArthur

2d Lt.

Wm. Montgomery.

Ensign.

Robt. Gray.

Serjts.

Michl. Limes.
Wm. Stewart.
Jas. Spence.

Corpls.

Jno. Dempsey.
Thos. Askin.
Jno. Page.
Jno. Miller.

Fifer.

George Smith.

1st Class.

Richard Carson.
Jno. Casle.
Wm. Duncan.
Wm. Lochrey.
Jacol Borman.
Jno. Buck.
Jno. Miller.
Hugh Robertson.

2d Class.

Abrah'm Eagly.
Peter Smith.
William McClure.

3d Class.

Martin Houser.
Jacob Miller.
Peter Pancake.
Jacob Limes.
George Sheets.
George Sample.
Jacob Syder.
George Carson.

4th Class.

Jos. Elder Esqr.
Jacob Awl.
Fred'k Casle.
George Dixson.
Wm. Ingram.
Barnabs Shupe.
Micl. Castle.
George Pile.
Adam Stong.

5th Class.

Valent. Baker.
Vandle Fockler.
Leonard Sheets.
Elijah Stewart.

Jacob Syder, Ser.
Adam Lampart.
Jno. McGarey.
Saml. Brown.

6th Class.

Danl. Cooper.
Jno. Gray.
Adm. Kitsmiller.
Josh Willson.

Jno. Davis.
Peter Brenar.
Jacob Houser.

7th Class.

Jno. Fritz.
Georg Page.
Jacob Beck.
Conrod Bob.
David Richey.
Jacob Pile.

Stophel Shupe.
Jacob Smith.
John Donaly.
Valent. Pancake.
Gabriel Davis.

8th Class.

Josh'h Shaw.
Mick'l Shaver.
David Shaw.
Allex'r Willson.
Jno. Sybourt.
Chrisly Page.
Jacob Millar.

Jacob Haldiman.
John Foy.
George Pancake.
Jas. Duncan.
Jas. Tagard.
John Wilson.

A RETURN OF CAPT. JONATHAN M'CLURE'S COMP'Y OF THE FOURTH CLASS OF THE FOURTH BATTALION LANCASTER COUNTY MILITIA FOR THE YEAR 1778.—(c.)

Captain.

Jonathan McClure.

1st Lt.

Fredk. Hubley.

2d Lt.

Daniel Dowdle

Ensn.

Dan'l Huffman.

First Class.

Henry Harris.
Martin Hemberly.
Henry Coldwell.
Fred'k Overlander.
Christian Shartz.
Adam Miller.
Mark Snider.
Simon Snider.
Jno. Barnutt.
Henry Stoner.

2d Class.

Christn. Spade.
Jno. Kissinger.
Jacob Snider.
Jno. Snider.
Jno. Stitt.
Valentine Walker.
Conrod Toot.
Rob't M'Whorter.
Jas. Harris.
Jacob Bargley.
Jno. Heflick.
Rickert Brodrick.

3d Class.

Adam Ritter.
John Mitsker.
Conrod Wolfley.
Christ'n King.
Jacob Miller.
Simon Rardon.
Thos. Reed.

4th Class.

Philip Wirrick.
Abraham Tarr.
George Frey.
Christ'n Sebaugh.
Saml. Parks.
George Lowman.
Will'm Walls.
Joseph Florey.
Wm. McWhorter.
Robt. Minshall.
Peter Florey.
George Millir.
David M'Cashland.

5th Class.

George Gross.
Samuel Searatzey.
Peter Rickert.
Jacob King.
John Miller.
Jas. Currey.
Laurene Smith.
Michael Pessinger.
Edward Brison.

6th Class.

Nicholas Castle.
Jacob Hetter.
Abraham Gross.
Henry M'Cann.
Jno. Backestoe.
Philip Shocking.

Philip Atley.
Philip Batemore.
Peter Shuster.
Henry Miller.
Henry Davis.
Wm. Widner.

7th Class.

Philip Grafft.
Vanetl. Wirrick.
Simon Snider, Wea'r.
Thos. Crall.
Peter Miller.
Christn. Hepeck.
Jno. Parks.
Doct'r Jno. Lenning.
Abner Wickersham.
Jno. King.
Thos. Foot.

8th Class.

George Mitsker.
Lodwick Hemberly.
Jno. Myers.
Conrod Tarr.
Fred'k Zebernick.
Michael Gross.
Christn. Gross.
Patrick Scott.
Jno. Snider, Potter.
Jacob Bowman.
David Toot, Junr.
Albright Skeer.
Jno. Steel.
Amanuel Bullinger.

JONATHAN McCLURE, Capt.

A RETURN OF CAPT. ANDW. STEWART'S COMP'Y OF THE SEVENTH CLASS OF THE FOURTH BATTALION LANCASTER COUNTY MILITIA COMMANDED BY COLO. ROB'T. ELDER. 1778. (c.)

Captain.

Andw. Stewart.

1st Lt.

Joseph Simpson.

2d Lt.

John Mathews.

Ensn.

John Whitehill.

First Class.

Felty Spangler.
Allexr. Hetherington.
Jacob Noss.
Nathl. Randolph.

Second Class.

James Cogley.
Paul Randolph.
Allexr. M'Cumpsey.
George Devibaugh.
George Fridley.
Fred'k Switzer

Third Class.

Chrisle Crawl.
Charles Grogan.
Thomas Miller.
Conrad Yauntz.
Allexr. Porter.

Fourth Class.

John Harris..
John Moore.
Peter Bobb.
Nathaniel Simpson.
John Parker.

Fifth Class.

John Hersha.
Abraham Brightfield.
Francis Yauntz.
John Gallaher.
Philip Fisher.
John Cogley.
Jas. Pinkerton.
Stophel Smith.

Sixth Class.

Allexr. McFadden.
Allexr. Berryhill.
Rob't Elder.
John Elder.
Wm. Kelso, Junr.
David Chambers.
Saml. Simpson, Sr.

7th Class.

Saml. Simpson, Jr.
Cornelius Cox.
John Cline.
James Johnston.
Wm. Carson.
Wm. Walker.
Robert Clark.
Adam Ekart.
Jas. Monteeth.
John Elder, Junr.

Eight Class.

David Montgomery.
Robert Cogley.
George Renniker.
Andw. Bell.
Patrick Heany.
Charles Stewart.
John Garber.
Wm. Kelso, Senr.

Arthur Bell.	Barney Fridley.
Jos. McKee.	Thos. Brynan.
Thos. More.	George Woods.
Robt. Fitzpatrick.	

A RETURN OF CAPT. JOHN GILLCHREEST'S COMP'Y EIGHT CLASS OF THE FOURTH BATTALION LANCASTER COUNTY MILITIA FOR THE YEAR 1778. (c.)

Captain.

John Gillchreest.

Lieutenants.

1st. Wm. Swan.	Math'w Gillchreest.

Ensign.

Andw. Berryhill.

Serjants.

Richard Swan.	Wm. McMillen.
Robt. Wiley.	John Grimes.

Court M. Men.

Robt. Gillchrist.	William Boyd.

First Class.

John McElheney.	Jacob Miller.
Robt. Smith.	John Meldor.

Second Class.

Andw. Smith.	John Kinsley.
George Shupe.	John Pottimore.
John Fleming.	Henry Achla.
David Patton, Jr.	

Third Class.

James Cochran.	Wm. Hogan.
Jas. Morrison.	Wm. Boyd.
Andw. Cochran.	Jno. Hatfield.

Fourth Class.

Robt. Ferrier.
Jas. Boggs.
Peter Shearer.
Jas. Caldwell.
Jas. McMillen.
Jas. Morrow.

Fifth Class.

Zachariah Stephen.
William Willson.
Will'm McRoberts.
Wm. Caldhoon.
John Boyd.
Andw. Berryhill, Jr.
Philip Jno. Burrows.
Saml. Barr.

Sixth Class.

James Finney.
Hugh Wray.
Jno. Cochran.
Jno. Hilton.
Abrm. Willson.
James Wiggens.
Thos. Gillchrist.
Saml. Martin.
Saml. Thomson.

Seventh Class.

Wm. Cochran.
Robt. Gillchrist.
David Caldwell.
Andw. Stephen.
Jas. Byers.
Robt. Douglas.

Eight Class.

Robt. Neel.
Jno. Miller.
John Murray.
Hugh Stephen.
Saml. Berryhill.
Edward Joice.
James Taylor.
James Cavet.
John Wright.

A RETURN OF CAPT. MARTIN WEAVERS COMPY. OF THE FOURTH BATTALION LANCASTER COUNTY MILITIA ROBT. ELDER COL. FOR THE YEAR 1778. (c.)

Capt.

Martin Weaver.

Lieut.

1st. Philip Rouscapt.
2d. John Cheesly.

Ens.

Daniel Steeber.

Serjts.

Jonathan Woodsides.
Mathias Divler.

Corpls.

John Matter.
George Radel.
Stophel Lerck.
Stophel Cheesley.

Privates.

1st Class.

Edward Willcocks.
John Philips.
Daniel Conn.
Jacob Cheesley.
Joseph Philips.
Fredrick Paul.
William Cline.

2d Class.

John Miller.
Henry Werfell.
Abraham Jura.
John Didey.
George Kilinger.
John Matter.

3d Class.

Philip Light.
Michl. Salendine.
Michl. Castle.
Abraham Neighbour.
Andw. Yeager.
Fredk. Bentz.
Leonard Snider.

4th Class.

John Hoffman.
Joseph Steeber.
Peter Mitz.
Detrick Stonbraker.
Adam Rubler.
George Divler.
George Shupe.

5th Class.

Francis Conaway.
Leonard Steeber.
John Hermon.
Henry Hains.
Robert Walker.
Henry Humbold.
Lodwick Shods.

6th Class.

Benjamin Buffington.
Peter Willer.
Jacob Bickel.
Jacob Hermon.
Henry normyer.
John Woodside.
Adam King.
John Wertz.

7th Class.

David Hermon.
Anthony Freely.
George Seel.
Adam Wertz.
Nicholes Hoffman.
George Menick.
Balstian Mitz.
Abraham Fishcr.
Henry Myer.

8th Class.

Michael Divler.
Henry Woolf.
Samuel Jura.
Christian Hoffman.
George Buffington.
Christian Wertz.
Philip Philips.

Court M. Men.

Lodowick Bretz.
Stephen Bentz.

(c.) I Do hereby certify that Micha Shuman of my Company did his tower of Duty in the year 1778 in the garreson of Lancaster pr me May the 10th 1781.

JOSEPH WRIGHT, Capt.

I do Certify that Peter Rummel a pravet of Capt. Wright's Company was out with a Waggon and Team when he was calld to march in the year 1778 pr me.

PAUL HAUSMAN.

CAPTAIN JOHN RUTHERFORD'S COMPANY. (a.)

Detachment under command of Captain John Rutherford, marched to Bedford county, April, 1779, for the protection of the inhabitants.

Captain.

John Rutherford.

Privates.

Capt. Murray's company.

John Cochran, Sr.
Michael Steever.
John Bunnel, 4th Sergt.
Samuel Pollock.
Philip Tinturff.
John Grames.
William Forster.
Samuel Cochran.

Capt. Collier's Company.

Stophel Earnest.
John Smith.
James McCord.
George Consor.
John Little.
John Brand.
Conrad Allcman.
Philip Newhouse.
Robert McWhortor.
Matthias Winagle.
Lodwick Dagon.
Abraham Brunson.

Capt. Rutherford's company.

Martin Houser.
Jacob Miller.
Peter Pancake.
George Pancake.
Barnabas Shoop.
Benjamin Jones
George Sheets.
Frederick Castle.
George Carson.
James Galley.

Capt. Crouch's company.

Adam Ritter.
John Minsker.
Conrad Wolfley.
Dr. Robert Kennedy.
Albright Swineford.
Christian King.
John Ritter.
Jacob Miller.
John Swineford.
George Segance.
Robert Harron.
George Williams.
Simon Rairdon.
Joseph Mark.

Capt. Clark's company.

Robert Kennedy.
Samuel Kisler.
Andrew Richardson.
Richard Allison.
John Chambers.
Jesse Packer.
Samuel Barnett.

Capt. Weaver's company.

Jonathan Woodside, Sergt.
Ludwick Light.
Frank Conway.
Lemuel Snyder.
Abraham Neighbour.
Andrew Yeager.
Michael Shattel.

Capt. Whitley's company.

Christian Crawl.
Jacob Weiser.
Charles Grogan.
Thomas Miller (sick).
William Gamble.
Conrad Yountz.
John Bell.
James Boyle.

Capt. Gilchrist's company.

James Cochran.
Samuel Cochran.
James Morrison.
William Boyd.
John Hatfield.
Dennis Dougherty.
William Hogan.

A RETURN OF CAPT. HENRY McKINNEY'S COMPY. OF THE 2D CLASS OF THE FOURTH BATTALION LANCASTER COUNTY MILITIA MAY 20TH, 1779. (c.)

Capt.

Henry McKinney.

Lt.

1st. Saml. Hucheson.
2d. Saml. Shearer.

Ensign.

Joseph Fulton.

Privates.

1st Class.

Henry Alleman.
Allexr. McClure.
Nicholas Alleman.
George Lerue.
Stophel Alleman.
Jacob Brand.
John Roop.
Ellial Neigley.
Jno. Knoop.
Robt. Caldwell.

2d Class.

John Winderley.
Christopher Roop.
Jacob Roop.
Barefoot Brunson.
John Mumma.
Wm. Murray.
Wm. Smith.
Gustavis Grimes.
Lodwick Dagon.

3d Class.

Stophel Earnish.
Jas. McCord.
George Consor.
Jno. Little.
Jno. Brand.
Conrad Alliman.
Mathias Winagle.
Abraham Brunson.
Wm. Steel.
Arthur Brisban.
Saml. Cochran.

4th Class.

Jacob Kerr. Andw. McClure.
Abraham Nidick. Hanteter Winderley.
Stephen Poorman. John Rennicks.
Jacob Fisher. John Postlewaite.
John Showmaker.

5th Class.

John Bowman. John Fleckiner.
John Consor. Samuel Wiley.
Christopher Temey. George Neveley.
William Wright. John McKinney.
Christopher Alleman. Arthur Chambers.
Henry Alleman.

6th Class.

Maxwell Chambers. John Alleman.
James Finney. Nicholas Neigh.
John Shearer. Peter Branard.
George Gray. Francis Lerue.
Adam Means.

7th Class.

Wm. McClure. Jugh Cunningham.
Michal Woolf. John Steel.
Richard McClure. Hugh Crocket.
Jacob Springer. Joseph Hucheson.
Wm. Kerr. John Fritz.
Joseph Smith. Felty Pancake.

8th Class.

Robt. Chambers. James McKinney.
Joseph Gray. Rowland Chambers.
Michael Boal. John Maxwell.
John Means. Conrad Buumback.
Rowan McClure. James Rutherford.
James Mahon .

A RETURN OF CAPT. MARTIN WEAVERS COMP'Y OF THE SIXTH CLASS OF THE FOURTH BATTN. LANCASTER COUNTY MILITIA, 4TH OCT. 1779. (c.)

Captain.

Martin Weaver.

1st Lieut.

Philip Rouscalp.

2nd Lieut.

John Cheesley.

Ensign.

Daniel Steeber.

Serjants.

Jonathan Woodsides.
Mathias Divler.

Corporals.

John Motter.
George Radle.
Stophel Cheisley.

1st Class.

Edward Wilcock.
John Phillips.
Jacob Cheesley.
Philip Philips.
Fredrick Paul.

2nd Class.

John Miller.
Henry Werfell.
Abraham Jura.
John Didy.
George Kilinger.
John Motter.

3d Class.

Michael Salendine.
Michael Shadle.
Leonard Snider.
Abraham Neighbour.
Andw. Yeager.
Fredrick Bentz.

4th Class.

John Huffman.
Joseph Steeber.
Peter Mitz.
Detrick Stonbraker.
Adam Ruber.
George Divler.
George Shupe.

5th Class.

Leonard Steeber.
John Hermon.
Henry Hains.
Michael Milecher.
Charles Bargar.
Henry Humholts.
Lodwick Shots.

6th Class.

Peter Willier.
Jacob Pickel.
Jacob Hermon.
Henry Normler.
John Woodsides.
Adam King.
John Wertz.

7th Class.

David Hermon.
Anthony Freeley.
George Seel.
Adam Wertz.
Nicholes Hoffman.
George Menick.
Sebastian Metz.
Henry Myer.

8th Class.

Michael Divler.
Henry Woolf.
Samuel Jura.
Christian Hoffman.
Joseph Philips.
George Buffington.
Christian Wertz.

Court M. Men.

Lodwick Bratz.
Stephen Bentz.

A RETURN OF CAPT. JONATHAN M'CLURE'S COMPY. OF THE FOURTH BATTN. OF LANCASTER COUNTY MILITIA AS THE STAND CLASSED OCTOBER 15TH 1779. (c.)

Captain.

Jonathan M'Clure.

1st Lieut.

Fredrick Hubley.

2nd Lieut.

Daniel Dondle.

Ensign.

Daniel Huffman.

1st Class.

Henrey Harris.
Fredrick Oberlander.
Mairtan Kemberly.
Christian Shartz.
Adam Miller.
Mark. Snider.
Henrey Stoner.
Daniel Coon.

2nd Class.

Christian Spade.
John Kissinger.
Jacob Snider.
John Snider.
John Stilt.
Valintin Walker.
Conrod Toot.
Robert McWartor.
James Harris.
Jacob Bargley.

3d Class.

Adam Ritter.
John Mitsker.
Conrod Wolfley.
Christan King.
George Snagance.
John Swinford.
Jacob Miller.
Simon Rardon.
Thomas Reed.
Robert Kennedy.
David M'Clure.
Henrey Moore.
Joseph Gregg.

4th Class.

Abraham Tarr.
Phillip Wirick.
George Frey.
Christopher Seabaugh.
Samuel Parks.
George Lowman.
William Walls.
Joseph Florey.
David M'Cashland.
George Miller.
Patrick Flannigan.
John Bowman.

5th Class.

George Gross.
Samuel Searatzey.
Petter Rekert.
Jacob King.
John Miller.
James Currey.
Larance Smith.
Micheal Pessinger.
Thomas Moore.
George Ammon.

6th Class.

Nicklous Castle.
Abraham Gross.
Henrey M'Cann.
Phillip Shoking.
John Backestos.
Phillip Atley.
Phillip Batamore.
Henrey Miller.
Petter Shuster.
Henrey Davis.
William Widner.
Robert Nailer.
Jacob Strikler.
John Holaback.
James Jackson.

7th Class.

Phillip Graft.
Valintin Wirick.
Thomas Crabb.
Petter Miller.
Christan Hepeck.
John Parks.
John Lenning.
John King.
Abner Wickersham.
Robert Watt.

8th Class.

George Mitsker.
Lodwick Hemberly.
John Mayers.
Conrod Tarr.
Fredrick Zebernick.
Micheal Gross.
Christan Gross.
Patrick Scoot.
John Snider.
David Toot.
Emanwell Bullinger.
Alexander Jameson.
William Crabb.

JONATHAN M'CLURE, Capt.

A RETURN OF CAPT. JAMES CLARKS COMPANY OF THE FIFTH CLASS OF THE FOURTH BATTALION LANCASTER COUNTY MILITIA, COMMANDED BY COL. ROBERT ELDER, 18TH OCT. 1779. (c.)

Capt.

James Clark.

Lieut.

1st. William Johnston. 2d. George Clark.

Ensign.

Elisha Chambers.

Serjeants.

1st. John Elder.
2d. Henry Leek.
3rd. George Selmons.
4th. Robert Kennedy.

Corpls.

1st. John Keys.
2d. Michael Herring.
3d. Hermon Leek.

Clerk.

Samuel Taylor.

Privates.

1st Class.

Isaac Jones.
William Henough.
Joseph McElwraith.
Ludwick Shelman.
John Swalgart.
James Black, Junr.
James Black.

2nd Class.

Robert George
Valentine Prough.
Joseph Little.
Isaiah Jones.
Andrew Ritchison.
John Chambers.
Adam Swalgard.
George McElyar.

3d Class.

Jacob Neese.
James McAll.
Malachia Powel.
Jacob Stricker.
Patrick Martin.
Archibald Muray.
John Mellon.
William Thomson.
Robert Boyd.

4th Class.

James Ireland.
James Speer.

5th Class.

William McComb.
Francis Conwey.

6th Class.

James Buchanan.
Alexander George.
Daniel Black.
Ritchard Gilmore.

7th Class.

John Gibson.
Samuel Oram.
George Waggoner.
Peter Swaigart.
John Gilmore.
Robert Crawford.
John Butler.

8th Class.

John McElheny.
James Black.
George McCandles.

Court Martial Men.

Thomas Oram.
George Taylor.

A RETURN OF CAPT. JAS. MURRAY'S COMPY. OF THE FIRST CLASS OF THE FOURTH BATTALION, LANCASTER COUNTY MELITIA OCT. 21ST, 1779. (c.)

Captain.

Jas. Murray.

1st Lieut.

Geo. Cochran.

2nd Lieut.

George Bell.

Ensign.

John Ryan.

1st Class.

Robt. McCord.
William Bell, Jr.
Daniel McCay.
James Watts.
George Johnston.
Robt. Gowdy.
Christn. Hettock.

2nd Class.

John Heirs.
John Bell, Senr.
Robert McGill.
Lawrence Hatton.
William Smith.
Patrick Lafferty.
Anthony Hoone.
Philip Newbacker.
John Lindsey.
Allexr. Givens.
Henry Hoone.
David Davis.

3d Class.

Michael Stiver.
John Barnett.
Samuel Pollouck.
Philip Tinturff.
William Forster.
Samuel Cochran.
Peter Kinter.

4th Class.

John Bell.
Jacob Eyeman.
John Bowland.
William Foulks.
Peter Sturgon.
John Duncan.
Elisha Lockart.

5th Class.

James Forster.
John Richmond.
Peter Duffey.
John Boyce.
John Kinter.
Hugh Watts.
John Bundel.
William Bell.
John Gartner.

6th Class.

John Simpson.
Henry McCloskey.
John Collegan.
John Thomas.
John Cochran, Jur.
William Boyce.
James Burney.
William Murray.
Thos. Burney.
Robert Armstrong.
John Stephenson.

7th Class.

Thos. Sturgon.
Martin Newbaker.
James Bell.
Thos. Kearns.
Christle Eyeman.
Thos. Gallaher.
Robert Smith.
James Reed.
Moses Lockert.
John Due.

8th Class.

John Brown.
Abraham Mooney.
John Bell, Jur.
Robert Joyce.
John Fisher.
Geo. Adam Gardner.
John Sloane.
Lodwick Mitsker.

A RETURN OF CAPT. JNO. GILLCHRIST'S COMPY. OF THE EIGHT CLASS OF THE FOURTH BATTN. LANCASTER COUNTY MILITIA 23D OCTR. 1779. (c.)

Captain.

John Gillchrist, Junr.

1st Lieut.

William Swan.

2nd Lieut.

Mathw. Gillchrist.

Ens.

Andw. Berryhill, Sr.

Serjants.

Richard Swan.
William McMillen.
Robert Willey.
John Grahams.

Fifer.

Wm. Hedrick.

First Class.

John McElheany.
Robert Smith.
Jacob Miller.
John Meider.

Second Class.

Andrew Smith.
George Shupe.
John Fleming.
David Patton.
John Kinsley.
John Pottimore.
Henry Achia.

Third Class.

James Cochran.
Andw. Cochran.
William Hogan.
William Boyde.
John Hatfield.
Anthony Witherill.

Fourth Class.

James Boggs.
Peter Shearer.
James Caldwell.
James McMillen.
William Hugh.
John M'Culley.

Fifth Class.

Zachrias Stephen.
William Willson.
William M'Roberts.
William Caldhoon.
Andw. Berryhill, Junr.
Philip Jno. Burres.
Samuel White.
John M'Caughan.
Thomas Murray.
John Allen.
George Dixon.

Sixth Class.

Hugh Wray.
John Cochran.
John Hilton.
Abraham Willson.
James Wiggins.
Thos. Gillchreest.
Samuel Martin.
John Whrite.
Samuel Thomson.

Seventh Class

William Cochran.
Robert Gillchrist.
David Caldwell.
Andw. Stephen.
James Byers.
Robert Douglas.
Thos. Bell.

Eight Class.

Robert Neel.
John Miller.
John Murray.
Hugh Stephen.
Saml. Berryhill.
James Calvet.
William Downing.
Allexr. Johnston.
Joseph Huffman.
Henry Pitner.

RETURN OF CAP'T. JNO. RUTHERFORD'S COMPY. OF THE THIRD CLASS OF THE FOURTH BATTALION LANCASTER COUNTY MILITIA OCT. 28TH 1779. (c.)

Captain.

Jno Rutherford.

1st Lieut.

Thos. McArthur.

2nd Lieut.

Wm. Montgumary.

Ensign.

Rob't Gray.

Serjts.

Michael Limes.
Wm. Stewart.
Jas. Spence.

Corpr.

Jno Dimpsey.
Thos. Eskin.
Jno. Page.
Jno. Miller.

Fifer.

George Smith.

Clerk.

Jno. Wilson.

1st Class.

Richard Carson.
Jno. Castle.
Wm. Duncan.
Wm. Lochrey.
Jacob Poorman.
Jno. Buck.
Jno. Miller. Sadler.
Hugh Robeson.
Michael Smith.

2nd Class.

Mathew Caldhoon.
Abraham Eagley.
Peter Smith.
Wm. M'Clure.

3d Class.

Martin Houser.
Jacob Miller, Junr.
Peter Pancake.
Jacob Limes.
George Sheets.
Jacob Snyder, Junr.
George Carson.
Joshua Elder, Esqr.
Jno. Boughman.

4th Class.

Jacob Awl.
Fredrick Castle.
Barnabus Shupe.
George Pile.
Thos. Gray.
Benjn. Duncan.

5th Class.

Valentine Baker.
Vandles Folkler.
Jacob Miller, Senr.
Leonard Sheets.
Elijah Stewart.
Jacob Syder, Senr.
Adam Lamphart.
Jno. McGary.
Saml. Brown.
Gabriel Bridegroom.
Francis Barley.

6th Class.

Danl. Cooper.
Jno. Gray.
Adam Kitsmiller.
Joseph Wilson.
John Davis.
Jacob Houser.
Peter Pankake, Junr.
Philip Firebaugh.

7th Class.

Milcham Miller.
George Page.
Jacob Beck.
Conrad Bobb.
David Ritchey.
Stophel Soop.
Jacob Smith, Senr.
John Donnelly.
Jos. Mark.

8th Class.

Jos. Shaw.
Michael Shearer.
David Shaw.
Alexr. Wilson.
Jno. Toy.
Jno. Sybort.
Jacob Smith, Junr.

A RETURN OF CAPT. JAMES MURRAY'S COMPY. OF THE FIRST CLASS OF THE FOURTH BATTALION LANCASTER COUNTY MILITIA FOR THE YEAR 1779. (c.)

Captn.

James Murray.

Lieut.

1st. Geo. Cochran.
2nd. Geo. Bell.

Ensign.

John Ryan.

Privats.

1st Class.

1. Robt. McCord.
2. Willm. Bell, jur.
3. Dan. McCay.
4. James Watts.
5. Geo. Johnston.
6. Robt. Goudey.
7. Christian Hallocks.

2nd Class.

8. John Ayers.
9. John Bell, Senr.
10. Robt. McGill.
11. Lorance Hatton.
12. Willm. Smith.
13. Patt. Lafferty.
14. Anthoney Hoone.
15. Philip Newbecker.
16. John Linsey.
17. Alexdr. Givins.
18. Henry Hoone.
19. David Davis.

3d Class.

20. Michl. Stiver.
21. John Barnet.
22. Saml. Plouge.
23. Philip Tintweff.
24. Willm. forster.
25. Saml. Cochran.
26. Peter Kinter.

4th Class.

27. John Bell.
28. Jacob Eyman.
29. John Boland.
30. Willm. foulks.
31. Peter Sturgeon.
32. John Duncan.
33. Elisha Lockard.

5th Class.

34. James forster.
35. John Richmond.
36. Peter Duffey.
37. John Boyce.
38. John Kinter.
39. Hugh Watts.
40. John Bundle.
41. John Gartner.

6th Class.

42. John Simpson.
43. Henry McCloskey.
44. John Colligan.
45. Joseph Colligan.
46. John Thomas.
47. John Cochran, jur.
48. Wm. Boyce.
49. James Birney.
50. Wm. Murray.
51. Thos. Birney.
52. Robt. Armstrong.
53. John Stephenson.

7th Class.

54. Thos. Sturgeon.
55. Martin Newbecker.
56. James Bell.
57. Thos. Kerns.
58. Christley Eyman.
59. Thos. Galachor.
60. Robt. Smith.
61. James Reed.
62. Moses Lockard.
63. John Due, jur.

8th Class.

64. John Brown.
65. Abraham Mooney.
66. John Bell, jur.
67. Robt. Boyce.
68. John fisher.
69. Geo. Adam Gartner
70. John Sloane.
71. Loudk. Minchker.
72. Willm. Bell.

5th Class.

Court Martial Men.

John Bell, jur. • Saml. Cochran.

A RETURN OF CAPT. HENRY McKINNEY'S COMPY. OF THE SECOND CLASS OF THE FOURTH BATTALION LANCASTER COUNTY MELITIA. FOR THE YEAR 1779. (c.)

Captain.

Henry McKinny.

1st Lieut.

Samuel Huchison.

2nd Lieut.

Samuel Sherer.

Ensign.

Joseph Fulton.

Privates.

Henry Alleman.
Allexander McCluwer.
Nicoles Alleman.
George Lerue.
Stophel Alleman.
Jacob Brand.
John Roop.
Eliab Neagly.
John Noop.
Robt. Caldwell.

2nd Class.

John Wonderly.	Willm. Murry.
Christopher Roop.	Willm. Smyth.
Jacob Roop.	Gustavis Graham.
Berefoot Brunson.	Ludwick Dagon.
John Mumma.	

3rd Class.

Stophel Ernest.	Mathias Winagel.
James McCord.	Abraham Brinson.
George Conser.	Willm. Steil.
John Little.	Arthur Brisbon.
John Brand.	Samuel Couhren.
Conrad Alleman.	

4th Class.

Jacob Kerr.	Andw. McCluwer.
Abraham Nidey.	Hanteter Wonderly.
Sophel Poorman.	John Penneck.
Jacob Teeher.	John Poselr.ght.
John Showmaker.	

5th Class.

John Boman.	John Flackenor.
John Conser.	Samuel Wyle.
Christopher Temmy.	George Nevly.
Willm. Right.	John McKinne.
Cristopher Alleman.	Arther Chambers.
Henry Alleman.	

6th Class.

Maxwell Chambers.	John Alleman.
James Finly	Necoles Negh.
John Sherer.	Petter Brenar.
George Gray.	Francis Lerue.
Adam Means.	

7th Class.

Willm. McCluer.	Hugh Cunningham.
Michel Woolf.	John Steil.
Richard McCluwer.	Hugh Crocket.
Jacob Springer.	Joseph Huchison.
Willm. Kerr.	John Frites.
Joseph Smyth.	Felty Pancack.

8th Class.

Robt. Chambers.
Jos. Gray.
Michel Bole.
John Means.
Rowan McCluer.
James Maghon.
James McKinney.
James Rutherford
Rowland Chamber.
John Maxwell.
Conred Bombach.

SAMUEL HUTCHISON, Lieut.

RETURN OF CAPT. JOHN RUTHERFORD'S COMPANY OF THE THIRD CLASS OF THE FOURTH BATTALION LANCASTER COUNTY MILITIA 1779. (c.)

Capt.

Jno. Rutherford.

Lieut.

1st. Thos. McArthur.
2nd. Wm. Montgumary.

Ensign.

Rob't Gray.

Serjants.

Michael Limes.
Wm. Stewart.
Jas. Spence.

Corporals.

John Dimpsey.
Thos. Esken.
Jno. Page.

Fifer.

Jno. Miller.
George Smith.

Clerk.

Jno. Wilson.

Privates.

1st Class.

Richard Carson.
John Castle.
Wm. Duncan.
Wm. Laughry.

Jacob Poorman.
John Buck.
Jno. Miller (Sadler).
Hugh Robeson.
Michael Smith.

2nd Class.

Mathew Calhoon.
Abraham Eagly.
Peter Smith.
Wm. McClure.

3rd Class.

Martin Houser.
Jacob Miller, Junr.
Peter Pankake, Sr.
Jacob Limes.
George Sheets.
Jacob Syder, Jun.
George Carson.
Joshua Elder, Esqr.
Jno. Baughman.

4th Class.

Jacob Awl.
Fredrick Castle.
Barnabas Supe.
George Pile.
Thos. Gray.
Benjn. Duncan.

5th Class.

Valentine Beaker.
Vandle folkler.
Jacob Miller, Snr.
Leonard Sheets.
Elijah Stewart.
Jacob Syder, Senr.
Adam Lampord.
Jno. McGary.
Saml. Brown.
Gabriel Bridegroom.
Francis Burley.

6th Class.

Danl. Cooper.
Jno. Gray.
Adam Kitsmiller.
Jos. Wilson.
Jno. Davis.
Jacob Houser.
Peter Pankake, Junr.
Philip firebaugh.

7th Class.

Milcham Miller.
George Page.
Jacob Beck.
Conrad Bobb.
David Richey.
Stophel Soop.
Jacob Smith, Senr.
Jno. Donnelly.
Jos. Mark.

8th Class.

Jos. Shaw.
Michael Shever.
David Shaw.
Allexr. Wilson.
Jno. Toy.
Jno. Sybort.
Jacob Smith, Junr.

A RETURN OF CAPT. MARTIN WEAVER'S COMPY. OF THE SIXTH CLASS OF THE FOURTH BATTALION LANCASTER COUNTY MILITIA FOR THE YEAR 1779. (c.)

Capt.

Martin Weaver.

Lt.

1st. Philip Rouscalp. 2d. Jno. Cheesley.

Ensign.

Danl. Steeber.

Serjts.

1st. Jonathn. Woodsides.
2d. Mathias Divler.
3d. Jno. Marten.

Corpls.

1st. George Ridle.
2d. Stophel Lark.
3d. Stophel Cheesley.

Privates.

1st Class.

Edwd. Wilcocks.
Jno. Philips.
Jacob Cheesley.
Philips Philips.
Fredrick Paul.

2nd Class.

Jno. Millar.
Henry Werfell.
Abrah'm Jura.
John Didy.
George Killinger.
Jno. Mortar.

3rd Class.

Michl. Salentine.
Michl. Shadle.
Leonard Snider.
Abrah'm Neibour.
Andw. Yeager.
Fred'k Bentz.

4th Class.

Jno. Hosman.	Adam Ruber.
Joseph Steber.	George Divler.
Peter Mitz.	George Shupe.
Detrick Stonebraker.	

5th Class.

Leonard Seeber.	Charles Bargan.
John Herman.	Henry Umholts.
Henry Hains.	Lodwick Shots.
Michl. Milehar.	

6th Class.

Peter Willer.	Jno. Woodsides.
Jacob Pickel.	Adm. King.
Jacob Harmon.	Jno. Wertz.
Henry Normler.	

7th Class.

David Harman.	Nicklous Hoofman.
Anthony Freyley.	George Mink.
George Seel.	Sebastian Mitz.
Adm. Wertz.	Henry Myer.

8th Class.

Michl. Divler.	Joseph Philips.
Henry Wolf.	George Buffington.
Saml. Jura.	Christ'n Wertz.
Christ'n Hoffman.	

Court Marshl. Men.

Lud'k Breats.	Stephen Bentz.

A RETURN OF CAPT. JOHN GILCHRIST COMPY. OF THE EIGHTH CLASS OF THE FOURTH BATALION LANCASTER COUNTY MILITIA FOR THE YEAR 1779. (c.)

Capt.

Jno. Gilchrist, Jun.

Lieut.

1st. William Swan.	2d. Mathew Gilchrist.

Ensign.

Andw. Berreyhill.

Serjts.

Richard Swan.
Robert Wylie.
Wm. McMillen.
Jno. Grahams.

Fifer.

Wm. Hederick.

Privates.

1st Class.

John McElheney.
Robert Smith.
Jacob Miller.
Jno. Medor.

2nd Class.

Andw. Smith.
George Shoap.
John Fleming.
David Patton.
Jno. Kinsley.
Jno. Pattimore.
Henery Achia.

3rd Class.

James Cochran.
Andw. Cochran.
Wm. Hogan.
Wm. Boyd.
John Hatfield.
Anthony Witherel.

4th Class.

James Boggs.
Petter Shearer.
James Caldwell.
James McMillen.
William Hughs.
Jno. McCulley.

5th Class.

Zacharia Stephen.
Wm. Wilson.
Wm. McRoberts.
William Calhoon.
Andw. Berreyhill, Junr.
Philip Jno. Burres.
Saml. White.
Jno. McCaughan.
Thos. Murray.
John Allen.
George Dixon.

6th Class.

Hugh Wray.
John Cochran.
John Hilton.
Abram. Wilson.
Jas. Wiggins.

Thomas Gilchrist.
Saml. Martin.
John Whrite.
Saml. Thompson.

7th Class.

William Cochran.
Robt. Gilchrist.
David Caldwell.
Andw. Stephen.

Jas. Buyers.
Robt. Doughlas.
Thos. Bell.

8th Class.

Robert Neel.
John Murray.
Hugh Stephen.
Saml. Berreyhill.
Jas. Cavett.

William Downing.
Alexr. Johnston.
Joseph Huffman.
Henery Pitner.

JOHN GILCHRIST, JUNR., Capt.

A CLASS ROLLE OF CAPTEN BEARDES COM. IN THE FOURTH BAT. COMMANDED BY COL. LUDWICK MARYES JN. HEMPFIELD TOWNSHIP LANCASTER COUNTY. (c.)

Privates.

1st Class.

Ander Kofman.
John Stamin.
Jacob Hestin.
Jacob Kerne, Jr.

John Honevir.
Christel Miller.
John Kofman.
Admin Moor.

2nd Class.

Martin Nisely.
John Nisely.
Martin Shafnir.
Gorg Morrey.

Frick Mory.
David Miller.
Christen Hidlir.
Petter Wanger.

3rd Class.

Petter Mouselman, jr.
Petter Mouselman, sen.
Samul Hofman.
Martin Boukir.
John Marys.
John Shwar, sen.
John Shwar, jr.
John Fang.

4th Class.

John Wilson.
Frick Hofman.
Youst. Millier.
Baston Hofman.
Ander Hofman.
Hindery Landes.
Christen Overhakir.
Abram Mills.
Ambris Newsim.

5th Class.

Martin Piperir.
Christel Houlris.
Ambram Frick.
Hugh Warkman.
Jacob Shirey.
Breny. McAnelye.

6th Class.

Jacob Ackir.
Petter Springir.
Jacob Shirey.
Petterir Goodshall.
Gocdlip Goodshall.
Mikil Goodshall.
John Heny.
Chrisly Herche.

7th Class.

Christin Berrick.
David Berrick.
Christel Sware.
Ludwick Teets.
John Morry.
Williamin Plets.
Christel Shirche.
Heneye Millir.
George Nirily.

8th Class.

Petterir Springer.
John Chroush.
Henrye Beekerir.
Christel Houir.
John Houir, senr.
Henrye Bouman.
John Plets.
Raburt Beard.
Williamen Petterson.

JAMES BEARD, Capt.

Of the 8th class bloingin to 4th Bet. in the county of Lancaster goun the 15th 1780.

A RETURN OF THE SEVENTH COMPANY OF THE FOURTH BATTALION OF LANCASTER COUNTY MILITIA COMMANDED BY COL. ROBERT ELDER. 1779. (c.)

Captain.

Andrew Stewart

Lieutenants.

1st. Joseph Simpson. 2nd. John Matthows.

Ensign.

John Whitehill.

1st Class.

Felty Spangler.
Alexd. Hetherington.
Jacob Noss.
Nathaniel Randolph.

2nd Class.

James Cogley.
Paul Randolph.
George Devibaugh.
George Fridley.
Frederick Switzer.
Wm. Dickey.

3rd Class.

Charles Grogan.
Thomas Miller.
Conrod Youtz.
Alexd. Porter.
John Bates.

4th Class.

John Harris.
John Moore.
Peter Bobb.
Nathanial Simpson.
John Parker.
Jacob Kisner.
Thomas Strahan.

5th Class.

John Hersha.
Frances Youtz.
John Galahur.
John Cogley.
Stophel Simeth.
John Fockler.
Hugh Montgomery.
Richard Hugh.

6th Class.

Alexd. Berryhill.
Robert Elder, Sr.
John Elder, Sr.
Wm. Kelso, Junr.
Samuel Simpson, Sr.
Wm. McConnold.

7th Class.

Samuel Simpson, Jr.
Cornelius Cox.
John Cline.
James Johnston.
Wm. Carson.
Robert Clark.
Adam Ekert.
Joseph Cog.ey.

8th Class.

Dav'd Montgomery.
Robert Cogley.
George Raniker.
Andw. Bell.
Patrick Heney.
Charles Stewart.
John Garber.
Wm. Kelso, Senr.
Arthur Bell.
James McKee.
Thomas Moore.
Robert Fitzpatrick.
Barney Fridley.
Thomas Brynon.
Henry Irvin.

Return'd by
AND'W STEWART, Capt. 7th Company.

OFFICERS OF FOURTH BATTALION. (a.)

Returned August 26, 1780.

Lieutenant Colonel.

Ludwig Meyer.

Major.

Nathan Siegler.

First Company.

Captain—Frederick Rodfong.
Lieutenant—Philip Baker.
Ensign—Henry Dietrich.

Second Company.

Captain—Jacob Brand.
Lieutenant—Jacob Miller.
Ensign—George Erisman.

Third Company.

Captain—Jacob Metzger.
Lieutenant—John Yanzer.
Ensign—Ulrich Fizit.

Fourth Company.

Captain—Christian Doman.
Lieutenant—Michael Heller.
Ensign—William Henry.

Fifth Company.

Captain—Alex. Scott, Jr.
Lieutenant—Jacob Gatz.
Ensign—James Jack.

Sixth Company.

Captain—Joseph Wright.
Lieutenant—Adam Fisher.
Ensign—Frederick Take.

Seventh Company.

Captain—James Patton.
Lieutenant—Christian Ferree.
Ensign—Christian Taylor.

Eighth Company.

Captain—James Beard.
Lieutenant—John Fisher.
Ensign—Jacob Murray.

MUSTER ROLL OF 2ND CLASS 4TH BATT. LANCR. COUNTY MILA. ON COMMAND AT LANCR. FOR PURPOSE OF GUARDG. OF BRITISH PRISS'RS, &c. (c.)

Names of persons who served a tour of duty.	Names of persons who furnished substitutes.	Time when duty commd.	Time when duty ended.
Capt.		1781	1781
Jacob Brandt,		June 22,	July 30.
Sergt.			
James Smith,	Fredk. Myer,		Aug. 24.
Wm. Thompson,	George Murray.		
Jno. Stineking,	Chris'r Newcomer.		
Corpl.			
Jaspar Sheets,	David Esteiman.		
Privates.			
Jno. Doam,			July 31.
Jaspar Shertzer,	Danl. Lintner,		Aug. 24.
Leenard Albright,	Jno. Helar.		
Joseph Stephenson,	Willm. Stephens.		
Jacob Hackenswiller,	Andw. Swank.		
Joseph Roner.			
Adm. Miller.			
Wm. Foulk,	Michl. Myer.		
Jacob Yost,			
Jno. Rimer.			
Frans Shover,	John Hare.		
Valentine Myer,			
Fredk. Murry.			July 31.
Wm. Moore.			Aug. 24.
Jno. Swartzer,	Frans. Hope.		
Jno. Kindler.			
Peter Wagner.			
John Ward,	Henry Zerger.		

July 30th, 1782. Then mustered Capt. Brandts Compy. as above specified.

AD'M HUBLEY, S. L. Lr. Cy.

MUSTER ROLL OF 3D CLASS 4TH BATALL. LANCR. COUNTY MILA. ON A TOUR OF DUTY AT LANCASTER. (c.)

Names of persons who served.	Names of persons who furnished substitutes.	Time when duty commd.	Time when duty ended.
Ensign.		1781	1781
George Errisman,		July 2.	Aug. 24.
Sergt.			
Daniel McIntire,	Henry Neff,	June 26,	
Fifer.			
Fred'k Hisely.			
Privates.			
Michl. Grider.*			
John Weaver,			July 29.
Peter Lavenwiler.			
John Mossla.			
Ludwig Shults,			Aug. 24.
Fredk. Myer,	Michl. Snyder.		
Jno. Cammel,	Henry Miller.		
Jno. Cheaply,			July 29.
George Smith,	John Myers,		Aug. 24.
John Orr,	John Eshleman,		Aug. 24.
Zacharia Houry,	Ad'm Kendrich.		
George Waggoner,			Aug. 24.
Jno. Swingle,	Isaac Miller.		
David Nollinger,	Henry Mumma.		
John Urich,	George Peck.		
Joseph Easter,			Aug. 24.
Mich. Merigner.			
Wm. Archer.			
Ad'm Riser.			
Jno. Armer.			
Jacob Risberger.			
Ad'm Elbesel.			

*Dischd. on acct. of sickness.

Lancr. 6th July 81. Then mustered above company as above specified.

AD'M HUBLEY, S. L. Lr. Cy.

MUSTER ROLL OF THE 4TH CLASS OF THE 4TH BATALION, LAN'R COUNTY MILITIA ON A TOUER OF DUTY AT LANCASTER, GUARDING BRITISH PRISONERS OF WAR. (c.)

Names of Persons who Perform a Touer of Duty.	What class.	Names of Persons wro Furnished Substitutes.	Time when duty commenced.	Time when duty ended.
Capt.			1781	1781
....	4th,	....	Aug't 22th,	Oct'r 20th.
Lieu't.				
John Yenser,	4th,	....	Aug't 22th,	Oct'r 20th.
Henry Dieterich,	4th,	....	Aug't 22th,	Oct'r 20th.
Serj't.				
John Stoneking,	4th,	Jacob Strickler,	Aug't 22th,	Oct'r 20th.
Casper Shietz,	4th,	Andrew Cofman,	Aug't 22th,	Oct'r 20th.
Corp'l.				
George Young,	4th,	Michael Shoeman,	Aug't 22th,	Oct'r 20th.
Drum.				
Christ'n Rineholl,	4th,	Christian Sieman,	Aug't 30th,	Oct'r 20th.

Fife.				
Frederick Mellinger,	4th,	Casper Holbrunner,	Aug't 22th,	Oct'r 20th.
Privates.				
John Herrgood,	4th,	John Wright,	Aug't 22th,	Oct'r 20th.
Joseph Rockhill,	4th,		Aug't 22th,	Oct'r 20th.
John Heable,	4th,		Aug't 22th,	Oct'r 20th.
Leonard Allbright,	4th,		Aug't 22th,	Oct'r 20th.
David Decker,	4th,		Aug't 22th,	Oct'r 20th.
Amos Moss,	4th,	George Brenner,	Aug't 22th,	Oct'r 20th.
Jacob Stephege,	4th,		Aug't 22th,	Oct'r 20th.
William Folk, Jun'r,	4th,		Aug't 22th,	Oct'r 20th.
William Folk,	4th,		Aug't 22th,	Oct'r 20th.
John Cash,	4th,	Henrey Neidick,	Aug't 22th,	Oct'r 20th.
John Oldham,	4th,	Christian Herr,	Aug't 22th,	Oct'r 20th.
William Meyer,	4th,	Jacob Coufman,	Aug't 22th,	Oct'r 20th.
John Clarck,	4th,	Abraham Hess,	Aug't 22th,	Oct'r 20th.

MUSTER ROLL OF THE 5TH, 6TH, & 7TH CLASS OF THE 4TH BATALION OF LAN'R COUNTY MILITIA ON A TOUER OF DUTY UNDER THE COMMAND OF. (c.)

Names of Persons who Perform a Touer of Duty.	What class.	Names of Persons wro Furnished Substitutes.	Time when duty commenced.	Time when duty ended.
Capt.			1781	1781
Alexander Scott,	5th,		Sep't 22d,	Oct'r 11d.
Lieu't.				
Joseph Tidball,			Sep't 22d,	Oct'r 11d.
Ens'n.				
Wm. Shaw,			Sep't 22d,	Oct'r 11d.
Serj'ts.				
John Smith,		Jacob Brand.		
Joseph Grey,				
William Arnet,		David Barrack.		
Corp'l.				
Wm. Moore,			Do.	
James Tack,		Joseph Hoober,	Do.	
Adam Warner,		John Funk,	Do.	

Name		Substitute	From		To	
Drum.						
Chris'n Widley,			Sep't	22d.	Oct'r	11d.
Fife.						
[illegible] Shindle,			Sep't	22d.	Oct'r	11d.
Privates.						
William [illegible],		Samuel Wright,	Sep't	22d.	[illegible]	11d.
Patrick Riely,			Sep't	22d.	[illegible]	11d.
Daniel [illegible],			Sep't	22d.	[illegible]	11d.
[illegible] [illegible],			Sep't	22d.	Oct'r	11d.
Edward Waterson,			Sep't	22d.	Oct'r	11d.
James Watt,			Sep't	22d.	Oct'r	11d.
John Monterbonck,		Andrew Hershey,	Sep't	22d.	Oct'r	11d.
Lawrence McCrady,		John Good,	Sep't	22d.	Oct'r	11d.
William Moorland,			Sep't	22d.	Oct'r	11d.
John Moorland,			Sep't	22d.	Oct'r	11d.
[illegible] Tolan,		James Kays,	Sep't	22d.	Oct'r	11d.
Leonard Albright,			Sep't	22d.	Oct'r	11d.
Jacob Hoffman,			Sep't	22d.	Oct'r	11d.
Charles [illegible],			Sep't	22d.	Oct'r	11d.
John McCawly,			Sep't	22d.	Oct'r	11d.
John [illegible],			Sep't	22d.	Oct'r	11d.
[illegible] [illegible],		Christ'n Kauffman,	Sep't	22d.	Oct'r	11d.
Christ'n Stouffer,			Sep't	22d.	Oct'r	11d.

CLASS ROLL OF CAPT. CORRS COMPANY 4TH BATTN. OF LANCASTER COUNTY MELITIA COMMANDED BY COLL. ZEIGLER. (c.)

Capt.

Conrad Coor.

Lieut.

Adam Fisher.

Ensing.

Fredk. Falk.

Sarjents.

George Waggonner.
Peter Cline.
John Manning.

Corporals.

Michel Shoeman.
Joseph Hinkle.
Adam Stake.

Privates.

Class 1st.

John Penter.
Chrn. Nestelraad, Jr.
Wm. Praat.
George Brenner.
John Hinkle.
Joseph Musser.
peter Snider.
Michel Baughman.

2d.

Wm. Moore.
Benjamin Hershey.
Jacob Goodman.
Benjamin Musser.
Chrisn. Martin.
Chrisn. Stoner.
Fred. Hofman.
Fred. Wiler.
John Hillir.

3d.

George Waggoner.
Chrisn. Hershey.
Richd. Whisler.
John Armer.
John Souder.
Henry Pauless.
John Ashleman.
Geo. Peck.
Michel Snider.
Rid. Funk.

4th.

John Ord.	John Stoner.
John Funk.	John Lowrey.
John Butt.	Edward Kelley.
Daniel Kendrck.	Peter Dunkle.

5th.

Michel Penter.	Abraham Stoner.
Chrisn. Correll.	Jacob Manning.
Saml. McDonnell.	Henry Miller.
Henry Souder.	

6th.

Chrisn. Bowman.	Obrick Rever.
Henry Litchty.	Jacob Brenner.
Cotleip Yelder.	Chrisn. Stopher.
John Kendrick.	peter Rommel.

7th.

Jacob Correll.	Wm. McMannimey.
peter Whitemore.	Isaac Martin.
philip Brenner.	James Wright.
Jacob Ashleman.	Isaac Kaufman.
Chrisn. Hare.	

8th.

Joseph Wenger.	Thomas Wright.
John Musser.	Garet Stake.
Henry Brenneman.	David Kaufman.
Henry Ashleman.	John Logan.
John Kremer.	

Certified by
CONRAD CORR, Capt.
for the year 1781.

A RETURN OF THE 5TH COMPANY OF THE FOURTH BATTALION OF LANCASTER COUNTY MILITIA COMMANDED BY COL. SEIGLER FOR THE YEAR 1781. (c.)

Capt.

Alex'd Scott, Jur.

Lieut.

Joseph Tidbal.

Ensign.

James Jacks.

Privates.

1st Class.

Adam Sheller.
David Mussleman.
Wilm. Brown.
Ludwig Frantz.
Joseph Martin.
Jacob Hossteter.
Wilm. Smith.
Jacob Springer.
Josep Charls.
Adam Take.
Christian Newcomer.
Jacob Hershey.
John Mosey.

2nd Class.

John Leman.
John Regal.
Jacob Carn.
Isaac Hershy.
Henry Bair, Jur.
Benjamin Bair.
Saml. Mockart.
John Knave.
Valen Myer.

3d Class.

John Segrist.
Jacob Prupacker.
Wm. Carn.
John Carn.
Benedick Esleman.
George Wolf.
Jacob Gansler.
Nicholas Sherick.
Ed. Waterson, serjt.
Christian Horst.
Mathias Hook.

4th Class.

Christian Kaufman.
David Mussleman.
David Miller.
Peter Mussleman.
Abraham Hershey.
Michael Riegal.
George Smith.
Henry Muma.
Tobias Miller.
Chris'n Morey.
Jacob Croner.

5th Class.

John Forrey.
Christian Kaufman.
Peter Lair.
David Forrey.
John Newcomer.
John Bonnet.
Jacob Carnman.
George Switzer.
Joseph Sherick.
Peter Nease.
Jam's Keys.
Wm. Moreland.
Richard McDonald.

6th Class.

Joseph Holler.	John Newcomer.
Jno. Hamacker.	Peter Leib.
John Woller.	John McAlly.
Andrew Hershey.	George Hauser.
John Weaver.	Melcher Walter.
Jacob Menigh.	George Bringwolt.

7th Class.

Bernart Riff.	Daniel Walty.
Christian Prubecker.	Jacob Switzer.
Jacob Getz, Jun.	John Bair.
Joseph Sherick, Jur.	Abraham Stephy.
Nicholas Segrist.	Jacob Newcomer.
Philip Lear.	John Moreland.
Peter Hornberger.	Philip Stecht.

8th Class.

Joseph Sherich.	David Prubecker.
Jacob Minige.	John Landes.
Stephen Hornberger.	Robt. Bines.
Frederick Barick.	Jas. Malony.
Michal Kaufman.	John George Bower.
Michael Ritsel.	Pilip Snyder.

Certyfyed by me,
ALEX. SCOTT, Capt.

A TRUE AND EXACT LIST OF THE NAMES OF EACH AND EVERY MALE WHITE PERSON INHABITING OR RESIDING WITHIN MY DISTRICT, IN THE SECOND COMPANY OF THE FOURTH BATTALION OF LANCASTER COUNTY MILITIA, BETWEEN THE AGE OF EIGHTEEN AND FIFTY-THREE YEARS. TAKEN FOR THE YEAR 1782. (c.)

Capt.

Jacob Brandt.

Lieu.

Jacob Miller.

Ens.

George Erisman.

Almonar.

Paul Houfman.

Privates.

Ist Class.

Jacob frantz.
Thomas krauter.
Isaac Kauffman.
Henry Neave, Jur.
Thomas Hyhard.
Jacob Sigrist.
George Dunckel.
Isaac Kuntz.
Michael Ryner.
George Fail.
John Diffenderfer.
Abraham Wittmer.

2nd Class.

Christian Steman.
John Herr.
Daniel Lindner.
John Kauffman.
John Hiller.
Thomas Meclany.
Peter Cuntz.
George Martin.
John Halbruner.

3d Class.

Jacob Charls.
John Shepply.
Christian Burgholder.
John Grob.
Henry Neave.
Henry Shop.
John Neave.
Christian Herr.
Jacob Graybeel.
Henry Smith.
Jacob Saneor.

4th Class.

Albertus Waller.
Casper Halbruner.
Jacob Barr.
Killian Boas.
Jacob Stibgen.
George Brenner.
John Kensimer.
Abra. Herr.
francis shober.
John Gandner.
Christian Yeniwine.

5th Class.

John Eberley.
Henry Eberley.
Christian Kauffman.
Abra. Herr, Jur.
John Ryst.
Jacob Stygleman.
Phillip Stech.
Christian Sinn.
Henry Hystand.
Jacob Kauffman.
Jacob Kindig.

6th Class.

Jacob Killheffer.	Henry Miller.
John Killheffer.	John Yessler.
John Hystand.	Stoffel Shertzer.
Rudolph Herr.	Mathias Dunkel.
Adam Loreman.	francis Miller.

7th Class.

Adam Martin.	Casper Shertzer.
Michael Shunk.	Jacob Manderbaugh.
Abraham Peter.	John Hirshy.
Fredrik Meanser.	John Dunkel.
Conrad Hyligas.	Paul Halbruner.
John Shertzer.	

8th Class.

Christian Funk.	Michael Shetterly.
Christian Shallenberger.	Andrew Kauffman.
John Saltzman.	Adam Bottsfield.
Godfrid Klug.	Christian Stoner.
Martin Oberholtzer.	

I do swear, on the Holy Evangelist of Almighty God: That the above list is a just and true state of the male white inhabitants residing in my District, agreeable to Law, and without any fraud to the State, to the best of my knowledge.

JACOB BRAND, Capt.

Sworn before me this 3d
day of August, 1782.
JAS. BARBER.

A TRUE AND EXACT LIST OF THE NAMES, OF EACH AND EVERY MALE WHITE PERSON, INHABITING OR RESIDING, WITHIN MY DISTRICT, IN THE FOURTH COMPANY, OF THE FOURTH BATTALON OF LANCASTER COUNTY MILITIA, BETWEEN THE AGE OF EIGHTEEN AND FIFTY-THREE YEARS. TAKEN FOR THE YEAR 1782. (c.)

Captain.
Barnard Mann.

Lieutenant.
Michael Heller.

Ensign.

Wm. Henry.

Almonar.

John Mann.

Serjeants.

John Alder.
John Alenton.
John Taylor.

First Class.

1. John Neaf.
2. Hery Kaufman.
3. Martin Gonter.
4. Isaac Kaufman.
5. Jacob Whitemore, Jn. son.
6. George Rutzel.
7. Peter Grayble.

Second Class.

8. Paul Ockerman.
9. Martin Funk.
10. Abraham Kaufman.
11. Conrad Zeigler.
12. Christian Newcommer.
13. David Frank, Hessian deserter.
14. John Allington.

Third Class.

15. Jacob Shock.
16. Jacob Bunn.
17. Balser Groe.
18. Leonard Reigart.
19. Henry Shank.
20. Jacob Stayman.
21. James Forsyth.
22. Christian Stoner.
23. David Mellenger.
24. Jacob Bixler.
25. Chrisn. Bixler.

Fourth Class.

26. Chris. Hare.
27. Jacob Kaufman.
28. Henry Neaf.
29. Abraham Miller.
30. Joseph Hobbecker.
31. Andrew Kaufman, M. son.
32. John Sherrick.
33. Isaac Kagey.
34. Joseph Sanders.
35. Mechel Funk.

Fifth Class.

37. Wm. Kennedy.
38. John Hosteller.
39. Andw. Kaufman, C. son.
40. Henry Shellenberger.
41. Henry Lighty.
42. John Funk.
43. Merkel Slot.
44. Jacob Mellenger.
45. Matheas Senger.
46. Thomas Bowland.

Sixth Class.

47. Jacob Sytz.
48 Jacob Shellenberger.
49. George Lutz.
50. Andrew Jacob.
51. Jacob Funk.
52. Abraham Hostetter.
53. Jacob Shellenberger.
54. Edward Gibons.
55. John Barnhart.
56. John Doman.

Seventh Class.

57. Benneduk Mellenger.
58. Christian Smith.
59. James Greenly.
60. Christian Kaufman, Sr.
61. Wm. McCormick.
62. Isaac Neaf.
63. Henry Hestand.
64. Jno. Whitmor, Jno. son.
65. Peter Reetzel.
66. Jno. Mann.
67. Joseph Kaufman.
68. George Nos.
69. John Sherreck.

Eighth Class.

70. Chrisn. Whisler.
71. Henry Funk.
72. Thomas Patten.
73. Benjamin Hostetter.
74. John Miers.
75. Michel Rubley.
76. George Oldwiler.
77. Jon. Whitemore, Jas. son.
78. Wm. Shue.
79. Samuel Funk.
80. Henry Gashaw.

I Do Swear, on the Holy Evangelist of Almighty God; That the above is a just & true state, of the Male white inhabitants, residing in my District, agreeable to Law, and without any fraud to the State, to the best of my knowledge.

BERNHART MANN, Capt.

Sworn before me this Day
of May 25th 1782.
JAMES BARBER, Sub. Lt. L. C.

A TRUE AND EXACT LIST OF THE NAMES OF EVERY MALE WHITE PERSONS INHABITING OR RESIDING WITHIN MY DISTRICT IN THE FIFTH COMPANY OF THE FOURTH BAT. OF LANCASTER COUNTY MILITIA BETWEEN THE AGE OF EIGHTEEN AND FIFTY-THREE FOR THE YEAR 1782. (c.)

Capt.

Alex'd Scott.

Lieut.

Jos. Tedbal.

Almonar.

Thos. Bires.

Privates.

1st Class.

Adam Shaller.
David Mussleman.
Ludwig Frantz.
Jos. Martin.
Jacob Hosteter.
Wil. Smith.
Jos. Charls.
Adam Tate.
Christian Newcomer, Junr.
Jacob Hershey.

2nd Class.

John Leman.
John Regal.
Isaac Hershey.
Henry Baer, Jur.
John Wilson.
John Knave.
John Bower.
Jacob Shrive.
John Newcomer, weaver.

3rd Class.

John Segrist.
Jacob Prupacker.
John Keesy.
John Carrs.
Jacob Gamler.
Nicholas Sherick.
Mathias Hook.
Henery Wolf.
Herman Whitmore.
Martin Bair.
John Getz.

4th Class.

David Musselman.
David Miller.
Peter Mussleman.
Abram Hershy.
Michael Regal.
Tobias Millar.
Jacob Croner.
Jonathan Jones.

5th Class.

Chris. Kaufman.	Peter Neafe.
Benjamin Prupaker.	James Keyes.
Peter Lair.	Wil. Moreland.
Jacob Caruman.	John Monterbank.
Joseph Shereck, Senr.	

6th Class.

John Hamacker.	Peter Lieb.
John Walter.	Melchar Walter.
Andw. Hershey.	Geo. Bringwolf.
Jacob Smith.	Thos. Bines.
John Newcomer, Stiller.	John Newcomer.

7th Class.

Bernart Rup.	Abram. Stephy.
Christian Prupacker.	Jacob Switzer.
Jacob Getz, Junr.	Jacob Newcomer.
Danl. Welty.	John Moreland.

8th Class.

Martin Bair, Junr.	John Landes.
Jacob Minigo.	Robt. Bines.
Fredk. Barreck.	John Lighty.
Michael Ritsel.	Michael Segrist, Junr.
David Prupacker.	Philip Snyder.

Sergt.

Edwd. Watterson.	John McCally.

I do swear by the Almighty God that the above list is a true state of the male white inhabitants residing in my district agreeable to law and without any fraud to the state to the best of my knowledge.

ALEXR. SCOTT, Capt.

Sworn before me this
25th day of May 1782.

JAMES BARBER, S. L. L. C.

A TRUE AND EXACT LIST OF THE NAMES, OF EACH AND EVERY MALE WHITE PERSON, INHABITING OR RESIDING, WITHIN MY DISTRICT, IN THE SEVENTH COMPANY, OF THE FOURTH BATTALION OF LANCASTER COUNTY, MILITIA, BETWEEN THE AGE OF EIGHTEEN, AND FIFTY-THREE YEARS. TAKEN FOR THE YEAR 1782. (c.)

Captain.

James Patten.

Lieutenant.

Christopher Taylor.

Ensign.

Joseph Hogantobler.

Almonar.

Jacob Stolze.

Serjants.

Jacob forry.
Jacob Libly.
John Taylor.

First Class.

1. John Newcomer.
2. Adam Stoneking.
3. Jack Smith.
4. Isaac Hogantobler.
5. Phillip fox.
6. Henry Arford.
7. Christian Moser.
8. Christian Garver, Junr.
9. David Shealinbargor.

Second Class.

10. David forry.
11. Henry Meldrim.
12. John Hogantobler.
13. William Stephens.
14. Christian Newcomer.
15. John Contz.
16. John Tombe.
17. John May.
18. William Carson.

Third Class.

19. Ludwick Shultz.
20. Samuel Carer.
21. John Mumer.
22. Henry Mumer.
23. John Neal.
24. John Weaver.
25. George Awmend.
26. John Arford.
27. John Mosey.

Fourth Class.

28. Joseph Rocknill.
29. George Mumer.
30. Conroad Ritzsal.
31. John Wright.
32. Jacob Strickler, Junor.
33. John Stoneking.
34. Andrew Garver.
35. John Hesinger.

Fifth Class.

36. Emaniel Spoor.
37. John Charles.
38. Peter Bruner.
39. James Watt.
40. Patrick Reyloy.
41. Robert Barber.
42. Joseph Jeffreys.
43. Peter Walter.
44. George Crabler.
45. John Reamley.

Sixth Class.

46. Samuel Wright.
47. Joseph Hoober.
48. John Sunn.
49. Christan Hartzler.
50. Jacob Shelenbargor.
51. Christan Laubenswler.
52. Charls Lockart.
53. Daniel Glazer.

Seventh Class.

54. Daniel forry.
55. Christan Mosey.
56. Anthony Awman.
57. Robert Patterson.
58. John Hartzler.
59. Daniel Hains.
60. John Smith.
61. John Beaver.
62. Samuel Barber.
63. Fredrick Clare.
64. John McGriger.

Eighth Class.

65. Stephen Cowlrick.
66. George Snyder.
67. William Birckman.
68. Thomas Barber.
69. Barnet Shupp.
70. Christan May.
71. John Barber.
72. Jacob Springer.
73. Abraham Colbert.
74. Jacob Arford.
75. Andrew Garver, J. G. son.

I Do swear, on the Holy Evengilist of Almighty God: That the above list is a just and true state, of the Male white Inhabitants, residing in my District, agreeable to Law, and without any fraud to the State, to the best of my knowledge.

JAMES PATTEN, Capt.

Sworn before me this
Day of June 15th, 1782.
JAS. BARBER, Sub. Lt. L. C.

A TRUE AND EXACT LIST OF THE NAMES, OF EACH AND EVERY MALE WHITE PERSON, INHABITING OR RESIDING WITHIN MY DISTRICT IN THE EIGHT COMPANY, OF THE FOURTH BATTALION OF LANCASTER COUNTY, MILITIA, BETWEEN THE AGE OF EIGHTEEN AND FIFTY-THREE YEARS.· TAKEN FOR THE YEAR 1782. (c.)

Capt.

James Beard.

Lieut.

John Fisher.

Ens.

Jacob Muorey.

Privates.

1st Class.

Handrew Coffman.
Jacob Hastend, Junr.
Michell Hibee, Senr.
John Coffman.
Christeen Miller.
Matheleas Hibe.
Jacob Hoverstat.
Henery Keezey.
Chrisstein Stoner.
Jacob Mussellman.

2nd Class.

Peter Hibe.
John Nissely.
Fridrich Muorey.
Dived Miller.
Habraham Hover.
John Schawsgood.
Daniell Keeler.
Martin Crider.

3d Class.

Peter Mussellman, jun.
Peter Mussellman, senr.
John Long.
John Schower, sen.
John Schower.
John Wissterd.
Martin Bocher.
Samueal Coffman.

4th Class.

John Willson.
Fridrick Hoffman.
John Keeler.
Henery Landes.
Christeen Hoveroltezer.
Ambres Newsen.
Georg Hover.
John Gray.

5th Class.

Martin Piper.
Henery Acker.
Abraham Frick.
Barney McEnely.
Christian Sigirest.
Peter Mussellman.
Isack Koffman.

6th Class.

Jacob Dock.
Peter Acker.
Peter Springer.
Jacob Schrick.
Goodlip Goodshall.
Michall Goodshall.
Chrissteen Harshey.
Henery Howerd.

7th Class.

Gorge Knissly.
John Stamen.
Gorge Muory.
David Bareek.
Ludwick Dites.
John Muory.
John Hover, juner.
Sepassteen Masster.
Simon Snider.
Willam Paterson.

8th Class.

Christen Breneman.
Henery Bowman.
Henery Smith.
Roberd Beard.
Nichlass Miller.
John Muyer.
Casper Stoner, livd. at Smith.
Joseph Goghnoower.
Samuel Magaret.

Serjts.

Hugh Workman.
Jacob Sherick.
Christian Hoober.

I do swear on the Holy Evangelist of Almighty God: That the above is a just and true state of the male white inhabitants, residing in my district agreeable to Law, and without any fraud to the State, to the best of my knowledge.

JAMES BEARD, Capt.

Sworn before me this
4th day of June 1782.

JAMES BARBER, S. L. L. C

A TRUE AND EXACT LIST OF THE NAMES, OF EACH AND EVERY MALE WHITE PERSON, INHABITING OR RESIDING, WITHIN MY DISTRICT, IN THE BATTALION OF LANCASTER COUNTY, MILITIA, BETWEEN THE AGE OF EIGHTEEN, AND FIFTY-THREE YEARS. TAKEN FOR THE YEAR 1782. (c.)

Captain.

Jacob Matzger.

Lieut.

John Yeanser.

Ens.

John Crummel.

Almonar.

John Stayman.

Privates.

First Class.

1. John Eshleman.
2. Abraham Miller.
3. Jacob Shoff.
4. John Folck.
5. Isaac Borckholder.
6. Edward Kelly.
7. Christian Nistebroe.
8. Samuel Neideg.
9. John Bauer.
10. Henry Eshleman.

Second Class.

11. David Eshleman.
12. Jacob Harnist.
13. Sammuel Hunder.
14. Martin Bare.
15. Henry Lersher.
16. Abraham Grafft.
17. John Werfel.
18. Peter Rummel.
19. Jacob Hess.
20. Michieal Mayer.

Third Class.

21. Michieal Herr.
22. John Sheaffer.
23. Jacob Mannert.
24. Adam Kendrick.
25. Danieal Brennemas.
26. Henry Miller.
27. Henry Pletsher.

Fourth Class.

28. John Mosser.
29. Benshaman Ehleman.
30. Isaac Miller.
31. Henry Neideg.
32. William Folck.
33. ——— ———.
34. Simon Brand.
35. John Shuster.
36. Jacob Shoff.
37. Henry Forer.
38. Alisa Foresia.
39. Peter Gonder.
40. William Harber.
41. Frantz Shober.

Fifth Class.

42. Daneal Mosser.
43. ——— ———.
44. Andrew Fale.
45. Martin Kuhn.
46. Fredrick Mannert.
47. Christian Kendrick.
48. Tehofelus Danning.
49. Jonas Newcommer.
50. Conrad Heable.
51. Jacob Stoner.
52. John Funck.
53. Dannnleal May.

Sixth Class.

53. Henry Shenck.
54. John Bare.
55. Ludwick Orbane.
56. Stofel Ort.
57. Jacob Hofman.
58. Fredrick Faver.
59. Lennert Albrihgt.
60. John Shoff.
61. Tobias Shanck.
62. John Rumble.
63. Abraham Fisher.

Seventh Class.

64. Fredrick Shoff.
65. Jacob Bacht.
66. Jacob Bare.
67. Dannleal Lingenfild.
68. Christian Shanck.
69. David Hess.
70. John Gut.
71. Malcher Hackman.
72. Antony Kline.
73. Tobias Stayman.
74. Harman Leeck.

Eighth Class.

75. Henry Stayman.
76. Micheal Shanck.
77. Christian Borckholder.
78. Henry Faltinbarger.
79. John Phillips.
80. Ritshard Borck.
81. George Miller.
82. Henry Gable.
83. Fredrick Polmer.
84. Simon Yeandas.
85. Henry Laudenshlager.
86. Lannerd Albright, Jr.

I do swear on the Holy Evangelist of Almighty God: That the above is a just and true state of the male white inhabitants, residing in my district agreeable to Law, and without any fraud to the State, to the best of my knowledge.

JACOB METZGER, Capt.

Sworn before me this
10th Day of August 1782.
JAMES BARBER.

OFFICERS OF FOURTH BATTALION. (a.)

Returned April 15, 1783.

Lieutenant Colonel.
Jacob Cooke.

Major.
Abraham Scott.

Adjutant.
Michael Peters.

Quarter Master.
Timothy Conner.

First company.
- Captain—James Anderson, Jr.
- Lieutenant—John Emmit.
- Ensign—John Shira.

Second company.
- Captain—John Bishop.
- Lieutenant—William Scott.
- Ensign—Conrad Shira.

Third company.
- Captain—George Ganttz.
- Lieutenant—Philip Arnold.
- Ensign—John Gerhart.

Fourth company.

Captain—David McQueen.
Lieutenant—Matthew Hays.
Ensign—Thomas Logan.

Fifth company.

Captain—Robert McKee.
Lieutenant—James Laird.
Ensign—Josiah Candour.

Sixth company.

Captain—James Cook.
Lieutenant—John Mercer.
Ensign—Joseph Galbraith.

Seventh company.

Captain—Patrick Hays.
Lieutenant—Benjamin Mills.
Ensign—James Sterrett.

Eighth company.

Captain—Thomas Robinson
Lieutenant—Andrew Shelley.
Ensign—James Miller.

A RETURN OF OFFICERS ELECTED IN THE FOURTH BATALLION OF LANCASTER COUNTY MILITIA—AGREEABLE TO ORDERS PUBLISHED FOR THAT PURPOSE ON THE 15TH DAY OF APRIL 1783. (c.)

Field Officers.

Lieut. Colonel.

Jacob Cook.

Major.

Abraham Scott.

Staff.

Michael Peters .... Adjut.
Timothy Connors .... Qur. Master.

Captains.

1. James Anderson, Junr.
2. John Bishop.
3. George Gantz.
4. David McQueen.
5. Robert McKee.
6. James Cook.
7. Patrick Hay.
8. Thomas Robeson.

Lieutenants.

1. John Emmit.
2. William Scott.
3. Philip Arnold.
4. Mathew Hay.
5. James Laird.
6. John Mercer.
7. Benjamin Mills.
8. Andrew Shell.

Ensigns.

1. Jacob Shire.
2. Conrad Shire.
3. John Gerhart.
4. Thomas Logan.
5. Josiah Candour.
6. Joseph Galbreath.
7. James Sterret.
8. James Miller.

I do hereby certify that the above Gentlemen were chosen officers in 4th Batal. Lancaster County Militia after returns made to me.

ADM. HUBLEY, JR., S. Lt. Lr. Cy.

GENERAL RETURN OF OFFICERS IN LANCASTER COUNTY MILITIA 15TH DAY OF APRIL 1783. (c.)

Fourth Battalion.

Field Officers.

Lieut. Colonel.

Ludwick Myer.

Major.

Nathanl. Siegler.

Captains.

1. Fred'k Rodfong.
2. Jacob Brand.
3. Jacob Metzger.
4. Christian Doman.
5. Alexr. Scott, Junr.
6. Joseph Wright.
7. James Patton.
8. James Beard.

Lieutenants.

1. Philip Baker.
2. Jacob Miller.
3. John Yanzer.
4. Michael Heller.
5. Jacob Gatz.
6. Adam Fisher.
7. Christian Ferree.
8. John Fisher.

Ensigns.

1. Henry Dietrich.
2. George Eresman.
3. Ulrich Fizil.
4. William Henry.
5. James Jacks.
6. Frederick Take.
7. Christopher Taylor.
8. Jacob Murray.

A TRUE & EXACT LIST OF THE NAMES OF EVERY MALE WHITE PERSON, INHABITING OR RESIDING WITHIN MY DISTRICT, IN THE FIRST COMPANY OF THE FOURTH BATTALION OF LANCASTER COUNTY MILITIA BETWEEN THE AGE OF EIGHTEEN & FIFTY THREE YEARS. TAKEN FOR THE YEAR 1783. (c.)

Captain.

Jas. Anderson.

Lieut.

John Emmuck.

Ensign.

Jacob Shereman.

Serjts.

Philip Clough.
Fred Stump.
John Wiand.

1st Class.

John Gorner.
Laurence Helman.
John Nighty.
Jacob Holsaple.
John Nicolas.
Daniel Elliot.
Petter Bowman.
James Clinghan.
Simon Cameron.
John Lang.
Fredrick Hope.
James Mase.
John Cook.
Christly Niesly.
John Whitehill.

2nd Class.

Adam Cline.
Christean Pestlar.
Jas. Macky.
Christly Grove.
Hendry Grove.
Jacob Grove.
John Grove, Jur.
Abraham Lang.
Arthur Vantz.
Jacob Hufman.
John Mase.
Jas. Karr.
John Black.
Thos. Bayly, Snr.
Nicolas Speck.
Thos. Bayly, Jur.
Martin Sieglar.
Hendry Naphaker.
Jas. McCam.
Joseph Work.
John McCallester.

3rd Class.

Christly Hegy.
Phillop Branner.
William Ginnen.
Jacob Clapper.
Fred. Yeigh.
Richard Keys.
Daniel Longaneckar.
Samuel Cook.
Jacob Long.
John Grove.
Petter Lindamore.
Martin Miley.
Richard Bishop.
Samuel Gennens.
David Vinegar.
Andrew Hershey.
Samuel Karr.
Christly Reignhart.
Phillop Morrison.
Joseph Hegle.

4th Class.

Christly Soudar.
Alexander Noble.
Thos. Thompson.
Petter Rutter.
Ulerick Engle.
Hugh Caldwell.
Christly Boocher.
George Barr.
George Fisher.
Wm. Mire.
Saml. McClun.
David Paughtel.
Adam Rosinberger.
Andrew Shirk.
Paul Gravner.
George Taniel.
George Reinhart.
Adam Clause.

5th Class.

Daniel Gilmore.
John Scott.
Martin Lindamore.
John Jurdin.
Robert Haselip.
Micael Nicolas.
George Clapper.
Robert Connal.

Wm. Rusko.
Nicolas Blasor.
Jacob Green.
Wm. Porter.
James Phegan.
Charles Aron.
John Rupe, Jur.
David Bowman.
John Logan.
James Cook.

6th Class.

Wm. Wilson.
Fredick Kelpaugh.
Wm. McGairy.
Robert Porter.
Anthony Hayns.
Jacob Wiand.
Micael Hufman.
Frances Stewart.
Felty Steer.
David Cook.
Richard Allison.
John Vantz.
John Brown.
Cornelus Fowlan.
Benjamin Tate.
John Albright.
Jas. Jacks.
Cornelus Higgans.
Martin Stoute.
Arthur Tigart.
Martin Jones.

7th Class.

John Tate.
Robert Cavan.
Ularick Tanner.
George Lindamore.
Samuel Thompson.
Jacob Harshey.
Fredrick Arden.
John Hourst.
Wm. Clinghan.
James Wilson.
Hendry Singlelope.
Thos. Hambleton.
Dominick Egle.
Patrick Oharoe.
George Kellar.
Wm. Maypowders.

8th Class.

Fredrick Kelpaugh, Snr.
Laughlin Ferree.
John Kelpaugh.
Walter Bell.
Heman Long.
John Defrance.
Conrade Albright.
Christean Vinegar.
Joseph Clapper.
Abraham Stowfer.
John Blasor.
Joseph Blatcher.
Daniel Stoute.
George Vantz.
Adam Niefe.
John Hollinger.
Jas. Michel.
John Bayly, Jur.
John Caron.
David Steel.
Jas. Gibbons.
Petter Sailor.
Richard McGarred.
Jacob Snider.

May ye 13th 1783.

A RETURN OF CAPT. ANDREW BOGGS COMPANY OF THE FOURTH BATTALION OF MILITIA IN LANCASTER COUNTY COMMANDED BY COLLN. JACOB COOK. (c.)

Captain.

Andrew Boggs.

Lieut.

James Cook.

Ens.

John Messer.

Serjants.

Nicholas Redsacker. George Snapper.

Corpls.

James Fiin. John Drivenstate.

Privates.

1st Class.

Joseph Galbreth.
John Eversole, Senr.
John Nicholas.
John Bower.
John Mummah.
Christian Blasor.
John Crill.
Jacob Earley.
John Grider, Junr.
William Gray.
Joseph Shank.
Thomas Scott.
Petter Stouts.

2nd Class.

Abraham Neesly.
Henry Cip.
Michale McCafferty.
George Root.
Jacob Neesly.
John Eversole, Junr, Big.
Thomas Hasson.
Robert Thompson.
John Frantz.
Andrew Bower.
George Newberry.

3rd Class.

Christian Horst.
John Bruniman.
Samuel Scott.
John Wiland, Junr.
John Earley.
Phillip Stam.
John Bruniman, Junr.

4th Class.

Phillip Holinger.	John Esleman, Senr.
Abraham Shaver.	John Nickey.
Benjamine Whisler.	Mathew Gray, Junr.
Jacob Barrick.	Petter Leighty.
Jacob Holinger.	

5th Class.

Martin Hisey.	Robert Connel.
Petter Hisey.	George Lindimore.
Robert Craig.	John Elder.
Bartrum Galbreth.	Christian Frantz.
Michale Neesly.	Randle McClure.

6th Class.

Samuel Wilson.	William Messer.
William Hawk.	Jacob Oldwiler.
Samuel Woods.	Jacob Brubacher.
Christian Bruniman.	George Hikes.
John Longnecker.	John Wilson.
Hugh Moore.	James Karr.
Petter Root.	Christian Stoner.
John Cook.	Nathan Woods.
Christian Bruniman, Junr.	Stophel Hollinger.
John Shank.	Abraham Albert.
John Grider.	George Counce.

7th Class.

Petter Hallsomer.	David Martin.
Jacob Angle.	Jacob Shimph.
John Horst.	Joseph Rheam.
Jacob Laver.	Jacob Bruniman.
Daniel Kinsinger.	Abraham Fredrick.
James Murphey.	Jacob Snider.
Zachariah Moore.	John Sleman, Junr.
Jacob Winecop.	Samuel Thompson.

8th Class.

Isack Rheam.	Robert Wilson.
John Brubacker.	John Angle.
Henry Wilhelm.	Thomas Messer.

Daniel Stramler.
John Wiland, Senr.
Abraham Scott.
Joseph Hisey.
Abrm. Carpender.
John Dukemineere.
Abraham Willislegle.
Henry Darr.
William Peck.
Andrew Hikes.
Christian Eversolc.
Henry Bruniman.
John Haldiman.

I Do Certify the above Return to be Just & True.
Certifyd.

ANDW. BOGGS, Capt.

May ye 13th 1783.

RETURNE OF THE MALE WITH INHABYTANS OF CAPT. DOMENYS COMPANY IN THE FOURTH BATILION COMMENDET BY COL. FREDERICK SIGLER. (c.)

Capt.

Christian Domen.

Let.

Michael Heller.

Ens.

William Henry.

St.

John Alter.
John Domen.
George Noss.

Privates.

1st Class.

1. John Kneef.
2. John Lip.
3. John Kaufman.
4. Martin Gonter.
5. Peter Grebiel.
6. John Kaufman.
7. Isaac Kaufman.
9. Michael Simer.
8. Jacob Witmore.
10. John McGriger.
11. Jacob Kaufman.

2nd Class.

12. Casper Loots.
13. Christian Newcomer.
14. Paul Acerman.
15. Martin Funck.
16. John Stopher.
17. Abraham Kaufman.
18. ——— ———.
19. ——— ———.
20. Conrad Sigler.
21. John Reiner.

3rd Class.

21. Jacob Shuck.
22. Jacob Bonn.
23. ——— ———.
24. Lenord Rickert.
25. Abraham Funck.
26. Henry Shank.
27. Jacob Stamen.
28. James Forsyth.
29. Christian Soner.
30. David Mellinger.
31. ——— ———.
32. William Archer.

4th Class.

32. Chirstian Herr.
33. Jacob Kaufman.
34. Samuel Funck.
35. Henry Kneef.
36. Abraham Miller.
37. Joseph Hobeger.
38. Andrew Kaufman.
39. John Sherck.
40. Christian Stamen.
41. Jacob Witmore.
42. Barny McLaglin.
43. William McCormick.
44. Adam Hanel.

5th Class.

44. William Kenedy.
45. John Hastater.
46. Andrew Kaufman.
47. Henry Shallenberger.
48. Henry Lighty.
49. John Funck.
50. Michael Shlot.
51. Jacob Hiller.
52. Mathis Singer.
53. Adam Shlot.
54. Mathis Bonn.

6th Class.

55. Jacob Sids.
56. Jacob Shallenberger.
57. George Loots.
58. Andrew Jacobs.
59. Christian Stoner.
60. Jacob Funck.
61. Abraham Hostater.
62. Abraham Stopher.
63. Jacob Shallenberger.
64. Edward Givins.
65. Jacob Shanck.

7th Class.

79. Benedict Melinger.
80. Christian Smith.
81. Jacob Mellinger.
82. James Grinly.
83. Christian Kaufman.
84. Henry Histant.

85. Isaac Kneef.
86. John Witmore.
87. Pitter Risel.
88.——— ———.
89. John Mann.
90. Joseph Kaafman.

8th Class.

66. Barny Mann.
67. Christian Wisler.
68. Christian Kaufman (Sen.)
69. Henry Funck.
70. Thomas Patton.
71. Benjamin Hostater.
72. John Miers.
73. Michael Ruply.
74. George Olwiller.
75. John Witmore.
76. Isaac Kaggy.
78. William Shoock.

Certyfy'd by me

CHRN. DOMEN, Capt.

RETURN OF CAPT. PATRICK HAYES COMP'Y OF THE 4TH BATTALION, LANCASTER CO. 1783. (c.)

Captain.

Pattrick Hayes.

Lieut.

Benjn. Mills.

Ensign.

James Sterret.

Corporals.

Jacob Arron.
William Williams.

First Class.

Christy Hoofman.
John Shank.
John Hayes.
Christy Erishman.
Phillip Gilman.
Baltzor Stake.
Hugh Haggerty.
Dewalt Shank.
James Corran.
Martin Ferr.
Abram Bear.
Allexr. Porter.

Second Class.

John Shelhorn. James Hayes.
Abram Kastle. Robert Sterret.
John Metz. John Strickler.

third Class.

Christy long. John Bayard.
Henry Strickler Jacob Walter.
Baltzor Walter. Petter Breilinger.
Henry Teesinger. Michael Pretz.

fourth Class.

Joseph Lytle. John Weigar.
Daniel Milloney. Ambrose Newsone.
Jacob Bender. Brice Clark.
Baltzor Shelhorn. George Snyder.
Abram Martin. Abram Holdeman.
Michael Stake. Saml. Brand.

fifth Class.

Hugh Grahams. Martin Niccely.
Michael Hoarst. Michael Hastler.
Petter Weigar. Saml. Mitten.
Jacob Hastater. Frederick Kistich.
Christy Longnecker. Henry Segrist.
Henry Aucher. John Broze.

Sixth Class.

Abram Motz. James Hutcheson.
Thomas Minto. William Cummins.
Mathias Kishler. Frederick Clair.
Isaac Gilman. James Moor.
Jacob Segrist. Petter Thomas.
James McCarvery. Christy Hoofman, Jr.
John McCalley.

Seventh Class.

Henry Hoobly. Christy Shelly.
Petter Heesten. John Boyd.
John Roara. Christy Shirk.
Ulley Strickler. John Templeton.
John Baker. Conrad Hoofman.
Phillip Baker. Frederick Sourer.
Jacob Kastle. Frederick Nauman.
Christy Metz.

Eighth Class.

Jacob Metz.	Petter Youts.
Jacob Erishman.	John Porter.
John Swenney.	Michael Rap.
Jacob Kinsler.	John Shellick.
Abram Erishman.	Petter Holderman.
William Sterret.	

Lancaster County.

I Do Swear the Return of the Persons Named herein Is Just and true.

Done before
me Oct. 23, 1783

PATRICK HAYES.

A MUSTER ROLE OF CAPTAIN THOMAS ROBINSON'S COMPANY BEING THE EIGHTH COMPANY OF THE FOURTH BATALION OF LANCASTER COUNTY MILITIA COMMANDED BY LEUT. COLN. JACOB COOK COMENSED ON THIS 21ST DAY OF APRIL 1783. (c.)

Captain.

Thomas Robinson.

Lieut.

Andrew Shell.

Ens.

James Miller.

Almonar.

Abraham Fredrick.

Sergt.

Henry Gepfert.	Jacob Wagler.
Michael Shell.	

1st Class.

Stophel Misenhelder.	John Schnyder.
Abraham Wolgonmuth.	Philip Sidenstricer.
John Stouffer.	James Carol.
Robert Robison.	Philip Beal.
Jacob Hummer.	

Second Class.

Robert Moorhead.	Fredrick Gantz.
John Peeter.	Jacob Eshelman.
John Leman, Junr.	Abraham Schnyder.
John Leman.	John Dinsman.

Third Class.

Christian Wolgomuth.	Ephraim Litle.
George Gepfert.	Philip Frederick.
William Moor.	Joseph Sherk.
Michael Hummer.	John Clark, Dead.
John Leman, Read.	Michael Over.
Philip Keiser.	Christian Cemerer.
Philip Kener.	Jacob Stopher.

Fourth Class.

Isaac Dettee.	Jacob Taubenberger.
Jacob Keener.	Jacob Hoffman.
Abraham Reesor.	John Eshelman.
Benjamin Benter.	Isaac Eshelman.
Meilhar Fortney.	Michael Black.
John Wagner.	James Breedy.
Anthony Shoemaker.	Christian Brand.
Jacob Conrad.	

Fifth Class.

James Moorhead.	John Brubaker.
William Allison.	John Kish, Dead.
Vallentine Hide.	Francis Grove, Junr.
David Flory.	Jacob Miller, Junr.
Jacob Shelly, Read.	Alexander Wiley.
John Springer.	Peter Frederick.
Christian Reesor.	Jacob (illegible).
Casper Lesher.	John Floory.

Sixth Class.

Christian Heer.	Joseph Wolf, Junr.
George Alspach.	Casper Coyer.
Andrew Robison.	Jacob Stopher, at Overs.
Philip Shoemaker, Junr.	William Connelly.
John Shelly.	Christian Sryar.
Abraham Flory.	Daniel Shoemaker.
Michael Ebby.	Michael Hoover.
Isaac Wagner.	Christian Bottenstone.
Conrad Springer.	

Seventh Class.

Fredrick Stober, Junr.
Jacob Holdeman.
Martin Griner.
Henry Limpert.
Jacob Grebil.
Peter Welker.
Isaac Boroway.
John Frederick.
John Peeter.
George Neeky.
Henry Over.
Sebastian Duncel.
Abraham Ettey.
John Heer.
John Benter.
Abraham Stollar, Dead.
Hugh McGlalin.
George Smith.
Jacob Segrist.
Jacob Reesor.
Peeter Eshelman.
Tobias Holinger.

Eighth Class.

David Misenhelder.
William Boal.
Daniel Conrad.
Michael Notz.
Larance Schneeringer.
George Shank.
Peeter Brubaker, junr.
John Holdiman.
William Mckain.
Abraham Geopfert.
Conrad Schreyer.
Philip Kemerer.
George Haventone.
Thomas Smith.

I Do Swear, On the Holy Evengalist of Almighty God: That the Within Roll is Just and true as it Stands Stated.
Sworn before me this first
Day of November 1783.

THOMAS ROBINSON, Capt.

A RETUREAN OF THE FIRST CLASS OF THE FOURTH BATN. IN LANCASTER COUNTY COMANDED BY COL. LUDWICH MUYER. (c.)

1st Company—Capt. Rodfanes Comp.

1st—Abraham Kindegh.
2d—fredrich buyear.
3d—Jacob Kindech.
4th—Jacob Lime.
5th—thomas McClaneghan.
6th—Jacob fouleat (?).
7th—Christen breneman.

2d Company—Capt. Brandes Comp.

1st—Jacob frantez.
2d—thomass Kratsor.
3d—Jacob Koofman.
4th—henery Knade, Jur.
5th—herman Wittmer.
6th—thomas hellord.
7th—Jacob Segelrest.
8th—george dunckle.

3d Company—Capt. Metzgar.

1st—Jacob borckeholder.
2d—John Cromewell.
3d—John Eshellman.
4th—Mechell Lormich (?)
5th—Heabrham millear.
6th—Mathew brown.
7th—george feawell.
8th—John fowelk.

4th Company comand by Capt. Doman.

1st—John Cofman.
2d—Jacob Witmear, son of John.
3d—henery Kofman.
4th—Martin Kander.
5th—petter grebell.
6th—Isack Koones.
7th—John Kofman.
8th—Isack Kofman.

5th Company—Capt. Scot Comp.

Ademe Shafer.
David Mossellman, junr.
Josepeh Martin.
Jacob hosetter.
Willeam Smith.
Jacob Springler.
Joseph Chaleres.
John Massey.
Jacob Hershy.

6th Company—Capt. Wright.

1st—John Bender.
2d—Christeen Neesteel Junr.
3d—george Braner.
4th—John Lincle.
5th—petter duncle.
6th—Jesoph Muser.
7th—petter Snider.
8th—Michell boughman.
9th—thomas Wright.

7th Comaney capt. patton.

1st—John Newcomar.
2d—William Stoneking.
3d—Jacob Simth.
4th ——— ———.
5th—phillip foox.
6th—Jacob Hoogendooblear.
7th—John taylor.
8th—david Shalleberger.
9th—henery harfoord.

8th company of capt. beardes.

1st—John Koofman.
2d — Christen Miller.
3d — Jhon Steman.
4th—Jacob hastend.
5th ——— ———.
6th—John hoover.
7th ——— ———.

LUDWICK MEYER, Col.

FIFTH BATTALION
LANCASTER COUNTY MILITIA.

THE MUSTER ROLL OF THE FIRST COMPANY OF THE FIFTH BATTALION, LANCASTER COUNTY, MILITIA, IN THE PROVINCE OF PENNSYLVANIA, COMMANDED BY COL. JAMES CRAWFORD AND CAPT. ROBERT BUYERS, BAERGEN TOWN CAMP, SEPT. 4TH., 1776:

Field and staff officers.

James Crawford, Colonel.
William Fullerton, First Major.
George Stewart, Second Major.
James Montgomery, St. Bearer.
John Whitehill, Q. M.
William Scott, Adjutant.
John Woodhull, D. D., Chaplain.
Leckey Murray, Surgeon.
James Wood, Sergt. Major.
James Forsyth, Q. M. Sergt.

First Company.

Robert Buyers, Capt. (sick).
Jno. Hopkins, First Lt.
James Armor, Second Lt.
James Houston, Ensign.
James Forsyth, 1st Sergeant.
John Hopper, 2d Sergeant.
John Wilson, 3d. Sergeant, promoted Sept. 5th, in place of William Holiday, discharged Sept. 1st.
Colin Martain, 4th Sergeant.
Charles Murray, 1st Corporal.
Jno. McMullin, 2d Corporal.
George Lynch, 3d Corporal.
Archibald McAfee, 4th Corporal.

Privates.

Michael Graham, dis. Sept. 3d, at Baergen.
William Camp.
Daniel Simons, dis. Aug. 12th.
Michael Jack.
John Runeba.
Wm. Cowan.
John Watson.

Wm. Boyd.
Wm. Wilson, dis. Aug. 18.
John Wilson, pro.Sergeant.
Ed. Runeha.
James Rodgers.
James Wilson.
Thomas Slemon, dis. Aug. 12.
Wm. Fleming, deceased at Baergen, Sept. 2.
John Armor.
J. T. Johnston.
J. T. Watson.
Arch. McCurdy, dis. at Trent Town Sept. 11.
Wm. Henry.
John Evans, dis. at Amboy Aug. 28.
Samuel Johnston.
John Wallace.
Adam Gault, dis. Aug. 12.
Thomas Johnston.
David McBride, dis. Trent Town Aug. 19.
James Mackey.
Wm. Richardson, dis. Amboy Aug. 25.
John McGowan, dis. Trent Town Aug. 19.
James Fleming.
Jacob Pee.
Samuel Hughes.
John Richardson.
J. T. McFadden.
T. Slemon, jr., dis. Trent Town Aug. 10.
James Gault.
Alex. Brown.
Wm. Brisban.
Robert Cowan.
Samuel Finley.
James Wilson.
Thomas Johnston.
John Herbison.
Robert Marshall.
Alex. Wilson.
Thomas Gault.
Wm. Patton.
Samuel Armor, dis. Amboy Aug. 27.
Jacob Martain.
David Guilkinson.
J. T. Borland.

Chas. McLean.
Thomas Henderson.
J. T. Patterson.
Daniel McAfee.
J. T. Dickey.
John Baxton.
Robert McNail.
Frank Holmes.
James Myers.
Moore Baggs.
David Withero, dis. Philadelphia Aug. 10.
J. T. McGaw.
Wm. Armstrong, dis. Philadelphia Aug. 10.
James Roach.
Wm. Codd.

"I do certify that this muster roll is a "true and correct statement of my company.

JAMES ARMOR, Lieut."

"Received December 2, 1776, of Capt. Robert Buyers the sum of twelve pounds, it being the money due to the men that enlisted into the Flying Camp ——— Received by Mr.

JAMES ARMOR, Lieut.

The Original of the foregoing in the possession of James Buyers, Esq., of Honey Brook, Chester county Penn.

A MUSTER ROLE OF CAPT. JAMES MERCERS COMP. OF THE 5TH BATTOLION OF LANCASTER COUNTY MILITIA COMMANDED BY COLN. JAMES CROWFORD. JANUARY 9TH 1777. (c.)

Capt.

James Mercer.

Lieut.

Henry Biggart.

Ensign.

Serjts.

Henry Smith. Andrew Moorland.

Privates.

Wm. McNabb.
James Henrey.
Patrick Corigan.
Hugh Woods.
John Turbatt.
John McFaden.
John Orr.
Mathew McClung.
James Hathorn.
Robt. Mathers.
Wm. Skiles.
Wm. Steward.

I do Declare on Honour that the Officers and men who Appeared this Day in my Compa are Bonafide Engaged in the Service of the United States, & Receive pay according to Rank they hold in this Role Likewise the time of Entring into & Present Service is Asscertained on & Face of this Role.

JAMES MERCER, Capt.

Mustred Then in Captn. Mecers Compa. The Captn one Lieutent, Two Serjants & Twelve Privates. This Muster Taken from Ninth January 1777 to Twenty Seventh Do Both Days Included.

NATH. DONNELL,
Dept. Must. Mast.

CAPTAIN JAMES MERCER'S COMPANY. (b.)

A Muster Roll of the Fifth Battalion of Lancaster County Militia, Commanded by Col. James Crawford, January 9, 1777.

Captain.

James Mercer.

Lieutenants.

Robert McCurdy.
Henry Biggart.

Ensign.

Hugh Duffy.

Sergeants.

Henry Smith.
Andrew Moorland.

Privates.

Wm. McNabb.	Wm. McCausland.
Sam'l Humes.	John Turbott, Jun'r.
James Henrey.	John Orr.
Patrick Corigan.	Mathew McClung.
Hugh Woods.	James Hathorn.
David Glen.	Robert Mathers.
John Turbott.	Wm. Skiles.
John McFaden.	Wm. Steward.

I Do Declare on Honour that the Officers and Men who appeared this Day in my Company are Bonafide Engaged in the Service of the United States, & Receive pay according to the Rank they hold in this Roll.

JAMES MERCER, Capt.

CAPTAIN ROBERT BUYERS' COMPANY. (a.)

A muster roll for Capt. Buyers' company of the 5th battalion of the Lancaster militia, commanded by Colonel Crawford. Philadelphia, January 27, 1777. Entered service January 13, 1777.

Captain.

Robert Buyers.

Lieutenant.

David Watson.

Sergeant.

John Campbell.

Privates.

William Wilson.	Robert Sharp.
John Armor.	John Hunter.
Thomas Johnston.	Samuel Smith.
Isaac Martin.	Daniel McAfee.
William Henrey.	John Wilson.

William McCashland. David Gleen.
John Calowell. Samuel Humes
Robert Miller.

I do Declare on Honour that the Officers a peared This Day in my company are Bonefid Service of the United States, and Receive P ye Rank they hold in this Roll. Likewise, th ing into ye Present Service is ascertained on Roll.

ROBERT BU

In Coun

Ja

Pay to the Order of Capt. Buyers Fifty- being one Month's pay for his company, to b Attlee, of Lancaster, to whom Capt. Buyers is the Money.

By Order of the Council,
THO. WHA

To J. M. NESBITT, ESQ.

Mustered then in Capt. Buyers' company t Lieutenant, one Serjeant, and Fifteen Privat is taken from the Thirteenth of January, 1777 seventh, Do, Boath Days Included.

NATH.
De

OFFICERS FIFTH LANCASTER COUNTY BA

Roll of part of Fifth Battalion, Lancaster Cou manded by Colonel James Crawford, who t teers at request of the Honourable Counc December 19, 1776, and marched to Philad ordered back the 26th of the same month b Putnam to bring the rest of the Battalio again to Philadelphia January 20, 1777.

Colonel.
James Crawford.

Major.

George Stewart.

Captain.

Robert Buyers.

Lieutenant.

David Watson.

Standard Bearer.

James Montgomery.

Quarter Master.

John Whitehill.

Sergeant.

Henry Smith.

Privates.

Thomas Johnson.
Thomas Johnston.
John Campbell.
James Johnson.
Isaac Martin.
John McFadden.

Passed in Council of Safety to be charged to William Atlee, Esq., to whom Major Stewart is to be accountable.

June 24, 1777.

THOMAS WHARTON, JR.
President.

To J. M. NESBITT, ESQ.

PAY ROLL OF PART OF 5TH BATTALION LANCASTER COUNTY MILITIA COMMANDED BY COL. JAMES CRAWFORD—WHO TURNED OUT VOLUNTEERS AT REQUEST OF THE HONORABLE COUNCIL OF SAFETY—ON THE 19TH DECEMBER 1776 & MARCHED TO PHILADA.—BUT WERE ORDERED BACK THE 26TH OF THE SAME MONTH BY MAJOR GENERAL PUTNAM TO BRING THE REST OF THE BATTALION—AND RETURNED AGAIN TO PHILA. THE 20TH JANUARY 1777. (c.)

Names.	Station.	Time in service.
George Stewart,	Major,	1 mo.
Robert Boyer,	Capt.,	1 mo.
David Watson,	Lieut.,	1 mo.
James Montgomery,	Std. Bearer,	1 mo.
John Whitehill,	Qr. Master,	1 mo.
Henry Smith,	Serjeant,	1 mo.
Thomas Johnson,	Private,	1 mo.
James Johnson,	Private,	1 mo.
Thomas Johnston,	Private,	1 mo.
Isaac Martin,	Private,	1 mo.
John Campbell,	Private,	1 mo.
John McFaddin,	Private,	1 mo.

Passed in Council of Safety to be charged to William Atlee Esq., of Lancaster to whom Major Stuart is to be accountable.

THOS. WHARTON, JR.,
President.

£78.S.17.d.6.

REPORT OF THE COMMISSIONED AND STAFF OFFICERS BELONGING TO THE FIFTH BATTALION OF MILITIA OF LANCASTER COUNTY, COMANDED BY COLONEL JACOB CLATZ, OCTOBER 25, 1777. (b.)

Colonel.
Jacob Clatz.

Lieutenant Colonel.
Philip Stouffer.

Major.
Jacob Richard.

Captains.

Mich'l App.
Ja's Krug.
John Graff.
George Francicus.
Peter Shaffner.
Ch'r Petrie.
Wm. Devis.
Adam Wilhelm.

First Lieutenants.

Ludw. Heck.
John Maurer.
Peter Diffedorfer.
Andrew Couningham.
George Bigler.
Henry Shauffer.

Second Lieutenants.

Jacob Shaefer.
Valentine Krug.
Ch'r Mayer.
George Leitaer.
John Bredyam.
John Griner.

Ensigns.

George Stragly.
Hen'r Giger.
Philip Witzel.
Henry Groff.
Geo. Koch.

Staff Officers.

Adjutant.

John Seelig.

Quarter Master.

Conrad Swartz.

Surgeon.

D. Huber.

Surgeon's Mate.

Andrew Walter.

Sergeant Major.

Leon'd Eichholtz, Q. M. Sergt.

REPORT OF THE COMMISSIONED AND STAFF OFFICERS BELONGING TO THE FIFTH BATTAL. OF MILITIA OF LANCASTER COUNTY, COMMANDED BY JACOB CLATZ, COL. OCTOBER 25TH, 1777. (c.)

Commissioned Officers.

Field Officers.

Jacob Clatz, Coll. Jacob Richard, Major.
Philip Boussel (?), Lt. Col.

Capts.

Mickl. App. Peter Shaffner.
Jas. Krug. Chr'st Petrie.
John Graff. Wm. Devis.
George Francisicis. Adam Wilhelm.

1st Lts.

Ludw. Heck. Andw. Conninghan.
John Maurer. George Bigler.
Peter Diffedorfer. Henry Stauffer.

2d Lts.

Jacob Shaefer. George Leitner.
Valent. Krug. John Bridyam.
Chr. Mayer. John Griner.

Ins'ns.

George Strayly. Henr. Graff.
Henr. Giger. Geo. Kock.
Philip Witzel.

Staff Officers.

John Seeley, Adjud. Andrw Walter, Surg. M.
Conrad Swartz, Qr. Master. Serjt. Major.
D. Huber, Surgeon. Leon't Eichholtz, Q. M. Sergt.

1777 October 25th. Recd. of Timothy Matlack esqr. Commissions agreeable to the above return of officers.

JACOB CLATZ, Col.

Certifyd by

BARTREM GALBRAITH,
Lieut. Lancr. County.

(c.) This is to certify that August Steiner Entterd as a substitute for a Drumer for John Long, Junr., to Serve in his Stead for tow monts according to Law in Capt. Samuel Davis Company in the Militia to go to the Camp in the 7 Class in the fifth Battalion for wich August Steiner is to have the Sum of Forty pounds & he the said August hath Rec'd on Demand the sum of Ten Pound for which I has a Rec'd for it and the Remander of the Ballunce he will Rec'd when he Gat his Hanestly Dischargh from his Captain & of his two monts.

Lancaster the 1 of
Novembr. 1777.

AUGUS STONER.

A LIST OF THE PERSONS NAMES THAT SERVED THEIR TOUR OF DUTY IN MY COMPANY AT CAMP IN THE YEAR. 1777. (c.)

Capt.
Joseph Jenkins.

Lieut.
1st. John Kilpatrick. 2d. Joseph Williamson.

Ensign.
James Vogan.

John Huston.	Jacob Mingos.
Thomas Eastburn.	Petter Miller.
Thomas Elliott.	John Cleeland.
Abraham Dolby.	John Harbeson.
Joseph Gilles.	Willm. Bell.
Francis Slay.	Alexander Tenant.
Jacob Ayres.	Jacob Nuthamer.
Daniel Ayres.	Chris'n Slough.
Robert Redman.	Hugh Harbeson
James Parks.	Jacob Hinkle.
Robert Good.	James McCoy.
John Maden.	Archibald McLeary.
John McMullen.	John Grist.
John McLean.	Alexander Clay.
Robert Hughes.	Patrick McGlocklin.
Jacob Silknitter.	Jacob Stoufer.

I do hereby certify the above to be a true return.

A RETURN OF LIEUT. SAML. ELLIOT COMPANIE FOR THE YEAR OF 1779. (c.)

1st Class.

Henry Good.
Peter Good.
Michal Stotts.
Henry Finfrock.
Rudy Fry.
Michael Troop.
Peter Lance.
Griffith Evans.

2d Class.

George Stoffer.
Henry Silknitter.
Martin Andsell.
Martin Greenplat.
Peter Funk.
Thomas Saychner.
Thomas Moor.

3d Class.

Peter Shirk.
Daniel Steever.
Richard Templin.
Vendle Cremer.
Johannes Guigley.
Cutlip Finkstock.
Robert Gaskin.

4th Class.

John Higer.
Peter Miller.
Samuel Good.
Nathan Evans.
Michael Keith.
Henry Yoter.
Jacob Couplance.
Philip Keith.

5th Class.

Malcolm Saychner.
Lance Goheen.
Robert Good.
George Snyder.
John Kattle.
Michael Funk.
Philip Troop.
George Hoofman.

6th Class.

Adam Shup.
Saml. Lance.
Jacob Good.
John Good.
Joseph Yoter.
Nichelas Moosen.
Adam Styer.

7th Class.

Nicholas Shup.
Christian Stofer.
Frederick Wallack.
George Slough.
Edward Goheen.
Androw Finfrock.
Christian Good.

8th Class.

William Snyder.
Mathias Muzleman.
Henrey Kern.
Jacob Burket.
Edward Kilpatrick.
Peter Weller.
Peter Peck.
John Cleeland.

A RETURN OF ALL THE NAMES OF ALL THE MAIL WHITE INHABITANTS OF THE FIRST COMPANY OF THE FIFTH BATTALION OF LANCASTER JUNE 15, 1780. (c.)

Capt.

William Crawford.

Livetenant.

Martin Bowman.

Ensign.

James Vogan.

Sargant.

Edward Good.

Privets.

Philip Shaffer.
Phillip Road.
Nicaloe trowdwine.
Richard Davis.
Fredreck Roadacre.
Christopher Sowr.
John Shaffer.
Petter Miller.
George Gaist.
Barnet Wolfe.
John Wolfe.
George Rine.
John Pinkerton.
William Randls.
Alexr. McCleare.
Adam Oberley.
Henry Bowman.
Samuel Bowman.
Henry Masoner.
Henry Otoe.
Johnathen Erwin.
Joseph Horst.

Barnet Lutz.
Marks grove.
James Erwin.
Alexa. Willson.
Abraham Rife.
Rudey Shaffer.
Petter Craps.
Jacob Sencennek, Jur.
Christion Sencennek.
Jacob Shovealter.
Jacob Stoffer.
Jacob Sensinigh, Ser.
John Widmor.
James Watson.
John Davis.
Robert Mathers.
John Diffenderfer.
Adam Diller.
Leonard Stone.
Jacob Stone.
George Stone.
George Maintzer.
Conrod Maintzer.
Abraham Groff.
Philip Sprecher.
Martin Groff.
Henry Groff.
Jacob Groff, Jur.
Christian Groff.
Casper Sherk.
Henry Lippart.
Jacob Summy.
Peter Summy.
Joseph Wolfe.
Michael Brubacker.
David Martin, Ser.
Marks Martin.
David Martin, Jur.
Christopher Martin.
Michael Sower.
Jacob Acre.
Philip Creak.
Jacob Weaver.
Christian Hole.
Jacob Hole.
Joseph Hole.
David Groff, Jir.
John Groff.
Peter Burkholder.
Christian Groff.
James Wallace.
Michael Kober.
Peter Dihl.
Henry Rohrer.
Peter Wyland.
John Smith.
Martin Shaffer.
Peter Ridenbaugh.
James Smith.
Willm. Miller.
Michael Sadler.
John Houser.
John at Marks Groves.

OFFICERS OF FIFTH BATTALION. (a.)

Returned August 26, 1780.

Lieutenant Colonel.
Jacob Carpenter.

Major.
Henry Markley.

First Company.

Captain—William Crawford.
Lieutenant—Martin Bowman.
Ensign—James Vogan.

Second Company.

Captain—Samuel Elliot.
Lieutenant—Robert Thompson.
Ensign—Andrew Finefrock.

Third Company.

Captain—Alexander McIlvaine.
Lieutenant—Alexander Martin.
Ensign—George Finefrock.

Fourth Company.

Captain—Joseph Jenkins.
Lieutenant—John Martin.
Ensign—Thomas Martin.

Fifth Company.

Captain—John Lutz.
Lieutenant—Abraham Zuber.
Ensign—George Stabbaugh.

Sixth Company.

Captain—Martin Bowman.
Lieutenant—John Ream.
Ensign—Valentine Varns.

Seventh Company.

Captain—Rudolph Statler.
Lieutenant—John Grim.
Ensign—John Alman.

Eighth Company.

Captain—Martin Holman.
Lieutenant—William Grove.
Ensign—John Kinser.

LIST OF THE FIRST CLASS 5TH BATT'N LA. COUNTY MILITIA ORDERED TO NORTHUMBERLAND OCTOBER 1780. (c.)

Capt. Elliots Compy.

Henry Good.
Peter Good.
Michl. Stoltz.
Henry Finefroch.
Michl. Troop.
Henry Lance.
John Davis.

Capt. Bowman's Compy.

John Gheer.
Joseph Zimmerman.
John Wanger.
Christ'n Swartzwelder.
Michael Handley.
John Shewwalter.
Michall Bitzer.
Benj. Sheneman.
Philip Swigert.
James Keemer.
Conrad Holtzinger.

Capt. Lutzes Compy.

Frederick Road.
Jacob Smith.
John Steigler.
Peter Good, Junr.
Beltzer Smith.
Jacob Cradler.

Capt. Jenkin's Compy.

Georg Weaver.
Jacob Nothamer.
Amos Evans.
Joseph Esington.
Jacob Yoder.
Daniel Stofer.

MAY THE 2, 1781. A RETURN OF ALL THE MAILE WHITE INHABETENS BETWENE THE EAGE OF EIGHTEEN AND FIFTY-THREE RESIDING WITHIN MY DISTRICK FIT TO BEARE ARMS. (c.)

Capt.
Samuel Elliott.

Lieut.
Robart Thomson.

Ins.
Androw Finfrock.

Shargens.

1st. Moses Cankead.
2d. James Hughes.
3d. Nathel Spencer.

Privates.

1st Class.

Henry Finfrock.
Henry Lance.
John Davis.
Peter Weller.

2d Class.

Gorge Stoffer.
Henry Silkniter.
Martin Ansel.
Peter Funck.
Philip Funck.
Adam Kyth.
James Rusel.

3rd Class.

Peter Shirk.
Vandel Cremer.
Joseph Shirk.
Abram Deal.
Abrham Eiselman, Fifer.

4th Class.

Peter Miller.
Nathan Evans.
Michel Kyth.
Jacob Longe.
Jacob Fulth.
Evan Rusel.

5th Class.

Lean Goheen.
Mickel Funch.
Philip Troop.
Androw Shimfasel.
Philip Castweller.
Richard Linsley.

6th Class.

Peter Peck.
Joseph Yoder.
Adam Stien.
William Glygle.

7th Class.

Mathias Stofer, Christ'r son.
Henry Sill.
James Castin.

8th Class.

William Syder.
James Douty.
Jacob Burket.
Edward Kirkpatric.
Christan Ludwick.
Isaak Rosburach.

I do sartyfy that this is a guste and true return to the best of my nolege.

SAMUEL ELIOTT, Capt.

A LIST OF THE FIRST COMPANY OF THE 5 BATTALION OF LANCASTER COUNTY MILITIA, MAY THE 11TH, 1781. (c.)

Captain.

Wm. Crawford.

Liuet.

John Davis.

Ensign.

James Vogan.

1st Class.

Philip Roade.
Christian Grove.
Rudolph Shaffer.
Adam Oberle.
Lenard Stone.
Nicalos troudwine.
Christopher Sowr.
David Grove.
Andrew ollipher.

2d Class.

John Wolfe.
Michael Kover.
Jacob Grove, Jur.
Peter Diller.
James Erwin.
Michael Brubacer.
Jacob Sencennek.
Jacob Stoufer.
Thomas Williamson.

3d Class.

Phillip Sprecher.
David Martin.
Christian Grove, Jur.
Abraham Rife, Jur.
Jacob Summey.
Richard Davis.
Abraham Grove.
James Wallace.
Henrey Bowman.
John Grove.

4th Class.

Alexander Willson.
Martin Grove, Jur.
Jacob Hole.
Petter Summey.
John Shaffer.
Marks Grove.
Henrey Grove.
Jacob Waver.
Thomas Erwin.
John Brenise.

5th Class.

Joseph Hole.	Peter Crap.
William Randels.	Michael Sowr.
Jacob Stone.	Petter Miller.
Casper Sherk.	Jacob Sencennek.
John Divedarver.	

6th Class.

Alexander McCleare.	Henrey Leppord.
Henrey Rorer.	John Baughman.
Johnathan Erwin.	James Watson.
George Gaist.	Daniel Ghare.
Petter Ridebaugh.	George Stone.

7th Class.

Samuel Bowman.	Henrey Otoe.
Phillip Shaffer.	Conrod Mainsor.
George Rine.	Barnet Wolfe.
Henrey Crim.	John Pinkerton.
Jacob Shovealter.	

8th Class.

Fredreck Roadeaker.	Christian Sencennek.
Michael Brubacer.	Adam Tiller.
Christian Hole.	Christopher Martin.
Marks Martin.	Daniel Grove.
Jacob Acer.	George Otoe.

WM. CRAWFORD, Capt.

A LIST OF ALL THE MANS IN WITHE AND HAVENTENCE OF CAPTIN JOHN LUTZES COMPENY IN BREEKNOCK TOWNSHIP MILITION IN THE YEAR 1781. 5TH COMPANY, 5TH BATTALION, LANC. CO. UNDER COMMAND OF COLONEL CARPENTER. (c.)

Capt.

John Lutz.

Leustennen.

Staffel Heft.

Ensign.

George Shlabach.

Sercents.

Michal Mesener.
Conerd Dehr.
John Shoup.

Corpral.

George Shnider.
Adam Behm.
Peter Fry.

Dromer.

Henry Shlabach.

Fyrer.

Philip Greber.

Klerck.

Samuel Enderen.

1st Class.

Jacob Shmith.
John Stigeler.
Peter Good, Ju.
Christian Shneder.
Henry Braunelet, Ju.
Baltzer Stone.
Benedick Mockel.
Peter Good, farmer.

2d Class.

Henry Wolfe.
Staffel Deerick.
Anderes Offenbach.
Peter Bohm.
John Zuber.
Abraham Zuber.
Jacob Weaver.

3d Class.

Henry Moser.
Jacob Stigeler.
Peter Franckhouser.
Danial Roth.
George Backer.
George Ranck.
Peter Good.

4tn Class.

Jacob Good, Ju.
Christian Mesener, Ju.
Friderick Houpt.
Henry Good.
Shem. Good.
Jacob Good, old.

5th Class.

Adem Weeber.
Jacob Roth.
Peter Kern.
Ludwick Fry.
Ludwick Shmith.
Peter Hosler.
Milchor Seynor.
Jacob Overholter.
Martin Cowel.
Christian Eickert.

6th Class.

John Stone. Christian Newshwamer.
Jacob Zeller. Jacob Good, Weeber.
Jacob Breidenstone. Henry Broumiller.
Jacob Fry, Ju. Leonard Mumma.
Stofel Wise. Balser Smith.
John Reseler.

7th Class.

Martin Myer. John Detvylor.
George Stigeler. John Shreek.
Philip Mesener. Christian Good.
Christian Shvartz. George Slaugh.
Michal Steffy. Philip Fensenach.
John Stover.

8th Class.

Abraham Martin. Ludwech Roth.
Samuel Martin. John Zuck.
Stoffel Kern. Mathias Holdry.
Henry Fry. Mathias Muselman.

JOHN LUTZ, Capt.

May 12th, 1781.

A RETURN OF THE MALE WHITE PERSONS FIT TO BER ARMS OF CAPT. RUTY STATTLER'S COMPY. BETWEEN EIGHTEEN & 53 YEARS OF AGE. (c.)

1 first Class.

Josept Rub. John Fesler.
Peter Brown. Christian forny.
Joel. Carpenter. John Meyer, Creeck.
Jacob Carpenter. Lenhart Conrad.

2 Second Class.

John Carpenter. Christian Meyer.
Abrham Forny, Junr. Niglaus Glaser.
Christian Garver. Friderick Smith.
Abraham Hunchberger.

3 Third Class.

Adam Alts. John Benter.
Henry Carpenter. Christian Wegner.
George Diderick. Micheal Wegner.
Martin Mawrer.

4 Fourth Class.

Adam Brown. John Ruty.
Henry Good. Martin Wolfart.
Christian Meyer. Chirstopher Reyer.
Peter Meyer. John Smith.
Christian Meyer, Junr. Jacob Roland.

5 fifth Class.

Enoch Abraham. Conrad Radman.
Abraham Forny, Senr. John Meyer, son of Elias.
Abraham Carpenter. Peter Wiland.
Samuel Grabile. Abraham Feig.

6 Sixt Class.

Diedrick Goched. Christian Harman.
John Grabile. John Shalenberger.
Solomon Harman. Peter Danner.
Christian Haas. Samuel Shenck.
Joseph Roland. Philip Hauge.

7 Seventh Class.

Andrew Fesler. Salomon Sigerift.
Micheal Forner. Valentin Gress.
Henry Garver. Jacob Eveneth.
Micheal Grosman.

8 Eight Class.

Micheal Altz. John Meyer, Junr.
Michael Capler. Elias Meyer.
Abraham Grabile. David Roland.
John Meyer, Christian's Son. John Rub.

The above Return is Certified by me this Second Day of June in the year one thousand Seven Hundred & Eighty one.

RUTY STATLER, Capt.

MUSTER ROLL OF THE 2ND CLASS 5TH BATT. LANC'R COUNTY MIL'A AND NOW DOING DUTY IN THE BOROUGH OF LANCASTER. (c.)

Names of Persons Who Served.	Names of Persons Who Furnished Substitutes.	Time when duty comm'd.	Time when duty ended.
Capt.		1781.	1781.
Samuel Elliot,		June 21,	Aug. 24.
Ensign.			
Wm. Smith.			
Cl'k.			
Nathl. Spencer,		June 26,	July 29.
Serjts.			
Mosses Kinkade,		June 21,	July 29.
James Hughes,		June 26,	July 29.
Drum.			
Joseph Williams,		June 21,	Aug. 24.
Fifer.			
Jacob Shirley.			
Privates.			
James Russel,		June 21,	July 29.
Jno. Markley,	Zacheus Pursell,		Aug. 22
Wm. Ditz,	Peter Becker.		
Christ'n Filebaum,			July 29.
Wm. Morgan.			
Mich'l Gillyan,	Peter Bence.		
Mich's Gillyan,	Abra. Andrews,		Aug. 22
Jacob Wyre.			
Jno. Groun,			July 29.
Edward Actison,		June 26,	
Nicholas Egges,	Mich'l Rhine,	June 21,	Aug. 22.
Mich'l Stever,		June 26,	July 29.
Abraham Zuber,		July 29,	July 29.
Ludwig Smith,	Staphel Ditrich,	June 28,	Aug. 24
Jacob Lutt,			July 29

Lanc'r June 26th, 81. Then mustered above company as specified in above roll.

AD'M HUBLEY, S. L. L'r C'y.

MUSTER ROLL OF 3D CLASS 5TH BATALLION LANC'R COUNTY MILA. ON DUTY AT LANCASTER. (c.)

Names of Persons Who Served.	Names of Persons Who Furnished Substitutes.	Time when duty comm'd.	Time when duty ended.
Lieut.		1781.	1781.
Jno. Martin,		July 1,	July 30.
Serj't.			
John McLeary,		July 2,	July 29.
Clerk.			
Fred'k Dity,		July 1,	July 30.
Privates.			
Jacob Hinkle,		July 2,	July 29.
Caspar Laurence,	David Harman,	July 4,	Aug. 24.
Michl. Rapp,	Peter Grimm.		
Fred'k Road,	George Beck,	July 2,	
Chris'n Long,	Jno. Diller,	July 3,	
Jno. Hinkle,	Jno. Rhine,	July 2,	
Ab'm Eisleman,		July 4,	
Eml. Pfeiffer,		July 4,	
Math's Colton,		July 4,	

Lanc'r July 10th, 81. Then mustered above company as above specified.

AD'M HUBLEY, S. L. L'r C'y.

ROLL OF THE 4TH, 5TH & 6TH CLASS OF 5TH BATALLION, LAN'R COUNTY MILITIA GONE ON A TOUER OF DUTY TO BUCKS COUNTY. (C.)

Names of Persons Who Perform a Toue of Duty.	What class.	Names of Persons Who Furnished Substitutes.	Time when duty commenced.	Time when duty ended.
			1781.	1781.
Capt.				
John Lutz,			Sept. 22d,	Oct'r 11d.
Lieut.				
John Ream,			Sept. 22d,	Oct'r 11d.
Ensign.				
John Kentzer,			Sept. 22d,	Oct'r 11d.
Privates.				
Evin Ressel,			Sept. 22d,	Oct'r 11d.
Allexarder Brown,		Henry Ritchwine,	Sept. 22d,	Oct'r 11d.
John Markley,		Andrew Brand,	Sept. 22d,	Oct'r 11d.
John Hinkle,		Nicholaus Yont,	Sept. 22d,	Oct'r 11d.
Jacob Dwenderffer,			Sept. 22d,	Oct'r 11d.
Jacob Verns,		Georg Hildebrand,	Sept. 22d,	Oct'r 11d.

ROLL OF THE 4TH, 5TH & 6TH CLASS OF 5TH BATALLION, LAN'R COUNTY MILITIA GONE ON A TOUER OF DUTY—Continued.

Names of Persons Who Perform a Touer of Duty.	What class.	Names of Persons Who Furnished Substitutes.	Time when duty commenced.	Time when duty ended.
			1751.	1781.
Abraham Forney,		John Rudey,	Spt. 22d,	Oct'r 11d.
Martin Wolfarth,			Sept. 22d,	Oct'r 11d.
Thomas Harris,		Henrey Skelles,	Sept. 22d,	Oct'r 11d.
Jacob Stone,			Sept. 22d,	Oct'r 11d.
John Miller,			Sept. 22d,	Oct'r 11d.
Enoch Abraham,			Sept. 22d,	Oct'r 11d.
Jacob Glsner,			Sept. 22d,	Oct'r 11d.
Martin Messner,		Abraham Carpenter,	Sept. 22d,	Oct'r 11d.
Joseph McCleary,			Sept. 22d,	Oct'r 11d.
Edward Eckison,		John Gordon,	Sept. 22d,	Oct'r 11d.
Michael Rap,		David Divenderffer,	Sept. 22d,	Oct'r 11d.
David felenbaum,			Sept. 22d,	Oct'r 11d.
Peter Keblinger,		James Watson,	Sept. 22d,	Oct'r 11d.
John Fox,		Henrey Kincer,	Sept. 22d,	Oct'r 11d.
Moses Kinked,		Frederick Seger,	[illegible] 22d,	Oct'r 11d.
James Evin,		Daniel Ehere,	Sept. 22d,	Oct'r 11d.

Peter Danner,			Sept. 22d,	Oct'r 11d.
Nicholaus Nothamer,		Adam Nothamer,	Sept. 22d,	Oct'r 11d.
Peter Donner,			Sept. 22d,	Oct'r 11d.
Josiah Brown,		Allex'r Collison,	Sept. 22d,	Oct'r 11d.
Jacob Bower,		John Shaleberger,	Sept. 22d,	Oct'r 11d.
James Cartner,			Sept. 22d,	Oct'r 11d.
John Zell,				

PROVISION RETURN OF THE 5TH BATAL OF LANCASTER COUNTY MILITIA COMMANDED BY COL. JACOB CARPENTER, FOR 2 DAYS COMMENCING THE 3D DAY OF OCTOBER, 1781. (c.)

	Col.	Major.	Cap.	Lieu.	Ens.	Adju.	Q. M.	Sur.	Q M. S.	Clark to Batal.	Privates.	Rate for each comp. per day.	Rations.
	1	1				1	1	1	1	1			22
Wm. Smith,			2	2	2						42	48	
Martain Huey,			2	2	2						42	48	
Jno. Fiel,			2	2	2						51	57	
Hugh Robinson,			2	2	2						41	47	
Noah Ceasey,			2	2	2						32	38	
David McQueen,			2	2	2						45	51	
Jno. Stone,			2	2	2						38	44	
Jno. Moore,			2	2	2						40	46	
Jos. Smith,			2	2	2						41	47	
												426	
												2	days,
												852	852
													874

Sr. Please issue above.
By order of J. Hanna, A. D. C.

Received eight hundred and seventy-four rations.
Alex'r Brown, Q. M.

MUSTER ROLL OF CAPT. RUDEY STADLER'S COMP'Y OF THE 7 CLASS OF THE 5 BATALION LAN'R *COUNTY MILITIA ON A TOUER OF DUTY AT LANCASTER.* (c.)

Names of Persons Who Perform a Touer of Duty.	What class.	Names of Persons who Furnished Substitutes.	Time when duty commenced.	Time when duty discharged.
			1781.	1781.
Capt.				
Rudy Stadler,	7th,		Oct'r 20th,	
Leiut.				
John Shelbly,	7th,		Oct'r 20th,	
Ensg'n.				
Valentine Wernts,	7th,		Oct'r 20th,	
Cl'k.				
Jacob Fohrney,	7th,		Oct'r 20th,	
Serj'ts.				
Conrad Ruty,	7th,		Oct'r 20th,	
Mathew Engil,	7th,		Oct'r 20th,	
Martin Bowman,	7th,		Oct'r 20th,	

MUSTER ROLL OF CAPT. RUDEY STADLER'S COMP'Y OF THE 7 CLASS OF THE 5 BATALION LAN'R COUNTY MILITIA—Continued.

Names of Persons Who Perform a Touer of Duty.	What class.	Names of Persons who Furnished Substitutes.	Time when duty commenced.	Time when duty discharged.
Corp'l.			81.	1781.
Henrey Steinbrink,	7th,		Oct'r [illegible],	
Conrad Menser,	7th,		Oct'r 20th,	
Daniel Hone,	7th,		Oct'r [illegible],	
Privates.				
James Gaston,	7th,		Oct'r [illegible],	
Elijah Hudson,	7th,		Oct'r [illegible],	
William Lee,	7th,	Nost. Ellmacher,	Oct'r 20th,	
Ludwick Smith,	7th,	Philip Maroner,	Oct'r 20th,	
Philip Bough,	7th,	Henrey Gerver,	Oct'r 20th,	
Isaac Oavis,	7th,		Oct'r 20th,	
Thomas Doglas,	7th,		Oct'r [illegible],	
Frederick Glass,	7th,		Oct'r [illegible],	
James Withrow,	7th,		Oct'r [illegible],	
John Pinckerton,	7th,		Oct'r 20th,	
Adam Leonard,	7th,	Michael Kindror,	Oct'r 20th,	

James Parcks,	7th,		Oct'r 20th,	
George [illegible]e,	7th,	Henrey Grim,	Oct'r [illegible],	
[illegible]ob Gillion,	7th,	Martin Myer,	Oct'r 30th,	
Jacob Bough,	7th,	George Ellin,	Oct'r 20th,	
Adam Ellin,	[illegible]th,	Andrew Fasler,	Oct'r 20th,	
Andrew Win,	7th,		Oct'r 20th,	
Jacob Warns,	7th,		Oct'r 20th,	
Frederick Mellinger,	7th,	Henrey Rudey,	Oct'r [illegible]0th,	
Jacob [illegible],	7th,	Philip Sheaffer,	Oct'r 20th,	
[illegible]es [illegible],	7th,	Barnard Wolf,	Oct'r 20th,	
Michael Ross,	7th,	[illegible]uel Bowman,	[illegible]t'r [illegible]th,	
Joseph Gillis,	[illegible],		Oct'r [illegible]th,	
Edward Attikison,	7th,	Henrey Zill,	Oct'r [illegible]th,	
John Zill,	7th,	Samuel Sttaffer,	Oct'r [illegible]th,	
John Markley,	7th,	Solomon Sichrist,	Oct'r 20th,	
George Divenderffer,	7th,	George Peiffer,	Oct'r [illegible],	
[illegible]ob Stone,	7th,	Isaac Ebey,	[illegible]t'r 20th,	
Thomas Edward,	7th,		Oct'r [illegible]th,	
John Shreck,	7th,		Oct'r [illegible]th,	
Jacob Roland,	7th,	Henrey Peter,	[illegible]t'r [illegible]th,	
Christopher Reinhill,	7th,	Mathis Springer,	Oct'r [illegible]th,	
Michall Reinhard,	7th,	Michael Grosman,	Oct'r 20th,	
James [illegible]y,	7th,		Oct'r 20th,	
Baltzer Haoener,	[illegible]th,	Jacob Sherk,	Oct'r 20th,	

A ROLL CALL OF CAPT. STATLER COMPY. THE 7TH OF THE 5TH BATT. L. C. MILITIA. (c.)

Capt.

Rudolph Statler.

Lieut.

John Grim.

Ensin.

Conrad Rudey.

Clerk.

Jacob Fohrney.

Serjts.

Mathise Engel.
Conrad Rudey.

Corp.

Wagoner.

Fife & Drum.

Jacob Werntz.
Henrey Rudey.

Privates.

1st Class.

Joseph Rup.
Petter Brown.
Joel Carpenter.
Jacob Carpenter.
John Fesler.
Christian Fahrney.
John Mayer, at the creek.
Bernhard Shriner.
Conhard Conrad.

2d Class.

John Carpenter.
Abraham Fohrney.
Christian Gerver.
Abraham Hunsperger.
Christian Meyer, Jun.
Niglaus Glasser.
Fridrik Smith.

3d Class.

Henrey Carpenter. John Banter.
George Digrick. Christian Wagoner
Adam Als. Mickel Wagoner.
Martin Masner.

4th Class.

Adam Brown. John Rudey.
Henrey Gooth. Martin Wolfart.
Christian Mayer, Vitzen son. Christian Rayer.
Petter Mayer. John Smith.
Christian Mayer, Juner. Jacob Roland.

5th Class.

Enoth Abraham. Conrad Radman.
Abraham Fohrney. Abrahan Fige.
Abraham Carpanter. John Mayer, Elis M'y son.
Samuel Grabil. Petter Wayland.

6th Class.

Dedreik Goshad. Christian Harmen.
John Grabil. John Shalenberger.
Salomon Harmen. Petter Donner.
Christian Hase. Samuel Shanck.
Joseph Roland. Phillip Hauck.

7th Class.

Andrew Fassler. Henry Gerver.
Mickel Forner. Mikel Grossman.

8th Class.

Mikel Alsts. John Mayer, Junner.
Mikel Capler. David Roland.
Abraham Grabil. John Roob.

December 22d, 1781.

RUDOLPH STATLER, Capt.

(c.) This is to Certify that Henry Rudy did play the Fife for the 7th Company in the 5th Battallion of Lancaster County Militia Eight Muster Days and Two Batallion Days in the year 1781 and Received no pay April ye 2d 1782.

JOHN KRIM, Lieut.

To MR. WILL'M SMITH,
Sub. Lieut.

(c.) I do hereby Certify that David Davis has served as a Drummer in the first Company in the fifth Batalion of Lancaster County Militia for ten days in the year 1781.

WM. CRAWFORD, Capt.

May 24th 1781.

To WILLIAM SMITH, Sub. Lieut.

(c.) I Do hereby Certify that Abram Esleman has Fifed for my Company eight Muster days and Two field days in the year 1781 in the 2d Comp'y in the 5th Batallion of Lancaster County Militia.

SAMUEL ELLIOTT, Capt.

December 26th 1781.

To COLO'L HUBLEY, Lieut. Lancaster County.

(c.) These are to Certify that Jacob Werts did Beat the Drum for the 7th Company in the 5th Batallion of Lancaster County Militia eight Muster days & Two Batalion days in the year 1781 and Rec'd no pay Aprile 2d 1782.

JOHN KEIM, Leut.

To WILLIAM SMITH, Sub. Lieut.

THE ROLL CALL OF CAP. ROODOLPH STATLERS COMPANY IN THE 7 COMPANY IN THE 5TH BATTELION OF LANCASTER COUNTY MILITIA, DECEMBER 28TH, 1782. (c.)

Captine.

Rudolph Statler.

Leithen.

John Grim.

Ensin.

Andree Roody.

Clarck.

Jacob fohrney.

Sarshant.

Mathis Engel.

Sarsh.

Conrad Roodey.

Corparel.

Barnd. Shriner.

Corpl.

Detrick Goshed.

Troomer.

Jacob Wernz.

Pfiffer.

Henrey Roody.

Privates.

1st Class.

Joseph Roop.
Petter Brown.
Joel Carpenter.
Jacob Carpenter.
John fasler.
Christian fohrney.
John Mayer at the Crik.
Lonhart Conrad.

2nd Class.

John Carpenter.
Abraham fohrney, junier.
Christian Gerwer.
Abraham Hunshberger.
Christian Mayer, Manit Son.
John fohrney.

3d Class.

Henry Carpanter.
George Ditrick.
Martin Masner.
Christian Wagner.
Michel Wagner.
Conrad Mayer.
Barnd. goshad.

4th Class.

Adam Brown.
Christian Mayer.
Peter Mayer.
Christian Mayer, Junr.
John Roodey
Martin Wolfart.
Stofel Rayer.
Jacob Rowland.
Ludwick Wolfart.
John Alleman.

5th Class.

Enogh Abraham. John Mayer, Elias Mayers Son
Abraham Carpanter. Harman Lorshpack.
Samuel Grebeel. Christian Heitler.

6th Class.

John Grebel. Peter Donner.
Salomon Harman. Phillip. Bachert.
Christian Hass. John Shallenberger.
Christian Harman.

7th Class.

Mickel Grosman. Emanuel Carpenter.
Henrey Gerwer. Henrey Bowman.
Jacob Roop.

8th Class.

Mickel Alts. John Mayer, Junier.
Adam Capler. John Roop.
Araham Grabel. Christian Sooke.

A Just and True Return of my Company in the 5th Batalion of Lancaster County Militia.

As Witness my hand.

RUDY STATLER, Capt.

A TRUE AND EXACT LIST OF THE NAMES OF EACH AND EVERY MALE WHITE PERSON INHABITING OR RESIDING WITHIN MY DISTRICT IN THE FIRST COMPANY OF THE FIFTH BATTALION OF LANCASTER COUNTY MILITIA BETWEEN THE AGE OF EIGHTEEN AND FIFTY-THREE YEARS. TAKEN FOR THE YEAR 1782. (c.)

Capt.

William Crawford.

Lieu.

John Davis.

Ens.

James Vogan.

Almonar.

William McClery.

1st Class.

Christian Grove.
Rudolf Shaffer.
Adam Overley.
Leonard Stone.
Nicholas Troudvine.
Christopher Soure.

David Grove.
Edward Ratchford.
Barnard Lutes.
Daniel Smith.
Adam Rumbarger.

2d Class.

John Wolfe.
Michalel Cover.
Jacob Grove, Junr.
Peter Dillar.
Michael Brubecer.

Jacob Sencennek.
Jacob Stofer.
Thomas Williamson.
Peter Springer.

3d Class.

Phillip Sprecher, Jun'r.
Abraham Rife, Junr.
Jacob Summy.
Richard Davis.
Abraham Grove.

James Wallace.
Henry Bowman.
John Grove.
Caspēr Kisinger, Rifs son in law.

4th Class.

Alexander Wilson.
Martin Grove, Junr.
Jacob Hole.
Peter Summy.
John Shaffer.

Marks Grove.
Henry Grove.
Jacob Weaver.
Thomas Ervin.
John Brenize.

5th Class.

Joseph Hole.
William Randals.
Jacob Stone.
Casper Sherk.
John Devedafer.
Peter Craps.

Michael Sour.
Peter Miller, Junr.
Jacob Senceneck, Senr.
George Oto.
David Harmon.
John Leopard.

6th Class.

Alexander McClery.
Henry Rorer.
Jonathan Ervin.
George Gaist.
Peter Ridebaugh.

Henry Leopard.
John Baughman.
James Watson.
Daniel Ghere.
George Stone.

7th Class.

Samuel Bowman.
Phillip Shaffer.
Jacob Shovealter.
Barnard Wolfe.
John Pinkerton.
Conrad Mainsor.
Nicholas Ridebaugh.
Peter Miller, Sen'r.
Jacob Waggoner.

8th Class.

Fredrick Rodacker.
Michael Brewbaker.
Christian Hole.
Marks Martin.
Jacob Ecer.
Christopher Martin.
Daniel Grove.
Abraham Mitts.

I do swear, on the Holy Evangelist of Almighty God: That the above is a just and true state of the male white inhabitants residing in my district agreeable to law and without any fraud to the state, to the best of my knowledge.

WILLIAM CRAWFORD, Capt.

Sworn before me this 5th day of July 1782.

WM. SMITH, Sub. Lt. L. C.

A TRUE AND EXACT LIST OF THE NAMES OF EACH AND EVERY MALE WHITE PERSON INHABITING OR RESIDING WITHIN MY DISTRICT, IN THE SECOND COMPANY OF THE FIFTH BATTALION OF LANCASTER COUNTY MILITIA BETWEEN THE AGE OF EIGHTEEN AND FIFTY-THREE YEARS. TAKEN FOR THE YEAR 1782. (c.)

Capt.

Samuel Elliott.

Lieu.

Robert Thomson.

Ens.

Moses Kincade.

1st Class.

Henry Finsrook.
Henry Lantz.
Christian Yoder.
Peter Weller.
Peter Good, farmer.
John Davis, carpenter.

2d Class.

George Staffey.	Adam Keyth.
Martin Ansil.	Henry Silknitter.
Philip Funk.	Peter Funk.

3d Class.

Peter Shirk.	Vandle Cremer.
Fredereck Weller.	Jo eph Shirk.
William James.	Abram Deal.

4th Class.

Peter Miller.	Jacob Long.
Hugh Coningham.	Jacob Fulst.
Robert Good.	Evan Russel.
Nathan Evans.	Samuel Good.
Micheal Keyth.	Peter Resler.

5th Class.

William Stolts.	Philip Troop.
Lane Gobeen.	Peter Good, Weaver.
Micheal Funk.	

6th Class.

Joseph Yoder.	John Kirkpatrick, Jur.
Adam Styer.	Philip Miller.
William Gigly.	Jacob Good.

7th Class.

Mathius Stofer.	Nicholas Soop.
Henery Zill.	George Slough.
Micheal Silknitter.	Chirstian Good.
James Casten.	

8th Class.

William Snyder.	Christian Loudwick.
James Douten.	Henry Kerns.
Jacob Burket.	Mathius Mussleman.
Edward Kirkpatrick.	Peter Lantz.
Peter Peck.	Henry Baker.
Henry Hoofman.	

I do swear, on the Holy Evangelist of Almighty God: That the above is a just and true state of the male white inhabitants residing in my district agreeable to law and without any fraud to the state, to the best of my knowledge.

SAMUEL ELLIOTT, Capt.

Sworn before me this 27th day of April 1782.

WM. SMITH, Sub. Lieut.

A TRUE AND EXACT LIST OF THE NAMES OF EACH AND EVERY MALE WHITE PERSON INHABITING OR RESIDING WITHIN MY DISTRICT IN THE FIRST COMPANY OF THE FIFTH BATTALION OF LANCASTER COUNTY MILITIA BETWEEN THE AGE OF EIGHTEEN AND FIFTY-THREE YEARS. TAKEN FOR THE YEAR 1782. (c.)

Capt.

Alexr. Mc Ilvain.

Lieu.

Allexr. Martin.

Ens.

Jacob Fox.

Almonar.

Robert Wallace.

Sargants.

1st. Jacob Widlor.
2d. Morgan Evans.
3d. Joseph Wright.

Corpl.

1st. Joseph Gillist.
2d. George Davis.
3d. Fredrick Glease.

Clark.

Evan Evans.

1st Class.

Casper Shirk.
Nathan Evans.
Edward Good.
James Keimer.
Valentine Mandle.
Henry Carpenter.
Christian Root.
Joseph Wilamson.

2d Class.

Daniel Burrel.
Loudwig Ranck.
George Martin.
John Sneder.
Daniel Staffer.
Edward Ackeson.
John Weaver, Jr., Jacob son.
Samuel Ranck.

3d Class.

Martin Martin.
Balser Bitzer.
Philip Sneder.
Jacob Weaver, Jo'n son.
Michal Sneder.
Michal Ranck.
Henry Weaver, Sn'r.
Peter Grim.
Daniel Stever.
Joseph Carpenter.
Jacob Glazer, Jur.

4th Class.

Peter Weaver.
Christian Sneder.
John Ranck.
Jacob Weaver, mil.
William Harvey.
Jacob Weaver, Jr., Jon. son.
George Weaver, Jo'n son.
Daniel Witman.
Stoffel Miller.

5th Class.

George Stoffer.
Henry Weaver, Stil.
Henry Wagner.
Michal Shirk, mil.
Andrew Lutter.
Peter Worst.
Daniel Stoffer, son.
George Fultz.

6th Class.

Jacob Ranck.
Abraham Aichard.
Daniel Aichard.
John Shirk.
Valintine Ranck.
Henry Weaver, hil.
Christian Carpenter.
John Goldon.
John Beaher.
Henry Root.

7th Class.

Jacob Hoover.
Peter Carpenter.
Mathias Springer.
Adam Ranck.
Jacob Matter.
John Higard.
John Kirpatrick.
Thomas Edwards.
John Spare.
John Houser.

8th Class.

Michal Shirk.	Christian Carpenter, Jun.
John Fultz.	George Weaver, fat Jon. son.
Samuel Stoffer.	James Mayers.
Adam .tock.	Adam Diller.
Henry Martin.	Henry Carpenter.

I do swear, on the Holy Evangelist of Almighty God: That the above list is a just and true state of the male white inhabitants residing in my district agreeable to law and without any fraud to the state, to the best of my knowledge.

ALEXR. McILVAIN, Capt.

Sworn before me this eight day of June, 1782.

WM. SMITH,
Sub. Lieut.

A TRUE AND EXACT LIST OF THE NAMES OF EACH AND EVERY MALE WHITE PERSON INHABITING OR RESIDING WITHIN MY DISTRICT IN THE FOURTH COMPANY OF THE FIFTH BATTALION OF LANCASTER COUNTY MILITIA BETWEEN THE AGE OF EIGHTEEN AND FIFTY-THREE YEARS. TAKEN FOR THE YEAR 1782. (c.)

Capt.

Joseph Jenkins.

Lieut.

John Martin.

Ens.

Thomas Martin.

Almonar.

John Evans.

1st Class.

Nicholass Narthomer.	Joseph Esington.
Jacob Narthamer.	Jacob Yoder, Junier.
Amos Evans.	

2d Class.

James Patterson.	William Morgan.
John Jenkins.	Thomas Eastbourn.
Thomas Ratue.	Michal Funk.

3d Class.

John Evans, Jun.	John Bowling.
Lott Evans.	James Davis.
John Wilson.	

4th Class.

John Piler.	James Morgan.
David Evans.	Francis Willmin.
Henry Weaver, miller.	George Hearst.
William Bell.	Christian Fisher.

5th Class.

Joseph Stearns.	Thomas Morgan.
James Watt.	John Reese.
John Zill.	William Fleming.

6th Class.

John Yoder.	David Jenkins.
Abram Dolby.	David Mongomery.
William Evans.	James Goheen.
Morris Hudson.	Jacob Lance.
Emanuel Nighswanger.	Jacob Blosor.
John Morgan.	Michal Bootner.
Thomas Jenkins.	William Lamus.

7th Class.

James Witherow.	Mathias Stofer.
Samuel Stofer.	Thomas Duglass.
Elijah Hudson.	Cromall McVity.
James Parks.	Edward Goheen.
Isaac Jenkin.	John Smith.
John Jenkins, Junier.	George Hudson.
William Hudson.	

8th Class.

John Zill, farmer.	Christian Curts.
Henry Weaver, Junr.	John Northamer.
Valentine Ronk.	John Yoder, Senr.
Theadcre Wilmin.	Christian Yoder.

William Meridith.	Samual Hidings	
Nathah Evans.	John Huston.	Serjants.
Jacob Stofer.	Thos. Fogarty.	
John Cleland.	Adam Northamer.	

I do swear on the Holy Evengilest of Almighty God: That the above is a just and true state of the male white inhabitants residing in my district agreeable to law and without any fraud to the state, to the best of my knowledge.

JOSEPH JENKINS, Capt.

Sworn before me this 4th day of June 1782.

WM. SMITH,
Sub. Lieut. L. C.

A TRUE AND EXACT LIST OF THE NAMES OF EACH AND EVERY MALE WHITE PERSON INHABITING OR RESIDING WITHIN MY DISTRICT IN THE 5TH COMPANY OF THE FIFTH BATTALION OF LANCASTER COUNTY MILITIA BETWEEN THE AGE OF EIGHTEEN AND FIFTY-THREE YEARS. TAKEN FOR THE YEAR 1782. (c.)

Capt.

John Lutts.

Lieu.

Stofel Heft.

Ens.

George Slabaugh.

1st Class.

Michael Masoner, 1st serjt.	Christian Snider.
Jacob Smith.	Henry Brownaller, Junr.
John Stigler.	Benedick Muchel.
Peter Good, Junr.	Emanuel Fifer.

2d Class.

Henry Wolf.	Peter Beam, Junr.
Christopher Ditterick.	John Zuber.
Andrew Offenbaugh.	Abram Zuber.

3d Class.

Peter Frankhouser.
Daniel Rode.
George Beck.
George Raunk.
Jacob Carpenter.

4th Class.

Jacob Good, Junr.
Christian Masoner, Junr.
Frederick Holt.

5th Class.

Adam Weaver.
Jacob Rode.
Peter Karn.
Ludwick Fry.
Ludwick Smith.
Peter Holler.

6th Class.

John Stone.
Jacob Zeller.
Jacob Fry, Junr.
John Resler.
Chirstian Newswanger
Palser Smith.
John Brindle.

7th Class.

Martin Myer.
George Stigler.
Jacob Masoner.
Chirstian Swarts.
Michael Staffey.
John Stofer.
John Ditwiller.
John Shruk.
Philip Fensenaugh.
Michael Carpenter.

8th Class.

Abram Martin.
Samuel Martin.
Stofel Karn.
Henry Fry.
Ludwick Rode.
John Soak.

I do affirm, on the Holy Evengileet of Almighty God: That the above list is a just and true state of the male white inhabitants residing in my district agreeable to law and without any fraud to the state to the best of my knowledge.

JOHN LUTTS, Capt.

Sworn before me this seventeenth day of April 1782.

WM. SMITH,
Sub. Lieut.

A TRUE AND EXACT LIST OF THE NAMES OF EACH AND EVERY MALE WHITE PERSON INHABITING OR RESIDING WITHIN MY DISTRICT, IN THE SIXTH COMPANY OF THE FIFTH BATTALION OF LANCASTER COUNTY MILITIA BETWEEN THE AGE OF EIGHTEEN AND FIFTY-THREE YEARS. TAKEN FOR THE YEAR 1782. (c.)

Capt.

Martin Bowman.

Lieu.

John Norton.

Ens.

Valentine Werntz.

Almonar.

John Martin.

Privates.

1st Class.

John Ghere.
Joseph Zimmerman.
Christian Schwartzwelder.
John Shuwalder.
Michael Bitzer.
Conrad Holtzinger.
Jacob Sneder.
Leonard German.
Philip Roth.

2d Class.

Jacob Weise.
Andrew Yount.
Peter Pence.
Jacob Swigert.
Abraham Wolfe.
Henery Sherk.
Jacob Wever.
James Shaw.
Abraham Andreas.

3d Class.

John McCleary.
George German.
Michiael Hause.
George Ghere.
John Evans.
Jacob Hinkle.
Wm. Parry.
Adam German.
Philip Rinmood.
Philip Wies.
John Getz.
Mathew Shaw.
George Glatze, farmer.

4th Class.

James Goult.
Andrew Wiese.
David Camssher.
John German.
John Muman.
George Wever.
Henery Roth.

5th Class.

John Yount.
Martin Wernce.
David Morgan.
John Bitzer.
Jonathan Roland.
Abraham Solenberger.
Ernst Miller.
Andrew Hipsher.
Philip Pence.
John McClen.
Henery Souder.

6th Class.

John Fautsnaught.
John Sids.
Alex'r Goult.
Philip Ronk.
Wm. McClen.
Christopher Miller.
John Cooper.
Wm. Culdin.
Henery Yeger.

7th Class.

James McClery.
George Clopper.
Isaac Davis.
John Campher.
John Wenger.
Jacob Sherk.
Mathias Wallig.
George Hessner.

8th Class.

John Roth.
Jacob Bratzor.
Valendin Britge.
Michiael Killian.
Willias Davis.
Wm. Shaw.
Melcher Brown.
John Fistenawer.
Thos. Kittera.
George Glatze Wever.

I do swear on the Holy Evengilest of Almighty God: That the above list is a just and true state of the male white inhabitants residing in my district agreeable to law and without any fraud to the state to the best of my knowledge.

MARTIN BOWMAN, Capt.

Affirmed before me this eleventh day of June in the year 1782.

WM. SMITH,
Sub. Lt. L. C. M.

A TRUE AND EXACT LIST OF THE NAMES OF EACH AND EVERY MALE WHITE PERSON INHABITING OR RESIDING WITHIN MY DISTRICT IN THE SEVENTH COMPANY OF THE FIFTH BATTALION OF LANCASTER COUNTY MILITIA BETWEEN THE AGE OF EIGHTEEN AND FIFTY-THREE YEARS. TAKEN FOR THE YEAR 1782. (c.)

Capt.

Roodolph Statler.

Lieu.

John Grim.

Ens.

Andreas Roodey.

Almonar.

Abraham Fohrney.

1st Class.

Josaph Roop.
Petter Brown.
Joel Carpenter.
John Fassler.
Jacob Carpenter.
Christian Fohrney.
John Mayer.
Lonhard Conrad.
Barnhard Shrinner.

2d Class.

John Carpenter.
Abraham Fohrney, Juneer.
Christian Gerver.
Abraham Hunshberger.
Christian Mayer.
Freidrick Smith.
John Fohrney.

3d Class.

Henry Carpenter.
George Ditrich.
Matrin Masner.
John Benter.
Christian Wagner.
Mickel Wagner.
Ludwick Fatriss.
John Drimbel.
Conrad Mayer.

4th Class.

Adam Brown.
Christian Mayer.
Petter Mayer.
Christian Mayer, Juneer.

John Roodey.
Martin Wolfart.
Stofel Rayer.
Jacob Rowland.
Ludwick Wolfart.
John Allamen.

5th Class.

Enogh Abraham.
Abraham Carpenter.
Samuel Grabel.
Abraham Fige.
John Mayer.
Herman Lorspach.
Christian Heistler.
Barnhart Goshad.

6th Class.

John Grabel.
Solomon Harman.
Christian Hass.
Chritian Harman.
Petter Donner.
Phillip Bachert.
William Otto.
Niclous Zaller.
John Shallanbegar.
Didrich Goshad.

7th Class.

Jacob Fohrney.
Mathias Engel.
Conrad Roodey.
Jacob Werns.
Henrey Roodey.
Andrew Fassler.
Mickel Grosman.
Henrey Gerver.
Jacob Roop.
Phillip Booch.
Emanuel Carpenter.

8th Class.

Henrey Bowman.
Mickel Als.
Adam Capler.
Abraham Grabel.
John Mayer, Junier.
David Rowland.
John Roop.
Adam Stoll.

I do affirm, on the Holy Evengiliest of Almighty God: That the above list is a just and true state of the male white inhabitants residing in my district agreeable to law and without any fraud to the state to the best of my knowledge.

ROODOLPH STATLER, Capt.

Affirmed before me this twenty-fifth day of June 1782.

WM. SMITH,
Sub. Lieut.

A TRUE AND EXACT LIST OF THE NAMES OF EACH AND EVERY MALE WHITE PERSON INHABITING OR RESIDING, WITHIN MY DISTRICT, IN THE EIGHT COMPANY OF THE FIFTH BATTALION OF LANCASTER COUNTY MILITIA BETWEEN THE AGE OF EIGHTEEN AND FIFTY-THREE YEARS. TAKEN FOR THE YEAR 1782. (c.)

Captain.

James McConnall.

Lieut.

John Shivly.

Ensign.

John Kindsor.

Almonar.

James Thompson.

First Class.

1. ulrick wisler.
2. Henry Stinbring.
3. Micheal Brows.
4. Emigh Snider.
5. Christan Primer.
6. Philiph Road.
7. John Davies.
8. John [illegible]enly.
9. Jacob Erick.
10. John Kurts.
11. Ludigh Kile.
12. Jacob Road.
13. Marten Road.
14. Henry Hildebrand.

Second Class.

Zachus Percal(?).
Jacob Lutt.
Petter Barker.
Christan Felenbaum.
Peter Smith.
Marten Huber, Jur.
Michael Rope.
John Barr.
Tobias Barr.

Third Class.

Michael Hildebrand.
John Rine.
John Huber, Jur.
John Diller.
Cutlip Paff.
Abraham Barr.
Soloman Deeds.
Isaac Diller.
John Light.
Hugh Speear.
Valintin Stover.
Jacob Hubor.

Fourth Class.

George Hildebrand.	Henry Road.
Sebaston Bower.	Michael Barr.
Andrew Marter.	Andrew Brand.
Henry Richwine.	George Dovendolpher.
Nichloos Yount.	Marten Grove.
Jacob Devenderver.	Joseph Rudolph.

Fifth Class.

John Linder.	Henry Skiles.
Michael Eackert.	John Miller.
John Perkenhauser.	Jacob Brubacker.
Michael Rine.	John Engle.
Samuel Grible.	William Marshel.
Christan Hubear.	John Grows.
Philip Brubacker.	

Sixth Class.

David Feienbaum.	Christopher wike.
Christan Musselman.	Peter Kurtes.
Nathanil Swaker.	Fredrick Seger.
Wendel Hinkle.	David Davender.
John Davendopher.	James Crawford.

Seventh Class.

Micheal Kindsor.	Isaac Ebey.
Petter Diller.	John Lower.
Valintin Kindsor.	Adam Eicholts.
Henry Petres.	James Dick.
George Eley.	John Hetzel.
Nathanil Ellmacker.	Henry Crim.
Joseph Musselman.	Valintin Petery.

Eighth Class.

Adam L.ller.	Christan Smoker.
Micheal Gribel.	Jacob Ellmacker.
James Marten.	Jacob Andrew.
Hugh Thompson.	Micheal Virly.
Micheal Marten.	John Grice.
Samuel Barr.	Marten Holman.

I do swear on the Holy Evengilest of Almighty God: That the above list is a just and true state of the male white inhabitants residing in my district agreeable to law and without any fraud to the state to the best of my knowledge.

JAMES McCONNALL, Capt.

Sworn before me this fifteenth day of June in the year 1782.

WM. SMITH,
Sub. Leret. L. C.

A ROLL CALL OF CAPT. ROODOLPH STADLER'S COMPANY AT THE 7TH CLASS THE 5TH BATTALION 1782. (c.)

Capt.

Roodolph Statler.

Lieut.

John Grim.

Ensine.

Andrew Roodey.

Clarck.

Jacob Fohrney.

Sarhant.

Mathise Engel. Conrod Rodey.

Corperal.

Barnhard Shriner. Ditrich Goshed.

Droomer.

Jacob Wernz.

Fifer.

Henrey Roodey.

Privates.

1st Class.

Joseph Roop. John Fassler.
Peter Brown. Christian Fohrney.
Joel Carpenter. John Mayer.
Jacob Carpenter. Lenhard Conrad.

2d Class.

John Carpenter.
Abraham Fohrney, Jun.
Chrstian Gerver.
Abraham Hunshberger.
Christian Mayer, Manis son.
Freidrick Smith.
John Fo: rney.

3d Class.

Henrey Carpenter..
George Ditrich.
Martin Masner.
John Benter.
Christian Wegner.
Mickel Wegner.
Ludwick Fatris.
John Drimbel.
Conrad Mayer.

4th Class.

Peter Springer.
Christian Mayer, Vizen son.
Petter Mayer.
Christian Mayer, Jun.
John Roodey.
Martin Wolfart.
Stofel Rayer.
Jacob Rowland.
Ludwick Wolfart.
John Allamen.
Adam Brown.

5th Class.

Enogh Abraham.
Abraham Carpenter.
Samuel Grebel.
Abraham Fige.
John Mayer, Elias M'y Son.
Herman Lorspach.
Christian Heiller.
Barnhart Gosbet.

6th Class.

John Grebel.
Solomon Herman.
Christian Hass.
Christian Herman.
Peter Donner.
Phillip Bachert.
William Otto.
Niclos Zeller.
John Shallenberger.

7th Class.

Andrew Fasler.
Michel Grosman.
Henrey Gerver.
Jacob Roop.
Phillip Booch.
Emen. Carpenter.
Henrey Bowman

8th Class.

Michel Abs.
Adam Capler.
Abraham Grebel.
John Mayer, Juner,
David Rowland.
John Roop.
Aadam Stoll,

OFFICERS OF FIFTH BATTALION. (a.)

Returned April 15, 1783.

Lieutenant Colonel.

Thomas Murray.

Major.

John Gilchrist, Jr.

First Company.

Captain—Jonathan McClure.
Lieutenant—Daniel Hoffman.
Ensign—Jacob Snider.

Second Company.

Captain—William McClure, Jr.
Lieutenant—Joseph Smith.
Ensign—William Steele.

Third Company.

Captain—William Murray.
Lieutenant—Thomas Sturgeon.
Ensign—John Brown, Jr.

Fourth Company.

Captain—Martin Weaver.
Lieutenant—Matthias Deibler.
Ensign—Daniel Stoever.

Fifth Company.

Captain—Andrew Stewart.
Lieutenant—Andrew Graybill.
Ensign—Thomas Forster.

Sixth Company.

Captain—George McMillen.
Lieutenant—William McMillen.
Ensign—Samuel Berryhill.

Seventh Company.

Captain—Hugh Robertson.
Lieutenant—Michael Simes.
Ensign—William Stewart.

Eighth Company.

Captain—William Johnson.
Lieutenant—George Cook.
Ensign—George Taylor.

GENERAL RETURN OF THE OFFICERS OF THE LANCASTER COUNTY MILITIA 15TH APRIL, 1783. (c.)

FIFTH BATTALION.

Field Officers.

Lieut. Col.

Jacob Carpenter.

Maj'r.

Henry Markley.

Captains.

1. William Crawford.
2. Samuel Elliot.
3. Alex'r McIlvaine.
4. Joseph Jenkins.
5. John Lutz.
6. Martin Bowman.
7. Rudolph Statler.
8. Martin Holman.

Lieutenants.

1. Martin Bowman.
2. Robert Thompson.
3. Alex'r Martin.
4. John Martin.
5. Abraham Zuber.
6. John Ream.
7. John Grim.
8. William Grove.

Ensigns.

1. James Vogan.
2. Andrew Finefrock.
3. George Finefrock.
4. Thomas Martin.
5. George Stabbaugh.
6. Valentine Verns.
7. John Alman.
8. John Kinser.

(c.) I, do hereby Certify that agreeable to orders by me issued for the purpose of Electing Field Officers, for the fifth Batallion Lancaster County Militia—The following two Gentlemen, were Duly and Unanimously Elected vizt.

Lieutenant Colonel—James Taylor.
and
Major—Robert King.

Witness my hand this 10th day of May 1783.

AD'M HUBLEY, J. L. L. C.

N. B.—A resegnation from Colo. Taylor, accompanies this. Council will please to take some order on it—Certificates for the Electing the several Company Officers of the 5th Bat. have not yet come to my hands.

A. HUBLEY, J. L. L. C.

(c.) At an Election for Militia officers held at Samuel Simpsons in Martlicks Township Lancaster County we the Judges appointed of sd. Election do certify that John Patton was chosen Captain, Peter Simpson for Lieut. and David McDermand Ensign.

Signed by us.

JAMES WHARRY }
JACOB HOOBER } Judges.

May 12th 1783.

The above named Capt. John Patton of the 5th Bat. commanded by Col. Taylor has declin'd accepting the same, and has for that purpose sent his resignation—Lanr. June 20th 1783.

AD'M HUBLEY, J. L. L. C'y.

MUSTER ROLL OF CAPT. MARTIN BOWMAN'S CO. 5TH BATTALION, LANCASTER COUNTY. (c.)

Captin.

Martin Bowman.

Leftenant.

1st. George Duck. 2d. John Reem.

Insign.

Jacob Swarshwelder.

Cort. Mershel Men.

John Norton.	Philip Duck.

1st Class.

Isack Cray.	Jacob Crim.
John Gheer.	Michial Hendly.
Peter Sensnich	John Showalder.
Jost Zimerman.	Michial Bitzer.
Christian Swartshwelder.	Benjeman Sheniman.
Christofel Rodaker.	John Wenger, Siner.

2d Class.

Philip Wever.	Henerery Miller.
George Otto.	Jacob Werns.
Engelhart Haltzinger.	Peter Resh.
Andrew Harter.	Abraham Andrews.
Jacob Oberlin.	Peter Pence.
Jacob Wisse.	Henery Wever.
Andrew Yont.	David Harman.

3d Class.

John McCleery.	George Werns.
George German.	Jacob Hinkle.
Michial Has.	William Berry.
George Gere.	Michial Sower.
Christian Danner.	Adam German, Juner.
John Beck.	Daniel Hane.
John Evans.	Philip Rinmood.

4th Class.

James Gault.	Sepastian Hower.
Peter Good.	Michial Oberlin.
Francis Hane.	John German.
Andrew Wisse.	John Mumma.
Henery Lippert.	John Soloberger.
David Kempher.	Jacob Roth.
John Resler.	George Wever.
Sepastian Hower.	

5th Class.

John Yoat.
Martin Werns.
Abraham Law.
Frederick Glaze.
David Morgan.
Joseph McCleery.
Conrad Brenizen.
John Swickert.
John Bitzer, Juner.
Dobias Medsger.
Philip Pence.
Ernst Miller.
Nicious Trout.

6th Class.

George Bowder.
Stofel Ily.
John Boyl.
John Hinkle.
John Fastnaught.
George Pifer.
Benjeman Harlager.
John Sids.
Alexander Gault.
Balser Smith.
Philip Rank.
Jacob Adam.
William McClane.
Henery Norton.

7th Class.

George Swickert.
Henery Nice.
James McCleery, Juner.
John Bitzer, Siner.
George Clopper.
Leonhart German.
George Hinkle.
Isace Davis.
Philip Fastnaught.
John Caupher.
Jacob Sherk.
Henery Snider.
Christian Wegner.

8th Class.

James McCleery.
Conrad Faustnaught.
Andrew Culp.
Joseph McCleery.
Christian Kinsely.
Henery Shultz.
Andrew Swickert.
John Roth.
Adam German.
Conrad Pence.
Henery Otto.
John Gunty.
William Gigly.

A RETURN OF THE NAMES AND SIRNAMES OF ALL THE MALE WHITE PARSONS RESIDING WITHIN MY DISTRIC BETWEEN THE AGES OF EIGHTEEN AND FIFTY THREE YEARS FIT TO BEARE ARMS. (c.)

Capt.

Alex. McIlvain.

Lieut.

Alex. Martin.

Ensign.

William Smith, Jun.

Clark.

Evan Evans.

Sarg.

1. Andrew Lutter.
2. Edward Akeson.
3. John Hover.

Class 1.

Casper Shirk.
Nathan Evans.
John Burrel.
Jacob Grim.
John Stopher.
Petter Light.
Antony Millar.
Chris.ian Root, Jun.
James Kimer.
Edward Good.

Class 2.

Daniel Burrel.
Loudwig Ranck.
Petter Stopher.
George Martin.
John Sneder.
Michal Stever.
Daniel Stopher.
John Weaver.

Class 3.

Martin Mart.n.
Philip Sneder.
Balzer Bitzer.
John Weaver, Jun.
Jacob Widler.
Michal Sneder.
Michal Ranck.
Henry Weaver, Sen.
Petter Grim.
Daniel Stever.
George Shikely.
Joseph Carpenter.

Class 4.

Petter Weaver.
Christain Sneder.
John Ranck.
Jacob Weaver, mill.
Henry Weaver.
William Harvey.
Jacob Weaver.
John Lender.
George Weaver.
Hugh Cuningham.

Class 5.

George Fultze.
Henry Weaver Stil.
Henry Wagner.
Michal Shirk (Mil).
Mathias Stopher.
Petter Springer.
George Davis.
Petter Worst.
George Matter.
Isaac Andrews.
George Stopher.
John Hoover.
Jacob Newman, gone off.

Class 6.

Jacob Ranck.
John Sherk.
Abraham Aichard.
Daniel Aichard.
Valintine Ranck.
Henry Weaver (hill).
Christain Carpenter.
John Golden.
Josaph Meredy.
John Becher.
Joseph Wright.

Class 7.

Joseph Gillis.
Jacob Hoover.
Petter Carpetner.
Mathias Springer.
Adam Ranck.
Jacob Matter.
Thomas Edwards.
John Higard.
Edward Goheen.
Fredrick Glase.
John Kirpatrick.

Class 8.

Michal Shirk.
Christian Weaver.
John Fultze.
Adam Stocke.
Henry Martin.
Christian Carpenter, Jun.
John Stevenson.
William Smith, Sin.
James Mayors.
George Weaver.

Certify'd

ALEX. McILVAIN, Capt.

A TRUE RETURN OF THE EIGHTH COMPANY THE FIFTH BATTALION OF LANCASTER COUNTY MILITIA. (c.)

1st Class.

Jacob Road.
Martin Road.
Ulrich Whisler.
Henry Hildebrand.
Henry Steinbring.
Michael Brows.
Emigh Snider.
Philip Road.
John Davis.
George Alexander.

2d Class.

Mchael Rine, Jun.
Jacob Lutt.
Peter Baker.
Christian Fellenbaum.
Martin Ritch.
Peter Smith.
Martin Huber, Jur.

3d Class.

Michael Hildebrand.
John Rine.
John Huber, Jur.
David Harman.
John Diller.
Isaac Ellmaker.
Abraham Barr.
Godliel Pauff.

4th Class.

George Hildebrand.
Sebastian Bower.
Andrew Matter.
Henry Richwine.
Nicholas Yunt.
Abraham Brubacker.
Henry Road.
Gabriel Davis.
Michael Barr.
Ludwigh Kyle.

5th Class.

Michael Eighart.
John Berkenhouser.
Michael Rine.
Samuel Grebill.
Christian Huber.
John Brubacker.
Henry Sckyles.
Peter Luther.
Philip Brubacker.

6th Class.

David Fellinbaum.
George Rine.
Christian Musselman.
John Diffenderfer.
John Hersh.
John Sheffer.
Christopher Wike.
Peter Kertz.
John Stoner.

7th Class.

Peter Diller.
Henry Peters.
Peter Ekerts.
George Ealy.
Nathaniel Ellmaker.
——— Musselman.

8th Class.

Adam Diller.
Michael Grebill.
James Martin.
Michael Martin.
Samuel Bar.
Christian Smucker.
Anthony Ellmaker.
George Barr.
Jacob Ellmaker.

A TRUE RETURN OF THE EIGHT COMPENY OF THE FIFTH BATTALION LANCASTER COUNTY MILITIA OF ALL THE MEAL WHITE INHABETENS OF THE SEAM. —(c.)

Major.
Henry Markley.

Captain.
James McConnall.

Letenent.
John Shivly.

Ensign.
John Kindsor.

Sergts.

John Fox.
John Grice.
Philip Fox.

1st Class.

Jacob Road.
Ulrick Wisller.
Henry Stinbring.
Michael Brong's.
Emegh Snider.
Christan Primer.
Philip Road.
John Deves.
Ludigh Kyle.
John Henly.

2d Class.

Micheal Rine, Jur.
Zauhus Pircal.
Anthony Hinkle.
Jacob Lutt.

Petter Backer.
Christian Fellenbam.
Marten Kitch.
Petter Smith.
Marten Huber, Jur.
John Grous.

3d Class.

Michael Hildebrand.
John Grove.
John Rine.
John Huber, Jur.
David Harmon.
Frederick Deeds, Jur.
John Diller.
Isaac Ellmacker.
Abraham Barr.
Cutlip Pauff.

4th Class.

George Hildebrand.
Sebastian Bower.
Andrew Marter.
Henry Richwine.
Nicholas Yount.
Abraham Brubacker.
Jacob Devenderfer.
Henry Road.
Gabriel Daves.
Michael Barr.
Andrew Barnd.
John Restlar.

5th Class.

Michael Eichart.
John Pirkenhouser.
Michael Rine.
Samuel Grebill.
Christan Huber.
John Brubacker.
Philip Brubacker.
Henry Skiles.
John Miller.
Jacob Brubacker.
Danial Morton.

6th Class.

David Fellenbaum.
Gorge Rine.
Christen Musselman.
Nathaniel Sweker.
Wendel Hinkle.
John Devenderfer.
Henry Kindsor.
Christopher Wike.
Petter Kurts.
Fredreck Seger.
David Devenderfer.
Adam Eohoholts.

7th Class.

Michael Kindsor.
Petter Diller.
Valentine Kindsor.
Henry Peters.
Petter Ehart.
George Eley.
Nathanial Ellmacker.
Joseph Musselman.
Jacob Cough.
Isaac Ebey.
John Lower.
George Pifer.
Adam Eicholtz.

8th Class.

Valentien Petrey.
Adam Diller.
Michael Gribill.
James Marten.
Hugh Thompson.
Michael Marten.
Samuel Barr.
Christan Smuker.
Antoney Ellmacker.
George Barr.
Jacob Ellmacker.
Jacob Andrew.
Michael Verly.

Total 67 privets.
1 Major.
1 Captain.
1 Letenent.
1 Insign.
and 3 sergents.

This is a true Return Certifid this 5th Day of July 1781.
By me.

JAMES McCONNALL, Capt.

A RETURN OF CAPT. ALEX'R MILVAINS COMPY. OF THE FIFTH BATT. OF LANCASTER COUNTY MILITIA COMMANDED BY COL. JACOB CARPENTER. c.)

Daniel Burrel.
Loudwick Ranck.
Petter Stopher.
George Martin.
Daniel Stopher.
Martin Martin.
Balser Bitzer.
John Weaver, Jun.
Mickel Ranck.
Henry Weaver, Sin.
John Herse.
George Shikely.
Joseph Carpenter.
Petter Weaver.
Christian Sneder.
John Ranck.
Jacob Weaver, mill.
Henry Weaver, turner.
William Harvey.
Jacob Weaver.
John Lender.
George Weaver, old, John son.
Henry Weaver, Still.
Henry Wanger.
Michal Shirk, mill.
Mathas Stopher.
Petter Springer.
Petter Worst.

Lenard Spigelmire.
George Stopher.
Jacob Ranck.
Samuel Ranck.
Abraham Aichard.
Daniel Aichard.
John Shirk.
Henry Weaver, hill.
Christain Carpenter.
Henry Root.
Jacob Hover.
Petter Carpenter.
Mathias Springer.
Jacob Matter.
John Higard.
Fredrick Glase.
Michal Shirk, P. son.
Christain Weaver.
Henry Martin.
Christain Carpenter, Jun.
Stophel Crush.
John Fultz.

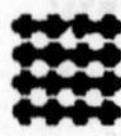

SIXTH BATTALION
LANCASTER COUNTY MILITIA.

RETURN OF THE THIRD CLASS OF MILITIA LANCASTER CO., COMMANDED BY COL. ALEXR. LOWRY. (c.)

Companies.	Officers Present.													
	Commissioned.						Staff.					Non-Com.		
	Colonel.	Lieut. Col.	Major.	Captains.	Lieutenants.	Ensigns.	Chaplain.	Adjutant.	Quarter Mas.	Surgeon.	Mate.	Serjeants.	Drummers.	Fifers.
Capt. John Johnson,	1	1		1	2	1			1			4		
Capt. John Rutherford,				1	2	1						4	1	
Capt. Thos. Kopenhever,				1	2	1						3	1	1
Capt. Joseph Work,				1	1	1						3	1	1
Capt. John Rolands,				1	1	1						3		
Total,	1	1	1	5	10	5			1			17	3	2

RETURN OF THE THIRD CLASS OF MILITIA LANCASTER CO., COMMANDED BY COL. ALEXR. LOWRY—(c.)

Companies.	Rank and File.						Alterations Since Last Return.			Total.	
	Fit for duty.	Sick present.	Sick absent.	On command.	On furlough.	Total.	Dead.	Discharged.	Deserted.	Substitutes.	Non-substit.
Capt. John Johnson,	43	....	....	....	....	43	....	....	....	....	....
Capt. John Rutherford,	31	2	....	4	....	37	....	....	1	....	....
Capt. Thos. Kopenhever,	34	....	1	4	1	40	....	....	....	....	....
Capt. Joseph Work,	44	....	3	9	1	57	....	....	....	....	....
Capt. John Rolands,	19	....	....	....	....	19	....	....	3	....	....
Total,	171	2	4	17	2	196	....	....	4	....	....

Chester, 28th Augst., 1777.

Lodk. Sprogell, M. M. G. of P.

CAPTAIN MARTIN WEAVER'S COMPANY. (b.)

Muster Roll of Captain Martin Weaver's Company of Lancaster County Militia, now in the Service of the United States, Commanded by Colonel John Rogers.

Captain.

Martin Weaver, July 1, 1777.

Lieutenants.

William Johnson. Mathew Gilchrist.

Ensign.

John Sheesley.

Sergeants.

John Sherer, Nov. 5, 1777.
George Semple, Nov. 5, 1777.
William McMillan, Nov. 5, 1777.
Mathias Deibler, Nov. 5, 1777.

Corporals.

John Matter, Nov. 5, 1777.
Nicholas Hoffman, Nov. 5, 1777.
Gotlieb Cline, Nov. 5, 1777.
Joseph Colligan, Nov. 5, 1777.

Privates.

Samuel Orrom, Nov. 5, 1777.
John Simpson, Nov. 5, 1777.
William Miller, Nov. 5, 1777; dis. Nov. 12, 1777.
James Black, Nov. 5, 1777.
John McIlhenny, Nov. 5, 1777.
Leonard Snyder Nov. 5, 1777; dis. Dec. 13, 1777.
Jacob Holdman, Nov. 5, 1777; dis. Dec. 13, 1777.
Anthony Fryly, Nov. 5, 1777.
George Seal, Nov. 5, 1777.
James Woodside, Nov. 5, 1777.
Abraham Phillips, Nov. 5, 1777.

Peter Stonebreaker, Nov. 5, 1777.
George Luffington, Nov. 5, 1777.
Valentine Pancake, Nov. 5, 1777.
Thomas Strachen, Nov. 5, 1777.
James Burney, Nov. 5, 1777.
John Butler, Nov. 5, 1777.
Thomas Hartine, Nov. 5, 1777.
Francis Canaway, Nov. 5, 1777.
Peter Sweigart, Nov. 5, 1777.
James Finney, Nov. 5, 1777.
Peter Willier, Nov. 5, 1777.
Michael Celler, Nov. 5, 1777.
John Frids, Nov. 5, 1777.
Adam Werts, Nov. 5, 1777.
Nicholas Cassel, Nov. 5, 1777.
Jacob Elder, Nov. 5, 1777; dis. Dec. 13, 1777.
William Witner, Nov. 5, 1777.
Henry Miller, Nov. 5, 1777.
John Bidel, Nov. 5, 1777.
Adam Meens, Nov. 5, 1777.
John Cline, Nov. 5, 1777.
Alexander Beryhill, Nov. 5, 1777.
Peter Shiels, Nov. 5, 1777.
Henry Myer, Nov. 5, 1777.
James Thom, Nov. 5, 1777.
Jacob Harman, Nov. 5, 1777.
Robert George, Nov. 5, 1777.
Henry McCann, Nov. 5, 1777.
John Milligan, Nov. 19, 1777.
Hugh Wray, December 2, 1777.
Stephen Bend, Nov. 5, 1777.
Valentine Brauch Nov. 5, 1777.
Jacob Bickel, Nov. 5, 1777.
Henry Normyer, Nov. 5, 1777.

Montgomery, Philadelphia Co., December 30, 1777.—Mustered then Captain Martin Weaver's company as specified above.

LOD'K SPROGELL,
M. M. G. of Pa.

[The time of discharge of the foregoing was January 1, 1777, with the exception of John Milligan, who is marked as "left in the service."]

A RETURN OF THE 6TH BATALLION OF LANCASTER COUNTY WITH THE NAMES AND RANKS OF THE OFFICERS OF THE SAID BATALLION WITH THE NUMBER OF THE CLASSES. AUG. 30, 1777. (c.)

Field Officers.

Col.
John Rogers.

Lieut. Co.
Robert Clark.

Major.
William Brown.

Staff Officers.

Adj't.
Anthony McCreigh.

Qr. Master.
James Sullivan.

1ST COMPANY.

Captain.
William McCullough.

1st Lieut.
Isaac Hannah.*

2nd Lieut.
John Barnet.*

Ensign.
James Willson.

Court Martial Men.

Timothy Green.
Wm. Allon.

Total number of men 79.

2ND COMPANY.

Captain.
Ambrose Crain.*

1st Lieut.
William Young.

2nd Lieut.
James Stewart.

Ensign.
John Armstrong.*

Court Martial Men.
George Aspy.
Jos. Aspy.

Total number of men 46.

3RD COMPANY.

Captain.
Thos. Copinhaffer.*

1st Lieut.
Abraham Latcha.*

2nd Lieut.
George Beasore.

Ensign.
John Beackel.*

Court Martial Men.
Adam Harper.
Michl. Strow.

Total number of men 88.

4TH COMPANY.

Captain.

James McCreight.

1st Lieut.

William Hill.*

2nd Lieut.

John Strain.*

Ensign.

John Thompson.

Court Martial Men.

Rob't. Hill.
Rich'd. Craford.

Total number of men 46.

5TH COMPANY.

Captain.

Paterick Hay.

1st Lieut.

Samuel Wier.

2nd Lieut.

James Willson.

Ensign.

James Willson.

Court Martial Men.

David Wray.
Benj. Boyd.

Total number of men 102.

6TH COMPANY.

Captain.

Joseph McClure.

1st Lieut.

James Johnson.

2nd Lieut.

James Wallace.

Ensign.

Joseph Willson.

Court Martial Men.

Wm. Catheart.
Jams. McCluer.

Total number of men 82.

7TH COMPANY.

Captain.

William Laird.

1st Lieut.

John McFarland.

2nd Lieut.

Michael Rham.

Ensign.

Jacob Reeker.

Court Martial Men.

Michel Ram.
Daniel Windlegh.

Total number of men 61.

8TH COMPANY.

Captain.
Michael Moyer.

1st Lieut.
Abraham Allis.

2nd Lieut.
Michael Brown.

Ensign.
Peter Lineaweaver.

Court Martial Men.
John Herkerider.

Total number of men 53.

Commissions dated the 31st July 1777.

Total—Field, Staff, Rank & file........................642 men.

1777 October 18th. Re'd of Timothy Matlack Esq. commissions for the Officers agreeable to the above Return (except those marked thus* which were delivered before).

ROBT. CLARK, Lt. Col.

A Return of the Officers of a Company of the Sixth Batalion of Lancaster County Militia Commanded by Coln. John Rogers, now under command of Coln. Alexr. Lowry of the third Batalion of Lancaster County now at Chester.

Captain.
Thomas Kopenhaver.

1st Lieut.
William Hill.

2nd Lieut.
John Barnet.

Ensign.
John Armstrong.

A Return of the Officers of a Co
alion of Lancaster County Militi
John Rogers, now under the command
the second class of Lancaster County

Capt.
Ambrose Crea

1st Lieut.
Isaac Hannal

Ensign.
John Beackel

2nd Lieut.
John Strain.

1st Lieut.
Abraham Latc

1777 August 30th. Received of
commissions for the within Officers
talion of Lancaster Co. Militia.

AMI

THE SEVENTH CC

SIXTH BATTALION, LANCAS

Captain.
William Lair

Lieut.
John McFarll

2nd Lieut.
Michal Ram

Ensign.
Jacob Righe

Sergens.

1st. Peter Fridly.
2nd. Jacob Spidel.
3rd. Philip Biesly.
4th. Ledwick Enrick.

Corporals.

George Peters.
Michal Spaid.
Henry Miller.
Barnut Fridly.

Clerk.

Valentine Humbel.

Fifer.

Tice Hover.

1st Class.

John Coffman.
Christy Boogner.
John Crimor.
Barnut Fults.
Philip Brand.
Christ'n Eversoal.
Adam Firebough.
Philip Brown.

2nd Class.

Peter Landes.
George Balshbought.
Adam Hamaker.
Christ. Hamaker.
John Brand.
Peter Groseloss, Jr.
Valintine Cinser.

3rd Class.

Fred'r Hass.
Fred'r Humbel.
Fred. Humbel, S'nr.
Daniel Tice.
Abraham Coppack.
Jacob Ram.
Michal Hooke.
Jacob Sider.

4th Class.

Casel Byers.
John Byers.
Philip Millor.
Christ Stoover.
Chris. Landes.
Makes Spidel.
John Hamaker.
Jacob Cisner.

5th Class.

Jacob Landes.
George Lower.
Adam Deam.
Daniel Bauhn.
Peter Perst.
John Snider.
John Eversoal.
David Hamaker.

6th Class.

John Landes.
George Emrick.
Jacob Fridly.
Martain Rouch.
Jacob Riker.
John Bringwolf.

7th Class.

Ludick Shirts.
Jos. Ferrer.
Jacob Hearroaf.
George Minnich.
Michal Bam.
Andrew Hentra.
Peter Eversole.

8th Class.

Henry Hise.
Jacob Riker.
Fred'k Stall.
Philip Hamaker.
Peter Crosselose.
Peter Eversole.
Henry Eater.
Andrew Horner.

THE EIGHTH COMPANY.

SIXTH BATTALION, LANCASTER CO. 1777. (c.)

Captain.

Michal Moyer.

1st Lieut.

Abraham Allis.

2nd Lieut.

Michal Brown.

Ensign.

Peter Lineaweaver.

Court Martalmen.

John Herkelrider.

Drumer.

Adam Heney.

Fifer.

Fred. Heney.

Sergens.

1st. Abraham Allis.
2nd. Stophel Heney.
3rd. Mathias Baker.
4th. John Hoover.

1st Class.

Jacob Pruner.
George Maire.
George Rumgarner.
George Minich.
Henry Seigler.

2d Class.

Peter Symon.
Adam Weiss.
George Heain.
Martain Long.
Casper Feeman.
Emanuel Toole.
John Reed.
Christy Sider.
George Sider.

3d Class.

George Wolf.
Chris'pr Mowra.
Jacob Allis.
Wm. Rough.
Martain Shoole.
George Mowra.

4th Class.

George Walmer.
Simon Minich.
John Baker.
John Millor.
John Carvary.
And'w Brown.
Jacob Sider.

5th Class.

Jacob Musser.
Henry Sharp.
Conrad Myer.
Martain Albright.
Peter Kelinger.
Christ. Richwine.
George Hooke.
John Poor.

6th Class.

Jacob Zercher.
Henry Fiten.
Daniel Millor.
Martain Miller.
John Shoole.

7th Class.

John Rough.
Henry Fencler.
Jacob Grass.
George Countz.
Andrew Kelinger.
Adam Poor.
George Sprigher.
Stofel Heney.

8th Class.

Jacob Seeant.
Stophel Brown.
Jacob Millor.
John Wolf.
Andrew Keefer.
Solomon Reed.
John Willson.

OFFICERS SIXTH BATTALION—1777. (a.)

Colonel.

John Rogers.

Lieutenant Colonel.

Robert Clark.

Major.

William Brown.

Adjutant.

Anthony McCreight.

Quarter Master.

James Sullivan.

First Company.

Captain—Thomas Kopenheffer.
First Lieutenant—William Hill.
Second Lieutenant—John Barnett.
Ensign—John Armstrong.

Second Company.

Captain—Ambrose Crain.
First Lieutenant—Isaac Hanna.
Second Lieutenant—James Stewart.
Ensign—John Bickel.

Third Company.

Captain—James McCreight.
First Lieutenant—Abraham Latcha.
Second Lieutenant—John Strain.
Ensign—James Wilson.

Fourth Company.

Captain—William McCullough.
First Lieutenant—William Young.
Second Lieutenant—George Beasor.
Ensign—John Thomson.

Fifth Company.

Captain—Patrick Hays.
First Lieutenant—Samuel Weir.
Second Lieutenant—James Wallace.
Ensign—James Willson.

Sixth Company.

Captain—Joseph McClure.
First Lieutenant—James Johnson.
Second Lieutenant—James Wilson.
Ensign—Joseph Willson.

Seventh Company.

Captain—William Laird.
First Lieutenant—John McFarland.
Second Lieutenant—Michael Rahm.
Ensign—Jacob Becker.

Eighth Company.

Captain—Michael Moyer.
First Lieutenant—Abraham Allis.
Second Lieutenant—Michael Brown.
Ensign—Peter Lineaweaver.

Court Martial Men.

First—Timothy Green, Esq., William Allen.
Second—George Espy, Josiah Espy.
Third—Adam Harper, Michael Straw.
Fourth—Robert Hill, Richard Crawford.
Fifth—David Wray, Benjamin Boyd.
Sixth—William Cathcart, Samuel McClure.
Seventh—Michael Rahm, Daniel Hindleogh.
Eighth—John Herkerider.

August 30, 1777—Captain Kopenheffer's company was stationed at Chester, under Colonel Alexander Lowrey.

August 30, 1777—Captains Crain and McCreight's companies at Chester, under command of Colonel James Watson.

A RETURN OF THE 1ST COMPY. OF THE 6 BITALLON OF MILITIA OF LANCASTER COUNTY FOR THE YEAR 1778 AND 1779. (c.)

Captain.

Wm. M'Cullough, Serv'd in Middlton.

1st Lieut.

Iaasac Hanna, Serv'd Volinteer.

2nd Lieut.

John Barnet, Serv'd North'd.

Ensign.

James Willson, Serv'd Volenteer.

1st Class.

1. David Mcquir, Serv'd Middleton.
2. Martin McClure, Serv'd Middleton.
3. Wm. Hune, Not Serv'd.
4. Wm. Miscimens, Serv'd Middeto.
5. Jas. McMillian, Constable.
6. David Davis, Serv'd Middelton.
7. Rob't. Barr, Serv'd Lebanon.
8. Wm. Patterson, Serv'd Middelton.
9. Rob't. Bedford, Serv'd Middelton.
10. John McNaughton, Serv'd Middelton.
11. David Maffet, Serv'd Middelton.

2nd Class.

13. John M'Cord, Serv'd Labanon.
14. Thomas M'Clure, Dead.
15. Lenard Umbarger, Not Serv'd.
16. Lenard Brisby, Dischargd.
17. John Forguson, Volunteer Nort.
18. Joseph Allen, Serv'd north tho.
19. Connard Smith, not Serv'd.
20. Thos. McMillan, Serv'd.
21. Jos. Barnet, Apeald.
22. Rob't. Lisk, not Serv'd.

3rd Class.

23. Wm. Allen, Serv'd Midlton.
24. Michal Vanlear, not Serv'd.
25. John Hume, Serv'd.
26. Francis Carson, Serv'd Labon.
27. David Caldwell, Serv'd North.
28. Rob't. Sturgon, not Serv'd.
2 David McCraken, not Serv'd.
30. Colen Campble, Serv'd dischard.
31. Josua Magus, Do Serv'd.

4th Class.

32. John M'Clure, not Serv'd.
34. Joseph Crean, Volenteer.
35. Danial Valley, Serv'd.
36. Saml. Sturgion, not Serv'd.
37. Hugh Ramssy, Discharged.
38. Richard Deyermond, Serv'd.
39. Jas. Connar, Serv'd.
40. Thomas Allen, Serv'd.
41. John Patterson, Volenteer Northd.

5th Class.

42. John Fearley, not Serv'd.
43. Wm. Cunningham, Serv'd.
44. Alexr. McElhaney, Volenteer.
45. John Carter, Serv'd.
46. Rob't. Kennedy, not Serv'd.
47. Wm. Wallace, Serv'd.
48. Jas. Stewart, Serv'd.
49. John Grahms, Serv'd.
50. Wm. Glen, Dicharg'd.
51. Saml. Forguson, not Serv'd.

6th Class.

52. David Watson, Discharged.
53. Robt. Dalton, Volenteer North'nd.
54. Neal McColgan, not Serv'd.
55. Timothey Green, Esqr., Apeald.
56. Saml. M'Cullough, Not Serv'd.
57 John Wright, Discharged.

58. John Snodgress, not Serv'd.
59. Jas. Hammel, Discharged.
60. David Hays, not Serv'd Apeald.
61. Rob't. Frekelton, Volenteer North'nd.

7th Class.

62. And'w Carr, Volenteer North'nd.
63. Henery Umbarger, not Serv'd.
64. Wm. Barnet, not Serv'd unfit for Duty.
65. Barnet McNutt, not Serv'd.
66. Wm. Wright, not Serv'd.
67. Thos. Finney, not Serv'd.
68 Wm. Crean, Volenteer North'nd.
69. Charles Barr, Volenteer North'nd.
70. John Johnston, Chester County.
71. Wm. Brisben.

8th Class.

72. Jas. Johnston, Volanteer North'nd.
73. Charles Brown, Disabled.
74. John Cooper, not Serv'd.
75. David Ramsey, Discharged.
76. Thomas McElhaney, not Serv'd.
77. John Howey, Above Age.
78. Rob't. Howey, not Serv'd.
79. Thomas Rowland, out of the Comp'y.
80. John Jameson, not Serv'd.
81. John Reed, Volenteer North'nd.

Sertifyd by Me,
WM. M'CULLOUGH, Capt.

A RETURN OF THE SECOND COMPY. OF THE 6TH BATTALION OF LANCASTER COUNTY WITH THIRE RESPECTIVE CLASSES AND A RETURN OF THOSE WHO HAVE SERVED IN THE YEARS 1778-1779. (c.)

Men's Names.	Remarks.
Capt.	
Ambrus Crain,	Serv'd Noththumberland.
Lieuts.	
Wm. Young,	Serv'd Midcltown.
Jas. Stuert,	No comand.
Ensign.	
John Armstrong,	No comand.
1st Class.	
David Young,	Serv'd Mideltown.
Archible Slowen,	Serv'd Mideltown.
Adam Vance,	Serv'd Mideltown.
Edward Ashcraft,	Serv'd Mideltown.
Robert Ewian,	Not served.
2d Class.	
John Cunningham,	Serv'd Norththumberland.
James Low.	
James Gleen.	
John Smily.	
John Willscn,	Gon to Cumberland.
Robert Young,	Serv'd Norththumberland.
James Young, Jnr.,	Serv'd Norththumberland.
Jos. Ridel,	Norththumberland.
3d Class.	
David Ramsy,	Serv'd Lebanon.
Dennis O. Brally,	Norththumberland.
James Slown,	Dead.
Wm. Ratford.	
Wm. Moor,	In the Contanental service.
Robt. McCann.	
Jas. Bickham.	
4th Class.	
Patt. Cunningham,	Discharged.
John Young,	Norththumberland.
Benjn. McKinsy,	
Wm. McFarlon,	Norththumberland.
Samuel Graims,	Norththumberland.
Jonah Espy,	Northumbeland.

A RETURN OF THE SECOND COMPY. OF THE 6TH BATTALION OF LANCASTER COUNTY—Continued.

Men's Names.	Remarks.
5th Class.	
Hugh Watt,	Lebanon.
Wm. Vance,	Lebanon.
Daniel McBride.	
Edward Taite.	
Robt. Kirkwood.	
Wm. Grahms,	Norththumberland.
George Young,	Norththumberland.
6th Class.	
Wm. Young,	Norththumberland.
Thos. McCoulogh.	
Thos. Smily.	
Jas. Young.	
Thos. Edmond.	
Jaret Nilson.	
Alex'd Young.	
7th Class.	
Robt. Bell,	Volinteer Northumberland.
George Stuert,	Volinteer Northumberland.
John Endwarth.	
Isaack Harison,	Volaintear at Northumberland.
John Graham,	Serv'd in second class.
8th Class.	
John Young,	Served.
Andrew Young.	
Gilbart Graham.	
Wm. Cunnigham,	Serv'd at Northumberland.
Thos. Clark.	
Wm. Donalson.	
George Espy.	

The above is a true state of said Compy. from the 24 of Aprile Ano Dom 1778 untill the 24 of October 1779.

AMBROSE CREAIN,
Capt.

A RETURN OF THE 3TH COMPANY OF THE 6TH BATALION OF LANCASTER COUNTY SHEWING EACH MENS NAMES—RESPECTIVE CLASS, ALSO A RETURN OF THOSE WHO HAVE SERVED IN THEIR CLASS IN THE YEAR AMO DOMI 1778 & 1779. (c.)

Capt.

Tho's Coppenhaver, Not Serv. Having no Command.

Lieut.

Abraham Latcha, Not Serv. Having no Command.
George Beasor, Not Serv. Having no Command.

Insgn.

Jo'n Bickel, Serv, Northumberl.

Drum & Fifer.

Jo'n Toops. Wm. Hedrich.

Men's Names.	Remarks.
1 Class.	
Daniel Weaver,	Serv. Mitletown.
Jacob Wolff,	Serv. Mitletown.
George Unger.	
Jacob Tibbine,	Serv. Mitletown.
Jacob Moser,	Serv. Mitletown.
Mich'l Straw,	Serv. Mitletown.
Wm. Carpenter.	
Abr'm Wingard.	
Jo'n Bomgartner.	
Andreas Carvery,	Serv. Mitletown.
Peter Peasore.	
Jo'n Steely,	Class A. D. 1779.
2 Class.	
Jo'n Bridbile.	
Nicholas Earhard,	Serv. Northumberl.
Jo'n Symon.	
Michael Feltin,	Serv. Northumberl.
Christian Perkey.	
Henry Hess.	
Leonard Widowmair,	Serv. Northumberl.
Jacob Stone,	Serv. Northumr.
Jo'n Peasore,	Class A. D. 1779.
Nicholas Titlor,	Class A. D. 1779.

A RETURN OF THE 3TH COMPANY OF THE 6TH BATALION OF LANCASTER COUNTY SHEWING EACH MENS NAMES—Continued.

Men's Names.	Remarks.
3	
Daniel Miller.	
John Fox.	
George Wilt,	Serv. Northum.
Joseph Pirkey.	
Conrad Road.	
Henry Peasore,	Serv. Northum.
Philip Bomgart'r.	
Jacob Graff.	
George Prouner,	Serv. Northum.
Lodwig Cearing,	Class A. D. 1779.
4 Class.	
Nicholas Snyder,	Serv. Northumbr.
Martin Mailey.	
Jas. Philips,	Serv. Mitletown.
Bolzer Bomgart'r.	
Peter Feltin.	
Jo'n Harper,	Serv. Northumbr.
Peter Gungrey.	
Henry Sowmiller,	Serv. Northumbr.
Jo'n Winder, Jun'r,	Class A. D. 1779.
Henry Latcha,	Class A. D. 1779.
George Hayn,	Class A. D. 1779.
5	
George Frank.	
Christopher Fox,	Serv. Lebanon.
Jo'n Rayer.	
Jo'n Prouner.	
Peter Fox,	Serv. Lebanon.
Frederick Peasore.	
Jacob Peasore.	
Nicholas Pruner,	Serv. Lebanon.
Henry Stone,	Serv. Lebanon.
Jo'n Carvery,	Serv. Lebanon.
Jo'n Guntrum,	Class A. D. 1779.
Jo'n Muser,	Class A. D. 1779.
6	
Jacob Cleaman.	
Peter Walmore.	
Henry Shuey.	
Adam Mark.	
Adam Titlor.	
Henry Pruner.	
Frances Alberthale.	
Jo'n Weaver.	
Adam Weaver.	

A RETURN OF THE 3TH COMPANY OF THE 6TH BATALION OF LANCASTER COUNTY SHEWING EACH MENS NAMES.—Continued.

Men's Names.	Remarks.
7th Class.	
Peter Bridbile.	
Jo'n Walmore.	
Mich'l Pilipey.	
Adam Wentling.	
Peter Rawer.	
George Hedrick.	
Jacob Henry.	
Bolzer Stone.	
8th	
Vallentine Sala.	
Peter Muser.	
Nicholas Alberthal.	
Conrad Helm.	
Nicholas Bobb.	
Adam Goodman.	
Lodwig Klick.	
Peter Stone.	
Jo'n Tibbing.	
Nicholas Poor.	
Peter Title.	
Phillip Frank.	
Conrad Mark.	

The above is a True State of S'd Comp. From the 24th Day of April Anno 1778 until this Day Oct'r 28th, 1779.

Certified by me,

THOS. COPPENHAVER, Capt.

A RETURN OF THE FOURTH COMPY. OF THE 6TH BATTALION OF LANCASTER COUNTY WITH THEIR RESPECTIVE CLASSES AND A RETURN OF THOSE WHO HAVE SERVED IN THE YEAR 1778 & 1779. (c.)

Men's Names. Commission'd Officers.	Who Have Served. Remarks.
Captain.	
James McCreight,	Not Serv'd having no command.
Lieutenant.	
1st William Hill,	Not Serv'd having no command.
Ensign.	
John Thomson,	Serv'd at Middleton.
Non Commiss'd Officers.	
John Todd,	Serv'd at Northumborland.
John Murphy,	Serv'd at Northumborland.
Robert Strain,	Serv'd Voluntier to North'beld.
1st Class.	
Robert Greenlee.	
John Knowling,	Serv'd at Midletown.
William Cloaky,	Serv'd at Midletown.
James Long.	
2d Class.	
James Breden,	Serv'd at Northumbr'ld.
John Pettyerew.	
3d Class.	
John Craig,	Serv'd at Northumbr'd by proxy.
Rich'd Finlay,	Serv'd at Northumbr'd by proxy.
George Ward,	Serv'd Vol. at Northumbr'ld.
William Ramage.	
4th Class.	
George Crain.	
John McQuown.	
James Andrew,	Serv'd at Northumb'rld.
Thomas Kennedy.	
William Thome.	
John Ward,	Class'd A. D. 1779.
Alexander Strain,	Class'd A. D. 1779.
5th Class.	
John French,	Serv'd at Lebanon.
William Strain,	Serv'd at Lebanon.
Samuel Brown,	Serv'd at Lebanon.
Robert McCully,	Serv'd at Lebanon.
Robert Porterfield,	Serv'd at Lebanon.
William Glenn,	Serv'd at Lebanon.
William Brandon,	Serv'd at Lebanon.

A RETURN OF THE FOURTH COMPY. OF THE 6TH BATTALION OF LANCASTER COUNTY—Continued.

Men's Names. Commission'd Officers.	Who Have Served. Remarks.
6th Class.	
Alexander Sloan.	
Thomas Wallace.	
Thomas Hume.	
John Ramage.	
William Brown.	
John Strain.	
Duncan Campbell.	
William McCally, ...	Serv'd at Lebanon.
7th Class.	
James Todd, ...	Serv'd Volunteer at Northumberland.
David Todd, ...	Serv'd Volunteer at Northumberland.
Samuel Robinson.	
Robert Hill.	
James Caldwell.	
John Templeton.	
8th class.	
Richard Crawford, ...	Serv'd Volunt'r at Northum'brid.
Edward Israelow.	
John Campbell.	
Hugh Morris.	

N. B.—Some of the above named persons mentioned to have served were Deficient in Serving in their Respective Classes in the Year A. D. 1778 have served A. D. 1779.

The above is A true state of s'd Comp'y from the 24th of April Ano. Dom. 1778 untill the 25th Day of October A. D. 1779.

Certify'd by

JAS. McCREIGHT, Capt.

To COL. JNO. ROGERS.

A COMPANY RETURN OF THE 5TH COMPANY AND 6TH BATALIAN OF LANCASTER COUNTY MILITIA COMMANDED BY CLO. JOHN RODGERS FOR THE YEAR 1778 AND 1779. (c.)

When Served.	Men's Names.	Where Served.	Volunteers up the River, 1779.
	1st Class.		
May the 1st, 1778,.....	Francis taylor.		
	Christopher Stoner.		
	Samuel Johnson, ...	Middletown.	
	Jacob Ballm, ...	[illegible]n.	
	o [illegible]h Carmony.		
	Daniel Longanecker.		
	Jab Rice.		
	Dewalk Shank, ...	Middletown.	
	Wm. Sands, ...	[illegible]town.	
	John [illegible]ilan, ...	[illegible]town, ...	Northumberland Volunteer.
	Vendel Henry.		
	Adem Dineager.		
	John Asewart, ...	[illegible]fted the 24th of May.	
	Abraham Mitchel, ...	Drafted the 2ith of May, 1779.	
	[illegible] Nowland, ...	Drafted tle 2ith of May, 1779.	
	Androw Duncan, ...	Drafted the 2ith of May, 1779,...	of Northumberland Volunteer.
	Daniel Weer, ...	Drafted the 27th of Sept., 1779.	
	2d Class.		
Sept'r the 1st, 1778,....	John Mayers.		
	Michael Ely.		
	Hendry hershy.		
	Wm. Ney.		

	Jerimyah Sulavan.	
	Peter Singer.	
	John Over.	
	John Landis.	
	John Canon.	
	Walter Clark, ...	Leabanon.
	Jacob Bowman.	
	Lowdwick ball.	
	Jacob Ney.	
	3d Class.	
Sept. the 1st, 1778,.....	Andrew Wallace.	
	John Michal Ely.	
	William Ballim.	
	Conrad Mishan.	
	thomas Mitchel.	
	Androw Byers.	
	philiph bitleon.	
	Daniel harshbarger.	
	Jacob longanecker.	
	henry Cregar.	
	Abraham Weitmore.	
	Nicholas Ballim.	
	Jacob Bowman.	
	John Rhea.	
	Adam Dinegar.	
	4th Class.	
Sept. the 1st, 1778,.....	John Harshbarger.	
	John Shuster.	
	David Hays, ...	Northumberland.
	James Dougherty, ...	Serv'd.
	John Blesly.	
	Conrod Crowl.	

A COMPANY RETURN OF THE 5TH COMPANY AND 6TH BATALIAN OF LANCASTER COUNTY MILITIA —Continued.

When Served.	Men's Names.	Where Served.	Volunteers up the River, 1779.
	Fourth Class—Continued.		
Sept. the 1st, 1778,.....	Henry Shell.		
	Jacob Plough.		
	Hanical Ball.		
	patrick Coyn.		
	William Sayers.		
	5th Class.		
Feb'ry the 1st, 1779,....	Samuel Brodly,	Lebanon.	
	thomas Aspy,	Lebanon.	
	John Weir,	Lebanon.	
	Phillup Deeds.		
	Christopher Early.		
	John Balim.		
	Peter Over.		
	John fleager,	Lebanon.	
	William Wat,	Lebanon.	
	George Bel,	Lebanon.	
	felx. Landise.		
	flavel Roan,	Volunteer, ...	Northumberland, Draft'd 24th May, 1779.
	John Eversoal,	Volunteer.	

	6th Class.		
May the 1st, 1779,......	Jacob Leaman.		
	Emanuel Kingrigh.		
	Peter Earter.		
	John Early.		
	John Sayers.		
	Benjamin Hearsy.		
	Joseph fearney.		
	Nicles Nay.		
	Robert McCallen.		
	Robert Dickey.		
	Archebald M'calister.		
	William Shaw.		
	George henry.		
	John Dougherty.		
	Martain Baira.		
	James Johnson.		
	7th Class.		
August ye 18th, 1779,..	John Willson.		
	Christopher beam.		
	William Sayers, Se'r.		
	John forney.		
	Joseph Mafoker.		
	Hendry bowman.		
	James McDonald.		
	Willery Weltmore.		
	John Pleshy.		
	Michael Katrien.		
	Christopher Carver.		
	John Bowman.		
	Robert Shearor, ...	24th of May, ...	Drafted.
	Daniel brough, ...	24th of May, ...	Drafted.

A COMPANY RETURN OF THE 5TH COMPANY AND 6TH BATALIAN OF LANCASTER COUNTY MILITIA —Continued.

When Served.	Men's Names.	Where Served.	Volunteers up the River, 1779.
	8th Class.		
August the 20th, 1779,.	John long.		
	Abraham longanecker.		
	Joseph Boyd, ...	Northumberland, ...	Volunteer.
	Robert Hays.		
	John White.		
	John humble.		
	Jacob Kensley.		
	Michael Carver.		
	Thomas M. Callin.		
	Everhart Katrien.		
	Robert Mecer.		
	Benjamin Sayers.		
	William Wilkeson.		
	George McMachon.		
	Phelty Katrien.		
	Peter Lynewever, ...	Drafted the 24th May.	
	George Gordon, ...	Drafted the 24th May.	
	Captain.		
February the 1st, 1779.	Patrick Hays, ...	Lebanon Serv'd, ...	Volunteer. Northumberland.

Lieutenant.

1st Samuel Weer.

2d James Willson.

Ensign.

James willson, Jur.

Certifyed by me this 25th of Oct'r, 1779.

PATRICK HAYS, Capt.

A RETURN OF THE SIXTH COMPANY OF THE 6TH BATALION OF LANCASTER COUNTY WITH THEIR RESPECTIVE CLASSES AND A RETURN OF THOSE WHO HAVE SERVED IN THE YEAR 1778 & 1779. (c.)

Men's Names. Commissioned Officers.	Who Have Served. Remarks.
Captain.	
Joseph McClure,	Not Serv'd having no command.
1st Lieutenant.	
James Johnston,	Served at Lebanon.
2d Lieutenant.	
James Wallace,	Served Volunteer at Northumberland.
Ensign.	
Joseph Willson,	Do. to Northumberland.
Non Commissioned Officers.	
Henry Laughlin,	Served Volunteer at Northumberland.
Duncan Sinckleer,	Serv'd at Lebanon.
Thomas Strain.	
Privates.	
1st Class.	
William Mitchel,	Served to Middletown.
William Snodgrass,	Served to Middletown.
Peter Balsbough,	
David Moffit,	Served to Middletown.
William Steawit,	Served to Middletown.
Samuel McCord,	Classed A. D. 1779.
William McFalls,	Do. This man ought to be in 7th class.
Phillip Bell,	Do.
Benjamin Finley,	gon to Virginia.
2d Class.	
John Dunlap,	Ser'd at Northumberland.
Patrick Gallant,	Class'd A. D. 1779.
Robt. Lewis,	Do.
Jas. Thompson,	Serv'd at Lebanon.
Jos. Willson.	
Peter Bell,	Class'd A. D. 1779.
William Black.	
3d Class.	
Thomas Martin.	
And'w Rogers.	
Samuel Stenart,	Serv'd Volunteer at Northumberland.
Felty Balsbough.	
Jas. Willson,	Ser'd Northumberland.
Jas. Rippeth,	Class't A. D. 1779.
Hugh Rippeth,	Do.
Henry O'Neal,	gon Virginia.

A RETURN OF THE SIXTH COMPANY OF THE 6TH BATALION OF LANCASTER COUNTY—Continued.

Men's Names. Commissioned Officers.	Who Have Served. Remarks.
4th Class.	
William Snody.	
John Sterit.	
William Rogers.	
Isaac Hodge.	
John Baird,	Serv'd Volunteer at Northumberland.
5th Class.	
Joseph Hutchison,	Serv'd at Lebanon.
Jeremiah Rogers,	Ser'd at Lebanon.
Francis McClure,	Ser'd at Lebanon.
Sam'l Swan,	Ser'd at Lebanon.
John Snody.	
James Willson,	Ser'd at Lebanon.
Wm. trousdale,	Ser'd at Lebanon.
Sam'l Boyd,	Class'd A. D. 1779.
John Ripeth,	Do.
6th Class.	
Thos. Walker.	
Robt. Moody.	
John Murry.	
William Hagerty.	
Christ. Bumberger.	
James Duncan.	
James Rogers,	Serv'd Volunteer at Northumberland & at Lebanon.
Edward Striddle,	Serv'd Boating with Geniral Sulifon.
James McClure.	
7th Class.	
Tho's McNair,	Ser'd Volentier at Northumberland.
Hugh Willson.	
John Cathcart,	Ser'd Volentier at Northumberland.
David Caldhoon.	
Andr'w Armstrong.	
David Kinging.	
Abram Flost.	
Wm. Robertson.	
8th Class.	
thos. McCord,	Served at Northumberland.
James Baird.	
Joseph Parks,	Sr'd Do. at Do.
And'r Willson.	
Patrick McNeight,	at turkey foot.
John thompson,	Ser'd at Northumberland.
Wm. Cathcart.	
Robt. Richey.	
Hugh Joley.	
Joseph Glen,	Ser'd Volunteer at Northumberland.

N. B.—Some of the Above Named Persons Mentioned to have

Served Were Deficient in Serving in their Respective Classes in the year A. D. 1778. Have Served A. D. 1779.

The Above is a true State of S'd Comp'y From the 24th of April Ano. Dom. 1778 untill the 25th Day of October A. D. 1779.

Certify'd By

JOS. McCLURE, Capt.

A RETURN OF THE SEVENTH COMPANY OF THE SIXTH BATALION OF LANCASTER COUNTY WITH THEIR RESPECTIVE CLASSES AND A RETURN OF THOSE WHO SERVED IN THE YEAR 1778 AND 1779. (c.)

Men's Names.	Remarks.
Commissioned Officers.	
Capt.	
William Laird,	No command.
Lieut.	
1st. John McFarland,	No command.
2d. Michael Ram,	Served Lebanon.
Ensign.	
Jacob Richar,	No command.
Non-Commissioned Officers.	
George Emmerick,	Volunteer to Northumberland.
Ludwick Emenck.	
George Peters.	
Michal Spade,	Served Lebanon.
Henry Miller.	
First Class.	
John Coffman.	
Barnet Fults.	
Philip Brand.	
Adam Firebaygh,	Served Middletown.
Philip Brown,	Served Middletown.
Christy Eversole.	
Second Class.	
peter Landis.	
George Speishbaugh.	
Adam Hammaker.	
Christy Hammaker.	
Phillip Richar,	Drafted Oct. Last, 1779.
Third Class.	
Frederick Hummel.	
Jacob Ram,	Serv'd Volunteer to Northumberland
Daniel Stover,	Not served.
James Laird,	Drafted Oct. last '79.
John Wetherhold,	Do. 1779.
James Donally.	
Philip Fishburn.	

A RETURN OF THE SEVENTH COMPANY OF THE SIXTH BATALION OF LANCASTER COUNTY—Continued.

Men's Names.	Remarks.
Commissioned Officers.	
Fourth Class.	
John Byars.	
Chrysty Stover.	
Christy Landis.	
Martin Fridly.	
Max Spidle.	
Peter Fishburn.	
Fifth Class.	
Jacob Landis.	
George Lower,	Served Lebanon.
Adam Deam,	Served Lebanon.
Daniel Baum.	
Peter Perst,	Served Lebanon.
John Snider.	
David Hammaker,	Serv'd Lebanon.
Ludwick Fishburn,	Serv'd Lebanon.
Philip Biesley,	Serv'd Lebanon.
David Brand,	Drafted Oct. Last—79.
Sixth Class.	
John Landis.	
Martin Rouse.	
Jacob Richar, Hanover.	
John Bringwolf.	
John Perst,	Drafted Oct. Last—79.
Seventh Class.	
Joseph Fever,	Volunteer to Northurberland.
George Minich.	
Michal Baum.	
Peter Eversole, Senior.	
Peter Fridly,	Volunteer to Northurberland.
Jacob Hereoff.	
Daniel Wonerly.	
Philip Nigh.	
James Clueney.	
Mathias Hoover.	
Eighth Class.	
Henry Eater.	
Henry Hesse.	
Frederick Stall.	
Philip Hammaker.	
Andrew Horning.	
John Brown.	
Edward Burges.	
David Hummel,	Drafted Oct. Last, 1779.
Jacob Spidle.	
Peter Eversole.	

The above is a true state of said company from the 24th of April 1778 untill this 7th day of December 1779.

Certifyed by

COL. JOHN RODGERS. WM. LAIRD, Capt.

A RETURN OF THE 8TH COMPANY OF THE 6TH BATTALION OF LANCASTER COUNTY SHEWING EACH MANS RESPECTIVE CLASS ALSO A RETURN OF THOSE WHO HAVE SERVED IN THEIR CLASS IN THE YEAR A. D. 1778 & 1779. (c.)

Commiss'd Officers.	Remarks.
Captain.	
Michael Moyer,	Not served, having no command.
1st Lieutenant.	
Abraham Allis,	Not serVed, haVing no command.
2d Lieutenant.	
Michael Brown,	Not served, having no command.
Non-Commiss'd Officers.	
Emanuel Toole.	
Mathias Baker.	
Jacob Allis, fifer.	
Class ye 1st.	
Jacob Pruner,	Served at Midletown.
George Minich.	
Henery Seigler.	
George Rumberger.	
2d Class.	
Peter Symon.	
Adam Weiss.	
George Haine.	
Martin Long.	
Casper Freeman,	Serv'd at Lebanon.
John Reid,	SerV'd at Lebanon.
George Cyder.	
Christophel Cyder.	
3d Class.	
George Wolf.	
Christophel Mowra.	
William Ranch,	Class'd A. D. 1779.
Martin Shoole.	
George Mowra.	
4th Class.	
George Walmer.	
Simon Minich.	
John Baker,	Serv'd at Northumberland.
John Carvary,	Served at Lebanon.
Andrew Brown.	
John Shupp.	
Conrad Moyer,	Served at Lebanon.
5th Class.	
Jacob Musser,	Served at Lebanon.
Henry Sharp.	
John Poor,	SerVed at Lebanon.
George Hoke,	Served at Lebanon.
John Hoover,	SerVed at Lebanon.

Y OF THE 6TH BAT-
UNTY—Continued.

ons Did not Serve A. D.
anon A. D. 1779.
Company from the 24th
th Day of October A. D.

CHAEL MOYER, Capt.

OMPANY 6TH BATTAL-
9. (c.)

opher Stoner.
Leman.
uel Kingerigh.

John Mires.
Philip Deeds.
John White.
John Michel Ealy.
Conrad Croul.
Peter Erter.
Christopher Early.
John Early.
John Balin.
Conrad Wishon.
Christopher Beam.
Martin Penogle.
Christopher Feder.
John Humble.
Hendry Hersey.
Benjamin Hersey.
Andrew Byars.
Joseph Forney, Jun.
John Forney.
Joseph Forney, Sen.
Philip Bittleon.
Joseph Naphskar.
William Nay.
Nicholas Nay.
Daniel Harshbarger.
Joseph Falgate, dead.
Hendry Bowman.
Peter Over.
Joseph Carminy.
James McDonnol.
Daniel Longnaker.
Hendry Shell.
(illegible) Weltmore.
Jacob Longaker.
Jacob Rice.
Peter Singer.
Jacob Bowman, Junr.
Hendry Creager.
Michael Carver.
Dewalk Shank.
John Biesly.
John Landice.
Vendal Hendry.
Everhart Katrine.
Michael Katrine.
John Cannon.
Jacob Plough.
Christopher Carver.
Loudwick Ball.
Hanicle Ball.
John Panter.
George Hendry.
Felix Landice.
Abraham Weltmore.
Peter Thomas.
Jacob Nay.
William Sayer.
Phelty Katrine.
John Bowman.
Jacob Bowman.

The above is a true account of the 5th Compy. of the 6th Battalion of Lancaster County Militia.

Anno Dom 1779 Each of the above named have been absent 5 days and the feild day certifyed the 24th day of May A. D. 1779 by

PATT. HAYS, Capt.

LIST OF MEN BETWEEN THE AGES OF 18 AND 53 YEARS OF CAPT. JOHN CALDWELL'S COMPANY, 6TH BATTALION, LANCASTER COUNTY. (c.)

James Herrin.
James Reed, Junr.
Charles Herrin.
Adam Moderwel.
John Reed, Jun'r.
Willam Porter.
Chrisly Horst.
Isaac Prubaker.
Sam'l Fisher.
Chrisly Graybil.
William Strahon.
John Evans, Junr
David Porter.
James McFarlin.
James Carson.
Sam'el Reed.
John Long.
Henry Heable.
Robert Williams.
Jam's Cunningham.
Daniel McReady.
Henry Hoover.
Sam'l McElroy.
George Moults.
James Cumings.
Casper Bowman.
John Rob.
Hugh Galaher.
George Oatman.
Spophel Bousman.
Robt. Farquer.
Sam'l Hyndman.
John Caldwel.
James Calhoon.
John Turner.
Henry Bear.
Stweart Hall.
Robt. Dunlap.
John Eackman.
John McCollough.
John Fleck.
Robt. Maxfield.
Thomas William.
William Kenadey.
Robt. Hillis.
John Feild.
James Porter.
Robert Petterson.
James Grier.
Robt. Kirkpatrick.
William Taylor.
John Jackson.
John Turher.
Jacob Buyers.
Joseph Lorimore.
Andrew Caldwel.
William Bigham.
William Hunter.
William Calhoon.
George Bleaps.
William Cumins.
Thom's Reed.
Will'm Quarl.
Jerom. Dunlap.
John Williamson.
John Cumins.
Joseph M'Clean.
George Glass.
William Fell.
David Chambers.
William Walker.
James Mitchel.
John Reed.
Jacob Bear.

John McMurry. James Moor.
George Taylor. James Gray.
William Strong. Hugh Hallaway.

Willam ,Miligon. James Reed.
James Marshal. David Gibson.
James Petterson. Joseph Haslet.
John McElroy.

The above Persons in my opinion are Persons unfit for Military Service.

The above is a List of names that are Between the ages of 13 and 53 years Living in the Bounds of the Eastran Company of Dromore Township to the best of My Knowledge and Information.

JOHN CALDWEL, Capt.

May 25th, 1780.

A MUSTER ROLE OF THE SIXTH COMPANY OF YE SIXTH BATALION OF LANCASTER COUNTY MILITIA COMMANDED BY COL. JAS. TAYLOR, AGUST 8TH, 1780. (c.)

Capt.
Jos. Walker.

Leut.
Jas. Noble.

Ensn.
Jno. Ross.

Sergts.
John McGraith. Jno. Crage.

Fifer.
John Calvin.

1st Class.
Nathan Thompson. Wim. Farr.
Ezekel Irwin. George Cooper.
John Tweed. John Moore.

2d Class.

Thos. Fullton.	Robt. Guy.
Thos. Watson.	Henery Pickle.
Gainer Peirce.	John porter, s'nr.
Jno. Watson.	Wm. Heerd.
Jacob Kerns.	John McFerson.

3d Class.

Jeremiah Moore.	Samuel Smith.
George Leach.	Samuel Simmins.
Jas. Hall.	George Money.
Andrew Moore.	Jonathan Cummins.
Robt. Moore.	

4th Class.

John Murry, junr.	Daniel Miller.
Wim. Loughead, S'nr.	Wim. Loughead, Junr.
Robt. Williams.	George Clark.
John Coventry.	Isaac Simpson.
George Oxer.	John Gribin.
Jas. Crage.	

5th Class.

Christephor Taffe.	John Lee.
Michal Gander.	Nathan Cope.
Robt. Wasson.	Robt. Evins.
Jas. Cooper.	John Crosbay.
John Heerd, Junr.	Robt. McClelen.
John porter, junr.	James Dun.

6th Class.

Leonard pickle.	Jas. Walles.
Thos. Hathorn.	Heironimus Miller.
John Donald.	David Bower.
Petter pickle.	Jonathan Simpson.
Robt. Gibson.	Jas. Wasson.

7th Class.

Ben. Irwin.	Jas. Gueist.
John Cummins.	Andrew Walker.
Jas. Rea, Junr.	Jacob Gander.
Stephen Herd, junr.	John Griffith.

8th Class.

Stephen Heerd, s'nr.
Wim. Tweed.
Isaac Irwin.
Joshua Chamberlain.
John Cooper.
Wim. Guy.
Philip Rokey.
Wim. Cummins.
Jas. Calvin.

A true Roole.

J. WALKER, Capt.

OFFICERS OF SIXTH BATTALION. (a.)

Returned August 26, 1780.

Lieutenant Colonel.

James Taylor.

Major.

Robert King.

First Company.

Captain—John Caldwell.
Lieutenant—James Calhoun.
Ensign—John Turner.

Second Company.

Captain—Robert Campbell.
Lieutenant—Isaac Walker.
Ensign—Daniel McCoomb.

Third Company.

Captain—John Duncan.
Lieutenant—John Neisser.
Ensign—Hugh McConkey.

Fourth Company.

Captain—Robert Miller.
Lieutenant—Robert Anderson.
Ensign—Matthew Park.

Fifth Company.

Captain—James Clark.
Lieutenant—Hugh McIntire.
Ensign—James Gribbon.

Sixth Company.

Captain—Joseph Walker.
Lieutenant—James Noble.
Ensign—John Ross.

Seventh Company.

Captain—John Patton.
Lieutenant—Peter Simpson.
Ensign—David McDermont.

Eighth Company.

Captain—Thomas Gormley.
Lieutenant—Henry Eackman.
Ensign—John Gouchey.

Little Brittain Township Lanc'r Co.

A CLASS ROLL OF THE 3RD COMPANY OF THE 6TH BATTALION OF LANC'R COUNTY MILITIA, COMMANDED BY CAPT. JOHN DUNCAN FOR 1780. (c.)

Capt.

John Duncan.

Lieut.

John Neiper.

Ens.

Hugh McConky.

Sergt.

Samuel Dilworth. Alexander Reed.
Robert Roy.

Clerk.

Thomas Carmichael.

1st Class.

William King.
Joseph McCreary.
Thomas Mooney.
James McCulley.
Abram Midcap.
Oliver Caldwell.
James Johnston.
William Holmes.
Stephen Lowrey.

2d Class.

Nathaniel Jenkins.
John Webster.
Samuel Cappock.
William Porter.
Samuel McCreary.
Thomas Cappock.
Larry Widowfield.
George Warden.
Benjamin Maul.
Robert Hannah.
David Burford.
Nath'l Breaddin.
Christian Neisely.
Caspar Tigart.
William Vint.

3 Class.

William Pennell.
George Ewing.
Robert Kill Chreest.
Jacob Gryder.
John Reed.
Andrew Dunning.
Jeremiah Brown.
Ephraim McMullen.
Andrew Sherraress.
Robert Barns.
James Cleney.
Samuel Neiper.
Alexander Carmichael.
James McElwain.
Andrew Dunn.

4th Class.

Christian Corpman.
William Money.
William Anderson.
Isaiah Brown.
Hugh Pennell.
John Glass.
George Mustard.
George Nicholson.
Abraham Russell.
Mark McDowell.
Atchison Blackwood.
John Scott.
Daniel Carmichael.
William Daviss.

5th Class.

David Killough.
Martin Gryder.
Samuel Rayough.
Joseph Stubbs.
George Henery.
James Young.
John Mills.
Luke McDowell.
James Leonard.
James McSparren.
William Beard.

6th Class.

Thos. Porter.
William McDowell.
James King.
John McCreary.
Samuel Caughey.

Robert Kief.
Alexander McKnight.
William Arbunckle.
Edward Earl.

7th Class.

Thomas Plummer.
Joseph Mills.
Vincent Stubbs.
John Perry.
Henry Lennox.

John McNight.
John Neil.
John Suitter.
James McDowell.

8th Class.

Joseph Robinson.
Joseph Harland.
Samuel McKinney.
James McDowell.
Josua Brown.

David Breaddin.
Michael Neisely.
John Donoho.
Robert Homer.
William Ferguson.

1780.

A CLESS ROLE OF THE FOURTH COMPANY OF THE SIXTH BATT'N OF LANCASTER COUNTY MILITIA COMMANDED BY JAMES TAYLOR, COLONEL. (c.)

Capt.

Robt. Miller.

Lt.

Robt. Anderson.

Ens.

Matt'w Parks.

Sergts.

Jno. Berry.
Jno. Hugh.

Clark.

John Baird.

1 Cless.

William Robison.
Jas. Walker, Senr.
Will'm Kire.
Jno. Semple.

2 Cless.

Jno. Briggs.
Stephen Mahen.
Hugh Willson.
Hugh McConnell.
Will'm Crain.
Robt. Grimes.
Jas. Gilmer.
Robt. Guy.
Jno. McClelan.
Hugh Cooper.
Sam'l McWilliams.
Abram Whiteside.

3 Cless.

Petter Hesten.
Jno. Geble.
Alex'd May.
Jas. Cunning'm Junr.
Robt. Paisley.
Jas. Cunning'm Senr.
Will'm Moore.
Jno. McCalley.
Will'm Fursythe.
Robt. McCalmont.
Jno. Bunting.

4 Cless.

Sam'l Galbreath.
Alexd. Morrison.
Matt'w Scott.
Jas. Glenn.
Jas. Walker, Junr.
Saml. Robison.
Henery Swisher.
Jno. Andrews, Jun'r.
Jas. McWhirter.
Alex'd Greer.

5 Cless.

And'n McGinnes.
Jno. Speer.
Jas. Finley.
Will'm Downey.
Jas. McKendrey.
Hugh Cummins.
Paul Raulston.
Will'm Carson.
Jacob Eayman.
Jas. Smith.
Rich'd Free.

6 Cless.

Robt. Ross.
Robt. Gregery.
Alex'd Huston.
Crisley Hess.
Will'm Anderson.
Jno. May.
Reynold Lee.
Benjamin Hasson.
Jno. Whiteside.
George Martain.
Jno. Andrews, Sen'r.

7 Cless.

Jas. Gallbreath.
Hugh Paisley.
Robt. Forth.
Jno. Brown.
Jas. Collance.
Jno. Teas.
Will'm Miller.

8 Cless.

And'w Parks.
Will'm McConnell.
Jno. Patterson.
Saml. McClelan.
Will'm Whiteside.
And'w Heney.
Jno. White.
Daniel McConnell.
Jno. McConnell.
Jno. Bamsey.
Jno. Fursythe.
George Thislow.
Saml. Greg.

Nov. 24th, 1780.

A CLASS ROLE OF THE 8TH COMPANY OF THE 6TH BATT'N OF LANC. C'Y MILITIA COMMANDED BY THOMAS GOURLY FOR 1780. (c.)

---

1 Class.

Martin Miller.
And'w Caughey.
Wm. McClure.
Arch'd McCready.
James Hainey.
Jacob Varnor.
James Leech.
Simon Ritz.

2d Class.

Rob't Karr.
David Hare.
Joseph Griffith.
John Caldwell.
Will'm Speer.
Jam's Sherard.
Robert Ramsey.
John Ramsey.
Will'm Ritchsison.
Sam'l McCartney.
John Keesacker.
John Myers.
Stophel Frievely.
Joseph Kine.
Abram. Newswanzer.
Rob't Ramsey, Ms.

3d Class.

Peter Sides.
Aaron Moore.
Jacob Young.
Henry Battlemy.
John Glass.
Martin Cokershire.
Malcom Millinger.
John Frunk.
David Carron.

4th Class.

John Maiger.
John Ramsey, Ms.
John McGrath.
Simon Ghost.
Wm. Kelly.
Arch'd McDowell.
Dan'l McCready.
Walter Davis.
Doring'n Willson.
Chris'n Black.
Wm. Maffett.
John Dowling.

5th Class.

James Givin.
John Shannon, Jun'r.
Wm. Cuncle.
Henry Nole, Jun'r.
John Thompson.
Henry Sides.
George Cuncle.
Thomas Dowing.
Robt. Falls.
Leonard Gross.
Wm. Brown.
Martin Bird.
Wm. Coulter.
Hierony Hickman.

6th Class.

Henry Warfield.
Jam's McKown.
Martin Bear.
Samuel Downing.
James Miller.
George Boughman.
John Richard.
George Rocky.
Conrad Tice.
John Hannah.
John Richadson.
William Sherrard.
William Hood.
John Paxton, Junr.
David Claghan.
James Shannon.
Patrick Brown.

7th Class.

Arnold Fite.
Andrew Frunk.
Frank McKnight.
John Mahen.
John Bean.
Jacob Whistler.
Samuel McDowel.
Mich'd Lingerfied.
John McClure.
Wm. Paxton.
Patrick Hoar.
Robt. McCumsy.
Wm. Ramsey.
Joseph Nole.
Adam Cremer.
John Barber.
John Clark.
Adam Johnston.

8th Class.

Henry Boughman.
Jacob Bolstone.
Caleb Hartman.
Moses Latta.
Mark McCord.
Henry Rockey.
John Liggit.
Henry Hocke.

John Campbell.	Nath'n Neely.
Robt. Hale.	John Paxton.
Robt. McClean.	Alex'd McBride.
Andrew Work.	Jams. McClure.
Nath. Coutter, Sen.	John Irwin.
Edw'd Wahab.	

Signed by me,

THOS. GOURLEY, Capt.

A RETURN OF THE SIXTH COMPANY OF THE SIXTH BATALION OF LANCASTER COUNTY MILITIA COMMANDED BY COLL. JAS. TAYLOR, MAY YE 12TH 1781. (c.)

Commissioned Officers.

Captain.

Joseph Walker.

Lieutenant.

James Noble.

Ensign.

John Ross.

Sergents.

John McGrath. John Craig.

Fifer.

John Colvin.

1 Class.

Nathan Thompson.	Jos. Curle.
Ezekel Irwin.	Stephen Hall.
George Cooper.	Jas. Heny.
John Moore.	

2nd Class.

Thos. Fullton.	Jacob Kerns.
Thos. Wasson.	Robt. Guy.
Gainer Peirce.	Henery Pickle.
John Wasson.	Wm. Heerd.

3d Class.

Jeremiah Moore.	Samuel Simins.
George Leech.	Job. Cooper (of 1st Class).
Andrew Moore.	Jonathan Cumins.
Robt. Moore.	John M'Cally.

4th Class.

John Murry.	Jas. Cuage.
Robt. Williams.	Daniel Miller.
John Coventry.	John Gribins.

5th Class.

Michal Gander.	Nathan Cope.
Robt. Wasson.	Robt. Evins.
Jas. Cooper.	John Crosbay.
John Heerd, junr.	Thos. Smith.
John Lee.	Jacob hill.

6th Class.

Leonard Pickle.	Jas. Wasson.
Thos. Hathorn.	Robt. Gibson.
John Donald.	Jonathan Simpsons.
Petter Pickle.	Sam'l Vogan.
Heironomus Miller.	Jas. Tweed.

7th Class.

Benjamin Irwin.	Andrew Walker.
John Cummins.	Jacob Gander.
Jas. Rea.	John Griffith.
Stephen Heerd, Junr.	James Cane.

8th Class.

Wim. Tweed.	John Cooper.
Isaac Irwin.	Wim Guy.
Joshua Cnamberlain.	Jas. Colvin.

Given under my hand the day and year above Writen.

JOS. WALKER, Capt.

A RETURN OF SIXTH COMPANY OF THE SIXTH BATTALION OF LANCASTER COUNTY MILITIA COMMANDED BY COL. JAMES TAYLOR—VIZ'T MAY 28TH, 1781. (c.)

Capt.

Joseph Walker.

Lieut.

James Noble.

Ens.

John Ross.

Sergts.

John McGrath.
John Craig.

Fifer.

John Colvin.

1st Class.

Nathan Tompson.
Ezekiel Irwin.
Geo. Cooper.
John Moore.
Joseph Curl.
Stephen Hall.
James Heany.

2d Class.

Thomas Fulton.
Thomas Wasson.
Gainer Peirce.
John Wasson.
Jacob Kerns.
Robert Guy.
Henry Pickle.
William Herd.
Jacob Hill.

3d Class.

Jerimiah Moore.
George Leech.
Andrew Moore.
Robert Moore.
Samuel Simmins.
George Mooney.
Jonathan Cummins.
John McCawley.
Job. Cooper.

4th.

John Murray.
Robert Williams.
John Coventry.
James Craig.
Daniel Miller.
John Grubbins.

5th Class.

Michael Gander.
Robert Wasson.
James Cooper.
John Herd, Junr.
John Lee.
Nathan Cope.
Robert Evans.
John Crosby.
Thomas Smith.

6th Class.

Leonard Pickle.
Thomas Hathorn.
John Donald.
Peter Pickle.
Hieronimus Miller.
James Wasson.
Robert Gibson.
Jonathan Simpson.
Samuel Vogan.
James Tweed.

7th Class.

Benjamin Irwin.
John Cummins.
Stephen Herd, Jun'r.
Andrew Walker.
Jacob Gander.
John Griffith.

8th.

William Tweed.
Isaac Irwin.
Joshua Chamberlain.
John Cooper.
William Guy.
James Colvin.

1781.

• LIST OF CAPT. JOHN PATTON'S BEING THE SEVENTH COMPANY OF THE 6TH BATTALION LANCASTER COUNTY COMMANDED BY COL. JAMES TAYLOR, MAY 1781. (c.)

Names.

Henry Byers.
Wm. Seabrooks.
Jas. McDonald.
Jacob Hoover.
Wm. Yorty.
George Kenrick.
Henry Keagy.
John Smith.
Wm. Turner.
Henry Bear.
John Grafft.
Martin plíman.
Jacob Beam.
Jacob Broobaker.
George Birdigg.
Daniel Collodon.
John Grafft.
Jacob Grafft.
Jas. Harra.
John Segal.

Jacob Hoover.	Christian Hoover.
Michael Shank.	Ulrich Hoover.
Patt. Kelly.	Andrew Pegan, Jr.
Sebastian Nize.	Michael Everly.
Samuel Lines.	Peter Stopher.
Jacob Kirgan.	Isaac Hare.
Jas. Pegan, Miller.	Henry Blucher.
John Hess.	Henry Kenrick.
Samuel Winter.	John Shank.
Ebrey Everly.	Jacob Grafft.
John Bond.	Cristian Lines.
Thos. Mackey.	Peter Good.
Abraham Keagy.	Cristian Good.
Petter Miller.	George Hess.
John Camp.	Willm. Biven.
Henry Hoover.	Fredrick hare.

JOHN PATTON, Capt.

William Tweed his hand and penn 1781.

MUSTER ROLL OF 2D CLASS 6TH BATAL. LANC'R COU'Y MILITIA ON A TOUR OF DUTY AT LANCR. (c.)

Names of Persons Who Serv'd.	Names of Persons Who Furnished Substitutes.	Time when duty commd.	Time when duty ended.
Lieut.		1781.	1781.
James Calhoon,		June 20,	July 30.
Serjt.			
Thos. Reed.			
Privates.			
Abraham Whiteside,		June 20,	July 28.
Robert Jones.			
Hugh McConnell.			
James Patterson.			
James Sheerer, Jr.,		July 7,	
Hugh Cooper,		June 20,	
David Porter.			
Wm. Atchison.			
Thos. Johnson,		June 23,	
Jas. Finley,	Jno. Briggs,	June 23,	
Stophel Byerly,	Jno. Myer.		
Jno. Ritchey.			
Danl. Craig,		June 20,	
And'w Walke,		June 23,	
Jno. Dennis,	James Dennis,	June 25,	July 29.
Alex'r Boggs,	John Boggs,		July 28.
Jno. Ritcheson,	Wm. Ritcheson,	June 20,	July 28.
Jno. Porter,	Wm. Porter,		July 28.
James Carter,	Gilbert Buchanan,	June 24,	Aug. 21.
Luke Harper,	Joseph Griffiths.		
Robert Trounsell,	James Black,	June 26,	Aug. 23.
Jno. Smith,	Saml. Willson,	June 20,	Aug. 24.
Geo. Mathiott,	James Neal,	July 6,	Aug. 24.
David Murphy,	Robert Ramsay,	June 22,	Aug. 24.
Wm. Anderson,		June 20,	
James Rach,	John Evans,	June 20,	

Lanc'r June 1781. Then mustered above compy. as above specified.

ADM. HUBLEY, S. L. L'r C'y.

A MUSTER ROLL OF CAPT. JNO. DUNCAN'S COMPANY OF THE SIXTH BET'N 1OF L'R CO. MELITIA, COMANDED BY LT. JAS. TAYLOR. JUNE YE 22D 1781. (c.)

Captain.

Jno. Duncan.

Lieutenant.

Jno. Neeper.

Ensign.

Hugh McConky.

Cleark.

Thos. Carmichael.

1st Class.

Wm. King.
Joseph McCreary.
Jas. McCully.
Olliver Caldwell.
Jas. Johnson.
Jno. Reagh.
Robt. Pennel.
Thos. Mooney.
Abraham Mid (illegible).

2d Class.

Wm.* Pint.
Alexr. Reed.
Wm. Porter.
Saml. McCreary.
Geo. Warden.
Robt. Hanna.
Nat. Breading.
Casper Tigart.
Christ. Nicely.
Benj'm Maule.
Nath'l Jinkine.
Jno. Webster.

3d Class.

George Ewing.
Robt. Gilgriest.
Jacob Gryder.
Jno. Reed.
And'w Dunning.
Robt. Barnes.
Sam'l Neeper.
Alexr. Carmichael.
Jerh. Brown.
And'w Sararas.

4th Class.

Wm. McCully.
Christ Coffman.
Wm. Mooney.
Hugh Pennel.

John Glass.
Geor. Mustard.
Mark McDowell.
Atchison Blackwood.
Jno. Scott.
Dan'l Carmichael.
Hugh Holliday.
Isacah Brown.
Casper Bowman.

5th Class.

David Killaugh.
Saml. Reagh.
Geor. Henery.
Frances Young.
Jno. Milles.
Luke McDowell.
Jas. Mcsparan.
Jno. McCleland.
Martin Grider.
Joseph Stubbs.
Wm. Baird.

6th Class.

Thos. Porter.
Wm. McDowell.
Jno. McCreary.
Saml. Cauchey.
Robt. Kief.
Alexr. McKnight.
Wm. Arbuckle.
Edwd. Earl.
Jas. King.

7th Class.

Joseph Milles.
John Perrey.
Henery Lynix.
Jno. McKnight.
Jas. McDowell.
John Sooter.
Wm. Davis.
Jehu Kay.
Vincent Stubbs.
James Clancy.
Robert Roy.

8th Class.

Joseph Robeson.
Saml. McKincy.
Jas. McDowell, smith.
David Breading.
Wm. Forguson.
Robt. Holmes.
Patrick McKeag, Junr.
Joseph Harling.
Joshua Brown, Jr.
Michael Niesley.

JNO. DUNCAN, Capt'n.

CLASS ROLL OF THE MALE WHITE INHABITANTS OF MARTICKS MILITIA BEING THE SEVENTH COMPANY OF THE SIXTH BATTALION OF LANCASTER COUNTY COMMANDED BY COL. JAMES TAYLOR—JUNE 1781. .(c)

Capt.

John Patton.

Lieut.

Peter Simpson.

Ensign.

Daniel McDermond.

Privates.

1st Class.

Archibald Pagon.
Alexander Boyd.
James Savage.
Jacob Markly.
Heney Beyers.
James Black.
David Gibson.
Phillip May.
William Moor.
Thomas Johnson.
Peter Fite.
William Seabrook.
Sebastian Swager.
James McDonald.
Andrew McGenis.
Jacob Hoover, Henry's son.
William Yorty.
George Kenricks.
James Morrow.
Jacob Myers.
David Hall.

2nd Class.

Hugh Caldwell.
Henry Kegay.
John Smith.
Loudwick Stouts.
John Cuncle.
Henry Bear.
John Graft.
Henry Alexander.
Joseph Myers.
Stophel Winter.
Daniel Crage.
Alexd'r Snodgrass.
William Steel.
Martin Isleman.
Jacob Beem.
Jacob Broobaker.
George Birdegg.
Daniel Collodon.
John Cooper.
Henry Cuncle.
James Glover.
Jacob Hart.
John Murphey.

3d Class.

James Snodgrass.
Gregory Harmar.
James Whary.
Valentine Hart.
John Caldwell.
Jacob Hoover, J'r.
Martin Byers.
Conrod Neble.
William Carr.
Thomas Dick.
John Grafft.
Jacob Grafft.
James Harra.
John Segat.
John Maphet.
John Reed.

4th Class.

Robert McColough.
Joseph Aird.
John McCreary.
Joseph Reagh.
Peter Lutes.
John Cunningham.
Samuel Ellot.
Jacob Hoover.
Michael Shank.
Patt Kelly.
Sebastian Nize.
Samuel Lines.
John Boyde.
John Pagon.
Alexander Brannon.
George Scriver.

5th Class.

James Johnson.
James Pegan, J'r.
Thomas Robinson.
Samuel Kirkpatrick, Jr.
James Pegan, miller.
Peter Poland.
John Clark, Jr.
Joseph McCollough.
John Ness.
George Ness.
Samuel Winter.
Ebrey Everly.
John Mitcheal.
John Douglass.
Joseph Gardner.
Samuel Ramsey.
John Patterson.
Patrick Campble.
John Bond.
Alexdr. Garrot.

6th Class.

Thomas Mackey.
Robert Long.
David McCollough.
Adam Moor.
Abram Heagy.
Samuel Wollson.
John Reed.
Peter Miller.
James Steel.
William Snodgrass.
William Brown.
Henrey Hoffman.
John Barr.
Thomas Boyde.
John Camp.
Henry Hoover.
Cristian Hoover.
Ulrick Hoover.

7th Class.

Robert Steen.	John Thomas.
John Pegan, Jr.	James Reed.
James Purdy.	Isaac McCowen.
John Robinson.	James Dick.
Andrew Pagon.	William McAdams.
James Long.	John Winter.
Mathias Horra.	John Blair.
John Hoover.	David Chambers.
George Teeter.	John Sulliman.
John Willy.	Samuel McCulough.
Michael Everly.	George Fockler.
John Albright.	John Rodgers.
Peter Stopher.	Alexander Orr.
John Smith, tanner.	

8th Class.

James Petterson.	John McCallister.
Valantine Gardner.	Samuel Simpson, Jr.
Fredrick Heble.	Thomas Wharry.
Isaac Hare.	Samuel Kirkpatrick, Sr.
Henry Blucher.	Peter Good.
Henry Kenricks.	Cristian Good.
John Shank.	William Simpson.
Jacob Grafft.	Benjamin Winter.
Cristian Lines.	Thomas Clark.

MUSTER ROLL OF 3D CLASS, 6TH BATALL. LANC'R CO'Y MIL'A ON A TOUR OF DUTY AT LANC'R. (c.)

Names of Persons Who Serv'd.	Names of Persons Who Furnished Substitutes.	Time when duty commd.	Time when duty ended.
		1781.	1781.
James Cunningham, ...	....	July 1,	July 30.
Peter Sides.			
Robert McCummon.			
Danl. McCrady.			
John Reed.			
Saml. Dilworth.			
John Frank.			
Collin Kirl, ...	John Atchison, ...	....	Aug. 22.
John Bally, ...	James Carson, ...	....	Aug. 24.
George Firestine, ...	Jno. Craft.		

1781, July 3d. Then mustered above company as above specified.

ADM. HUBLEY, S. L. L'r C'y.

A CLASS ROLE OF THE FOURTH COMPANY OF THE SIXTH BATT'N OF LANCASTER COUNTY MILITIA COMMANDED BY COL. JAMES TAYLOR. (c.)

Capt.

Robt. Miller.

Lt.

Robt. Anderson.

Ens.

Matt'w Parks.

Sergts.

Jno. Berry. | Jno. Huss.

1 Class.

Will'm Robison.	Henery Addams.
Jas. Walker, Sen'r.	Arch'd Cook.
Will'm Kire.	

2 Class.

James Carter.	Hugh Cooper.
Jno. Briggs.	Sam'l McWilliams.
Stephen Mahen.	Abram. Whiteside.
Hugh McConnell.	Will'm Anderson, Junr.
Will'm Crain.	Jno. Ritchey.
Robt. Grimes.	

3 Class.

Petter Hesten.	Robt. Paisley.
Jno. Geble.	Jas. Cuming'm, Sen'r.
Alex'd May.	Robt. McCalmont.
Jas. Cuming'm.	

4 Class.

Sam'l Gallbreath.	Jno. Andrews, Junr.
Alex'd Morrison.	Arthur May.
Matt'w Scott.	Will'm Barcley.
Jas. Glenn.	Jos. Miller.
Jas. Walter, Jun'r.	Sam'l Entrican.
Sam'l Robison.	And'n Parks, Jun'r.
Jno. Baird.	John berry.
Henery Swisher.	

5 Class.

And'w McGinnes.	Will'm Carson.
Jas. Finley.	Jas. Smith.
Will'm Downing.	Rich'd Free.
Hugh Cummins.	Jno. Dely.
Paul Rauiston.	Jno. Roddy.

6th Class.

Robt. Ross.	Jno. Whiteside.
Robt. Gregery.	George Martain.
Alex'd Huston.	Jno. Andrews, Sen'r.
Crisley Hess.	Saml. McConnell.
Will'm Anderson, Sen'r.	Jno. Ryburn.
Jno. May.	

7th Class.

Randol lee.	Will'm Miller.
Jas. Galbreath.	Addam Johnston.
Hugh Paisley.	Phillip Swisher.
Jno. Brown.	Rynard Weaver.
Jas. Collance.	Duncan Kenan.

8th Class.

Will'm McConnell.	Jno. McConnell.
Jno. Patterson.	George Thislow.
Sam'l McClelan.	Jno. Craford.
Will'm Whiteside.	Rich'd Mackey.
And'n Heney.	Sam'l Bunting.
Jno. White.	Paterson bell.
Daniel McConnell.	John Conhaven.

Aug't —th, 1781.

ROLL OF THE 4TH, 5TH & 6TH CLASS OF THE 6TH BATALION LAN'R COUNTY MILITIA ON A TOUER OF DUTY AT BUCKS COUNTY. (c.)

Names of Persons Who Perform a Touer of Duty.	What class.	Names of Persons Who Furnished Substitutes.	Time when duty commenced.	Time when duty ended.
Capt.			1781.	1781.
John Neeper,			Sept. 22d,	
Lieut.				
John Turner,			Sept. 22d,	
Serjts.				
William [illegible]lley,			Sept. 22d,	
John [illegible]b,			Sept. 22d,	
Privates.				
[illegible]w Parck,			Sept. 22d,	
Samuel Neeper,			Sept. 22d,	
Atkinson [illegible],			Sept. 22d,	
Marck McDowell,			Sept. 22d,	
John Grubbin,			Sept. 22d,	
William [illegible]y,			Sept. 22d,	

ROLL OF THE 4TH, 5TH & 6TH CLASS OF THE 6TH BATALION LAN'R COUNTY MILITIA—Continued.

Names of Persons Who Perform a Touer of Duty.	What clas'	Names of Persons Who Furnished Substitutes.	Time when duty commenced.	Time when duty ended.
			1781.	1781.
Al-x'r Ferguson,			Sept. 22d,	
Hugh Pennon,			Sept. 22d,	
Lucke McDowell,			Sept. 22d,	
William Henrey,			Sept. 22d,	
James Walker,			Sept. 22d,	
Henrey Swisher,			Sept. 22d,	
William Bartley,			Sept. 22d,	
Joseph Miller,			Sept. 22d,	
Daniel Craig,		George Hess,	Sept. 22d,	
Samuel Entrican,			Sept. 22d,	
John Scott,			Sept. 22d,	
James Snodgress,			Sept. 22d,	
Arther Mease,			Sept. 22d,	
Henrey Free,			Sept. 22d,	
William Maffet,			Sept. 22d,	
Samuel McElroy,			Sept. 22d,	

Name			Date	
Capt.				
James Clerk,			Sept. 22d,	
Lieut.				
James Noble,			Sept. 22d,	
Ensign.				
John Caughey,			Sept. 22d,	
Serjt.				
Hugh Long,			Sept. 22d,	
Privates.				
John Robison,			Sept. 22d,	
William Coulter,			Sept. 22d,	Oct. 11th.
Robert Falls,			Sept. 22d,	
Hugh Weir,			Sept. 22d,	
Alex'r Snodgrass,		John McClelen,	Sept. 22d,	
Hugh Harris,			Sept. 22d,	
James Ferguson,			Sept. 22d,	
James McSparon,			Sept. 22d,	
Samuel Logan,			Sept. 22d,	
Paul Ralston,			Sept. 22d,	
Henrey Sides			Sept. 22d,	
James Finley,			Sept. 22d,	
John Shennon,			Sept. 22d,	
James Miller,			Sept. 22d,	
James Beatty,			Sept. 22d,	
Alex'r Scott,			Sept. 22d,	
James Catagan,			Sept. 22d,	
Samuel Reach,			Sept. 22d,	

ROLL OF THE 4TH, 5TH & 6TH CLASS OF THE 6TH BATALION LAN'R COUNTY MILITIA—Continued.

Names of Persons Who Perform a Touer of Duty	What class.	Names of Persons Who Furnished Substitutes.	Time when duty commenced.	Time when duty ended.
Capt.			1781.	1781.
Joseph Walker,			Sept. 22d,	Oct'r 11th.
Leiut.				
James Gribon,			Sept. 22d,	
Ensign.				
David McDarmon,			Sept. 22d,	
Serjt.				
John McGrath,			Sept. 22d,	
Samuel McHollan,			Sept. 22d.	
Privates.				
James Paterson, Jr.,		John Patterson,	Sept. 22d,	
John Richison,			Sept. 22d,	
Henrey Linecks,		Edward Arrall,	Sept. 22d,	
Daniel McCredey,		John McColech,	Sept. 22d,	

John Culvin,			Sept. 22d,	
John Hill,			Sept. 22d,	
Robert [illegible]y,			Sept. 22d,	
[illegible]ert Ross,			Sept. 22d,	
Robert [illegible]ire,			Sept. 22d,	
Hugh [illegible]el,			Sept. 22d,	Oct'r 11th.
George [illegible]n,			Sept. 22d,	
William Ervin,			Sept. 22d,	
James Shanon,			Sept. 22d,	
Alex'r McConnel,			Sept. 22d,	
William McGlaghlen,			Sept. 22d,	
John Ervin,			Sept. 22d,	
John May,			Sept. 22d,	
Samuel McConnel,			Sept. 22d,	
Leonhard Pickle,			Sept. 22d,	
Robert [illegible]th,			Sept. 22d,	
John McCreary,			Sept. 22d,	
Samuel Caughey,			Sept. 22d,	
Jonathan Simpson,			Sept. 22d,	
Alex'r [illegible]night,			Sept. 22d,	
Samuel Vogan,			Sept. 22d,	
Alex'r Snodgrass,		William Snodgrass,	Sept. 22d,	
John Scott,			Sept. 22d,	
Walter Davis,			Sept. 22d,	
John Whitside,			Sept. 22d,	
Robert Jones,		Hugh Maters,	Sept. 22d,	
Alex'r Houston,			Sept. 22d,	
Thomas Makey,			Sept. 22d,	
William Penny,			Sept. 22d,	
Sam'l Logan,		James Patterson,	Sept. 22d,	

MUSTER ROLL OF THE 7TH CLASS OF THE 6TH BATALION LANC'R COUNTY MILITIA ON A TOUR OF DUTY AT LANCASTER. (c.)

Names of Persons Who Perform a Touer of Duty.	What class.	Names of Persons Who Furnished Substitutes.	Time when duty commenced.	Time when duty ended.
Capt.			1781.	1781.
John Patton,	7th,		Oct'r 20th,	
Leiut.				
Henrey Heakman,	7th,		Oct'r 20th,	
Ensg'n.				
John Ross,	7th,		Oct'r 20th,	
Serj'ts.				
James McConnel,	7th,		Oct'r 20th,	
James Reed, Clerk,	7th,		Oct'r 20th,	
John Craige,	7th,		Oct'r 20th,	
Corp'l.				
John McKnight,	7th,		Oct'r 20th,	
Simon Hastings,	7th,		Oct'r 20th,	
John Glass,	7th,	William Ramsey,	Oct'r 20th,	

Privates.				
Robert Patterson,	7th,		Oct'r 30th,	Oct'r 25th.
James Greer,	7th,		Oct'r 30th,	Oct'r 25th.
Robert Kirkpatrick,	7th,		Oct'r 30th,	Oct'r 25th.
John Jaxon,	7th,		Oct'r 30th,	Oct'r 25th.
Joseph Lowramor,	7th,		Oct'r 30th,	Oct'r 25th.
William Bigam,	7th,		Oct'r 30th,	Oct'r 25th.
George Low,	7th,	Andrew Caldwell,	Oct'r 30th,	
William Graham,	7th,		Oct'r 30th,	
Thomas Hill,	7th,		Oct'r 30th,	
Robert Johnston,	7th,		Oct'r 30th,	
James Walker,	7th,		Oct'r 30th,	
John Nesbit,	7th,		Oct'r 30th,	
Jacob Moats,	7th,		Oct'r 30th,	
John Alexander,	7th,		Oct'r 30th,	
Collin Carl,	7th,		Oct'r 30th,	
David Powell,	7th,		Oct'r 30th,	
Joseph Miles,	7th,		Oct'r 30th,	
Fred'k Doers,	7th,	John Perry,	Oct'r 30th,	
Henrey Lynix,	7th,		Oct'r 30th,	Oct'r 25th.
Robert Fals,	7th,	James Calbrecht,	Oct'r 30th,	
Hugh Paisley,	7th,		Oct'r 30th,	
John Brown,	7th,		Oct'r 30th,	
James Collins,	7th,		Oct'r 30th,	
William Miller,	7th,		Oct'r 30th,	
Adam Johnson,	7th,		Oct'r 30th,	
Philip Shwisher,	7th,		Oct'r 30th,	
Reinard Weaver,	7th,		Oct'r 30th,	
Duncan Kinon,	7th,		Oct'r 30th,	
Samuel Ramsy,	7th,	James Knox,	Oct'r 30th,	
Stephan Long,	7th,		Oct'r 30th,	
John Kelley,	7th,		Oct'r 30th,	
David Bigham,	7th,		Oct'r 30th,	
Alexander Boyd,	7th,		Oct'r 30th,	

MUSTER ROLL OF THE 7TH CLASS OF THE 6TH BATALION LANC'R COUNTY MILITIA—Continued.

Names of Persons Who Perform a Touer of Duty.	What class.	Names of Persons Who Furnished Substitutes.	Time when duty commenced.	Time when duty ended.
			1781.	1781.
Fred'k Minger,	7th,	Thomas Neal, Jr.,	Oct'r 20th,	
Andrew Walker,	7th,		Oct'r 02th,	
Jacob Gander,	7th,		Oct'r 08th,	
John Pigon,	7th,		Oct'r 02th,	
James Purdey,	7th,		Oct'r 20th,	
John Robertson,	7th,		Oct'r 02th,	
Andrew Pigon, Jun'r,	7th,		Oct'r 20th,	
John Wiley,	7th,		Oct'r 20th,	
Fibir Row,	7th,	John Albright,	Oct'r 6th,	
John Cuningham,	7th,	John Thomas,	Oct'r 02th,	
Isaac McCowen,	7th,		Oct'r 20th,	
James Dick,	7th,		Oct'r 20th,	
William McAdams,	7th,		Oct'r 20th,	
David Chambers,	7th,		Oct'r 02th,	
Samuel McCulough,	7th,		Oct'r 08th,	
George Fokler,	7th,		Oct'r 08th,	
John Rogers,	7th,		Oct'r 8th.	Oct'r 25th.
Thomas Makey,	7th,	Alexander Oar,	Oct'r 20th,	

Andrew Frank,	7th,		Oct'r 20th,	
John Melvin,	7th,		Oct'r 20th,	Oct'r 25th.
James McDowel,	7th,		Oct'r 20th,	Oct'r 25th.
John McCluer,	7th,		Oct'r 20th,	
Patrick Sloan,	7th,		Oct'r 20th,	
Hugh McCashlin,	7th,		Oct'r 20th,	
Joseph Nolls,	7th,		Oct'r 20th,	
Adam Creamer,	7th,		Oct'r 20th,	
John Barber,	7th,		Oct'r 20th,	
Joseph Ross, Jun'r,	7th,		Oct'r 20th,	
John Bucanin,	7th,		Oct'r 20th,	
Robert Roy,	5th,		Oct'r 20th,	

A CLASS ROLE OF THE FIRST COMPY. OF THE SIXTH BATTN. LANCASTER COUNTY MILITIA. 1781. (c.)

1st Class.

George Oatman.
James Herron.
James Reed, Jur.
Charless Heron.
Adam Moderwell.
Wilm. Steel.
John Reed, Sergt.
Jams. Anderson.
Jams. Cunningham, clark.

2d Class.

Lieut. Jams. Calhoon.
Wm. Porter.
Chrisly Horch.
Isaac prupacker.
Chrisly Graybill.
Wilm. Strahon.
John Evans.
David Porter.
Thos. Mace.

3d Class.

Jams. McFarlin.
Jas. Carson.
Saml. Reed.
Henry Heable.
Wilm. Milligon.
Robt. Williams.
Daniel McReady.
Aaron Moor.

4th Class.

Ensign, John Turner.
Serjnt., John Rob.
Saml. McElroy.
Geoge Moults.
Jams. Petterson.
Jas. Cummins.
Thos. Law.

5th Class.

Robt. Farguar.
Samuel Hyndman.
Henry Bear.
Robt. Dunlap.
Henry Whistick.
Robt. McCleland.
Hugh Harris.
James Calahon.

6th Class.

John Eackman.
Patrick Brown.
John McCollough.
John Fleck.
Robt. Maxfeild.
Robt. Hillis.
John Feild.
Jacob Bear.

7th Class.

Jams. Porter.	John Jackson.
Wm. Bleecher.	Joseph Lorimore.
Robt. Petterson.	Andw. Caldwell.
Jas. Grier.	Wilm. Bigham.
Robt. Kirckpatrik.	Willm. Graham.
Wilm. Taylor.	

8th Class.

Wm. Calhoon.	John Williamson.
George Bleeks.	John Cummins.
Wm. Cummins.	John McMurry.
Thos. Reed.	John Forseythe.
Willm. Quarl.	Saml. Buyers.
Jerom Dunlop.	John Cochran.

The above is a true state of the company as the stand clased for the year 1781.

Is certifyed pr. me,

JOHN CALDWELL,
Capt.

A RETURN OF CAPT. ROBT. CAMPBLE'S COMPANY OF MILITIA OF LITTLE BRITAIN. (c.)

Officers.

Captain.

Robt. Campble.

Lieutenant.

Isaac Walker.

Ensign.

David McComb.

Privates.

1st.

Jno. Walker.	Jas. Millor.
Jno. Camron.	Thos. Finley.
Jno. Patton.	

2d.

Gilt Buchanan. Allr. Snodgress.
Jno. Brooks. Danl. Copple.
Andw. Walker. Petter Hill.
Jas. Petterson, Junr. Thos. Loid.

3d.

John Atchison. Jno. Brown.
Saml. Reynolds. Joseph Walker.
Joseph Heans. Hugh Weir.
John Powel, Junr. Wm. Pennol.

4th.

Wm. Henery. Allr. Ferguson.
Joshua Heans. Th's Badgor.

5th.

David Allexander. Jas. Beaty.
Allr. Scott. Hugh Johnson.
Jas. Petterson, Senr.

6th.

John Petterson. Thos. Grist.
Francis Henery. Robt. Allison.
Wm. Brown. Thos. Petterson.
Wm. Irwin. George Nelson.
Jno. Hill. Will'm Ewing.
Robt. Allexander. Robt. Moore.

7th.

Thos. Hill. Wm. Leetch.
John Gibson. Jacob Moats.
Robt. Johnson. John Alexander.
Jams Walker. Collon Kerrol.
Saml. Reynolds. David Powel.
Jno. Nesbit. John Buchanan.
Abso'm Camron. Mart'n Ickman.

8th.

Sam'l Mitchel. Wm. Grist.
Henery Reynolds. David Mitchel.
Thos. Campble. Jam's Jamison.
Isaac Reynolds. Jno. Campble.
Sam'l Logon. Jam's Osburn.

ROBT. CAMPBELL, Capt.,

For fall 1781.

A CLASS ROLE OF THE 2D COMPANY OF MILITIA & 6TH BATTALION FOR LANCASTER COUNTY, COMMD. BY CAPT. ROB'T. CAMPBELL FOR THE YEAR 1781. (c.)

Captain.

Robt. Campbell.

Lieut.

Isaac Walker.

Ensn.

David McComb.

Privates.

1st Class.

John Patton.
John Walker.
John Cammeron.
William Dunlap.
William Johnston.

2d Class.

Gilbert Buchanan.
John Brooks.
Andrew Walker.
James Patterson, Junr.
Daniel Copple.
Peter Hill.
Thomas Loyd.
Alexander Snodgrass.

3d Class.

John Atcheson.
Joseph Haines.
John Powell.
John Brown.
Joseph Walker.
Hugh Weir.
William Pennell, Jur.

4th Class.

James Black.
William Henery.
Hugh Glover.
Jacob Reynolds.
Joshua Haines.
David Beard.
Thomas Badger.
Alexander Ferguson.

5th Class.

David Alexander.
Alexander Scott.
James Patterson, Sen.
Daniel Burkard.
James Beatty.
Hugh Johnston.

6th Class.

Abraham Whiteside.
John Patterson.
Francis Henery.
William Brown.
William Ervine.
John Hill.
Robert Alexander.
Thomas Grist.
Robert Allison.
Thomas Patterson.
John Grist.
George Neilson.
William Ewins.
Robert Moore.

7th Class.

Thomas Hill.
John Gibson.
Robert Johnston.
James Walker.
Samuel Reynolds.
John Nesbitt.
Absolom Cameren.
William Leech.
Martin Eackman.
Jacob Moates.
John Alexander.
Colla Carroll.
David Powell.

8th Class.

Samuel Mitchell.
Henry Reynolds.
Thomas Campbell.
Isaac Reynolds.
Saml. Logan.
William Grist.
David Mitchell.
James Jameson.
John Campbell.
James Osbourn.

JOSEPH ALLISON, Clk.

A MUSTER ROOLE OF THE SIXTH COMPANY OF THE SIXTH BATALION OF LANCASTER COUNTY MILITIA COMMANDED BY COL. JAS. TAYLOR FOR 1781. (c.)

Capt.
Jos. Walker.

Lieut.
Jas. Noble.

Ensn.
Jno. Ross.

Serg'ts.

John McGraith. John Craig.

Fifer.

John Colvin.

1 Class.

Nathan Thompson. Jos. Curle.
Ezekel Irwin. Stephen Hall.
George Cooper. Jas. Heny.
John Moore.

2d Class.

Thos. Fullton. Jacob Kerns.
Thos. Wasson. Rob't Guy.
Gainer Peirce. Henry Picple.
John Wasson. Wim. Heerd.

3d Class.

Jeremy Moore. George Mooney.
George Leech. Jonathan Cummins.
Andrew Moore. John McCaly.
Robt. Moore. Job. Cooper.

4th Class.

Robt. Williams. Daniel Miller.
John Coventry. George Clark.
Jas. Crage. John Gribins.

5th Class.

Michal Gander. Nathan Cope.
Robt. Wasson. Robt. Evins.
Jas. Cooper. John Throsbay.
John Heerd, Jun'r. Jacob Heil.
John Lee.

6th Class.

Leonard Pickle. Jas. Wasson.
Thos. Hathorn. Robt. Gibson.
John Donald. Jonathan Simpson.
Petter Pickle. Samuel Vogan.
Heironomis Miller. Jas. Tweed.

7th Class.

Benjamin Irwin.
John Cumins.
Stephen Heerd, Jun'r.
Andrew Walker.
Jacob Gander.
John Griffith.
Jas. Kean.

8th Class.

Wim. Tweed.
Isaac Irwin.
John Cooper.
Wim. Guy.
Jas. Colvin.

JO'S WALKER, Capt., 1781.

RETURN OF THE EIGHT COMPANY OF MILITIA IN THE SIXTH BATTALION OF LANCASTER COUNTY COMMANDED BY CAPT. ROBERT RAMSEY FOR THE YEAR 1781. (c.)

Commis'd Officers.

Capt.

Robt. Ramsey.

Lieut.

Henry Hickman.

Ensign.

John Caughey.

John Paxton, Senr.
Will'm Ramsey.
Will'm Brown.
Andrew Caughey.
Will'm McClure.
Archebald Mc ready.
Robert Karr.
David Hare.
Joseph Griffith.
John Caldwell.
James Shearrer.
Will'm Richardson.
John Keesacker.
Jno. Ramsey, mino.
Archebald McDowel.
John Shannon.
Simmon Ghost.
Daniel McReady.
John Ramsey.
James Geeven.
Willm. Cuncle.
Henry Sides.
Nenry Noll.
George Cuncle.
Martain Bare.
Samuel Downing.

John Thompson.
George Boughman.
John Ritchard.
George Rockey.
Conrad Rice.
John Hannah.
Andrew fronk, senr.
Francis McKnaught.
John Malbeen.
John Bare.
Jacob Whisler.
Samuel McDowel.
Henry Baughman.
Jacob Boylston.
Thomas Downing.
Moses Latta.
Mark McCord.
Henry Rockey.
John Ligget.
Henry hook.
Martain Miller.
Walter Davis.
Will'm Paxton.
Jno. Ritchardsons.
Leonard Ghost.
Nathaniel Coulter.
Andrew Work.
Henry Bartholomew.
Jacob Young.
Christian Black.
William Hood.
Joseph Noll.
Will'm Maffet.
Edward Wahob.
Peeter Oatman.
John Clark.
Jacob Varner.
Martain Bird.
John Glass.
Martain Coherspire.
John Paxton, Junr.
John Dowlan.
John Myer.
Stophel Freivly.
James Leech.
Willm. Coulter.
Maher Millinger.
John Fronk.
Adam Creamer.
Simonon Ritz.
Henry Russell.
James McClure.
Heronamas Eackman.
James Shannon.
Joseph King.
Robt. Ramsey, mins.
Robert Willson.
James Climson.
Willm. Loughead.
James Gilmore.
Allexander McConel.
Joseph Otman.
William Keely.
Samuel Kitts.
James McConel.
Adrew fronk, Junr.
Joseph Ross.
Joseph Welch.
John Modrell.
Robt. Patterson.
Samuel Willson.
Jacob Cuncle.
Robert hannah.
Mathew Jones.
William forsyth.
Petter Garner.
John Miller.
Jno. Erwine, Jun'r.
John Morrison.
Hugh McCashlin.
Patrick Sloane.
Peeter Sides.
Robert Hall.
John McClure.
John Ramsey.
Samuel Sharon.
John Tease.
John Erwine.

David Layhead.
John Karr.
John hostater.
Francies Lerland.
James Thompson.
James Duncan.
Samuel McCartney.
John Barber.

A MUSTER ROOLE OF THE SIXTH COMPANY OF THE SIXTH BATALION OF LANCASTER COUNTY MILITIA COMANDED BY COLL. JAS. TAYLOR. FOR THE 1782 (c.)

Captain.

Jos. Walker.

Leu.

Jas. Noble.

Ens.

John Ross.

1st Class.

Nathan Thompson.
Ezekle Irwin.
Sthephen Hall.
John Moore.
Jas. Heny.
Wim. Pease.

2nd Class.

Thos. Fulton.
Thos. Wasson.
Gainer Pierce, S'nr.
John Wasson.
Jacob Kerns.
Rob't. Guy.
Henry Pickle.
Wim. Heerd, S'nr.
John Climins.
Wim. Foster.
Wim. Rea.

3rd Class.

Jeremiah Moore.
George Leech.
Andrew Moore.
Robert Moore.
George Money.
Jonathan Cumins.
John M'Cally.
Job. Cooper.
John Kesacker.
Archibald Griffith.
Jos. Welch.
John Donnel.
Jas. Heerd.
Thos. Baldon.

4th Class.

Barnard Martin. John Gribins.
John Murry. Wm. Loughead.
Rob't Williams. Jeremiah Staar.
John Coventry. Jos. Tweed.
Jas. Craig.

5th Class.

Rob't Wasson. John Throsbay.
Jas. Cooper. Jacob Hill.
John Lee. David Loughead.
Nathan Cope. Wim. Heerd, Junr.
Rob't Evens.

6th Class.

Leonard Pickle. Jonathan Simpson.
Thos. Hathorn. Samuel Vogan.
Petter Pickle. Jas. Tweed.
Jas. Wasson. Wim. Boon.
Rob't Gibson. John Foster.

7th Class.

Ben. Irwin. John Griffith.
John Cumins. Jas. Cain.
Stephen Heerd. Gainer Peirce, junr.
Andrew Walkr. John Craig.

8th Class.

Wim. Tweed. Jas. Colvin.
Isaac Irwin. John Livingston.
John Cooper. Jas. Loughead.
Wim. Guy. Hugh McCahan.

Given under my hand 27th May 1782.

JOS. WALKER, Capt.

LIST OF CPT. JOHN PATTONS COMPY. BEING THE SEVENTH COMPANY OF THE SIXTH BATT. OF LANCASTER COUNTY MILITIA COMMANDED BY COL. JAS. TAYLOR MAY 1782. (c.)

George Kenricks. Martin phenan.
Loudwick Stouts. Michael Wood.
Henry Bear. John Cooper.
John Grafft. Joseph Conghnour.

John Everson.
Rudy Keagy.
Valantine Hart.
John Grafft.
Jacob Grafft.
John Segalt.
Jacob Hart.
Peter walter.
John Stopher.
Alex'dr Garrat.
Andrew Serarah.
Jacob Hoover.
Patt. Kelly.
Sebastian Neize.
Isaac Reid.
John Hess.
Ebrey Everly.
John Bonn.
George Counter.
John Hook.
John Mouser.
Abram. Kegy, Jr.
Henry Hoover.
Job Vancard.
Cornelias Khoon.
Henry Everly.
Michael Everly.
John Hoover.
John Everhart.
John Miller.
Jacob Grafft.
Cristian Lynes.
McDonald Mannage.
Mathew Brown.
Jacob Winter.
Jacob Broobaker.
John Gold.

JOHN PATTON, Capt.

RETURN COMPARED WITH CAPT. HENRY GREGLOWS MUSTER ROLL FIRST PART OF THE 4TH CLASS 6TH BATALLION ORDERED IN SEVICE THE 27TH DAY OF JULY 1782. (c.)

Capt.

Henry Greglow.

Sergt.

Michael Finstermacker.

Corpl.

Conrad Beebelhymer.

Drum.

Jacob Horner, Junr.

Fifer.

Andw. Knerr.

1. Michael Wertman.
2. Paul Hertzog.
3. Charles Stroub.
4. Adam Miller.
5. Jno. Baltauff.
6. Jacob Sander.
7. Wm. Moyer.
8. Jacob Hanse.
9. Jno. Delong.
10. Michael Hemebach.
11. Jno. Edmunds.
12. Jno. Heath.
13. Nathanl. Edmunds.
14. Joseph Everitt.
15. Christian Wise.
16. Abraham Greenwalt.
17. Christopher Dresher.
18. Michael Rishell.
19. Jacob Musgenug.
20. Christian Marburger.
21. Bernhard Trees.
22. Henry George.
23. Mardin Kopp.
24. Peter Knoedler.
25. John Wuchter.

RETURN COMPARED WITH LIEUT. GEORGE GREENWALT'S MUSTER ROLL SECOND PART OF THE 4TH CLASS, 6TH BATALLION, ORDERED OUT IN SERVICE SEPT. 21ST, 1782. (c.)

Lieut.

Geo. Greenwalt.

Ensign.

Wm. Yett.

Corp.

• Daniel Rise.

Casper Hunsicker.
Dewalt Peter.
Geo. Rex.
Gerret Rittenhouse.
Abraham Rex.
Christian Swobenland.
Henry Snyder, Junr.
Jno. Kistner.
Jacob Rex.
Mathias Delong.
Jacob Billman.
Jacob Wanemaker.
Jacob Riniesmith.
Michael Weaber.
Andw. Gittner.
Bernhard Gittner.
Jacob Peter.
Christian Smith, Junr.
Jacob Hartman.
Jacob Barrall.
Mathias Snyder.

RETURN OF THE FIRST COMPANY SIXD. BATTALION LANCASTER COUNTY MILITIA 1783. (c.)

Capt.

John Shonhower.

Liet.

Casper Shimp.

Ens.

George Rock.

Ser.

Conrad Radman.
Casper Jordan.

1st Class.

Herman Ernst.
Christian Balmer.
Adam Bietz.
Abraham Musselman.
Peter Christ.
Jacob Musselman.
Casper Giddinger.
Daniel Habecker.
Henry Hackman.
John Erb (son of Christain).
Samuel Steinecke.
Henry Duliban.

2d Class.

Jacob Eby.
Daniel Christ.
Peter Becker.
John Fautz.
Peter Kreider.
Greenbere Betlcooet.
Christian Erb (son of ditto).
Henry Franck.
Peter McMullen.
Peter Sheffer.
Jacob Unger.
Christian Grub.
Joseph Stotzens.
Peter Furman.

3d Class.

Mickel Balmer.
Christian Blickensderfer.
Christian Musselman.
John Mickel.
Abraham Huber.
John Seyler.
Jacob Brown.
Adam Ernst.
John Shneider.
Lenord Westheffer.
Henry Netzly.

4th Class.

Jacob Cassler.
Christian Hess.
Christian Erb.
Mickel Kreider.
Christian Stucke.
Peter Bessinger.
Fridrich Lehman.
John Brubacher.
Etward More.
Christian Blauch.
George Reyer.
Henry Fry.
Conrad Westheffer.
George Grafft.
Peter Lenhard.

5th Class.

Jacob Shmuck.
Jacob Erb (Brother son).
Henry Wanner.
Christian Habecker.
John Erb.
George Rode.
Lenhard Widder.
Andrew Betz.
John Oblinger.
Fridrich Stober.
Jacob Rode.
Peter Shneider.
Nicholaus Klein.
Daniel Klein.
Christian Lesher.
George Meyer.

6th Class.

Abraham Dirdorff.
Andrew Kreider.
Jacob Habecker.
Simon Dantz.
Christian Becker.
John Bietz.
Lenhard Miller.
Jacob Dirdorff.
Daniel Shaller.
Nicolaus Zeller.
Peter Bessinger, Juner.
George Fertig.
Jacob Shneider, Juner.
Christian Gruber.

7th Class.

Peter Ricker.
George Fierling.
Andrew Wissler.
Michel Meyer.
Christian Eby.
Christian Huber.
Peter Eby.
John Sensenig.
Joseph Gembold.
George Geldner.
Anton Ronner.
George Stoler.
Adam Bender.
Jacob Rudy.
Lorentz Herchelrode.
John Buch.
John Shumacher.

8th Class.

Henry Foltz.
Martin Shenck.
Jacob Hackman.
George Geyer.
Jacob Shneider.
Peter Kreider.
Wilhelm Cassler.
Christian Eby (uper).
Daniel Erb (son of Chr.).
John Dirdorff.
Joseph Shenck.
Abraham Hiestand.
George Widder.
Peter Holle.
Jacob Metzel.
Peter Bruner.
John Enck.
Daniel Erb.
John Frymeyer.

I do swear on the Holy Evengilest of Almighty God: That the above return is a just & true state of the company agreeable to law and without any fraud to the state to the best of my Knowledge.

JOHN SPONHOWER, Capt.

Sworn before me this
27th day of November 1783.

JOHN HUBER, Lt. Col.

RETURN OF MY SECOND COMPANY AND 3D BATTL. NOW BELONGING TO THE 8TH COMPY. AND 6TH BATT. LANCASTER COUNTY MILITIA. (c.)

Capt.

Andrew Ream.

Lt.

Henry Ream.

Ensign.

Christian Baltzley.

Serj.

Casper Shrite.
Abraham Killian.
Martin Mohler.

Privates.

1st Class.

Nicholas Wolff.	Jacob Mohler.
Daniel Bethálome.	Peter Graff.
Nicholas Snydor.	Adam Kingmaker.
Daniel Bowman.	Andrew Histler.
Jacob Lesher.	

2d Class.

Nicholas Duck.	Jacob Bucher.
Michael Sherck.	Abraham Landes, miller.
Abraham Bixler.	Henry Leeder.
David Meltzer.	Fredrick Ream.
Leonhard Keller.	David Graff.
Samuel Bowman.	Andrew Ream, Jr.

3d Class.

Henry Mohler.	Tobias Ream.
Christian Waggoner.	Jacob Ream.
Abraham Kline.	Jacob Landis.
Christian Knup.	Frantz Brunbach.
David Meredith.	Valentine Showalder.
John Mohler.	Jacob Sunday.
Wm. Mellinger.	John Mellinger.
Jacob Sensmeier.	Ditrick Walck.
Joseph Groff.	

4th Class.

Adam Nees, Esqr.	Frederick Leeder.
Michael Reiter.	Joas Miller.
Ulry Sherck.	Jacob Hagy.
Jacob Showalder.	Philip Krig.
George Spade.	Samuel Keller.

5th Class.

George Kuntz.	John Ream, Jur.
Abraham Landes.	John Heaffer.
Adam Musser.	Peter Eberley.
Joseph Leisy.	Martin Miller.
Peter Brubaker.	George Sprigle.
Jacob Keller, Se'r.	John Ream, Shoemaker.
Samuel Graff.	Fredrick Shlott.
John Landes, Jur.	

6th Class.

Berned Geiger.
Joseph Mishler.
Henry Hershberger.
Jacob Killian.
Jacob Rohland.
Jacob Witmer.
David Ream.
Abraham Hershberger.
Abraham Kneisley.
John Heck.
Casper Keiper.

7th Class.

Godlieb Mock.
John Martin.
Michael Bare.
John Bucher.
Isaac Hershberger.
Jacob Conrod.
Joseph Sprigle.
Daniel Groff.
Wm. Shoemaker.
Nicholas Wilt.
Christian Frantz.
Henry Good.
Henry Keiper.
Daniel Firestone.
Joseph Flickinger.

8th Class.

Peter Reyer.
David Sherck.
Abraham Ream, miller.
John Musleman.
Abraham Bare.
Abraham Rohland.
Samuel Meder.
Berned Gets.
Jacob Frantz.
Abraham Ream.
John Mohler, Jur.
Adam Weitzel.
Marcus Montelius.
David Hershberger.
Adam Hoh.
Ludwick Leaman.

I, the subscriber do hereby certify that the above & within is a just and true return to the first field day A. D. 1783 of the persons reciting and belonging to my late compy. without any fraud to the state of Pennsylvania as witness my hand this 3d day of July A. D. 1783.

ANDREW REAM,
Capt.

Affirmed & subscribed before me this 3d day of July 1783.
ADAM NEES, ESQR.

RETURN OF MY 4TH COMPANY OF THE 6TH BATTALION OF LANCASTER COUNTY MILITIA 1783. (c.)

Capt.

Joseph Gear.

Lieut.

George Bruner.

Ens.

William Snyder.

Almon'r.

Fredrick Kerber.

Sergants.

Jermias Miller.
John Bruner.
Casper Bossert.

Corpr.

Baltzer Hoffman.
David Heckernel.
Philip Hoffman.

Fife & Drum.

Peter Snyder.
Conrad Snyder.

First Class.

George Frantz.
Daniel Solleberger.
Jonathan Sheoneman.
Jacob Sherb.
Jacob Blanck.

The 2d Class.

Jost. Miller.
Fredrick Kissinger.
Christian Flickinger.
John Ober.
Bastian Gagly.

The 3d Class.

Samuel Eby.
Jacob Eberly.
David Gagly.
John Stover.
Mathias Bitner.
Philip Shiveigart.
Henry Smith.
Henry Henshy.

The 4th Class.

Martin Glever. Stophel Kline.
Jacob Bare. George Mose.
John Keller. Henry Eberly.
John Flickinger. John Kumer.
Christian Hernly. Mathias Featherhoff.

The 5th Class.

Henry Binckley. Christian West.
Daniel Riech. John Acho.
John Noftzgar. Michael Walter.
Christian Harnish. John Gearhart.
Adam Sherb. Gerrad Walter.
John Flickinger. Christian Ely.
William Walter. Peter Bricker.
John Conrad. Frantz Pumbach.
Abraham Hossler.

The 6th Class.

Joseph Jacob. David Bricker.
Peter Snyder. Peter Geistwut.
Stophel Sherb. John Kerber.
Andrew Gear. John'Gagly.
Jacob Hildebidle. Fredrick Walck.
George Long.

The 7th Class.

John Bricker. George Kissinger.
Abraham Soffel. Peter Shoemaker.
Henry Borgholter. John Hoshar.
Christian Kuntzy. Christian Conrad.
Joseph Conrad. John Zuger.
Fredrick Reinholt. Michael Keller.
Henry Reinholt. George Bargholter.

The 8th Class.

David Gagly. Lorrantz Ludwick.
Philip Shenckle. John Jacob.
Christian Shenckle. Jacob Disler.
Jacob Dwinbach. Adam Frantz.
Paul Fuhrman. Henry Walter.

I do swear on the Holy Evengilest of Almighty God: That the above and within is a Just & True return of the Persons reciding and belonging to my company agreeable to Law and Without any Friend to the State to the Best of my Knowledge.

JOSEPH GEHR.

Sworn before me this
25th Day of November, A. D. 1783.

JOHN HUBER, Lt. Col.

A TRUE AND EXACT RETURN OF THE SIXTH COMPANY AND SIXTH BATTALION LANCASTER COUNTY MILITIA FOR THE SPRING 1783 COMMANDED BY JOHN HUBER, LIEUT. COL. (c.)

Lieut.

Andrew Ehrman.

Ens.

Nicklaus Unger.

Drumar.

John Huber.

Pfeiver.

Jacob Unger.

Sert.

John Ehrman.
Peter Huber.
John Kiesel.

1st Class.

John Ricksecker.
Barthel Hock.
John Geib.
George Haffert.
Joseph Gingrig.
Joseph Buger.
Abraham Reist.
Jacob Hostather.
David Frey.
John ohlmaier.
Jacob Borckholser.
Henry Gibbel.

2d Class.

John Erb.
Christel Hershy.
Daniel Gingrich.
Felty Greiner.
Silvester Gruber.
Bernd Coutzman.
Martin Greiner.
Christel Eshelman.
John Dusinger.

3d Class.

Michel Guthetel.
Joseph Bamberg.
John Bucher.
Christian Grebiel.
John Staufer.
George Maier.
Jacob Gilbert.
Wendel Gilbert.
Henry Maier.
Jacob Leiderd.
Mathaw Marat.
Christian Frey.
Casper Fischter.
Christof Suis.

4th Class.

John Langonecker.
Martin Baeler.
Mathaw Ramra.
Christian Reist.
Peter Armstrong.
John Hanss.
Michel Baem.
Fridrich Kiesel.
John Kiesel.
Jacob Eberle.
Felty Witmaier.
John Meier.
Christel Hersby.

5th Class.

John Shneider.
Henry Leib.
Jacob Armishong.
Gotfrid Gutjahr.
Nicklaus Stroh.
Fridrick Armishong.
Henry Miller.
George Ruhl.
John Noecker.
Mathew Armishong.
Andrew Lansz.
Mathew Hofart.
Joseph Erb.
John Hofferd.
David Zug.

6th Class.

John Spickler.
John Eby.
John Sumy.
John Amishong.
John Gibbel.
Martin Spickler.
Peter Jung.
Jacob Dusinger.
Adam Hollinger.
Peter Reist.
John Mercke.
Daniel Hefelbauer.
Jacob Oberholtzer.

7th Class.

Christel Zug.
Jacob Gingrich.
Jonathan Gingrich.
Michel Wilmer.
George Kisel.
Ruthy Baem.
Jacob Gibbel.
John Eby.
Salomon Langenecker.
Daniel Basler.
Marthin Martzal.

8th Class.

Jacob Bamberger.
Christian Staufer.
John Bamberger.
Mickel Gross.
Jacob Wolf.
Nicklaus Spickler.
Lutwig Gutjahr.
Stofel Gibbel.
George Mengel.
John Lauman.
Christel Spickler.
Jacob Maier.

I do swear that the above return is just and to the best of my knowledge.

Witness my hand.

PETER HUBER, Ser.

MUSTER ROLL OF ALL THE MALE WHITE INHABITANTS OF MARTICKS TOWNSHIP LANCASTER COUNTY BEING THE SEVENTH COMPANY OF THE SIXTH BATTALION COMMANDED BY COL. JAS. TAYLOR. (c.)

Captain.

. John Patton

Lieut.

Petter Simpson.

Ensign.

David McDermant.

Privates.

1st Class.

Archibald Pegan.
Alexdr. Boyde.
Jas. Savage.
Jacob Markley.
Henry Byers.
James Black.
David Gibson.
Philip May.
John Smith, Jr.
William Moor.
Thomas Johnson.
Peter Fite.
Wm. Seabrooks.
Sebastian Swager.

James McDonald.	George Kenricks.
Andrew McGinnis.	Jacob Bear.
Jacob Hoover.	Wm. Boyles.
Henry Stopher.	Jas. Morrow.
Wm. Yorty.	Jas. Snodgrass.

2d Class.

Hugh Caldwell.	Joseph Myers.
Henry Cauggey.	Stophel Winter.
John Smith.	Daniel Crage.
John Hart.	Alexander Snodgrass.
John Kuncle.	Wm. McAdams.
James Ramsey.	Wm. Steel.
	Martin Pleman.
Loudawick Stouts.	Jacob Beem.
Wm. Turner.	Jacob Brookbaker.
Henry Bear.	George Birdegg.
John Graft.	Danile Collodon.
Henry Alexander.	Alexdr. Lighton.

3d Class.

James Snodgrass.	John Graft.
Gregory Farmer.	Jacob Graft, swamp.
John Snodgrass.	James Harra.
James Wharry.	John Segat.
Valentine Hart.	George Leaman.
John Caldwell.	Sebastian Frank.
Jacob Hoover.	Saml. McCullough.
Martin Byers.	John Maphet.
Martin Shock.	John Boyde, Taylor.
John Heble.	George McGuire.
William Carr	Ulrich Hoover.
Thomas Dick	

4th Class.

Robert McCollough.	James Duncan.
Joseph Aird.	Jacob Hoover.
John McCreary.	Michael Shank.
Joseph Leaugh.	Patt Kelly.
Peter Lutes.	Sebastian Nize.
John Cunningham.	Samuel Lines.
Samuel Ellot.	John Boyde, Sen'r.

John Pegan, Jr.
Thomas White.
Alexr. Brannon.
George Fockler.
Thos. Reed.
John Sandalin.
Peter Gardner.
George Seriver.
George Wallace.
James Harris.

5th Class.

Jas. Johnson.
Jas. Pagan, Jur.
Thos. Robinson.
Sam'l Kirkpatrick, Jr.
Jas. Pegan, miller.
Peter Poland.
John Clark, Jr.
Joseph McCollough.
Samuel Snodgrass.
John Hess.
Samuel Winter.
Micheal Louder.
Jacob Hoover.
James Kellachan.
Ebrey Everly.
Samuel Keech.
John Mitchal.
John Douglass.
Joseph Gardner.
Samuel Ramsey.
John Petterson.
Patrick Campble.
Jas. Dick.

6th Class.

Thomas Mackey.
William White.
Robert Long.
David McCollough.
Adam Moor.
Abram Cagguy, Jr.
Samuel Wilson.
Joseph Neal.
John Reed.
Peter Miller.
James Steel.
Wm. Snodgrass.
Wm. Brown.
Henry Hoffman.
Martin Byers.
Henry Cable.
Edward Feel.
John Barr.
Thomas Boyde.
John Camp.
Henry Hoover.
Robert Snodgrass, Jr.
Ulrich Hoover.

7th Class.

Rob't. Steen.
John Reban, Sr.
James Purdey.
Thomas Culley.
John Robinson.
Andrew Pegan.
James Long.
James Moor.
Martias Horra.
Cristian Murphey.
Jacob Stigal.
John Callaehan.
Jacob Winger.
George Teeter.
Alexander Orr.
Thomas Stonrod.

Micheal Everly.
John Albright.
John Patton, miller.
Peter Stopher.
Daniel Steward.
John Smtih.
John Thomas.

8th Class.

James Petterson.
John Crage.
Valentine Gartner.
Fredrick Heble.
Jacob Rees.
Isaac Hare.
Martin Myers
Henry Bleecher.
Henry Kendrick
John Shank.
Jacob Graft.
Cristian Lines.
John McCallister.
Samuel Simpson, Jr.
Thomas Wharry.
Samuel Kirkpatrick, Sr.
Alexander McCollough.
Peter Good.
Cristian Good.
Benjamin Winter.
Thomas Clark.
Robert Pendrey.
James Reed.

GENERAL RETURN OF THE OFFICERS OF THE LANCASTER COUNTY MILITIA 15TH APRIL 1783. (c.)

SIXTH BATTALION.

Field Officers.

Lieut. Col.

James Taylor.

Maj'r.

Robert King.

Captains.

1. John Caldwell.
2. Robert Campbell.
3. John Duncan.
4. Robert Miller.
5. James Clerk.
6. Joseph Walker.
7. John Patton.
8. Thos. Gourley.

Lieutenants.

1. James Calhoon.
2. Isaac Walker.
3. John Neisser.
4. Robert Anderson.
5. Hugh McIntire.
6. James Noble.
7. Peter Simpson.
8. Henry Eackman.

Ensigns.

1. John Turner.
2. Daniel McComb.
3. Hugh McConkey.
4. Mathew Park.
5. James Gribbon.
6. John Ross.
7. David McDormont.
8. John Gouchey.

A RETURN OF THE MILITIA OF CAPT. ROBERT CAMPBELL COMPY. IN LITTLE BRITTAIN. (c.)

Officers.

Robert Campbell.
Isaac Walker.
David McComb.

1st Class.

John Walker.
John Camron.
Wm. Dunlap.
Wm. Johnston.
Thomas Loyde.

2d Class.

Gilb. Buckhanon.
John Brooks.
Andrew Walker.
James Petterson, Junr.
Samuel Littel.
Alex'dr Snodgrees.
Denel Copple.
Peter hill.

3d Class.

John Atchison.
Samuel Randoles.
Joseph Heans.
Baxter Long.

4th Class.

Jas. Black.
Wm. Henery.
Hugh Glover.
Jacob Reighknoolos.
Jos. Heans.
Wm. McCollough.
Alexander forguson.

5th Class.

David Alexander.
Alx'r Scoot.
Samuel gillgreest.
Jas. Petterson, sener.
Denal Burkard.

6th Class.

Abram Witside.
John Petterson.
frances Hennery.
Wm. Brown.
John Hill.
Wm. Irwin.
Robert Alexander.
Thomas Geist.
Robert Alison.
Thomas Petterson.
Joseph Alison.
John Geist.
Gorge Neilson.
Wm. Ewing.

7th Class.

Thomas Babston.
Thos. hill.
John Gibson.
James Walker.
Samuels Randoles.
John Nisbut.
Abesolam Cambron.
Wm. Leetch.
John Powel.
Jacob Moots.
John tannehill.
John Alexander.
John McClain.
Wm. Brice.
Benjamin Zoo.

8th Class.

Samuel Mickel.
Henery Ranoldes.
Patrick Mutton.
Jos. Carswell.
Wm. Grist.
David Mitchel.
Wm. McAlhatton.

The above is just and true return of my company.

ROBT. CAMPBELL,
Capt.

A RETURN OF THE FIRST CLASS OF THE SIXTH BATT'N OF LANCASTER COUNTY MILITIA MET AT COX'S TOWN, MADE BY JOHN CALDWELL, CAPT. (c.)

Capt.
John Caldwell.

Lieut.
Isaac Walker.

Ensign.

Mathew Parks.

Sergt.

John Reed.
Willm. Johnson.

Privates.

Archy Pagon.
Wilm. McClure.
Wilm. Moor.
Jno. Sample.
Alexr. Boyd.
Nathaniel Kely.
James Morrow.
Wm. Strong.
James Walker.
Jno. Walker.
Simon Ritz.
George Glass, for Adam Moderwell.

SEVENTH BATTALION

LANCASTER COUNTY MILITIA.

A MUSTER ROLL OF A PART OF CAPTAIN FRIEDRICH. ZIGLER'S COMPANY OF MILITIA OF COLONEL MATHIAS SLOUGH'S BATTALION (THIS PART MISSING) DESTINED FOR THE CAMP IN THE. (d.)

Captain.

Fredrich Sigler.

1st Lieutenant.

John Gessler.

2nd Lieutenant.

Adam Martin.

Ensign.

Conrad Hilleg (illegible).

Serjeant.

Abraham Fisher.

Drummer.

John Immel.

Privates.

No.
1. John Monteback.
2. George Brenner.
3. Jacob Miller.
4. Henry Peter.
5. Philip Peel.
6. Casper Shertzer.
7. Paul Housman.
8. Adam Ulrich.
9. John Shepley.
10. Nicholas Mousser.
11. Melchior Dunc (rest missing).
12. John Ditty.
13. George Erisman.
14. Thomas Crowter.

15. Philip Litty.
16. Mathias Bensinger.
17. John Krats.
18. Gabriel Beam.
19. Francis Hope.

19 Privates 50 shillings.
1 Serjeant.
1 Drummer. } this part missing.
—
21 Men adv.

Mustered and passed before the Committee of Obeservation and Inspection in Lancaster the 21st of August & 5th of September 1776. And the above fifty two pounds & ten shillings paid to Captain Fredrich Sigler to enable him to pay the above advance to his Men.

Test. WILL'M ATLEE, Chairman of Commitee,
FREDRICH ZIGLER, Coupt.

A MUSTER ROLL OF CAPT. JACOB KRUG'S COMPANY OF LIGHT INFANTRY OF COLONEL MATHIAS SLOUGH'S BATTALION OF LANCASTER COUNTY, DESTINED FOR THE CAMP IN THE JERSEYS, SEPTEMBER 9TH 1776. (d.)

Captain.

Jacob Krug.

Lieutenants.

2d. Philip Baker.
3d. Daniel Frank.
4th. Mathias Snider.

Serjeants.

Jacob Young.
Leonard Eichholtz.
Jacob Shaffer.

Corporals.

John Reishling.
John Sheaffer.
John Fisher.
John Lechler.

Drummer.
Sebastian Shirk.

Fifer.
Godleip Eberman.

Privates.

1. Peter Bugh.
2. John Shaffner.
3. Peter Seffrentz.
4. Adam Hirshberger.
5. Francis Lambert.
6. George Reitsell.
7. George Marquart.
8. Joseph Shiff.
9. Jacob Heffer.
10. John Kock.
11. Fredrick Metzer.
12. Michael Kremer.
13. Jacob Amend.
14. Christian Liebpe.
15. Michael Trebert.
16. Joseph Walter.
17. Melchior Hill.
18. Anthony Welty.
19. John Alsbach.
20. Adam Hirshman.
21. John Henneberger.
22. Fredrick Doghterman.
23. Christopher Demuth.
24. Andrew Adam Lutz.
25. Francis Heger.
26. Henry Fortiner.
27. Joseph Banks.
28. Dominie Clip.
29. Conrad Burg.
30. Fredrick Kercher.
31. Conrad Disher.
32. Andrew Backenstoss.
33. John Hiester.
34. Christian Liebpe, junr.
35. George Swope.
36. William Waggoner.
37. Christian Isch.

4 Officers, 3 Serjeants, 4 Corporals, 1 Drummer, One Fifer and 37 effective Men—no advance paid.

Mustered and passed before the Committee of Observation and Inspection in Lancaster the 9th of September 1776, except Anthony Welty who with their leave is gone forward to provide necessarys for the Company & will join the Company.

Test. WILLE. ATLEE, Chairman of Committee &
JACOB KRUG, Capt.

A MUSTER ROLL OF CAPTAIN JASPER YEATE'S COMPANY OF MILITIA OF COLONEL MATHIAS SLOUGH BATTALION OF ASSOCIATORS—LANCASTER COUNTY, DESTINED FOR THE CAMP IN THE JERSEYS, SEPTR. 9TH, 1776. (d.)

Lieutenants.

1st, Christian Petree.
2d. Michael Musser.

Ensign.

Peter Walter.

Serjeants.

Fredrick Mann.
George Streabley.
Henry Geiger.

Corporals.

George Lightner.
John Ream.
Adam Hart.
Simon Snider.

Drummer.

Daniel St. Clair.

Fifer.

Michael Rinehart.

Privates.

1. John Daub.
2. Fredrick Swentzell.
3. Mathias Dehuff.

4. Jacob Miller.
5. George Hoff.
6. Conrad Swartz.
7. Philip Waggoner.
8. Peter Reitsell.
9. Charles Klugh.
10. Valentine Brenenen.
11. Henry Gross.
12. Lorence Burst.
13. Valentine Hoffman.
14. Christopher Reitsell.
15. Thomas Doyle.
16. John Deredinger.
17. Nicholas Leib.
18. Daniel Riblet.
19. George Young.
20. Jacob Etenier.
21. Jacob Frey.
22. Morgan Shee.
23. Henry Frankfurter.
24. George Messersmith.
25. Daniel O'Mullen.
26. Michael Oxer.
27. Henry Winon.
28. Fredrick Sheffer.
29. Nicholas Long.
30. Gerhard Bubach.
31. John Anderson.
32. Michael Hess.
33. Peter Lantz.
34. Jacob Backenstose.
35. Casper Singer.
36. John Franciseus.

3 Officers.
3 Serjeants.
4 Corporals.
1 Drummer.
1 Fifer.

36 effective Men.—no advance paid.

Mustered and passed before the Committee of Obeservation and Inspection at Lancaster the 9th of September 1776.

Test. WILLE. ATLEE, Chairman of Committee &
CHRISTIAN PETRIE, Lieut.

A MUSTER ROLL OF CAPTAIN BARNARD ZIMMERMAN'S COMPANY OF MILITIA OF COLONEL MATHIAS SLOUGH'S BATTALION OF ASSOCIATORS—LANCASTER COUNTY—DESTINED FOR THE CAMP IN THE JERSEYS SEPTR. 10TH 1776. (d.)

Captain.

Barnard Zimmerman.

Lieutenants.

1st. Stephen Hornberger.
2d. Samuel Macker.

Ensign.

John Fisher

Serjeants.

Jacob Murray.
John Pletz.
Enoch Hilliard.

Corporals.

Philip Foox.
Jacob Miller.
Michael Frey.

Drummer.

Philip Zimmerman.

Privates.

1. Daniel Wendle.
2. Henry Alspach.
3. Michael Gotschall.
4. Peter Springer.
5. Jacob Shirick.
6. Daniel Wolf.
7. Henry Ditter.
8. Conrad Seigrist.
9. Jacob Shaffner.
10. Christian Lehr.

11. George Eby.
12. Michael Groob.
13. James Jackson.
14. David Eyden.
15. William Myer.
16. Peter Angstet.
17. Casper Shitz.
18. John Reitlinger.
19. Jacob Kirchman.
20. William Marshall.
21. Adam Stoneking.
22. Melchior Walter.
23. Jacob Walter.
24. John Bonnet.
25. George Stermer.
26. William Pletz.
27. Conrad Fromen.
28. John Sohn.
29. Jacob Rensler.
30. Jacob Levick.

30 Privates at 50 shillings each	£75.. 0..0
3 Serjeants at 50 shillings each	7..10..0
3 Corporals at 50 shillings each	7..10..0
1 Drummer	2..10..0
37 Men's advance	£92..10..0

Mustered and passed before the Committee of Obeservation & Inspection in Lancaster on the 23d & 26th of August and 2d & 10th September 1776. And the above ninety two Pounds and ten Shillings paid to Captain Barnard Zimmerman to enable him to pay the advance of 50 shillings each to his Men above mentioned.

Test. WILLE. ATLEE, Chairman of Committee &
BARNARD ZIMMERMAN, Capt.

A MUSTER ROLL OF CAPTAIN NATHANIOL PAGE'S COMPANY OF MILITIA OF COLONEL MATHIAS SLOUGH'S BATTALION OF LANCASTER COUNTY DESTINED FOR THE CAMP IN THE JERSEYS—SEPT'R 11TH 1776. (d.)

Captain.

Nathaniel Page.

1st Lieutenant.

George Rathfong.

2nd Lieutenant.

Thomas McClenaghan.

Ensign.

John Stoffer.

Serjeants.

William Smith.
John Cromwell.
John Hardt.

Corporal.

George Waggoner.
Henry Seyler.

Drummer.

Peter Smith.

Privates.

1. William Brown.
2. Jacob Miller.
3. Henry Platcher.
4. John Logan.
5. Ulrich Fissel.
6. William Folk, Junr.
7. Michael Pitz.
8. Lawrence Connoly.
9. Jacob Rathfong.
10. Leonard Allbright.

11. Rinehart Weaver.
12. John Kealer.
13. Philip Urbon.
14. Patrick Burk.
15. Henry Loudenslager.
16. Benjamin Carpenter.
17. John Miller.
18. Fredrich Feagh.
19. Jacob Hoffman.
20. William Gonder.
21. John Slighter.
22. James Smith.
23. Edward Kelley.
24. Daniel Yendes.
25. Martin McDonald.
26. William McCormick.
27. Jacob Landmesser.
28. Joseph Cowan.
29. Roger Offarran.
30. Christian Henry.
31. John Albert.
32. Cornelius Taylor.
33. John Gennet.
34. Henry Feltenberger.

34 Privates 50 shillings each	£85.. 0..0
3 Serjeants 50 shillings each	7..10..0
2 Corporals 50 shillings each	5.. 0..0
1 Drummer	2..10..0
40 Mens advance	£100.. 0..0

Mustered and passed before the Committee of Obeservation & Inspection in Lancaster on the 24th of August & 5th & 9th of September 1776—and the above One Hundred Pounds paid to Captain Nathaniel Page to enable him to pay the advance of 50 shillings each to his men.

Test. WILL'M ATLEE, Chairman of Commitee,
NATHANIEL PAGE, C'p't.

A MUSTER ROLL OF A DETACHMENT OF CAPTAIN JOSEPH WRIGHT'S COMPANY OF MILITIA OF COLONEL MATHIAS SLOUGH'S BATTALION, LANCASTER COUNTY. DESTINED FOR THE CAMP IN THE JERSEYS—SEPTEMBER THE 11TH 1776. (d.)

Captain.

Joseph Wright.

Ensign.

Jacob Rupley.

Serjeant.

Fredrick Finstermacher.

Corporal.

Fredrick Oldweiler.

Fifer.

Jacob Winter.

Privates.

1. Henry Myer.
2. Martin Gander.
3. John Weigart.
4. Jacob Brenner.
5. William McMannamy.
6. Thomas Wright.
7. Michael Shutt.
8. Fredrick Carpenter.
9. Michael Kline.
10. James Pratt.
11. George Nass.
12. John Manning.
13. Conrad Raeger.
14. James Maxwell.
15. James McElwain.

15 Privates, 50 shillings each	£37..10..0
1 Serjeants.	2..10..0
1 Corporal	2..10..0
1 Fifer	2..10..0
19 Men's advance	£45.. 0..0

Mustered and passed before the Committee of Obeservation & Inspection in Lancaster the 3d & 9th of September 1776. And the above Forty five pounds paid to Captain Joseph Wright to enable him to pay the above advance to his people—the 11 Sept. 1776.

Test. WILLE. ATLEE, Chairman of Committee &
JOSEPH WRIGHT, Capt.

A REPORT OF THE OFFICERS OF THE SEVENTH BATTALION OF THE LANCASTER COUNTY MILITIA COMMANDED BY COLONEL JOHN BOYD WHO WAS ELECTED THE DAY OF MAY 1777. (c.)

Field Officers.

Colonel.
John Boyd.

Lieut. Colo.
George Stewart.

Major.
James Mercer.

Staff Officers.
Thomas Boyd, Adjutant.

Qr. Master.
John Turbett.

Chaplain.
John Woodwell.

Surgeon.

John Duglas.

1st Company.

Captain—James Brown.
1st. Lieut.—Alex'dr Hunter.
2nd. Lieut.—Alex'dr Campbell.
Ensign—James Campbell.

2nd Company.

Captain—David Whitehill.
1st Lieut.—John Caldwell.
2nd Lieut.—Jas. Henderson.
Ensign—Jno. Whitehill, Jur.

3rd Company.

Captain—John Rowland.
1st Lieut.—James Hamilton.
2nd Lieut.—John Moore.
Ensign—Abraham Line.

4th Company.

Captain—Samuel Heans.
1st Lieut.—James Davis.
2nd Lieut.—John Scott.
Ensign—John Sclater.

5th Company.

Captain—Jno. Slaymaker.
1st Lieut.—Geo. McElvaine.
2nd Lieut.—Daniel Hughston.
Ensign—Saml. Hathorn.

6th Company.

Captain—Wm. Brisben.
1st Lieut.—John Hopper.
2nd Lieut.—John McGowen.
Ensign—Saml. Hews.

7th Company.

Captain—Robt. McCurdy.
1st Lieut.—Jas. Woods.
2nd Lieut.—Jacob Herbert.
Ensign—Robert Young.

8th Company.

Captain—Henry Kendrick.
1st Lieut.—Jno. Carpenter.
2nd Lieut.—Geo. Deffeybough.
Ensign—Danl. Lemmon.

1777 Dec. 8th, Rec'd of Timothy Matlack, Esq., commissions agreeable to the above return dated the 8th Dec.

JAMES MERCER, Maj.
JOHN BOYD, Col.

Certifyed Pr.

BARTRAM GALBRAITH,
Lieut. for Lancaster County.

A TRUE ACCT. OF THE MILITIA DRAUGHT MADE IN THE WEST END OF STRASBURGH TOWNSHIP. (c.)

Captain.

James Brown.

Lieutenants.

1st. Allexr. Hunter. 2nd. Allexr. Campble.

Ensign.

James Campble.

Court Martial Men.

John Brackbill. George Ritchman.

Privates.

1st Class.

John Hickman.	Sam'l Hynold.
John Werner.	Thos. Tomey.
Abram Bowman.	Peter Rush.

Dan'l Ehler.
John Hare, Junr.
George Heckman.
Wm. Fell.
Jacob Miller.
Jacob Bear.
John White.
Phillip Kessler.
George Smith.
John Rasar.
Christian Huber.

2d Class.

Thos. Lackey.
John Glass.
Andw. Sercrous.
Marten Hickman.
Henrey Miller.
James Shaw.
George Fisher.
Christian Wendtz.
Peter Musser.
Allexr. Work.
Saml. Hawthorn.
Nicholas Hool.
Abrm. Butshy.
Balser Bergman.
John Brun.
Conrad Shaver.
John Henrey.
Sam'l Coeswell.

3d Class.

Jacob Fritz.
Joseph Miller.
John Rush.
Wm. Logan.
James Patton.'
Jacob Rush.
Marten Bear.
Wm. Bell.
Christley Byers.
Christian Sharp.
Sam'l Finley.
Henry Hare.
Nicholas Sercrous.
John Vandersmith.
Everard Grubber.
Wm. Hoggins.
Sam'l Hoggins.

4th Class.

Jacob Shitterhelm.
Marten Kindrick.
Joseph Otterbough.
John Brubaker.
Jacob Sides.
Jacob Hubber.
Nic's Hart.
Dan'l Miller.
John Campble.
Christley Morten.
Jacob Hickman.
Dan'l Deans.
Christley Lighternaught.
Hans Miller (carpenter).
Wm. Davis.
Henry Neave.
Wm. Cimmins.
Hyronimus Byerly.

5th Class.

Christopher Culp.
Conrod Hook.
Phillip Wigard.
John Walter.
Robt. Carlton.
John Firll.

Christ'n Baker.
Henry Huber.
Andw. Spitzer.
John Cremer.
Henry Hevel.
Edmond Lindner.
John Simpson.
Abm. Hare.
Conrad Smith.
Michael Fout.

6th Class.

John Kindrick.
Bernard Kowser.
Jacob Vancord.
Jacob Feelick.
Jacob Neave.
Francis Row.
Charles Level.
Henry Rush.
Marten Bird.
Jacob Miller.
Saml. Miller.
John Moor.
Charles Phillips.
Noah Hogee.
Jacob Young.
Phillip Bear.

7th Class.

John Wither.
Valentine Vondersmith.
Jacob Hubber, Junr.
John Miller.
George Markly.
Henry Bowman.
John Bear.
Jacob Heckman.
Danl. Bowman.
Wm. Hunter.
Wm. Walter.
George Myer (nailer).
Henry Bushman.
Nicholas Mocky.
Peter Shupstable.
Marten Hare.
Henry Kindrick.
Fredrick Smith.

8th Class.

John Stoutsberger.
Matthias Miller.
Jacob Miller.
Henry Bowman.
George Wither.
James Fisher.
Michael Wither.
John Bear.
Wm. Kiney.
Christley Shultz.
Conrad Houshup.
Marten Stall.
James Mony.
George Bright.
Jacob Kindrick.
Henry Stoner.
Jacob Foutz.
Fredrick Romige.

SAULSBURY TOWNSHIP. (c.)

Captain.

David Whithill.

Lieutenants.

1st, Jno. Caldwell.
2nd, Jas. Henderson.

Ensign.

Court Martial Men.

Robert Byers.
Jos. Whithill.

Privates.

1st Class.

Hugh McBride.
Dan'l Campbell.
Thos. Withrow.
Wm. Chamberlain.
James Douglas.
Joseph Dickinson.
Yost Yoder.
Sam'l Johnston.
James Sterret.
Thos. Ervin.
Joseph Hoare.
James Allison.
John Hasten.

2nd Class.

John Whithill.
James Rodgers.
John McClure.
Joseph Holl.
James Allison, Senr.
James Barret.
Thos. Leviston.
George Burns.
Andrew Allison.
Stewart Monteeth.
Robt. Sharp.
David Walker.

3rd Class.

Thos. Boyd.
John McColley.
John Rummans.
Isaac McDill.
Enoch Hastings.
John Darrough.
James McColley.
George McDill.
Charles McCalley.
Wm. Hamilton.
Fredrick Baker.

4th Class.

James Henderson.
James Allison (S'c M.).
John Harris.
John Walker.
Isaac Marten.
Allex'r Sterret.
John Anderson.
John Shaffer.
John Howit.
George Lee.
Andrew Croiser.
Wm. Fullerton.
James Climpson.
Robt. Caldwell.

5th Class.

James Boyd.
Wm. Wallace.
John Clempson, Ju'r.
Joseph Warner.
Isaac Taylor.
Jcseph Miller.
Robt. Ray.
John Clempson, S'r.
Sam'l Smith.
John Hannah.
Wm. Alley.
Thomas Johnson.

6th Class.

David Harris.
Danil McAfee.
John Reed.
Wm. Linvil.
Benj'n Crawford.
Thos. Green.
James Clendenin.
Dan'l McGee.
Wm. Armstrong.
John Addleman.
James Clempson, Sen.
John Allison, Ju'r.
Robt. McNeal.

7th Class.

Sam'l Worrel.
Wm. Marshall.
James McDill.
Edward Berry.
Robt. Cooper.
John McCloy.
Robt. All.
Josiah Ervin.
Moses All.
Thos. Douglas.
Dan'l Miller.
Jonothan Hoar.
John Young.

8th Class.

Arch'd Montgomery.
Wm. Romage.
Arch'd Henderson.
John Campbel.
James Agnew.
John Harkens.
James Huston.
John Addlman, Jun'r.
Thomas Henderson.
Wm. Leviston.
Leonard Ellmaker.
Thos. Simpson.
Dan'l Harkins.

A TRUE ACC'T OF A MILITIA DRAUGHT MADE IN THE NORTH WEST END OF LEACOCK TOWNSHIP. (c.)

Captain.

John Rowland.

Lieutenants.

1st, James Hamilton.
2nd, John Moor.

Ensign.

David Lyne.

Court Martial Men.

James Scott.	William Quinn.

Privates.

1st Class.

Jacob Shons.	Jacob Hammer.
Henry Bear.	Samuel Eby.
Adam Rumberger.	George Fenfrock.
William Shealer.	Abram Myer.
Henry Fults.	John Kilheffer.
Sam'l Biggart.	John Hiller.
Henry Shivaly.	John McGreger.
Phillip Shower.	

2nd Class.

Jacob Myer.	Henry Swab.
Jacob Swoab.	Jacob Eby.
Sam'l Smith.	Michael Widler.
Peter Eby, Jun'r.	John Snoots.
Matthias Fisher.	George Ekert.
John Painter.	Thomas Pinkerton.
Peter Ekert.	Jacob Shearer.
Adam Hoostater.	

3rd Class.

Adam Miller.	Honical Barnet.
Sam'l Mchatton.	John Shons.
Christian Hase.	Patrick Connel.
Christian Winger.	Makom McNeal.
And'w Bear, Jun'r.	Painters Miller.
James Harkens.	Joseph Brinton.
Matthias Ault.	Henrey Eby.
John Snevly.	

4th Class.

Joseph Piggart.	David Bair.
Abram Garver.	Isaac Garver.
Marten Eare.	John Buckwolter.
John Ross.	John Willson.
Baltzer Pumberger.	John Enoch.
John Curts.	Marten Maxwell.
John Stalter.	Abraham Eby.
Ephraim Bair.	

5th Class.

John Eby, Jun'r.	Stofel Weaver.
Hugh Calhoun.	Allexander Lemmon.
Marten Hiller.	Peter Garver.
William Lyne.	Nicholas Claser.
Dan'l Swoab.	Henry Winger.
Jacob Lyne.	Isaac Rife.
And'w Bear.	James Wallace.
Michael Gaver.	

6th Class.

And'w Tauge.	And'w Scott.
John McCollaster.	Jacob Garver.
Peter Kilkeffer.	Marten Bear.
Peter Eby (shoemaker).	Jacob Maxwell.
Jacob Kittle.	Abram Haistens.
Robt. Crab.	Henrey Fults.
James Remsey.	Michael Vancanan.

7th Class.

John Maxwell.	Abram Shons.
George Bourd.	Sam'l McOhlley.
Michael Sholaberg.	George Allexander.
Wm. Brinton.	John Garver.

John Pots.
Marten Hervey.
Fra's Buckwalter.
Sam'l McOlilley, Jun'r.
Peter Eby, Sen'r.
Mic'l Hause.

8th Class.

Julius Rock.
Jonathan Owens, Ju'r.
David Rife.
Adam Swoab.
Elias Stump.
George Lamberg.
Jacob Snively.
Jacob Shively.
Mathias Fisher.
Christian Myer.
Anthony Willson.
And'w Maxwell.
Charles Stewart.
John Rider.
David Painter.
Sickman Shower.

LAMPETER TOWNSHIP. (c.)

Captain.
Sam'l Heans.

Lieutenants.
1st, James Davis.
2nd, John Scott.

Ensygn.
John Sleater.

Court Martial Men.

John Whitmore.
Robert Roddack.

Privates.

1st Class.

Christians Rorars, Miller.
Martin Grove.
Daniel Keeports.
Thomas Evans.
Henry Landis.
William Hains.
Jacob Musser.
Marten Beam.
Jacob Rorah.
Andrew Hiller.
David Rorah.
Christian Rorah.
Henry Buckwalter.
George Keetle.
Christian Hartman.
John Burkholder.

2nd Class.

Gorge utz.
John Keneday.
George on John Miller's place
Jacob Yerdey.
Moses Eaten.
John Miley.
Joseph Buckwalter.
Peter Lawrence.
Daniel Keeports.
Fredrick Windle.
Peter Musser.
David Whitmore.
Isaac Peters.
Jacob Pickle.
Benjamin Whitmore.

3rd Class.

Isaac Rorah.
Felix Bingley.
David Hoover.
Jacob Crider.
Isachar Baurd.
Daniel Wier.
Jacob Grove.
Thons at old Crawf'd place.
Morten Musser.
Jno. Willson.
Isaac Lefever.
Abraham Buckwalter.
John Davis.
Abraham Buckwalter.
Benj'n Landes.

4th Class.

John Hornest.
Phillip Mack.
Henry Eyman.
Isaac Kindrick.
Jacob Stopher.
Christian Rorah, M Creek.
Robert Weir.
Patrick Conel.
Dan'l Whitmore.
Jno. Miller.
Abram Toner.
Marten Miley.
Jno. Bingley.
George Irish.
Sam'l Watt.

5th Class.

Benj'n Bowman.
Henry Hartman.
Jam's George, at Kindrick.
Nicholas Mack.
George Truckabroade.
Jacob shons.
Jno. Crider.
Henry Marten.
Jno. Busham.
Adam Limans.
John Kirk.
Joseph Bowman.
Fredrick Palmer.
Jno. Beam.
Jno. Mileys, Stiller.
Jno. Eyebright.

6th Class.

Jno. Stopher.
Leonard Benter.
George Baurd.
James Knox.
Jacob Landis.
Thomas Reed.

George Shingle.
Jno. Wanner.
Robt. Knox.
Adam Miller.
Dan'l Miller.
Henry Whitmor.
Jacob Kirk.
Abraham Peters.
Millinger Shuma.

7th Class.

Nicholas Keeports.
W'm Mathers.
Geo. Kindrick.
And'w, at John Millers.
David Grove.
Jno. Snively.
Henry Eckman.
James Henry.
Henry Grove.
James Gibbons.
Henry Whitmore.
Jno. Buckwalter.
Tobias Crider.
Jeremiah Kirk.
James Reece.

8th Class.

Arch'd Campble.
Jno. Farrow.
Jno. Shons.
Dan'l Tub.
Adam Lefever
Abram Landes.
Christian Yordey.
Marten Millinger.
Nicholas Scriner.
Ulrich Hoover.
George Kimberlin.
Baltzer Thumb.
Phillip Baurd.
Dan'l Hoover.
Phillip Busham.
Henry Hartman.

A TRUE ACC'T OF A MILITIA DRAUGHT MADE IN EAST END OF STROUSBURG TOWNSHIP. (c.)

Captain.
John Slaymaker.

Lieutenants.
1st, George McElvain.
2nd, Daniel Huston.

Ensygn.
Sam'l Hawthorn.

Court Martial Men.

Moses Beard.
John Bower.

Privates.

1 Class.

Peter Holl. Sam'l Lefever.
John Smith. Christian Stutsberry.
Thos. White. Henry Slaymaker.
Peter Taylor. Richard Copland.
Andrew Bird. Balser Barthman.
Francis McMin. Amos Slaymaker.
Conrad Gram. Abraham Carpenter.
John Miller.

2 Class.

George Carpenter. Fredrick White.
Robert Crossby. Matthias Slaymaker.
Ludwick Miller, Sen'r. John Richardson.
George McCulloch. David Firee.
Allex'r White. Joseph White.
John Slaymaker. Malcom McCarter.
George Walk. Ludiwick Road.

3 Class.

John Kerr. William McCandless.
Jacob Elsman. Robert Beard.
Henry Bragoner. David Foster.
Thomas Kennoy. John Firee.
Jacob Stoutsberry. Jacob Stambough.
Dan'l Peck. Robt. McElvain.
Ellis Treter.

4 Class.

Nicholas Nesor. Jacob Beckman.
John Taylor. Paul Trout.
Tobias Hartman. William Snowden.
Benj'n Brackbill. Peter Lefever.
Dan'l Firee. Cronomus Miller.
Robert Murduch. Allex'r Gallagher.
Marten Elsman. James Allison.
Fredrick Den.

5th Class.

Jacob Shirts. William Slaymaker.
John Shirts. David Bower.
Phillip Firee. Isaac Firee.

Thos. Love.
Henrey Engle.
Torrence Duffy.
Charles McGowan.
Matthias Slaymaker.
Hugh Woods.
Robt. McCleland.
Jacob Hill.
Michael Fernor.

6th Class.

Jacob Miller.
John Coulter.
John Clark.
Wendle Trout.
James Kannay, Sen'r.
George Hort.
Christian Bower.
Thos. Buffentown.
Cronimus Cane.
Henry Stambach.
Cronimus Biorly.
Geo. Swortsly.
John Groff.
John Lefever.
John Gibboney.

7 Class.

Jacob Bower.
Cornelius Firee.
John Carpenter.
Robert Marten.
Michael Buch.
Neal Kenney.
Thos. Lockry.
John Hare.
Adam Drogger.
Jacob Buccof, Jun'r.
Marten Cochberger.
John Cashaday.
James Brown.
Thos. Craig.

8 Class.

William Rondler.
Abram Bower.
Benj'n Groft.
Abram Lemmon.
Nicholas Hall.
Isaac Firee, Sen'r.
Dan'l Slaymaker.
William Firee.
Valentine Gates.
James Hawthorn.
James Kenney.
John Foster.
Robt. Neel.
Michael Bower.
James Quigley.
Andrew Firee.

A TRUE ACC'T OF A MILITIA DRAUGHT MADE IN SAULSBURY TOWNSHIP. (c.)

Captain.

Wm. Brisban.

Lieutenants.

1st, Jno. Hopper.
2nd, John McGowan.

Ensign.

Samuel Hues.

Sergts.

Colin Marten. William Henrey.

Court Martial Men.

John Willson. Isaac McCalmont.

Privates.

1st Class.

Hugh Rochford. Arch'd McCurdy.
Thos. McNeal. John Wallace.
Henrey Cowan. Jacob Kiser.
Edw'd Rochford. Joshua Heans.
Isaac McCalmont. Jacob Kiser, Jun'r.

2nd Class.

Michael Graham. Mich'l McCloskey.
James Majrs. Charles Murrey.
Henry Skiles. James Gault.
James Douglas. James Siemmons.
John Watt. James Willson.
David Haket. Colin Marten.

3rd Class.

James Collin. Hugh Forgy.
Thos. Gault. Jacob Curtz.
Patrick Carigan. John Richardson.
James Johnson. Mich'l Jack.
Geo. Wike. Robt. Mathers.
Andw. Little.

4th Class.

Jno. Douglas. Thos. Siemons.
And'w Hosoh. Wm. Gault.
William Armstrong. John Baxter.
Christian Curtz. Jno. Cope.
Thos. Patton. John Armor.
Henry Calahan. Jas. Morison.
William Patton.

5th Class.

Jno. Plank.
Joseph Shannon.
Jos. Belford.
James Marten.
Joshua Roberts.
George Rutter.
Adam Gault.
And'w Collin.
George Boyd.
Matthew Henderson.
James Borland.
Wm. Henrey.
Wm. Willson.

6th Class.

Joseph Welch.
James Gault.
Charles Caldwell.
Edw'd Runchey.
James Watson.
Wm. Begs.
Thos. Slemons.
Sam'l Holaday.
Allex'r Brown.
Robt. Huey.
John Hopkin.
James Anderson.
Arch'd McAfee.

7th Class.

Jas. Mcfadden.
Wm. Richardson.
Jacob Heans.
Wm. Holeday.
Jno. Whithill.
John Hamilton.
Jacob Pee.
Wm. Cowan.
Jno. Willson.
John Holey.
John Willson.
Jacob Miller.
Jas. McCalmont.

8th Class.

Henrey Willson.
Jacob Jack.
Wm. Boyd.
Thos. Henderson.
Robt. Cowan.
John McComb.
James Dunlap.
John Watson.
Wm. Adair.
James Willson.
John Murphy.
Sam'l Armer.
John Cowan.
Robt. Smith.
Capt. Stewart.
John McKinley.
Henry Mesoner.
John Rutter.

A TRUE ACCT. OF MILITIA DRAUGHT MADE IN LOWER END OF LEACOCK TOWNSHIP. (c.)

Captain.

Robt. McCurdy.

Lieutenants.

1st, James Woods.
2nd, Jacob Herbert.

Ensign.

Robt. Young.

Serjts.

Allex'r Mchorrey.
James Abraham.
Rich'd Woods.
Abraham Henrey.

Corporals.

John Orr.
James McEnall.
Sam'l McGilley.
John Campble.

Court Martial Men.

William Porter.
Hugh Hamilton.

Privates.

1st Class.

Robt. Stuart.
Denis Cane.
Dan'l McCanechy.
Dan'l Balar.
Robt. Anderson, Jun'r.
Allex'r Miller.
George Shofer.
Allex'r Skiles.
Christian Sharp.
Wm. Wallace.
John Eaby.
Wm. Barns.
John Barr.

2nd Class.

Honicle Weaver.
John Stewart.
Little Hugh Hamilton.
Joseph Evits.
Henrey Musser.
Robt. Anderson.

William Whithjll. | And'w McCowan.
Joel Firee. | Allex'r Ray.
William Beans. | Wm. Skiles.
David Glen. | Jacob Firee.
Peter Kline.

3rd Class.

Jacob Sensinich. | Henry Cox.
Benj'n Crawford. | James Cooper.
James McNeal. | And'w Caldwell.
Wm. Montgomery. | Robt. Simpson.
Benj'n Varner. | Wm. Abraham.
Wm. McCausland. | Thomas Pinkerton.
Jos. Rutter. | Dan'l Huston.
William Watson.

4th Class.

Henrey Rutter. | Rutter Givven.
Matthew McClung. | John Turbott.
James Skiles. | Allex'r McMullon.
Isaac Firee. | Thos. Skiles.
Wm. Reed. | Henry Rutter, Jun'r.
Jno. Rush. | Henry Skiles.
Arch'd Gormley. | James Dunlap.
James McClung. | Emanuel Firee.
Jos. Rice.

5th Class.

John Anderson. | Adam Woods.
John McCay. | Henry Skiles, Jun'r.
John Abraham. | Wm. Lee.
Thos. Woods. | Joseph McMullon.
Sam'l Humer. | Jacob Myer.
James Moor. | Robt. Forsyth.
James Watson. | John Underwood.
John Turbott. | Sam'l Biggart.

6th Class.

Geo. Seldomridge. | Abram Sensnick.
Allex'r Ligget. | Geo. Lerew.
Robt. Douglas. | Hugh McCoy.
Sam'l Biggart. | Wm. Donaldson.
David Watson. | Peter Miller.
John Lightner. | Geo. Carnighon.
Peter Sharp. | Allex'r McGongin.
John Johson.

7th Class.

Dan'l Mc fadden.
John Woods.
Jas. Montgomery.
Abram Gibbons.
Balzer Basser.
Wm. Rutter.
John McCausland.
James Keneday.
John Mc fadden.
Dan'l McCalaster.
Wm. Lightner.
James Hamilton.
Henry Smith.
Adam Lightner.
John Hansey.
Sam'l McGilley.
James Peel.

8th Class.

Ephraim McColm.
Adam Weever.
Wm. Presley.
Thos. Lyon.
Wm. McCausland.
John Dublin.
Jno. Campble.
Dan'l McCausland.
Jacob Ludwick.
William Hamilton.
Phillip Aker.
And'w Givin.

123 privates.

A TRUE ACC'T OF A MILITIA DRAUGHT MADE IN THE EAST SIDE LAMPETER. (c.)

Captain.

Henry Kendrick.

Ensign.

Daniel Lemon.

Lieutenants.

1st, John Carpenter.
2nd, George Diffeybough.

Court Martial Men.

William Smith.
Isaac Kindrick.

Privates.

1st Class.

Christian Harre.	George Prisler.
Joseph Smith.	Robt. Sheerman.
John Bowman.	John Harmon.
Henry Diffebough.	Robt. Finley.
Abra'm Longinaker, Ju'r.	Jacob Hore.
John Deffeybough.	Dan'l Lemmon, Sen'r.
Abram Whitmore.	John Yoner.
James Smith, Jun'r.	Thomas McManas.

2nd Class.

Sam'l Hains.	Abra'm Snively.
Jacob Hoover.	William McNabb.
Marten Kindrick.	Jacob Lutman.
Petter Miller.	Christian Miller (weaver).
John Bowman.	James Norton.
Anthony Pruner.	Christian Stoner.
James Smith.	John Segar.
Abr'h Hair.	Benj'n Bowman.
Henry Hoober.	Michael Rife.

3rd Class.

Dan'l McLoney.	Jacob Beacht.
John Hare.	John Souder.
Dan'l Hains.	Christian Hemerly.
Barney Feggan.	Benj'n Hair.
Thos. Williams.	Conrad Speicher.
Peter Heckman.	Francis Smith.
Chas. Rinehart.	Phillip Bernard.
Dan'l Lefever.	Peter Hoarsh.
Jacob Musser.	

4th Class.

John Graham.	William Finley.
John Shofstall.	Henry Kuhn.
Ludwick Rinehart.	Peter Prisler.
And'w Sides.	Brice Clark.
John Miller.	Robt. Fletcher.
John Pots.	Henry Spiteer.
And'w Hicks.	Hugh Woods.
John Hoarch.	David Miller.

lass.

bra'm Longinaker.
ohn Neal.
Randle Leess.
Michael Kline.
George Lemmon.
ohn Fowler.
John Tonlinger.
Henrey Biggart.

lass.

Abra'm Tanlinger.
Isaac Lemmon.
Jacob Stoner.
Nicholas Prisler.
David Brown.
Dan'l Caran.
Patrick Brown.
Joseph Trimble.

lass.

aco Tanlinger.
Allex'r McGongan.
Dan'l McCook.
David Hare.
Peter the Taylor.
Lives at David Firees.
James Caldwell.
Thomas Hart.

lass.

Michael at Diffebough's
Meadow.
Jacob Hains.
Thomas Evans.
Fredrick Smith.
Thomas Bowman.
Isaac Means.
James Henry.
George Oyrich.

133.

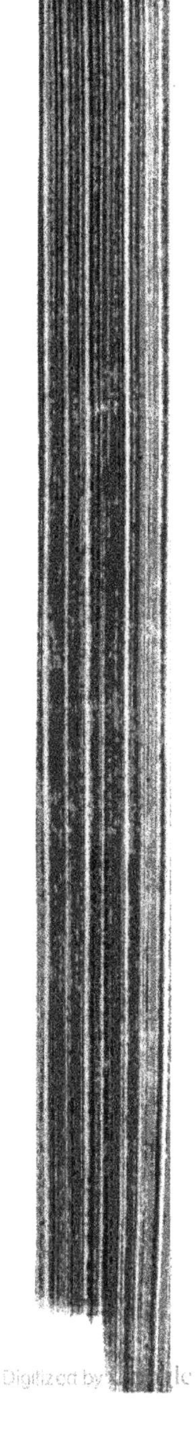

(c.) This is to certify that Allbright Miller Served part of his with Capt. David McQueen in the 5th Class of Lancaster County Militia and the rest of his time with me. December the 26th, 1777.

JOHN SLEAMAKER.

I do Certify that John hay Sarved a tower of two months in the Melitia in my Companey in the year 1777. (c.)

March the 2th, 1781.

Certifyed By

ROBT. McKEE, Capt.

I Do Certify that John hays Sarved a tower of two months in my Companey in Middletown in the year 1778 when I had the Command of the hersfon Prisners there.

March the 2th, 1781.

ROBT. McKEE, Capt.

To home may Consern.

(c.) I Do hereby Certify that Robt. Shearman has served a Tower of Duty of Two months in the 7th Batalion Lancaster County Militia Com'd by Con'l John Boyd and s'd Shearman has Deliver one gun & catock Box I say.

ROBT. McCURDY, Capt.

I Do hereby Certify that Jacob Baker has served as Drummer in my Comp'y the Space of Forty six days Given under my Hand Northwales Camp, January 18th, 1778.

ROBT. McCURDY, Capt.

(c.) ENLISTMENT PAPERS OF PENN'A MILITIA—1777.

JOHN BOYD'S REGIMENT OF MILITIA IN LANCASTER COUNTY.

I George Alexander aged Twenty Three years, five Feet five Inches high, fair Hair, Fair Complexion, born in Ireland do voluntarily agree, to serve as a Substitute in the Room and Stead of John Devibaugh in the First Class of Captain Hendry Kendricks Company, of Colonel John Boyd's Regiment of Militia in the County of Lancaster, for and in Consideration of Forty pounds, during the space of Two months as agreed with.

JAMES CRAWFORD.

Sub. Lieutenant for the County of Lancaster. Witness my Hand, this Third Day of September, 1777.

GEORGE his X mark ALEXANDER.

I, William Alley, aged Twenty one years, Five Feet eleven Inches high, Fair Hair, Fair Complexion, born in Pennsylvania, do voluntarily agree to serve as a Substitute in the Room and Stead of W'm Chamberlain in the First Class of Captain David Whithill's Company, of Colonel John Boyd's Regiment of Militia, in the County of Lancaster, for and in Consideration of Forty Pounds during the space of Two Months as agreed with.

JAMES CRAWFORD.

Sub. Lieutenant for the County of Lancaster. Witness my Hand, this First Day of September, 1777.

WILLIAM ALLEY.

I,Robert Anderson, Jun'r, aged Seventeen years, Six Feet 1 Inches high, Black Hair, Black Complexion, born in Pensylvania, do voluntarily agree to serve as a Substitute in the Room and Stead of Benjamin Brackbel in the 4th Class of Captain John Slaymaker's Company, of Colonel John Boyd's Regiment of Militia, in the County of Lancaster, for and in Consideration of Forty pounds, the Receit of Ten pounds I acknowledge, during the Space of Two Months as agreed with

JAMES CRAWFORD,
Sub. Lt.

Sub. Lieutenant for the County of Lancaster. Witness my Hand, this 20th Day of September, 1777.

ROBERT ANDERSON.

I,Christopher Andover, aged Twenty-two years, five Feet Eight Inches high, fair Hair, fair Complexion, born in

Amarica do voluntarily agree to serve as a Substitute in the Room and Stead of Abraham Carpenter in the first Class of Captain John Slaymaker's Company, of Colonel John Boyd's Regiment of Militia, in the County of Lancaster, for and in Consideration of Forty pounds, during the Space of Two months as agreed with.

JAMES CRAWFORD.

Sub. Lieutenant for the County of Lancaster. Witness my Hand, this Eight Day of September, 1777.

CHRISTOPHER his X mark ANDOVER.

I, William Armstrong, aged Twenty two years, Five Feet Six Inches high, Brown Hair, fair Complexion, born in Ireland do voluntarily agree, to serve as a Substitute in the Room and Stead of George Wike, in the Second Class of Captain David Whitehill's Company of Colonel John Boyd's Regiment of Militia, in the County of Lancaster, for and in Consideration of Forty pounds, during the Space of Two Months as agreed with.

JAMES CRAWFORD.

Sub Lieutenant for the County of Lancaster. Witness my Hand, this Seventeenth Day of September, 1777.

W'M ARMSTRONG.

I, Robert Bell, aged Thirty Years, five Feet Eight Inches high, fair Hair, fair Complexion, born in Ireland do voluntarily agree to serve as a Substitute in the Room and Stead of Henry Buckwalter, in the first Class of Captain John Craig's Company, of Colonel John Boyd's Regiment of Militia, in the County of Lancaster, for and in Consideration of Forty pounds, during the Space of Two months as agreed with.

JAMES CRAWFORD.

Sub. Lieutenant for the County of Lancaster. Witness my Hand, this 11th Day of September, 1777.

ROBERT BELL.

I, Edward Burk, aged forty five years, five Feet eight Inches high, Black Hair, Black Complexion, born in Ireland do voluntarily agree, to serve as a Substitute in the Room and

Stead of Joshua Hains in the first Class of Captain John hopkin's Company, of Colonel John Boyd's Regiment of Militia in the County of Lancaster, for and in Consideration of Forty pounds, during the Space of Two months as agreed with.

JAS. CRAWFORD.

Sub. Lieutenant for the County of Lancaster. Witness my Hand, this fifth Day of September, 1777.

EDWARD BURK.

I, Archabel Cambell, aged Twenty one years, five Feet Three Inches high, Fair Hair, fair Complexion, born in Ireland do voluntarily agree, to serve as a Substitute in the Room and Stead of Christian Hair, Lampeter, in the First Class of Captain Hendry Kendrick's Company, of Colonel John Boyd's Regiment of Militia, in the County of Lancaster, for and in Consideration of Forty pounds during the Space of Two months as agreed with.

JAS. CRAWFORD.

Sub. Lieutenant for the County of Lancaster. Witness my Hand this Third, Day of September, 1777.

ARCHIBALD CAMPBELL.

I, John Campble, aged Forty Years, Five Feet eight Inches high, Black Hair, Black Complexion, born in Ireland do voluntarily agree to serve as a Substitute in the Room and Stead of Abraham Myer in the First Class of Captain John Rowland's Company, of Colonel John Boyd's Regiment of Militia, in the County of Lancaster, for and in Consideration of Thirty two pounds Ten shillings during the Space of Two months as agreed with.

JAMES CRAWFORD.

Sub. Lieutenant for the County of Lancaster. Witness my Hand, this Thirtyeth Day of August, 1777.

JOHN his X mark CAMPBLE.

I, John Campbell, aged Twenty four Years, Five Feet Eight Inches high, Dark Hair, Fair Complexion, born in Ireland do voluntarily agree, to serve as a Substitute in the Room and Stead of Jacob Curtz in the Second Class of Captain David

Whitehill's Company, of Colonel John Boyd's Regiment of Militia, in the County of Lancaster, for and in Consideration of Forty pounds during the Space of Two Months as agreed with.

JAMES CRAWFORD.

Sub. Lieutenant for the County of Lancaster. Witness my Hand, this Seventeenth Day of September, 1777.

JOHN his X mark CAMPBELL.

I, Samuel Cauchy, aged Twenty Two Years, five Feet Three Inches high, fair Hair, fair Complexion, born in Ireland do voluntarily agree, to serve as a Substitute in the Room and Stead of Thomas Erinn in the first Class of Captain David Whitehill's Company of Colonel John Boyd's Regiment of Militia, in the County of Lancaster, for and in Consideration of Forty pounds during the Space of Two months as agreed with.

JAS. CRAWFORD.

Sub. Lieutenant for the County of Lancaster. Witness my Hand, this Eight Day of September, 1777.

SAMUEL his X mark CAUGHEY.

I, Nicholas Conaly, aged Twenty one Years, five Feet Eight Inches high, fair Hair, fair Complexion, born in Ireland do voluntarily agree, to serve as a Substitute in the Room and Stead of John Eaby in the first Class of Captain Roland's Company of Colonel John Boyd's Regiment of Militia, in the County of Lancaster, for and in Consideration of Forty pounds during the Space of Two months as agreed with.

JAS. CRAWFORD.

Sub. Lieutenant for the County of Lancaster. Witness my Hand, this Eight Day of September, 1777.

NICHOLAS his X mark CONALY.

I, Patrick Connally, aged twenty eight years, five Feet seven Inches high, Sandy Hair, fair Complexion, born in Ireland, do voluntarily agree, to serve as a Substitute in the

Room and Stead of Andrew Bird in the First Class of Captain John Slaymaker's Company, of Colonel John Boyd's Regiment of Militia, in the County of Lancaster, for and in Consideration of ——— ———, during the Space of Two months as agreed with.

JAMES CRAWFORD.

Sub. Lieutenant for the County of Lancaster. Witness my Hand, this Third Day of September, 1777.

PATRICK his X mark CONNALLY.

I, Robert Crabb, aged Twenty six Years, Five Feet six Inches high, Black Hair, Black Complexion, born in Ireland do voluntarily agree, to serve as a Substitute in the Room and Stead of Christian Hare, in the First Class of Captain Henry Kendrick's Company of Colonel John Boyd's Regiment of Militia, in the County of Lancaster, for and in Consideration of Forty pounds during the Space of Two months as agreed with.

JAMES CRAWFORD.

Sub. Lieutenant for the County of Lancaster. Witness my Hand; this First Day of September, 1777.

ROBERT CRABB.

I, Samuel Crawford, aged Twenty Years, five Feet five Inches high, Black Hair, Black Complexion, born in Ireland do voluntarily agree, to serve as a Substitute in the Room and Stead of Jacob Eselman, in the Third Class of Captain John Slaymaker's Company, of Colonel John Boyd's Regiment of Militia, in the County of Lancaster, for and in Consideration of Forty Pounds during the Space of Two Months as agreed with.

JAS. CRAWFORD.

Sub. Lieutenant for County of Lancaster. Witness my Hand, this 6th Day of October, 1777.

SAMUEL CRAWFORD.

I, William Cummins, aged Twenty Years, Five Feet Eleven Inches high, Black Hair, Dark Complexion, born in Pennsylvania do voluntarily agree to serve as a Substitute in the

Room and Stead of John Hickman in the First Class of Captain James Brown's Company of Colonel John Boyd's Regiment of Militia, in the County of Lancaster, for and in Consideration of Forty pounds during the Space of Two Months as agreed with.

JAMES CRAWFORD.

Sub. Lieutenant for County of Lancaster. Witness my Hand, this First Day of September, 1777.

W'M CUMMINS.

I, William Davis, aged Twenty Years, Five Feet nine Inches high, Brown Hair, Fair Complexion, born in Ireland, do voluntarily agree to serve as a Substitute in the Room and Stead of Jacob Johnce (?) in the First Class of Captain Jas. Brown's Company of Colonel John Boyd's Regiment of Militia, in the County of Lancaster, for and in Consideration of Forty pounds during the Space of Two Months as agreed with.

Sub Lieutenant for the County of Lancaster.
Witness my Hand, this First Day of September 1777.

WM. DAVIS.

I, Henry Dickover, aged Nineteen Years, five Feet nine Inches High, Black Hair, Black Complexion, born in Germany, do voluntarily agree to serve as a Substitute in the Room and Stead of James Smith Junr. in the First Class of Captain Henry Kendrick's Company, of Colonel John Boyd's Regiment of Militia, in the County of Lancaster, for and in Consideration of Forty pounds during the Space of Two Months as agreed with.

JAMES CRAWFORD.

Sub. Lieutenant for the County of Lancaster.
Witness my Hand, this First Day of September 1777.

HENRY DICKHOVER.

I, James Fisher, aged Thirty Years, Five Feet Seven Inches high Fair Hair, Fair Complexion, born in Ireland, do voluntarily agree, to serve as a Substitute in the Room and Stead of Abraham Longnecker in the First Class of Captain

Henry Kendrick's Company, of Colonel John Boyd's Regiment of Militia, in the County of Lancaster, for and in Consideration of Forty pounds during the Space of Two months as agreed with.

JAMES CRAWFORD,

Sub. Lieutenant for the County of Lancaster.

Witness my Hand, this Third Day of September, 1777.

his
JAMES X FISHER.
mark

I, John Fullerton, aged Twenty five years, five Feet five Inches high, fair Hair, fair Complexion, born in Ireland, do voluntarily agree, to serve as a Substitute in the Room and Stead of Jacob Kiser, Jun'r in the first Class of Captain John hopkin's Company, of Colonel John Boyd's Regiment of Militia, in the County of Lancaster, for and in Consideration of Forty pounds during the Space of Two months as agreed with.

JAS. CRAWFORD.

Sub. Lieutenant for the County of Lancaster.

Witness my Hand, this Eight Day of September 1777.

his
JOHN X FULLERTON.
mark.

I, george gammel, aged Twenty five years, five Feet eight Inches high, fair Hair, fair Complexion, born in Ireland, do voluntarily agree, to serve as a Substitute in the Room and Stead of Conrad Grum in the First Class of Captain John Slaymaker's Company, of Colonel John Boyd's Regiment of Militia, in the County of Lancaster, for and in Consideration of Forty pounds during the Space of Two months as agreed with.

JAMES CRAWFORD,

Sub. Lieutenant for the County of Lancaster.

Witness my Hand, this Third Day of September, 1777.

his
GEORGE X GAMMEL.
mark.

I, Jacob Gibson, aged Twenty two Years, five Feet nine Inches high, fair Hair, fair Complexion, born in Amarica, do voluntarily agree, to serve as a Substitute in the Room and Stead of Martin Grove, in the first Class of Captain John Craig's Company, of Colonel John Boyd's Regiment of Militia, in the County of Lancaster, for and in Consideration of Forty pounds during the Space of Two months as agreed with.

JAS. CRAWFORD.

Sub. Lieutenant for the County of Lancaster.

Witness my Hand, this Eight Day of September 1777.

JACOB GIBSON.

I, Robert Gibson, aged Twenty one Years, five Feet four Inches high, fair Hair, fair Complexion, born in Amarica do voluntarily agree, to serve as a Substitute in the Room and Stead of Peter Taylor in the First Class of Captain John Slaymaker's Company, of Colonel John Boyd's Regiment of Militia, in the County of Lancaster, for and in Consideration of Forty pounds during the Space of Two months as agreed with.

JAS. CRAWFORD.

Sub. Lieutenant for the County of Lancaster.

Witness my Hand, this Eight Day of September, 1777.

ROBERT GIBSON.

I, William Griffin, aged Twenty five Years, five Feet Ten Inches high, Black Hair, Black Complexion, born in Ireland do voluntarily agree, to serve as a Substitute in the Room and Stead of Thomas Eavins, in the first Class of Captain John Craig's Company, of Colonel John Boyd's Regiment of Militia, in the County of Lancaster, for and in Consideration of Forty pounds during the Space of Two Months as agreed with.

JAS. CRAWFORD.

Sub. Lieutenant for the County of Lancaster.

Witness my Hand, this Eight Day of September, 1777.

WILLIAM GRIFFEY.

I, John harkin, aged twenty three Years, five Feet ten Inches high, Brown Hair, black Complexion, born in Amarica do voluntarily agree, to serve as a Substitute in the Room and Stead of Samuel Eabby, in the first Class of Captain John Roland's Company, of Colonel John Boyd's Regiment of Militia, in the County of Lancaster, for and in Consideration of Forty pounds Ten Shillings during the Space of Two Months as agreed with.

JAMES CRAWFORD.

Sub. Lieutenant for the County of Lancaster.

Witness my Hand, this First Day of September, 1777.

his
JOHN X HARKEN.
mark

I, Jacob Herbert, aged Twenty one Years, five Feet eight Inches high, Black Hair, Black Complexion, born in Amarica do voluntarily agree, to serve as a Substitute in the Room and Stead of Francis M'Fmin in the first Class of Captain John Slaymaker's Company, of Colonel John Boyd's Regiment of Militia, in the County of Lancaster, for and in Consideration of Forty pounds during the Space of Two Months as agreed with.

JAS. CRAWFORD.

Sub. Lieutenant for the County of Lancaster.

Witness my Hand, this fifteenth Day of September 1777.

JACOB HERBERT.

I, James Jacks, aged Fifty four Years, Five Feet Eight Inches high, Gray Hair, Black Complexion, born in Ireland do voluntarily agree, to serve as a Substitute in the Room and Stead of Christian hartman, Jun'r, in the first Class of Captain John Craig's Company of Colonel John Boyd's Regiment of Militia, in the County of Lancaster for and in Consideration of Forty pounds during the Space of Two months as agreed with.

JAMES CRAWFORD.

Sub. Lieutenant for the County of Lancaster.

Witness my Hand, this Second Day of September 1777.

his
JAMES X JACKS.
mark.

I, Ritchard Kenady, aged 18 Years, 5 Feet 4 Inches high, Brown Hair, fair Complexion, born in Ireland do voluntarily agree, to serve as a Substitute in the Room and Stead of Abraham Sensinack in the 6th Class of Captain Robert McCurdey's Company of Colonel John Boyd's Regiment of Militia in the County of Lancaster, for and in Consideration of Forty pounds during the Space of Two Months as agreed with.

JAS. CRAWFORD.

Sub. Lieutenant for the County of Lancaster.

Witness my Hand, this 5th Day of Dec. 1777.

his
RITCHARD X KENADY.
mark

The Receit of ten pounds (£10) I acknowledge.

I, Robert Keney, aged Twenty two Years, five Feet ten inches high, Black Hair, Black Complexion, born in Ireland, do voluntarily agree to serve as a Substitute in the Room and Stead of Jacob Howney in the Second Class of Captain Jas. Brown's Company of Colonel John Boyd's Regiment of Militia, in the County of Lancaster, for and in Consideration of Forty pounds during the Space of Two Months as agreed with.

JAS. CRAWFORD.

Sub. Lieutenant for the County of Lancaster.

Witness my Hand, this first Day of October 1777.

I, Neal Kenny, aged Twenty one Years, five Feet five Inches high, Black Hair, Black Complexion, born in Ireland, do voluntarily agree to serve as a Substitute in the Room and Stead of Jacob Rush in the Third Class of Captain Jas. Brown's Company of Colonel John Boyd's Regiment of Militia, in the County of Lancaster, for and in Consideration of Forty pounds during the Space of Two Months as agreed with.

JAS. CRAWFORD.

Sub. Lieutenant for the County of Lancaster.

Witness my Hand, this Twenty Third Day of September 1777.

his
NEAL X KENNEY.
mark.

I, Barnabas Laffarty, aged Twenty Seven Years, Five Feet Six Inches high, black Hair, black Complexion, born in Ireland do voluntarily agree, to serve as a Substitute in the Room and Stead of John Eckman in the first Class of Captain James Brown's Company of Colonel John Boyd's Regiment of Militia, in County of Lancaster, for and in consideration of Thirty two pounds five shillings during the Space of Two Months as agreed with.

JAMES CRAWFORD.
Sub. Lieutenant for the County of Lancaster.

Witness my Hand, this first Day of September 1777.

his
BARNABAS X LAFFERTY.
mark

I, Robert Laurance, aged Twenty one Years, five Feet Eight Inches high, Brown Hair, fair Complexion, born in Ireland do voluntarily agree to serve as a Substitute in the Room and Stead of Peter Eakert in the Second Class of Captain John Roland's Company, of Colonel John Boyd's Regiment of Militia in the County of Lancaster, for and in Consideration of Forty pounds during the Space of Two Months as agreed with.

JAS. CRAWFORD.
Sub. Lieutenant for the County of Lancaster.

Witness my Hand, this 26th Day of Sept. 1777.

ROBERT LAURANCE.

I, Thomas Mackhey, aged Forty four Years, five Feet Eight Inches high, Black Hair, Black Complexion, born in Ireland do voluntarily agree to serve as a Substitute in the Room and Stead of Thomas Witter in the first Class of Captain John hopkin's Company, of Colonel John Boyd's Regiment of Militia in the County of Lancaster, for and in Consideration of Forty pounds during the Space of Two Months as agreed with.

JAMES CRAWFORD.
Sub. Lieutenant for the County of Lancaster.

Witness my Hand, this Eight Day of September 1777.

THOS. MACKEY.

I, Isack Martin, aged Twenty one Years, Six Feet — Inches high, fair Hair, fair Complexion, born in Ireland do voluntarily agree to serve as a Substitute in the Room and Stead of John penter in the first Class of Captain John Roland's Company, of Colonel John Boyd's Regiment of Militia, in the County of Lancaster during the Space of Two Months as agreed with

JAS. CRAWFORD.

Sub. Lieutenant for the County of Lancaster.

Witness my Hand, this Thirteenth Day of September 1777.

ISAAC MARTIN.

I, Alexander McBride, aged Twenty four Years, six Feet— Inches high, Black Hair, Dark Complexion, born in Ireland do voluntarily agree to serve as a Substitute in the Room and Stead of Peter Rusly in the First Class of Captain James Brown's Company, of Colonel John Boyd's Regiment of Militia in the County of Lancaster, for and in Consideration of Forty pounds during the Space of Two Months as agreed with.

JAMES CRAWFORD,

Sub. Lieutenant for the County of Lancaster.

Witness my Hand, this First Day of September 1777.

ALEX. McBRIDE.

I, John McCalestor, aged Twenty three Years, five Feet seven Inches high, Sandy Hair, fair Complexion, born in Ireland do voluntarily agree to serve as a Substitute in the Room and Stead of Daniel Beasor in the First Class of Captain Robert McCurdey's Company of Colonel John Boyd's Regiment of Militia in the County of Lancaster, for and in Consideration of Forty pounds during the Space of Two Months as agreed with.

JAMES CRAWFORD,

Sub. Lieutenant for the County of Lancaster.

Witness my Hand, this Third Day of September, 1777.

his
JOHN X McCALESTOR.
mark

I, Francis McCay, aged Fifty six Years, five Feet five Inches high, fair Hair, fair Complexion, born in Ireland do voluntarily agree to serve as a Substitute in the Room and Stead of Jas. Allison in the First Class of Captain John Roland's Company, of Colonel John Boyd's Regiment of Militia in the County of Lancaster, for and in Consideration of Forty pounds during the Space of Two Months as agreed with.

JAMES CRAWFORD,

Lieutenant for the County of Lancaster.

Witness my Hand, this Third Day of September 1777.

his
FRANCIS X McCAY.
mark

I, Addam Mcferson, aged Twenty four Years, five Feet Eight Inches high, Brown Hair, Brown Complexion, born in Ireland do voluntarily agree to serve as Substitute in the Room and Stead of Benjman Varner in the 3d Class of Captain Robert McCurdey's Company of Colonel John Boyd's Regiment of Militia, in the County of Lancaster, for and in Consideration of Forty pounds during the Space of Two Months as agreed with.

JAS. CRAWFORD.

Sub. Lieutenant for the County of Lancaster.

Witness my Hand, this 13th Day of october 1777.

ADDAM McFARSON.

I, John Mcgauhoon, aged Eighteen Years, five Feet five Inches high, Black Hair, Black Complexion, born in Ireland, do voluntarily agree to serve as Substitute in the Room and Stead of George Ritchman, in the first Class of Captain James Brown's Company, of Colonel John Boyd's Regiment of Militia, in the County of Lancaster, for and in Consideration of Forty pounds during the Space of Two Months as agreed with.

JAS. CRAWFORD.

Sub. Lieutenant for the County of Lancaster.

Witness my Hand, this First Day of September, 1777.

his
JOHN X McGAUHOON.
mark.

I, Daniel McGee, aged Thirty Two Years, Five Feet six Inches high, Brown Hair, Fair Complexion, born in Ireland do voluntarily agree to serve as Substitute in the Room and Stead of John Miller, in the First Class of Captain John Hopkin's Company, of Colonel John Boyd's Regiment of Militia in the County of Lancaster, for and in Consideration of The sum of Thirty Two Pounds Two Shillings during the Space of Two Months as agreed with.

JAMES CRAWFORD,

Sub. Lieutenant for the County of Lancaster.

Witness my Hand, this Thirtyeth Day of August 1777.

DANIEL MAGEE.

I, Charles McGowan, aged Nineteen Years, Five Feet seven Inches high, Fair Hair, Fair Complexion, born in Ireland do voluntarily agree to serve as Substitute in the Room and Stead of Baltzer Barkman, in the First Class of Captain John Slaymaker's Company, of Colonel John Boyd's Regiment of Militia, in the County of Lancaster, for and in Consideration of Forty pounds during the Space of Two Months as agreed with.

JAMES CRAWFORD.

Sub. Lieutenant for the County of Lancaster.

Witness my Hand, this First Day of September 1777.

his
CHARLES X McGOWAN.
mark

I, Peter M'Chollane, aged Thirty Three Years, five Feet Eight Inches high, fair Hair fair Complexion, born in Ireland do voluntarily agree, to serve as a Substitute in the Room and Stead of Jacob Stoutsabary in the Third Class of Captain John Slaymaker's Company, of Colonel John Boyd's Regiment of Militia, in the County of Lancaster, for and in Consideration of Forty pounds during the Space of Two Months as agreed with.

JAS. CRAWFORD.

Sub. Lieutenant for the County of Lancaster.

Witness my Hand, this 23th Day of September, 1777.

his
PETER X MEHOLLANE.
mark

I James McKnight aged Forty seven years, Five Feet six Inches high, Brown Hair, Fair Complexion, born in Ireland do voluntarily agree, to serve as a Substitute in the Room and Stead of Christian Sharp in the First Class of Captain Robert McCurdey's Company of Colonel John Boyd's Regiment of Militia, in the County of Lancaster, for and in Consider-tion of Thiryt two pounds Ten Shillings during the Space of Two Months as agreed with.

JAMES CRAWFORD.

Sub. Lieutenant for the County of Lancaster.

Witness my Hand, this Thirtyeth Day of August 1777.

his
JAMES X McKNIGHT.
mark

I, William Meacumson, aged seventeen Years, five Feet seven Inches high, brown Hair, fair Complexion, born in Maryland do voluntarily agree, to serve as a Substitute in the Room and Stead of——— ——— in the second Class of Captain David Whitehill's Company, of Colonel John Boyd's Regiment of Militia, in the County of Lancaster, for and in Consideration of forty pounds during the Space of two Months as agreed with.

JAMES CRAWFORD.

Sub. Lieutenant for the County of Lancaster.

Witness my Hand this twenty seven Day of Septr. 1777.

his
WILLIAM X MEACUMSON.
mark

I, Alexander Meclain, aged forty years, five Feet eight Inches high, Black Hair, Black Complexion, born in Ireland do voluntarily agree, to serve as a Substitute in the Room and Stead of Mathias Slaymaker, in the Second Class of Captain John Slaymaker's Company, of Colonel John Boyd's Regiment of Militia, in the County of Lancaster, for and in Consideration of Forty pounds during the Space of Two Months as agreed with.

JAS. CRAWFORD.

Sub. Lieutenant for the County of Lancaster.

Witness my Hand, this 28th Day of Sept. 1777.

his
ALEXANDER X MECLAIN.
mark

I, Alexander Meharry, aged twenty three Years five Feet ten Inches high, Brown Hair, fair Complexion, born in Ireland do voluntarily agree, to serve as a Substitute in the Room and Stead of henrey Shibley, in the first Class of Captain hendry Kendrick's Company, of Colonel John Boyd's Regiment of Militia, in the County of Lancaster, for and in Consideration of Thirty Two pounds Ten Shillings during the Space of Two Months as agreed with.

JAMES CRAWFORD.

Sub. Lieutenant for the County of Lancaster.

Witness my Hand, this First Day of September 1777.

ALEX. MEHARG.

I, Jas.Meneliy, aged Twenty one Years, five Feet nine inches high, fair Hair, fair Complexion, born in Ireland do voluntarily agree, to serve as a Substitute in the Room and Stead of hendry Landis in the first Class of Captain John Craig's Company, of Colonel John Boyd's Regiment of Militia, in the County of Lancaster, for and in Consideration of Forty pounds during the Space of Two Months as agreed with.

JAS. CRAWFORD.

Sub. Lieutenant for the County of Lancaster.

Witness my Hand, this Eight Day of September 1777.

JAMES MENEELY.

I, Jas. Merleyry, aged Twenty four Years, five Feet 9 inches high, fair Hair, fair Complexion, born in Ireland do voluntarily agree, to serve as a Substitute in the Room and Stead of Adam Lightner, in the Seventh Class of Captain Robert McCurdy's Company, of Colonel John Boyd's Regiment of Militia, in the County of Lancaster, for and in Consideration of Forty pounds during the Space of Two Months as agreed with.

JAS. CRAWFORD.

Sub. Lieutenant for the County of Lancaster.

Witness my Hand, this 24th Day of Nov. 1777.

JAMES MERLEYRY.

I, Robert Miller, aged Twenty one Years, Six Feet 0 inches high, Brown Hair, Brown Complexion, born in America do voluntarily agree, to serve as a Substitute in the Room and Stead of Jacob Galver in the ——— Class of Captain John Roland's Company, of Colonel John Boyd's Regiment of Militia, in the County of Lancaster, for and in Consideration of Forty pounds during the Space of Two Months as agreed with.

JAS. CRAWFORD.

Sub. Lieutenant for the County of Lancaster.

Witness my Hand, this 17th Day of November 1777.

ROBT. MILLER.

I, John Morrison, aged Eighteen Years, five Feet Two Inches high, fair Hair, fair Complexion, born in Amarica do voluntarily agree, to serve as a Substitute in the Room and Stead of George Smith in the first Class of Captain James Brown's Company, of Colonel John Boyd's Regiment of Militia, in the County of Lancaster, for and in Consideration of Forty pounds during the Space of Two Months as agreed with.

JAS. CRAWFORD.

Sub. Lieutenant for the County of Lancaster.

Witness my Hand, this Ninth Day of September 1777.

JOHN MORRISON.

I, Thomas Norras, aged Twenty-five Years, five Feet, 10 Inches high, Black Hair, Black Complexion, born in Amarica, do voluntarily agree, to serve as a Substitute in the Room and Stead of John Perree, in the Third Class of Captain John Slaymaker's Company, of Colonel John Boyd's Regiment of Militia, in the County of Lancaster, for and in Consideration of Forty pounds during the Space of Two Months as agree with Jas. Crawford.

Sub. Lieutenant for the County of Lancaster.

Witness my Hand, this 11th Day of October 1777.

his
THOMAS X NORRAS.
mark

I, John Patterson, aged Thirty Six Years, five Feet Six Inches high, Black Hair, Black Complexion, born in Ireland do voluntarily agree, to serve as a Substitute in the Room and Stead of Jacob Rorra, in the first Class of Captain John Craig's Company, of Colonel John Boyd's Regiment of Militia, in the County of Lancaster, for and in Consideration of Forty pounds, during the Space of Two Months as agreed with.

JAS.^r CRAWFORD.

Sub. Lieutenant for the County of Lancaster.
Witness my Hand, this Eleventh Day of September 1777.

his
JNO. X PATTERSON.
mark

I, John Pinkerton, aged Eighteen Years, five Feet four inches high, fair Hair, fair Complexion, born in America do voluntarily agree, to serve as a Substitute in the Room and Stead of John Rush in the Third Class of Captain Jas. Brown's Company of Colonel John Boyd's Regiment of Militia, in the County of Lancaster, for and in Consideration of Forty pounds, during the Space of Two Months as agreed with.

JAS. CRAWFORD.

Sub. Lieutenant for the County of Lancaster.
Witness my Hand, this Day of 1777.

JOHN PINKERTON.

I, John Poukley, aged Twenty seven Years, five Feet eight inches high, Black Hair, Black Complexion, born in Ireland do voluntarily agree to serve as a Substitute in the Room and Stead of Joseph Brantan in the Third Class of Captain John Roland's Company, of Colonel John Boyd's Regiment of Militia, in the County of Lancaster, for and in Consideration of Forty pounds, during the Space of Two Months as agreed with.

JAS. CRAWFORD.

Sub. Lieutenant for the County of Lancaster.
Witness my Hand, this 27th Day of September 1777.

I, John Redman, aged Eighteen Years, five Feet four Inches high, Brown Hair, Brown Complexion, born in Ireland do voluntarily agree to serve as a Substitute in the Room and Stead of Philip Kesler, in the first Class of Captain Jas. Brown's Company of Colonel John Boyd's Regiment of Militia, in the County of Lancaster, for and in Consideration of Forty pounds, during the Space of Two Months as agreed with.

JAS. CRAWFORD,

Sub. Lieutenant for the County of Lancaster.

Witness my Hand this First Day of September 1777.

his
JOHN X REDMAN.
mark

I, Henrey Renken, aged Twenty one Years, Five Feet Ten Inches high, Fair Hair, Fair Complexion, born in Ireland, do voluntarily agree to serve as a Substitute in the Room and Stead of Jacob Miller, Junr., in the First Class of Captain James Brown's Company, of Colonel John Boyd's Regiment of Militia, in the County of Lancaster, for and in Consideration of Forty pounds, during the Space of Two Months as agreed with.

JAMES CRAWFORD,

Sub. Lieutenant for the County of Lancaster.

Witness my Hand, this First Day of September 1777.

HENRY RENKIN.

I, John Rose, aged Twenty Two Years, Five Feet Nine Inches high, fair Hair, fair Complexion, born in Germany do voluntarily agree to serve as a Substitute in the Room and Stead of Andrew Bair in the Third Class of Captain John Roland's Company, of Colonel John Boyd's Regiment of Militia, in the County of Lancaster during the Space of Two Months as agreed with

JAS. CRAWFORD,

Sub. Lieutenant for the County of Lancaster.

Witness my Hand, this Twenty Third Day of Sept. 1777.

JOHN ROSE.

I, Robert Roy, aged Twenty Years, five Feet Eight Inches high, fair Hair, fair Complexion, born in Ireland do voluntarily agree, to serve as a Substitute in the Room and Stead of Martain Reeam, in the First Class of Captain John Craig's Company of Colonel John Boyd's Regiment of Militia, in the County of Lancaster, for and in Consideration of Forty Pounds, during the Space of Two Months as agreed with.

JAS. CRAWFORD,

Sub. Lieutenant for the County of Lancaster.

Witness my Hand, this Eight Day of September, 1777.

ROBERT ROY.

I, Andrew Scot, aged Twenty Years, five Feet 9 Inches high, Brown Hair, fair Complexion, born in Ireland, do voluntarily agree, to serve as a Substitute in the Room and Stead of John Jonse in the Third Class of Captain John Roland's Company, of Colonel John Boyd's Regiment of Militia, in the County of Lancaster, for and in Consideration of Forty Pounds, during the Space of Two Months as agreed with.

JAS. CRAWFORD,

Sub. Lieutenant for the County of Lancaster.

Witness my Hand, this 13th Day of October 1777.

ANDREW SCOTT.

I, John Simson, aged Twenty five Years, five Feet Ten Inches high, fair Hair, fair Complexion, born in Ireland do voluntarily agree, to serve as a Substitute in the Room and Stead of Peter Musser in the Second Class of Captain Jas. Brown's Company, of Colonel John Boyd's Regiment of Militia, in the County of Lancaster, for and in Consideration of Forty pounds during the Space of Two Months as agreed with.

JAS. CRAWFORD,

Sub. Lieutenant for the County of Lancaster.

Witness my Hand, this 28th Day of Sept. 1777.

JOHN SIMSON.

I, Jas. Smith, aged Thirty Seven Years, five Feet Seven Inches high, fair Hair, fair Complexion, born in Ireland do voluntarily agree, to serve as a Substitute in the Room and Stead of Martian Bear in the Third Class of Captain Jas. Brown's Company, of Colonel John Boyd's Regiment of Militia, in the County of Lancaster, for and in Consideration of Forty pounds during the Space of Two months as agreed with.

JAS. CRAWFORD.

Sub. Lieutenant for the County of Lancaster. Witness my Hand, this Twenty fourth Day of Sept., 1777.

JAMES SMITH.

I, Charls. Stewart, aged Twenty Seven Years, Six Feet —— Inches high, Sandy Hair, Fair Complexion, born in Amarica, do voluntarily agree to serve as a Substitute in the Room and Stead of Joseph Hoar, in the first Class of Captain John Roland's Company, of Colonel John Boyd's Regiment of Militia, in the County of Lancaster, for and in Consideration of Forty pounds during the Space of Two months as agreed with.

JAMES CRAWFORD.

Sub. Lieutenant for the County of Lancaster. Witness my Hand, this Second Day of September, 1777.

CHARLES his X mark STEWART.

I, John Stewart, aged twenty four Years, five Feet five Inches high, Black Hair, Black Complexion, born in Ireland, do voluntarilly agree to serve as a Substitute in the Room and Stead of Jacob Kiser in the First Class of Captain John Hopkin's Company, of Colonel John Boyd's Regiment of Militia, in the County of Lancaster, for and in Consideration of Forty pounds during the Space of Two months as agreed with.

JAMES CRAWFORD.

Sub. Lieutenant for the County of Lancaster. Witness my Hand, this Third Day of September, 1777.

JOHN STUART.

I, Elis Teeder, aged Twenty five Years, five Feet Ten Inches high, Fair Hair, Fair Complexion, born in Amarica, do voluntarily agree to serve as a Substitute in the Room and Stead of Hendry Devibaugh, in the First Class of Captain Hendry Kendrick's Company, of Colonel John Boyd's Regiment of Militia, in the County of Lancaster, for and in Consideration of Forty pounds during the Space of Two months as agreed with.

JAMES CRAWFORD.

Sub. Lieutenant for the County of Lancaster. Witness my Hand, this Third Day of September, 1777.

I, Alexander Thomson, aged Seventeen Years, five Feet six Inches high, fair Hair, fair Complexion, born in Newcastle County, do voluntarily agree, to serve as a Substitute in the Room and Stead of Daniel Swob, in the 5th Class of Captain Roland's Company, of Colonel John Boyd's Regiment of Militia, in the County of Lancaster, for and in Consideration of Forty pounds during the Space of Two months as agreed with.

JAS. CRAWFORD.

the Receit for Ten pounds I acknowledge.

Sub. Lieutenant for the County of Lancaster. Witness my Hand, this 17th Day of November, 1777.

ALEXANDER his X mark THOMSON.

I, Phillip Varnim, aged Twenty four Years, five Feet Six Inches high, Brown Hair, fair Complexion, born in Germany, do voluntarily agree to serve as a Substitute in the Room and Stead of Fredrick White, in the Second Class of Captain John Slaymaker's Company of Colonel John Boyd's Regiment of Militia, in the County of Lancaster, for and in Consideration of Forty pounds during the Space of Two months as agreed with.

JAS. CRAWFORD.

Sub. Lieutenant for the County of Lancaster. Witness my Hand, this 28th Day of Sept., 1777.

PHILLIP VAERNEN.

I, Samuel Vogan, aged Twenty Years, five Feet Eight Inches high, fair Hair, fair Complexion, born in Amarica do voluntarily agree to serve as a Substitute in the Room and Stead of Mich. Widler in the first Class of Captain John Roland's Company, of Colonel John Boyd's Regiment of Militia, in the County of Lancaster, for and in Consideration of Forty pounds during the Space of Two months as agreed with.

JAMES CRAWFORD.

Sub. Lieutenant for the County of Lancaster. Witness my Hand, this 15 Day of September, 1777.

SAMUEL VOGAN.

I, John Walter, aged Eighteen Years, five Feet Ten Inches high, Fair Hair, Fair Complexion, born in Pennsylvania do voluntarily agree to serve as a Substitute in the Room and Stead of John Hare in the First Class of Captain James Brown's Company, of Colonel John Boyd's Regiment of Militia, in the County of Lancaster, for and in Consideration of Forty pounds during the Space of Two months as agreed with.

JAMES CRAWFORD.

Sub. Lieutenant for the County of Lancaster. Witness my Hand, this First Day of September, 1777.

JOHN his X mark WALTER.

John Watt, aged nineteen Years, five Feet, Six Inches high, fair Hair, fair Complexion, born in Ireland, do voluntarily agree to serve as a Substitute in the Room and Stead of John Harman in the First Class of Captain Hendry Kendrick's Company, of Colonel John Boyd's Regiment of Militia, in the County of Lancaster, for and in Consideration of Forty pounds during the Space of Two months as agreed with.

JAMES CRAWFORD.

Sub. Lieutenant for the County of Lancaster. Witness my Hand, this Third Day of September, 1777.

JOHN WATT.

I, George Young, aged Nineteen Years, five Feet Six Inches high, Brown Hair, Brown Complexion, born in Scotland do voluntarily agree to serve as a Substitute in the Room and Stead of Andrew Little in the 3d Class of Captain John hopkin Company of Colonel John Boyd's Regiment of Militia, in the County of Lancaster, for and in Consideration of Forty pounds during the Space of Two months as agreed with.

THOMAS SMITH.

Witness my Hand, this Thirtyeth Day of September, 1777.

GEORGE his X mark YOUNG.

A RETURN OF CAPT. HUGH PEDEN'S COMPY. OCTOBER 28TH, 1778. (c.)

Captain.

Hugh Peden.

Lieutenant.

Patrick Hayes.

2d Lieutenant.

Benjamin Mills.

Ensign.

John Bogs.

1st Class.

Christy Hoffman.
John Shanks.
Edward Waterson.
John Hayes.
Christy Erishman.
James Cloon.
Patrick Bowins.
William Allison.
William Patterson.

2nd Class.

John Shelhorn.
John Scott.
Abraham Cassel.
John Mattz.
John McCalla.
Cornelius Toland.
Joseph Titball.
Ludwick Mattz.

3rd Class.

Cristian Long.	Henry Strickler.
David Hayes.	James Melony.
Henry Strickler.	David Moore.
Balser Walter.	John Beard.
Sam'l Robison.	John Ishbach.

4th Class.

James Patterson.	Jacob Panter.
Joseph Litle.	James Sterret, Ju'r.
Samuel Corrin.	Balser Shelhorn.
Joseph flatcher.	John Scott.
Robert Alice.	

5th Class.

Hugh Grimes.	Christian Longnecor.
Michael Horst.	Henry Ocker.
Jacob Hosteter.	Jacob Berns.
William Cummins.	John Wilson.
Peter Walter.	John Meshe.

6th Class.

James Hucheson.	Thos. Mento.
Cristy Haldeman.	Sam'l McCreeking.
Abraham Mattz.	William Wilson.
Samuel Hesse.	George the Miller to Abraham Casel.
Isaac Gilmore.	John Vance.
John Chambers.	

7th Class.

John Rora.	John Beard.
Samuel Brand.	Daniel Slain.
Henry Houbley.	John Miller.
Peter Hesten.	Sam'l Patterson.
Abraham Haldemn.	Olery Strickler.
James Sterret, Sen'r.	Jacob Erishman, Ju'r.
Neal Welch.	

8th Class.

Jacob Matz.	Jacob Kensler.
Joseph Brand.	Ebenezer Berty.
Jacob Erishman, Sen'r.	James Beard.
John Sweny.	William Campbell.

CAPT. HUGH PEDEN'S CO. RAPHO TOWNSHIP, MAY 24, 1779. (c.)

Capt.

Hugh Peden.

Lieuts.

Patrick Hays.
Benjamin Mills.

Insin.

John Boggs.

1st Class.

Christian Hufman.
John Shanck.
John Hays.
Edward Waterson.
Christan Eieresman.
Patrick Borns.
Pillip Gilmer.
Jacob Aren.

2nd Class.

John Shilhorn.
John Scott.
Abraham Castle.
John Matts.
Cornelus Tolan.
Joseph Tidball.
Neil a Boayl.

3rd Class.

Ludwick Matts.
Christan Laung.
Henry Strickler.
Balser Walter.
Samuel Robeson.
Henry Strickler.
John Beard.
John Ishbach.
Petter Funck.

4th Class.

James Petterson.
Joseph Littel.
Samuel Corran.
Joseph Flacher.
Robart Aless.
Jacob Penter.
James Dortter.
John Toumey.
Balser Shilhorn.
James Starat, Junr.

5th Class.

Hugh Grins.	Christan Loungnecker.
Michal Hirst.	Henry Ocker.
Petter Walter.	John Meshey.
Jacob Hostater.	Charles Newcom.

6th Class.

James Hucheson.	Thomas Minto.
Christan Holdeman.	Samuel McCracken.
Abraham Matts.	William Wilson.
Samuel Hesse.	Alrick Hacket.
Isaac Gilmer.	William Portter.
John Chembers.	

7th Class.

Samuel Brand.	John Rora.
Henry Hubly.	John Miler.
Petter Hesten.	Samuel Petterson.
Abraham Holdiman.	Alrick Strickler.
James Starret, Senr.	John Gray.
Neil Welch.	

8th Class.

Jacob Eresman.	Jacob Kensler.
Jacob Matts.	Ebenezer Bettey.
Joseph Brand.	James Beard.
Jacob Erisman.	Abraham Cobart.
John Sweney.	Thomas Grerer.

Certifyd the above pr me.

HUGH PEDEN, Capt.

OFFICERS OF SEVENTH BATTALION. (a.)

Returned August 26, 1780.

Lieutenant Colonel.

Alexander Lowrey.

Major.

Jacob Cook.

First company.

Captain—Andrew Boggs.
Lieutenant—James Cook.
Ensign—John Mosser.

Second company.

Captain—Abraham Scott.
Lieutenant—Robert Cunningham.
Ensign—Abraham Scott.

Third company.

Captain—Thomas Robinson.
Lieutenant—Andrew Shell.
Ensign—James Miller.

Fourth company.

Captain—David McQuown.
Lieutenant—Matthew Hays.
Ensign—Thomas Logan.

Fifth company.

Captain—Noah Keesey.
Lieutenant Christian Hacklewood.
Ensign—Christian Detter.

Sixth company.

Captain—William Willson.
Lieutenant—James Cook.
Ensign—James Willson.

Seventh company.

Captain—Robert McKee.
Lieutenant—[Vacant.]
Ensign—[Vacant.]

Eighth company.

Captain—Hugh Pedan.
Lieutenant—Patrick Hays.
Ensign—Benjamin Wills.

A MUSTER ROLL OF CAPTAIN THOMAS ROBINSONS COMPANY, BEING THE THIRD COMPANY OF THE SEVENTH BATTALION OF LANCASTER COUNTY MELITIA COMMENTED BY LT. COL. ALEXANDER LOWRY. BEGAN ON THE 23RD DAY OF APRIL A. D. 1781. (c.)

Capt.

Thomas Robinson.

Lt.

Andrew Shell.

Ensn.

James Miller.

Serts.

Henry Goepfert.
Michael Shell.
Jacob Wagler.

Privates.

1st Class.

Stoffel Meisenhelder.
Abraham Wolgamuth.
John Staufer.
Mathias Blantz.
Robert Robinson.
John Stern.
Andrew Moor.
Jacob Hummer.
John Snyder, Junr.
John Forry.
Philip Seitnenstriker.
John Noll.

2nd Class.

Robert Moorhead.
John Peler.
John Leman, Junr.
Michael Royer.
John Leman, in Rapho.
Frederick Gantz.
Lorance Kuns.
Jacob Eshelman.

3rd Class.

John Goepfert.
Christian Wolgamuth.
George Goepfert.
William Moor.
Michael Hummer.
John Leman.
Anthony Bratz.
Philip Keiser.
Philip Keener.
Ephraim Little.
Philip Frederick.
William Weyley.
Andrew Walles.

4th Class.

Isaac Dettey.
Jacob Keener.
Abraham Reeser.
Benjamin Benter.
Melcher Fortney.
John Wanger.
Anthoney Shoemaker.
Isaac Eshelman.
Jacob Conrad.
Jacob Fauvenberker.

5th Class.

James Moorhead.
William Allison.
Valentine Hide.
David Flory.
Jacob Shelly.
John Springer.
John Flory.
Christian Reeser.
Casper Lesher.
John Whitmer.
John Brubaker.
Peter Frederick.
John Gisch.
France Grove, Junr.
John Kemrer.

6th Class.

Christian Herr.
Andrew Robinson.
Jacob Kuns.
Thomas Welley.
Philip Shoemaker, Junr.
Christian Witmer.
John Hummer, Junr.
John Shelly.
Abraham Flory.
Michael Eby.
Isaac Wenger.
Conrad Springer.
Jacob Stauffer (at Obers).
Joseph Wolff, Junr.
John Grove.
James Wilson.
George Alspaugh.

7th Class.

Frederick Stolar, Jn.
Jacob Haldiman.
Henry Limbert.
Peter Welker.
Abraham Eshelman.
Jacob Shelly (Black).
Abraham Eckert.
Isaac Boraway.
John Frederick.
George Nickey.
Henry Ober.
Abraham Ettey.
John Bentter.
Daniel Hoover.
James Carns.
Sebastian Dunkel.
Jacob Krebill.
Martin Griner.
John Herr.

8th Class.

John Beard.
Philip Kemrer.
David Meisenhelder.
William Boal.
Daniel Conrad.
Abraham Wolff.

John Gould.
Michael Notz.
Abraham Grove.
George Kuns.
Lorance Schneeringer.
Peter Brubaker.
Nicklous Hide.
George Shanke.
Jacob Forry.
Peter Brubaker, Jur.
John Holdiman.
John Hoffman.

Certified by me the 29th day of May, 1781.

THOMAS ROBINSON, Capt.

MAY YE 30TH, 1781.

A RETURN OF CAPT. ANDREW BOGG'S COMPANY OF THE SEVENTH BATTALION OF MILITIA IN LANCASTER COUNTY COMMANDED BY COL. ALEX'R LOWREY. (c.)

Capt.

Andrew Boggs.

Leut.

James Cook.

Ens.

John Messer.

Serjts.

1st, Nicholas Redsacker.
2d, Phillip Clugh.
3d, George Snapper.

Corp.

1st, John Tison.
2d, James Flinn.
3d, John Drivenstate.

1st Class.

Joseph Galbreth.
John Eversole, Sr.
John Nicolas.
John Haldiman.
John Bower.
John Mumah.
Christian Blasor.
Joseph Shirk.
John Crill.
Jacob Earley.
John Smith.
John Grider, Junr.
William Gray.

2nd Class.

Abraham Neesly.
Henry Cip.
Michal McCaferty.
John Gray.
George Root.
Jacob Bosler.
Jacob Neesly.
John Eversole, Junr.
Thomas Hasson.
Robart Thompson.
John France.
Andrew Bower.
George Newbery.
Fredrick Batts.

3rd Class.

Christian Horst.
John Bruniman.
John Cooble.
Samuel Scott.
John Wiland, Junr.
John Laver.
John Early.
Phillip Stam.
John Cornhors.
Jacob Claper.

4th Class.

John Sharp.
Phillip Holinger.
Abraham Sheaver.
Benjamin Whisler.
Jacob Barrick.
Arthur Tagert.
Jacob Holinger.
John Esleman.
John Neesly.

5th Class.

Alexander Boggs.
Martin Hisey.
David Cooble.
Randle McClure.
Jacob Eversole, Jr.
Petter Hisey.
Robert Craig.
James Young.
Bartrim Galbreth.
David Jamison.
Michal Neesly.
Robert Connel.
John Elder.
Abraham Whitmor.
John Coal.
Hugh McBride.
John Beech.

6th Class.

Samuel Wilson.
William Hawk.
Samuel Woods.
Christian Bruniman.
John Longnecker.
Hugh Moore.
Petter Root.
John Cook.
Christian Bruniman, Jr.
John Shank.
John Grider.
Adam plats.
William Messer.
Jacob Oldwiler.
Jacob Brubacker.
Christian Fisher.
George Hikes.
John Wilson.

7th Class.

Petter Hailsomer.
Jacob Angle.
Henry Kintick.
John Horst.
Jacob Laver.
Daniel Kinsinger.
James Murphey.
Zachariah Moor.
Jacob Winecop.
David Martin.
Jacob Shimph.
Joseph Rheam.
Jacob Bruniman.
George Edmond.
Abr'm Fredrick.
Jacob Snider.
Hug Donoly.

8th Class.

Isack Rheame.
Jno. Brubacker.
Henry Wilhelm.
Robert Wilson.
John Angle.
John Neesly.
Thomas Messer.
Daniel Stamler.
Petter Blasor.
Jno. Wiland, Senr.
Abr'm Scott.
Joseph Hisey.
Jac'b Carpenter.
Jno. Dukenineer.
Abrm. Wilsiegal.
Mathew Gray, Junr.
Henry Darr, Junr.
Willm. Peck.
Thomas McGee.
Petter Trayor.

I certify the above return to be just and true.
Certyd. be

AND'W BOGGS, Capt.
June ye 9th, 1781.

to COL. LOWEY,
7th B. L. C. M.

A RETURN OF CAPT. PATTRICK HAYES' COMPANY OF 7TH BATT'N FOR MAY 31TH, 1781. (c.)

Capt.

Pattrick Hayes.

Lieut.

Benjamin Mils.

In'n.

James Hutcheson.

Sergents.

Robert Corry.
James Steret.
Arthur Patterson.

Corpalers.

Barnard Martin.
Jacob Aaron.
William Williams

1 Class.

Christy Hoofman.
John Shank.
John Hayes.
Christy Erishman.
Philip gilman.
Robert Mears.
Edward Watterson.
Baltzor Stake.
Pattrick Burns.
John grise.

2 Class.

John Shelhorn.
Abraham Kastle.
John Metz.
Caust Weyble.
Michael goodal.
Petter Willer.

3 Class.

Ludwick Metz.
Christy Long.
Henry Strickler.
Baltzer Watter.
Wendal Martzel.
Michael Hostler.
Henry Teesinger.
John Beard.

4 Class.

Samuel Robinson.
James Patterson.
Joseph Lytle.
Robert Ellis.
Jacob Bender.
Baltzer Shelhorn.
John Somy.
Abraham Martin.
Daniel Shits.
John Lisher.
Michael Stake.
John Welgar.
Samuel McClun.

5 Class.

Hugh grahms.
Michael Hosst.
Petter Watter.
Jacob Hostater.
Christy Longnecker.
Henry Okes.
John Mesba.
Charles Welger.
Martin Neisly.
Michael goodadle.
george gambler.
Jonathan Joans.

6 Class.

Christy Holdeman.	John Vance.
Abraham Metz.	Michael Segrast.
George Bergalbrough.	Mathias Kister.
Thomas Minto.	Isack gilman.

7 Class.

William Porter.	William Mears.
Henry Hoobly.	John Baker.
Petter Hasten.	Philip Baker.
James Sterrat.	John Speckler.
Neal Welsh.	Jacob Kastle.
John Rora.	Christy Mets.
Ully Strickler.	Jacob McKinney.

8 Class.

Jacob Erishman.	David Moore.
Jacob Metz.	Michael Lisher.
Jacob Erishman.	Abraham Erishman.
John Sweny.	William Sterret.
Jacob gantster.	Petter Youts.
Abraham Cubert.	John Porter.
John Brown.	James Buchanan.
John Boggs.	

I do Certify on Honor the above to be a true State of my Comp'y.

PATTRICK HAYES, Capt.

MUSTER ROLL OF 2ND CLASS, 7TH BATALL. ON A TOUR OF DUTY AT LANCASTER. (c.)

Names of Persons Who Served.	Names of Persons Who Furnsd. Substit's.	Time when duty comm'd.	Time when duty ended.
Capt.		1781.	1781.
Abraham Scott,		June 26.	Aug. 25.
Lieut.			
Mathew Hay,			
Ens.			
James Miller,			
Clerk.			
Thos. Bally,			July 31.
Sergt.			
James Defrance,			Aug. 25.
James Smith,			July 23.
Jacob Wagle,	Philip Hipler,		Aug. 25.
Corpl.			
Martin Pitts,			July 28.
George Snapper,			
Jno. Musser,		July 2.	July 28.
Privates.			
Thos. Bally, Jur.,	David Lindon,	June 26.	Aug. 25.
James Macky,			July 28.
Saml. Kerr,			
Philip Morrison,			
John Mays,			July 28.
Thos. McClung,			
Eseklel Fleming,	John Barber,		Aug. 25.
Alex'r McClintick,	Wm. Moore,		
Robert Hunter,			July 29.
Cornelius Green,			July 28.
Fred'k Strouse,			July 23.
Mathew Gray,	Jno. Gray,		July 29.
Jacob Carbough,			Aug. 25.
Nicholas Sprill,	Archur Vance,	June 26.	Aug. 25.
Jno. Witherbolts,	James Fox,	June 26.	Aug. 25.
Chris'r Fisher,	And'w Bower,		July 23.
Philip Sellers,			Aug. 25.
Jno. Nixtorff,	John Holts,		Aug. 25.
Jno. Little,	Benjamin Nauman,		Aug. 25.
Danl. Myers,	Philip Stone,		
Alex'r Hunter,			July 15.
Wm. Hay,			July 29.
Wm. Smith,	Nich's Pack,		Aug. 25.

Lanc'r, July 1st, 81. Then mustered above Company as specified in above roll. AD'M HUBLEY, S. L. L'r C'y.

MUSTER ROLL OF 3D CLASS 7TH BATALL. LANC'R COUNTY MIL'A ON A TOUR OF DUTY AT LANC'R. (c.)

Names of Persons Who Served.	Names of Persons Who Furnsd. Substit's.	Time when duty comm'd.	Time when duty ended.
Lieut.		1781.	1781.
James Cook,		July 1.	Aug. 4.
Wm. Wiley,			Aug. 23.
Michl. Ween,	Philip Keener,		
Wm. Innis,			July 30.
Henry Hines,			July 29.
Joseph Brown,	John Flack,		Aug. 25.
Wm. Moore,			July 30.
Chris'n Kap,			July 24.
Saml. Cook,			July 30.
Wm. Siprill,	Ulry Tanner,		July 21.
Rich'd Donel,	Richard Kays,		Aug. 25.
Jno. Camaghan,	John Leman,		Aug. 25.
Henry Gibford,	say George,	July 2.	July 30.

A RETURN OF CAPTAIN NOAH CEASEY'S COMPANY, BEING THE FIFTH COMPANY OF THE SEVENTH BATTALION OF LANCASTER COUNTY MILITIA COMMADED BY CONNELL ALEXANDER LOWREL AUGUST 2ND, 1781. (c.)

Captain.

Noah Ceasey.

Lieut.

Christian Herkelrod.

Ensign.

Christian Detter.

Sergnts.

Jacob [illegible]yar. Marten Fore.
Philip Bretz.

Corpreis.

Mathias Helton.
Marten Betz.
Abraham Trotey.

Drummer.

Fredrick Drukamiller.

Fifer.

Emanuel Dyar.

1st Class.

John Wetmore.
George Hatz.
Daniel Lamon.
Henrey Hershey.
Abraham Kobel.
Jaob Snyder.
Christian Longneker, Jr.
Joseph Eversol.
Jacob Drukamilor.

2nd Class.

Adam Minich.
Peter Fooks.
Christian Wenger, Sen'r.
John Garhart.
Abraham Longneker.
Henrey Lesher.
Fredrick Spekler.
Casper Werner.
Jacob Myar.

3rd Class.

John Hatz.
Henrey Hines.
Abraham Laman.
John Gorman, Ju'r.
Christian Earhart.
Benj. Nowman.
Jacob Earhart.
Daniel Lamon, Ju'r.

4th Class.

John Rudey.
George Secrist.
Fredrick Korager.
John Fritz.
Christian Hernly.
Daniel Longonker.
Jacob Rife.
John Bumgardner.
John Brand.
John Shorer.
Adam Worfell.
Adam Rease.
John Menshell.
Christian Eversol.
Christian Snyder.
Joseph Hummer.

5th Class.

Soloman Longoneker.
Jacob Keller.
Thomas Hollinger.
Peter Fisher.

Andras Betz.	Jacob Heagey.
Abraham Gipel.	Thomas Stonrod.
Henrey Werley.	Peter Kaberly.
Abraham Heastand.	John Boroway.
	6th Class.
Conrod Wert.	Daniel Earhort, Jur.
Jacob Lithey.	John Gorman, Ju'r.
Henrey Longoneker.	Abraham Fooks.
Adam Motzaboch.	Wm. Turner.
George Hounstone.	Peter Platenbarger.
John Rupart.	
	7th Class.
Nicklos Lebrey.	John Dyar.
Matheus Long.	Fredrick Sousar.
Peter Humer.	Tobias Hollnger.
Peter Rule.	Michal Gudey.
John Nourman.	John Hernly.
Christian Kobel.	Christian Martin.
	8th Class.
Jacob Shole.	Jacob Gudey.
George Werner.	John Eabey.
Michall Huber.	Fredrick Nouman.
Andras Halter.	Adam Panter.
Eanas Henry.	George Fishoak.
John Huber.	John Rupert.

RETURN OF CAPT'N DAVID McQUEEN'S COMPANY OF THE SEVENTH BETALLON OF LANCASTER COUNTY COMMENCING OCTOBER 1ST, 1781. (c.)

Captain.
David McQueen.

Lieut.
Mathew Hay.

Ensign.
Thos. Logan.

Serjts.

Robt. Rhea.
William Moore.
Robt. McCleany.

First Class.

Jno. Hay.
Michael Prats.
Mathew Montgomery.
William Hall.
James Kelly.
Abrim Evil.
Michael Shenk.
Andrew Wallas.
Michael Brand.
Allex'r Kennady.
James Kilpatrick.
Philip Shoop.

Second Class.

William Hay, Jun'r.
Barnet McGlahlin.
Patrick Kelly.
Sam'l Wolf.
Rob't Buck, discharged.
Jno. Cansinger.
Mark Worst.
Rob't Hunter.
Abrim Stevick.
Jno. Linck.
Cornelus Green.
Will'm Carnaghan.
Christ'n Buck.
Henry Wolf.
Hen'y Eseleman.

Third Class.

James Morison.
Wm. Crossler.
Jno. Reasor.
Mich'l Frances.
Dewalt Grim.
Flawel Rowan.
George Null.
Mich'l Shirts.
Jacob Stopher.
James Smith.
Jno. Herion, discharged.
Jno. Belch.
Anth'y Buck.

Fourth Class.

Jno. Stickley.
Pat'k Lynch.
Jno. Stevick.
Hen'y Rowland.
James Kennady, dead.
James Donelson.
Abrim Reamer.
Arch'd Eliot.
Jno. Duncan.
Christ'n Brand.
Mat'w Wolf.
Wm. Simonton.
Allex'r Long.
Paul Sigg.

Fifth Class.

Christ'n Null.
Christ'n Snyder.
Stophel Bishop.
David Foster.

Conrod Wolf.
Will'm Hay, Sin'r.
Christ'n Stevick.
Sam'l McCleary.
Will'm Foster.
Sam'l Hess.
Philip Reamer.
Jno. Leach.
Peter Reesor, Jun'r.

Sixth Class.

And'w Foster.
Stophel Shenk.
Philip Bughman.
Peter Reesor, Sin'r.
Jno. Rhea.
Jacob Shire.
Jno. Thompson.
Rob't McQueen.
Joseph McClintock.
Clemis Shire.
Jno. Carnaghan.
Jno. Garret.
Joseph Stevick.

Seventh Class.

Peter Poorman.
Christian Dolobagh.
Jno. Johnston.
Charles Johnston.
Mich'l Pheltebarger.
Abrim Longneker.
Hanlin Painter, discharged.
James Kernaghan.
Will'm Buck.
Sam'l Pennel.
Rob't Allen, discharged.
James Hay.
James Beghim, discharged.
Jno. Allexander.
Jno. Shoop.
Adam Henry.

Eighth Class.

Allex'r McClintock, discharged
Dan'l Plough, discharged.
Jacob Meckley.
Jno. Meckley.
James Huey, discharged.
Fredrick Buck.
Patrick Cain.
Jno. Kennady.
And'w Hunter.
Peter Beeker.

Certifed December 4, 1781.

DAVID McQUEEN, Capt.

RETURN OF CAPT. THOMAS ROBINSONS COMPANY OF THE SEVENTH BETALLON OF LANCASR. COUNTY COMANDED BY COLN. ALLEXR. LOWRY, COMENCING OCTOBER 1ST, 1781. (c.)

Cap.
Thomas Robinson.

Lt.
Andrew Shell.

In.

James Miller.

Serts.

1. Henry Goepfert.
2. Michael Shell.
3. Jacob Wagler.

Privates.

1st Class.

Stoffel Meisenhelder.
Abraham Wolgamuth.
John Stauffer.
Robert Robinson.
John Stern.
Andrew Moor.
Jacob Hummer.
John Shnyder, Junr.
John Forry.
Philip Seidenstricker.
John Noull.

2nd Class.

Robert Moorhead.
John Peter.
John Leman, Junr.
Michael Royer.
John Leman, Rapho.
Frederick Gantz.
Lorance Kuntz.
Jacob Eshelman.
Jacob Walter.

3rd Class.

John Goepfert.
Christian Wolgamuth.
George Goepfert.
William Moor.
Michael Hummer.
John Leman.
Anthony Bratz.
Philip Keiser.
Philip Keener.
Ephraim Little.
Philip Frederick.
Andrew Walles.
William Heyley.

4th Class.

Samuel Gracham.
Isaac Detty.
Jacob Keener.
Benjamin Benter.
Melcher Fortney.
John Wanger.
Anthoney Shoemaker.
Isaac Eshelman.
Jacob Conrad.
Jacob Taubenberker.

5th Class.

James Moorhead.
William Allison.
Vallentin Hide.
David Flory.
Jacob Shelly.
John Springer.

John Flory.
Christian Reeser.
Casper Lesher.
John Whitmer.
John Brubaker.
Peter Frederick.
John Gisch.
France Grove, Junr.
John Kamrer.

6th Class

Christian Herr.
George Alspach.
Andrew Robinson.
Philip Shoemaker, Jr.
Christian Whitmer.
John Hummer, Junr.
John Shelly.
Abraham Flory.
Michael Eby.
Isaac Wanger.
Conrad Springer.
Jacob Stauffer, at Obers.
Joseph Wolff, Jr.
John Grove.
Thomas Weyley.

7th Class

Frederick Stolar, Junr.
Jacob Haldiman.
Henry Limbert.
Peter Weiker.
Abraham Eshelman.
Jacob Shelly.
Abraham Eckert.
Isaac Boraway.
John Frederick.
George Nicky.
Henry Ober.
Sebastian Duncle.
Abraham Etty.
John Herr.
John Benter.
Daniel Hoover.
James Carnes.
Jacob Grebill.
Martin Greiner.
Wm. McKinly.

8th Class.

John Beard.
Philip Kaemrer.
David Meisenhelder.
William Boal.
Daniel Conrad.
Abraham Wolff.
John Gould.
Michael Notz.
Abraham Grove.
Lorance Schneeringer.
Peter Brubaker.
Nicklous Hide.
George Shank.
Jacob Forry.
Peter Brubaker, Junr.
John Hoffman.
William Buck.
William Mc kain.

The Within Return Certifyed November 27th, 1781. By
THOMAS ROBINSON, Capt.

A RETURN OF CAPT. ANDREW SCOTT'S COMPANY 7TH BATT. LANCASTER COUNTY COMMENCING THE 1ST OF OCTOBER, 1781. (c.)

Captain.

A'm. Scott.

Lieut.

R't Cunningham.

Ensign.

A'm. Scott.

Serjeants.

David Scott.
Thos. Philips.
Jacob Petters.

1st Class.

Henry Hine.
A'm Black.
Leonard Negly.
F'd Strow.
A'm Sharer.
Jno. Albert.
Sam'l Smith.
A'm Stricler.
Jno. Black, Jun.
C'r Wiland.
Petter Stuts.
A'm Ream.
Jno. Waddle.
Henry Hise.
Jno. Black, Sen'r.

2nd Class.

Jno. Gray.
Petter Bishop.
Patt. Hackett.
Geo. Rumbah.
Petter Bredy.
Jno. Linch.
Henry Metzler.
Ab'm Herr.
Jacob Kensly.
Jacob Carbah.
George Williams.
Ja's Defrance.
Dan'l Ream.
A'r Hunter.
Jno. Marten, C's son.

3rd Class.

Jo's Ekenroad.
Jno. Musser.
Christian Cap.
Ab'm Miller.
Geo. Hoke.
Chris'n Nisly.
Sam'l Cochran.
Jno. Coble.
Jacob Leman.

4th Class.

W'm Bishop.
Cotleip Bishop.
Jacob Cofman.
Jno. Fistle.
C'n Martian.
F'd Keaty.
Jno. Nisly.
Rudy Pesam.
C'n Eater.
Jacob Frear.
Jos. Jones.
Fk. Bealor.
Ja's Bready.

5th Class.

Ja'ob Stofer.
David Boyd.
Philip Bishop.
W'm Poorman.
Mel'r Poorman.
Jno. Cofman.
Geo. Ridsaker.
Fim Conner.
France Swope.
Philip Smith.
M'l Oxor.
Jno. Kinsly.
Jno. Bishop.
C'tn Whitmore.
Jacob Shelly.
A'm Speck.
Daved Coble.
Jacob Eversole.
Jno. Martain, J'r.
Conrad Shire.
Conrad Moyer.

6th Class

Ct'n Martian, Sen.
Fred. Batz.
Petter Ereston.
A'r Barnet.
C'n Black.
Peter Shafer.
Jacob Palmore.
Leo'd Petters.
Ja's Conner.
C'n Ekinroad.
J'b Foglesong.
Geo. Stake.
An'w Grose.
Sam'l Batsler.
George Blasor.
Jno. Shomaker.

7th Class

Petter Leman.
W'm Scott.
Henry Penter.
Jno. Foreman.
Antony Snider.
Jno. Singer, Jur.

Samson Babb.
Dan'l Murfy.
A'm Kish.
Ja'b Sharer.
Isaac Hernly.
W'm Smith.
C'n Martlan.
A'r Barr.

8th Class.

M'l Petters.
Jno. Martlan.
Petter Cap.
A'm Shelly.
Jacob Shafer.
Jno. Onger.
Mar'n Nisly.
Sam'l Ream.
Jacob Shelly.
Jno. Kinsinger, Sen.
Isaac Gruber.
Dun. Leviston.
Petter Blasor.
Henry Cu'p.
R't Gilleland.

ROLL OF THE 4TH, 5TH & 6TH CLASS OF THE 7TH BATALION LAN'R NTY MILITIA ON A TOUER OF DUTY IN BUCKS COUNTY. 1781. (c.

Names of Persons who perform a touer of Duty.	What Class.	Names of Persons who fuished Substitutes.	Time when Duty Commenced.	Time when Duty ended.
Capt.				
David McQueen,	4th,			
Noah Keasey,	5h,			
Lieut.				
Andrew Shell,	4th,			
James Kook,	6th,			
Ensgn.				
John Messer,	4th,			
Jas. [illegible]on,	7th,			
Serjt.				
Thomas Payn,	4th,			
Robert Rhey,	4th,			
Michael Shell,	4th,			
Drumer.				
Henry Stouffer,				

ROLL OF THE 4TH, 5TH & 6TH CLASS OF THE 7TH BATALION LAN'R COUNTY MILITIA ON A TOUER OF DUTY IN BUCKS COUNTY. 1781.—Continued.

Names of Persons who perform a touer of Duty.	What Class.	Names of Persons who furnished Substitutes.	Time when Duty Commenced.	Time when Duty ended.
Privates.				
John Shape,	4th,			
William Hall,	4th,			
Ezichiel Fleming,	4th,	ohn Esleman.		
James Karns,	4th,	William Bishop.		
Joseph Sink,	4th,	John Fitzall.		
Peter Kerbach,	4th,	Christian hn.		
James Breadey,	4th,			
John Crimes,	4th,	Samuel Crimes.		
ohn Duncan,	4th,			
Luke Jolly,	4th,	Joseph Lightel.		
Robert Allis,	4th,			
Samuel McLeenn,	4th,			
Thomas Mentow,	4th,			
John Vance,	4th,			
Henrey Stauffer,	4th,	Samuel Robison.		
Frederick Waggoner,	4th,			
John Bomgardner,	4th,			
Adam Wiefel,	4th,			

Samuel Mis,	4th,	John Myer, Junr.
Patrick Burns,	4th,	James Patterson.
Jacob Toffnberger,	4th,	
Serjts.		
Daniel Learey,		
Mathias Min,		
Privates.		
John Ck,	5th,	Tim Conner.
bert Connel,	5th,	
John Elder,	5th,	
John Gl,	5th,	
Philip Bisp,	5th,	
John Gan,	5th,	
Michl. Oxer,	5th,	*John Bishop.
Henry Maycrantz,	5th,	
William Scott,	5th,	
Christian Bausser,	5th,	
William Foster,	5th,	
Samuel McClearey,	5th,	
Henry Kock,	5th,	Stephen Bishop,
Hml Dyar,	5th,	
William Raske,	5th,	
Mic Rods,	5th,	
John I Mr,	5th,	John Kinkey.
Henrey Oker,	5th,	
Charles Walker,	5th,	
Jonathan Ie,	5th,	
William McKinley,	5th,	
Philip Koutz,	5th,	
Thomas Hollinger,	5th,	
Serjt. Frek. Kilbrue,	6th,	
Imes Duff,	6th,	Samuel Wilson

ROLL OF THE 4TH, 5TH & 6TH CLASS OF THE 7TH BATALION LAN'R COUNTY MILITIA ON A TOUER OF DUTY IN BUCKS COUNTY. 1781.—Continued.

Names of Persons who perform a touer of Duty.	What Class.	Names of Persons who furnished Substitutes.	Time when Duty Commenced.	Time when Duty ended.
John Wilson,	6th,			
Alexr. Barnett,	6th,			
Peter Shaffer,	6th,			
Leanard Peters,	6th,			
Christian Ekenrods,	6th,			
Jacob Togulson,	6th,			
Dommlnic Eagle,	6th,	Andrew Gross.		
John Shoemaker,	6th,			
John Rhey,	6th,			
Robert McQueen,	6th,			
John Thompson,	6th,			
Clemt. Shire,	6th,			
James Bayley,	6th,	Christian Swarts.		
Matw. McGomerey,	6th,	Stauffer Shank.		
Andrew Foster,	6th,			
Joseph McClintick,	6th,			
William Williams,	6th,			
James Crethers,	6th,	Jacob Detweiler.		
Cornelius Losartis,	6th,			

Edward Long,	6th,	Frederick Caregan.
Philip Britz,	6th,	
Peter Blattenberger,	6th,	
Andrew Robison,	6th,	
William McGearey,	6th,	
Jacob Shire,	6th,	
Arther Patterson,	6th,	
George Hawnslown,	6th,	
David Cook,	6th,	
John Beard,	5th,	
Joseph Wolf,		No pay to be drawn.

MUSTER ROLL OF THE 7TH CLASS OF THE 7TH BATALION OF LANC'R COUNTY MILITIA ON A TOUER OF DUTY AT LANCASTER. (c.)

Names of Persons who perform a touer of Duty.	What Class.	Names of Persons who furnished Substitutes.	Time when Duty Commenced.	Time when Duty ended
Capt.			1781.	1781.
Robert Mc Cay,	7th,		Octr. 15,	Dec. [illegible]
Leiut.				
Benjamin Mills,			Octr. 20th,	
Ensgn.				
[illegible] Willson,			Octr. 20th.	
Serjts.				
James Patton,	7th,		Octr. 20th.	
James Starrett,	7th,		Octr. 20th.	
Daniel Leary,	7th,	Philip Branner,	Octr. [illegible]	
Corpl.				
Jacob Arndt,	7th,		Octr. 20th.	
Drum.				
Christn. Bl[illegible]nill,	7th,	Martin Griner,	Octr. 20th.	

Fife.			
Peter Thindley,	7th,	John Frederick,	Octr. [illegible]
Privates.			Discharged.
Adam Keller,	7th,	James Hay,	Octr. [illegible]
John McLaughlin,	7th,		Octr. [illegible]
Jacob Winecoop,	7th,		Octr. 20th.
William Porter,	7th,		Octr. 20th.
John Cook,	7th,	John Soop,	Octr. [illegible]
Robert McCleery,	7th,		Octr. 20th.
James [illegible],	7th,	James Scott,	Octr. 20th.
William Allison,	7th,	Jacob Crebill,	Octr. [illegible]
Elder Breden,	7th,		Octr. 20th.
Neal Welsh,	7th,		Octr. 20th,
[illegible] McKinley,	7th,		Octr. [illegible]
Michael Judy,	7th,		Octr. 20th.
James Cerns,	7th,		Octr. 20th.
Adam Matzebacher,	7th,	Nicholas Librigh,	Octr. 20th.
[illegible] Cample,	7th,		Octr. 20th.
William Leard,	7th,	James Leard,	Octr. 20th.
John Cain,	7th,		Octr. 20th.
Josias Kender,	7th,		Octr. 20th.
John Neseman,	7th,		Octr. 20th.
John Noble,	7th,		Octr. 20th.
John Dyar,	7th,		Octr. 20th.
Chrisn Fisber,	7th,	[illegible] Frederick,	Octr. 20th.
John Hood,	7th,	John Allexander,	Octr. 20th.
John [illegible]r,	7th,		Octr. 20th.
Alexr. Russell,	7th,	James I [illegible]ell,	Octr. 20th.
Henrey Hoover,	7th,	Philip Baker,	Octr. [illegible]
John Acord,	7th,	Abraham Acord,	Octr. [illegible]
Robert [illegible],	7th,	Peter Poorman,	Octr. [illegible]
Daniel [illegible]r,	7th,		Octr. [illegible]
Samuel Smith,	7th,	Isaac Burroway,	Octr. [illegible]

MUSTER ROLL OF THE 7TH CLASS OF THE 7TH BATALION OF LANC'R COUNTY MILITIA ON A TOUER OF DUTY AT LANCASTER.—Continued.

Names of Persons who perform a touer of Duty.	What Class.	Names of Persons who furnished Substitutes.	Time when Duty Commenced.	Time when Duty ended.
			1781.	1781.
Frederick Sousser,	7th,		Octr. 20th.	
John Long,	7th,		Octr. [illegible]	[illegible]
John Bender,	7th,		[illegible] 20th.	
George Hounstain,	7th,	Mathias Long,	[illegible] 20th.	
Abraham Eaton,	7th,		Octr. 20th,	[illegible]
Robert Wilson,	7th,	Robert Ballers,	Octr. 20th.	
John Poorman, Corpl.,	7th,		Octr. [illegible]	
Samuel Thompson,	7th,		Octr. 20th.	
Henrey Hubley,	7th,		[illegible] 20th,	[illegible] 25th.
James Kiel,	7th,		[illegible] 20th,	Oct. 25th.
Joseph Sinck,	7th,		[illegible]	
James Kilpatrick,	7th,	Frederick Steber,	Octr. 20th.	
Sebastian Duncan,	7th,		Octr. 20th.	
Thomas Wiley,	7th,	Adam Cover,	Octr. 20th.	
Henrey Shaffner,	7th,		Octr. [illegible]	
Anthony Snyder,	7th,		[illegible] 20th.	
John Trevenstat,	7th,		Octr. 20th,	[illegible] 25th.
Daniel Murphy,	7th,		Octr. 20th.	

John Earley,	7th,	John Crebill,	Mtr. 20th.	
Charles Johnson,	7th,		Qtr. 20th.	
James Alison,	7th,	George Alison,	Octr. 20th.	
Jacob Carbough,	7th,	Sampson Babb,	Octr. 20th.	
Jacob Shump,	7th,		Octr. 20th,	Dec. [illegible]
Robert Connel, Corpl.,	7th,	William Clingan,	Octr. 20th.	
John Wilson,	7th,	Zacharias Moor,	Octr. 20th.	
Jacob Jones,	7th,	Frederick Miller,	Qtr. 20th,	Dec. 25.
James Johnson,	7th,		Octr. 20th.	
William Mears,	7th,		Octr. 20th.	
James Kernahon,	7th,		Octr. 20th.	
Daniel Ellet,	7th,		Qtr. 20th.	
John McKee,	7th,		Qtr. 20th.	
Jared Penwell,	7th,	Say Samuel,	Octr. 20th,	Decr. 1st.
William Smith,	7th,		Qtr. 20th.	

NOVEMBER 27, 1781.

A RETURN OF CAPT. ANDREW BOGG'S COMPANY OF THE 7TH BATTALION OF MILITIA IN LANCASTER COUNTY COMMANDED BY COL'N ALLEXANDER LOWREY. (c.)

Captain.

Andrew Boggs.

Lieut.

James Cook.

Ensign.

John Messer.

Serjents.

Nicolas Redsacker.
George Snaper.

Corporals.

John Tison.
John Drivenstate.
James Flin.

1st Class.

Joseph Galbrreth.
John Eversole, Sen'r.
John Nicholas.
John Holdiman.
John Mummah.
Christian Blaser.
Joseph Shirk.
John Crill.
Jacob Earley.
John Smith.
John Grider, Jun'r.
William Gray.
Joseph Shank.

2nd Class.

Abraham Neesly.
Henry Clp.
Michale McCaferty.
John Gray.
George Root.
Jacob Bosler.
Jacob Neesly.
John Eversole, Jun'r.
Thomas Hasson.
Robert Thompson.
John France.
Andrew Bower.
George Newbery.

3rd Class.

Christian Horst.	John Laver.
John Bruniman.	John Earley.
Sam'l Scott.	Phillip Starn.
John Wiland, Jun'r.	John Cornhors.

4th Class.

John Sharp.	Jacob Barrick.
Philip Holinger.	Jacob Holinger.
Abraham Shearer.	John Esleman.
Benjamin Whisler.	John Nickey.

5th Class.

Allexander Boggs.	Robert Connel.
Martain Hisey.	John Elder.
Randle McClure.	John Beech.
Jacob Eversole, Ju'r, Smith.	Abraham Whitmer.
Petter Hisey.	John Coal.
Rober Craig.	Hugh McBride.
James Young.	Martin Lindamore.
Bartrim Galbreth.	Jacob Horine.
Michal Neesly.	

6th Class

Sam'l Wilson.	John Grider.
William Hawk.	Adam Plats.
Sam'l Woods.	William Messer, Jun'r.
Christian Bruniman.	Jacob Oldwiler.
John Longnecker.	Jacob Brubacher.
Hugh Moore.	Christian Fisher.
Petter Root.	George Hiks.
John Cook.	John Wilson.
Christian Bruniman, Jur.	Christian Stoner.
John Shank.	James Karr.

7th Class

Petter Hailsomer.	Zachariah Moore.
Jacob Angle.	Jacob Winecop.
Henry Kintick.	David Martin.
John Horst.	Jacob Shimph.
Jacob Laver.	Jacob Bruniman.
Daniel Kinsinger.	George Ammon.
James Murphey.	Abraham Fredrick.

8th Class.

Jacob Snider.
Isack Rheam.
John Brubacher.
Henry Wilhelm.
Robert Wilson.
John Angle.
John Neesly.
Thomas Messer.
Daniel Strambler.
John Wiland, Sen'r.
Abraham Scott.
Jacob Carpender.
John Dukemineer.
Abraham Wilslegle.
Mathew Gray, Jun.
Henry Darr.
William Peck.

The within return is certified by

ANDREW BOGGS, Capt.

RETURN OF THE 5TH COMPNEY OF THE 7TH BATTALION OF LANCASTER COUNTY MILITIA, NOVEMBER 27TH, 1781. (c.)

Captain.

Noah Ceasey.

Lieut.

Christian Herkelrod.

Ensign.

Christian Detter.

Sargents & Corporals.

Mathias Helton.
Jacob Myar.
Philip Bretz.
Marten Fare.
Marten Betz.
Abraham Trotey.

1st Class.

John Witmore.
George Hatz.
Daniel Laman.
Henrey Henrey.
Abraham Kobel.
Jacob Snyder.
Christian Longnkr, Jr.
Joseph Eversoal.
Jacob Drukamiller.
Jacob Galaden.
Jacob Srite.

2nd Class.

Adam Minich.
Peter Fooks.
Christian Wenger.
John Garhart.
Abraham Longnkr.
Henrey Lesher.
Fredrick Spickler.
Casper Warner.
Jacob Myar.
William Mattsiner.

3rd Class.

Jacob Eversoal.
John Camran.
John Hatz.
Henrey Hines.
Abraham Laman.
John Garman, Ju'r.
Jacob Earhart, discharged.
Benjamin Nowman.
Steven Chambers.
Adam Reek.
Mich'l Longnecor.
Henrey Trite.
Joseph Shock.

4th Class.

John Rudey.
George Secrist.
Frederick Karager.
John Fritz.
Christian Hemly.
Daniel Longankr.
Jacob Rife.
John Bomgardner.
John Brand.
John Sharer.
Adam Warffel.
John Minshall.
Christian Eversoal.
Christian Snyder.
Joseph Hummer.
Morgen Ginkins.

5th Class.

Andrew Shimp.
Andras Bortroff.
Christian Mumma.
Jacob Keller.
Thomas Hollinger.
Peter Fisher.
Andras Betz.
Abraham Gipell.
Henrey Warley.
Abraham Heastand.
Jacob Hagey.
Thomas Stonrod.
Peter Kuckerly.
John Boraway.
Emanal Dyer.
Daniel Laman, Jr.
Fredrick

6th Class

Conrod Wert.
Jacob Lithey.
Henrey Longanker.
Adam Motzaboch.
George Hounstone.
Daniel Earhart, Jr.
John Gorman.
Abraham Fooks.
John Keller.
William Turner.
Peter Platenborger.
Thomas Willimson.
Michal Fogelsonger.
Henrey Kling.

7th Class

Nickloas Lebrey.	Fredrick Souser.
Mathias Long.	Tobias Holinger.
Christian Martin.	Michal Gudey.
Peter Rule.	John Hernley.
John Nowman.	John Minich.
Adam Kober.	Henrey Bordelma.
John Dyar.	John Shumaker.

8th Class.

Jacob Shobe.	Christian Earhart.
George Werner.	Christian Wenger.
Michal Huber.	Fredrick Nawman.
Andras Halter.	Adam Pander.
John Rooport.	John Skalley.
Eanas Murrey.	Abraham Ramer.
John Hubar.	Peter Crumbane.
Jacob Gudey.	George Fishoak.

This is to certify that this is a gust and true Return of my Company Certifyd by me November 27th; 1781.

NOAH CEASEY, Capt.

A RETURN OF THE MEAL WHITE INHABITANCE OF THE FIRST COMPY, SEVENTH BATTALION LANC'R COUNTY MILITIA. (c.)

Capt.

Andw. Boggs.

Lieut.

James Cook.

Ensn.

John Messer.

Serjts.

Nichos Redcakor.	Geo'r Snaper.
Phillip Clugh.	

Corpl.

John Tison.	John Drivenstate.
James Flin.	

1st Class.

Joseph Galbreath.	Joseph Shirk.
John Eversole, senr.	John Crill.
John Nicholes.	Jacob Early.
John Holdeman.	John Smith.
John Bower.	John Grider, Junr.
John Mumah.	William Gray.
Christ'n Blasor.	

2nd Class.

Abram Neesly.	John Eversole.
Henry Cip.	Thos. Hasson.
Michl. McCaferty.	Robt. Thomson.
John Gray.	John France.
George Root.	Andw. Bower.
Jacob Bosler.	George Newbry.
Jacob Neesly.	Fredk. Batts.

3rd Class.

Christ'n Horst.	John Early.
John Bruneman.	Philip Starn.
John Cooble.	John Cornhorse.
Saml. Scott.	Jacob Claper.
John Daver.	

4th Class.

John Sharp.	Arthur Tigart.
Philip Holinger.	Jacob Holinger.
Abrm. Sharer.	John Eshelman.
Benjn. Whisler.	John Neegly.
Jacob Berrick.	

5th Class.

Alex'r Boggs.	Davd. Jameson.
Martin Hisey.	Michl. Neesly.
David Cooble.	Robt. Connel.
Randl. McClure.	John Elder.
Jacob Eversole.	Abrm. Whitmore.
Peter Hisey.	John Coal.
Rob't Crage.	Hugh McBride.
James Yong.	John Beach.
Bart'm Galbreath.	

6th Class.

Saml. Wilson.	John Shank.
William Hawk.	John Grider.
Saml. Woods.	Adam Plats.
Christ'n Brunlman.	Wm. Messer, Junr.
John Longnecker.	Jacob Oaldwiler.
Hugh Moore.	Jacob Brubacker.
Peter Root.	Christ'n Fisher.
John Cook.	George Hicks.
Christ'n Bruneman, Jur.	John Wilson.

7th Class.

Peter Hilsemore.	David Martin.
Jacob Angle.	Jacob Shimph.
Henry Kintick.	Joseph Rheam.
John Horst.	Jacob Bruneman.
Jacob Laver.	George Emmond.
Danl. Kinsinger.	Abram Fredrick.
James Murphy.	Jacob Snider.
Zacharia Moore.	Hugh Donely.
Jacob Winecop.	

8th Class.

Isack Rheam.	Abrm. Scott.
John Brubacker.	Joseph Hisey.
Henry Welhelm.	Jacob Carpenter.
Robt. Wilson.	John Dicker.
John Angle.	Abram Wilslegal.
John Neesly.	Math'w Gray, Junr.
Thos. Meeser.	Henry Darr, Junr.
Danl. Strimpler.	William Peck.
Peter Bleasor.	Thos. McGee.
John Wiland, Senr.	Peter Trayer.

I do certify the within is just and true return of my compy. for the year 1781.

Certifyed by

ANDW. BOGGS, Capt.

1781.

A RETURN OF THE MEAL WHITE INHABETANCE OF THE SECOND COMP'Y SEVENTH BATTALLION LANCA'R COUNTY MILITIA. (c.)

Capt.

Abra'm Scott.

Lt.

Rob't Cunningham.

Ensin.

Abra'm Scott, Jun'r.

Serjents.

David Scott.
Thos. Phillips.
Simes Chambers.
Jacob Petters.

1st Class.

Henry Hine.
Abra'm Black.
Leanord Negly.
Fredk. Strous.
Abra'm Shara.
John Àlbert.
Sam'l Smith.
Abram Strikler.
John Black, Jun'r.
Christ'n Wiland.
Peter Stuts.
Abra'm Reem.
George Wadle.
Henry Hise.

2nd Class.

John Gray.
Peter Bishup.
Patrick Hacket.
Geo. Rambach.
Peter Bready.
John Linch.
Hendry Metzler.
Abram Hear.
Jacob Kinsly.
Jacob Carbach.
James Defrance.
Danl. Reem.
John Martin.

3rd Class.

Joseph Econrode.
John Muser.
Christ'n Cap.
Abr'm Miller.
George Hoke.
Christ'n Neesly.
Jacob Lehman.

4th Class.

William Bishop.
Cutlip Bishup.
Jacob Cofman.
John Fisel.
Christian Martin.
Fred'k Kattey.
John Neesly.
Rudy Peasum.
Christ'n Eater.
Jacob Treaer.
Joseph Jones.
Fredk. Bealer.
James Bready.

5th Class.

Jacob Stoper.
Dav'd Boyd.
Sam'l Sims.
Phillip Bishop.
Wm. Poorman.
Michel Poorman.
John Coffman.
Geo. Redsacker.
Thim's Conner.
Frances Swope.
Phillip Smith.
Mich'l Oxer.
John Kinsly.
Jacob Shelly.
John Bishup.
Christ'n Whitmor.
Adam Spike.
David Coble.
Jacob Ebersole.
Conrod Shire.
Conrod Myer.
John Martin, Jun'r.

6th Class.

Christ'n Martin, Ju'r.
Fredk. Batts.
Peter Earston.
Alx'r Barnit.
Christ'n Black.
Peter Sheaver.
Jacob Palmore.
Leanord Peters.
David Swarts.
James Conner.
Christi'n Ekinrode.
Jacob Foglesong.
Christ'n Whitmor.
Geo. Stake.
Andw. Gross.
Sam'l Batsler.
Geo. Bleazer.
John Shoemaker.

7th Class.

Peter Leman.
W'm Scott.
John Alexander.
Henry Penter.
John Foreman.
Ant'y Snyder.
John Singer.
Samson Babb.
Dan'l Murphy.
Abram Guish.
Jacob Shara.
Isack Harnly.
W'm Smith.
Christ'n Martin.
Alex'r Barr.
David Guish.

8th Class.

Mich'l Peters.	John Holdeman.
John Martin.	John Long.
Peter Cap.	Isack Gruber.
Ab'rm Shelly.	Dunikan Leaveston.
Jacob Sheaver.	And'w Keriger.
John Onger.	Peter Bleasor.
Martin Neesly.	Henry Culp.
Sam'l Reem.	Rob't Gillelon.
John Kensinger.	

Certified by me

ABR'M SCOTT,Capt.
1781.

A TRUE RETURN OF THE MEAL WHITE INHABITANTS OF THE THIRD COMP'Y SEVENTH BATTALION LAN'R COUNTY MILITIA FOR THE YEAR 1781. (c.)

Capt.

Thos. Robenson.

Lieut.

And'w Shell.

Ens'n.

James Miller.

Sergeants.

Henry Geepfert.	Jacob Wagler.
Mich'l Shele.	

1st Class.

Stop'l Meisenhelter.	And'w Moor.
Abra'm Wolgomuth.	Jacob Hummer.
John Stofer.	John Snyder, Jun'r.
Mathias Blank.	John Furry.
Robert Robenson.	Phil. Stetenstreker.
John Stern.	John Null.

2nd Class.

Rob't Moorhead.	John Leaman, Rapho.
John Peter.	Fred'k Gantz.
John Leaman.	Larance Kuns.
Mich'l Royer.	Jacob Eshelman.

3rd Class.

John Goepfert.	Philip Keiser.
Christ'n Wolgomuth.	Philip Keener.
Geo. Goepfert.	Ephram Little.
William Moor.	Philip Fredrick.
Mich'l Hummer.	W'm Wiley.
John Leaman.	And'w Walles.
Anthny Bratz.	

4th Class.

Isack Dettey.	John Wanger.
Jacob Keener.	Anto'y Shoemaker.
Abra'm Reesor.	Isack Eshelman.
Benja'n Penter.	Jacob Conrade.
Mich'l Fortney.	Isack Foufenbarg'r.

5th Class.

James Moorhead.	Casper Lesher.
W'm Allison.	John Whitmore.
Vallentine Hide.	John Brubacker.
David Florry.	Peter Fredrick.
Jacob Shelly.	John Guish.
John Sprenger.	Frances Grove.
John Flory.	John Kemer.
Christ'n Reesor.	

6th Class.

Christ'n Herr.	Abram Flory.
And'w Robenson.	Mich'l Eaby.
Jacob Kuns.	Isack Wenger.
Thos. Wiley.	Conrad Springer.
Philip Shoemaker.	Jacob Staufer.
Christ'n Whitmore.	Joseph Wolf.
John Humer, Jun'r.	John Grove.
John Shelly.	James Dilson.

7th Class.

Fred'k Stolar.
Jacob HolDeman.
Henry Limpert.
Peter Welter.
Abram Eshelman.
Jacob Greable.
Jacob Shelly.
Martin Griner.
Abram Ecert.
Isack Boraway.
John Fredrick.
George Nickey.
Henry Ober.
Abram Etty.
John Herr.
John Benter.
Daniel Hoover.
James Carns.
Sabast'n Dunckel.

8th Class.

John Beard.
Philip Kenner.
David Misenhelter.
W'm Bowl.
Dan'l Conrade.
Abram Wolf.
John Gould.
Mich'l Notz.
Abram. Grove.
Geo. Kuns.
Larn. Sneeringer.
Philip Brubacker.
Nich's Hide.
Geo. Shank.
Jacob Furry.
Peter Brubacker.
John Holdeman.
John Hoffman.

The within Certified by me.

THOS. ROBINSON, Capt.
1781.

A RETURN OF THE MEAL WHITE INHABITANTS OF THE FOURTH COMP'Y SEVENTH BATTALION LAN'R COUNTY MILITIA IN THE YEAR 1781. (c.)

Capt.

David McQueen.

Lieut.

Math'w Hay.

Ins'n.

Thos. Logan.

Serg'ts.

Robert Rea.
William Moor.
Robert McCleary.

1st Class.

John Hay.
Mich'l Pratz.
Math'w Montgomery.
W'm Hall.
James Kelly.
Abram Evill.
Mich'l Shank.
And'w Wallis.
Mich'l Brand.
Alex'r Kennaday.
Wm. Carnahan.
Phillip Shope.
James Kilpatrick.

2nd Class.

W'm Hay.
Hen'y Eshelman.
Pat'k Kelly.
Sam'l Wolf.
Mark Worst.
John Cansinger.
Abram Stevick.
Rob't Hunter.
Corn. Green.
John Link.
Christ'n Buch.
Henry Wolf.

3rd Class.

Jas. Morrison.
Mich'l Frances.
John Reesor.
Flavel Rowan.
Dav'd Grim.
Mich'l Shirts.
Geo. Null.
James Smith.
Jacob Stopher.
John Beilh.
And'y Buck.

4th Class.

John Stickly.
Pat'k Linch.
John Stevick.
Henry Rowland.
James Kenaday.
James Donelson.
Abram Remer.
Arch'l Eliot.
John Duncken.
Christ. Brand.
Mat'w Woolf.
W'm Simonton.
Alex'r Long.
Paul Sigg.

5th Class.

Christ'n Null.
Sam'l McCleary.
Stoph'l Bishop.
W'm Forster.
Chris't Snider.
Sam'l Hess.
David Forster.
Philip Reamer.
Con'd Wolf.
John Leach.
Wm. Hay.
Peter Reaser.
Christ. Stevick.

6th Class.

And'w Forster.	Rob't McQueen.
Stoph'l Shank.	Joseph McClintock.
Phil'p Boughman.	Clemence Shire.
Peter Reeser.	John Carnahan.
John Reah.	John Garrett.
Jacob Shope.	Joseph Stevick.
John Shier.	

7th Class.

Peter Poorman.	W'm Buck.
Chris'n Dolebocb.	Sam'l Pennel.
John Johnston.	Rob't Allen.
Char's Johnston.	James Hay.
Mich'l Felteberger.	John Allexander.
Abram Longnecor.	John Shoop.
Hanlin Penter.	Adam Henry.
James Carnehan.	

8th Class.

Alex'r McClintock.	John Kenneday.
Dan'l Plough.	Pat'k Coyn.
Jacob Mickly.	Alex'r Hunter.
John Mickly.	W'm Crowzer.
James Hughey.	Barny McLaughlen.
Fred'k Buck.	

The within Certified by me.

DAV'D McQUEEN, Capt.

1781.

A RETURN OF THE MEAL WHITE INHABITATS OF THE FIFTH COMP'Y SEVENTH BATT'N LANC'R COUNTY MILITIA FOR THE YEAR 1781. (c.)

Capt.

Noah Ceasey.

Lieut.

Christ'n Herkelrode.

Ensign.

Christ'n Detter.

Sergts.

Jacob Messer.
Martin Forry.
Phillip Bretz.

Drummer.

Fredk. Drunkamiler.

Fifer.

Eman Dyer.

1st Class.

Mathias Helton.
Martin Betz.
Abram. Troty.
John Whitmore.
Geo. Hatts.
Danl. Leaman.
Henry Herskey.
Abram Kable.
Jacob Snyder.
Christ'n Longnaker.
Joseph Eversole.
Jacob Druckamiler.

2nd Class.

Adam Menick.
Peter Fawks.
Christ'n Wenger.
John Goarhart.
Abrm. Longnaker.
Henry Leaker.
Fred'k Speckler.
Gasper Werner.
Jacob Myer.

3rd Class.

John Hatz.
Henry Hines.
Abrm. Leamon.
John Gorman.
Christ'n Earhart.
Benj'n Nowman.
Jacob Earheart.
Danl. Leaman.

4th Class.

John Rudey.
Geo. Seecrist.
Fred'k Kereger.
John Fritz.
Christ'n Hernly.
Danl. Longnecker.
Jacob Rife.
John Bumgarner.
John Brand.
John Shearer.
Adam Warfel.
Adam Reall.
John Mincher.
Christ'n Eversole.
Christ'n Snyder.
Joseph Humer.

5th Class.

Solom'n Longnacker.
Jacob Heller.
Thos. Holenger.
Andw. Betz.
Abrm. Gipple.
Henry Werley.

Abrm. Heston.
Jacob Heagey.
Thos. Stonerode.
Peter Cookerly.
John Boraway.
Peter Fisher.

6th Class.

Conrod Worst.
Jacob Leythey.
Henry Longnecker.
Adam Metzebach.
George Hounstone.
Danl. Earhart.

John Gorman.
Abram Fowks.
John Keller.
Wm. Turner.
Peter Plateberger.

7th Class.

Nichos. Leborey.
Maths. Long.
Peter Humer.
Peter Rule.
John Nowman.
Chris'tn Kable.

John Dyer.
Fred'k Souser.
Tobias Hollnger.
Michl. Getty.
John Hernly.
Christ'n Martin.

8th Class.

Jacob Shole.
George Werner.
Michl. Hobrer.
Andw. Halter.
Enas Murry.
John Hubar.

Jacob Gadey.
John Eabry.
Fred'k Newman.
Adam Penter.
George Fishook.
John Ruport.

Certifyed by me.

NOAH CEASEY, Capt.
1781.

A RETURN OF THE MEAL WHITE INHABITANTS OF THE SIXT COMPY. SEVENTH BATL'N LANC'R COUNTY MILITIA IN THE YEAR 1781. (c.)

Captain.
Wm. Wilson.

Lieut.
James Cook.

Ensn.

James Wilson.

Serjeants.

William Comens. Philip Braner.
Fred'k Kelbough.

Fifer.

Henry Heans.

1st Class.

Fred'k Albright, John Gorner.
Peter Bowman. John Nighty.
Danl. Eliot. James Allison.
Fred'k Mumer. Larans. Fauntz.
John Dunlap. Jacob Lavenswiler.
Jacob Shireman. Jacob Hoseaple.
Phillip Wiant. John Grove, Ser.
James Clingen.

2d Class.

Adam Cline. James Karr.
John Mease. John Barber.
Nichols Peck. Christopher Long.
Thos. Bayly. Chrisly Pesler.
Simon Camron. Abrm. Long.
James Mackey. Henry Grove.
Thos. McClun. Henry Graft.
Jacob Hufman. Henry Grove, Junr.
Phillip Morrison. Thos. Bayly, Jur.
Arthur Vance.

3rd Class.

John Grove. Martin Miley.
Christ'n Heagy. Fred'k Yeach.
Peter Lindemore. Wm. Ginens.
Saml. Cook. Ulery Taner.
Danl. Longnacker. Martin Bougher.
Rich'rd Keys.

4th Class.

Thos. Thomson. Hugh Caldwel.
Uley Angel. Peter Leighty.
Saml. Stouver. John Emock.

George Fisher.	Christ'r Souder.
George Barr.	Chrisly Bugher.
John Bullon.	Adam Wiand.
Saml. Karr.	Thos. Pean.
Patrick M'Cormick.	John Hartman.

5th Class.

Joseph Kirkpatrik.	John Jordon.
Martin Lindemore.	John Scott.
Rob't Heslip.	Phillip Kuntz.
Jas. Anderson.	Geo. Claper.
Wm. Ruske.	Danl. Gilman.
Michl. Nicholes.	John Wiant.
Ludwick Rienhart.	James Gibens.
Hugh M'bride.	Danel Leary.

6th Class.

Christ'n Vineger.	John Yeach.
Abrm. Albert.	Rob't Porter.
Nichos. Hoffman.	Christ'n Mosey.
Jacob Wiant.	Wm. M'Geary.
Jacob Fantz.	Francs. Stuart.
Richard Allison.	Arthur Chamberlain.
David Cook.	Valintin Steer.
Adam Wantz.	John Brown.

7th Comp'y.

Jacob Hersha.	Peadon Cook.
Robt. Ballence.	Moses Moreland.
John Greable.	Saml. Thomson.
John Horst.	John Tate.
Wm. Clingen.	Fred'k Miller.
Rob't Caven.	Joseph Sink.
Peter Sellers.	

8th Class.

Abrm. Stouver.	Wm. Peck.
John Blesor.	John Kelbough.
Mathias Ipe.	Danl. Kenaday.
John Fisher.	Wm. Mckean.
Laughlan Ferree.	Harman Long.

Walter Bell.
Frad'k Bower.
Fred'k Siprell.
Jas. Feagon.
Nichlos Blasor.
Adam Nees.
John Holinger.

Certifiedby me

WM. WILSON, Capt.

1781.

A RETURN OF THE MEAL WHITE INHABITANTS OF THE SEVENTH COMP'Y SEVENTH BATTAL'N LANC'R COUNTY MILITIA IN THE YEAR 1781. (c.)

Capt.

Robt. McKee.

Lieut.

Hugh Hall.

Ens.

James McCleaster.

Sergents.

James Paton.
Mich'l Hain.
John Hannah.

1st Class.

Wm. Gray.
Henry Booser.
Jacob Causs.
Henry McGee.
George Allison.
Josep Rife.
Phillip Sellers.
John Frey.
John Ritsell.
Alex'r Rusell.
Jacob Shelly.

2nd Class.

Jacob Rife.
John Pifer.
James Coyl.
Geo. Booker.
Fred'k Shoat.
Stephen Phelix.
Jacob Hashbarger.
Conrad foutz.
Barny Thrum.
Jacob Neesly.
Patrick Laferty.
Christ'n Plough.
John Miller.
[illegible]

3rd Class.

John Reesor.	Henry Bricker.
William Jameson.	Barny Manly.
David Tatwiler.	David Allison.
John Sharr.	Phillip Shoat.
Abram Gingery.	Henry Alliman.
Jacob Metzker.	

4th Class.

Jacob Smith.	Fred'k Wagner.
John Branser.	Dines Stall.
James Hineman.	Jacob Books.
Thos. Oagle.	Robt. Henderson.
John Myers.	Geo. Crabner.
Henry Sharer.	Henry Booser.
Peter Booker.	Henry Ridly.
Conrad Crabner.	

5th Class.

Sam'l Clark.	John Campble.
Joseph Prim.	Abrm. Shuney.
John Whitmore.	John Simerman.
Mich'l Road.	John Booser.
John Gingery.	Wm. Scott.

6th Class.

Christ'n Branser.	Jacob Breacker.
Wm. Mills.	Peter Rodrock.
Jacob Tatwiler.	Geo. Bower.
Christ'n Burkholder.	Abram. Sherare.
Dan'l Boninc.	Corn's Laverty.
Peter Yeatz.	George Coons.

7th Class.

Danl. Eliot.	John Noble.
James McKee.	John Long.
Fred'k Sellers.	Henry Shafner.
John McKee.	James Johnston.
Elder Breadon.	James Scott.
John McGlachlon.	James Leard.
Josias Cander.	James McGines.
James Rusell.	John Kean.

8th Class.

Dav'd Thrum.	John Grimes.
Saml. Hanah.	John Jackson.
Fred'k Shafner.	Thos. Caleb.
Dan'l Shelly.	James Hughey.
Adam Thomas.	John Funk.

The above Certified by me.

ROBT. McKEE, Capt.

1781.

A RETURN OF THE MEAL WHITE INHABITANTS OF THE EIGHTH COMP'Y SEVENTH BATT'N LAN'R COUNTY MILITIA IN YEAR 1781. (c.)

Capt.

Pat'k Hay.

Lieut.

Benja'n Mills.

Ensn.

James Patterson.

Sergeants.

Rob't Curry.	Arthur Patterson.
James Starrit.	

Corporl.

Barn'd Martin.	Will'm Williams.
Jacob Aron.	

1st Class.

Christy Huffman.	Robt. Mears.
John Shank.	Edward Waterson.
John Hay.	Balser Stake.
Christy Earshman.	Pat'k Brines.
Philip Gilman.	John Grise.

2nd Class.

John Shelhorn.
Abr'm Cassel.
John Metz.
Mich. Goodel.

Castel Wible.
Peter Willer.
Jacob Speiles.

3rd Class.

Ludwig Metz.
Christ'n Long.
Henry Strickler.
Baltz'r Walter.

Wendel Metsel.
Mich'l Hostler.
Hen'y Teesinger.
John Beard.

4th Class.

Sam'l Robenson.
James Paterson.
Joseph Little.
Robt. Elies.
Jacob Penter.
Balzer Shelhorn.
John Suny.

Abr'm Martin.
Dan'l Shitz.
John Leasher.
Mich'l Stake.
John Weiger.
Saml. McClun.

5th Class.

Hugh Grimes.
Mich'l Horst.
Peter Walker.
Jacob Hostater.
Christ'n Longnecor.
Henry Oa-or.

John Meashea.
Charl's Weiger.
Martin Neisly.
Mich'l Goodel.
Geo. Gamel'r.
Jonath'n Joans.

6th Class.

Christ'n Holdeman.
Abrama Metz.
Thos. Minto.
Geo. Berglebough.

John Vance.
Mich'l Segrost.
Mathias leasler.
Isack Gilman.

7th Class.

Wm. Porter.
Henry Hubley.
Peter Herston.
James Starrit, Sen'r.
Neal Welsh.
John Rora.
Ubey Strickler.
Wm. Mears.

John Beacor.
Philip Beacor.
John Speckler.
Jacob Casel.
Christy Metz.
Jacob McKenny.
James Buchanan.

8th Class.

Jacob Erishman.	John Baggs.
Jacob Metz.	David Moor.
Joseph Brand.	Mich'l Leasher.
Jacob Erishman, Senr.	Abram. Erishman.
John Sweany.	Wm. Starret.
Jacob Gonsler.	Peter Yeats.
Abram Cubert.	John Porter.
John Brown.	

The above Certified by me.

PAT'K HAY, Capt.

1781.

These are to Certify that Chrisly Hear did the Duty of a Clark in my Comp'y for the year Eighty one. Given from under my hand this 20th of March 1782. (c.)

THOMAS ROBENSON, Capt.

May ye 28th 1782.

A RETURN OF CAPT. ANDREW BOGGS COMPANY OF THE SEVENTH BATTALION OF MILITIA IN LANCASTER COUNTY COMMANDED BY COLLN. ALXR. LOWERY, VIZ. (c.)

Capt.

Andrew Boggs.

Leut.

James Cook.

Ens.

John Messer.

Serjents.

Nicholas Redsaker.	Petter Leighty.
George Snapper.	Thom. Hason.

Corpls.

James Flin.	John Drivenstate.

Privates.

1st Class.

Joseph Galbreth.	Jacob Earley.
John Eversole, Senr.	John Grider, Junr.
John Nicholas.	William Gray.
John Bcwer.	Joseph Shank.
John Mummah.	John Neesly, Junr.
Christian Blaser.	Thomas Scott.
John Crill.	Petter Stouts.

2nd Class.

Abraham Neesly.	John Eversole, Junr.
Henry Cip.	Thomas Hasson.
Michale McCaferty.	Robert Thompson.
John Gray.	John France.
George Root.	Andrew Bower.
Jacob Neesly.	George Newberry.

3rd Class.

Christian Horst.	Jno. Earley.
John Bruniman.	Phillip Starn.
Saml. Scott.	Jno. Cornhors.
John Wiland, Junr.	Jacob Clapper.
John Laver.	Jno. Bruniman, Jur.

4th Class.

John Sharp.	Jacob Hollnger.
Phillip Hollnger.	John Esleman.
Abrm. Sheaver.	John Nickey.
Benjm. Whisler.	Mathew Gray, Junr.
Jacob Carrick.	Petter Leighty.

5th Class.

Martin Hisey.	Robert Connel.
Jacob Eversole, Junr., smith.	George Lindimore.
Petter Hisey.	John Elder.
Robert Craig.	Abrm. Whitmore.
Bartrim Galbreth.	Randle McClure.
Michale Neesly.	Christian Frantz.

6th Class.

Saml. Wilson.
William Hawk.
Saml. Woods.
Christn. Bruniman.
John Longnecker.
Hugh Moore.
Petter Root.
John Cook.
Christn. Bruniman, Junr.
John Shank.
John Grider.
Wilm. Messer, Junr.
Jacob Oldwiler.
Jacob Brubacher.
George Hikes.
John Wilson.
James Karr.
Christn. Stoner.
Nathan Woods.
Jacob Fuglesong.
George Counce.
Stophel Holinger.
Abrm. Albert.
John Grider, Sonr.

7th Class.

Petter Hailsomer.
Jacob Angle.
John Horst.
Jacob Laver.
James Murphey.
Zacharia Moore.
Jacob Winecop.
David Martin.
Jacob Stumph.
Joseph Rheame.
Jacob Bruniman.
Abrm. Fredrick.
Jacob Snider.
John Steman.
Saml. Thompson.
Abrm. Nessonger.

8th Class.

Isack Rheame.
Jno. Brubacher.
Henry Wilhelm.
Robert Wilson.
Jno. Angle.
Jno. Neesly, sn.
Thms. Messer.
Danl. Stramler.
John Wiland, sen.
Abrm. Scolt.
Joseph Hisey.
Jacob Carpender.
Jno. Dukemineer.
Abrm. Wilsiegle.
Mathew Gray, Senr.
Henry Darr.
Wilm. Peck.
Andrew Hikes.
Christn. Eversole.
Jno. Haldiman.
Henr. Bruniman.

The Within Return is Just & True Certifyd—

ANDREW BOGGS, Capt.

May ye 30th 1782.

A MUSTER ROLE OF CAPTON THOMAS ROBISON'S COMPANY BEING THE THIRD COMPANY OF THE SEVENTH BATTALION OF LANCASTER COUNTY MILITIA COMMANDED BY LIEUT. COL. ALEXANDER LOWRY COMMENCED ON THIS SEVENTH DAY OF OCTOBER 1782. (c.)

Capt.

Thomas Robinson.

Lieut.

Andrew Shell.

Ens.

James Miller.

Almanas.

Abraham Fredrick.

1st Class.

Henry Goepfert.
Michael Shell.
Jacob Wagler.
Stophel Meisenhelder.
Abraham Wolgomwith.
John Stouffer.
Robert Robison.
John Stern.
Andrew Moor.
Jacob Hummer.
John Schnyder.
John Forry.
Philip Seidenstricker.
John Null.
Philip Beill.
Andrew Hoover.

2d Class.

Robert Moorehead.
John Peter.
John Leman, Junr.
Michael Royer.
John Leman, in Rapho.
Fredrick Gantz.
Jacob Eshelman.
Jacob Walter.
Abraham Schnyder.

3rd Class.

John Geapfert.
Christian Wolgamwith.
George Geopfert.
William Moor.

Michael Hummer.
John Leman, Read.
Anthony Bretz.
Phillip Keiser.
Phillip Keener.
Ephraim Litle.
Philip Frederick.
Weilliam Weyley.
Joseph Sherk.
John Clark.

4th Class.

Isaac Dettee.
Jacob Keener.
Abraham Reeser.
Meilhar Fortney.
John Wagner.
Anthony Shoemake.
Isaac Eshelman.
Jacob Conrad.
Jacob Tubenbarger.
Jacob Hoffman.
Samuel Smith.
John Eshelman.
Benjamin Benter.

5th Class.

James Moorhead.
William Allison.
David Flory.
Vallentine Hide.
Jacob Shelley, Read.
John Springer.
John Flory.
Christian Reeser.
Casper Lesher.
John Brubaker.
Peter Frederick.
John Kish.
Francis Grove, Jur.
Jacob Miller, Jur.
Jacob Leman, moved.
John Bowman.

6th Class.

Christian Herr.
George Alspah.
Philip Shoemaker, Jur.
John Hummer, Junr.
John Shelley.
Abraham Flory.
Michael Ealy.
Isaac Wanger.
Conrad Springer.
Joseph Wolf, Junr.
John Grove.
David Roland.
Casper Keler.
Jacob Stouffer, at Over's.
William Connely.
George Bleazor.

7th Class.

Frederich Stolar, Junr.
Jacob Holdiman.
Martin Greiner.
Henry Limbert.
Jacob Grebill.
Peter Welker.
Abraham Eshelman.
Jacob Shelley.
James Carnes.
Abraham Eckert.
Isaac Boraway.
John Frederick.
William Smith.
George Nicky.

Henry Over.
Sebastian Duncle.
Abraham Ettey.
John Herr.
John Benter.
Daniel Hover.
William McKinley.
Abraham Stollar.
Martin Johan.
Hugh McGlaulin.

8th Class.

David Meisenhelder.
William Boal.
Daniel Conrad.
Abraham Wolf.
Michael Notz.
Larance Schneeringer.
George Shank.
Peter Brubaker, Jur.
John Holdiman.
John Hoffman.
William Mckain.
Abraham Goepfert.
Conrad Schreyer.
Jacob Conrad, Junr.
Philip Keemerer.
Henry Bell.
John Lemmon.

I do certify the within to be a just & true return as stated pr. me.

THOMAS ROBINSON, Capt.

Nov. 30th, 1782.

A RETURN OF THE FOURTH COMPANY OF THE SEVENTH BETALLION OF LANCASTER COUNTY COMMANDED BY COL'N ALLEXANDER LOWRY COMMENCING OCTOBER. 1782. (c.)

Captain.

David McQueen.

Lieut.

Mat'w Hay.

Ensign.

Thos. Logan.

1st Class.

John Hay.
Mathew Montgomery.
Jemes Kelly.
Michel Brand.

Michel Shenk.
James Kilpatrick.
Michael Prats, discharged.
Abrim Evill.
William Hall.
Philip Shoop.
Conrod Hembagh.
John M'Cleary.

2nd Class.

William Hay, Jun.
Patrick Kelly.
Mark Worst.
Abrim Stevick.
Cornlus Green.
Christian Buck.
Henny Alliman.
Barnet M'Glaghlin.
John Cansinger.
Robert Hunter.
John Linck.
Henry Wolf.
Robert Humes, discharged.

3rd Class.

William Moore, Serjt.
James Morison.
Dewalt Grim.
Michael Frances.
Flowel Rowan, discharged.
John Reesor.
Henry Coak.
Henry Asleman.
Fredrick Flinchbagh.

4th Class.

Robt. Rhea, Serjt.
David Hay.
James Defrance.
John Burnetor.
John Stukley.
John Stevick.
Abrim. Reamer.
John Duncan.
Archab'd Eliott.
Christian Brand.
Paul Segg.

5th Class.

Andrew Kelly.
James Duncan.
Christian Snyder, discharged.
Christian Null.
Stophel Bishop.
David Foster.
William Hay, Senr.
Christian Stevick.
Samuel McCleary.
William Foster.
Samuel Hess.
Peter Reesor, Junr.
Conrod Wolf, discharged.

6th Class.

John Craig.
Andrew Foster.
Philip Boughman.
Peter Reesor, Senr.
John Rhay.
John Thompson, discharged.
Robert M'Queen.
Joseph M'Clintock.
Clemes Shire.
Jacob Shire.
John Cornaghan.
John Garrit.
Joseph Stevick.

7th Class.

Robert M'Cleary, Serg't.
John Kellar.
Jacob Worst.
Peter Poorman.
Christian Dolobagh.
John Johnston.
Charles Johnston.
Abrim Longneker.
James Carnaghan.
James Hay.
John Allexander.
John Shoop.
Adam Henry.
William Allison.

8th Class.

Charles Dougherty.
Jacob Mickley.
John Mickley.
Fredrick Buck.
John Kennady.
Patrick Cain.
Andrew Hunter.
George Jordan.
Peter Beaker, discharged.
John Farmer.
Daniel Plough.
James Huey.

RETURN OF CAPT. NOAH CEASEYS BEING THE 5TH OF SEVENTH BATTALION OF LANCASTER COUNTY MILLITIA COMMANDED BY COL. ALEXANDER LOWREY NOVEMBER THE 26TH, 1782. (c.)

Capt.

Noah Ceasey.

Lieut.

William Smith.

Ens.

Christian Dettear.

1st Class.

John Witmore.
George Hatz.
Daniel Laman.
Martin Fare.
Henry Hershey.
Jacob Snyder
Christian Longankr, Jr.
Joseph Eversoal.
Jacob Druckinmelor.
Abraham Trotey.
John Kinkaly.

2d Class.

Adam Meneeh.	Jacob Myar.
Peter Foaks.	William Macksiner.
John Garbart.	Henry Winger.
Christian Wenger.	Peter Hagey.
Henary Lesher.	Thomas Spencer.
Casper Werner.	Jacob Nicklour.

3d Class.

John Camaron.	John Garman, Jr.
John Hatz.	Jacob Earhart.
Henry Hines.	Benjeman Nowman.
Gotleap Spone.	Peter Risht.
Abraham Laman.	Abraham Steigenwalt.
Michal Longanecker.	

4th Class.

Fred'r Karager.	John Sharon.
John Radey.	John Brand.
George Secrist.	Adam Worfel.
John Fritz.	Christian Snyder.
Christian Hernly.	Joseph Humer.
Daniel Longanker.	Morgen Jenkins.
Jacob Rife.	Tabias Ruster.
John Bomgardner.	Abraham Reamer.

5th Class.

Andrew Bartruff.	Peter Kuckerly.
Mathias Helton.	John Boraway.
Jacob Myar.	Daniel Laman, Jur.
Philip Bretz.	Henry Trite.
Fred'k Drukmeilr, Drumr.	Joseph Shock.
Emanal Dyar, fifer.	Michal Godadel.
Jacob Keller.	Jonas Hamer.
Abraham Heastand.	Christian Toner.
Jacob Hagey.	Charls Welker.

6th Class.

Conrod Wert.	George Hounstone.
Jacob Lithey.	Christian Herkelrod.
Henory Longnecker.	Jacob Earhart, Jur.
Adam Motzabocher.	John Garman, Jur.

Abraham Fooks.	Nickalos Hide.
William Turner.	Ulrich Kisear.
Peter Plotenborger.	Adam Keek.
Thomas Williamson.	Philip Arnold.
Michal Fogelsonger.	John Hagey.
Martin getter.	Fred'r platenbarger.

7th Class.

Nickalos Lebary.	John Hernly.
Matheas Long.	John Minich.
Martin Becker.	John Shumaker.
Peter Rule.	Abraham Eversoal.
John Nousman.	Abraham Humer.
Adam Rober.	Christian Martin.
John Dyar.	George Pifer.
Fred'r Souser.	John Humer.
Tobias Holinger.	David Fogelsonger.
Mickal Gudey.	

8th Class.

George Gantz.	Jacob Gudey.
George Werner.	Christian Wenger.
Michal Hubar.	Fred'r Nowman.
Andrew Halter.	George Ferhoah.
Jacob Shole.	Jeams Clune.
Eanas Murrey.	Christian Earhart.
John Eabey.	John Rupart.
John Habar.	Fred'r Roston.

I do certify the within to be a true return as stated pr. me.

NOAH CEASY, Capt.

Nov. 28th, 1782.

MUSTER ROAL FOR THE YEAR 1782. NOV. 26TH SEVENTH BATTALION, LANCASTER CO. (c.)

Captain.

Abram Scott.

Lieut.

Robt. Cuningham.

Ensign.

Abram Scott.

Serjts.

Thos. Phillips.
Jacob Peters.

1st Class.

Henry Hine.
Chr'n Holdiman.
Abr'm Black.
Leon'd Negly.
Fred. Strouse.
Abrm. Sharrer.
Jno. Albert.
Saml. Smith.
Abrm. Struklar.
Jno. Black, Junr.
Chrn. Wiland.
Abram. Ream.
Henry Hisse.
Wm. Hood.

2nd Class.

John Leman.
John Gray.
Peter Bishop.
Patr. Hacket.
Geor'e Rambach.
Peter Bredy.
Jno. Lynch.
Henry Metzlar.
Abram. Hear.
Jacob Kinsley.
Jacob Carbaugh.
Gorge Williams.
Jas. Defrance.
Danl. Ream.
Jno. Martin.
Henry Poorman.

3rd Class.

Jas. Ekenrode.
John Mussar.
Chrn. Cap.
Abrm. Millar.
Chrn. Neesley.
Jno. Coble.
Jacob Leman.
Jas. Chesnut.
Peter Carbach.

4th Class.

Nat'l Nilson.
Wm. Bishop.
Cotlip Bishop.
Jacob Coffman.
Jno. Fissal.
Crsn. Martin.
Fred. Ritey.
John Neesley.
Rudy Pesum.
Chrn. Eater.
Dad. Coble.
Jas. Jones.
Fred. Bilghear.
Jas. Breadey.
Syms. Chambers.
Jas. Carrethers.
Henry Mygrants.

5th Class.

Chrn. Brunlmen.
Jacob Stofer.
Dad. Boyd.
Philip Bishop.
Wm. Poorman.
Jno. Cofman.
Geor. Redsacker.
Timo. Conner.
Da'd Hamhacker.
Chrn. Keener.
Fran's Swope.
Philip Smith.

Mike Oxer.
Jno. Kinsley.
Jon. Bishop.
Crn. Whitman.
Jacob Shelley.
Adam Specke.
Da'd Cooble.
Jacob Eversole.
Jno. Martin, Jr.
Conrad Myor.
Arnold Baker.

6th Class.

Chrn. Patiston.
Jno. Stofer.
Chrn. Martin.
Fred. Bats.
Alex. Barnet.
Chrn. Black.
Peter Shaffer.
Jacob Palmar.

Leon'd Peters.
Jon'e Bard.
Jas. Conner.
Chrn. Ekenroad.
Andw. Groce.
Saml. Batslar.
George Bleasor.
John Hood.

7th Class.

Peter Leman.
Wm. Scott.
Henry Panther.
Chrn. Hide.
Jno. Poorman.
Domink Eagle.
Anthony Snider.
John Snider.
Phillip Braner.
Danl. Murphey.

Robt. Hood.
Abrm. Kish.
Isaac Hernly.
Wm. Smith.
Chrn. Martin.
Alexr. Barr.
Robt. Balance.
Jas. Brown.
Thos. Howard.

8th Class.

Abrm. Shelley.
Mikl. Peters.
Jno. Martan.
Peter Cap.
Jacob Shaffer.
Jno. Ungar.

Mart. Neessley.
Saml. Ream.
Jno. Kinsingar.
Isaac Gruver.
Duncan Livingston.
Henry Culp.

Robt. Gilliand.	Paul Grabler.
Peter Blaser.	Jacob Eberly.
Jno. Jamison.	Gorge Stake.
Crn. Shoemaker.	Jacob Hanneberger.

The above is a true Return of Capt. Ab'm Scott's. Certifyd Montjoy N'r 26, 1782.

R'T CUNNINGHAM, Lt.

A RETURN OF CAPT. ABR'M SCOTTS COMPANY FOR YE YEAR 1782 OF THE SEVENTH BATALION LANCASTER COUNTY MILITIA, COMMANDED BY COLL. ALEXD'R LOWREY. (c.)

Captain.

Abrm. Scott.

Lieut.

Robt. Cuningham.

Ensign.

Abrm. Scott.

Serjants.

Thos. Philips.	Jacob Peters.

1st Class.

John Holdeman.	Christian Wiland.
Hendry Hine.	Abraham Reem.
Abrm. Black.	Hendry Ilise.
Lenard Negly.	John Black, Sen.
Fredrick Strouce.	Adam Grocehart.
Abram. Sharar.	William Hood.
John Albart.	Abram Stricklar.
John Black, Jr.	

2nd Class.

John Liman, Junr.	Patrick Hackis.
John Gray.	George Rambach.
Peter Bishop.	Peter Bredin.

John Lench.
Hendry Mitzlar.
Abram Hear.
Jacob Kinsley.
Jacob Carback.
George Williams.
James Defrance.
Daniel Reem.
John Martin.
Hendry Poorman.

3rd Class.

Joseph Ekinrode.
John Mussar.
Christian Cap.
Abrm. Millar.
George Hoke.
Christian Neesly.
Saml. Cochran.
John Coble.
Jacob Leman.
James Chesnut.
Peter Carbach.

4th Class.

Nathaniel Nilson.
William Bishop.
Cotlip Bishop.
Jacob Cofman.
John Fissal.
Christian Martin.
Fredrick Ritty.
John Nisley.
Rudy Peasum.
Christian Eater.
Joseph Jonas.
Fredrick Bealer.
Jas. Bredy.
Sims Chambers.
Jas. Corithers.
Hendry Magrants.
David Eaby, Jur.

5th Class.

Christ. Pruniman.
Jacob Stofer.
David Boyd.
Philip Bishop.
William Poorman.
Melcher Poorman.
John Cofman.
George Ridsacher.
Timothy Conner.
David Hamaker.
Christian Keen.
France Swope.
Philip Smith.
Michael Oxer.
John Kinsley.
John Bishop.
Christian Whitmore.
Jacob Shelly, Jur.
Adam Speck.
David Cable, Senr.
Jacob Eversole.
John Martin, Jur.
Conrod Myer.
Arnold Baker.

6th Class.

Cristian Patestone.
John Stofer.
Christian Martin, Sen.
Phredrick Bats.
Alexr. Barnet.
Christian Black.
Peter Shafer.
Jacob Palmore.

Lenard Peters.	Andrew Groce.
John Biard.	Saml. Batsler.
Jas. Connor.	George Bleaser
Christian Ekinrode.	John Hood.
George Stake.	

7th Class.

Domenick Eagle.	Robt. Hood.
Peter Leman.	Abrm. Kish.
William Scott.	Isaac Harnly.
Hendry Penther.	Wim. Smith.
Christian Hide.	Christian Martin.
John Foreman.	Alexr. Baar.
Anthony Snider, Jr.	Robt. Balance.
John Singar.	Jas. Brown.
Philip Brannan.	Thos. Howard.
James Murphy.	

8th Class.

Abram Shelly.	Isaac Gruber.
Michael Peters.	Duncan Levingstone.
John Martin.	Hendry Culp.
Peter Sap.	Robt. Gihland.
Jacob Shafer.	Peter Bleaser.
John Onger.	John Jameson.
Martin Neasley.	Christian Shomaker.
Saml. Reem.	Paul Grabler.
John Kinsinger.	Jacob Eberly.

I do certify the above to Just and true to the best of my knowledge.

ABRM. SCOTT, Capt.,
In ye 2nd Co. 7 B. L. Col.

A TRUE AND EXACT LIST OF THE NAMES, OF EACH AND EVERY MALE WHITE PERSON, INHABITING OR RESIDING WITHIN MY DISTRICT, IN THE FIRST COMPANY, OF THE SEVENTH BATTALION OF LANCASTER COUNTY, MILITIA, BETWEEN THE AGE OF EIGHTEEN, AND FIFTY-THREE YEARS. TAKEN FOR THE YEAR 1782. (c.)

Capt.

Andrew Boggs.

Lieu.

James Cook.

Ens.

John Messer.

Almonar.

Hendry Cipe.

Sergents.

Nicholas Redsaker.
George Snaper.
Petter Leightey.

Corporals.

James Fline.
John Drivenstats.
Thomas Hasson.

Privates.

1st Class.

Joseph Galbreath.
John Eversole, Sr.
John Nickloss.
John Bower.
John Mummah.
Christian Blasor.
John Crill.
Jacop Earley.
John Grider, Jur.
Wm. Gray.
Joseph Shank.
John Neesley, Senr.
Thomas Scott.
Petter Stouts.

2nd Class.

Abraham Neesley.
Hendrey Cip.
Michal McCaster.
John Gray.
Gorge Roat.
Iasak Neesley.
John Eversol, Junr.
Robert Thompson.
John France.
Andrew Bower.
George Newberry.

3d Class.

Christian Horst.
John Bruniman.
Saml. Scott.
John Wiland, Jur.
John Laver.
John Earley.
Phillip Starn.
John Cornbas.
Jacop Claper.
John Bruniman.

4th Class.

John Shape.
Phillip Hollnger.
Abrm. Sheaver.
Benjm. Wislar.
Jacob Barrick.
Jacop Hollngar.
John Esleman.
John Nickey.
Mathew Gray, Jur.

5th Class.

Jacop Eversole, Jur., smith.
Marlaim Hisay.
Peter Hisay.
Robert Craig.
Bartrim Galbreath.
Michale Nesly.
Robert Connel.
Gorge Lendemore.
John Elder.
Randle McClure.
Christian Frantz.

6th Class.

John Longnecker.
Hugh Moor.
Petter Root.
John Cook.
Christn. Bruniman, Senr.
John Shank.
John Grider.
Wm. Messer, Jur.
Jacop Oldwilder.
Jacop Brubacker.
Gorge Hickes.
John Wolson.
James Karr.
Christn. Stoner.
Nathan Woods.
Jacop Faulssong.
Gorge Counce.
Stophel Hollnger.
Abram. Albert.

7th Class.

Petter Hallsomer.
Jacop Angle.
John Horst.
Jacop Laven.
Daniel Kissinger.
James Murphey.

Zacharia Moor.
Jacop Windcop.
David Martin.
Jacob Shimple.
Joseph Reem.
Jacop Bruniman.
Abrm. Fredrick.
Jacop Snider.
John Steman.
Saml. Thompson.

8th Class.

Robert Wilson.
John Angle.
John Nessley, Junr.
Thom. Messer.
Danl. Stramler.
John Willand, Snr.
Abrm. Scott.
Joseph Hisey.
Abrm. Carpender.
John Dickminer.
Abrm. Milsiegle.
Mathew Gray, snr.
Hendery Darr.
Wm. Peck.
Andw. Hikes.
Christn. Eversole.
John Holdiman.
Hindrey Bruniman.
Isack Rheeme.
John Brubacker.
Hendrey Wilhelm.

I Do swear, on the Holy Evengilest of Almighty God: That the above list is a just and true state, of the Male White Inhabitants, residing in my District, agreeable to law, and without any fraud to the State, to the best of my knowledge.

ANDW. BOGGS, Capt.

Sworn before me this 5th Day of June 1782.
WILLIAM KELLY, Sub. Lt.

A TRUE AND EXACT LIST OF THE NAMES, OF EACH AND EVERY MALE WHITE PERSON, INHABITING OR RESIDING WITHIN MY DISTRICT IN THE SECOND COMPANY, OF THE SEVENTH BATTALION OF LANCASTER COUNTY, MILITIA, BETWEEN THE AGE OF EIGHTEEN, AND FIFTY-THREE YEARS. TAKEN FOR THE YEAR 1782. (c.)

Capt.

Abrm. Scott.

Lieu.

Robert Cuningham.

Ens.

Abrm. Scott.

Almonar.

John Black.

1st Class.

Abrm. Black.
Christian Haldeman.
Hendry Hine.
Lenord Negley.
Fredrick Strouce.
Abraham Sharah.
John Albart. .
Samuel Smith.
Abraham Stricklar.
John Black, Junr.
Christian Wiland.
Abram Reem.
Hendry Hise.
Adam Grosehart.
William Hood.

2d Class.

Thomas Philips.
Jacob Peters.
Conrode Shire.
John Leman.
John Gray.
Peter Bishop.
Patrick Hackit.
George Ramback.
Peter Bredin.
John Linch.
Hendry Mitzlar.
Abram Hare.
Jacob Kinsley.
Jacob Carback.
James Defarnce.
Daniel Reem.
John Martin.
Hendry Poorman.

3d Class.

Joseph Ekinrode.
John Musser.
Christian Cap.
Abram Millar.
Christian Neesley.
Samuel Couchran.
John Cable.
Jacob Leman.
James Chesnut.
Peter Cacback.

4th Class.

Nathanial Nelson.
William Bishop.
Cutlip Bishop.
Jacab Cafman.
John Fissal.
Chritian Martin.
Fredrick Ketty.
John Neesley.
Rudy Pesum.
Christian Eater.
Joseph Jonas.
Fredrick Bealer.
James Bredy.
Sims Chambers.
James Corathers.
Hendry Megrants.

5th Class.

Christian Bruniman.	Francis Swope.
Jacob Stofer.	Philip Smith.
David Boyd.	Michael Oxer.
Philip Bishop.	John Kinsley.
William Poorman.	John Bishop.
Conrode Myer.	Christian Whitmore.
John Cofman.	Jacob Shelly.
Ernal Beaker.	Adam Speek.
George Ridsacher.	David Cable.
Timothy Connar.	Jacob Eversole.
David Hamaker.	John Martin, Junr.
Christian Kinsley.	

6th Class.

Christian Potastone.	John Beard.
John Stofer.	James Conner.
Christian Martin, Sen.	Christian Ekinrode.
Alexander Barnit.	george Stake.
Christian Black.	Andrew Grove.
Peter Shafer.	Samuel Batzlar.
Jacob Palmore.	George Bleazer.
Lenard Peters.	John Hood.

7th Class.

Peter Leaman.	Robert Hood.
William Scott.	Abram Kish.
Hendrey Penther.	Isaac Harnly.
Charles Hide.	William Smith.
John Foreman.	Christian Martin.
Anthony Snider, Jun.	Alexander Barr.
John Singar.	James Brown.
Philip Brannar.	Thos. Howard .
Daniel Murfy.	

8th Class.

William Kelly.	Samuel Reem.
Michal Peters.	Isaac Gruber.
John Martin.	Duncan Levingstone.
Peter Cap.	Hendry Culp.
Jacob Shefer.	Robt. Gilliand.
John Kinsinger.	Peter Bleaser.
Abram Shelly.	John Jamison.
Martin Neesley.	Christian Sheomaker.

I Do swear, on the Holy Evengilest of Almighty God: That the above list is a just and true state, of the Male White In-

habitants, residing in my District, agreeable to law, and without any fraud to the State, to the best of my knowledge.

RT. CUNNINGHAM, Lt.

Sworn before me this 15th day of May 1782.

WILLIAM KELLY,
Sub. Lieut.

A TRUE AND EXACT LIST OF THE NAMES, OF EACH AND EVERY MALE WHITE PERSON, INHABITING OR RESIDING, WITHIN MY DISTRICT, IN THE THIRD COMPANY, OF THE SEVENTH BATTALION OF LANCASTER COUNTY, MILITIA, BETWEEN THE AGE OF EIGHTEEN, AND FIFTY-THREE YEARS. TAKEN FOR THE YEAR 1782. (c.)

Capt.

Thomas Robison.

Lieu.

Andrew Shell.

Ens.

James Miller.

Almonar.

Abraham Frederick.

Privates.

1st Class.

Henry Goepfert.
Michael Shell.
Jacob Wagler.
Stoffel Meisenhelder.
Abraham Wolgamuth.
John Stauffer.
Robert Robison.
John Stern.
Andrew Moor.
Jacob Hummer.
John Schnyder, Junr.
John Forry.
Philip Seidenstriker.
John Noull.
Philip Beill.
Andw. Hoover.

2nd Class.

Robert Moorhead.
John Peter.
John Leman, Junr.
Michael Royer.
John Leman, in Rapho.
Frederick Gantz.
Jacob Eshelman.
Jacob Walter.
Abraham Schnyder.

3d Class.

John Goepfert.
Christian Wolgamuth.
George Goepfert.
William Moor.
Michael Hummer.
John Leman.
Anthony Bretz.
Philip Keiser.
Philip Keener.
Ephraim Little.
Philip Frederick.
William Wegley.
Joseph Sherk.
John Clark.

4th Class.

Isaac Dettee.
Jacob Keener.
Abraham Reeser.
Benjamin Benter.
Melchar Fortney.
John Wanger.
Anthony Shoemaker.
Isaac Eshelman.
Jacob Conrad.
Jacob Faubenberker.
Jacob Hoffman.
John Eshelman.
Saml. Smith.

5th Class.

James Moorhead.
William Allison.
Vallentin Hide.
David Florey.
Jacob Shelley.
John Springer.
John Florey.
Christian Reeser.
Casper Lesher.
John Brubaker.
Peter Frederick.
John Gisch.
France Grove, Junr.
Jacob Miller, Junr.
Jacob Leman.
John Bowman.

6th Class.

Christian Herr.
George Alspach.
Andrew Robison.
Philip Shoemaker, Junr.
John Hummer, Junr.
John Shelley.
Abraham Flory.
Michael Eaby.
Isaac Weanger.
Conrad Springer.
Joseph Wolff, Junr.
John Grove.
David Rowland.
Casper Keler.
Jacob Stauffer, at Obers.
William Connely.
George Blosser.

7th Class.

Frederick Stolar, Junr.
Jacob Holdiman.
Martin Greiner.
Henry Limbert.
Jacob Greebill.
Peter Weiker.
Abraham Eshelman.
Jacob Shelley.
James Carnes.
Abraham Eckert.
Isaac Boraway.
John Frederick.
Hugh McClaughlin.
George Nickey.
Wm. Smith.
Henry Ober.
Sebastian Duncle.
Abraham Ettey.
John Herr.
John Benter.
Daniel Hoover.
William Mckinly.
Abraham Stollar.
Martin Johann.

8th Class.

Philip Kemrer.
David Meisenhelder.
William Boal.
Daniel Conrad.
Abraham Wolff.
Michael Notz.
Abraham Grove.
Lorance Schneeringer.
George Shanke.
Henry Bell.
John Leman.
Peter Brubaker, Junr.
John Holdiman.
John Hoffman.
William Mckain, Junr.
Abraham Goepfert.
Conrad Schryer.
Jacob Conrad, Junr.

I Do swear, on the Holy Evengilest of Almighty God: That the above list is a just and true state, of the Male White Inhabitants, residing in my District, agreeable to law, and without any fraud to the State, to the best of my knowledge.

THOMAS ROBINSON, Capt.

Sworn before me this 27th Day of June 1782.
WILLIAM KELLY, Sub. Lt.

A TRUE AND EXACT LIST OF THE NAMES, OF EACH AND EVERY MALE WHITE PERSON, INHABITING OR RESIDING WITHIN MY DISTRICT IN THE FOURTH COMPANY, OF THE SEVENTH BATTALION OF LANCASTER COUNTY, MILITIA, BETWEEN THE AGE OF EIGHTEEN, AND FIFTY-THREE YEARS. TAKEN FOR THE YEAR 1782. (c.)

Capt.

David McQueen.

Lieut.

Mathew Hay.

Ens.

Thomas Logan.

Almonar.

John Logan.

1st Class.

John Hay.
Mathew Montgomery.
James Kelly.
Michael Shenk.
Michael Brand.
James Kilpatrick.
Michael Prats.
William Hall.
Abrim Evil.
Philip Shoop.
Conrd. at McFrances.
John McCleary.

2nd Class.

Sergt. Willm. Moore.
William Hay, Junr.
Patrick Kelly.
Mark Worst.
Abrim Stevick.
Cornelius Green.
Christian Buck.
Henry Esleman.
Barnet McGlaghlin.
John Cansinger.
Robert Hunter.
John Linch.
Henry Wolf.
Robert Humes.

3d Class.

James Morison.
John Reasor.
Dewalt Grim.
Michael Frances.
Flawel Rowan, discharged.
John Belch, discharged.
Heny. Coah.
Heny. Alleman.

4th Class.

Serjt. Robt. Rhea.
John Stickley.
John Stevick.
John Duncan.
James Donelson, disc.
Archibald Eliot.
Christian Brand.
Paul Sigg.
Daved Hay.
John Bumeaters.
Abrim Reamer.
James Defrance.

5th Class.

Christian Null.
Christian Snyder.
Stophel Bishop.
David Foster.
Conrad Wolf.
William Hay, Senr.
Christian Stevick.
Saml. McCleary.
Willm. Foster.
Saml. Hess.
Peter Reesor, Junr.
Andw. Kelly.
James Duncan.

6th Class.

Andw. Foster.
Philip Bughman.
Peter Reesor, Sin.
John Rhea.
Jacob Shire.
John Thompson.
Robert McQueen.
Joseph M'Clintock.
Clemins Shire.
John Carnaghan.
John Garret.
Joseph Stevick.
John Craig.

7th Class.

Sergt. Robert McCleary.
Peter Poorman.
Christian Dolobagh.
John Johnston.
Charles Johnston.
Abrim Longneker.
James Carnaghan.
James Hay.
John Allexander.
John Shoop.
Adam Henry.
John Kellar.
Jacob Worst.
Wm. Allison.

8th Class.

Jacob Meckley.	Charles Dougherty.
John Meckley.	George Jordan.
Fredrick Buck.	Peter Beaker.
John Kennady.	John Farmer.
Patrick Coin.	James Huey.
Andrew Hunter.	Danl. Kennady.

I Do swear, on the Holy Evengileet of Almighty God: That the above list is a just and true state, of the Male White Inhabitants, residing in my District, agreeable to law, and without any fraud to the State, to the best of my knowledge.

DAVED McQUEEN,
Capt.

Sworn before me this 5th day of May 1782.

WILLM. KELLY, Sub. Lieut.

A TRUE AND EXACT LIST OF THE NAMES, OF EACH AND EVERY MALE WHITE PERSON, INHABITING OR RESIDING WITHIN MY DISTRICT, IN THE FIFTH COMPANY, OF THE SEVENTH BATTALION OF LANCASTER COUNTY, MILITIA, BETWEEN THE AGE OF EIGHTEEN, AND FIFTY-THREE YEARS. TAKEN FOR THE YEAR 1782. (c.)

Captain.
Noah Ceasey.

Lieut.
William Smith.

Ensign.
Christian Detter.

Almonar.
Jeramia Miller.

1st Class.

John Witmore.	Marten Fare.
Gorge Hatz.	Henry Hershey.
Daniel Lemon.	Jacob Snyder.

Christian Longaneker.
Joseph Eversole.
Jacob Druekenmiller.
Jacob Srite.
Abraham Troley.
George Snyder.
Young Kerkly.

2nd Class.

Adam Minich.
Petter Fooks.
Christian Wenger.
John Gerhart.
Henry Lesher.
Casper Werner.
Jacob Myar.
William Macksimer.
Henry Wenger.
Peter Hagey.
Thomas Spencer.

3rd Class.

Marten Betz.
John Camran.
John Hatz.
Henry Hinns.
Ootlep Spone.
Abraham Laman.
Michal Longneker.
John Garman, Jun.
Jacob Earhart.
Benj. Nowman.
Peter Risht.
Steven Chambers.

4th Class.

Fredrick Karayer.
John Rudey.
George Secrist.
John Fritz.
Christian Hernly.
Danial Longneker.
Jacob Rife.
John Bomgardnar.
John Brand.
John Shearer.
Adam Warffel.
John Minshall.
Christian Eversoal.
Christian Snyder.
Joseph Humer.
Morgen Jinkens.
Tobias Kuster.
Abraham Reamer.

5th Class.

Andrew Bartruff.
Jacob Myar, Serjt.
Mathias Hilton, Serjt.
Philip Bretz, Serjt.
Emanuel Dyer.
Fredrick Drukenmiller.
Jacob Keller.
Abraham Heastand.
Jacob Hagey.
Peter Kuckerly.
John Boraway.
Daniel Laman, Junr.
Henry Srite.
Joseph Shock.
Michal Godadel.
Jonos Humer.

6th Class.

Conrad Wert.
Jacob Lithey.
Henry Longneker.
Adam Motzaboch.
Gorge Hounstone.
Frantz Gipe.
Jacob Earhart, Jun.
Abraham Fooks.
John Hagey.
Nickloas Hide.
Wm. Turner.
Peter Blatenberger.
Thomas Williamson.
Michal Fogelsonger.
John Cline.
Marten Yetter.
John Garmon, Junr.

7th Class.

Nicklas Librey.
Abraham Humer.
Mathias Long.
Marten Becker.
Peter Rule.
John Nousman.
Adam Kober.
John Dyar.
Fredrick Sousar.
Tobias Hollinger.
Michal Gudey.
John Hernly.
John Minick.
John Shumaker.
George Krider.
Abraham Eversowl.
Christian Marten.

8th Class.

Gorge Gantz.
George Werner.
Michal Hubar.
Andrew Halter.
Jacob Shole.
Eanas Murry.
John Hubar.
Jacob Gudey.
Christian Wenger.
Fredrick Nowman.
Adam Pender.
John Eabey.
Peter Crumbane.
Georg Fishoake.
Jeams Clunn.
Christian Earhart.
John Rupart.

I Do swear, on the Holy Evenglilest of Almighty God: That the above list is a just and true state, of the Male White Inhabitants, residing in my District, agreeable to law, and without any fraud to the State, to the best of my knowledge.
Sworn before me this
15 Day of April 1782.
WILLIAM KELLY, Sub. Lieut.
NOAH CEASEY, Capt.

A TRUE AND EXACT LIST OF THE NAMES, OF EACH AND EVERY MALE WHITE PERSON, INHABITING OR RESIDING WITHIN MY DISTRICT, IN THE SIXTH COMPANY, OF THE SEVENTH BATTALION OF LANCASTER COUNTY, MILITIA, BETWEEN THE AGE OF EIGHTEEN, AND FIFTY-THREE YEARS. TAKEN FOR THE YEAR 1782. (c.)

Captain.

William Wilson.

Lieut.

James Cook.

Ensign.

James Wilson.

Almonar.

Nathaniel Megim.

1st Class.

Petter Bowman.
Daniel Elliott.
Jacob Shireman.
Philip Wiant.
James Clingen.
John Gorner.
John Nighty.
Laurence Fontz.
Jacob Holsaple.
John Grove, Jur.
Lawrence Heiman.
Edward Cook.
Fredrick Swisher.
Simeon Camron.

2nd Class.

Adam Clyn.
John Mays.
Nicholas Peck.
Thomas Bayly.
James Mackey, Jur.
Thomas McCun.
Jacob Hoofman.
Arthur Vance.
James Karr.
John Barber.
Christian Long.
Christipher Pestler.
Abraham Long.
Hendry Grove.
Hendry Graft.
Christly Grove.
Thomas Bayly, Jur.
Samuel Karr.
Joseph Whitmore.
Jacob Grove.

3rd Class.

Chrisly Heagy.	Fredrick Yeach.
Fetter Lindimott.	William Ginnins.
Samuel Cook.	John Grove, Junr.
Daniel Longnecker.	Rich'd Bishop.
Richard Keays.	Jacob Long.
Martin Miley.	John Fleck.

4th Class.

Ulrich Angle.	Chrisly Boohar.
Hugh Caldwell.	Adam Wiant.
Petter Lightey.	Thomas Pain.
John Emmauck.	William Myor.
George Fisher.	Petter Rutter.
George Barr.	Samuel McCun.
Christy Souder.	

5th Class.

Fred'k Kilbough, Serjt.	Philip Koutz.
Martin Lindemott.	George Clapper.
Robert Haslip.	Daniel Gilman.
James Anderson, Jur.	John Wiant.
William Rusko.	Robert Connell.
Michael Nicholas.	Sam'l Ginnins.
Loudwick Rineheart.	Cornelius Toulon.
John Scott.	William Williams, Corpl.

6th Class.

William Cumming, Serjt.	William Megery.
Hendry Hains, Fifer.	Frances Stewart.
Philip Gorner, Drumer.	Arthur Chamberlin.
Abraham Albert.	Valentine Steer.
Michael Hoofman.	John Brown.
Jacob Wiant.	Anthony Hains.
Jacob Fontz.	Fredrick Kelbough, Jur.
Richard Allison.	John Vance.
David Cook, Jur.	Lazy Lowrey.
Robert Porter.	George Roupe.

7th Class.

Lieut. Col. Mr. Alexander Lowrey.	Jacob Hersha.
	Robert Ballance.
Ulrich. Tanner, 3d Sergt.	John Gribill.

John Herst.
William Clinger.
Samuel Thompson.
Dr. John Tate.
Moses Morland, discharged 9th April 1782.
Philip Clough.
Jacob Miller.
Nicholas Sipprell.

8th Class.

John Hollinger.
Adam Nees.
Abraham Stoufer.
John Blasor.
Laughland Ferree.
John Kilbough.
Conrad Albrigh.
Herman Long.
Walter Bell.
Fredrick Bower.
Fredrick Sipprell.
Nicholas Blasor.
John Defrance.
Joseph Blacher.
John Scully.
John Baird.
Joseph Clapper.
Daniel Stout.
Christian Rinehart.
Christian Vinigar.

I Do swear, on the Holy Evengliest of Almighty God: That the above list is a just and true state, of the Male White Inhabitants, residing in my District, agreeable to law, and without any fraud to the State, to the best of my knowledge.

WILLIAM WILSON,
Capt.

Sworn before me this
11th Day of April 1782.
WILLIAM KELLY, Sub. Lieut.

A TRUE AND EXACT LIST OF THE NAMES, OF EACH AND EVERY MALE WHITE PERSON, INHABITING OR RESIDING, WITHIN MY DISTRICT, IN THE SEVENTH COMPANY, OF THE SEVENTH BATTALION OF LANCASTER COUNTY, MILITIA, BETWEEN THE AGE OF EIGHTEEN, AND FIFTY-THREE YEARS. TAKEN FOR THE YEAR 1782. (c.)

Captain.
Robert McKee.

Lieut.
Hugh Hall.

Ensign.

James McClesler.

Almonar.

Joseph Condour.

1st Class.

Henry Booser.	John Fry.
Jacob Coss, Jun.	John Ritzel.
Henry M'Gee.	Alexander Russel.
Gorge Allison.	Jacob Shelley.
Joseph Rife.	John Smith (Taylor).
Philip Sellers.	Gorge Hood.

2nd Class.

Jacob Rife.	Stephen Felix.
John Fifer.	Jacob Hansbarger.
James Kile.	Barney Thrum.
Gorge Books.	Christopher Plough.
Fredrick Shoat.	William Bredon.

3rd Class.

John Riser.	Jacob Mitzer.
William Jamison.	Henry Bricker.
Jacob Nesley.	Philip Righer.
David Tatwiler.	Philip Shoat.
Abraham Gingrey.	Joseph Gregg.

4th Class.

Jacob Smith.	Dines Stall.
John Branser.	Jacob Books.
Thomas Ogle.	Jenry Booser, Jun.
John Myers.	Henry Ridley.
Henry Sherer.	John Smith.
Peter Books.	Gorge Null.
Fredrick Waggner.	James McCaley.

5th Class.

Joseph Prim.	John Booser.
John Gingrey.	Peter Bruniman.
John Camel.	James Yong.
Honikel Simerman.	Runimus Heney.

6th Class.

Christopher Branser.	Peter Yeats.
William Mills.	Jacob Bricker.
Jacob Tatwiler.	Peter Rodrock.
Cristopher Burkholder.	Gorge Bower.
Daniel Bonine.	David Pruniman.

7th Class.

Daniel Elliott.	John Long.
James McKee.	Henry Shoffmen.
Fredrick Sellors.	James Johnston.
John McKee.	James Scott.
Elder Bredon.	James Laird.
John McLaughlen.	James McGines.
Josias Candour.	James Allison.
James Russel.	John Blair, Jun.
Moses Campbel.	Charels Colgan.
John Nobel.	James Patton.

8th Class.

David Thrum.	Henry Sherer, Jun.
Samuel Hannan.	William Armstrong Jackson.
Fredrick Shaffner.	Nicklous Lighty.
Daniel Shelley.	Jacob Rife, Jun.
Adam Thomas.	Jonn Man.
John Grimes.	Henry Hes.
John Jackson.	Henry Hamaker.
John Funk.	Jacob Ginrey.
Jacob Sherer.	Conrod Books.
David Allison.	Michael Hain.

I Do swear, on the Holy Evengilest of Almighty God: That the above list is a just and true state, of the Male White Inhabitants, residing in my District, agreeable to law, and without any fraud to the State, to the best of my knowledge.

Sworn before me this
7th Day of May 1782.
WILLIAM KELLY, Sub. Lieut.

A TRUE AND EXACT LIST OF THE NAMES, OF EACH AND EVERY MALE WHITE PERSON, INHABITING OR RESIDING, WITHIN MY DISTRICT, IN THE EIGHT COMPANY, OF THE SEVENTH BATTALION OF LANCASTER COUNTY, MILITIA, BETWEEN THE AGE OF EIGHTEEN, AND FIFTY-THREE YEARS. TAKEN FOR THE YEAR 1782. (c.)

Capt.

Pattrick Hayes.

Lieu.

Benjamin Mils.

Ens.

James Hutcheson.

Almonar.

William Corran.

1st Class.

James Sterret.
Arthur Patterson.
Jacob Aaron.
Christy Hoofman.
John Shank.
John Hayes.
Chrisly Erishman.
Philip Gilman.
Robert Mears.
Edward Waterson.
Baltzor Stake.
Patrick Burns.
Hugh Hagerty.
Dewalt Shank.
James Corran.

2d Class.

John Shelhorn.
Abraham Kastle.
John Metz.
Michael goodle.
Petter willes.
John Hoofman.
Joseph Miller.

3rd Class.

Christy Long.
Henry Strickler.
Baltzer walter.
wendal mertzel.
Henry Teesinger.
John Beard.
Allexander McClean.
Fredrick Aaron.
Ludwig Metz.

4th Class.

Samuel Robinson.
Joseph Lytle.
Robert Allis.
Jacob Bender.
Baltzer Shelhorn.
Abraham martin.
John Lisher.
Michael Stake.
John welger.
Samuel McClun.
Michael marshal.
Stephen Pike.
Fredrick Blotenberger.
Ambrose Neusham.
Samuel Milton.

5th Class.

Hugh grahms.
Michael Horst.
Petter walter.
Jacob Hostater.
Christy Longnecker.
Henry Acker.
John Meashy.
Charls welger.
Martin Neisly.
Michael Harsler.
Dinnes Cleary.
John Ashbougher.

6th Class.

Abraham Metz.
Thomas Minto.
George Bergelbough.
Michael Segrist.
Mathias Kishler.
Isack gilman.
John jordan.
Joseph Porter.
William Cumins.
Chrisly Holdeman.

7th Class.

Henry Hoobly
Petter Hesten.
John Rora.
Ullrick Strickler.
William Mears.
John Baker.
Philip Baker.
John Speekler.
Jacob Kastle.
Christy metz.
Christy Shelly.
Samuel Porter.

8th Class.

Jacob Metz.
Jacob Erishman.
John Sweeny.
Jacob Kensler.
John Brown.
John Boggs.
Abraham Erishman.
William Sterret.
Petter Youts.
John Porter.
James Bochanon.

I Do swear, on the Holy Evengilest of Almighty God: That the above list is a just, and true state, of the Male White In-

habitants, residing in my District, agreeable to law, and without any fraud to the State, to the best of my knowledge.

PATRICK HAYES,

Sworn before me this
3d day of May, 1782.
WILLIAM KELLY, Sub. Lieut.

GENERAL RETURN OF THE OFFICERS OF THE LANCASTER COUNTY MILITIA APRIL 15TH, 1783. (c.)

SEVENTH BATTALION.

Field Officers.

Lieut. Col.

Alex'r Lowry.

Maj'r.

Jacob Cook.

Captains.

1. Andrew Boggs.
2. Abraham Scott.
3. Thos. Robinson.
4. David McQueen.
5. Noah Keesy.
6. William Willson.
7. Robt. McKee.
8. Hugh Peaden.

Lieutenants.

1. James Cook.
2. Robert Cunningham.
3. Andrew Shell.
4. Mathew Hay.
5. Christ'n Hackelwood.
6. James Cook.
7.
8. Patrick Hays.

Ensigns.

1. John Messer.
2. Abraham Scott.
3. James Miller.
4. Thomas Lowgan.
5. Christ'n Detter.
6. James Willson.
7.
8. Benj'n Wills.

MUSTER ROAL FOR THE YEAR 1783. 7TH BATTALION LANC. CO. (c.)

Capt.

Abraham Scott.

Lieut.

Robt. Cunningham.

Ens.

Abraham Scott.

Sar.

Thomas Phillips.
Jacob Petters.

Privates.

First Class.

Henry Hine.
Chrsn. Holdiman.
Abram. Black.
Leonard Neagly.
Fredrick Strouse.
Abraham Sharer.
John Albert.
Samuel Smith.
Abraham Stricklar.
John Black.
Christian Wiland.
Abraham Rheam.
Henry Hise.
Adam Grosheart.
William Hood.
Peter Stouts.

Second Class.

John Lheman.
John Gray.
Peter Bishop.
Patrick Hacket.
George Rambaugh.
Peter Bready.
John Lynch.
Henry Mitzlar.
Abraham Hear.
Jacob Kinsly.
Jacob Carbaugh.
George Williams.
James Defrance.
Danial Rheam.
John Martin.
Henry Poorman.
Leonard Grouse.

Third Class.

Joseph Eakenroad.
John Musar.
Christian Cap.
Abraham Millar.
Christian Neesly.
John Cooble.
Jacob Lheman.
James Chesnut.
Peter Carbaugh.
Saml. Cochran.

Fourth Class.

Nathan Nilson.
William Bishop.
Cotlip Bishop.
Jacob Cofman.
John Fissal.
Christian Martain.
Fredrick Ketty.
John Neesly.
Rudy Pessum.
Christian Eater.
David Cooble.
Joseph Joans.
Fredrick Bailghar.
James Bready.
Syms Chambers.
Henry Migrants.

Fifth Class.

Christian Pruniman.
Jacob Stoffer.
David Boyd.
Phillip Bishop.
William Poorman.
John Cofman.
George Ridsacker.
Timothy Conner.
David Hambacker.
Christian Keener.
Frans. Swope.
Phillip Smith.
Michal Oxer.
John Kinsly.
John Bishop.
Christian Whitmore.
Jacob Shelly.
Adam Speck.
Jacob Eversole.
John Martian.
Conrod Myar.
Arnold Baker.

Sixth Class.

Christian Patistone.
John Stoffer.
Christian Martin, Snr.
Fredrick Botz.
Alexander Barnet.
Christian Black.
Peter Shaffer.
Jacob Palmore.
Leonard Petters.
John Bard.
James Conner.
Christian Ekenroad.
Andrew Groce.
Samuel Patzlar.
George Blaser.
John Hood.
Jacob Tindore.
Abraham Whitmore.

Seventh Class.

Peter Lheman.
William Scott.
Henry Panther.
Christian Hide.
John Foorman.
Dominick Eagle.
Anthony Snider.
John Singar.
Phillip Braner.
Daniel Murphy.
Robert Hood.
Abraham Kish.
Isaac Hernly.
William Smith.
Christian Martin.
Alexander Barr.
Robert Balance.
James Brown.
Thomas Howard.

Eighth Class.

Abraham Shelly.
Michal Petters.
John Martin.
Peter Cap.
Jacob Shaffer.
John Unger.
Martain Neesly.
Samuel Rheam.
John Kingsinger.
Isaac Gruvar.
Duncan Livingstone.
Henry Culp.
Robert Gilliland.
Peter Blaser.
Christian Shoemaker.
Paul Gravler.
Jacob Everly.
George Stake.
Jacob Hunibarger.
William Peck.

That the Within Return is true to the Best of my knowledga is Certifyd By me.

RT. CUNNINGHAM, Lieut.

Spring 1783.

A RETURN OF THE 4TH, 5TH, 6TH AND 7TH CLASSES OF THE FIRST COMPANY OF THE 7TH BATTALION OF LANCASTER COUNTY MILITIA COMMANDED BY COLO. ALEXANDER LOURY—ANDREW BOGGS, Captain, (c.)

4th Class.

John Sharp.
Philip Holinger.
Abraham Shaver.
Benjamin Whister.
Jacob Barrick.
Arthur Tagert.
Jacob Holinger.
John Eslinger.
John Neegly.

5th Class.

Alexander Boggs.
Martin Hisey.
David Cooble.
Randal McClure.
Jacob Eversole, Junr.
Peter Hisey.
Robert Craig.
James Young.
Bartrim Galbreath.
David Jamison.
Michall Neesly.
Robert Connels.
John Elder.
Abraham Whitmer.
John Coal.
Hugh McBride.
John Beech.

6th Class.

Samuel Wilson.
William Hawk.
Samuel Woods.
Christian Bruniman.
John Longnecker.
Hugh Moore.
Petter Root.
John Cook.
Christian Bruniman, Junr.
John Shank.
John Grider.
Adam Platts.
William Messer, Junr.
Jacob Oldwiler.
Jacob Brubacker.
Christian Fisher.
George Hikes.
John Wilson.

7th Class.

Peter Hadsomer.
Jacob Angle.
Henry Kintick.
John Horst.
Jacob Laver.
Daniel Kinsinger.
James Murphey.
Zachariah Moor.
Jacob Winccop.
David Martin.
Jacob Shimph.
Joseph Rheam.
Jacob Bruniman.
George Emmond.
Abraham Frederick.
Jacob Snider.
Hugh Donoly.

A RETURN OF THE 4TH, 5TH, 6TH AND 7TH CLASSES OF THE SECOND COMPANY OF THE 7TH BATTALION OF LANCASTER COUNTY MILITIA COMMANDED BY COLO. ALEXANDER LOURY. (c.)

ABRAHAM SCOTT, Captain.

4th Class.

William Bishop.
Cuttlip Bishop.
Jacob Cofman.
John Tissal.
Christian Marten.
Frederick Kattey.

John Neesly.
Rudy Pissum.
Christian Ettar.
Jacob Frear.
Joseph Jones.
Frederick Bealer.
James Bready.

5th Class.

Jacob Stopher
David Boyd.
Samuel Sims.
Philip Bishop.
William Poorman.
Melchar Poorman.
John Cofman.
George Ritsacker.
Timothy Connor.
Francis Swope.
Philip Smith.
Michael Oxer.
John Kinsley.
Jacob Shelly, Junr.
John Bishop.
Christian Whitmore.
Adam Spike.
David Coble.
Jacob Eversole.
Conrad Shire.
Conrad Myar.
John Marten, Junr.

6th Class.

Christian Marten, Junr.
Frederick Batts.
Peter Earstone.
Alexander Barnitt.
Christian Black.
Peter Shafer.
Jacob Palmore.
Leonard Peters.
David Swarts.
James Connor.
Christian Ekinrode.
Jacob Foguison.
Christian Whitmore.
George Stake.
Andrew Gross.
Samuel Batzler.
George Blazer.
John Shoemaker.

7th Class.

Peter Leman.
William Scott.
John Alexander.
Henry Painter.
John Foreman.
Anthony Snider.
John Singer.
Samson Babb.
Daniel Murphy.
Abram Kish.
Jacob Shara.
Isaac Harnley.
William Smith.
Christian Marten.
Alexander Barr.
David Gish.

A RETURN OF THE 4TH, 5TH, 6TH AND 7TH CLASSES OF THE THIRD COMPANY OF THE 7TH BATTALION OF LANCASTER COUNTY MILITIA COMMANDED BY COLO. ALEXANDER LOURY. (c.)

THOMAS ROBINSON, Captain.

4th Class.

Isaac Dettey.
Jacob Keener.
Abraham Reeser.
Benjamin Benter.
Melcher Fortney.
John Wanger.
Anthony Shoemaker.
Jacob Krebill.
Isaac Eshelman.
Marten Greiner.
Jacob Conrad.
Jacob Fauvenberker.

5th Class.

James Moorhead.
William Allison.
Valentine Hide.
David Flory.
Jacob Shelly.
John Springer.
John Flory.
Christian Reeser.
Casper Lesher.
John Whitmer.
John Brubaker.
Peter Frederick.
John Gish.
France Grove, Jur.
John Kemrer.

6th Class.

Christian Herr.
Andrew Robinson.
Jacob Kuns.
Thomas Weiley.
Philip Shoemaker, Jur.
Sebastian Dunkel.
Christian Whitmer.
John Hummer, Junr.
John Shelly.
Abraham Flory.
Michael Ebby.
Isaac Wenger.
Conrad Springer.
Jacob Staufer, at Over's.
Joseph Wolf, Junr.
John Grove.
James Wilson.

7th Class.

Frederick Stolar, Junr.
Jacob Haldeman.
Henry Limbert.
Peter Welker.
Abraham Eshelman.
Jacob Shelly, Black.
Abraham Eckert.
Isaac Boroway.
John Frederick.
George Nickey.
Henry Ober.
Abraham Etty.
John Herr.
John Bentter.
Danl. Hoover.
James Carns.

A RETURN OF THE 4TH, 5TH, 6TH AND 7TH CLASSES OF THE 4TH COMPANY OF THE 7TH BATTALION OF LANCASTER COUNTY MILITIA COMMANDED BY COLO. ALEXANDER LOURY, LONDONDERRY. (c.)

DAVID McQUEEN, Captain.

4th Class.

John Stickley.
John Stevick.
James Kennedy.
Abraham Reamer.
John Duncan.
Mathew Wolf.
Alexander Long.
Patrick Lynch.
Henry Rowland.
James Doneldson.
Archibald Ellott.
Christian Brand.
William Simonton.
Paul Sigg.

5th Class.

Christian Null.
Stophel Bishop.
Christian Snyder.
David Foster.
Conrod Wolf.
William Hay, Senr.
Christian Stevick.
Samuel M'Clary.
William Foster.
Samuel Hess.
Philip Reamer.
John Leach.
Peter Reaser.

6th Class.

Andrew Foster.
Stophel Shenk.
Philip Bughman.
Peter Reiser, Senr.
John Rhea.
Jacob Shire.
John Thompson.
Robert McQueen.
Joseph M'Clintock.
Clemis Shire.
John Carnahan.
John Garrett.
Joseph Stevick.

7th Class.

Peter Poorman.
Christian Dolobagh.
John Johnston.
Charles Johnston.
Michael Felteberger.
Abraham Longnecker.
Hanlin Painter.
James Carnaghan.
William Buck.
Samuel Pennel.
Robert Allen.
James Hay.
John Alexander.
John Shoop.
Adam Henry.

A RETURN OF THE 2D AND 3D CLASSES OF THE 5TH COMPANY OF THE 7TH BATTALION COMMANDED BY COLO. ALEXANDER LOURY. (c.)

NOAH KEASY, Captain, Rapho.

2nd Class.

Peter Fowks.	Henry Lesker.
Christian Winger.	Frederick Speckler.
John Gorhort.	Casper Werner.
Abraham Longnecker.	Jacob Myer.

3rd Class.

John Hatz.	Christian Earheart.
Henry Hines.	Benjamon Nowman.
Abraham Lemon.	Jacob Earheart.
John Gormon, Junr.	Daniel Lemon, Junr.

A RETURN OF THE 4TH, 5TH, 6TH AND 7TH CLASSES OF THE 5TH COMPANY OF THE 7TH BATTALION OF LANCASTER COUNTY MILITIA COMMANDED BY COLO. ALEXANDER LOURY. (c.)

NOAH KEASY, Captain, Rapho.

4th Class.

John Rudey.	John Brand.
George Secrist.	John Shorer.
Frederick Kerager.	Adam Worsell.
John Fretz.	Adam Kease.
Christian Hernley.	John Minshell.
Daniel Longnecker.	Christian Eversoll.
Jacob Rife.	Christian Snyder.
John Bumgardner.	Joseph Hummer.

5th Class.

Solomon Longnecker.	Peter Fisher.
Jacob Keller.	Andrew Betz.
Thomas Hollinger.	Abraham Gipel.

Henry Werley.
Abraham Heastand.
Jacob Heagey.
Thomas Stonrod.
Peter Koberley.
John Boroway.

6th Class.

Conrod Wert.
Jacob Lithey.
Christian Marten.
Henry Longnecker.
Adam Mutseberger.
George Hounstone.
John Ruport.
Daniel Earhort.
John Gormon.
Abraham Fooks.
John Keller.
William Turner.
Peter Platenberger.

7th Class.

Nicholas Lebrey.
Mathias Long..
Peter Humer.
Peter Rule.
John Nousman.
Christian Kobel.
John Dyar.
Frederick Sousar.
Tobias Holinger.
Michael Gadey.
John Hernley.

A RETURN OF THE 4TH, 5TH, 6TH AND 7TH CLASSES OF THE SIXTH COMPANY OF THE 7TH BATTALION OF LANCASTER COUNTY MILITIA COMMANDED BY COLO. ALEXANDER LOURY.

WILLIAM WILLSON, Captain, Donegal. (c)

4th Class.

Thomas Thompson.
Ulrich Angle.
Samuel Stopher.
Hugh Caldwell.
Peter Lighley.
John Emmauch.
George Fisher.
George Barr.
John Bullion.
Samuel Kan.
Patrick McCormick.
Chrisley Souder.
Chrisley Boohar.
Adam Wiant.
Thomas Pain.
John Hartman.

5th Class.

Joseph Kirkpatrick.
Martin Lindlmore.
Robert Haslip.
James Anderson, Jun.
William Rusko.
Michael Nicholas.

Loudwick Reinheart.
Hugh McBride.
John Jordon.
John Scott.
Philip Koutz.
George Clapper.
Daniel Gilman.
John Wiant.
James Gibbins.
Daniel Leary.

6th Class.

Christian Vinegar, Junr.
Abraham Albert.
Michael Hoofman.
Jacob Wiant.
Jacob Foutz.
Richard Allison.
David Cook.
Adam Wance.
John Yeach.
Robert Porter.
Adam Neice.
John Hollingar.
Christian Mosey.
William Megery.
Frances Stewart.
Artr. Chamberlin.
Valentine Steer.
John Brown.

7th Class.

Jacob Harsha.
Robert Ballance.
John Grible.
John Hoest.
William Clingen.
Robert Caren.
Peter Sellers.
Pedon Cook.
Moses Morland.
Samuel Thompson.
John Tate.
Frederick Abraham Stophers (Stiller).
Joseph Sink.

A RETURN OF THE 4TH, 5TH, 6TH AND 7TH CLASSES OF THE SEVENTH COMPANY OF THE 7TH BATTALION OF LANCASTER COUNTY MILITIA COMMANDED BY ALEXANDER LOURY, COLO., DERRY. (c.)

ROBERT McKEE, Captain.

4th Class.

Jacob Smith.
John Branser.
James Hinman.
Thomas Ogle.
John Myers.
Henry Sherer.
Peter Books.
Conrod Crabner.
Frederick Wagner.
Denis Stall.
Jacob Books.
Robert Henderson.
George Crabner.
Henry Booser, Jur.
Henry Ridley.

5th Class.

Samuel Clark.	John Camell.
Joseph Prim.	Abraham Shunney.
John Whitmor.	John Simerman.
Michael Roads.	John Booser.
John Ginrey.	William Scott.

6th Class.

Christian Branser.	Jacob Bricker.
William Mills.	Petter Redrock.
Jacob Tatwiler.	George Bower.
Christian Burgholder.	Abraham Sherers.
Daniel Bonine.	Cornelius Laferty.
Petter Yeats.	George Coons.

7th Class.

Daniel Elliot.	John Noble.
James McKee.	John Long.
Frederick Sellers.	Henry Shafner.
John McKee.	James Johnston.
Elder Bredon.	James Scott.
John McLaughlan.	James Laird.
Josias Candour.	James McGines.
James Russel.	John Cain.

A RETURN OF THE 4TH, 5TH, 6TH AND 7TH CLASSES OF THE 8TH COMPANY OF THE 7TH BATTALION OF LANCASTER COUNTY MILITIA COMMANDED BY ALEXANDER LOURY, COLO.

PATRICK HAY, Captain, Rapho. (c.)

4th Class.

Samuel Robinson.	Abraham Marten.
James Patterson.	Daniel Shitz.
Joseph Lyttle.	John Leeshar.
Robert Ellis.	Michael Stake.
Jacob Render.	John Welgar.
Baltzer Shelhorn.	Samuel McLane.
John Sunny.	

5th Class.

Hugh Grimes.
Michael Horst.
Peter Waltar.
Jacob Hostater.
Chris'y Longnecker.
Henry Oaker.
John Mesha.
Charles Welger.
Martin Neesley.
Michael Goodadle.
George Gambler.
Johnathon Jones.

6th Class.

Chrisley Holdeman.
Abraham Metz.
Thomas Minto.
George Bargalbrough.
John Vance.
Michael Segrost.
Mathias Kisler.
James Bochanan.
Isaac Gilman.

7th Class.

William Porter.
Henry Hoobly.
Peter Heasten.
James Sterratt.
Neal Welsh.
John Rora.
Ully Strickler.
William Mears.
John Baker.
Philip Baker.
John Specklar.
Jacob Castle.
Chrisly Metz.
Jacob McKenney.

A MUSTER ROLL OF CAPTAIN THOMAS ROBINSONS COMPANY BEING THE THIRD COMPANY OF THE SEVENTH BATTALION OF LANCASTER COUNTY MILITIA COMPA. COMMENCED BY LIT. COL. ALEXANDER LOWRY. (c.)

Captain.

Thomas Robison.

Lieu.

Andrew Shell.

Ens.

James Miller.

Almonar.

Abraham Frederick.
Henry Goepfert.
Michal Shell.
Jacob Wagler.

Privates.

first Class.

Stoffel Misenheldar.
Abraham Wolgamuth.
John Stauffer.
Robert Robinson.
John Stern.
Andrew Moor.
Jacob Hummer.
John Schnyder.
John Forry.
Philip Seidenstricer.
John Noull.
Philip Balll.
Andw. Hoover.

Second Class.

Robert Moorhead.
John Peter.
John Leman, Junr.
Michael Royer.
John Leman, in Rapho.
Frederick Gantz.
Jacob Eshelman.
Jacob Walter.
Abraham Schnyder.

Third Class.

John Goepfert.
Christian Wolgamuth.
George Goepfert.
William Moor.
Michael Hummer.
John Leaman.
Anthony Bratz.
Philip Keiser.
Philip Keener.
Ephraim Litle.
Philip Frederick.
William Weyley.
Joseph Sherk.
John Clark.

fourth Class.

Isac Detter.
Jacob Keener.
Abraham Reeser.
Benjamin Benter.
Milhcer Fortney.
John Wagner.
Anthony Shoemaker.
Isaac Eshleman.
Jacob Conrad.
Jacob Tubenbarger.
Jacob Hoffman.
Samuel Smith.
John Eshelman.

fifth Class.

James Morehead.
William Allison.
Vallentin Hide.
David Flery.

Jacob Shelley.	Peter Frederick.
John Springer.	John Eirich.
John Flory.	Frances Grove, Jun'r.
Christian Reeser.	Jacob Miller, junr.
Casper Lesher.	Jacob Leman.
John Brubacker.	John Bowman.

Sixth Class.

Christian Herr.	Conrad Springer.
George Alspuh.	Joseph Wolff, Junr.
Andrew Robinson.	John Grove.
Philip Shoemaker, Jr.	David Rowland.
John Hummer, Jur.	Casper Keicer.
John Shelly.	Jacob Stouffer.
Abraham Flory.	William Connely.
Aichal Eaby.	George Blazor.
Isaac Wenger.	

Seventh Class.

Frederick Stolar, jun.	Isac Borroway.
Jacob Holdiman.	John Frederick.
Martin Greiner.	George Nicky.
Henry Limpert.	Henry Ober.
Jacob Grebill.	Sebastian Duncle.
Peter Wilker.	Abraham Ettey.
Abraham Eshelman.	John Herr.
Jacob Shelly.	John Benter.
Wm. Smith.	Daniel Hover.
James Carnes.	William Mc kinly.
Hugh McGlaughlen.	Martin Johan.
Abraham Eckert.	Abraham Stollar.

Eighth Class.

David Meisenhelter.	John Huffman.
William Boal.	William Mc kain.
Daniel Conrad.	Abraham Goepfert.
Abraham Wolff.	Conrad Schreyer.
Michael Nutz.	Jacob Conrad, Junr.
Larance Snearinger.	Philip Kemror.
George Shank.	Henry Bell.
Peter Brubacker, Junr.	John Leman.
John Holdaman.	Abram Grove.

I do Certify the above is a true Return of my Compy̆. pr me
THOMAS ROBINSON, Capt.

A RETURN OF THE FOURTH COMPANY OF THE SEVENTH BATALION OF LANCASTER COUNTY MILITIA COMMANDED BY COLONEL ALEXANDER LOWRY. (c)

Capt.

David McQueen.

Lieut.

Mathew Hay.

Ensn.

Thomas Logan.

Serjts.

Robert Rhea.
Robert McClary.
William Moore.

1st Class.

John Hay.
Mathew Montgomery.
James Kelly.
Michael Shank.
Michael Brand.
William Carnahan.
James Killpatrick.
Michael Pratt.
William Hale.
Abrim Evil.
Andw. Wallas.
Alexd'r Kennedy.
Philip Shoop.

2d Class.

William Hay, Junr.
Patrick Kelly.
Mark Worst.
Abram Stevick.
Cornelius Green.
Christ'n Buck.
Henry Esleman.
Samuel Wolf.
John Cansinger.
Robt. Hunter.
John Linck.
Henry Wolf.

3d Class.

James Morrison.
John Reesor.
David Grim.
George Nule.
John Herron.
Jacob Stopher.
Ant'y Buck.
Mic'l Frances.
Flaw'l Rowen.
Michael Shirts.
James Smith.
John Belch.

4th Class.

John Stickley.	Patrick Lynch.
John Stevick.	Henry Rowland.
James Kennedy.	James Donaldson.
Abrim Reamer.	Archd. Ellott.
John Duncan.	Cht'r Brand.
Mathew Wolf.	William Simonton.
Allexander Long.	Paul Sigg.

5th Class.

Cht'n Nule.	Samuel McClary.
Stophel Bishop.	William Foster.
Cht'n Snyder.	Samuel Hess.
David Foster.	Philip Reamer.
Cond. Wolf.	John Leach.
William Hay, senr.	Peter Reesor.
Cht'n Stevick.	

6th Class.

Andrew Foster.	Robt. McQueen.
Stophel Shenk.	Josh. McClintock.
Philip Bughman.	Clemis Shire.
Peter Reaser, senr.	John Carnahan.
John Rhea.	John Garrets.
Jacob Shire.	Joseph Stevick.
John Thompson.	

7th Class.

Peter Poorman.	James Carnaghan.
Cht'n Dolobagh.	Samuel Pennel.
John Johnston.	Robt. Allen.
Charles Johnston.	James Hay.
Mich'l Pheltebeger.	John Alexander.
Abrm Longnecker.	John Shoop.
Hanlin Painter.	Adam Henry.

8th Class.

Alex'dr McClintock.	Patrick Coin.
Daniel Plough.	Andrew Hunter.
James Hughey.	William Crossor.
Fred'k Buck.	Bar'd McLaughn.
John Kennedy.	

RETURN OF CAPT. NOAH CEASEY'S COMPNEY BEING THE 5TH OF THE 7TH BATTALION OF LANCASTER COUNTY MILLITIA COMMANDED BY COL. ALEXANDER LOWREY. (c.)

Capt.

Noah Ceasey.

Lieut.

Wm. Smith.

Ens.

Christian Detter.

1st Class.

John Witmore.
George Hatz.
Daniel Laman.
Marten fare.
Henry Hershey.
Jacob Snyder.
Christian Longnker.
Joseph Eversoal.
Jacob Druckinmelor.
Jacob Trite.
Abraham Trotey.
John Kinkaly.

2d Class.

Adam Moneeh.
Peter fooks.
John Garhart.
Christian Wenger.
Henry Lesher.
Casper Werner.
Jacob Myar.
Wm. Macksiner.
Henry Wenger.
peter Hagey.
Thomas Spencer.

3d Class.

Marten Betz.
John Camaron.
John Hatz.
Henry Hines.
Gotlepe Spone.
Abraham Lamon.
Michal Longaneker.
John Garman.
Jacob Earhart.
Benjeman Nowman.
peter Risht.
Steven Chambers.

4th Class.

Frederick Karager.
John Rudey.
George Seacrist.
John fritz.
Christian Hernly.
Daniel Longancker.
Jacob Rife.
John Bomgardner.
John Brand.
John Sharer.
Adam Warfell.
John Minshall.
Christian Eversoul.
Christian Snyder.
Joseph Humer.
Morgen Ginkens.
Tobias Kuster.
Abraham Ramer.

5th Class.

Andrew Bartruff.
Jacob Myars. }
Mathias Helton. } Serjt.
philip Bretz. }
Fredrick Druckinmeler, D.
Emanul Dyar, fifer.
Jacob Keller.
Abraham Heastand.
Jacob Hagey.
peter Kuckerly.
John Boraway.
Daniel Laman, Jur.
Henry Trite.
Joseph Shock.
Michal Goadadel.
Jonas Hamer.

6th Class.

Conrad Wert.
Jacob Lithey.
Henrey Longanker.
Adam Motzabocher.
George Hounstone.
Christian Herkelrod.
Jacob Earhart, Junr.
John Garman, Junr.
Abraham fooks.
William Turner.
peter platenbarger.
Thomas Willmson.
Michal fogelsonger.
John Cline.
Marten getter.
Nicklos Hide.
Ulrich Reaser.
Adam Ruk.

7th Class.

Nickloas Leabary.
Mathias Long.
Martan Becker.
peter Rule.
John Nowsman.
Adam Kobar.
John Dyar.
Fredrick Sousar.
Tobias Hollnger.
Michal Gudey.
John Hernly.
John Minich.
John Shumaker.
Abraham Eversoal.
Abraham Humer.
Christian Marten.
George pifer.
John Humer.
David Fogelsonger.

8th Class.

George Gantz.
George Werner.
Mickal Hubar.
Andrew Halter.
Jacob Shole.
Cunas Murrey.
John Eabey.
John Hubar.
Jacob Gudey.
Christian Wenger.
Fredrick Nowman.
George . fishoake.
Jeames Clune.
Christian Earhart.
John Rupart.
Fred'r Ruston.

A RETURN OF CAPT. ANDREW BOGGS COMPANY OF THE SEVENTH BATTALION OF MILITIA IN LANCASTER COUNTY COMMANDED BY COL'N ALEX'R LOWERY. (c.)

Captain.

Andrew Boggs.

Lieut.

James Cook.

Ensign.

John Messer.

Serjents.

Nicholas Redsacker.
George Snapper.

Corporals.

James Flin.
John Drivenstate.

1st Class.

Joseph Galbreth.
John Eversole, Sen'r.
John Nicholas.
John Bower.
John Mummah.
Christian Blasor.
John Crill.
Jacob Earley.
John Grider, Jun'r.
William Gray.
Joseph Shank.
Thomas Scott.
Petter Stouts.

2d Class.

Abraham Neesly.
Henry Cip.
Mich'l McCafferty.
George Root.
Jacob Neesly.
John Eversole, Jun., big.
Thomas Hasson.
Robert Thompson.
John France.
Andrew Bower.
George Newberry.

3d Class.

Christian Horst
John Bruniman.
Sam'l Scott.
John Wiland, Jun'r.
John Laver.
John Earley.
Phillip Starn.
John Cornhorst.
Jacob Clapper.
John Bruniman, Jun'r.
George Ammond, Jun.

4th Class.

John Sharp.
Phillip Holinger.
Abraham Shaver.
Benjamin Whisler.
Jacob Barrick.
Jacob Holinger.
John Esleman.
John Nicky.
Mathew Gray, Jun'r.
Petter Leighty.

5th Class.

Martin Hisey.
Petter Hisey.
Robert Craig.
Bartrim Galbreth.
Michale Neesly.
Robert Connel.
George Lindimore.
John Elder.
Christian Franc.
Randle McClure.
Jacop Eversole, Ju'r.

6th Class.

Sam'l Wilson.
William Hawk.
Sam'l Woods.
Christ'n Bruniman.
John Longnecker.
Hugh Moore.
Peter Root.
John Cook.
Cha's Bruniman, Jun'r.
John Shank.
John Grider.
Wil'm Messer, Jun'r.
Jacob Oldwiler.
Jacob Brubacher.
George Hikes.
John Wilson.
James Karr.
Christian Stonr.
Nathan Woods.
Stophel Holinger.
Jacob Fuglesong.
Abraham Albert.
George Counce.

7th Class.

Petter Hailsomr.
Jacob Angle.
John Horst.
Jacob Laver.
Dan'l Kinsinger.
James Murphey.
Zacharia Moore.
Jacob Winecop.
David Martin.
Jacob Shimph.
Joseph Rheam.
Jacob Bruniman.
Abr'm Fredrick.
Jacob Snider.
John Steman, Jun'r.
Sam'l Thompson.

8th Class.

Isack Rheam.
John Brubacher.
Henry Wilhelm.
Robert Wilson.
John Angle.
Thommas Messer.
Dan'l Stramler.
John Wiland, Sen'r.
Abr'm Scott.
Joseph Hisey.
John Dukeminer.
Abr'm Willislegle.
Mathew Gray, Sen'r.
Henry Darr.
Wil'm Peck.
Andrew Hikes.
Chris Eversole.
Henry Bruniman.

The Above Retorn is Just & true.
Certifyd by

AND. BOGGS. Capt.

RETURN OF CAPT. NOAH CEASEY'S COMPNY BEING THE FIFTH OF THE SEVENTH BATTALION OF LANCASTER COUNTY MILLITIA UNDER COMMAND OF LUT. COL'N ALEXANDER LOWRY, ESQR., FOR THE YEAR 1783. (c.)

Capt.

Noah Ceasey.

Lut.

Wm. Smith.

Es.

Chris't Dettear.

First Class.

1 John Whitmore.
2 George Hatz.
3 Daniel Laman.
4 Martin Fare.
5 Henry Hershea.
6 Christian Longanker.
7 Joseph Eversole.
8 Jacob Druckinmiller.
9 Abraham Trottey.
10 John Kinkell.
11 Steven Showar.
12 Jacob Koover.
13 Christian Byar.
14 George Seaver.

Second Class.

15 Adam Minnich.
16 Peter Fooks.
17 John Garhart.
18 Christian Wenger.
19 Casper Werner.
20 Henrey Lesher.
21 Jacob Myar.
22 Henry Wengar.
23 Petar Hagey.
24 Thomas Spencer.
25 Fred'k Risht.
26 Abm. Karver.

Third Class.

27 John Camaron.
28 John Hatz.
29 Henrey Higns.
30 Gotleep Spone.
31 Ab'm Laman.
32 Michal Longneker.
33 John Gorman.
34 Benjamin Nowman.
35 Peter Risht.
36 Ab'm Stigenwald.
37 Charls. Smith, Ju'r.
38 Peter Dineius.

Fourth Class.

39 Fred'k Karager.
40 John Rudey.
41 George Secrist.
42 John Fritz.
43 Christian Hernly.
44 Daniel Longaneker.
45 John Bomgardner.
46 John Sharer.
47 Jacob Rife.
48 Adam Werffell.
49 Christian Eversoal.
50 Christian Snyder.
51 Joseph Hummer.
52 Morgen Jinkens.
53 Tobias Kuster.
54 Peter Frey.
55 John Grove.

Fifth Class.

56 Andrew Bartruff.
57 Matheas Helton, Sarjt.
58 Phelip Bretz, Sarjt.
59 Jacob Myar, Sarjt.
60 Fred'k Druckinmeilr, Drum
61 Emanaul Dyar, fifer.
62 Jacob Kellor.
63 Peter Bream.

64 Jacob Hagey.
65 Peter Kockerly.
66 Ludawick Kaslear.
67 Daniel Laman, Ju'r.
68 John Florey.
69 Joseph Shock.
70 Michael Goodadel.
71 Jonas Hummer.
72 Christian Tanner.
73 David Rollen.

Sixth Class.

74 Conrod Wert.
75 Jacob Lithey.
76 Henry Longnecker.
77 Adam Matzabocher.
78 George Hounstone.
79 Christian Herkelrode.
80 Jacob Earhart, Ju'r.
81 John Garman, Ju'r.
82 Abraham Fooks.
83 Peter Platenborager.
84 Michael Fogelsonger.
85 Nickaloas Hide.
86 Ularaik Kinser.
87 Adam Keek.
88 Philip Arnold.
89 Fred'k Platenbaroger.
90 John Shuck.
91 Jacob Saltzar.

Seventh Class.

92 Nickalous Lebary.
93 Mathias Long.
94 Martin Becker.
95 Peter Rule.
96 John Nousman.
97 John Dyar.
98 Fred'r Sousear.
99 Michal Gudey.
100 George Graber.
101 John Hernly.
102 Achelborager John.
103 John Minnich.
104 John Shumacker.
105 Ab'm Eversoal.
106 Christian Marten.
107 Ab'm Hummer.
108 George Pefer.
109 John Hummer.
110 David Fogelsonger.

Eighth Class.

111 George Gantz.
112 Andrew Halter.
113 John Eabey.
114 John Huhar.
115 Jacob Gudey.
116 Christian Wenger.
117 George Fishoak.
118 Christian Earhart.
119 John Rapart.
120 Fred'r Raston.
121 George Stake.
122 Jacob Marten.
123 Henrey Hergood.

Lancaster County—

Personaly came Noah Keasy before me the Subscriber and Made Oath that the Within Return is Just and true.

NOAH CEASEY, Capt.

Sworn & Subscribed before me May 6th, 1784.

JACOB COOKE.

(c.) This is to Certify that William Hay procured a Substitute, named Philip Arnold to Serve his Tour of Duty in the fifth Class of the 7th Battalion of Lancaster County Militia, which Substitute passed muster and did his Duty as others from me.

November 27th.

NOAH CEASEY, Capt. 5 C. Y.

EIGHTH BATTALION

LANCASTER COUNTY MILITIA.

CAPT. DAVID MORGAN'S COMPANY.

A Muster Roll of the Eighth Battalion of Lancaster County, from Earl Townshin, Commanded by Colonel Peter Grubb, Destined for the Defence of Philadelphia, June 1, 1776. (b.)

Captain.
David Morgan.

First Lieutenant.
John Norton.

Second Lieutenant.
Peter Miller.

Ensign.
Nicholas Fought.

Privates.

Edward Good.
John White.
Henry Hambright.
Lenhart Giest.
William Runnals.
James Irwin.
Christopher Horne.
John Showalter.
John Shearer.
John Rhoads.
Rudy Sheaver.
James Vogan.
Philip Shearer.
William Heidler.
James Martin.
George Hinkle.
James Kimes, Jr.
Henry Norton.
George Ryan.
William Crawford.
Robert Monroe.
Thomas Moore.
George Giest.
Fred'k Rodaker.
Nicholas Troutwine.
Jacob Weams.
Abraham Andrew.
Jonathan Irwin.
Phillip Rhoads.
Barnard Wolf.
Thomas Davis.
Francis Hanne.
Michael Ellick.
Martin Werns.
John Rusler.
Isaac Greay.
Jacob Rhoads.
Michael Bronse.
Conrad Fasnocht.
Jacob Shirk.
Jacob Aker.
Jacob Hinkle.

CAPTAIN JOHN HUBER'S COMPANY.

A Muster Roll of Company of Associators of the Eighth Battalion of Lancaster County, Commanded by Colonel Peter Grubb, Ordered for the Defence of Philadelphia, June 24th, 1776. (b.)

Captain.
John Huber.

Lieutenant.
Christian Hollinger.

Privates.

Conrad Mark.
John Sheets.
Henry Mark.
Michael Kenrick.
John Kenrick.
Jacob Hollinger.
Daniel Hollinger.
Andrew Messersmith.
Abraham Bollman.
Casper Egle.
John Jones.
Jonathan Kingray.
John Ringe.
John Russel.
Henry Miller.
Conrad Mark.
Mathias Weimar.
Nicholas Schroph.
Martin Cromar.
Thomas Hauley.

A MUSTER ROLL OF CAPTAIN ALEXANDER MARTIN'S COMPANY OF MILITIA OF COLO. PETER GRUBB'S BATTALION OF LANCASTER COUNTY ON THEIR MARCH FOR THE CAMP IN THE JERSEYS. (d.)

Captain.
Alexander Martin.

Lieuts.
1st. Conrad Laub.
2d. Henry Merckley.

Ensign.

Valentine Kinzer.

Serjeants.

James Blair. Henry Erter.
Thos. McMullen. Samuel Craig.

Drummer.

John Shoe.

Corporals.

Zacheus Piersoll. Christian Romig.
Emigh Snider. Jacob Lud.

Privates.

1. Alexander McElwain.
2. James Martin.
3. Charles Stewart.
4. Alexander McBride.
5. Henry Rankin.
6. Andrew Moreland.
7. Lawrence Shultz.
8. Thomas Bennet.
9. Thomas Norris.
10. John Henley.
11. Hugh Harbeson.
12. Michael Rogers.
13. Josiah Kittera.
14. John Kochran.
15. John Davis.
16. Charles Oldwine.
17. William McElwain.
18. John Houser.
19. Henry Peters.
20. George Reifeild.
21. Tarrance Talls.
22. Andrew Morter.
23. John Lippert.
24. Philip Rode.
25. Daniel Johnston.
26. James Rice.
27. John Stewart.
28. Henry Reichwine.
29. Roger McGee.
30. Francis Nolen.
31. John Berckenhouser.
32. Michael English.
33. William Jennings.
34. John Mast.
35. Jacob Rode.
36. John Carlton.
37. Philip Stikleman.
38. Jacob Kinnard.
39. Thomas Brown.
40. John McMullen.
41. Robert Kenney.

41 privates, 50 shillings each	£102.10.0
4 Serjeants, 50 shillings each	10. 0.0
6 Corporals, 50 shillings each	10. 0.0
1 Drummer	2.10.0
	£125. 0.0

Mustered and passed by & before the Committee of Observation & Inspection in Lancaster the 13th August 1776—And the £125.0.0 advance money paid to Capt. Alexander Martin to pay to his private Serjeants, Corporals & Drummer as p. Rect.

Test. WILL. ATTLEE, Chairman of Com. &c.
ALEXD. MARTIN, Capt.

A MUSTER ROLL OF CAPTAIN JOHN JONES'S COMPANY OF MILITIA OF COLONEL PETER GRUBB'S BATTALION OF ASSOCIATORS IN LANCASTER COUNTY DESTINED FOR THE CAMP IN THE JERSEYS. (d.)

Captain.

John Jones.

Lieutenants.

Jacob Wideman.
John Martin.
George Stober.

Serjeants.

John Sensiman.
Stophel Weidman.
Philip Beck.
Jacob Gorges.

Corporals.

George Coffroad.
John Ream.
Adam Oberley.
Christian Oberley.

Drummer.

Stophel Travinger.

Fifer.

John Bassler.

Privates.

1. George Long.
2. Valentine Stober.
3. Adam Frantz.
4. Francis Brumbach.
5. Hannes Eberley.
6. Hannes Appel.

7. Conrad Herman.
8. John Graff.
9. Henry Landes.
10. Christopher Bricker.
11. Tietrick Walch.
12. Bernhart Grauss.
13. Conrad Rathman.
14. Michael Long.
15. John Arndies.
16. William Stober.
17. John Wacker.
18. Ludwig Lehman.
19. David Meinzer.
20. George Kettig.
21. Fredrick Hacher.
22. Michael Pitz.
23 Barnard Gardner.
24. Fredrick Riem.
25. John Balmer.
26. Conrad Hass.
27. Daniel Witman.
28. John Travinger.
29. Casper Travinger.
30. Michael Scherley.
31. Fredrick Adam.
32. Leonard Spitsnagle.
33. Hannes Hildebrand.
34. Christopher Gold.
35. John Vertrees.

35 privates, 50 shillings each	£ 87.10.0
4 Serjeants, 50 shillings each	10 .0.0
4 Corporals, 50 shillings each	10 .0.0
1 Drummer	2.10.0
1 Fifer	2.10.0
	£112.10.0
3 more privates	7.10.0
48 men	£120 .0.0

Mustered and passed before the Committee of Observation & Inspection in Lancaster the 15th of August 1776. And the above £120.0.0 advance money paid to Capt. John Jones to pay the above men's advance.

Test: WILL J. ATLEE, Chairman of Committee &c.
JOHN JONES, Capt.

36. William Heidler.
37. John Heffer.
38. Jacob Oberley.

A MUSTER ROLL OF CAPT. ISAAC ADAMS' COMPANY OF LIGHT INFANTRY OF MILITIA OF COLONEL PETER GRUBB'S BATTALION OF ASSOCIATORS IN LANCASTER COUNTY—DESTINED FOR THE CAMP IN THE JERSEYS. (d.)

Captain.

Isaac Adams.

Lieutenants.

Thomas Holmes.
John Bechtol.
Henry White.
Peter Feasor.

Serjeants.

John Houpt.
Henry Eichholtz.
Adam Eichholtz.
Christopher Heft.

Corporals.

George Urey.
Peter Blaser.
Nicholas Shoner.
George Feasor.

Drummer.

Philip Slabbach.

Fifer.

Jacob Zinn.

Privates.

1. Peter Rine.
2. Henry Loush.
3. George Slabbach.
4. Andrew Lutz.
5. John Milleisor.
6. Peter West.
7. Wendle Weinholdt.
8. John Lesher.
9. Henry Brindel.
10. John Holtery.
11. Abraham Eshelman.
12. John Hoffman.
13. John Shoup.
14. Peter Kern.
15. Henry Lisher.
16. George Killer.
17. George Eberhart.
18. Lorentz Steffer.
19. Peter Smith.
20. Abraham Bower.

21. John Grill.
22. John Colman.
23. Michael Weinhold.
24. George Weinhold.
25. Michael Hortmer.
26. David Barrener.
27. George Coppes.
28. Henry Snyder.
29. Henry Gier.
30. Hector Pain.
31. Philip Valentine.
32. Jacob Leed.
33. George Valentine.
34. Michael Young.
35. William Witman.
36. Conrad Derr.

36 Privates, 50 shillings each	£ 90 .0.0
4 Serjeants, 50 shillings each	10 .0.0
4 Serjeants, 50 shillings each	10 .0.0
1 Drummer	2.10.0
1 Fifer	2.10.0
46 men	£115 .0.0

Mustered and passed before the Committee of Observation & Inspection in Lancaster the 15th of August 1776—And the above One Hundred & fifteen pounds advance Money paid to Capt. Isaac Adams to pay his men.

Test: WILLE ATLEE, Chairman of Committee &
ISAAC ADAMS, Captn.

A MUSTER ROLL OF CAPT. DAVID MORGAN'S COMPANY OF MILITIA OF COLNEL PETER GRUB'S BATTALION IN LANCASTER COUNTY, AUGUST THE 16TH 1776—DESTINED FOR THE CAMP IN THE JERSEYS. (d.)

Captain.

David Morgan.

Lieutenants.

1st. John Norton.
2nd. Peter Miller.

Ensign.

Philip Road.

Serjeants.

John Sheafer.	James Erwin.
William Jones.	Fred. Rodecker.

Corporals.

Jonathan Erwin.	Wm. Reynolds.
Isaac Gray.	Jacob Sherk.

Drum Major.

Christopher Sower.

Privates.

No.

1. Henry Norton.
2. Francis Haun.
3. John Erwin.
4. Rudolph Sheafer.
5. James Keimer.
6. Wm. Crawford.
7. Thos. Davis.
8. Edward Good.
9. Abraham Andrews.
10. Michael Sauer.
11. Michael Brause.
12. Martin Wertz.
13. Nicholas Troutwine.
14. James Wogan.
15. Jacob Stiegler.
16. Joseph Hardy.
17. Andrew Colp.
18. John Fasnacht.
19. Jacob Ecker.
20. Michael Eley.
21. Benja. Shenniman.
22. Jacob Werntz.
23. Henry Nise.
24. John Evans.
25. Peter Creps.
26. Leonard Geist.
27. Michael Nockton.
28. Richard Davis.
29. Barnard Wolf.

29 privates, 50 shillings each	£ 72.10.0
4 Serjeants, 50 shillings each	£ 10 .0.0
4 Corporals, 50 shillings each	10 .0.0
Drum Major	2 .0.0
	£ 95 .0.0

Mustered and passed before the Committee of Observation & Inspection in Lancaster the 16th of August 1776—And the above Ninety-five pounds paid to Captain David Morgan to enable him to advance to the Serjeants, Corporals, Drum & privates 50 shillings p. man.

Test: WILLM. ATLEE, Chairman of Com. &c.
DD. MORGAN, Captn.

A MUSTER ROLL OF CAPTAIN JOSHUA EVANS' COMPANY OF MILITIA OF COLONEL PETER GRUBB'S BATTALION OF ASSOCIATORS IN LANCASTER COUNTY—DESTINED FOR THE CAMP IN THE JERSEYS—17TH AUGUST 1776. (d.)

Captain.

Joshua Evans.

Lieutenants.

1st. Thomas Elliot.
2nd. John Martin.

Ensign.

James Watson.

Serjeant Major.

John Evans.

Serjeants.

Thomas Martin.
Joseph Williamson.
Lott Evans.

Corporals.

Nathaniel Spencer.
William Smith.

Drummer.

John Virgin.

Fifer.

Adam Northeimer.

Privates.

No.
1. John Killpatrick.
2. James Miller.
3. Daniel Miller.
4. Patrick McLaughlin.
5. Griffith Evans.
6. Hugh Love.
7. Thomas Rattew.
8. John Martin.
9. William Hudson.
10. Joseph Martin.

11. James McConnel.
12. Amos Evans.
13. Michael Engle.
14. Jacob Northeimer.
15. John Thornbury.
16. John Boling.
17. James Watt.
18. Daniel Ayers.
19. William Nelson.
20. Jacob Ayers', junr.
21. George Hudson (carter).
22. George Hudson (Farmer).
23. James Joy.
24. Henry David.
25. Daniel Shay.
26. Charles Smith.

26	privates, 50 shillings each	£65.0.0
4	Serjeants, 50 shillings each	10.0.0
2	Corporals, 50 shillings each	5.0.0
1	Drummer	2.0.0
1	Fifer	2.0.0
34	Men	85.0.0

Mustered and passed before the Committee of Observation & Inspection in Lancaster the 17th of August 1776 And the above Eighty-five Pounds paid to Captain Joshua Evans to enable him to advance to the Serjeants, Corporals, Drum, Fife and privates 50 shillings p. man.

Test: WILLI. ATLEE, Chairman of Committee &
JOSHUA EVANS, Capt.

A MUSTER ROLL OF PART OF CAPTAIN WILLIAM PARRY'S COMPANY OF MILITIA OF COLONEL PETER GRUBB'S BATTALION OF ASSOCIATORS IN LANCASTER COUNTY—DESTINED FOR THE CAMP IN THE JERSEYS—19TH AUGUST 1776. (d.)

Captain.

William Parry.

Lieutenants.

1st. William Shaw.
2d. Christopher Miller.

Ensign.

Thomas Law.

Serjeants.

William Smith. William McClean.

Corporals.

John Shaw. Martin Felix.

Drummer.

Morgan Evans.

Privates.

1. Joseph Carpenter.
2. James McCleary.
3. William Moody.
4. Henry McLaughlin.
5. James McCleary, junr.
6. William Golding.
7. Robert Miller.
8. John Stunkard.
9. Abraham Law.
10. Hugh Colvin.

10 privates, 50 shillings each	£25 .0.0
2 Serjeants, 50 shillings	5 .0.0
2 Corporals, 50 shillings	5 .0.0
1 Drummer	2.10.0
15 Mens advance	£37.10.0

Mustered and passed before the Committee of Observation & Inspection in Lancaster the 19th August 1776—And the above Thirty seven Pounds and ten Shillings paid to Captain William Parry to advance to his Men 50 shillings each.

Test: WILLE ATLEE, Chairman of Committee &
WILLIAM PARRY, Cpt.

A MUSTER ROLL OF CAPTAIN HENRY WEAVER'S COMPANY OF MILITIA OF COLONEL PETER GRUBB'S BATTALION—29TH AUGUST 1776—DESTINED FOR THE CAMP IN THE JERSEYS. (d.)

Captain.

Henry Weaver.

Lieutenants.

1st. George Fisher.
2d. Conrod Pope.

Ensign.

William Livingston.

Serjeants.

1. Michael Messner.
2. Jacob Gray.
3. John Ludwick.

Corporals.

John Giegley.
Joseph Wright.
James Conner.
Andrew Finefrock.

Drummer.

John Wright.

Fifer.

Valentine Petree.

Privates.

1. Alexander McElwain.
2. Christian Slough.
3. Michael Perkihouse.
4. Robert Christy.
5. Joseph Gillis.
6. James Stonherd.
7. Daniel Steever.
8. David Montgomery.
9. William Snider.
10. William Turndorf.
11. George Steffa.
12 William Zell.
13. Peter Miller.
14. Philip Sidertrecher.
15. John Merner.
16. Roger McLaughlin.
17. Mathias Wallick.
18. Joseph Carver.
19. Wendle Creamer.
20. James Patterson.
21. Adam Styer.
22. Abraham Soffel.
23. Henry Siltneider.
24. Michael Siltneider.
25. Michael Funk.
26. Benjamin Mucle.
27. Philip Funk.
28. John Dunlap.
29. George Fouts.

29 Privates, 50 shillings each	£72.10.0
3 Serjeants, 50 shillings each	7.10.0
4 Corporals, 50 shillings each	10 .0.0
1 Drummer	2.10.0
1 Fifer	2.10.0
38 Men's Advance	£95 .0.0

Mustered and passed before the Committee of Observation & Inspection in Lancaster the 20th of August 1776—And the above Ninety five Pounds to Capt. Henry Weaver to advance to his Men fifty Shillings each.

Test: WILLE ATLEE, Chairman of Committee &
HENRY WEAVER, Capt.

A MUSTER ROLL OF PART OF CHRISTIAN HOLLINGER'S COMPANY OF MILITIA OF COLONEL PETER GRUBB'S BATTALION OF LANCASTER COUNTY, DESTINED FOR THE CAMP IN THE JERSEYS—26TH AUGST. 1776. (d.)

Captain.

Christian Hollinger.

Ensign.

John Gingerich.

Privates.

1. Philip Miller.
2. John Shitz.
3. Michael Gingerich.
4. Daniel Hollinger.
5. John Ink.
6. Daniel Hollinger, junr.
7. Jonn Jones.
8. Henry Miller.
9. Valentine Howalter.
10. William Maypowder.
11. William Smith.
12. Thomas Hollinger.
13. Henry Custer.
14. Thomas Scott.

14 Privates, 50 shillings each.......................... £35.0.0

Mustered and passed before the Committee of Observation & Inspection in Lancaster the 26th August 1776—And the above Thirty five Pounds paid to Captain Christian Hollinger to enable him to pay the advance of fifty Shillings to his Men above named. 26 August 1776.

Test: WILLE. ATLEE, Chairman of Committee.
CHRISTIAN HOLLINGER, Captain.

CAPTAIN ROBERT GOOD'S COMPANY. (a.)

A Muster Roll of Captain Robert Good's Company of the 8th Battalion of Lancaster County, Commanded by Col. Peter Grubb, Ordered for the defence of Philadelphia.

Captain.

Robert Good.

Privates.

David Jenkins.
Joshua Evans.
John Martin.
Joseph Jenkins.
Thomas Martin.
Thomas Eastburn.
John Watt.
Isaac Tenbins.
Daniel Shay.
Abraham Danbey.
James Watson.
John Tenbins.
Jacob Ayres.
Thomas Elat.
Joseph Williamson.
Thomas Rutter.
Thomas Edwards.
William Smith.
Joseph Martin.
John Evans.
John Thornbury.
Daniel Ayres.
George Hudson.
Isaac Eyris.
James Walsan.
Samuel McConla.
Joshua Evans.
S. Evans.
Amos Evans.
Nathaniel Shener.
Robert Hugh.
John Clendening.
John Martin.
Hugh Lore.
John Kirkpatrick.
James Parke.
William Jenkins.
John Norakemer.
John Baland.
Jacob Norakemer.
Joseph Esenton.
Wm. McQuaid.
John Huston.
John Clelan.
Henry Dowe.
Thomas Hurst.
James McClelland.
Griffith Evans.

(c.) 1777, Nov'r 18th. I do hereby certify that Alex'r Noble and Nathaniel Barber are appointed Adjutant and Quarter Master of the eighth battlion of the County of Lncaster and that the following persons are appointed Officers of he sixth company of the said battalion, vizt.

Captain ....James Barber.
First Lieutenant ....Robert Barber, junr.
Second Lieutenant ....John Barber.
Ensign ....James Patton.

JNO. BAYLY.

Com. made out by order of the President dated 18th Nov'r.

Received of Timothy Matlack Esqr. comm's for the above officers.

JAMES BARBER, Capt.

OFFICERS OF EIGHTH BATTALION. (a.)

Returned August 26, 1780.

Lieutenant Colonel.

James Ross.

Major.

Frederick Hubley.

First Company.

Captain—John Hubley.
Lieutenant—George Trisler.
Ensign—George Lightner.

Second Company.

Captain—John Ewing.
Lieutenant—Daniel Newman.
Ensign—Jacob Bayley.

Third Company.

Captain—Joseph Hubley.
Lieutenant—Thomas Cuthbert.
Ensign—Christian Lenhart.

Fourth Company.

Captain—William Wirtz.
Lieutenant—Thomas Meloney.
Ensign—Adam Keller.

Fifth Company.

Captain—Samuel Boyd.
Lieutenant—Jacob Hubley
Ensign—Simon Snider.

Sixth Company.

Captain—John Miller.
Lieutenant—John Offner.
Ensign—James Davis.

Seventh Company.

Captain—James Davis.
Lieutenant—Valentine Ede.
Ensign—S. Wilkes Kittera.

Eighth Company.

Captain—Jacob Wilhelm.
Lieutenant [Vacant].
Ensign—Joseph Whitmore.

(c.) This is to certify that Charles Klug Private of my Company belongs to the 8th Class: and the following Men Privates of my Company have removed out my district with the Years annexed when they did remove viz:

Peter Steffan, in the Spring of the Year 1781.
David Pine, in the Year..................1780.
John Gansemar, in the Year..............1781.
Michael Crawford died the Year..........1781.
& John Kellor Marched in the fifth Class...1781

Lancastr decr 2d, 1782.

JOHN EWING, Capt'n 2d Class 8th Batt.

MUSTER ROLL OF THE 2ND CLASS 8TH BATALION LANCASTER MILITIA COMANDED BY CAPT. JNO. EWING ON A TOUR OF DUTY AT LANCASTER. (c.)

Names of those whose tour it was.	Names of those who hired as substitutes.	When duty commd.	When duty ended.
Capt.		1781.	1781.
Jno. Ewing,		Apr. 21,..	June 21.
Lieut.			
Geo. Trissler,		Apr. 21,..	June 21.
Ens.			
Chris. Leonard,		Apr. 21,..	June 21.
Serjt.			
Jno. Trissler,		Apr. 21,..	June 21.
Jacob Barr,		Apr. 25,..	June 21.
Jno. Frick,		Apr. 25,..	June 21.
Corpl.			
Danl. Ayler,		Apr. 21,..	June 21.
Adm. Keller,	Chrisr. Herr,	Apr. 26,..	June 21.
Peter Riblet,		Apr. 23,..	June 21.
Drum.			
Joseph Jacobs,	John Musser(farmer),..	Apr. 21,..	June 21.
Fifer.			
Peter Shindle,		Apr. 23,..	June 21.
Private.			
Fredk. Shaeffer,		Apr. 21,..	June 21.
Jno. Jones,		Apr. 21,..	June 21.
Henry Hook,		Apr. 21,..	June 21.
Nicholas Martin,		Apr. 21,..	June 21.
Adm. Stockslener,		Apr. 21,..	June 21.
Jacob Bakestoes,		Apr. 21,..	June 21.
Isaac Bargle,		Apr. 21,..	June 21.
Jno. Shaeffer,		Apr. 21,..	June 21.
Jno. Fisher,		Apr. 21,..	June 21.
Chris. Knees,	Simon Brant dischd. at muster May 6th by Col. Hubley.	Apr. 21,..	May 6.
Michl. Greendaker,	Michl. Rynehart,	Apr. 21,..	June 21.
George Kessel,	Fred. Myer,	Apr. 21,..	June 21.
Michl. Musser,	Mark Thea, Dischgd. at muster May 6th; Geo. Young comd. for do.	Apr. 21,..	June 21.

MUSTER ROLL OF THE 2ND CLASS 8TH BAT'N—Continued.

Names of those whose tour it was.	Names of those who hired as substitutes.	When duty commd.	When duty ended.
		1781.	1781.
Fredk. Fainot, ...	Nicholas Gerlock, discharged at muster May 6th; Geo. Gerloch comd. for him same day.	Apr. 21,..	June 21.
Gotleb Naumar, ...	Felix Bough, dischd. at muster May 6th the 22nd J. Metzker comd. for do.		
Peter Bolinger, ...	Peter Weill, ...	Apr. 21,..	June 21.
Jacob Glatz, ...	Jno. Deredinger.		
Mathias Young, ...	Chris. Keller dischd. 6, May.	Apr. 21,.	May 6.
Andw. Bakestoes, ...	Danl. McIntire, ...	April 21,.	June 21.
Jacob Reigart, ...	Conrad Gelder dischd. 6 May; Andw. Libely comd. 10 & dischd. 18th, under age; Wm. Thompson Comd. 18.	Apr. 22,.	June 21.
Casper Laurence, ...	....	Apr. 22,..	June 21.
Stophel Uxx, ...	Mathias Smith, ...	Apr. 21,..	June 21.
Peter Litsaberger, ...	Michl. Algyer, dsichd. May 6th; Danl. Myer commd. 8th of do. for do.	Apr. 22,..	June 21.
Henry Hain, ...	Joseph Brown, ...	Apr. 22,..	June 21.
Jno. Graeff, ...	Jno. Nixtorf, ...	Apr. 22,.	June 21.
David Lauck, ...	Jno. Lauck, ...	Apr. 22,..	June 21.
Jno. Lutman, ...	Jno. Kreeger, ...	Apr. 22,..	June 21.
Geo. Musser, ...	Jacob Tawers, ...	Apr. 22,..	June 22.
Adam Weaver, ...	Samuel Penn, ...	Apr. 22,..	June 21.
Geo. Koch, ...	Ferdihand Kenay, dischd. May 6th; Geo. Koch Comd. his self the 12th.	Apr. 22,..	June 21.
Peter Conn, ...	Jno. Litener, ...	Apr. 22,..	June 21.
Henry Lutz, ...	Stephen Lutz, ...	Apr. 21,..	June 21.
Peter Miller, ...	Michl. Rynehart, ...	Apr. 23,..	June 21.
Jno. Palmer, ...	Jacob Peterman, ...	Apr. 21,..	June 21.
Jno. Orr, ...	....	Apr. 23,..	June 21.
Casper Brooner, ...	Philip Thomas, ...	Apr. 21,..	June 21.
Joseph Thornbery, ...	....	Apr. 23,..	June 21.
Adm. Shitz, ...	Jno. Deredinger commd. ser do. did duty till the 11 May.	Apr. 23,..	June 21.
Fredk. Byrade, ...	....	Apr. 22,..	June 21.
Jno. Immell, ...	....	Apr. 23,..	June 21.

MUSTER ROLL OF THE 2ND CLASS 8TH BATTALION—Continued.

Names of those whose tour it was.	Names of those who hired as substitutes.	When duty comm'd.	When duty ended.
		1781.	1781.
Jacob Knale,		Apr. 23,..	June 21.
Valentine Bossler,	Jno. Sell,	Apr. 23,..	June 21.
Jacob Mederd,		Apr. 23,..	June 21.
Geo. Klyne,	Geo. Kurtz,	Apr. 24,..	June 21.
Jacob Bear,	Danl. Shyreman,	Apr. 24,..	June 21.
Jno. Kurtz,		Apr. 25,..	June 21.
Jacob Nininger,	Isaac Peter,	Apr. 33,..	June 21.
George Keller,		Apr. 25,..	June 21.
Fredk. Keller,		Apr. 25,..	June 21.
Thomas McManus,		Apr. 25,..	June 21.
Peter Sipe,	Michl. Rautmakor,	Apr. 25,..	June 21.
Martin Myers,	Samuel Davis,	Apr. 23,..	June 21.
Henry Cryder,			
Stophel Haiger,	Peter Long,	Apr. 25,..	June 21.
Abram,	Chris. Eberman,	Apr. 29,..	June 21.
Jno. Miley,	Geo. Leonard,	Apr. 29,..	June 21.
Jno. Lauman,	Geo. Smith,	Apr. 29,..	June 21.
Jno. Johnson,	Henry Taeff,	May 2,...	June 21.
Fred. Stoneman,	Michl. Gumph,	May 2,...	June 21.
Andrew Mentzer,	Sebastian Marquart,	Apr. 21,..	June 21.
James Kain,	Michael House,	Apr. 23,..	June 21.
Henry Pinkerton,	Jno. Booch,	Apr. 22,..	June 21.
Chrisr. Oxer,		May 7,...	June 21.

Lan'r, April 30th, '81. Then mustered above company as above specified.

ADM. HUBLEY, S. L. Lr. Cy.

MUSTER ROLL OF 3D CLASS 8TH BATALL LANCR. COUNTY MILITIA ON A TOUR OF DUTY AT LANCASTER, COMD. BY. (c.)

Names of persons who served.	Names of persons who furnished substitutes.	Time when duty commd.	Time when duty ended.
Capt.		1781.	1781.
Jos. Hubley,		June 25.	Aug. 23.
Lt.			
Jno. Offner,			
Ensign.			
Jacob Baily,			July 30.
Clerk.			
George Witzell,			Aug. 23.
Serjt.			
James Boyd,			
Jacob Long,			
Jno. Shartle,			
Corpl.			
Chrisr. Apple,			
Drum.			
Joseph Jacobs,			
Fifer.			
Peter Shindle,			
Privates.			
Ludwig Hoover,			July 29.
Jno. Rishling.			
Ludwig Dennut.			
Jno. Eppele.			
Jno. Jordan.			
Peter Razor.			
Adm. Hirshberger.			
Fredk. Swindle,			Aug. 23.
Jno Lutz,			July 29.
Adm. Dembach.			
Jacob Flubacher,			Aug. 23.
Jno. McGuire,			July 29.
Jno. Brandt.			
Jacob Shrotl, say Saml.,			Aug. 23.
Ludwig Wiland.			
Milchier Snyder,			July 29.
Henry Myer.			
Anthony Genter,		June 25.	July 29.
Maths. Sawnelsen,			Aug. 23.

MUSTER ROLL OF 3RD CLASS 8TH BATALL. LANCR. COUNTY.

Names of persons who served.	Names of persons who furnished substitutes.	Time when duty commd.	Time when duty ended.
		1781.	1781.
Jno. Bickham,			July 29.
Maths. Dehuff.			
Jno. Franciscus,			Aug. 23.
Jno. Pinkerton,			
Jacob Doubentour,			July 29.
Jonas Mitzgar.			
Geo. Eichholtz,			Aug. 23.
Jno. Lightner,			
Philip Bottenstine,			
Jacob Lauman,	Henry Geiger,		July 29.
Geo. Baker,			Aug. 23.
Sebast Marquart,	Michl. App.		
Chrisn. Stitle,	Martain Bard.		
Jno. Keller,	Abr. Peters.		
Fredk. Bausman,			
Geo. Young,	Milchr. Rudesell.		
Jacob Wien,	Geo. Lutman.		
Fredk. Cows,	Geo. Moore.		
Wm. Myer,			
Henry Taeff,	Anthoy. Welty.		
Saml. Davis,	Geo. Kurtz.		
Jno. Landy,	Aaron Levy.		
Michl. Sander,	Peter Lewis.		
Fredk. Byroth,	Jacob Schner.		
Peter Long.			
John Wier.			
Chrisr. Good.			
Jacob Grove,	George Graeff.		
George Lenhan,	Josiah Lockert.		
Adm. Koeller,	Jaspar Yeates.		
Jno. Criner,	Jacob Ricksager.		

Lanc'r, June 26th, 81. Then mustered above company as above specified.

ADM. HUBLEY,
S. L. L'r Cy.

A PROVISION RETURN FOR THE 4TH DRAUGHT OF LANCR. COUNTY MILITIA COMMD. BY COL. JAMES ROSS FOR FOUR DAYS COMMD. THE 4TH & ENDING THE 7TH OF OCTR. 1781 BOTH DAYS INCLUDED. (c.)

Companies.	Lt. Colonel.	Majors.	Capt.	Subalterns.	Adjutant.	Qr. Master.	Serjt. Major.	Qr. Mr. Sergt.	Clerks.	Serjents.	Drum & Fifer.	Waggoners.	Rank & file.	Total of rations p day.	No. of Days drawn for.	Total of Rations.
Field and Staff officers,	1	1	......	......	1	1	......	......	......	......	......	......	......	8	4	32
Capt. Wirtz's,	......	......	1	2	......	......	1	1	1	3	3	2	36	53	4	212
Capt. Boyd's,	......	......	1	......	......	......	......	......	1	3	2	......	31	39	4	156
Capt. Scott's,	......	......	1	2	......	......	......	......	1	2	2	1	57	69	4	276
Capt. Clark's,	......	......	1	2	......	......	......	......	1	3	......	1	35	46	4	184
Capt. Willson's,	......	......	1	2	......	......	......	......	1	3	......	1	45	56	4	224
Capt. Walker's,	......	......	1	2	......	......	......	......	......	3	......	......	36	45	4	180
Capt. Allen's,	......	......	1	2	......	......	......	......	......	3	......	......	47	55	4	220
Capt. Bradley's,	......	......	1	1	......	......	......	......	1	3	......	......	39	47	4	188
Total,	1	1	8	13	1	1	1	1	6	22	7	5	326	48	......	1,672

JAMES ROSS, Lt. Col. 4th Draught,
Lancr. Cty. Mila.

MUSTER ROLL OF THE 4TH, 5TH & 6TH CLASS OF THE 8TH BATALION LANCASTER COUNTY MILITIA ON A TOUER OF DUTY UNDER THE [illegible]D OF LT. COL. JAMES ROSS. (c.)

Names of Persons who perform a touer of Duty.	What Class.	Names of Persons who furnished Substitutes.	Time when Duty Commenced.	Time when Duty ended.
Lt. Col.				
James Ross,			1781	1781.
Capt.				
William Wirtz,				
Samuel Boyd,				
Leiut				
Philip Weltzel,				
Ensgn.				
William B[illegible]n,				
George Lightner,				
Staff Offir. Qu. Mr.				
Andrew Graff,				
Qu. Mr. Serjt.				
Michael Grubb,				

MUSTER ROLL OF THE 4TH, 5TH & 6TH CLASS OF THE 8TH BATALION LANCASTER COUNTY MILITIA ON A TOUER OF DUTY UNDER THECOM'D OF LT. COL. JAMES ROSS.—Continued.

Names of Persons who perform a touer of Duty.	What Class.	Names of Persons who furnished Substitutes.	Time when Duty Commenc'd.	Time when Duty ended.
			1781	1781.
D. Majr.				
Christian Weldley,				
Fife Maj.				
Peter Shindel,				
Clark.				
Philip [illegible],				
Gottlib Eberman,				
Serjt.				
Jacob Grubb,				
[illegible] [illegible],				
George Burkhart,				
Philip Lenhare,		Peter Hufnagle.		
Drum.				
Christian Furry,		John Wilson.		
James Mosher,		Ludwick Shell.		

Fife.	
Frederick Heisley,	
William Holleday,	Frederick Hiess
Privates.	
Henrey Hook,	George Cryder
George Smith,	
Martin Ayler,	John Burck.
Frederick Smith,	William Hencel
George Leonard,	Math. Marckle
Thimothy Sullivan,	
Michael Gaff,	Christn. Sheak, Senr.
Casper Remey,	
Mi haal Reinhart,	
Ekr. Kincaid,	
Christian Zorn,	
Peter Long,	Michael Ballard.
John Dalinger,	Henry Landis.
Samuel Shrote,	Jab Metzgar.
Georg Folz,	Daniel Hontsh.
George Kistler,	
Jab Dowenhauer,	Henry Turckney.
John Clelenon,	Jacob Shaffer.
Jacob Metzgar,	Jhn Swarr.
Joseph Ean,	Frank Sanderson.
John Seelig,	
Michael Greamer,	
Christain Odenwald,	
Francis Lambert,	
John Remley,	
Jacob Ris,	Leonard Eigholts.
Michael Spanseler,	
Christian Levey,	
John Nigh,	

ROLL OF THE 4TH, 5TH & 6TH CLASS THE 8TH BATALION LANCASTER COUNTY MILITIA ON A TOUER OF DUTY UNDER THE COM'D OF LT. COL. JAMES ROSS.—Continued.

Names of Persons who perform a touer of Duty.	What Class.	Names of Persons who furnished Substitutes.	Time when Duty Commenced.	Time when Duty ended.
			1781	1781.
Henry Nagle,				
Elias [illegible],				
[illegible] Mydinger,				
[illegible] Girlocke,				
Jacob Marks,				
Christian Eberman,		George Hoofnagle.		
John Grimer,		Daniel Frank.		
[illegible] Lorentz,		Jacob Fry.		
Frederick Lazarus,		Michael Heisley.		
[illegible] [illegible],		Jacob Fetter.		
Martin Jordan,				
Christian Oxer,		Conrad Haas.		
Martin [illegible],				
Peter Deiler,				
Michael Ayler,				
John Blattenberger,				
Thomas Koutz,				
Frederick Shaffer,				
John Goosman,				

[illegible] [illegible],		Jacob Maureau.
[illegible] Grisinger,		
[illegible] Beegler,		
[illegible] [illegible],		Joseph Waggoner.
Henrey [illegible],		
George [illegible],		John Fisher.
Charles [illegible],		
John Pinkerton,		Balser Startzer.
Philip [illegible],		Geremiah Mosher.
[illegible] Carr,		Andrew Lutz.
Christn. Bottenstone,		
George Baker,		Frederick Fritk.
John Lind,		John Getz.
John [illegible],		Casper Micenfelder.
Daniel [illegible],		Chrisn. Shenk, Senr.
Peter Messersmith,		Henrey Hottenstone.
Joseph [illegible],		George Ross.
Henrey [illegible],		
John Bower,		
John Hambright,		William Thompson
[illegible] Lindon,		Andw. Gise.
Peter Wiley,		
Peter Welle,		Peter Bear.
Peter Retneer,		Jacob Graeff.

A LIST OF THE MALE WHITE INHABITANTS BETWEEN THE AGES OF EIGHTEEN AND FIFTY THREE YEARS. RESIDING WITHIN CAPTAIN JOHN HUBLEY'S DISTRICT OF THE 8TH BATTALION LANCASTER COUNTY MILITIA, SUBJECT TO THE MILITIA LAW, AND ALSO THE RESPECTIVE CLASSES TO WHICH EACH OF THEM BELONG. APRIL 21ST, 1781. (c.)

Major.

Frederick Hubley.

Captn.

John Hubley.

Lieut.

George Trisler.

Ensign.

George Leitner.

Sergts.

Anderw Sprecher. Frederick Deorsh.

Corpl.

George Matheot.

Fifer.

Frederick Mellinger.

First Class.

Philip Lenhare Junr.
Frederick Hartafel.
Casper Egle.
Peter Shaffner.
Frederick Lazarus.
Martin Ehler.
Charles Drum.
peter protsman.
John pinkerton.
Christopher Zehan.
Matthias Shipe.

Second Class.

Matthias Slough A member of Assembly.

Jacob Glatz.	John Musser.
David Louch.	Adam Stocksleger.
Philip Thomas.	Christophel Kinass.
Peter Miller.	Peter Kann.
Isaac Bargee.	

Third Class.

Henry Dehuff.	George Ludman.
Conrad Ferree.	John Leitner.
John Epply.	George Bard.
Melchor Rudishill.	Henry Pinkerton.
John Franciscus.	William Tanner.

Fourth Class.

John Mesencope.	Henry Musser.
Francis Fortney.	Michael Reinhart.
Jacob Metzgar.	John Matheot.
Daniel Ehler.	Alexander Kincaid.
Lawrence Burst.	James Crawford.
Adam Hart.	Andrew Tryer.
Adam Britzins.	

Fifth Class.

Leonard Eicholtz.	George Wiss.
George Greisinger.	Michael Spanseiler.
Conrad Koenig.	Michael Heissley.
John Selig.	Ludwick Mettinger.

Sixth Class.

George Yentz.	John Lichly.
Peter Row.	John Maffet.
John Blottenberger.	Frederick Sheffer.
John Metzgar.	Henry Geiger.
Joseph Waggoner.	

Seventh Class.

Francis Heger.	Adam Messencope.
Jacob Mesersmith.	John Walter.
Michael Kuntz.	Michael Sauter.
Ulrick Lampartle.	Henry Etter.
Jacob Fortiney.	Jacob Britges.
Michael Lightner.	Frederick Bausman.

Eighth Class.

Conrad Swartz.
Martin Foutz.
Charles Hinitz.
Jacob Yentz.
David King.
Caleb Johnson.
John Beam.
John Quash.
Almoner, Nicholas Job.

A true & exact List by me

JOHN HUBLEY,
1st Capt. 8th Batt'n,
Lan'r County Militia.

Lancaster Ap 21st 1781.

1781.

RETURN OF THE MALE WHITE INHABITANTS BETWEEN THE AGES OF EIGHTEEN AND FIFTY THREE YEAR, RESIDING IN MY WARD WITH THE CLASSES THEY BELONG TO VIZ:—SECOND COMPANY, 8TH BATTALION. (c.)

First Class.

Vallentine Hoffman.
Christian Levi, Sen'r.
Hinry Maurer.
Joseph Sheaff.
Peter Geedy.
Dewald Smith.
Abraham Steigerwald.
Jacob Idenouer.
John Leibley.
Jacob Krug.
Philip Heidy.
Emanuel Singer.
Peter Bugh.
John Ritesell.
Christian Crawford.
George Millsoch.
John Shaffner.
Rudy Herr.
Christian Ritesell.
Henry Seybold.

Second Class.

Henry Kryder.
Nicholas Martin.
Valentine Bossier.
Christopher Oxer.
John Trisler.
Jacob Reigard.
Henry Hook.
Henry Lutz.
Henry Hain.
Andrew Backenstose.
Christian Herr.
Jacob Backenstose.
George Kessel.
John Palmer.
Casper Lorentz.
Frederick Stoniman.
George Leonard.
John Frick.
Jacob Barr.

Third Class.

Peter Cazor.
Adam Hirshberger.
Frederick Wensel.
Jasper Yeates.
Gottlieb Felter.
John Lutz.
Adam Hirshman.
Addam dambach.
Jacob Flubacher.
aron Levi.
Henry Geyer.
John McGuire.
George Eicholtz.
Emanuel Herr.
Michael App.
John Brandt.

Fourth Class.

George Kryder.
Gottlieb Blemler (over age).
John Burke.
Christian Shenk, Jan'r.
John davidinger.
William Hensel.
Marke Gus (over age).
Philip Messenhope.
Henry deringer, Senr.
Michael Horn.
Mathias Marckel.
John Ganumar.
adam Wilhelm.
Christian Zorm.
Henry Barnetheysels.

Fifth Class.

Francis Lambert.
Christian Levi, Junr.
Jacob Zank.
Charles Klug, Senr.
John Kellar.
Christian Shenk, Senr.
John Kryder.
John Remly.
George Gerloch.
Jacob Kryder (son of Michael Kryder).
Peter Stefan.
David Pem.
Michael Crawford.

Sixth Class.

Peter Beer.
Theophilus Goseart.
Martin Geedy.
John Getz.
Jacob Kryder, Son of Jno. Kryder.
Martin Kryder.
Thomas Cautz.
Frederick Frick.
John Weitlle.
Christian Mattheot.
Jacob Shuler.
Henry Bennet.
Philip Brewsel.
Valentine Krug.

Seventh Class.

Bernard Wolff.
daniel Fetter.
daniel Chrisman.
John Shertz.
John Schwenke.
John Hoffstater.

Michael Shenk, Junr.
andrew Bowman.
Valentine Brennison.
Joseph Walter.
Henry deringer, Junr.
Ludwick Holesworth.
Peter Walter.
John Mawrer.
daniel Blottenberger.
Joseph Huber.
Robert Campbell.
George Edder.
John Smith.
John Moore.
George Hukelwiller.

Eighth Class.

George Murquort.
Charles Klug, Junr.
Paul Zantzinger.
Christopher demuth.
John Shenk.
Casper Tribble.
Jasper Ewing.
Thomas duncan.
Jacob Schwartz.
Jacob Marks.
adam Paul.
John Switzer.
Frederick Witman.
Henry Kaufman.
Jacob Genser.

Signed at Lancaster Jun. 27th 1781.

JOHN EWING, Capt. 2d Class,
8th Batt. L. C. M.

A LIST OF THE MALE WHITE INHABITANTS, BETWEEN THE AGES OF EIGHTEEN AND FIFTY THREE YEARS RESIDING WITHIN CAPTAIN JOSEPH HUBLEY'S DISTRICT, OF THE 8TH BATTALION LANCASTER COUNTY MILITIA, SUBJECT TO THE MILITIA LAW TO WHICH EACH OF THEM BELONG: AND ALSO THE RESPECTIVE CLASSES. APRIL 21ST, 1781. (c.)

Col. of the 8th Battalion.
James Ross.

Capt. of the 3d Company.
Joseph Hubley.

Lieut. of the 3d Company.
Philip Weitzel.

Ensign of the 3d Company.
Christ'n Lenhare,

Clerk of the Company.

George Weitzell.

Sergeants.

Jacob Long.
John Shartle.

Corporals.

Peter Long.
Christ'n Apple.

First Class.

Michael Klein.
Isaac Peters.
George Ilger.
John Roberts.
Levy Andrew Levy.
John Henneberger.
Christopher Myers.
John Griner.
Frederick Weaver.

Second Class.

Stophel Hager.
John Lauman.
Mathias Young.
John Graff.
Michael Gundaker.
Jacob Dieler.
John Lutman.
Fredrick Keller.
George Keller.
Jacob Nininger.
Frederick Falnot.

Third Class.

George Moore.
Ludwig Denick.
John Reishling.
Abraham Peters.
Ludwig Hoover.
John Musser.
Caleb Coope.
Anthony Syfert.
John Jordan.
Josiah Lockert.

Fourth Class.

Isaac Solomon.
John Bowsman.
Jacob Graeff.
George Gundaker.
Henry Stuber.
William Rowell.
Francis Sanderson.
Timothy Sullivan.
John Coope.
John Brenneman.

Fifth Class.

Levy Soloman.
Peter Hoofnagle.
Frederick Heiss.
Baltzer Stertzer.

William Webb.
Jacob Fetter.
Nicholas Groll.
John Eberman.
William Thompson.
Jacob Kagy.

Sixth Class.

George Ross.
Peter Deeler.
David Diffenderfer.
Jacob Mourer.
Samuel Wylie.
Jacob Sando.
Adam Fontrout.
Peter Wile.
William Weiss.
Andrew Lutz.
George Good.
Conrad Hass.
John Getz.

Seventh Class.

Christian Wirtz.
John Witmer, Junr.
John Kip.
John Houston.
Joshua Isaacs.
Nicholas Long.

Eighth Class.

Myer Soloman.
Thos. Cuthbert.
Philip Diffenderfer.
Philip Klein.
Nicholas Smous.
George Sands.
Andrew Graff.
Ludwig Fritz.
Christian Neff.
Jacob Killer.
John Cook.
Almoner, Ludwig Lauman.

A true & Exact List by me

J. HUBLEY,
Capt. 3d Comp'y.

Lancaster, 21st April 1781.

1781.

A LIST OF THE NAMES & SIRNAMES OF THE MALE WHITE INHABITANTS, BETWEEN THE AGES OF EIGHTEEN AND FIFTY THREE YEARS SUBJECT TO THE MILITIA LAW, INHABITING IN THE BOROUGH OF LANCASTER WITHIN CAPT. WILLIAM WIRTZ'S DISTRICT OF THE EIGHTH BATTALION OF LANCASTER COUNTY MILITIA COMMANDED BY COL. JAMES ROSS. (c.)

Capt.

William Wirtz.

Lieut.

Thomas Meroney.

Ensign.

William Bandon.

Serjeants.

George Shafer. Jacob Grubb.

Clerk of the Company.

Philip Dean.

Privates.

First Class.

1. Tobias Barrett.
2. John Earnest.
3. Philip Arnold.
4. Baltzer Martin.
5. Martin Darewart.
6. Henry Sibole.
7. Henry Teaf.

Second Class.

8. Gotlieb Nauman.
9. Jacob Mederd.
10. George Foltz.

Third Class.

11. Samuel Shrode.
12. Jacob Dowers.
13. George Curtz.
14. Jacob Zehner.

Fourth Class.

15. Casper Remey.
16. Henry Tuckney.
17. Gotlieb Zehner.
18. Henry Kushler.

Fifth Class.

19. Abraham Reigar.
20. Elias Albright.
21. John Farmwalt.
22. George Hcofnagle.
23. Cornelius Sweitzer.
24. George Weideley.
25. Christian Odenwalt.
26. Henry Nagle.
Peter Lehr.

Sixth Class.

27. Henry Lechler.
28. Christian Weidley, Jur.
29. Peter Fetter.
30. Gerhard Bambach.
31. John Gilliard.
32. David Miller.
33. Henry Weenore.
34. Charles Boyd.
35. Philip Hast.
36. Caspar Michenfelder.
37. Christian Weidley, Senr
Jacob hecketswiler.

Seventh Class.

38. John Koch.
39. Joseph Nagle.
40. John Kuhns.
41. Fredk. Weidley.
42. Fredk. Anspach.
43. George Lindeberger.
44. Michail Huber.
45. Bernhard Greider.
46. Jacob Stahl.
Mathias Koch.

Eighth Class.

47. Jacob Hefer.
48. Jacob Miller.
49. John Albright.
50. William Myer.
51. John Pflugir.
52. Dietrich Heiss.
53. Henry Zehmer.
54. Robert Purdy.
lodwick Koch.

The following have been classed. They being out of Town has prevented my Returning them in their proper Classes.

55. Mathias Koch in the 7th.
56. Lodwick Koch in the 8th.
57. Jacob Heckltswiller in the 7th.
58. Philip Lehr, in the 5th.

WILLIAM WIRTZ, Capt.,
4th Class 8th Batta. L. C. M.

A LIST OF ALL THE MALE WHITE INHABITANTS IN MY DISTRICT, BETWEEN 18 & 53 YEARS OF AGE & EACH CLASS THEY BELONG TO—TAKEN 28TH JUNE A. D. 1781. SAML. BOYD 5TH, CAPT. 8TH BATT. L. C. MILITIA. (c.)

First Class.

Charles Hall, Esqr.
Jacob Kraft.
Mathias Kéhler.
George Graff.
Christ'n Eberman.
John White.

2 Class.

Lewis Heck.
George Musser.
George Koch.
Adam Weaver.
William Bell.
Mich'l Musser.
Jno. Fisher Shoemaker.
John Immel.

3 Class.

Nicholas Miller.
Conrad Graff.
Melhor Snyder.
Matt'w Dehoff.
Anthony Weldy.
Jonas Metzger.
George Becker.

4 Class.

Peter Gonter.
Jacob Sheffer.
Andrew Keiss.
Christian Ish.
Step'n Porter, Esqr.
Nathaniel Hanch.
Mich'l Orndorf.

5 Class.

John Ney.
Jacob Frey.
Frederick Boyer.
Fred'k Heisly.
Fred'k Yeiser.
Fred'k Man.
Jacob Reiger, Doc'r.
Jacob Marx.

6 Class.

Geo. Yost.
Ludwick Schell.
Adam Reigart.
Daniel Frank.
Jacob Shingle.
Jacob Young.
John Fisher.
Geo. Ackerman.
And'w Kramer.

7 Class.

William Cooper.
Jacob Kehler.
Lewis Peter.
Thos. Yeidler.
Jacob Britges.
Lowdon Alliburton.
Matt. Hehl.
John Doyle.

8 Class.

Casper Shafner.
John Lehler.
Casper Fortney.
Peter Walter.
William Flick.
William Henry Esq. (?)
Francis Walter.
Mich. Crawford.

Not Class.

Tobias Musser.
James Cain.

John Dehuff is Ajudant to the third Battalion.

A RETURN OF THE SIXTH COMPANY IN THE EIGHT BATTALION OF LANCASTER COUNTY MILITIA COMMANDED BY COL. JAMES ROSS. (c.)

First Class.

Conrad Lind.
Henery Fortney.
Jacob Dickers.
Casper Bruner.
Joseph Stephenson.
Henery Subil.
Adam Keller.

Second Class.

Peter Bollinger.
Frederick Shaffer.
John Shaffer.
James Kean.
Christopher Ux.
Frederick Byroad.
Henery Oyster.
John Shriver.
Philip Mining.
Thomas Thornbury, dead.
Peter Hitzelberger.
Thomes McManes.
John Jones.

Third Class.

Casper Orman.
Mathias Stonizen.
Anthony Kinter.
John Bickham.
Geo. Graeff.
Henery Myer.

Fourth Class.

Michael Reinhart.
Daniel Glazier.
Jacob Stuff.
Michael Ballard.
William Ruell.
Martin Feigner.

Fifth Class.

Michael Kremer.
Henery Stouffer.
Daniel Keighler.
Martin Capp.
Matthias Smith.
Jacob Brubacker.
Abraham Brown.
Geo. Messersmith.
Henery George.

Sixth Class.

Geo. Beighler.
Geo. Eichelberger.
John Hotts.
Martin Jourdan.
John Wilson.
Leonard Benedict.
Nicholas Hitzelberger.
John Goosman.
John Lint.
Jeremiah Mossea.
Christoph Crawford.
Peter Mourer.

Seventh Class.

Samuel Davis.
Henery Durn.
Henery Rung.
Christopher Deobler.
Jacob Hubert.
Jacob Linde.
John Witcraft.
Jacob Denlinger.
Michael Bower.
John Quash.
Chris Petre.
F. Myer.
Hy. Oster.
William Wallace.
Sebastian Marckwart.

Eighth Class.

Daniel Riblett.
Frederick Doughterman.
Rudolph Cámfor.
Samuel Humbs.
John Alsbaugh.
Philib Mossea.
James Ramsey.
Henry Grap.
Peter Ritner.

A True copy.

JOHN MILLER, Capt. 6th
L. C. M. Lancaster July 24, 1781.

SEVENTH COMPANY MISSING.

1781.

RETURN OF THE MALE WHITE INHABITANTS OF CAPT. JACOB WILHELMS CO'Y. (c.)

First Class.

John Brubacher.
David Stoner.
Jno. Kneissley.
John Myer.
William Geiger.
Jno. Brown.

Second Class.

Peter Seip.
Henry Brubacher.
Peter Bachman.
Jno. Bassler.
Conrad Segrist.
Andrew Mentzer.
Jno. Ore.

Third Class.

Jno. Leib.
Peter Lewigh, over age & marched.
Jno. Kaufman.
Geo. Rickel.
Christian Myer.
Christian Shenck.
Jacob Ricksecker.
Jacob Sener.
Philip Bodenstone.
Martin Bard.

Fourth Class.

Jno. Shreiner.
Jacob Grub.
Andrew Kehler.
Geo. Utz.
Peter Bachman, Jr.
Abraham Huber.
Jacob Huber.
Jacob Good.

Fifth Class.

Christian Brubacher.
Jacob Kaufman.
Geo. Huber.
Peter Grebill.
Jno. Brubacher, Jr.
Christian Bamberger.
Christian Hartman.
Fredk. Staufer.
Peter Flory.

Sixth Class.

Philip Lauer.
Daniel Weigel.
Michael Rickel.
Jno. Schwarr.
Jno. Bower.
George Cummings.
Jacob Myer.
Christian Bodenstone.
Jno. Hubert.

Seventh Class.

Abraham Leib.
Jno. Snyder.
Jos. Brubacher.
Jos. Streit.
Francis Gardner.
Jacob Peifer.
Peter Angstadt.
Martin Myer.

Eighth Class.

Christian Frick.
Christian Streit.
Chris'n Byermeister.
Christian Huber.
Hugh Hackerty.
Henry Hoff.
Henry Seitensticker.
Abraham Fries.

I certify on honor the above is a just & true state of my Company as above Specify'd.

JACOB WILHELM, Capt.

A CLASS ROLL OF CAPTEN HENRY COMY FOR THE YEAR 1781 OF THOSE THAT WAS TO MARCH. (c.)

Class.

Jn. Campie.
Isaac Climson.
Robert Chesnot.
Geret Elwin.
David Henderson.
John Withrow.
Wm. McLaghlin.
Henry Gray.
John Wilson.
Wm. Jones.

Class 7.

Alx. Davidson.
Jno. Fleming, Jur.
Brian McCune.
James Entrican.
Barny Cain.
Wm. Wiley.
Thomas Richardson.

Class 8.

William Shearer.
Patrick Sheels.
Caleb Way.
Charles Kinkead.
Joshua Stewens.
Patrick Cochran.
George Marton.
Wm. Eaiches.
Serg. Bartholomew Coleman.
Henry Hannah.
John Crucher.

Class 1.

Peter Babb.
John Davison.
Isaac Taylor.
Jno. Fleaming, Sen.
James Blelock.
Ezecal Keary.
Hugh Jurdon.
Jese Pears.
James Lovedon.
Samuel Wilson.

A RETURN OF CAPT. JOHN SMITH'S COMPANY THAT DID MARCH IN THE YEAR 1781. (c.)

JOHN SMITH, Capt.

Henry Young.
Wm. Murry.
Robt. McElheny.
Wm. McElheny.
David Brooks.
John Arnold.
Tobias Shields.
Charles Shields.
David Conar.
Jno. McClemmts.
Wm. Barret.
Charles Wallace.
James Smith.
Wm. Bruce.
Patrick Harvey.
Jno. Adams.
Frances Peoples.
——— Waggoner Near the Compas.
——— Skiles Near the Compas.
Wm. Dickey.
Jno. Caruthers.
Jas. Banks.
Ranken.
Robt. Campble.
Robt. Gray.

MUSTER ROLL OF THE 7TH CLASS 8TH BATTALION LANC'R C'Y MILITIA ORDERED ON A TOUR OF DUTY IN LANCASTER FOR THE PURPOSE OF GUARDING PRISONERS OF WAR SEP'R 25TH 1782. (c.)

Names of those Who done duty.	Stations.	Names of those who Hired Substitutes.
Martin Wibrecht,	Capt.	
Danl. Bord,	Lieut.	
James Davis,	Ens.	
Wm. Bandan,	Adjt.	
Sebastian Graff,	Clk.	
Saml. Davis,	Q. M. S.	
Fredk. Bausman,	Serjt.,	Nicholas Bausman.
Peter Shindle,	Serjt.,	Jno. Quash.
Andrew Fultz,	Serjt.	
Adm. Messincop,	Corpl.	
Peter Long,	Corpl.,	Isaac Long.
Robt. Traunsel,	Corpl.,	Jacob Denlinger.
Jacob Fovecy,	Drum,	Jno. Snyder.
Fredk. Melenger,	Fife,	Fredk. Weedley.
Jacob Messersmith,	Privt.	
Michl. Kuntz,	Privt.	
Jacob Kensler,	Privt.,	Ulrich Lombartle.
Jacob Fortney,	Privt.	
Michl. Lightner,	Privt.,	Dischargd.
Michl. Rensler,	Privt.,	Jno. Walter.
Henry Etter,	Privt.	
Fredk. Hook,	Privt.	
Bernd. Wolff,	Privt.,	Dischargd.
Danl. Fetter Senr.,	Privt.,	Dischargd.
Adm. Powell,	Privt.,	Danl. Erisman.
Jno. Shartz,	Privt.	
Henry Hook,	Privt.,	Jacob Hoshter.
Jno. Gerlock,	Privt.,	Vale. Brenizer.
Ludk. Holsworth,	Privt.,	Sick.
Mathias Baker,	Privt.,	Jno. Maurer.
Robt. Camble,	Privt.	
David Snyder,	Privt.,	Saml. Bear, Jr.
Jno. Parcell,	Privt.,	Henry Kevell.
Peter Wyle,	Privt.,	Philip Royer.
Wm. McElhaney,	Privt.	
Henry Myer,	Privt.,	Joseph Streiht.
Francis Gardner,	Privt.	
Jno. Smith,	Privt.	
Alexr. McKoy,	Privt.,	Jno. Moor.
Anw. Lubley,	Privt.	
Jacob Keller,	Privt.,	Jno. Kepp.
Nichl. Long,	Privt.,	Dischargd.
Chris. Gumph,	Privt.,	Francis Haiger.
Jacob Cook,	Privt.	
Jno. Kuntz,	Privt.,	Dischargd.
Jno. Kough,	Privt.	
Michl. Hoover,	Privt.	

MUSTER ROLL OF THE 7TH CLASS 8TH BATTALION LANC'R C'Y MILITIA—Continued.

Names of those Who done duty.	Stations.	Names of those who Hired Substitutes.
Geo. Lindeberger,	Privt.,	Dischargd.
Henry Dearn,	Privt.	
Fredk. Mayer,	Privt.	
Henry Oster,	Privt.	
Jacob Hubert,	Privt.	
Bastion Marquart,	Privt.,	Dischargd.
Chris. Doebber,	Privt.	
Joseph Brown,	Privt.,	Jacob Lindey.
Michl. Bower,	Privt.	
Wm. Thompson,	Privt.,	Isaac Whiteroft.
Wm. Wallace,	Privt.	
Jacob Shartz,	Privt.,	Jacob Keeler.
Lewis Peter,	Privt.,	Dischargd.
Chris. Apple,	Privt.,	London Ally Burton.
Wm. Cooper,	Privt.	
Thomas Yiedler,	Privt.,	Dischargd.
Jno. Bough,	Privt.,	Henry Lane.
Henry Crytzer,	Privt.,	Mn. Shelleberger.
Fredk. Byrode,	Privt.,	Jno. Long Junr.
Henry Sugar,	Privt.,	Dischargd.
Peter Anstat,	Privt.,	Dischargd.
Bernard Cryder.		

MARTIN WEYBRIGHT,
Capt. of the 7th Class 8th Batt.

I do solemnly sincerely declare & Affirm that the Within Muster Role is a just & true state of the Company, under my Command, being 7th Class of 8th Batt., ordered in Command at Lancaster for the purpose of Guarding British Prissoners, without any fraud to the states or any individual thereof to the bist of my knowledege.

MARTIN WEYBRIGHT,
Capt.

Affirmed before me this
6th day of March 1783.
A. HUBLEY.

THE FOLLOWING IS A LIST OF PERSONS WHO (IN CONSEQUENCE OF BEING ALLOW'D A FULL TOUR DUTY), GUARDED TO ELIZABETH TOWN A NUMBER OF BRITISH OFFICERS, PRISONERS OF WAR, TO BE EXCHANG'D VIZT.—(c.)

Lieut. Merrony.	Jacob Stuff.
Ludwig Heck.	Conrad Fisher.
Jacob Zank.	Adam Hart.
Conrad Ferree.	George Yost.
John Weidly.	Jacob Shindle.
Conrad Graff.	Danl. Miller.
Peter Maurer.	George Buch.
Peter Genter.	

I do Certify that the above Men of my Battallion, perform'd a tour of Duty Voluntarily, on being promised that they, when call'd upon in their respective class's should be Credited for a full tour of Duty.

Witness my hand this 29th day of November 1782.

JAMES ROSS, Lt. Col.,
8 B. L. C. M.

To COLO. HUBLEY, or whom it may concern.

THE FOLLOWING MEN ENROLL'D IN MY COMPANY OF THE EIGHTH BATTALION OF LANCASTER COUNTY MILITIA ARE ACCOUNTED FOR IN THE FOLLOWING MANNER, VIZ. (c.)

George Foltz of the 2nd Class	Served as a Seven Months man and on his return remov'd from the District.
*Henry Keesler of the 4th Class.	Mistake in the Name, is George Keeshler, he marched to New Town.
Peter Lehr of the 5th Class.	Enroll'd in Captain Willhelms Company, did not belong to my District, and appears he was not notified, to march.

*The Mistake in Keeshlers Names must have been made in Transcribing of the class Roll, as no such person as Henry Keesler resided within the Bounds of my District.

David Miller	Marched to East Town with prisoners in Col. AtLee's Time, and was allowed a Tour of Duty for the same.—
Henry Weenon	Belongs to the Seventh Class & had notice in the last Call accordingly.
Philip Hart & Jacob Heckitswiller	Are Appealents as will appear by Certificate from the members of the Court of Appeal.
Cornelius Sweitzer.	In Custody for his Fine.

I do certify the above is a true and exact State of those Men enroll'd in my Company belonging to the Eighth Battalion of Lancaster County Militia, s'd not accounted for in the class Roll without Fraud to the State or any Individual.

WILLIAM WERTZ, Capt. 4th Class
of the 8th Batt. Lan. Co'y Militia.

Lancaster December 1st 1782.
To COL. ADAM HUBLEY,
Lieutenant of Lancaster County.

A TRUE AND EXACT LIST OF THE NAMES, OF EACH AND EVERY MALE WHITE PERSON, INHABITING OR RESIDING WITHIN MY DISTRICT, IN THE FIRST COMPANY OF THE EIGHTH BATTALION OF LANCASTER COUNTY MILITIA, BETWEEN THE AGE OF EIGHTEEN AND FIFTY THREE YEARS TAKEN FOR THE YEAR 1782. (c.)

Capt.

John Hubley.

Lieu.

George Trissler.

Ens.

George Leitner.

Almoner.

Nicholas Jobe.

Sergeants.

Frederick Dorsh.
Andrew Tryer.
John Wien.

First Class.

Frederick Mellinger, Fif.
Philip Lenhere.
Casper Egle.
Martin Ehler.
John Pinkerton.
Mathias Shipe.
George Ilger.
Stophel Gumpf.
Michael Wein.

Second Class.

Jacob Glatz.
David Lauch.
Philip Thomas.
Peter Miller.
Isaac Bargee.
John Musser (Farmer).
Adam Stockslagler.
John Frick.
Robert Willson.
George Yost.
Thomas Pinkerton.
Stophel Heger.

Third Class.

Henry Dehuff.
Conard Ferree.
John Eppele.
Melchion Rudisill.
John Franciscus.
George Lutman.
John Leitner.
Henry Pinkerton.
William Tanner.
Frederick Bausman.
Jacob Dowers.
John Tanner.
Jacob Hoffman.
Jacob Gable.

Fourth Class.

John Mesencope.
Francis Fortinee.
Jacob Metzgar.
Daniel Ehler.
Lawrence Burst.
Adam Hart.
Adam Britins.
Henry Musser.
Michael Reinhart weaver.
John Matheot.
Alexander Kinkade.
Philip Gallacker.
William Hensel.
Philip Mesencope.
Devalt Lisinger.

Fifth Class.

Leonard Eicholtz.
Conrad Koenig.
John Selig.
George Weis.
Michael Sponseller.
Michael Heiseley.
Ludwig Mittinger.
George Shenk.
Daniel Witmer.
David Atlee.
Michael Rinehart, skinner
Elias Albright.

Sixth Class.,

George Yentz.
Peter Row.
John Plottenberger.
John Metzgar.
Joseph Waggoner.
John Lighty.
Frederick Sheffer.
Michael Ehler.
Frederick Boyer.
John Lauch.
Daniel Henig.
Robert Moore.

Seventh Class.

Jacob Mesersmith.
Michael Kuntz.
Ulrich Lampartel.
Jacob Fortunee.
Michael Litner.
Adam Mesencope.
John Walter.
Henry Etter.
Joshua Isaacs.
Joseph Ash.
Samuel Davis.
Frederick Hoke.

Eighth Class.

Conrad Swartz.
Martin Foutz.
Charles Hinitz.
Jacob Yentz.
David Koenig.
Martin Cooper.
Michael Trebert.
Michael Hoke Jur.
Isaac Elemaker.
Alexander McCoy.
Caleb Johnson (doubtful whether he be not above 53)

I Do swear, on the Holy Evengilest of Almighty God: That the above list is a just and true state of the male white inhabitants, residing in my District, agreeable to Law, and without any fraud to the State, to the best of my knowledge.

JOHN HUBLEY, 1' Capt.

Sworn before me this
10 Day of July 1782.

ABRAHAM DEHUFF,
S. L. L. Co

A TRUE AND EXACT LIST OF THE NAMES, OF EACH AND EVERY MALE WHITE PERSON, INHABITING OR RESIDING WITH MY DISTRICT, IN THE SECOND COMPANY OF THE EIGHTH BATTALION OF LANCASTER COUNTY MILITIA, BETWEEN THE AGE OF EIGHTEEN, AND FIFTY THREE YEARS. TAKEN FOR THE YEAR 1782. (c.)

Capt.

John Ewing.

Lieut.

Daniel Newman.

Ens.

Jacob Bailey.

Almoner.

John Hopson.

First Class.

Valentine Hoffman.
Henry Mawrer.
Christian Levi, Seur.
Joseph Sheaff.
Peter Geedy.
Dewald Smith.
Everhart Stygerwald, Senr.
Jacob Idenouer.
John Leibley.
Peter Bugh.
John Shaffner.
Rudy Herr.
Christoph Ritesell.
Henry Seybold.
John Ritesell.
Jacob Kinsol.

Second Class.

John Trisler, Sergt.
Jacob Barr, Sergt.
Joseph Walter, Corp.
Henry Hook.
Henry Lutz.
George Kesster.
Henry Hain.
Christopher Oxer.
Nicholas Martin.
Andrew Backenstose.
Jacob Shenk.
John Schliehter.
Michael Kryder.
Christian Herr.
Henry Kryder.
Valentine Bosster.

John Palmer.
Casper Lorentz.
George Hecketwiller.
Frederick Stoneman.
Jacob Medderd.
Jacob Knoll.
Adam Shitz.
Christopher Levi, Junr.
George Leonard.
George Geiger.
Daniel Fetter.
John Gerlock.
Frederick Stubal.
Peter Meyrs.

Third Class.

Michael App.
Peter Razor.
Jacob Flubacher.
Frederick Swensel.
Adam Hirshberger.
Adam dambach.
John Brandt.
John McGuire.
Charles Leederson.
Jacob Musser.
Emanuel Herr.
Michael Klepfer.
Abraham Henneberger.
Aron Levi.
Thomas Roberts.
Jasper Yeates.
Gottlieb Fetter.
John McCormick.
Peter Beer, Junr.

Fourth Class.

Thomas Turner.
Adam Wilhelm.
Christian Zornn .
John Burke.
Christian Shenk.
John Kryder, Junr.
Mathias Marckel.
John dardinger.
Henry Barntheisel.
John Myer.
John Bugh.
Daniel Switzer.
Christian Wolff.

Fifth Class.

Francis Lambert.
Christian Levi, Junr.
Jacob Zank.
John Keller.
John Kryder, Senr.
Lorentz Klepfer.
George Gerloch.
Jacob Kryder (son of Mich. Kryder).
John Rukenbach.
Jacob Shertz.
Lodwick New.
John Bonnat.
Frederick Stone.
Jacob Shafer.

Sixth Class.

Peter Beer, Senr.
Jacob Kryde (Son of Jn's Kryder).
Martin Kryder.
John Getz.
Thomas Cautz.
Frederick Frick.
John Weidele.
Christian Mattheot.
Jacob Shuler.

Henry Bennet.
Philip Brewsel.
Valentine Krug.
Peter Starn.
William Fitz.
Henry Shenk (Son of Mich. Shenk).
peter Lutz.
Martin Geedy.
abraham Stygerwald, Junr.
peter Getz.
adam Kellor.
Frederick Kautze.
Mahtias Fetter.
William Weiss.
Michael Kinsoi.

Seventh Class.

Bernard Wolff.
Daniel Fetter.
Daniel Arisman.
John Shertz.
Jacob Hoffstater.
Velentine Brennisin, Senr.
Lodwick Holesworth.
John Mawrer.
Daniel Blottenberger.
Joseph Huber.
Robert Campbell.
George Edder.
John Smith.
John Moore.
Bernard Craws.
Nicholas Bawsman.
Andrew Leibley.
Frederick Remley.
Jacob Arisman.
Jacob Ritesell.
david Gairey.

Eighth Class.

John Schwenk.
George Murquart.
Charles Klug, Junr.
Paul Zantzinger.
Christopher Demuth.
John Shenk.
Casper Tribble.
Jasper Ewing.
Jacob Marks.
Adam Paul.
Henry Kauffman.
John Koch.
Robert Boyde.
Valentine Brennisen, Junr.
Jacob Peterman.
Christopher Barntheisel.
Archibald Steel.

I Do swear, on the Holy Evengilest of Almighty God: That the above is a just and true state, of the Male White Inhabitants, residing in my District, agreeable to Law, and without any fraud to the State, to the best of my knowledge.

JOHN EWING, Capt'n 2d Comp. 8th Bat.
La. Cy. Ma.

Sworn before me this
2 Day of July 1782.

ABRAHAM DEHUFF,
S. L. L. Co.

A TRUE AND EXACT LIST OF THE NAMES, OF EACH AND EVERY MALE WHITE PERSON, INHABITING OR RESIDING WITHIN MY DISTRICT, IN THE THIRD COMPANY, OF THE EIGHTH BATTALION OF LANCASTER COUNTY, MILITIA, BETWEEN THE AGE OF EIGHTEEN, AND FIFTY-THREE YEARS. TAKEN FOR THE YEAR 1782. (c.)

Capt.

Joseph Hubley.

Lieu.

Philip Weitzel.

Ens.

Christian Lenbare.

Almoner.

Ludwig Lauman.

Sergeants.

Jacob Long. John Shartle.

Corporals.

Peter Long Christian Apple.

Clerk of the Comp.

Geo. Weitzel.

First Class.

Michael Klein. Christopher Myers.
Isaac Peters. John Griner.
John Roberts. Andrew Sprecher.
Levy Andrew Levy.* Peter Brotzman.
John Henneberger. Adam Keller.*

Note.—That Levy And'w Levy has inlisted a Man for the Continental Army Agree able to Law.

Note that Ad'm Keller is appointed Ensign of Capt. Wilhelm's Company.

Second Class.

John Lawman.
Mathias Young.
John Graeff.
Michael Gundaker.
Jacob Dieler.
John Lutman.
Frederick Keller.
George Keller.
Jacob Mininger.
Isaac Peters, Junr.
James Ferguson.
John Ferguson.
Christian Wertz, Junr.

Third Class.

George Moore.
Ludwig Denig.
John Reishling.
Abraham Peters.
Ludwig Hoover.
John Musser.
Caleb Coope.
Anthony Syfert.
John Jordan.
Josiah Lockert.*
George Baird.

Note that Josiah Lockert his Inlisted a Man in the Continental Service agreeable to Law.

Fourth Class.

Timothy Sullivan.
John Bowsman.
Jacob Graeff.
George Gundaker.
Henry Stuber.
John Brenneman.
John Coope.
Henry Huttenstine.
Francis Sanderson.
Henry Dering.
Abraham Witmer.

Fifth Class.

Levy Soloman.
Peter Hoofnagle.
Frederick Heiss.
William Bowsman, Junr.
Baltzer Stertzer.
William Webb.
Jacob Fetter.
Nicholas Groll.
John Eberman.

Sixth Class.

George Ross.
Peter Bieler.
Jacob Mourer.
Samuel Wylie.
Jacob Sando.
Adam Fontrout.
Peter Wile.
William Weiss.
Andrew Lutz.
Conrad Hass.
Daniel Crainor.

Seventh Class.

John Kip.
John Houston (Surgeon to 4th Batt).
Nicholas Long.
George Hoch.
Francis Haiger.
Henry Dering Junr.
Jacob Cook.
Jacob Kagey.*

Note that Jacob Kagey has Inlisted a Man agreeable to an Act of Assembly.

I shall add him to this class he nor I knowing what class he properly belongs to.

Eighth Class.

Myer Soloman.
Philip Diffenderfer.
Philip Klein.
Charles Sando.
And'w Graff 2n Mart'n 8th Batt'n.
Ludwig Fritz.
Christian Neff.
Jacob Keller.

Memo.—That a Number of American Officers & Soldiers and British Prisoners of War Exclusive of the above Male White Inhabitants, Also Peter Weitzel an Ideot & Blizart McCruder a Lunatic reside within the limits of my District.

I Do swear, on the Holy Evengilest of Almighty God: That the above list is a just and true state, of the Male White Inhabitants, residing in my District, agreeable to Law, and without any fraud to the State, to the best of my knowledge.

J. HUBLEY, Capt. 3d Comp'y,
8th Batt'n.

Sworn before me this
8 Day of July 1782.

ABRAHAM DEHUFF,
S. L. L. Co.

A TRUE AND EXACT LIST OF THE NAMES, OF EACH AND EVERY MALE WHITE PERSON, INHABITING OR RESIDING, WITHIN MY DISTRICT, IN THE FOURTH COMPANY, OF THE EIGHTH BATTALION OF LANCASTER COUNTY, MILITIA, BETWEEN THE AGE OF EIGHTEEN, AND FIFTY-THREE YEARS. TAKEN FOR THE YEAR 1782. (c.)

Capt.

William Wertz.

Lieu.

Thomas Maroney.

Ens.

William Bandon.

Sergts.

Joseph Nagle.
George Kushler.
Jacob Shaffer.

Clerk.

Philip Dean.

First Class.

Martin Dowart.
John Stormbach.
John Earnest.
Isaac Keehns.

Second Class.

Gotlieb Nauman.

Third Class.

George Kurtz.
John Nixdorf.
Samuel Shrode.
Nicholas Miller.

Fourth Class.

Gotlieb Lehner.
George Kryder.
Jacob Grubb.

Fifth Class.

George Hoofnagle.	Christian Weidle.
John Formwalt.	Henry Harcoot.
Christian Odewalt.	Jacob Fetter.
Daniel Koyler.	

Sixth Class.

Gerhart Bumbach.	Charles Boyd.
Henry Lecther.	Daniel Whitelock.
Casper Michenfilder.	John Gilliard.
Philip Hart.	

Seventh Class.

Frederick Weidile.	George Lindeberger.
Frederick Arnspach.	Michael Huber.
John Kuntz.	Henry Weenow.
John Koch.	

Eighth Class.

Jacob Heffer.	Jacob Miller.
Jacob Stalh.	John Albright.
John Hennelberger.	William Myers.
Henry Zehmer.	George Grusinger.

I Do swear, on the Holy Evengilest of Almighty God: That the above list is a just and true state, of the Male White Inhabitants, residing in my District, agreeable to Law, and without any fraud to the State, to the best of my knowledge.

WILLIAM WERTZ,
4th Class 8th Batt.

Sworn before me this
15 Day of August 1782.

ABRAHAM DEHUFF,
S. L. L. Co.

A TRUE AND EXACT LIST OF THE NAMES, OF EACH AND EVERY MALE WHITE PERSON, INHABITING OR RESIDING, WITHIN MY DISTRICT, IN THE FIFTH COMPANY, OF THE EIGHTH BATTALION OF LANCASTER COUNTY, MILITIA, BETWEEN THE AGE OF EIGHTEEN, AND FIFTY-THREE YEARS. TAKEN FOR THE YEAR 1782. (c.)

Capt.

Saml. Boyd.

Lieut.

Jacob Hubley.

Ensign.

John Fisher.

First Class.

Chas. Hall.
George Groff.
Ephraim Butler.
Jacob Kraft.
Matt. Kehler.

Second Class.

Lodwick Heck.
Chris'n Kenison.
Jacob Pakestoes.
Michl. Musser.
John Fisher, Shoe.
George Musser.
Geo. Koch.
John Immel.
James Kain.
Geo. Krebs.
Jacob Hoffman.

Third Class.

Conrad Graff.
Jonas Metzger.
Anthony Weldy.
Matt. Deboff.
Mether snider.
Geo. Becker.
Geo. Eigholtz.

Fourth Class.

Jacob Sheffer.
Peter Ganter.
Andw. Kiefs.
H. Porter.
Chas. Brandon.
Chris. Ish.
Nath'l Haneh.
Henry Tuekney.
John Wilborne.

Fifth Class.

Jacob Frey.	John Ney.
Fred Man.	Jacob Slaughter.
Jacob Marks.	

Sixth Class.

Lodw'k Shell.	Jacob Shingle.
A. Riegart.	Jacob Young.
Dan. Franch.	Simon Snider.

Seventh Class.

Jacob Kehler.	Wm. Cooper.
Jno. Doyle.	Matt. Hehl.
Lewis Peter.	James Edgar.
Lowdon Alleburton.	Tho. Yudler.

Eighth Class.

Cas'n Fordney.	Wm. Flick.
Francis Walter.	Jas. Mosher.
Cas'n Shaffner.	Nich. Smous.
Jno. Lehter.	——— Brenisen.
Peter Walter.	

I Do swear, on the Holy Evengilest of Almighty God: That the above list is a just and true state, of the Male White Inhabitants, residing in my District, agreeable to Law, and without any fraud to the State, to the best of my knowledge.

SAML. BOYD, 5th Capt.,
8th Batt.,
L. Co. Militia.

Sworn before me this
first Day of August 1782.

ABRAHAM DEHUFF,

A TRUE AND EXACT LIST OF THE NAMES, OF EACH AND EVERY MALE WHITE PERSON, INHABITING OR RESIDING, WITHIN MY DISTRICT, IN THE SIXTH COMPANY OF THE EIGTH BATTALION OF LANCASTER COUNTY, MILITIA, BETWEEN THE AGE OF EIGHTEEN, AND FIFTY THREE YEARS. TAKEN FOR THE YEAR 1782. (c.)

Captain.

John Miller.

Lieutenant.

John Offner.

Ensign.

James Dalves.

Almonar.

George Bweckerd.

Sargents.

Michgael Groff.
John Hambricth.
George Birckert.

Pif (fifer.)

Peter Shindal.

First Class.

1. Peter Shaffner.
2. Jacob Dickart.
3. Cunrad Lind.
4. Martin Fichner.
5. Henerich Fardny.

Second Class.

1. Peter Bullinger.
2. Frederick Sheffer.
3. Frederick Bayrod.
4. Peter Hitzelberger.
5. Joseph thorenbery.
6. John Jons.
7. Adam Wever.
8. thomas Crason.
9. John Sheffer.

Third Class.

1. Cristor Craffort.
2. Casper Erman.
3. Mathias Q(?)aneson.
4. Henrich Mayer.
5. Antony Ginter.
6. John Bickham.
7. George Graff.
8. Samuel Benn.

Fourth Class.

1. Jacob Motzger.
2. Jacob Stover.
3. Jacob Boss.
4. Casper Remy.
5. John Hambrichgt.
6. George Groff.
7. Michgael Ballart.

Fifth Class.

1. Michgael Kremmer.
2. Michgael Gross.
3. Martin Capp.
4. Robert Transul.
5. Jacob Browbacher.
6. Josep Hampfil.
7. George Mesershmith.
8. John Word.
9. Philib Mimih.

Sixth Class.

1. Peter Maurar.
2. George Eigelberger.
3. John Hotz.
4. Martin Jordan.
5. Mathius Bigler.
6. Peter Bruner.
7. Henrich Yentzer.
8. Nichlaus Hutzleberger.
9. John Wilson.
10. John Gusman.
11. Lanhard Benetick.
12. John Lind.
13. Jeremius Mosher.
14. Frederich Ston.
15. John Geiger.

Seventh Class.

1. John Qash.
2. Cristor Petery.
3. Henrich Dern.
4. Friderich Mayer.
5. Henrich Oster.
6. Jacob Hubert.
7. Sebastian Margart.
8. Christor Devler.
9. Jacob Lindy.
10. Michgael Bower.
11. Jacob Denling.
12. Isack Whithcraft.
13. William Wolles.

Eighth Class.

1. Daniel Ribler.
2. John Alspach.
3. Samuel Humes.
4. Peter Ritner.
5. Rutolve Cuper.
6. Henerich Gross.
7. Adam Moscatnus.
8. Philib Moshar.

I Do swear, on the Holy Evengilest of Almighty: That the above list is a just and true state, of the Male white Inhabitants, residing in my District, agreeable to Law, and without any fraud to the State, to the best of my knowledge.

ABRAHAM DEHUFF, S. L. L. County.

Sworn before me this 24 Day of June, 1782.

JOHN MILLER, Capt. 6th 8 B.
L. C. M.

A TRUE AND EXACT LIST OF THE NAMES, OF EACH AND EVERY MALE WHITE PERSON, INHABITING AND RESIDING, WITHIN MY DISTRICT, IN THE 7TH COMPANY, OF THE 8TH BATTALION OF LANCASTER COUNTY, MILITIA, BETWEEN THE AGE OF EIGHTEEN AND FIFTY THREE YEARS. TAKEN FOR THE 1782 (c.)

Capt.

Martin Weybright.

Lieut.

Gorge Hambright.

Ens.

Jacob Conrad.

First Class.

Benjamin Long.
Peter Lean.
Baltzer Sheling.
Samuel Mayer.
Abraham Royer.
Nicolaus Huhn.
Peter Hess.
John Mayer.
Conrad Shisler.
John Line.

Second Class.

Abraham Hershy.
Gorge kline.
Christian Pinckly.
Jacob Baer.
Martin Mayer, Son of Chris.
John Janstin.
Jonathan Royer.
John kurtz, son of Jacob.

Third Class.

Benjamin Lindes Jur.
Benjamin Hersby.
Henry Bugh.
John Metsler.
Jost Strow.
Jacob kaufman.
Henry Lindes.
Abraham Mayer, son of Mart.

Fourth Class.

Jacob Metsler.
Gorge Bugh.
David Mayer.
John Kurtz, son of Chris.
Peter Fass.
Casper Peter.
Maichel grenewald.
Henry Brentzer.

Fifth Class.

William Cavel.
John Huhn.
John Michel Shriner.
Daniel Reudy, Ju.
Martin Hambright.
Henry Line.
Thomas Davis.
Ludwick Bard.
Andrew Shenow.

Sixth Class.

Phillip Hass.
John Phillip Shriner.
Henry Landis.
John Master.
Michel Reudesill.
Jacob Weidler.
Isac Baer.
Samuel kaufman.

Seventh Class.

Henry Lane.
Martin Shallenberger.
Henry Metzler.
John Long, Ju.
Phillip Bugh.
Isaac Long.
Henry Shuger.
Samuel Baer.
Henry Cevel.
Phillip Boyer.
William Mockleheny.

Eighth Class.

Barnd Fultz.
george Michel Shriner.
gorge Huhn.
Androw Billemayer.
David Shnyder.
John Stalter.

I Do swear, on the Holy Evengilest of Almighty God: That the above list is a just and true State, of the Male white Inhabitants residing in my District, agreeable to Law, and without any fraud to the State, to the best of my knowledge.

ABRAHAM WEYBREGHT, Cap. 7th Company
Lancaster 8th Battalion.

Sworn before me this 24 Day of June, 1782.

ABRAHAM DEHUFF, S. L. L. Co.

A TRUE AND EXACT LIST OF NAMES, OF EACH AND EVERY MALE WHITE PERSON, INHABITING OR RESIDING WITHIN MY DISTRICT, IN THE EIGHTH COMPANY, OF THE EIGHTH BATTALION OF LANCASTER COUNTY, MILITIA, BETWEEN THE AGE OF EIGHTEEN AND FIFTY-THREE YEARS. TAKEN FOR THE YEAR 1782. (c)

Capt.

Jacob Wilhelm.

Lieu.

Daniel Bart.

Ens.

Adam Keller.

First Class.

John Brubaker.
David Stoner.
John Kneisly.
John Myer.
William Geiger.
Christian Brown.
Michael Grub.

Second Class.

Henry Brubaker.
Peter Bachman, Sen.
Conrad Sichrist.
Andrew Mentzer.

Third Class.

John Leib.
Peter Lebick.
John Kaufman.
George Rickle.
Christian Myer.
Christian Shank.
Jacob Ritsecher.
Martin Bart.
John Huber.

Fourth Class.

John Shreiner.
Jacob Grub.
Andrew Kehler.
Christian Lehr.
Peter Bachman, Junr.
Abraham Huber.
Jacob Huber.
Jacob Good.
David Bechtel.
Robert Hutchins.

Fifth Class.

Christian Brubaker.
Jacob Kaufman.
Peter Graybill.
John Brubaker, Junr.
Christian Bomberger.
Christian Hartman.
Frederick Stouffer.
George Bennet.

Sixth Class.

Philip Lower.
Daniel Weichel.
Michael Richel.
John Swarr.
George Cummins.
Jacob Meyer.
John Hubert.
George Folk.
George Luke.

Seventh Class.

Abraham Leib.
John Sneider.
Joseph Brubaker.
Joseph Streit.
Francis Gardner.
Jacob Peifer.
Peter Angstat.
Adam Seits.

Eighth Class.

Christian Frick.
Christian Streit.
Christopher Beyermeister.
Christian Huber.
Henry Hoff.
Henry Seidensticker.
Abraham Frick.
George Minick.
Christian Shertzer.

I Do swear, on the Holy Evengiliest of Almighty God: That the above list is a just and true state, of the Male white Inhabitants, residing in my District, agreeable to Law, and without any fraud to the State, to the best of my knowledge.

JACOB WILHELM, Capt. 8th Comp. 8th Be.

Sworn before me this 22 Day of July, 1782.

ABRAHAM DEHUFF, S. L. L. County.

GENERAL RETURN OF THE OFFICERS OF THE LANCASTER COUNTY MILITIA APRIL 15TH, 1783. (c.)

Eighth Battalion.

Field Officers.

Lieut. Col.

Jas. Ross.

Majr.

Fredk. Hubley.

Captains.

1. John Hubley.
2. John Ewing.
3. Joseph Hubley.
4. William Wirtz.
5. Samuel Boyd.
6. John Miller.
7. James Davis.
8. Jacob Wilhelm.

Lieutenants.

1. George Trisler.
2. Daniel Neuman.
3. Thomas Cuthbert.
4. Thomas Meroney.
5. Jacob Hubley.
6. John Offner.

Ensigns.

1. George Lightner.
2. Jacob Bayley.
3. Christian Lenhare.
4. Adam Kellar.
5. Simon Snider.
6. James Davis.

RETURN OF THE FIFTH COMPANY THE EIGHTH BATTALION LANCASTER COUNTY MILITIA, 1783. (c.)

No. 1.

Peter Good.
Henry Brauneler.

No. 2.

Henry Woolfe.
Christoper Ditrich.
Andrew offenbag.
Peter Pame.
Emanel Piffer.
Mathias Mosser.
Peter Mosser.

No. 3.

John Bame.
Samuel good.

No. 4.

Jacob good.
Adam Bame.
Christian Messner.
Fridig Haupt.
John Mosser.

No. 5.

Peter Kern.
Peter Haller.

No. 6.

John Stein.
Christian Neyswander.

No. 7.

John Stover.
John Detwiler.
Michael Killan.

No. 8.

Samuel Marden.
Christoper Kern.
Marthers Roberd.
George Sneider.

I to hereby afirm that the above Return to the best of my Knowleg is just and true Return.

CHRISTOPHEL HEFT, Capt.
JOSEPH JENKINS, Col.

A RETURN OF CAPT. MT. WEYBRIGHT'S COMPANY BEING THE SEVENTH OF THE 8TH BATTALION OF LANCASTER COUNTYE MILITIA COMMANDED BY COL. JAMES ROSS. (c.)

Captain.

Wm. Weybright.

Lieutenant.

Georg Hambe.

Clerk of Company.

Sebastian Graff.

Privates.

1st Class.

Benjamin Long.
Peter Lean.
Baltzer Sheling.
Samuel Myers.

Abrham Royer.
Nicholas Haun.
Peter Hess.
John Mayers.
Conrad Shisler.
John Line.

2nd Class.

Abraham Hersby.
george kleine.
Christian pinkly.
Jacob Bear.
Martin Myer.
John Janston.
John Kurtz.

3rd Class.

Benjamin Landis, Jur.
Benjamin Hersby.
Henry Bugh.
John Metsler.
Henry Landis.

4th Class.

Jacob Metsler.
george Bugh.
Michael gerber, Jur.
David Mayers.
David Bechely.
John Kurtz.
Peter Fass.
Casper Peter.

5th Class.

William Cavel.
John Huhn.
Michael Shriner.
Daniel Rudy, Jur.
Martin humbright.
Henry Line.
Damas Devis.
Joseph Stump.

6th Class.

Ephram Bear.
Philip Hess.
John philip Shriner.
Henry Landis.
John Mester.
Michael Ridysill.
Jacob Weitler.
Isac Bear.
Androw Foltz.
Samuel Bausman.
Jacob Conrad.

7th Class.

Henry Lane.
Martin Shallenberger.
Henry Metsler.
John Long, Jur.
Philip Bugh.
Isaac Long.
Henry Shuger.
Samuel Bear, jur.
Henry Cevel.
Philip Royer, Jur.

8th Class.

Barm. Fultz.
George Michel Shriner.
George bahn.
Andrew Billmrer.
David Shnyder.
George Minnich.
Nicholaus Reydehboy.
John Stalter.

I do declare on honor the above to be just & true State of my Company as above specified.

WM. WEYBRIGHT, Capt

RETURN OF THE MALE WHITES BETWEEN THE AGES OF EIGHTEEN AND FIFTY THREE YEARS RESIDING IN THE DISTRICT OF THE SECOND COMPANY OF THE EIGHT BATALION OF LANCASTER COUNTY MILITIA COMMANDED BY COL'O JOHN ROGERS. (c.)

Captain.
Patrick Hay.

Lieutenant.
Samuel Weir.

Ensign.
John Ebersole.

Non. Commissd. Officers.
Thomas Espy.
James Johnston.
David McDonnald.

First Class.

James Campbell.
Vendle Henry.
Christopher Stoner.
John McCallen.
Joseph Carminy.
Jacob Ballim.
Jacob Rice.
Frances Taylor.
John Morrison.
Robert Crocket.
Abram Mitchell.
Nicholas Musser.
William Maffet.
John Sheckle.
Michael Nowland.
Christopher Weyland.
William Clark.

Second Class.

Walter Clark.
Loudwick Ball.
John Landice.
John Myres.
Martin Long.
John Over.
William Nay.
Jacob Bowman, Jun.
James Fox.
Michael Ealy.
Hendry Hoover.
John Mitchell.
John Plesly.

Third Class.

Thomas Mitchell.
Michael Kreager.
Martin Miller.
Abram Weltnor.
Jacob Bowman.
Adam Dinangar.
Andrew Byars.
Daniel Harshbarger.
William Ballim.
Nicholas Ballim.
Conrad Wishon.
John Hoover.
Dewalt Henry.
Jacob Lehman, Jun.
Abraham Betleon.

Fourth Class.

William Sayer, Sen.
Jacob Plough.
David Hays.
Dewalt Kreager.
Phelty Rode.
Daniel Weir.
George Killinger.
Christopher Forney.
John Nay.
James Low.

Fifth Class.

Samuel Brodley.
Benjamin Boyd.
John Fleagar.
Felix Landice.
Philip Deeds.
Martin Penogle.
Christopher Earley.
Peter Over.
John Ballim.
John O'Neil.
Christopher Erwin.
Flavel Roan.
George Bell.
John Weir.
Joseph Sayers.
Christopher Keatly.
George Geegy.

Sixth Class.

George Henry.
Robert McCallen.
John Early.
Benjamin Hersey.
Joseph Forney.
Nicholas Nay.
John Sayers.
Emanuel Kingrigh.
William Shaw.
James Donnaldson.
Jacob Lehman, Sen.
Archd. McAlister.

John Fairleigh.
Jacob Hoover.
James Sayers.
Wm. Hunter.
Frederick Miller.
Charles Dougherty.
James Mitchell.

Seventh Class.

Michael Katrine.
Williry Weltnor.
John Forney.
Joseph Naphsker.
Henry Bowman.
William Sayers, Jun.
Christopher Ream.
James McDonnal.
Christopher Tanner.
James Willson.
Jacob Eirly.
Peter Rodebaugh.
Peter Forney.

Eighth Class.

Robert Hays.
Martin Hoover.
Thomas McCallen.
John White.
Jacob Kinsley.
Joseph Falgate.
Peter Lineweaver.
Benjamin Sayer.
John Lehman.
Joseph Boyd.
James Willson, Sen.
Phelty Katrine.
William Ball.
David Mitchell.
William Sayer (orphan).
Daniel Braught.
Phelty Sterger.
Peter Balim.
John Carithers.

A just Return certified by me.

PATRICK HAY. Capt.

NINTH BATTALION
LANCASTER COUNTY MILITIA.

NINTH BATTALION 1777. (a.)

Colonel.
John Huber.

Lieutenant Colonel.
Samuel Jones.

Major.
Adam Bower.

Adjutant
Stophel Whiteman.

First Company.

Captain—John Gingrich.
First Lieutenant—[Vacancy.]
Second Lieutenant—[Vacancy.]
Ensign—Andrew Ehrman.

Second Company.

Captain—Bernard Gardner.
First Lieutenant—Conrad Haase.
Second Lieutenant—John Senseman.
Ensign—Philip Beck.

Third Company.

Captain—George Feather.
First Lieutenant—Ludwick Hoffer.
Second Lieutenant—[Vacancy.]
Ensign—[Vacancy.]

Fourth Company.

Captain—Isaac Adams.
First Lieutenant—Adam Eichholtz.
Second Lieutenant—John Bechthold.
Ensign—Philip Broadstone.

Fifth Company.

Captain—Joseph Gehr.
First Lieutenant—[Vacancy.]
Second Lieutenant—Peter Geistwite.
Ensign—Abraham Bower.

Sixth Company.

Captain—Christian Hollinger.
First Lieutenant—Michael Horner.
Second Lieutenant—Christian Garman.
Ensign—John Jones.

Seventh Company.

Captain—John Smuller.
First Lieutenant—John Moeller.
Second Lieutenant—John Hoffer.
Ensign—Andrew Ream.

Eighth Company.

Captain—George Foulke.
First Lieutenant—John Martin.
Second Lieutenant—Daniel Parrey.
Ensign—Joseph Bemersderfer.

(c.) Chosen by the officiers of the Secund Class of Coll. Hubers Battalion, Charis Harlacher, to be overcier ober the Said families as Such as are in their own Service in the Militia, in Captin Gardners District ordered By the Genrall Assembly given under our hands.

Lancaster County November 2th 1777.

The Lieut. of Lancaster County is to pay Charis Harlacher teen Shillings per Week for the use of the poor Wemen Wich ther Husbands has ben in thir our Service, in the Militia, as Wittnes our band.

BERNHARD GARNER, Capt.
CONRAD HASE, Lieut.
JOHAN SENSEMAN, Lieut.
PHILIP BECK, Ens.
JOHAN BALMAR, Cort martial man.

Received of Charls Harlacher Each of us We the untermontined Each of our Wife's for ouer Time bieng at Camp, for their Sub Sistans.

Henrich Smidt ....four pounds.
Niclos vogel Sang ....four pounds.
Willhelm Stober ....four pounds
Michel Franz ....four pounds.
Deater Walk ....four pounds.
Willim Wuker ....four pounds.

£24..0..0

this money paid Capt. Gartner 21st May 1778 to pay unto Harlacher.

MUSTER ROLL OF CAPT. GEORGE FEATHERS COMPANY IN THE NINTH BATTALION OF MILITIA OF LANCASTER COUNTY COMMANDED BY COLO. JOHN HUBER FOR THE YEAR 1778. (c.)

Captain.

George Fether.

Lieutenants.

1. Latwick hafer. 2. Casper Shimpf.

Ensign.

John Gyer.

First Class.

Herman Ernst.
Renades Keller.
Christian Ballmer.
Abraham Widder.
Christian Brown.
Conrad Long.
Daniel Habacker.
Jacob Bleckensderffer.
Jacob Youngman.
Jacob Erb, Jur.
Adam Bletz.
Jacob Ballner.
Philip Michael.
Abraham Musselman.
Stoffel Widder.
Peter Christ.
Willlamat Vanshack.
Christian Eby (uper).

Second Class.

Jacob Farling.
Peter Weyland, Jur.
Lenhard Dullpon.
Henry Fronck.
Jacob Eby.
Michael Stoffer.
Peter McMullen.
George Engel.
Greenberg Peticoats.
Lenhard Kline.
John Sheffel.
Daniel Christ.
Joseph Whitmore.
David Daneberger.
Peter Backer.
Henry Rough.
John Foutz.
Peter Krider.
Lanhard Shertzer.
John Snutz.

Third Class.

Abraham Snider.
Adam Ernst.
Jacob Brown.
Henry Netzley.
Jacob fether.
Michael Ballmer.
Christian Lincoln.
Michael Bitzman.
Christian Blickensderffer.
Mathias Sam.
Christian Musselman.
Peter Miller.
Martin Hird.
John Michael.
Jacob Gyer.
God Lob yungman.
Abraham Huber.
Christian Hess.
Conrad Westheffer.
George Rock.
Fredrick Leman.
Nicklouss unger.
Jacob siger Lander.

Fourth Class.

John thomes.
Jacob Miller.
Norts Ernst.
Arnolt Backer.
Jacob Casler.
John Shontz.
Christian Stuckey.
Peter Eiser.
Joseph Erb.
John Karg.
Peter Martick.
Jeremia Wolff.
Christian Eyer.
Christian Erb.
Michael Krider.
Peter Stutz.
John thames.

Fifth Class.

Jacob Rod.
Jacob Erb (brother Son).
Christian Eby.
Henry Wanner.
Christian Erb, Jun.
Peter Sniter.
John Brubacher.
Lotwick Gidner.
Christian Habecker.
Nicklous Kline.
John Erb.
Henry Erder.

Georg Rode.
Henry Hackman.
Lenhard Widder.
Jacob Alter.
Christian Lesher.
John Unger.

Sixth Class.

William Smith.
Michael Cromer.
Henry Fether.
Lenhard Miller.
Andony Ronner.
Ludwick Castler.
Conrad Wolff.
Jacob Habecker.
Samuel Huber.
Jacob Snider, Jur.
Abraham Dirdorff.
Henry Dirdorff.

MUSTER ROLL OF CAPT. BARNARD GARDNER'S COMPANY OF THE NINTH BATTALION OF LANCASTER COUNTY COM'D BY COL. JOHN HUBER FOR THE YEAR 1778. (c.)

Captain.

Barnard Gardner.

Lieutenant.

1st. Conrod hoase.
2nd. John Sensan.

Ensign.

Philip Beck.

Serjeants.

1st. John Cromer.
2nd. Jacob Beck.
3rd. Jacob Firestone.
4th. Micaal Oberly.

Corprils.

1. Adam France.
2. Adam Irish.

Drummer and Fifer.

Court Martial Men.

John Bolmar.
John Jones.

First Class.

Jonathan Kelh.
Conrod fether.
Abraham Bare.
Ludwick Weber.
Christian Weland.
Elias Wolf.
Henry Cofroad.
Peter Fanistock.
Micaal Snearly.
Christopher Westanbager.
Micaal Pitz.
Peter Cellar.

Second Class.

Christian Weinland.
John Fanistock.
Jacob Gorgas, Juniar.
Danial Bollinger.
John Urich.
John Sheafer.
Georgh Houk.
Adam Kell.
Henry Bare.

Third Class.

Fredrick Wolk.
Jacob Landas.
Jacob Oberly.
Matain Lawber.
Jacob Gorgas.
John Witmar.
Jacob Cofroad.
John Frimayer.
Jacob Eberly.
Henry Smith.
Peter Fether.
Benjaman Bowman.

Fourth Class.

Martain Bare.
George Ellick.
John Bare.
Peter Bollinger.
Peter Wise.
Jacob Weidman.
Fredrick fanistock.
Henry Brendle.
Rudolf Bollingar.
Abraham Searfoss.
Abraham Bollingar.

Fifth Class.

George Weetter.
Christian Lutter, Juniar.
William Stober.
John Millar.
Peter Millar.
Henry fether.
Christopel Strigle.
William Dishon.
Jacob Witmer.
David Landas.

Sixth Class.

Jacob Kimel.
Benjaman Landas.
Leonard Spitsnagle.
Abraham Vertz.
John Fredrick.
Johnthan Ruland.
John Snearar.
Christian Bolsely.
Durst Ome.
Benjaman Bare.

Seventh Class.

John Royar.
Joh Lutter.
John Cees.
Christian Loutter.
Martain Mayar.
Conroad Mainser.
Jacob Wolf.
Joseptb Ebenit.
Christopher Trovingar.
Micaal Weber.
Jacob Andrass.
Henry Milar.
William Kezel.

Eighth Class.

John Trovinger.
Fredrick Hockar.
Philip Ronk.
Abraham Pruppacker.
Henry Millar.
Fredrick Adam.
Lodwick Kebel.
Samual Harlochar.
Danial Royar.
Casper Trovingar.

MUSTER ROLL OF CAPT. JOSEPH GEARS COMPANY OF NINTH BATTALION OF LANCASTER COUNTY. COMMANDED BY COLL. J. HUBER FOR THE YEAR 1778. (c.)

Captain.

Joseph Gear.

Lieutenants.

1st. Martin Burcholter.
2nd. Peter Geistweit.

Ensign.

Abraham Bower.

Serjeants.

1. John Achy.
2. George Achy.
3. Adam oberly.
4. John Brunner.

Corporals.

1. Christoph oberly.
2. Willem Snyder.
3. Abraham Hassler.
4. Jost Miller.

Fiffer and Drummer.

Peter Snyder.
Cunrad Snyder.

1st Class.

John ober.
Danl. Solleberger.
Philip Hoffman.
George Brunner.
Jacob Frantz.
George Frantz.
Christian Bricker.
Jacob Blanck.

2nd Class.

John Furhman.
John Harnish.
Herman Philp.
Christian Flickinger.
Jacob Fuhrman.
Steephan Bolender.
Willem Beker.

3rd Class.

Henry Henshy.
Henry Hubshman.
Saml. Eby.
George Eby.
Dav'd Kackly.
Jacob Eberly.
Matheis Buttner.
Balthes Hoffman.
Henry Henshy, Jnr.
George Sydebender.

4th Class.

Jacob Bear
John Blanck.
Jacob amwey.
Peter Blanck.
John Keller.
Bastian Kackly.
Jacob Hornly.
Fredrich Eahly.

5th Class.

Henry Binckly.
Will'm Walter.
Gottfried Eberhard.
John Cunrad.
Danl. Riech.
Christian Wist.
John Naffscer.
Jonn Gerhard.
David Heckenell.
Michl. Walter.
Lenhard Keatig.
Gerhard Walter.
Adam Sherp.

6th Class.

Thom's Simon.
John Kunss.
Henry Rohrer.
Christoph Sherp.
Joseph Jacob.
Marx Binckly.
Peter Snyder.
Chasper Boszert.
John Funck.

7th Class.

Henry Burckholter.
Christian Cinssy.
Joseph Cunrad.
Georg Wolfarth.
John Bricker.
Henry Rheinhold.
Fridrick Kerper.
Georg Kissinger.
Ludwich Borry.
Peter Shumaker.
Philip Hefft.

8th Class.

Chasper Hassler.
Dav'd Kackly.
Henry Walter.
Martin Kissinger.
Jacob Dornbach.
Paul Fuhrman.
Lorentz Ludwich.
John Jacob.
Jacob Deathwiler.
Jacob Dissler.

I do hereby certify that these is a true List.

JOSEPH GERE, Capt.

A RETURN OF CAPT. JOHN GINGERY'S COMPANY IN THE NINTH BATTALION OF LANCASTER COUNTY MILITIA COMMANDED BY COLO. JOHN HUBER FOR THE YEAR 1778. (c.)

Capt.

John Gingery.

first Class.

John Ricksacre.
John Gipe.
Bartel Hock.
Mathias Hoffer.
George Hock.
George Hoffer.
John amweg.
Jacob Ricksacre.
Joseph Bucher.
Joseph Gingery.
Abraham Rist.
Wendle Gilbert.
Jacob Hochsteter.
Henry Giple.
Jacob Burckholdor.
David Frye.

2d Class.

Martin Keller.
John Painter.
Abraham Fredrick.
John Bucher.
Christian Fryes.
Christian Graybill.

George Martin.
Henry Hogh.
John Stauffer.
Martin Gross.
Daniel Gingery.
Jacob Michal.
Adam Garber.
Henry Kinsey.
Pettor Eip.
Casper Lair.

3d Class.

Christian Rule.
George Moyer, S'nr.
Jacob Hershy.
John Erb.
Philip Shertzer.
Henry Sidinsticker.
Martin Griner.
Christian Bomberger.
Mathias Weller.
Abraham Giple.
Christian Goodyear.
Jacob Doubenberger.
Lowrence Keener.
Henry Sipe.
Valentine Griner.
Petter Huber.

4th Class.

Martin Eby.
Andrew Eby.
John Dud.
John Longenecker.
George Moyer, Jnr.
Martin Beiler.
Henry Homacker.
Mathias Comerer.
Christian Riste.
Jacob Holdeman.
Nicholas Morret.
Andrew Lantz.
Jacob Eberly.
Petter Armstrong.
John Hans.
Henry Miller.
Christian Weaver.

5 Class.

John Riste.
John Hersby.
Nicholas Blei.
Henry Liep.
John Riste, Jnr.
John Fredrick.
George Hollinger.
Jacob Armstrong.
John Ingle.
Godfrid Goodyear.
Nicholas Strow.
Mathias Eip, dead.
Philip Griner.
Fredrick Armstrong.
Petter Lipe.
Henry Miller, Jnr.
George Rhul.

6 Class.

Michal Huber.
Adam Hollinger.
John Eby.
Christian Bomberger.
John Sumy.
John Armstrong.
Petter Young.
John Snider.
Phillip Smith.
John Spickler.

George Alspoch.
Jacob Eby.
Martin Spickler.
Andrew Shover.
Fredrick Toosing.
John Gipple.
Daniel Weller.
Daniel Hefelbower.

7th Class.

John Kiseli.
Daniel Miller.
Jacob Bomberger.
Adam Kriner.
Abraham Long.
John Bomberger.
Lodwick Goodyear.
Jacob Longenecker.
Ulry Eshelman.
John Lowman.
Christian Stouffer.
Petter Huber.
Stoffel Gipple.
Fredrick Stouffer.
Micheal Beam.
George Mongel.

8th Class.

Daniel Erb.
Henry Painter.
Petter Frye.
Jacob Haller.
Christian Zook.
Jacob Kingery.
Rudy Beam.
Jonathan Gingery.
Jacob Gipple.
Hardman Morret.
George Giger.
Michal Witmore.
George Kissel.
Henry Shompino.
Lonhard Hersh.
Adam Sytz.

MUSTER ROLL OF CAPTAIN CHRISTIAN HOLLINGER'S COMPANY OF THE NINTH BATTALION, OF LANCASTER COUNTY MILITIA, COMMANDED BY COL. HUBER IN THE YEAR 1778. (c.)

Capt.

Christian Hollinger.

First Lieu.

Michael Horning.

Second Lieu.

Christian german.

Ens.

John Jonse.

Serg.

John Shitz. Tomas owns.

Drumr.

Dan. Hollinger.

Fifer.

Thomas Hollinger.

1th Class.

John Hare.
Andrew Fale.
Jacob Kaber.
Conrad Marck Sen.
William Wite.
John Eby.
Jacob Kinsy

2th Class.

George Miller, Stiller.
David Jonse.
Xander Lartman, Sen.
Daniel Stauffer.
Fredrick witmeyer.
Peter Eby.
Jacob Muselman.
William old.

3th Class.

John Rudy.
Adam Kaner.
Conrad Marck, Jr.
Stofel fover.
George Same.
Samuel Wisler.
Christian Stauffer.
Joseph Moyer.
William Shmith.

I Do here Cartify That this is a true Returne.

CHRISTIAN HOLLINGER, Capt.

MUSTER ROLL OF CAPT. SMULLERS COMP'Y FOR THE YEAR 1778. (c.)

Captain.

John Smuller.

Lieutenants.

1st. Jno. Mohler. 2d. Jno. Heaffer.

Ensign.

Andw. Ream.

Serjeants.

1st. Jacob Ream.
2nd. Joas Miller.
3rd. Nichls. Killian.
4th. Jno. Klein.

Drummer.

Andrew Ream.

Fiffer.

Henry Ream

1st Class.

Mich'l Sayler.
Abraham Killian.
Nichlaus Wolff.
Nichlaus Snyder.
Christian Schowalter, Senr.
Danl. Bowman.
Jacob Dock.
Joseph Heaffly.
Jacob Leasher.
Lenhard Cunrad.
Jacob Mohler.
Henry Heyple.
Jacob Deathwiller.
Peter Groff.
Henry Eberly.
George Hiltebrand.
Adam Kingmaker.
Andw. Heagler.

2nd Class.

Nichlaus Dock.
Mich'l Scherg
Joseph Bear.
Abraham Byxler.
David Meinzer.
Georg Wittman.
Lenhard Keller.
Christian Guth.
And'w Ream, Sen'r.
Sam'l Bowman.
Jacob Hagy.
Peter Ceander.

3rd Class.

Henry Mohler.
Christian Bowman.
Abraham Klein.
Christian Knopp.
David Meredy.
Jhon Mellinger.
Jhon Mohler.
Abraham Wolff.
Jacob Sontag.
Will'm Mellinger.
Jacob Zentmyer.
Joseph Groff.
Tobias Ream.
Jacob Landes.
Cunrad Miller.

4th Class.

Mich'l Reuter.
John Gusswiller.
Georg Merckle.
Uly Scherg.
Jacob Snyder.
Casper Kelper.
Dewald Meder.
Jacob Schowalter.
Philp Krieg.
Georg Speath.
Georg Miller.

5th Class.

Georg Kunss.
Abraham Landes.
Adam Mosser.
Jhon Miller.
Joseph Leypy.
Peter Brubacher.
Foelix Borchart.
Jacob Keller.
Sam'l Groffe.
Frantz Brumbach.
Casper Walter.
John Landes, Jur.
Jacob Mischler.
John Ream, Jur.
Fridrick Leader.

6th Class.

David Ream.
Jhon Hershberger.
Bernhart Geiger.
Joseph Mischler.
Adam Ebrecht.
Henry Herschberger.
Peter Snyder.
Martin Mohler.
George Hohe.
Abraham Hershberger.
Jacob Wantz.
Jacob Killian.
Tobias Ream.
Jacob Rholand.
Abraham Groff.
Vallent'n Brikman.

Class 7.

Vallent'n Wolff.
John Martin.
Christian Cunrad.
Casper Schryth.
John Holtry.
John Bucher, Jur.
Math'w Ream.
Isack Herschberger.
Wendel Hubschman.
Simon Stetecorn.
Henry Miller.
Georg Sheaner.
John Becker.
Jacob Cunrad.
Gotlieb Mack.
Joseph Spegle.
Mich'l Bear.

8th Class.

Peter Reyer.
David Sherg.
Abraham Ream.
Abraham Ream, Mill'r.
John Mussleman.
Michl. Wolff.
Christian Showalter.
Mich'l Kneysly.

Andrew Ream, Jur.
Abraham Bear.
Jacob Groffe.
Abraham Rebland.
Jacob Schryt.
Fridrick Ream.

I do hereby Certify that this is a true Return.
JOHN SMULLER, Capt.

A RETURN OF CAPTAIN GEORGE VOLICKS IN THE 9TH BATALION OF LANCASTER COUNTY, MILITIA, COMMANDED BY COLLONEL JOHN HUBER FROM MAY 25 TO OCTOBER 26, 1778. (c.)

Capt.

John Volicks.

Lieut.

John Martin.
John Gesander.
Henry Willy.

1 Class.

Conrad Critzinger.
John Stucky.
Balser Gantz.
Thomas Megomery.
Christian Royer.
Christian Willy.
George Graff.
John Gantz.
John Bowman.

2 Class.

Peter Eberley.
Fred'k Iasius (?).
Peter Bernhard.
Henry Good.
George Hildebrand.
Bernhard Grows.
Herman berger.
Neil Leman.

3 Class.

John Hearth.
Frederick Moler.
John Brown.
Adam Shiner.
Stofel Gesel.
James Jacobs.
John Flemming.

4 Class.

Martin Barr. Jacob Shiner.
Solomon Shread. Peter Bowman.
Mathias Grall. George Hornberger.
Christian Grall. Alick Jegg (?).

5 Class.

Ullerick Grall. Christian Swally.
Henry Shindler. Michael Shoare.

6 Class.

George Barr. John Ruth.
Balser Hetzler. Jacob Welman.
Joseph Juncker. Jacob Gesander, Junr.
Jost Martin. John Leman.
Christian Staley. George Plantz.

7 Class.

Joseph Mathews. David Smith.
Robert Coleman. Jacob Miller.
George Caucher. John Sents.

8 Class.

David Merckle. Frederick Hetzler.
Jacob Beeker. Bernhard Meglouglin.
George Gantz. Mathias Bafemoyer.

A True Return from the Roll.
October 26, 1778.
By order of

CAPT. GEO. VOLICK.
HENRY WM. STIEGEL.

MUSTER ROLL OF CAPT. JNO. SMULLER'S COMP'Y. NINTH BATTALION OF LANCASTER COUNTY MILITIA COMMANDED BY COLL. JNO. HUBER FOR THE YEAR 1779 OF APRIL & MAY. (c.)

Capt.
Jno. Smuller.

Lieut.

John Mohler. John Haeffer.

Ens.

Andrew Ream.

Serjeants.

Jacob Ream.
Joas Miller.
Nichlaus Killian.
John Klein.

Corps.

Henry Landes.

Drumor & Fiffer.

Andrew Ream.
Henry Ream.

Class 1.

Abraham Killian.
Nichlaus Wolff.
Nichlaus Snyder.
Christian Showalter, Jur.
Dan'l Bowman.
Jacob Dock.
Jacob Leasher.
Lenhare Kunrad.
Jacob Mohler.
Jacob Deathwiller.
Peter Groffe.
Henry Eberly.
Georg Hildebrand.
Adam Kingmaker.
Andrew Heagler.

Class 2.

Nichlaus Dock.
Mich'l Schirg.
Joseph Bear.
Abraham Byxler.
Dav'd Meintzer.
Georg Wittman.
Lenhard Keller.
Andres Ream, Sen'r.
Sam'l Bowman.
Jacob Hagy.
Peter Seander.
Peter Shoener.
William Cramm.

Class 3.

Henry Mohler.
Abraham Klein.
Christ. knopp'e.
Dav'd Meredy.
John Mellinger.
John Mohler.
Abraham Wollff.
Jacob Suntag.
Willem Mellinger.
Jacob Zentmeyer.
Joseph Groffe.
Tobias Ream.
Jacob Landes.

Class 4.

Mich'l Reuter.
John Gusswiller.
Georg Merckel.
Ulrich Scherg.
Jacob Snyder.
Casper Keiper.
Dewald Meder.
Jacob Showalter.
Philip Kreeg.
Georg Spathe.
Georg Miller.
Philip Ream.
John Shiote.
Henry Hartman.
Georg Firestone.
Daniel Wittman.

Class 5.

George Kunss.
Abraham Landes.
Adam Mosser.
Joseph Leipy.
Peter Brubacher.
Jacob Keller.
Sam'l Groffe.
John Landes, Jur.
Jacob Mishler.
John Ream, Jur.
Frantz Brumbach.

Class 6.

Dav'd Ream.
Berhard Geiger.
Joseph Mishler.
Adam Ebrecht.
Henry Hershberger.
Peter Snyder.
Martin Mohler.
George Hoe.
Abraham Hershberger.
Jacob Wantz.
Jacob Killian.
Jacob Rholand.
Abraham Groffe.
Vallentine Brickman.

Class 7.

John Martin.
Mich'l Bear.
Christian Cunrad.
Casper Schryt.
John Holtry.
John Bucher.
Matheis Ream.
Isack Hersberger.
Wendel Hubshman.
Henry Miller.
George Shoener.
John Beaker.
Jacob Kunrad.
Gottlib Mack.
Joseph Spregel.
John Schryt.
John Sloth, Jur.
Simon Stetecorn.

Class 8.

Peter Ryer.
David Scherg.
Abraham Ream.
Abraham Ream, miller.
John Mussleman.
Mich'l Wolff.

Christ. Schowalter.	Abraham Rholand.
Mich'l Kneissly.	Matheis Mohler.
Andrew Ream, Jur.	Mich'l Killian.
Abraham Bear.	Bernhard Getz.
Jacob Graff.	Mich'l Wittman.

1779. I do herby certify that this is a true List of my Comp'y.

JOHN SMULLERS, Capt.

A RETURN OF THE SEVENTH CLASS OF THE NINTH BATT. LANCASTER COUNTY MILITIA COMD. BY COL. JOHN HUBER UNDER MARCHING ORDERS TO SUNBURRY 11TH AUG. 1779 AT CAPT. GARTNERS. (c.)

1st Company.

Capt. John Gingry's Co.

None.

2nd Company.

Capt. Gartner's Co.

William Winckert.

3rd Company.

Capt. Feather's Co.

None.

4th Company.

Capt. Adams's Co.

None.

5th Company.

Capt. Ghear's Co.

Henry Reinhold.

6th Company.

Capt. Hollinger's Co.

None.

7th Company.

Capt. Smuller's Co.

John Martin.
Vendal Hebshman.

8th Company.

Capt. Zwaly's Co.

None.

by me, JOHN SMULLER, Capt.

A RETURN OF ELIZABETH TOWNSHIP MILITIA COMPANY AS CALLED PR. ORDERS TO CAPT. VOLCK AND LIEUTENANT JOHN MARTIN, VIZN. (c.)

Sergant.

John Gesander. Henry Willy.

Corporal.

George Humer.

Privates.

1st Class.

John Humer. Christian Willy.
Conrad Critzinger. George Graff.
John Stucky. John Gantz.
Balser Gantz. John Bowman.
Thomas Megomery. Christian Royer.

2nd Class.

Peter Eberley. Georg Hildebrand.
Peter Bernhard. Bernhard Grous.
Henry Good. Neal Leman.

3rd Class.

Fredrick Moler. Adam Shiner.
Jacob Beringer. Stofel Gesel.
George Weyman. James Jacobs.
John Brown. Jacob Kissinger.

4th Class.

Martin Bare. Peter Bauman.
Salomon Shroad. Alick Clack.
Matthias Grall. George Druck.
Jacob Shiner. Christian Crull.

5th Class.

Matthias Betz. Christian Zwally.
Ullery Grall. Michael Beringer.
Henry Shingler.

6th Class.

George Bare. John Ruth.
Conrad Engel. Jacob Weyman.
Joseph Juncker. Jacob Gesander, Junr.
Jost Martin. George Plantz.
Christian Staley.

7th Class.

Joseph Mathews. David Shmit.
Robert Coleman. Jacob Miller.
George Caugher. John Sentz.

8th Class.

David Merckly. Michael Palmer.
Jacob Becker. Andrew Cristy.
George Gantz. Bernhard Meglouglin.
John Carson.

Elizabeth Township.
October 9th 1779.

JOHN MARTIN,
first Lieutenant.

A RETURNE OF CHRISTIAN HOLLINGERS COMPANY FORE THE YEARE 1779 IN THE NINTH BATTALION OF LANCASTER COUNTY COMMAND BY COL. JOHN HUBER, OCT. 25, 1779. (c.)

Capt.

Christian Hollinger.

Leuts.

Michael Horning. **Christian German.**

Insine.

John Jones.

Sergents.

John Shitz. **Tom. Owens.**

Drumer.

Daniel Hollinger.

Fif.

Tom. Hollinger.

Corprals.

Nicklos Shroff. **George Day.**

Privates.

Clase 1.

Andrw. fale.
John Hare.
Jacob Keaber.
Conrad March, Sen.
Whiliam White.
John Eby.
Jacob Kinsy.

Clase 2.

Georg Miller, Stiller.
Xander Zartman, Sen.
Daniel Stauffer.
Friedrich Witmeyer.
Peter Eby.
Jacob Musselman.
Whilliam Old.
Henry Good.

Clase 3.

George Zame.
John Rudy.
Adam Kaner.
Conrad Marck.
Stoffel faver.

Georg Same.
Samuel Whisler.
Christian Stauffer.
Joseph Moyer.
Wm. Smith.

Clase 4.

John Gromer.
Nicklos Bàle.
Tom. Handly.
Peter Crotser.
Georg fox.

Michael Zartman.
Georg Hoverter.
Jacob Moyer.
Henry Rudy.
Casper Sieger.

5th Class.

John Brubacker.
Martin gromer.
Abraham Stauffer.
John Musselman.

Manuel Sease.
Jacob Bordner.
Georg Bets.
Mich. Berringer.

Clase 6.

Friedrich Shitz.
Oly Keyser.
Philip Enters.
Mathias Weimer.
Conrad Plasterer.

David Fourdene.
Michael Hochlender.
Georg Witcraft.
Carle Smith.

Clase 7.

georg Miller.
John Whinter.
Allexander Zartman.
Leonard Smith.
Christian Zug.

John Trump.
Henry Marck.
Georg Potser.
Christian Kemmerer.
William Shumacker.

Clase 8.

Ernst oberman.
Marx Nagule.
Samuel Russel.
Friedrick Hare.
Jacob Brubacher.

Peter grubb.
John Petter.
Adam Miller.
Christian Smith.

A True Returne of the Role of Capt. Christian Hollinger's Compy.

MUSTER ROLL OF CAPTAIN ISAAC ADAMS COMP'Y OF THE NINTH BAT'N OF LANCASTER COUNTY COMMANDED BY COL'N J. HUBER'S FOR THE YEAR 1779. (c.)

Capt.
Isaac Adams.

1 Lieu.
Adam Eighols.

2 Lieu.
John Beehtols.

3 Lieu.
Philip Broadingstone.

Sergiants.

David Baringer.
Henry Eigholds.
Michael Young.
George Urey.

Corporalls.

Nicholas Shower.
Henry Laush.

Drum & fiffers.

Court Merchel Men.

Richard Adams.
John Miller.

Class 1.

Geo. Westheffer.
Jacob Huber, Jur.
Jacob Hershe.
Nichaless Lutz.
Adam Grill.
Philip Lutz.
John Lininer.
John Palls.
Nichlass Lesher, Jur.

Class 2.

John Lutz.
Mathews Kolten.
Peter Steffa.

Class 3.

Peter Johns.
John Westheffer.
Christel Weavor.
John Lesher.
Michel Hardiner.
Geo. Cappes.
Ruddy Miller.
John Geetts.
Adam Leed.

Class 4th.

Matheis Wallck.
Henry Brandel..
Peter Felzor.
Henry Galer.

Mertlen Fenslor.
Henry Bosteon.
Jacob Bower.
Michael Windholds.

Class 5th.

Joseph Wingard.
Jacob Tzin, Junr.
Henry Lead.
Jacob Beehard.

John Krill.
Christen Brouer.
John Rouch.

Class 6th.

John Shays.
Adam Witsel.
Frederick Gardner.

Ruddy Bear.
Jacob Kimberlen.
Simmon Kochel.

Class 7th.

Davied Titlo.
Peter Binkly.
Jacob Fanneda.
John Huber.

Nichlass Rup.
John Kalman.
Youst Spengler.
Adam Kissiner.

Class 8th.

Christian Hardinor.
Christan Cimmerman.
Peter Cimmerman.
Isaac Pettecover.
John Pettecover.

Charles Irich.
John Youst.
Bosten Nageal.
Geo. Bemal.
Christen Iseman.

I Do Hereby Certfey that this is a true Stete of My Company.

ISAAC ADAMS, Capt.

MUSTER ROLL OF CAPT. GEORGE FEATHER'S COMPANY IN THE NINTH BATTALION OF LANCASTER COUNTY COMMANDED BY COLONEL JOHN HUBER FOR THE YEAR 1779. (c.)

Captain.
Georg Fether.

Lieutenant.
2d, Chasper Shimph.

Ensign.

John Gyer.

1st Class.

Herman Ernst.
Renades Keller.
Abraham Wider.
Christian Brown.
Conrad Long.
Daniel Habecker.
Jacob Blekensderffer.
Jacob Youngman.
Jacob Erb, Jur.
Adem Bletz.
Jacob Ballmer.
Abraham Musselman.
Stoffel wither.
Peter Christ.
John Deller.
William at Shonhocks mill.
Christian Eby (uper).

Second Class.

Jacob Farling.
Peter Weyland, Jur.
Lenhard Dullepon.
Henry Fronck.
Jacob Eby.
Michael Stoffer.
Peter McMullin.
George Engel.
Greenbery Beticoats.
John Sheffel.
Daniel Christ.
Joseph witmore.
Peter Backer.
Henry Rough.
John Foutz.
Peter Krider.
Lenhard Shertzer.

Third Class.

Abraham Snider.
Adem Ernst.
Jacob Brown.
Henry Netzly.
Jacob Fether.
Michael Balmer.
Christian Lineboch.
Michael Bitzman.
Christian Blickensderffer.
Mathias Same.
Christian Musseman.
Peter Miller.
Mardin Hird.
John Michael.
Jacob Gyer.
God Leb Youngman.
Abraham Huber.
Christian Hess.
Conrad wesdhaffer.
Georg Rock.
Fredrick Layman.
Nicklouss unger.
Jacob Sigerlender.

Fourth Class.

John Thomes.
Jacob M. Miller.
Arnolt Backer.
Norts Ernst.
Jacob Cassler.
Christian Stucky.

Peter Eiser.	Christian Eyer.
Joseph Erb.	Christian Erb.
John Korg.	Michael Krider.
Peter Mardick.	Peter Stutz.
Joramia woolf.	John Thomes.

Fifth Class.

Jacob Rode.	John steess.
Jacob Erb brothers son.	Henry Erder.
Christian Erb	George Rode.
Henry Wonner.	Henry Hackman.
Christian Erb, Jur.	Lenhard wither.
Peter Snider.	Jacob Alder.
Lodwick Gidner.	John Backer.
Christian Habecker.	Christian Lisber.
Nicklous Kline.	John unger.

6th Class.

William Smith.	Jacob Snider.
Michael Cramer.	Abraham Dirdorff.
Henry fether.	Henry Dirdorff.
Lenhard Miller.	Godfrid Thomas.
Lutwick Casler.	Andrew Krider.
Conrad woolff.	Michael Eichelberger.
Jacob Habocker.	Christian Backer.
Samuel Huber.	Simon Dontz.

7th Class.

Jacob Roody.	Christian Ricksecker.
John Sanck.	Christian Huber.
Larantz hargelrod.	Henry Snider.
John Bugh.	Mathias Sriner.
Geo. wiss.	Christian Erb.
Casper Grub.	John Sensenigh.
Peter Ricksecker.	George wither.
Adrew wissler.	John Gyer.
Geo. Groberger.	Daniel Shierman.
Michael Myer.	Christian Eby.
John Sponhower.	

8th Class.

Henry Foultz.	Jacob Steess.
Michael Groff.	Daniel Sheller.
Stoffel Miller.	Mardin Shanck.

Jacob Hackman.
Jacob Smuck.
Elias Jordon.
John wither.
Samuel Krauss.
George Gyer.
Jacob Snider.
Peter Krider.
Jacob Sponhower.
William Castler.
Peter Bruner.
Joseph Gambolt.
Jacob wisler.
John Eng.
Jacob Gyer.

MUSTER ROLL FOR CAPT. GEAHRS COMPANY FOR THE YEAR 1779 IN THE NINTH BATTALION OF LANCASTER COUNTY, COMMANDED BY COLONEL JOHN HUBER. (c.)

Captain.

Joseph Geahr.

Lieutenants.

1. Martin Borkholter.
2. Peter Geistweit.

Ensign.

Abraham Bower.

Serjeants.

1. Jno. Achy.
2. George Achy.
3. Adam oberly.
4. Jno. Brunner.

Corprals.

1. Christoph oberly.
2. Willem Shuyder.
3. Abraham Hassler.
4. Jost Miller.

Drumer and Fifter.

Cunrad Snyder.
Peter Snyder.

1st Class.

John ober.
Philip Hoffman.
Danl. Soleberger.
George Frantz.
Jacob Blanck.
Christian Briker.
George Brunner.
Michl. Huber.
Christian Snyder, removed.

2nd Class.

Jno. Furhrman.
Herman Philip, dead.
Stephen Bolender.
Fridrich Wagner.
Christian Flickinger.
Jno. Harnish.
Jacob Furhrman.

3rd Class.

Henry Hensby.
Henry Henshy, Jur.
Saml. Eby.
David Gackly.
Matheis Bittner.
George Eby, gone.
Jacob Eberly.
Baltzer Hoffman.
George Sydebenter.

4th Class.

Jacob Bear.
Jacob amweg.
Jno. Keller.
Jacob Hornly.
Jno. Blank.
Peter Blanck.
Bastian Kackly.

5th Class.

Joseph Flickinger.
Henry Binkly.
Gotfried Eberhard.
Jno. Naffscer.
Danl. Riech.
Lorentz Ludwig.
Lenhard Retig.
Adam Sherp.
Willem Walter.
Jno. Kunrod.
Christian Wist.
Jno. Gerhard.
Michl. Walter.
Gerhard Walter.
Christ Ely.

5th Class.

Thomas Simon.
Henry Rhorer.
Joseph Jacob.
Peter Snyder.
Jno. Philipy.
Christoph Sherpp.
Marx Binckly.
Casper Bossart.
David Heckenell.
Jno. Gackly.

7th Class.

Christian Kinsy.
Joseph Cunrad.
Jno. Bricker.
George Kissinger.
Peter Schoemaker.
Philip Hefft.
Jeremies Miller.

8th Class.

Casper Hassler.
David Gakly.
Henry Walter.
Paul Fuhrman.
Martin Kissinger.
Jacob Deathwieler.
Jacob Dissler.
Cunrad Cuhnrad.
Jacob Dornbach.
Lorentz Ludwick.
John Jacob.

I do hereby certify this to be a true Return.

JOSEPH GEHR, Captain.

A RETURN OF CAPT. CHRISTIAN HOLLINGER'S COMPANY FOR THE YEAR 1779 IN THE NINTH BATTALION OF LANCASTER COUNTY COMMANDED BY COL. JOHN HUBER. (c.)

Capt.

Christian Hollinger.

Lieu.

Michael Horning.
Christian German.

Ensine.

John Jonse.

Serjeants.

Peter Grubb.
John Sheets.
Tom Owens.

Corprals.

Nicklos Throve.
George Day.

Clark.

Daniel Hollinger.

Drumer.

Daniel Hollinger.

fifer.

Tomas Hollinger.

Class 1.

Andrw fale. William Wite.
Jacob Kieber. John Eby.
Conard Marck, Sen. Jacob Kinsy.

Class 2.

George Miller, stiller. Frederick Witmier.
David Jonse. Peter Eby.
Xander Zartman, Sen. Jacob Musselman.
Daniel Staffer. William old.

Class 3.

John Ruty. Samuel Wisler.
Adam Kinner. Christian Stauffer.
Conrad Marck, Jr. Joseph Moyer.
Stoffel fover. William Smith.
georg Same.

Class 4.

John gromer. Michael Zartman.
Niclos Bale. george Hovarter.
Tomas Handly. Jacob Moyer.
Peter Crotser. Henry Ruty.
georg fox. Casper Sieger.

Class 5.

John Brubacker. John Crise.
Martin gromer, Jr. Manuel Sease.
Abraham Stouffer. Jacob Bordner.
John Musselman. george Bets.

Class 6.

Fredrich Shitz. David Furdny.
oly Kyser. Michael Hochlender.
Philip Enters. georg Witcraff.
Mathias Wimer. Charles Smith.
Conrad Resterer.

Class 7.

georg Miller, Sen. John Trump.
John Winter. Henry Marck.
Xander Zartman, Jr. Georg Petser.
Leonhaod Smith. Christian Kemmerer.
Christian Zug. William Shumacker.

Class 8.

Ernst. oberman.
Marx Nagule.
Samuel Russel.
Friedrich Here.
Jacob Brubacker.
Peter grubb.
John Peter.
Adam Miller.
Christian Smith.

I Cartify that this is a True Return of the Role of Capt. Christian Hollinger's Company of May 24th 1779 by order of the Capt. Christian Hollinger.

MUSTER ROLL CAPT. SMULLERS COMP'Y FOR THE YEAR 1779. (c.)

Captain.

John Smuller.

Lieutenants.

1st. Jno. Mohler.
2nd. Jno. Heaffer.

Ensign.

Andres Ream.

Rank and File.

Jacob Ream.
Joas Miller.
Nicklaus Killian.
Jno. Klein.
Henry Landes.
Henry Ream.
Andreas Ream.

1st Class.

Abraham Killian.
Nicklaus Woolff.
Nicklaus Snyder.
Christ Showalter, Jur.
Danl. Bowman.
Jacob Dock.
Jacob Leasher.
Jacob Deathwiller.
Peter Groff.
Henry Eberly.
George Hildebrand.
Adam Kingmacker.
Andreas Hegler.

2nd Class.

Nicklaus Dock.
Mich'l Sherg.
Joseph Bear.
Abraham Byxler.

David Meintzer.
George Wittman, removed.
Lenhard Keller.
Andreas Ream, Senr.
Saml. Bowman.
Jacob Hagy.
Peter Seander, removed.
Peter Shoner.

3rd Class.

Henry Mohler.
Christian Knop.
Abraham Klein.
Dav'd Meredy.
Jno. Mellinger.
Hanes Mohler.
Abraham Woolff.
Jacob Suntag.
William Mellinger.
Jacob Zentmeyr.
Joseph Groff.
Tobias Ream.
Jacob Landes.

4th Class.

Mich'l Reuter.
George Merkle, removed.
Ulrich Sherg.
Jacob Snyder.
Casper Keyper.
Dewald Meder.
Jacob Showalter.
Philip Kreeg removed.
George Spathe.
George Miller.
Philip Ream.
Jno. Sloth, Jur.
George Firestone.
Henry Hartman.
Jno. Guswiller.

5th Class.

George Kunss.
Abraham Landes.
Adam Mosser.
Jno. Miller, removed.
Joseph Leisy.
Peter Brubacher.
Jacob Keller.
Saml. Groff.
Jno. Landes, Jur.
Jacob Mishler.
Jon. Ream, Jnr.
Frantz Brumbach.
Fredrik Leeder.

6th Class.

Dav'd Ream.
Bernhard Geyger.
Joseph Mishler.
Adam Ebrecht.
Henry Hersberger.
Peter Snyder.
Martin Mohler.
George Hohe.
Abraham Hershberger.
Jacob Wantz.
Jacob Killian.
Jacob Rhuland.
Abraham Groff.
Valentin Brikman.

7th Class.

George Shoener, removed.
Jno. Martin.
Michl. Bear.
Christian Cunrad.

Casper Shryth.	Jno. Becker.
Jno. Holtry.	Jacob Kunrad, removed.
Isack Hershberger.	Gottlieb Mack.
Simon Stotecorn, removed.	Joseph Spregle.
Henry Miller.	

Court Marshal Men.

Jno. Sholtb, Senr.	Jno. Shryth.

8th Class.

Peter Reyer.	Jacob Shryth, Jur.
Dav'd Sherg.	Abraham Bear.
Abraham Ream.	Jacob Groff.
Abraham Ream, mill'r.	Abraham Rhuland.
Jno. Musselman.	Michl. Killian.
Christian Showalter, Jur.	Bernhard Getz.
Mich'l Knyssly.	Jno. Bucher, Jur.
Andreas Ream, Jur.	Willem Cram.

I do certify this a true Return of my Company.

JOHN SMULLER, Capt.

A RETURN OF CAPT. GEORGE VOLICKS IN THE 9TH BATT'N OF LANCASTER COUNTY MILITIA COMMANDED BY COLL. JOHN HUBER FOR THE YEAR 1779. (c.) Made by Lieut. John Martin.

Capt.
George Voilcks.

Lieu.
John Martin.

Lieu.
Daniel Parry.

Ensign.
John bemesderfer.

Sergeant.

John Gesaner.	Henry Willy.

Corporal.

George Hamer.

1

John Hummer.
conrad critzinger.
John Stucky.
Balser Gants.
Thomas Megomery.
Christian Royer.
Christian Willy.
George Graff.
John Gants.
John Bowman.

2

Peter Eberly.
Peter Bernhard.
Henry good.
George Hildebrand.
Bernhard grous.
Neal Ceman.

3

Frederick Moler.
Jacob Beringer.
George Weyman.
John Brown.
Adam Shiner.
Stofel Gesel.
James Jacob.
Jacob Kissinger.

4

Martin Bare.
Salomon Shroad,
Mathias Grull.
Jacob Shiner.
Peter Bauman.
Alick Cluck.
Thomes Calaughan.

5

Mathias Betz.
Ullery Grall.
Henry Shingeler.
Christian Zwally.
Michael Beringer.

6

George Bare.
Conrad Engel.
Joseph Juncker.
Jos. Martin.
Christian Staley.
John Ruth.
Jacob Weyman.
Jacob gesander, Junior.
George Plantz.

7

Joseph Mathews.
Robert Coleman.
George Caugher.
David Smith.
Jacob Miller.
John Sents.

8

David Markly.
Jacob Beeker.
George Gants.
John Carson.
Michael Palmer.
Andrew Crisby.
Frederick Hetzler.
Bernhard Meglaughlin.

1779.

OFFICERS OF NINTH BATTALION. (a.)

Returned August 26, 1780.

Lieutenant Colonel.

John Rogers.

Major.

Abraham Latcha.

First Company.

Captain—William Allen.
Lieutenant—John Barnett.
Ensign—James Willson.

Second Company.

Captain—Patrick Hays.
Lieutenant—Samuel Weir.
Ensign—John Eversol.

Third Company.

Captain—Ambrose Crain.
Lieutenant—William Young.
Ensign—Henry Graham.

Fourth Company.

Captain—John Harkenrider.
Lieutenant—Emanuel Ferree.
Ensign—Jacob Pruder.

Fifth Company.

Captain—James McCreight.
Lieutenant—William Hill.
Ensign—William. Brandon.

Sixth Company.

Captain—James Willson.
Lieutenant—James Rogers.
Ensign—James Johnston.

Seventh Company.

Captain—Daniel Bradley.
Lieutenant—Adam Mark.
Ensign—Baltzer Stone.

Eighth Company.

Captain—William Laird.
Lieutenant—John McFarland.
Ensign—George Lower.

JOHN LIDIG, SURO'N OF 9TH POTALION, L. C. M. THE 4TH MAY 1780. (c.)

Dr. Robert Clark, Sub. Lieut.

1st Company.

2d Class.

Allen's Comp.

Joseph Barnett of the 7 Class.
Leonard Umbarger, marched by Subt.

2d Compy.

2d Class.

Hay's Co.

John Plesley, of the 8th Comp'y.
James Fox, march. by Subt.

3d Comp'y.

2d Class.

Cranes Co.

John Cunningham, marcht.
Robert Young, marcht.
Peter Rambo, marcht by Subt.
James Young, Senr, Gon Aprivetering.

5th Comp'y.

2d Class.

John Petigrew, marcht.

7th Comp'y.

2nd Class.

Peter Millar, marcht.
Henry Heoss, marcht.
Benjamin Clark, marcht.
Peter Ventlen, marcht.
Jacob River, marcht.

1st Class.

Philip Stone, marcht.

8th Comp'y.

2d Class.

Philip Richart, marcht.
Adam Spidle, marcht.

1st Comp'y.

3d Class.

John Humes, marcht.
David Caldwell, marcht by Subt.
Robert Sturgin, marcht by Subt.
George Simons, marcht.

2d Compy.

3d Class.

William Balim, serv'd in the 6th.
Nicholas Balim, serv'd in 5th.

4th Comp'y.

3d Class.

George Wolf, march't.
Henry Baker, march't.

5th Comp'y.

3d Class.

John Craige, marcht.
Rſchard Finley, marcht.

7th Comp'y.

3d Class.

Michael Selcer, marcht.
John Carvory, marcht.
John Murcer, marcht 7 Class.

8th Comp'y.

3d Class.

Jacob Rahm, marcht.
James Laird, marcht.
Jacob Millar, marcht.
James Donely, marcht.
John Weatherhold, marcht.
Jacob Hoak, of 8 Class, Exon'd.

1st Comany.

4th Class.

Samuel Sturgeon, marcht.
Richard Dearman, Quarter master.
James Ablen, marcht.
Patrick Linch, marcht.
Samuel Finney, marcht.

2 Comp'y.

4th Class.

David Hays, march't.
George Killinger, march't.
James Sullivan, Gon to Virginia. Exon'd.

3d Comp'y.

4th Class.

Murte Burns, marcht.
Robert Kirkwood, marcht.

5th Company.

4th Class.

Samuel Petigrew, marcht.
Richard Dixon, Sergt. Major.

6th Comp'y.

4th Class.

William Snodgrass, marcht.
John Sterrett, marcht.
William Rodgers, marcht.
Daniel Vailaly, marcht.
Samuel McCord, marcht.
Alexander Swan, marcht.
Robert Templeton, marcht.
Isaac Hodge, gon to York County.
John Johnson, 1st Compy.

7th Company.

4th Class.

Casper Graver, marcht.
John Winter, marcht.
John Harper, marcht.

8th Comp'y.

4th Class.

John Buyers, marcht.
Martin Fridley, marcht.

1st Comp'y.

5th Class.

John Graham, marcht.
Robert Dolton, marcht.
Neal Colgin, marcht.

6th Class.

John Snodgress, marcht.
David Hays, Drum major.
Hugh Ramsey, marcht.
John Fleming, Refugee from Northum.
Andrew Karr, marcht.
Jacob Youngman, of the 1st Class.

7th Class.

William Right, mårcht.
Thomas Finnay, marcht.
William Crean, marcht.
John Johnston, marcht.
James Tagert, marcht.
William Brown, member of assembly.

2nd Company.

5th Class.

Samuel Brodley, marcht.
Benjamin Boyd, marcht.
Martin Penogle, marcht.
Chrislay Earley, marcht.
Chrislay Irwin, marcht.
Flavel Roan, of the 7th Battalion.
Joseph Sawer, marcht.
Christ. Keatley, marcht.
George Gigga, marcht.

6th Class.

John Sayer, marcht.
James Donalson, marcht.

7th Class.

William Sawer, Senr, marcht.
James McDonald, marcht.
James Willson, marcht.
Peter Rodebaugh, marcht.

3d Company.

5th Class.

William Grahams, marcht.

6th Class.

Garret Wilson, marcht.
James Robertson, marcnt.
Robert Caldwell, marcht.

7th Class.

Robert Bell, marcht.
George Stuart, marcht.
John Ensworth, marcht.
Isaac Harrison, marcht.
David Robertson, marcht.

4th Company.

5th Class.

John Poor, marcht.
Charles Spiker, marcht.

6th Class.

Henry Fiting, marcht.
Daniel Millar, marcht.
Martin Millar, marcht.

7th Class.

Jacob Kisner, marcht.
John Weaver, marcht.
George Ranke, marcht.

5th Company.

5th Class.

Robert Poterfield, marcht.
James Petigrew, marcht.
John Todd, marcht.
William Carson, marcht.

6th Class.

Alexander Sloan, marcht.
Thomas Wallace, marcht.
John Ramage, marcht.
Duncan Campbell, marcht.
Robert Ramage, marcht.
John Robison, Quarter M. Serjent.
Arch'd Roan, marcht.

7th Class.

James Todd, marcht.
David Todd, marcht.
Samuel Robison, marcht.
Robert Hill, marcht.
Robert Strain, marcht.

6th Comp'y.

5th Class.

Joseph Hutchison, marcht.
Robert Maxell, marcht.
William McCormick, marcht.
Jeremiah Rodgers, marcht.
Francis McClure, marcht.
James Willson, marcht.
William Trousdale.

6th Class.

Thomas Walger, marcht.
Robert Moody, marcht.
William Hagerty, marcht.
James McClure, marcht.
Mathew McGrier, Gon to fort pitt.

7th Class.

Thomas McNair, marcht.
John Kithkart, marcht.
David Calhoon, marcht.
William Robison, marcht.
David Caldwell, marcht.
Joseph Willson, of 8th Class.
Anthony Donlevy, of 1st Class.

7th Company.

5th Class.

John Pruner, Jun'r, marcht.
Peter Fox, marcht.
Nicholas Pruner, marcht.
Nicholas Titler, marcht.

6th Class.

Adam Titler, of the 2d Battalion.
Nicholas Poor, marcht.
John Weaver, marcht.
Jacob Toops, marcht.

7th Class.

Peter River, marcht.
Balser Stoner, marcht.
Henry Swarts, marcht.
Thomas McCullough, marcht.
John Stone, marcht.
Alexr. Young, marcht.
James Stuart, of the 10th Battalion.
John Shultz, marcht.
John Pickley, marcht.
Henry Winter, marcht.
James Young, marcht.

8th Company.

5th Class.

Adam Deam, marcht.
Peter Pearst, marcht.
David Hamaker, of the 7 Battalion.
Philip Plesley, marcht.
George Weatherhold, marcht.
John Plesley, marcht.

6th Class.

David Rowland, marcht.

7th Class.

Joseph Feaver, marcht.
George Peters, marcht.
Jacob Heroof, marcht.
Daniel Wonderly, marcht.
Philip Nigh, Gon to 2 Battalion.
James Cluney, marcht.
Stofel Bower, marcht.
Peter Eversole, Sen'r, marcht.

The above is the State of the Severeal Classes as near as I can discover.

Certified by

ROBT. CLARK, S. Lt. L. Co.

NOVEMBER 1ST, 1780, CAPT. CRAFFORDS FIRST CLASS OF THE FIRST COMPANY. (c.)

Capt. Craffords first class.

Philip Road.
Christian Grove.
Rudolph Shafer.
Adam Oberley.
Lenard Stone.
Nicholas Troudwine.
Christian Sour.
John Smith.
Barnet Lutes.
David Grove, Jur.
Edward Good.

Capt. McCelwane's first Class.

Casper Shirk.
Christ Snider, Jur.
Nathan Evans.
Jacob Snider, Jur.
John Weaver, fat.
Hugh Harbeson, a sergent.
Jacob Grim.
John Stofer, run away.
Peter Lite, run away.
Christian Root, jun., under age.
Antony Miller, gone away.
John Purrel.
Jacob Fox.

Capt. Statlers first Class.

Peter Brown.
Joel Carpenter.
Jacob Carpenter.
John Fiser.
Christian Farney.
John Myer.
Barnet Shrinet, not yet found.

Capt. Holmans first Class.

Jacob road.
Martin Road.
Ulerich Wisler.
Henry Hildebrand.
Henry Steinbring.
Michael Brous.
Enigh Snider.
Christian Brimmer.
Philip Road.
John Davies, Gabriels son.
George Alexander.

(c.) I do Certify that Richard Dixon was appointed Sergen Majr of the Ninth Battallion of Lancaster County in the Year 1780 and has ever since acted as such To this Deat. Given this 17th May 1786.

JOHN RODGERS.

A RETURN OF CAPT. DANL. BRADLEY COMPANEY OF THE NINTH BATILION OF LANCASTER COUNTY MILITIA COMMADED BY COLLR. JON. RODGERS FROM THE FIST DAY OF MARCH 1781. (c.)

Jon Bomgartner.
Matine Miley.
Jon. Muser.
Jacob Wolf.
Georg Unger.
Abraham Winger.
petter Beasore.
Jon. Brighbill.
Jon. Simon.
Christion pirkey.
Danl. Miller.
Jas. pirkey.
Henry Moyer.
Jacob Moyer.
Gabril Shope.
Jacob Graff.
Boiser Bomgartner.
petter Kingrey.
Jon. Royer.
fredrick Beasore.
Jacob Beasore.
petter Wolmer Jur.
Henry Shue.
Henry Bruner.
Jon. Weaver.
Adam Weaver.
petter Brighbill.
Jon. Wolmer.
petter River.
Georg hedrick.
Jacob Henry.
Nicolas Abertoll.
Adam Goodman.
Jon. Stelly.
Ludwick Sering.
Christion Winger.
Christion fronk.
Georg Mese.
Adam Carpender.
Jon. Bougher.

A true Return Certified by me.

D. BRADLEY, Capt.
of the Seventh Class of the Ninth Batilion.

MUSTER ROLL OF THE EIGHT COMPANY OF COL. RODGERS BATALION COMMANDED BY CAPTAIN WILLIAM LAIRD. MAY 1781. (c.)

Captain.
William Laird.

Lieutenant.
John McFarland.

Ensign.

George Lower.

John Coffman.
Philip Brand.
Henry Cooper.
Adam Copaugh.
Henry Miller.
Abraham Strickler.
Henry Landes.
Petter Landis.
George Spelsbaugh.
Adam Hamaker.
Christopher Hamaker.
Christopher Stover.
James Carnachan.
Christopher Nover.
Christopher Landis.
Max Spidle.
John Books.
Valentine Kinsler.
Jacob Catrine.
Jacob Landis.
Daniel Baum.
Petter Perst.
John Snider.
David Hamoker.
David Brand.
John Blesley.
John Landis.
Jacob Richer, Hanovèr.
John Perst.
Abraham Landis.
Simon Singer.
George Minich.
Petter Eversol.
George Peetters.
Phillip Nigh.
Henry Eater.
Fredrick Stall.
Philip Hamaker.
Petter Eversol.
Samuel Hamaker.
Jacob Strickler.

A True acount of the above from April 23 to May 31. Certifyed by

WM. LAIRD, Capt'n.

MUSTER ROLL OF 2ND CLASS 9TH BATALL. LANC'R COUNTY MILITIA ON A TOUR OF DUTY AT LANCASTER. (c.)

Names of Persons who compleated a tour of duty.	Names of persons who furnished substitutes.	Time when duty commd.	Time when duty ended.
Ensign.		1781.	1781.
Henry Graham,		June 27,	Aug. 13.
Drumer.			
Danl. Wiley,			Aug. 26.
Privates.			
Wm. Ratchford,	Michl. Straw.		
Jno. Potts,	Henry Hess.		
Conrad Herger,	Jacob River.		
Jno. Peter,	Archd. Stone.		
Jno. Clark,	Peter Miller.		
Christn. Odenwalt,	Peter Vendle.		
Robert Young,			
Danl. Myer,	Philip Stone.		
Philip Richart.			
Dan'l Wentler,	Leonard Umberger.		
John Boyer,	Peter Bump.		
Jno. Hagler,	Benj. Clark.		
Thos. Evans,	John Fox.		
Jno. Weatherholt,	James Fox.		

Lanc'r July 2nd 1781. Then mustered the above Compy. as above specified.

AD'M HUBLEY, S. L. L'r C'y.

MUSTER ROLL OF 3D CLASS OF 9TH BATAL. LANCASTER COUNTY MILITIA ON A TOUR OF DUTY AT NORTHUMBERLAND. (c.)

Names of Persons Who Served.	Names of persons who furnished substitutes.	Time when duty commd.	Time when duty ended.
Serjt.		1781.	1781.
Robert Maxwell, ...	Jaspar Freeman, ...	July 9, ...	Aug. 21.
Thomas Crawford, ...	John Humes.		
Danl. Mathias, ...	Robert Sturgeon.		
Jno. Huey, ...	Henry Baker.		
Jno. Cunningham.			
Henry McHenry, ...	Richd. Finley.		
James Laird.			
Jacob Miller.			
Jacob Youngman, say for....	Jacob Pham.		
James Donaly.			
Jno. McHenry, ...	Jno. Craig.		

Certify'd by Wm. Johnston Capt. & mustered by Col. Hunter on the 21st Aug. 81.

N. B. 6 days allow'd in above for marching to & from home the whole service 50 days.

MUSTER ROLL OF THE 5TH, 6TH & 7TH CLASS OF THE 9TH BATALION LANCASTER COUNTY MILITIA ON A TOUER OF DUTY (c.)

Names of Persons who perform a touer of Duty.	What Class.	Names of Persons who [illegible] Substitutes.	Time when Duty Commenced.	Time when Duty ended.
Capt.				
William Allen,	5th,			
Leiut.				
John Barnet,	5th,			
Ensgn.				
George [illegible]er,	5th,			
Serjts.				
Robert Greenlee,	5th,			
Philip Lesly,	5th,			
Drum.				
John O'Neal,	5th,			
Fife.				
Andrew Hearof,	5th,			

Privates.					
Alexr. Sloan,	5th,				
Hugh Jelly,	5th,				
Thomas Dunlap,	5th,				
John Johnson,	5th,				
David McDonnell,	5th,				
John Spence,	5th,				
Robert Allen,	5th,				
John McCanderick,	5th,				
Michael Drury,	5th,				
Christopher Ervin,	5th,				
William Montgomery,	5th,				
John [illegible]b,	5th,				
James Sawyer,	5th,				
John Clark,	5th,	Benjamin Boyd.			
[illegible]mes Barnett,	5th,				
William [illegible]d,	5th,	Samuel Bradley.			
William McCormick,	5th,				
George Giggy,	5th,				
James Queen,	5th,				
John Pettycrew,	5th,				
William Carson,	5th,				
John Shuster,	5th,				
Henry Beasor,	5th,				
Gabriel Davis,	5th,				
David Rowland,	5th,				
Simon Singer,	5th,				
Charles Spricher,	5th,				
[illegible]am Tim,	5th,	Adam Tim, Senr.			
[illegible]el [illegible]k,	5th,				
Peter Fox,	5th,				
John Poor,	5th,				
Murty Burns,	5th,	William Graham.			
John Todd,	5th,				

MUSTER ROLL OF THE 5TH, 6TH & 7TH CLASS OF THE 9TH BATALION LANCASTER COUNTY MILITIA ON A TOUER OF DUTY—Continued.

Names of Persons who perform a touer of Duty.	What Class.	Names of Persons who furnished Substitutes.	Time when Duty Commenced.	Time when Duty ended.
Jacob Youngman,	5th,	Conrad Smith.		
[illegible] Mura,	5th,	William Weiss.		
James Low,	5th,			
George Carvery,	5th,			
Henrey Fitting,	5th,			
Duncan Campbell,	5th,			
William Glen,	5th,			
Joseph [illegible]n,	5th,	William Troustle.		
Thomas Espy,	5th,			
Robert Moorhead,	5th,			
Joshua Maugra,	5th,			
Daniel Miller,	5th,			
[illegible]r Hearof,	5th,	Daniel Wintedinger.		
William Davis,	5th,			
William Davis,	5th,			

MUSTER ROLL OF THE 5TH, 6TH & 7TH CLASS OF THE 9TH BATALION LANCASTER COUNTY MILITIA ON A TOUER OF DUTY—Continued.

Names of Persons who perform a touer of Duty.	What Class.	Names of Persons who furnished Substitutes.	Time when Duty Commenced.	Time when Duty ended.
Capt.				
James Willson,	6th,			
Leiut.				
William Hill,	6th,			
Ensgn.				
Jacob Stone,	6th,			
Serjts.				
Henrey Laughlin,	6th,			
John Ward,	6th,			
Archibel Rowan,	6th,			
Privates.				
James Donnelson,	6th,			
John Hutchison,	6th,			
William Robertson,	6th,			
Samuel Finning,	6th,			

MUSTER ROLL OF THE 5TH, 6TH & 7TH CLASS OF THE 9TH BATALION LANCASTER COUNTY MILITIA ON A TOUER OF DUTY—Continued.

Names of Persons who perform a touer of Duty.	What Class.	Names of Persons who furnished Substitutes.	Time when Duty Commenced.	Time when Duty ended.
William McElheney,	6th,			
Robert McCully,	6th,			
William Hagerty,	6th,			
John Sawyers,	6th,			
Robert Ramage,	6th,			
John McCully,	6th,			
John Ramage,	6th,			
Thomas Maffit,	6th,			
James Taggert,	6th,			
John Cathcart,	6th,			
[illegible]bert Freekelton,	6th,	Thomas Wallace.		
Robert Dean,	6th,			
Thomas Walker,	6th,			
Robert [illegible]ll,	6th,			
Thomas Dougherty,	6th,			
Archibel [illegible]e,	6th,			
[illegible] Ramsey,	6th,			
Peter Mellon,	6th,	Robert Dallow, Say Dalton.		
John Morrison,	6th,			
Anthony Donlevy,	6th,	Michael Kilener.		

James Mitchel,	6th,			
Robert Moody,	6th,			
James Wilson,	6th,			
James Pinkerton,	6th,			
David Miskins,	6th,	William Crow.		
Ephraim Spencer,	6th,			
Hugh Morris,	6th "			
Robert McCanery,	6th,	Robert Porterfield.		
James Bigs,	6th,			
Robert Warnock,	6th,			
Joshua Magull,	6th,			

MUSTER ROLL OF THE 5TH, 6TH & 7TH CLASS OF THE 9TH BATALION LANCASTER COUNTY MILITIA ON A TOUER OF DUTY—Continued.

Names of Persons who perform a touer of Duty.	What Class.	Names of Persons who furnished Substitutes.	Time when Duty Commenced.	Time when Duty ended.
Capt.				
Daniel Bradley,	7th,			
Leiut.				
William Young,	7th,			
Ensgn.				
James Johnston,	7th,			
Sergts.				
William McFarland,	7th,			
Stophel Fox,	7th,			
Privates.				
Thomas McCulough,	7th,			
James Willey,	7th,	Balzer Stone.		
Henrey Swartz,	7th,			
John Toner,	7th,	David Toner.		
Alexr. Young,	7th,			

John Shuller,	7th,	
Gilbert Samuel,	7th,	John Pickle.
Henrey Wr,	7th,	
John Swartz,	7th,	
James Young,	7th,	
Henrey Stone,	7th,	
John Hughes,	7th,	John Weacers, say Weaver
David Todd,	7th,	
John Weatherhold,	7th,	
Christopher Huber,	7th,	Jacob Keiner.
Alexr. Moore,	7th,	James Fary.
Robert Bell,	7th,	
Andrew Armstrong,	7th,	
Isaac Keiner,	7th,	Daniel Weaver.
Henrey Pesone,	7th,	Nicholas Bruner.
John Skringer;	7th,	Isaac Harrison.
George Stewart,	7th,	
Robert Strain,	7th,	
David Robison,	7th,	
James Young,	7th,	
Jared Nilson,	7th,	
George Shoke,	7th,	George Barck.
William Bonday,	7th,	
Henrey Gr,	7th,	
David Hill,	7th,	
James Hoger,	7th,	
James Robison,	7th,	
William McCormick,	7th,	Thomas McCormick.
Joseph Porter,	7th,	James Clarey.
John Hall,	7th,	
Torris Cox,	7th,	Peter Eversole.
Nicholas Titlor,	7th,	
Michael Nowland,	7th,	James Willson.
John Corrathers,	7th,	Geoge Peters.

MUSTER ROLL OF THE 5TH, 6TH & 7TH CLASS OF THE 9TH BATALION LANCASTER COUNTY MILITIA ON A TOUER OF DUTY—Continued.

Names of Persons who perform a touer of Duty.	What Class.	Names of Persons who furnished Substitutes.	Time when Duty Commenced.	Time when Duty ended.
Philip Bomgartner,	7th,			
[illegible]h Romsey,	7th,			
John Rithcart,	7th,			
John Muser,	7th,			
John Petre,	7th,			
Peter Radelbough,	7th,			
John Winter,	7th,	William Titler.		
[illegible]ert Hill,	7th,			
William Ferguson,	7th,			
William [illegible]ht,	7th,			
[illegible] [illegible]le,	7th,			
David Hains,	7th,	William Sawyer.		
James Hains,	7th,	Andrew Carr.		

RETURN OF THE FIRST COMPANY OF THE NINTH BATALION OF LANCASTER COUNTY MILITIA COMMANDED BY LIEUT. COL. JOHN RODGERS. (c.) 1781.

Capt.
Wm. Allen.

Lieu.
John Barnet.

Ens.
Jas. Wilson.

First Class.

Mat. Crowser.
Jas. Barent.
David McGuire.
Wm. Hume.
David Miskimmens.
Jas. McMillen.
David Moffet.
John Mckendry.
John Stuart.
Robt. Moorhead.
Wm. McCullough.
John McAully.

Second Class.

John McCord.
Leonard Umbarger.
John ferguson.
Joseph Allen.
Conrad Smith.
Robt. Lusk.
Hugh Graham.

Third Class.

Michael Vanlear.
John Hume.
Frances Carson.
David Couldwell.
Robt. Sturgeon.
David McCraken.
George McMillen.
John Martin.
Wm. Ramsey.
George Simmons.
John Elder.

fourth Class.

Jas. Crean.
Saml. Sturgeon.
Jos. Allen.
John Patterson.
Thos. Allen, idiot and unfit for service.
Robt. forstor.
Jas. Moffet.
Patrick Linch.
Saml. finey.
Robt. McCullough.

Fifth Class.

Wm. Cuningham.
Alexdr. McElheney.
John Carter.
Robt. Kenaday.
Jas. Stuart.
John Graham.
Robt. dolton.
Neal Colgan.
Robt. Wily.
Wm. Wilkeson.

Sixth Class.

Tim'y Green Esq., excused.
Saml. McCullough, removed.
John Snodgrass.
David Hay, 1 Drum Major.
Robt. frecelton.
Hugh Ramsey.
John fleming, refugee from Northumberland.
Andrew Carr.
Barnerd McNutt.
——— Modral.
——— Youngman.

Seventh Class.

Wm. Right.
Thos. finney.
Wm. Crean.
John Jonson.
Jas. Taggert.
John Dunlap.
Adam Harbyson.
Wm. Brown, member of Assembly.
Joseph Barnet.

Eighth Class.

Jas. Jonson.
John Cooper.
Thos. McElheney.
Robt. Aughy.
Jas. Green.
Jas. McMillen.
Robt. McCord.
Wm. Crawford.
Frances ferguson.
Jas. McCullough.
Thos. Ward.
Wm. hadun.

Certified by me

WM. ALLEN, Capt.

A RETURN OF THE SECOND COMP'Y OF THE NINTH BATALION OF LANCASTER COUNTY MILITIA COMMANDED BY COLO. JOHN ROGERS THIS 17TH DAY OF NOVEMBER 1781. (c.)

Captain.
Patrick Hays.

Lieutenant.
Samuel Weir.

Ensign.

John Eversole.

Serjeants.

Thomas Espy.
James Johston.
David McDonnal.

1st Class.

Vendal Henry.
Christopher Stoner.
John McCallen.
Joseph Carmony.
Jacob Ballim.
Jacob Rice.
Francis Taylor.
Frederick Weyman.
Robert Crocket.
Abram Mitchell.
Nicholas Musser.
William Moffit.
John Sheckle.
Michel Nowland.
Chrisly Weyland.
William Clark.

2d Class.

Hendry Hoover.
John Myres.
Michael Ealy.
William Nay.
John Over.
John Landice.
Walter Clark.
Jacob Bowman.
Loudwick Ball.
Jacob Ney.
Martin Long.

3d Class.

Thomas Mitchell.
Michael Kreager.
Martin Millar.
Abram Weltmore.
Jacob Bowman, Sen.
Adam Dinangar.
Andrew Byars.
Daniel Harshbarger.
William Ballim.
Nicholas Ballim.
Conrod Wishon.
John Hoover.
Dewalt Henry.
Jacob Lehman, Jun.
Abram Pitleon.

4th Class.

William Sayer, Jun.
Jacob Plough.
David Hays.
Dewalk Kregaer.
Phelty Rhode.
Daniel Weir.
George Killinger.
Christopher Forney.
John Nay.
James Low.
John Shuster.
John Brought.
Joseph Swertswell.

5th Class.

Samuel Brodley.
Benjamin Boyd.
John Fleagar.
Felix Landice.
Philip Deeds.
Martin Penogle.
Christopher Early.
Peter Over.
John Ballim.
John O'Neal.
Christopher Erwin.
George Bell.
John Weir.
Joseph (missing).
Christopher Keatly.
George Guiggy.
John Harshbarger.

6th Class.

George Henry.
Robert McCallin.
John Early.
Benjamin Hersey.
Joseph Forney.
Nicholas Nay.
John Sayers.
Emanuel Kingrigh.
William Shaw.
James Donnalson.
Arch'd McAlister.
Jacob Hoover.
James Sayers.
William Hunter.
Jacob Longnaker.
Tetrach Millar.
Charles Dougherty.
James Queen.

7th Class.

Michael Katrin.
Williry Weltmore.
John Forney.
Joseph Naphsker.
Henry Bowman.
William Sayer, Sen.
Christopher Beam.
James McDonnal.
Christopher Taner.
James Willson.
Peter Rodebaugh.
Jacob Earley.
Peter Forney.

8th Class.

Robert Hays.
Martin Hoover.
Thomas McCallen.
John White.
Jacob Kensley.
Joseph Falgate.
Peter Lineweaver.
Benjamin Sayers.
John Lehman.
John Fairley.
James Willson.
Phelty Katrin.
William Ball.
David Mitchell.
Wm. Sayer (orphan).
Phelty Sterger.
Daniel Brought.
Peter Ballim.
John Carithers.
Henry Wray.

Certify'd by me.

PATT HAYS, Capt.

A TRUE AND EXACT LIST OF THE NAMES AND SIR-NAMES OF EACH AND EVERY MALE WHITE PERSON INHABITING OR RESIDING WITHIN THE BOUNDS OF THE THIRD COMPANY DISTRICT BETWEEN THE AGES OF EIGHTEEN AND FIFTY THREE, THE NINTH BATTALION UNDER THE COMMAND OF COL. JOHN RODGERS, LANCASTER COUNTY MILITIA THIS 5TH DAY OF APRIL 1781. (c.)

Capt.

Ambros Creain.

Lieut.

William Young.

Ensign.

Henry Graham.

Class 1st.

Robt. Ewing.
Archibald Man.
James Stewart, Senior.
William Campbell.

Class 2d.

John Cuningham.
Robt. Young.
Peter Rambow.
James Young, Junr.
John Stewart.
James Young, Senior.

Class 3d.

David Ramsey.

Class 4th.

Samuel Keasly.
Josiah Espy.
Thomas Smily.
Murtagh Burn.
William Bundy.
Andrew Young.
Robt. Kirkwood.

Class 5th.

James Stewart, Junior.
John Armstrong.
William Graham.
George Young.

Class 6th.

Patrick McLane, absconded.
William Young.
Jared Nelson.
John Young, Senior.
Michael Polce.
James Robertson.
Robert Caldwell.

Class 7th.

Will'm Gilbert, absconded .
Robert Bell.
George Stewart.
John Endsworth.
John Campbell, dead.
Isaac Herrison.
William Sloan.
David Robertson.

Class 8th.

John Young.
George Espy.
John Graham.
William Donnelson.
Robt. Warnock.

1781.

RETURN OF THE FOURTH COMPANY OF THE NINTH BATTALION OF LANCASTER COUNTY MILITIA COMMANDED BY LIEUT. COL'N JOHN ROGERS, APRIL 11TH 1781. (c.)

Capt.

John Herkerider.

Lieut.

Emanuel Duey.

Ensn.

Jacob Pruner.

Serts.

Henry Sharp.
Conrad Meyer.
Mathias beaker.

fifer.

Michael Pruner.

1 Class.

Henry Sigler.
georg Romberger.
Jacob Hauser.
Conrad Suey.
Jacob Youngman.

2 Class.

Adam Woul.
Casper feeman.
georg Sider.
Christy Sider.
John Rigard.
Peter Wirick.

3 Class.

georg Wolf.
Christoffer Mourd.
Wm. Rough.
Martin Suey.
george Moura.
Henry beaker.
Christy Huver.

4 Class.

John Serker.
george Wallmer.
Simon Minock.
John Carbary.
Andrew Brown.
John Shup.

5 Class.

John Poor.
Charles Spricker.
george Hooke.
Daniel Huffnogel.
John Simerman.
Stoffel Richwine.
John Hoover, Jur.

6 Class.

Henry fitting.
Daniel Miller.
Peter killinger.
Michael Brown.
Valuntin hufnogel.
Jacob Serker.
Martin Miller.
Henry glevey.

7 Class.

John Rough.
Jacob kisner.
John Weaver.
Jacob Grose.
Andrew killinger.
georg Spricker.
georg Rank.

8 Class.

Jacob Sent.	Andrew kiffer.
Stofel brown.	Michael Moura.
Bernet Rough.	John Stover.
Jacob Miller.	Joseph Miller.
John Wolf.	

The truth of the Within Return to the Best of My Knowledge Sworn and Subscribed the 11th Day of April A. D. 1781.
Certified by

JOHN HERKERIDER,
Capt.

A RETURN OF ALL THE MALE WHITE INHABITANTS BETWEEN THE AGE OF 18 & 53 YEARS OF AGE RESIDING WITHIN THE BOUNDS OF THE 5TH COMP'Y OF THE 9TH BATA'LA OF LANCASTER COUNTY MILITIA COMMANDED BY S. COL. JOHN ROGERS; AS THEY STAND IN THEIR RESPECTIVE CLASSES. (c.)

Capt.

Jas. McCreight.

Lieu.

Wm. Hill.

Ensn.

Wm. Brandon.

Sergts.

Robert Greenlee.	Wm. Jones.
John Ward.	

1 Class.

Wm. Cloaky.	John Seringer.
Dr. John Knowling.	

2d Class.

John Hume.	John Pettycrew.
Alex'dr Kidd.	James Low.

8 Class.

John Craig.
Rich'd Finlay.
George Ward.

4th Class.

George Crain.
John McQuown.
Thos. Kennedy.
Alex'dr Strain.
Rich'd Dixon.
Sam'l Pettycrew.
Wm. Thome.

5th Class.

John French.
Wm. Strain.
Sam'l Brown.
Robt. McCully.
Robt. Porterfeild.
Jas. Pettycrew.
John Todd.
Jas. Breden.
William Carson.

6th Class.

Alex'dr Sloan.
Thos. Wallace.
John Ramage.
Wm. Brown.
Duncan Campbell.
Robt. Ramage.
Wm. McCally.
Jas. Hammel.
John Robinson.
Arch'd Roan.
John Dunlap.

7th Class.

James Todd.
David Todd.
Sam'l Robinson.
Robert Hill.
Jas. Caldwell.
Robert Strain.

8th Class.

Rich'd Crawford.
Edward Israelow.
Hugh Morris.
Hugh Jelly.

Samuel Bells, class not known.

Refugees.

David Hay.
John Moor.
Robt. McNeal.

The truth of the within Return to the Best of my knowledge is sworn and subscribed the 11th Day of April A. D. 1781.

By

JAS. McCREIGHT, Capt.

COL. ROBERT CLARK, ESQ.,
S. L. L. County.

1781.

A RETURN OF ALL THE MALE WHITE INHABITANTS AND RESIDENTS BETWEEN THE AGES OF 18 AND 53 YEARS LIVING OR RESIDING IN THE DESTRICT OF THE 6TH COMPANY OF THE NINTH BATALION OF LANCASTER COUNTY MILITIA. (c.)

Captain.

Jas. Willson.

Lieutenant.

Jas. Rogers.

Ensign.

Jas. Johnston.

Serjeants.

Duncan Sinckleer.
Henry Laughlin.
James Ripith.

First Class.

John Spencer.
Wm. Mitchel.
Peter Balsbough.
Patrick flin.
William Steuart.
John Anderson.
Philip Bell.
Adam Firebough.
William Ripeth.
Will'm Snodgrass.
John McCleland.

2d Class.

Robt. Lewis.
Peter Bell.

Third Class.

thos. Martin.
Andrew Rogers.
Samuel Steuart.
Felty Balsbough.
Wm. Willson, removed to York Co.

Fourth Class.

Will'm Snody.
John Sterrit.
Will'm Rogers.
John Baird.
Daniel Validay.
John Johnston.

John Miller.
Alex'r Swan.
Sam'l McCord.
James Porter, Jr.
Isaac Lodge.
Joshuah Magus.

Fifth Class.

Jos. hutchison.
Robt. Maxwell.
Wm. McCormick.
Jeremiah Rogers.
Frances McClure.
Sam'l Swan.
James Willson.
Wm. Tronsdale.
John Ripeth.

Sixth Class.

Thos. Walker.
Robt. Moody.
Wm. Hagerty.
Christ Bumberger.
James Duncan.
Jas. McClure.
Hugh Ripeth.
Edward Striddle.
Matthew McGregor.

Seventh Class.

thos. McMair.
Hugh Willson.
John Cathcart.
David Caldhoon.
Andrew armstrong.
Abraham host.
Wm. Robertson.
David Kingring.
Benjamin Fulton.
David Caldwell.
Jos. Willson.
anthony Deleny.

Eighth Class.

thos. McCord.
Jas. Bayrd.
Jos. Parks.
John thompson.
William Cathcart.
Joseph Glen.
Andrew Willson.
Jas. Wallace.
Felex McCluskey.
Benjamin Sterrit.
Phillip Walthower.
John Morison.

Certified By

JAS. WILLSON, Capt.

A MUSTER ROLL OF CAPT. BRADLEY'S COMPANY OF THE NINTH BATILION OF LANCASTER COUNTY MILITIA. APRIL THE 10TH 1781. (c.)

Captain.
Danl. Bradley.

Lieutenant.
Adam Mark.

Ensign.

Jacob Stone.

Sergeants.

William McFarland. Jacob Muser.
Christian fox.

Corporals.

Anthoney fox. peter Roddy.
John Swartz.

Drummer.

John tups.

Fifer.

William Hedreck.

First Class.

John petre.
Jacob Wolf.
peter Beasore.
Abraham Wingar.
George Beasore.
George unger.
William Corpender.
John Bomgortner.
Michael Straw.
John Tibings, Jur.

Second Class.

Gabril Shop.
Ludwick Searing.
Christian wingar.
John Brilbill.
John Symon.
Christian pirkey.
Henry Heose.
Bejamen Clark .
petter ventling.
Jacob River.
philip Stone.

Third Class.

Dan'l Miller.
Conrad Road.
Michel Selcer.
Joseph Birkey.
George Wilt.
Jacob tibings.
Dan'l weaver.
Henry Beasore.
philip Bomgartner.
vendle Bartlemay.
John Carvery.
Jacob Grave.
John Steley.
John Muser.

Fourth Class.

vendle fortney.
Martine Miley.
Philip Bomgartner.
peter felty, Jr.

George Haine.
petter kingrey.
Henry Lowmiller.
John Winter, Jur.
Casper Graser.
Jacob Carpender.
John harper.
Adam Carpender.

Fifth Class.

John Roger.
John Bruner, Jur.
peter fox.
fredrick Beasore.
Jacob Beosore.
Nicholas Bruner.
John Lose.
Henry houser.
Jacob Moyer.
Nicholas titler.

Sixth Class.

peter wolmer, Jur.
Henry Shue.
Adam titler.
Henry Bruner.
frances Abbertall.
Nicholas poor.
John Weaver.
petter Symond.
George Mouran.
John Bougher.
Jacob tups.
George Man.
Adam Weaver.

Seventh Class.

petter Brightbill.
John Walmer.
Michael fillphey.
petter River.
George Hedrick.
Jacob Henry.
Balzer Stone.
Henry Swarz.
thomas McCullouch.
Dan toner.
John toner.
Alexander Young.
James Stewart.
John Shultz.
John pickle.
Moyer Michael.
Henry Moyer.
Henry Winter.
George Lose.
Jacob Lose.
James Young.

8th Class.

Ludwick klick.
Valintine Sala.
Nicholas Abbertall.
Conrade Helm.
Adam Goodman.
petter Stone.
petter title.
philip frank.
Michael Singer.
John Young.
Andrewas Young.
Christian frank.

Jacob Creomer.
Jacob Carvery.
John Hedrick.
Christian harshbarger.
John Stone.
Roger Brolly.
John McBride.

This is to Certify that the within is a true State of my Company.

Certified by me.

BRADLEY, Capt.

A LIST OF THE NAMES AND SIRNAMES OF THE MALE WHITE INHABITANTS, BETWEEN THE AGES OF EIGHTEEN AND FIFTY THREE, LIVING OR RESIDING WITHIN THE BOUNDS LIMITS OR LINES OF THE EIGHT COMPANY OF THE NINTH BATALION OF LANCASTER COUNTY MILITIA COMMANDED BY COL. JOHN RODGERS. (c.)

Commissioned officers.

Captain.

William Laird.

Lieutenant..

John McFarland.

Ensign.

George Lower.

Non Commissioned officers.

Sergts.

1st. George Emmerick.
2nd. Ludwick Emerick.
3rd. William Whigam.

Corporals.

Edward Burges.
John Gaul.
Michael Spade.

firs Class.

John Coffman.
Barnet Foults.
Philip Brand.
Henry Cooper.

Adam Coupaugh. Abraham Strickler.
Henry Miller. Henry Landes.
John Fox. Frederick Blessly.

Second Class.

Petter Landis. Adam Spidle.
George Spalsbaugh. Christopher Noover.
Adam Hammaker. William Breden.
Christly Hammaker. James Carns.
Phillip Richar.

Third Class.

Frederick Hummel. John Weatherhold.
Jacob Rham. James Donally.
Phillip fishbourn. Jacob Miller.
James Laird.

Fourth Class.

John Byers. Martin Fridley.
Christian Stopher. Petter Fishbourn.
Christly Landis. John Books.
Max Spidle. Valentine Kensler.

Fifth Class.

Jacob Landis. Phillip Blessley.
Adam Deam. David Brand.
Daniel Baum. George Weatherhold.
Petter Perst. Andrew Heroof.
John Snider. John Blessley.
David Hammaker. Jacob Kathoring.
Ludwick Fishbourn.

Sixth Class.

John Landis. Abraham Landis.
Martin Rhouse. David Rowland.
Jacob Richar, Hanover. Jacob Richar.
John Furst. James Kennedy.
Andrew Gamble.

Seventh Class.

Joseph Fever. James Cluenie.
George Minich. Stople Bower.
George Petters. John Myers.
Petter Fridley. Valentine Hummel.
Jacob Heroof. Petter Eversole, Senr.
Daniel Wonderly. Simon Singer.
Phillip Nigh.

Eight Class.

Jacob Hook.	Michael Rham.
Henry Eater.	Rober Breden.
Henry Hesse.	John Martin.
Frederick Stall.	Jacob Strickler.
Phillip Hammaker.	George Chapman.
Andrew Horning.	Martin Rice.
John Brown.	Henry Hammaker.
David Hummel.	Teetrick fishbourn.
Jacob Spidle.	Peter Eversole, Jr.
Samuel Hammaker.	Andrew Alexander.

Certifyed By me

WILLIAM LAIRD, Capt.

April 11th 1781.

1781.

(c.) To His Excellency the President & the Honorable the Supreme Executive Council of the Commonwealth of Pennsylvania.

The Representation and Memorial of the Officers and Privates of the 9th Battalion of Lancaster County Militia, Humbly Shewith—

That your Petitioners beg leve to Represent, that under the former and presant Militia Laws, the Eight Classes of Militia of the County of Lancaster have been called out and performed two full Tours, and the 7th Class of thé third tour is now upon Duty—we Conceive (Councel however are better aquainted with the details of the Militia of the State) that the County of Lancaster has don considerably more than thire proportion of Duty. Several of the Adjecant Counties we are Creditably informed, are not less than 6th Clas's Short of us.

This we consider directly contrary to the intent and meaning of the 29th Sect: of the Militia Law, as well as a Grivance as it is imposeing an unequal burden not only on those who render there Personal Service, but alsso on such as pay fines for Delinquincy money of whome we know are well affected, but from perticular and unavoidable Circumstances cannot give thire Personal Attendance.

Your Memorialists therefore pray Your Excellency and the Honl. Council will take the Premisses into Concidiration and redress our Grivances.

And they as in duty bound will pray &c.

JAS. McCREIGHT, Capt.
WM. LAIRD, Capt.
JOHN McFARLEN, Lieut.
GEORGE LOAR, Ensign.
JOHN RODGERS.
TIMY GREEN, ESQR.
SAMUL BREDLY.
JOHN HERKERIDER, Capt.
JAMES ROGERS, Lut.
EMANUEL DUEY, Leut.
JACOB PRUNER, Ens.
WM. ALLEN, Capt.
AMBROS CREAIN, Capt.
JAS. WILLSON, Capt.
LUT. WM. YOUNG.
LUT. ADAM MARK.
INS. JACOB STONE.
DANL. BRADLEY, Capt.
JOHN BARNETT, Lut.
LUT. WILLIAM HILL.
WM. BRANDON, Ensign.

MUSTER ROLL OF CAPT. PATRICK HAY'S COMPANY LANCASTER COUNTY MILITIA FOR JUNE 1782. (c.)

Capt.

Patrick Hays.

Lieu.

Benjamin Mills.

Ens.

James Hutchison.

Sergeants.

James Sterret.
Arthur Patterson.

Corpler.

Jacob Aaron.

First Class.

Christy Hoofman.
John Shank.
John Hayes.
Christy Erishman.

Philip Gilman.	Hugh Haggerty.
Robt. Mears.	Dewalt Shank.
Edward Watterson.	James Corran.
Baltzor Stake.	

Class 2.

John Shelhorn.	Joun Metz.
Abraham Castle.	John Hocfman.

Class 3.

Christy Long.	Henry Teesinger.
Henry Strickler.	John Beard.
Baltzer Walter.	Allex'r McClean.
Wendel Martzel.	Frederick Arrond.

Class 4.

Saml. Robinson.	Michael Stake.
Joseph little.	John Welger.
Robt. Ally.	Saml. McClun.
Jacob Bender.	Mick. Marchel.
Baltzer Shilhorn.	Stephen pike.
Abram Martin.	Frederick Blettenberger.
John Lisher.	Ambrose Newsorn.

Class 5.

Hugh Grahms.	John Masha.
Michael Horst.	Charles Welger.
Peter Walter.	Martin Niesley.
Jacob Hostater.	Michael Horsler.
Christian Loognecker.	Jinis Cleary.
Henry Acker.	John Ashbaugher.

Class 6th.

Abram Matz.	John Jorden.
Thomas Minto.	Joseph Porter.
George Berglebough.	Jacob Sigrist.
Mathias Kishler.	James McCarvary.
Isaac Gilman.	

Class 7th.

Henry Hoobly.	Wolvey Strickler.
Peter Hasten.	Will'm Mears.
John Rorra.	John Baker.

Philip Baker.	Christian Metz.
John Speckler.	Christian Shelly.
Jacob Kestle.	Saml. Porter.

Class 8th.

Jacob Metz.	Abram Erishman.
Jacob Erishman.	Will'm Sterret.
John Sweney.	Peter Utts.
Jacob Kensler.	John Porter.
John Brown.	

Certifyed to be a true return This 7th Day of June 1782.
PATRICK HAYES, Capt.

(c.) Dier Sir..

these are to certify that the bearor Christeant Erley hierd two Different Substitutes for the old Delinquency. The one was John Torrans, Serv'd under me at white Marchh or Chestnut hill, the other was Wm. Sands Serv'd at Leabanon, the Reason why he is charg'd for Delinquency be owing to his not making Report at the Apail, for said towrs of Duty, these from—Dier—Sir..

Your friend
PATT. HAYS, Capt'n.

Febr'y the 27th 1782.
To COL. ADAM ORTT.

(c.) I do hereby Certify that Samuel Kersley of the Ninth Batalion of Lancaster County has served as a light horse man well Equipt under the late Militia law Certified by me this 22d Day of November 1782.

JOHN RODGERS, Lieut. Col'n.

(c.) I Do Hereby Certify that David Hays of the Ninth Batalion of Lancaster County Militia is Appointed Drum Major of the aforesaid Batalion and has served as such Certifyed by me this 22d Day of November 1782.

JOHN RODGERS, Lieut. Coln.

A TRUE AND EXACT LIST OF THE NAMES, OF EACH AND EVERY MALE WHITE PERSON, INHABITING OR RESIDING, WITHIN MY DISTRICT, IN THE FIRST COMPANY, OF THE NINTH BATTALION OF LANCASTER COUNTY MILITIA, BETWEEN THE AGE OF EIGHTEEN AND FIFTY-THREE YEARS. TAKEN FOR THE YEAR 1782. (c.)

Capt.

William Allen.

Lieu.

John Barnett.

Ens.

James Willson.

Almonar.

Joseph Barnet.

First Class.

William McColough.
David Maffat.
James Barnett.
William Hume.
David McGuier.
John McCullay.
John Stewart.
James McMillan.
Jacob Youngman.
David Miscomins.
Robert Frahelton.

Second Class.

Lenard Umbargar.
Conrad Smith.
John McCord.
Hugh Graham.
John Forguson.

Third Class.

George Simons.
John Hume.
John Elder.
Robert Sturgon.
Michal Vanlear.
Francis Carson.
David Caldwell.

Fourth Class.

Joseph Crain.
John Paterson.
James Allen.
Saml. Sturgeon.

Fifth Class.

Alax'r McElheany.
Samuel Finnay.
James Stewart.
William Cunningham.
John Graham.
Robert McColough.
James Pinkerton.
Alax'r Forster.
Robt. Dotton.
Neal Colgam.
Robt. Wiley.
Wm. Wilkeson.

Sixth Class.

William McElheaney.
John Snodgrass.
James Tagart.
Robert Madorville.
Timothy Greene.
Robert Allen.
David Hays.
Hugh Ramsy.
Andy Carr.
Barnerd McNitt.
Adam Harbyson.

Seventh Class.

William Wright.
Thomas Finney.
Hugh Ramsey.
Thomas Barnett.
William Creane.
Frances Forguson.
Joseph Barnet, Junior.
John Dunlap.

Eighth Class.

George Ramsey.
William Crawford.
James McMillan, Jun'r.
Joseph Green.
William Haddon.
Robert McCord.
John Coosser.
Thomas McElheaney.
James Johnson.
John Miller.
William Brown.
Jas. McCollough.

I Do swear, on the Holy Evenglieet of the Almighty God: That the above list is a just and true state, of the Male White Inhabitants, residing in my District, agreeable to Law, and without any fraud to the State, to the best of my knowledge.

WM. ALLEN, Capt.

Sworn before me this
first Day of May 1782.

ROBT. CLARK, S. L.

A TRUE AND EXACT LIST OF THE NAMES, OF EACH AND EVERY MALE WHITE PERSON, INHABITING OR RESIDING WITHIN MY DISTRICT, IN THE SECOND COMPANY, OF THE NINTH BATTALION OF LANCASTER COUNTY MILITIA, BETWEEN THE AGE OF EIGHTEEN AND FIFTY-THREE YEARS. TAKEN FOR THE YEAR 1782. (c.)

Capt.

Patrick Hays.

Lieu.

Samuel Weir.

Ens.

John Eversole.

Almonar.

David Wray.

First Class.

Vendal Henry.
Christ. Stoner.
John McCallen.
Jacob Ballm.
Jacob Rist.
Francis Taylor.
Frederick Wayman.
Robert Crocket.
Abram Mitchell.
Nicholas Musser.
Wm. Moffit.
John Shekle.
Michael Nowland.
Christ. Weyland.
Wm. Clark.
James Minsker.
Christ. Beam.
Samuel Johnson.
Anthony Donlevy.

Second Class.

John Myre.
Michael Eaby.
Wm. Nay.
John Over.
John Landice.
Walter Clark.
Jacob Bowman.
Londwig Ball.
William Earley.
Peter Neigh.
James Fore.
Henry Hoover.

Third Class.

Thos. Mitchell.
Abram. Weltmore.
Jacob Bowman.
Adam Dinangar.
Daniel Harshbarger.
Wm. Balim.
Nicholas Balim.
Dewalt Henry.
Jacob Lehman, Jun'r.
John Minsher.
Peter Carshnets.
Andrew Wallace.
Robert Rhea.

Fourth Class.

Wm. Sayer, Jun.
Jacob Plough.
David Hays.
George Killinger.
Christ. Forney.
John Shuster.
John Brought.
Joseph Swartsel.
John Neigh.
Lowdwick Heroff.
Christian Weisbaugh.

Fifth Class.

Samuel Brodley.
Benjamin Boyd.
John Fleager.
Felix Landice.
Martin penogle.
Peter Over.
John Ballim.
David McDonnal.
George Bell.
Thos. Espy.
John Weir.
Joseph Sayer.
Christ. Keatly.
George Guiga.
John Hershbarger.
Daniel Wray.
William Thomson.
William Watt.

Sixth Class.

George Henry.
Robert McCallen.
John Earley.
Benjamin Hersey.
John Sayer.
Emanuel Kingrigh.
William Shaw.
Jas. Donnalson.
Arch'd McAllister.
James Johnston.
William Hunter.
Jacob Hoover.
James Queen.
Frederick Swarts.
John Gibb.
John Fairley.
James Sullavan.
William McCalley.
Stophel Shank.
John Miskely.
Christean Bumbarger.

Seventh Class.

Williny Weltmore.
John Forney.
Joseph Napsher.
Henry Bowman.

Wm. Sayer, Sen'r.
Christ. Beam.
Christ. Tanner.
James Willson, Jun'r.
Peter Rodebaugh.
Henry Earhart.

Eighth Class.

Robert Hays.
Thos. McCallen.
John White.
Jacob Kinsley.
Joseph Falgate.
Peter Lineweaver.
Benjamin Sayer.
James Willson, Sen'r.
Felty Katrin.
William Ball.
David Mitchell.
Wm. Sayer, orphan.
Felty Starger.
Peter Ballim.
John Carithers.
Frederick Hetsler.
Martin Hoover.

I Do swear, on the Holy Evengilest of Almighty God: That the above list is a just and true state, of the Male White Inhabitants, residing in my District agreeable to Law, and without any fraud to the State, to the best of my knowledge.

PATRICK HAYS, Capt.

Sworn before me this
30 Day of May 1782.

ROBT. CLARK, S. L.

A TRUE AND EXACT LIST OF THE NAMES, OF EACH AND EVERY MALE WHITE PERSON, INHABITING OR RESIDING WITHIN MY DISTRICT, IN THE THIRD COMPANY, OF THE NINTH BATTALION OF LANCASTER COUNTY MILITIA, BETWEEN THE AGE OF EIGHTEEN AND FIFTY-THREE YEARS. TAKEN FOR THE YEAR 1782. (c.)

Capt.
Ambros Creain.

Lieu.
william Young.

Ens.
Henery Grahams.

Almonar.

William Robertson.

First Class.

James Steart, Sener.
William Campble.
John Cremger.
Henery Miller.
George Espy, Junior.

Second Class.

Robert young.
Petter Rambo.
James Young, Jun.
John Stewart.
James Young, Sen'r.

Third Class.

David Ramsey.
Stephen Boyers.
Henery Smelser.

Fourth Class.

Josiah Espy.
Thomous Smiley.
Murty Burns.
Andrew Young.
Robert kirkwood.
William Coningham.
Samuel kearsley.
Patrick Coningham.

Fifth Class.

James Stewart, Jun'r.
John Armstrong.
William Grahams.
George Young.
Jacob Hubler.

Sixth Class.

William Young.
Jaramiaha Neelson.
John Young, Sen'r.
Michal Polce.
James Robertson.
Robert Calwell.
Thomous Craford.
Thomous Foster.
Andrew Foster.

Seventh Class.

Robert Bell.
george Stewart.
John Ensworth.
Isaac Heareson.
William Slown.
David Robartson.
Robert Foster.
James willes.

Eighth Class.

John Young.
George Espy.
John grahams.
Robert warnar.
William Ramsey.

I Do swear, on the Holy Evengilest of Almighty God: That

the above list is a just and true state, of the Male White Inhabitants, residing in my District agreeable to Law, and without any fraud to the State, to the best of my knowledge.

AMBROS CREAIN, Capt.

Sworn before me this
30 Day of May 1782.

ROBT. CLARK, S. L.

A TRUE AND EXACT LIST OF THE NAMES, OF EACH AND EVERY MALE WHITE PERSON, INHABITING OR RESIDING WITHIN MY DISTRICT, IN THE FOURTH COMPANY, OF THE NINTH BATTALION OF LANCASTER COUNTY MILITIA, BETWEEN THE AGE OF EIGHTEEN AND FIFTY-THREE YEARS. TAKEN FOR THE YEAR 1782. (c.)

Capt.

John Herkerider.

Lieu.

Emanuel Duey.

Ens.

Jaccb Pruner.

Almonar.

Michael brown, Sen'r.

Sert.

Henry Sharp.

fifer.

George Pruner.

First Class.

Henry Sigler. George Romberger.

Second Class.

Adam Woice. Christy Sider.
Casper feeman. John Rigard.
George Sider. Peter Wirick.

Third Class.

George Wolf. George Moura.
Stoffel Moura. Henry Baker.
Wm. Rough. Christy Hoover.

Fourth Class.

John Serker. Andrew Brown.
George Wallmer. John Shup.
Simon Minoch. John Rank.
John Carvary.

Fifth Class.

John Poor. John Simerman.
Charles Spricker. Christian Early.
Daniel Huffnogel. Conrad Moyer.

Sixth Class.

Henry fitting. Michael Brown.
Daniel Miller. Valluntine Huffnogel.
Peter killinger. Bernet Eisenhuth.

Seventh Class.

John Rough. George Spricker.
Jacob kisner. George Rank.
John Weaver. Henry Minock.
Jacob Gross.

Eighth Class.

Jacob Sent. andrew kiffer.
Stoppel Brown. Michael Moura.
Barnet Rough. John Stover.
Jacob Miller. Joseph Miller.
John Wolf. Michael Moyer.

I Do swear, on the Holy Evengilest of Almighty God: That the above list is a just and true state, of the Male White Inhabitants, residing in my District agreeable to Law, and without any fraud to the State, to the best of my knowledge.

JOHN KERKERIDER, Capt.

Sworn before me this
first Day of May 1782.

ROBT. CLARK, S. L.

A TRUE AND EXACT LIST OF THE NAMES, OF EACH AND EVERY MALE WHITE PERSON, INHABITING OR RESIDING WITHIN MY DISTRICT, IN THE FIFTH COMPANY, OF THE NINTH BATTALION OF LANCASTER COUNTY MILITIA, BETWEEN THE AGE OF EIGHTEEN AND FIFTY-THREE YEARS. TAKEN FOR THE YEAR 1782. (c.)

Capt.

James McCreight.

Lieu.

William Will.

Ens.

William Brandon.

Almonar.

William Thome.

Sergt. major.

Richard Dixon.

Q. M. Serg.

John Robinson.

First Class.

William Cloaky.

Second Class.

Alexander Kidd.
John Pettycrew.
John Hume.

Third Class.

John Craig.
Richard Finlay.
George Ward.
James Donnally.

Fourth Class.

George Crain.
John McQuown.
Alexander Strain.
John Tully.
Samuel Pettycrew.
Daniel Wier.

Fifth Class.

Robert Greenlee.
John French.
William Strain.
Samuel Brown.
Robert McCully.
Robert Porterfeild.
James Pettycrew.
William Carson.
John Todd.
John Thomson.
James Breden.
William Cunningham.

Sixth Class.

Alexander Sloan.
Thomas Wallace.
John Ramage.
William Brown.
Duncan Campbell.
James Hamble.
John Dunlap.
Archibald Roan.
Hugh Andrew.
John Ward.
Thomas Ward.
John Darby.

Seventh Class.

James Todd.
David Todd.
Robert Hill.
Robert Strain.
James Caldwell.

Eighth Class.

Richard Crawford.
Samuel Bell.
Edward Israelow.
Hugh Morris.
Hugh Jelly.
Robert Allen.

I Do swear, on the Holy Evengliest of Almighty God: That the above list is a just and true state, of the Male White Inhabitants, residing in my District agreeable to Law, and without any fraud to the State, to the best of my knowledge.

JAMES McCREIGHT.

Sworn before me this
30th Day of May 1782.

ROBT. CLARK.

Refugees.

David Hay.
John Moor.
Robert McNeal.

A TRUE AND EXACT LIST OF THE NAMES. OF EACH AND EVERY MALE WHITE PERSON, INHABITING OR RESIDING, WITHIN MY DISTRICT, IN THE SIXTH COMPANY, OF THE NINTH BATTALION OF LANCASTER. COUNTY MILITIA, BETWEEN THE AGE OF EIGHTEEN AND FIFTY-THREE YEARS. TAKEN FOR THE YEAR 1782. (c.)

Capt.

James Willson.

Lieu.

James Rodgers.

Ens.

James Johnson.

Almonar.

William Cathcart.

First Class.

Wm. Stewart.	Adam Firebough.
William Snodgrass.	William Rippeth.
William Mitchel.	John Spence.
Peter Balsbough.	

Second Class.

Robert Lewis.	John Martin.
William M'Cormick, Jn'r.	Hugh Swan.
Robert Mcfarlin.	

Third Class.

Thomas Martin.	Valentine Balsbough.
Andrers Rodgers.	Neal Maddon.
Samuel Steuart.	

Fourth Class.

Williám Snody.	Samuel McCord.
John Sterrit.	Alexander Swan.
William Rodgers.	Robert templeton.
John Baird.	John Cathcart.
Daniel Validay.	William Willson.

Fifth Class.

Joseph Hutchison.
Jeremiah Rodgers.
Francis McClure.
James Willson.
William Trousdale.
William McCormick.
William Glen.
Joshua Magus.
Henry Laughlin.
Alexander Mcgee.
John Ripeth.

Sixth Class.

Thomas Walker.
Robert Moody.
William Hagerty.
James Duncan.
James McClure.
Edward Striddle.
Hugh Rippeth.
John Morrison.
Duncan Sinckleer.
George Chapman.
James Long.

Seventh Class.

James Rippeth.
Thomas McNair.
John Cathcart, Jn'r.
David Caldhoon.
Andrew Armstrong.
Abraham Host.
William Robertson.
David Caldwell.
John Fleming.

Eighth Class.

Thomas McCord.
Joseph parks.
John Thompson.
Joseph Glen.
James Wallace.
Felix McCluskey.
Andrew Willson.
Joseph Willson.
Phillip Woolever.
John Herrin.

I Do swear, on the Holy Evenglilest of Almighty God: That the above list is a jus' and true state, of the Male White Inhabitants, residing in my District agreeable to Law, and without any fraud to the State, to the best of my knowledge.

JAS. WILLSON, Capt.

Sworn before me this
Second Day of May 1782.

ROBT. CLARK, S. L.

A TRUE AND EXACT LIST OF THE NAMES, OF EACH AND EVERY MALE WHITE PERSON, INHABITING OR RESIDING, WITHIN MY DISTRICT, IN THE 7TH COMPANY, OF THE 9TH BATTALION OF LANCASTER COUNTY MILITIA, BETWEEN THE AGE OF EIGHTEEN AND FIFTY-THREE YEARS. TAKEN FOR THE YEAR 1782. (c.)

Capt.

Danl. Bradley.

Lieu.

Adam Mark.

Ens.

Jacob Stone.

Almonar.

Wm. McCullouch.

First Class.

Wm. Mcfarland, Ser.
Christian fox.
Jacob Muser.
John petre.
Jacob Wolf.
petter Beasore.
Abraham Wingart.
George Beasore.
George unger.
John Bomgartner.
Michael Straw.
petter Miller.
Ludwick Sering.
Christian Wingart.
John tibings.
Archabald Slone.

Second Class.

John Britbill.
John Simon.
Christian perkey.
Henry Nease.
Benjaman Clark.
petter ventling.
Jacob River.
philip Stone.
Jacob ouran.

Third Class.

Michael Selcer.
Joseph perkey.
Henry Beasore.
Philip Bomgartner.
John Carvery.
Jacob Graff.
John Muser.
James Connor.
Martin Bougher.
John Bear.

Fourth Class.

Vendal fortney.
Balzer Bomgartner.
George Haine.
petter Kingrey.
Henry Lowmiller.
John Winter.
Gasper Craser.
Jacob Carpender.
John harper.
Martine Miley,

Fifth Class.

John Royer.
John Bruner, Jur.
petter fox.
frederick Bresore.
Nicholas Bruner.
John Lose.
Henry Houser.
Jacob Moyer.
Nicholas titler.
Henry Connor.

Sixth Class.

Petter Walmer, Jur.
Henry Shue.
Adam titler.
Henry Bruner.
frances Albertali.
Nicholas poor.
John Weaver.
Adam Weaver.
Petter Simond.
George Mowran.
John Bougher.
Jacob tups.
George Weaver.

Seventh Class.

Petter Britbill.
John Walmer.
Petter River.
George Hedrick.
Jacob Henry.
Balzer Stone.
Henry Swartz.
Thomas McCullouch.
Dan'l toner.
Alex'r Young.
John Shultz.
John Bickle.
Henry winter.
George Lose.
Jacob Lose.
James Young.
Jacob Latchas.

Eighth Class.

Ludwick klick.
Nicholas Albertall.
Conrade Helm.
Adam Goodman.
Petter Stone.
Petter Title.
Jacob Creamer.
Jacob Carver.
John Hedrick.
Christian Harsbarger.
John Stone.
Rodger Brolly.
John Mcbride.
Michael Singar.
John, Young.
Andrew Young.
George Mease.

I Do swear, on the Holy Evengilest of Almighty God: That the above list is a just and true state, of the Male White Inhabitants, residing in my District agreeable to Law, and without any fraud to the State, to the best of my knowledge.

D. BRADLEY, Capt.

Sworn before me this
30th Day of May 1782.

ROBT. CLARK, S. L.

A TRUE AND EXACT LIST OF THE NAMES, OF EACH AND EVERY MALE WHITE PERSON, INHABITING OR RESIDING WITHIN MY DISTRICT, IN THE EIGHTH COMPANY, OF THE NINTH BATTALION OF LANCASTER COUNTY MILITIA, BETWEEN THE AGE OF EIGHTEEN AND FIFTY-THREE YEARS. TAKEN FOR THE YEAR 1782. (c.)

Capt.
William Laird.

Lieu.
John McFarland.

Ens.
George Lower.

Almonar.
Milchi Rham.

First Class.

Philip Brand.
Adam Compaugh.
Abraham Strickler.
Frederick Blessley.
John Hoover.
Abraham Brand.
John Richar.
John Been.
John Bower.
John Cofman.

Second Class.

Peter Landis.
George Spelsbaugh.
Adam Hamaker.
Christly Hamaker.
Philip Richar.
Adam Spidle.
Christly Hoover.
Henry Switzer.
Frederick Walter.
Mathew Calhen.

Third Class.

Frederick Hummel.
Jacob Rham.
Philip Fishbourn.
James Laird.
Jacob Miller.
George Brindle.
John Stopher.
Jacob Hesse.
Jacob Plucher.

Fourth Class.

John Buyers.
Christly Stopher.
Christly Landis.
Max Spidle.
Martin Fridly.
Peter Fishbourn.
John Books.
Valentine Kinsler.
Peter Gundy.

Fifth Class.

Jacob Landis.
Adam Deam.
Daniel Baum.
Peter First.
John Snider.
Philip Blessley.
David Brand.
George Wetherhold.
John Blessley.
Ludwick Fishbourn.
Gabrael Davis.
Michael Spade.
John fox.

Sixth Class.

John Landis.
Martin Rhouse.
Jacob Richar Hanover.
John First.
Abram Landis.
Jacob Richar.
Henry Singer.
James Hinman.
John Moody.

Seventh Class.

Joseph Fever.
Peter Eversole.
Peter Fridley.
Jacob Heroof.
James Clunie.
Stophel Bower.
John Myers.
Valentine Hummel.
John Wetherhold.
John Gaul.
Michael Baum.
James Stinson.

Eighth Class.

Henry Hesse.
Frederick Stall.
Philip Hamaker.
Peter Eversole.
Martin Rice.
Andrew Horner.
John Brown.
Jacob Spidle.
Samuel Hamaker.
Michael Rham.
Jacob Strickler.
Fetrick Fishbourn.
Andrew Alexander.
Daniel Robison.

Jacob Hoak.
William Whigam.
Edward Burges.
Andrew Heroof.
David Hummild.

I Do swear, on the Holy Evengileet of Almighty God: That the above list is a just and true state, of the Male White Inhabitants, residing in my District agreeable to Law, and without any fraud to the State, to the best of my knowledge.

WM. LAIRD, Capt.

Sworn before me this first Day of May 1782.

ROBT. CLARK, S. L.

GENERAL RETURN OF THE OFFICERS OF THE LANCASTER COUNTY MILITIA APRIL 15, 1783. (c.)

NINTH BATTALION.

Lieut. Col.

Jno. Rodgers.

Maj.

Abra'r Latcha.

Captains.

1. William Allen.
2. Patrick Hays.
3. Ambrose Crain.
4. Jno. Harkenrider.
5. James McCright.
6. James Willson.
7. Daniel Brodley.
8. William Laird.

Lieutenants.

1. John Barnet.
2. Samuel Weir.
3. William Young.
4. Emanuel Ferey.
5. William Hill.
6. James Rodgers.
7. Adam Mark.
8. John McFarland.

Ensigns.

1. James Willson.
2. John Eversol.
3. Henry Graham.
4. Jacob Pruder.
5. William Brandon.
6. James Johnston.
7. Baltzer Stone.
8. George Lour.

MUSTER ROLL OF THE SEVANTH COMPANEY AND NINTH BATTALION OF LANCASTER COUNTY MILITIA COMMANDED BY COL'N FREDRICK ZIGLER FOR THE YEAR 1783. (SPRING). (c.)

Captain.

Godfried Klugh.

First Glass.

Isaac Kaufman.
Jacob Sechrist.
Henry Neff.
Abraham Witmer.

Second Glass.

Jacob Karly.
Henry Neff, long.
Henry Shop.
Christian Here.
Jacob Grebiel.
Henry Smith.
Jacob Zeaner.

Thirt Glass.

Abraham Here.
John Reist.
Henry Hestand.
Jacob Kaufman.
Jacob Kindig.

Fifth Glass.

Christian Steman.
John Kaufman.
Peter Kuntz.

Sixth Glass.

Casper Heilbruner.
Jacob Bear.
Abraham Here, Jun'r.

Seventh Glass.

Jacob Killhefer.
John Killhefer.
John Hestand.
Rudy Here.
France Miller.

Eight Glass.

Christian Funck.
Martin Oberholtzer.
Andrew Kaufman.
Christian Stoner.
Henry Funck.

Certifyed by me this 20 day of May 1783.

GODFRIED KLUGH, Capt'n.

I do Swear on the Holy Evengelist of Almighty God that the above Return is a true Return Agreeable to the Law without Eny fraud to the State to the best of my Knowledge.

GODFRIED KLUGH, Capt.
FRIEDERICH ZIEGLER, Colon.

TENTH BATTALION

LANCASTER COUNTY MILITIA.

LANCASTER COUNTY.

CAPTAIN JOHN ROLAND'S COMPANY.

Associators of Leacock Township Belonging to Captain Roland's Company, Associated 5th day of July, 1775. (b.)

James Scott (Leacock).
John Roland.
Henry Swope.
John Moor.
George Lyne.
Adam Swope.
Abraham Lyne.
Henry Foltz.
Stofle Weaver.
George Finfrock.
Siemont Shower.
Marteen Hillar.
Daniel Swope.
Adam Rombarger.
Joseph Bigart.
Jacob Bear (enlisted).
David Benter.
John Botts.
William Lyne.
Adam Hoofstetter.
Peter Eby.
Samuel Eby.
Jacob Barngut.
David Lyne.
Aphraem Bear.
Henry Foltz, Jun'r.
Phillip Shower.
John Maxvel.
Hugh McDonel.
Bolsar Rombarger.
Peter Eby, Jun'r.
John Hiller.
Jacob Hamer.
Henry Eby.

Emanuel Carpenter (Earl township).
Patrick Conel (Leacock township).
William McCormeck (enlisted).
John Scott (Lampeter township).
John Creake (Lampeter township).
David Crawford (Lampeter township).
William Shelar (Leacock township).
George Lambart.
John Eby.
John Snavly.
Jacob Swope.
Jacob Maxvel.
Marteen Maxvel, Jun'r.
George Bard.
James Hamilton.
James Kearns (enlisted).
Henry Wenger, Sen'r.
John Foltz.
Peter Barngut.

Certified by

JOHN FREE, Colonel.

A LIST OF THE POOR ASSOCIATORS IN STRAUSBURG TOWNSHIP, LANCASTER COUNTY, WHO WENT TO THE CAMPS IN THE JERSEYS IN COL. JOHN FERREE'S BATT'N IN THE MONTH OF AUGUST, 1776, AND RELIEF EXTENDED TO THEIR DISTRESSED FAMILIES. (c.)

John Botts, left a wife and five small children.
John Mace, left a wife and several small children.
Martin Kochersberg, left a wife and two small children.
Abraham Bowman, left a wife and children.
John Glass, left a wife and several small children.
Jacob Miller, left a wife and children.
Nicholas Mackey, left a weakly wife.
Martin Burd, left a wife and several small children.
Robert Charlton, left a sickly wife and child.
Valentine Myer, left a wife and two children.
William Dowland.
Ludwig Stotz, left a wife and children.

John Kraemer, left a wife and child.
James Patton, left a wife and child.
Samuel Finley, left a wife and child.
John Manley, left a wife and large family.
Jacob Froelich, left a wife and children.
Jacob Young, left a wife and two children.
Peter Hall, left a wife and several children.
David Kinger, left a wife and several children.
Mathias Truckebrod, left a large family.
John White, left a wife and five children.
James Cavanaugh, left a wife and children.
James Trum } Went to Flying Camp and left their old
Charles Trum } and lame father and mother.
William Logan, left a wife and child.

EVERHARD GRUBER.

CAPTAIN SAMUEL BOYD'S COMPANY. (a.)

A list of Captain Boyd's company, August 14, 1776.

Captain.

Boyd, Samuel.

Lieutenant.

Hall, Charles.

Ensign.

Krugh, Valentine.

Sergeants.

Pflieger, John.
Booskirk, Lawrence.

Corporals.

Helm, John.
Hunter John.

Privates.

Allison, John, Flying Camp.
Bartges, Mathias.
Biffort, William.
Boop, Adam.
Bowsman, Nicholas.
Brandon, Charles.

Criswell, Samuel, locksmith.
Davis, Gabriel.
Ehler, Michael, Flying Camp.
Hubert, Jacob.
Mars, Alexander, Flying Camp.
Bradley, Thomas.
Kain, John.
Lamb, John.
Mencer, Jacob.
Michael, Eberhard.
Mininger, Jacob.
Reed, John, Flying Camp.
Roberts, John.
Smith, John, cooper.
Smith, John.
Snyder, Joseph.
Snyder, Melchior.
Sullivan, Timothy.
Yeidler, Thomas.
Lanisen, Matthew.
Michenfeler, Casper.
Stutsman, John.

4 of y'e above privates went for Flying Camp as is above mentioned.

A MUSTER ROLL OF CAPTAIN JOHN WITHER'S COMPANY OF MILITIA OF COLONEL JOHN FERREES BATTALION OF ASSOCIATORS IN LANCASTER COUNTY, DESTINED FOR THE CAMP IN THE JERSEYS. (d.)

Captain.

John Withers.

Lieutenants.

1st, David Pine.
2nd, George Withers.
3rd, John Miller.

Serjeants.

Michael Fouts.
Lodwick Stoltz.
John Vernon.
John Quick.

Corporals.

Jacob Fouts.
Henry Hoke.
Bernard Houser.
Vincent Williams.

Drummer.

Herman Benning.

Fifer.

Thomas Toomey.

Privates.

1 Alexander Campbell.	19 John Casedy.
2 Mathew Sutton.	20 Casper Dicker.
3 Henry Stoner.	21 Peter Fite.
4 William Hunter.	22 Daniel Deans.
5 John Mace.	23 John Dowling.
6 Jacob Young.	24 Jacob Frelick.
7 Henry Dickoven.	25. Isaac Farlow.
8 Henry Heynold.	26 Jacob Heckman.
9 Andrew Sererons.	27 Abraham Bowman.
10 Jacob Miller.	28 Samuel Finley.
11 Jacob Drum.	29 John Heckman.
12 Andrew Myers.	30 Joab Vancourt.
13 Mathias Drybread.	31 David Kingin.
14 Joseph Otterbough.	32 William Kile.
15 John Morrison.	33 Martin Bird.
16 John Glass.	34 Wm. Pendergrast.
17 James Cavanaugh.	35 Joseph Miller.
18 John Manley.	

35 privates, 50 shillings each	£87.10.0
4 Serjeants, 50 shillings each	10. 0.0
4 Corporals, 50 shillings each	10. 0.0
1 Drummer	2.10.0
1 Fifer	2.10.0
45 Men's Advance,	£112.10.0

Mustered and passed before the Committee of Observation & Inspection in Lancaster the 19th of August, 1776. And the above One Hundred & twelve pound & ten Shillings paid to Captain John Wither to enable him to advance his Company 50 shillings a man.

Test WILLE. ATLEE, Chairman of Committee &

JOHN WITHERS, Capt.

A RETURN OF THE OFFICERS OF 10TH BATTALION OF MILITIA OF LANCASTER COUNTY AS FOLLOWS. (c)

Colonel.

David Jenkins.

Lieu't Col'l.

Jacob Karpenter.

Major.

Henry Mercle.

John Lutts, ...1st Cap't.
Christopher Heft, ...1st Lieu't.
Henry Wite, ...2 Lieut.
Peter Bleaser, ...Ensign.

James Davies, ...2d Cap't.
Samuel Elliot, ...1st Lieu't.

Martin Bowman, ...3d Cap't.
George Duck, ...1st Lieu't.
John Ream, ...2d Lieu't.
Jacob Swartswelder, ...Ensign.

George Rees, ...4th Capt.
Valentine Kinser, ...1st Lieu't.
John Diffenderffer, ...2d Lieu't.
John Shiverly, ...Ensign.

Joseph Jenkins, ...5th Capt.
Tho's Elliot, ...1st Lieu't.
Joseph Williams, ...2d Lieu't.
James Patterson, ...Ensign.

James Watson, ...6th Cap't.
John Kirkparick, ...1st Lieu't.
Alexander McIlwain, ...2d Lieu't.
Thomas McMullen, ...Ensign.

Emanuel Carpenter, ...7th Cap't.
Rudy Statfor, ...1st Lieu't.
John Rudy, ...2d Lieu't.
James Harber, ...Ensign.

William Crawford, ...8th Cap't.
John Davies, ...1st Lieu't.
James Wallace, ...2d Lieu't.
James Vogan, ...Ensign.

SIMON SNYDER, Sub. Lieut.
CHRISTOPHER CRAWFORD, Sub. Lieut.

1777, Dec. 6th. Rec'd of Timothy Matlack, Esq'r., commissions for the following officers viz't: John Lutts; Christopher Heft; John Reem; Peter Bleasier; Joseph Jenkins; John Kirkpatrick; Joseph Williamson; James Vogan.

DAVID JENKINS.

RETURN OF THE 10TH BATTALION OF MILITIA IN LANCASTER COUNTY COMMANDED BY COL: DAVID JENKINS, WITH THE OFFICERS AND PRIVETS OF EACH COMPANY AS THEY WERE RESPECTIVELY CLASS'D. 1777. (c.)

FIRST COMPANY.

Captain.

John Lutts.

Lieutenants.

1st, Christopher Heft.
2d, Henry White.

Ensign.

Peter Bleaser.

Court Martial Men.

Martin Myre. Peter Hacker.

1st Class.

Frederick Road. Benedict Morrel.
George Sickly. William Goldin.

Jacob Smith.
Michael Messener.
John Grove.
Conrod Miller.
Conrod Derr.

2nd Class.

George Steegler.
Henry Woolf.
Jacob Weaver.
Christian Deeter.
Andrew Ovenbough.
Peter Beam.
Peter Staffy.
Abraham Suber.
John Overholser.

3rd Class.

Matthias Dick.
Adam Beam.
Henry Moser.
Peter Good.
Jacob Steegler.
Peter Frankhouser.
Daniel Road.
George Pecker.
George Ronk.

4th Class.

Abraham Essleman.
Jacob Good.
Jacob Good, Jun'r.
Christian Messener.
Adam Beam, Jun'r.
Frederick Howseker.
Frederick Hope.
Henry Good.
Thomas Law.

5th Class.

Christian Broadstone.
Jacob Oberholser.
Adam Weaver.
Frederick Staffen.
George Slaybouch.
Peter Smith.
Jacob Road.
Peter Kern.
Nicholas Holler.

6th Class.

Henry Brownelder.
John Stone.
Jacob Seller.
Philip Slaybouch.
Christian Nyswanger.
Jacob Broadstone.
Jacob Fry, Jun'r.
Christopher Wise.
Leonard Momey.

7th Class.

Martin Myre.
George Steegler.
Christian Essleman.
Jacob Messener.
Christian Swarts.
Jacob Fry.
Michael Steffy.
John Stofer.
Henry Becker.

8th Class.

Abraham Martin.
Henry Good, Jun'r.
George Fry.
Samuel Martin.
Christian Kern.
Peter Hackart.
Jacob Follintine.
Henry Fry.
Daniel Geman.
Nicklas Musser.

SECOND COMPANY.

Captain.

James Davies.

Lieutenant.

1st, Samuel Elliot.

1st Class.

Henry Good.
Peter Good.
Michall Stolts.
Henry Finfrock.
Rudy Fry.
Michael Troop.
Peter Lance.
Griffith Evans.

2nd Class.

George Staffen.
Henry Silknitter.
Martin Andsel.
Martin Greenplat.
Peter Funk.
Thomas Saychner.
Thomas Moore.

3rd Class.

Peter Shirk.
Daniel Steever.
Richard Templin.
Vendle Cremer.
Johannes Guigley.
Cutlip Finkstock.
Robert Gaskin.

4th Class.

Peter Miller.
Samuel Good.
Nathan Evans.
Michael Keith.
Henry Yoter.
Jacob Couplance.
Philip Keith.
John Ficher.

5th Class.

Malcolm Saychner.
Lane Goheen.
Robert Good (a Substitute).
George Snyder.
John Kattle.
Michael Funk.
Philip Troop.
George Huffman.

6th Class.

Adam Shup.
Samuel Lance.
Hugh Love.
Jacob Good.
John Good.
Joseph Yoter.
Michael Moser.
Adam Styre.

7th Class.

Nicholas Shup.
Christian Stofer.
Benjamin Gilmore.
Frederick Wallick.
George Slough.
Edward Goheen.
Andrew Finfrock.
Christian Good.

8th Class.

William Snyder.
Matthias Muzleman.
Henry Kern.
Jacob Burket.
Edward Kilpatrick.
Peter Weller.
Peter Peck.
John Cleeland.

THIRD COMPANY.

Captain.

Martin Bowman.

Lieutenants.

1st, George Duck.
2nd, John Raem.

Ensign.

Jacob Swartswelder.

Court Martial Men.

John Norton.
Philip Duck.

1st Class.

Isaac Gray, gone to the English.
John Geer.
Peter Sensinick.
Joseph Zimmerman.
Christian Swartswelder.
Christopher Rodaker.
Jacob Grim.
Michael Handly.
John Sheewalter.
Michael Bitzer.
Benjamin Sheniman.
John Wenger, Sen'r.

2nd Class.

Philip Weaver.
George Otto.
Englehart Holtzinger.
Andrew Harter.
Jacob Oberlin.
Jacob Wise.
Henry Miller.
Jacob Werns.
Peter Rush.
Abraham Andrews.
Peter Pence.
Henry Weaver.
David Hamon.
John Kittera.

3rd Class.

John McCleery.
George German.
Michael Hays.
George Gere.
Christian Tanner.
John Beck.
John Evans.
George Werns.
Jacob Hinkle.
William Parry.
Michael Sower.
Adam German, Jun'r.
Daniel Hane.
Philip Ringmood.

4th Class.

James Gault.
Peter Good.
Francis Hane.
Andrew Wise.
Henry Lippert.
David Kempher.
John Resler.
Sebastian Hower.
Michael Oberlin.
John German.
John Mumma.
John Soloberger.
Jacob Roth.
George Weaver.

5th Class.

John Yont.
Martin Werns.
Abraham Law.
Frederick Glaze.
David Morgan.
Joseph McCleery.
Conrod Brenizer.
John Swickart.
John Bitzer, Jun'r.
Tobias Medsger.
Philip Pence.
Erastus Miller.
Nicholas Troutwine.
Josiah Kittera.

6th Class.

George Powder.
Christopher Fly.
John Boyle.
John Fosanouch.
George Pifer.
Benjamin Harlager.
John Sides.
Alexander Gualt.
Palser Smith.
Philip Ronk.
Jacob Adam.
William McClane.
Henry Norton.

7th Class.

George Swickert.
Henry Nice.
James McCleery, Jun'r.
John Bitzer, Sen'r.
George Clopper.
Leonard German.
George Hinkle.
Isaac Davies.
Philip Fosanouch.
John Campher.
Jacob Sherk.
Henry Snyder.
Christian Wenger.

8th Class.

James McCleery.
Conrod Fosanought.
Andrew Culp.
Joseph Melinger.
Christian Kinsly.
Henry Shults.
Andrew Swickart.
John Roth.
Adam Garman.
Conrod Pence.
Henry Otto.
John Gunty.
William Guigley.

FOURTH COMPANY.

Captain.

George Rees.

Lieutenants.

1st, Valentine Kinser.
2nd, John Divedaver.

Ensign.

John Shiverly.

Court Martial Men.

James Thomson.
John Brenbaker.

1st Class.

John Grise.
Michael Brewbaker.
Jacob Ellmaker.
Adam Diller, Jun'r.
Henry Sherk.
Michael Greybill.
Ameck Snyder.
Peter Smith.
Henry Hildebrand.
Anthony Ellmaker.
Martin Keith.
John McMullen.
Jonathan Rowland.
George Rine (Carter).

2nd Class.

George Leoner.
Michael Hildebrand.
Henry Stinbrink.
Michael Rine, Ju'r.
Andrew Morter.
Joseph Road, Ju'r.
John Lippert.
George Bear, Jun.
John Brewbaker.
Valentine Bower.
Jacob Bear.
Michael Rine (Geo. Son).

3rd Class.

George Ealy.
Deitrick Coshet.
Adam Road.
Martin Hoover.
Reynard Sheebler.
Jacob Road.
George Leoner, Jun.
Philip Stickleman.
Samuel Bear.
Valentine Petry.
Nicholas Yont.
Michael Kinser.
Martin Steever.

4th Class.

Martin Hoover (Jno.'s Son).
Jacob Koonts.
Michael Bear.
George Rine.
Peter Sheaver.
James Thompson.
Christian Smoker, Jun.
Jacob Ludel.
Christian Musselman.
George Bear.
Peter Baker.
Henry Kinser.
Thomas Morgan.
George Morter.

5th Class.

Jacob Earick.
Christopher Wike.
Christian Hoover.
James Martin.
Godlip Poff.
Martin Bear.
Conrod Laub.
Nathaniel Ellmaker.
Elias Peters.
Alexander Martin.
Christian Getz.
Christian Eckert.
George Burket.

6th Class.

John Ritter.
Joseph Eby.
Henry Richevine.
Jacob Ringwalt.
Christian Primmer.
John Hoover, Jun'r.
Robert Filson.
Sam Greybil.
Anthony Hinkle.
David Harman.
John Kinser.
John Bolick.
George Steever.

7th Class.

Michael Eicher.
Gabriel Davies.
Christian Smoker.
George Hildebrand.
Bernard Coshet.
Philip Road.
Isaac Coshet, Jun.
Matthias Coshet.
John Sheaver.
Felix Snyder.
Henry Peters.
Leonard Earick.
William Marshel.

8th Class.

Michael Hildebrand, Jun'r.
Henry Road.
Jacob Bersher.
John Rine.
Nathaniel Swecker.
Michael Martin.
Leonard Diller.
John Berkinhiser.
Christian Musselman.
Christopher Frederick.
Frederick Diets.
Sebastian Bower.
Moses McIlvain.

FIFTH COMPANY.

Captain.

Joseph Jenkins.

Lieutenants.

1st, Tho's Elliot.
2nd, Joseph Williamson.

Ensign.

James Patterson.

Court Martial Men.

John Martin.
John Jenkins.

1st Class.

George Weaver.
Nathaniel Spencer.
Jacob Nurthamer.
Thomas Hurst.
Amos Evans.
Joseph Essington.
Jacob Yoter, Jun'r.
Hugh Allen, gone to Maryland
John Boland.

2nd Class.

John Martin, Jun.
James Patterson (weaver).
Jacob Ayres, Sen'r.
Joshua Evans.
Jacob Bleaser.
John Jenkins.
Thomas Rattew.
James Old.
Philip Baker.
William Morgan.
Thomas Eastburn.

3rd Class.

James Gaskin.
Christian Slough.
Edward Hughes.
John Evans, Jun'r.
Lott Evans.
Christian Lodowick.
Alexander Clay.
Robert Hughes.
Joseph Wright.
David megumery.

4th Class.

John Watt.
Thomas Fogerty.
William McQuead.
John Piler.
Thomas Martin.
Robert Brown.
David Evans.
James Withrow.
Henry Weaver.
William Bell.

5th Class.

Jacob Silknitter.
Daniel Ayres.
John Gill.
Jacob Minges.
Henry Zill.
Thomas Morgan.
John Thornbury.
Christian Summers.
John Evans (Carp'r).

6th Class.

John Yoter.
Jacob Ayres, Jun'r.
John Madden.
Abraham Dolby.
William Evans.
Morris Hudson.
Emanuel Nyswanger.
John Morgan.
Christian Overhoker.

7th Class.

Alexander Tennant.
Samuel Stofer.
Elijah Hudson.
George Fisher, gone to Virginia.
James Parks.
Joseph Gillis.
Emanuel Nyswanger, Ju'r.
Robert Redman.
Isaac Jenkins.
James McConnel, lives in New Holland.

8th Class.

Valentine Ronk.
Theodore Willmin.
Gerardus Clarkson.
Christian Curts.
John Nurthamer.
John Yoter, Sen'r.
John Higer.
Christian Yoter.
Nathan Evans.
Wi. .am Meredith.
Charles Jacobs.
James Watt.

SIXTH COMPANY.

Captain.

James Watson.

Lieutenants.

1st, John Kirkpatrick.
2nd, Alexander McIlvain.

Ensign.

Thomas McMullen.
Robert Wallace.

Court Martial Men.

Robert Wallace.
Alex. McIlvain.

1st Class.

Andrew Closer.
Casper Shirk.
Christian Snyder, Jun'r.
Nathan Evans.
Jacob Snyder.
John Weaver.
Henry Stofer.
John Purril.
Hugh Harbison.

2nd Class.

Michael Rogers.	William Smith, Ju'r.
Daniel Purril.	James Kare.
Lodowick Ronk.	William Kare.
Jacob Weaver.	Samuel Ronk.
Peter Stofer.	George Steely.
Daniel Stofer.	John Senseny.

3rd Class.

Martin Martin.	Willis Davies.
Philip Snyder.	Michael Ronk.
Christian Root.	Henry Weaver, Sen.
Polser Pitsor.	Jacob Stofer.
John Weaver, Jun.	John Wright, moved to the River.
Jacob Widler.	Henry Weaver (Turner).
Michael Snyder.	

4th Class.

John Weaver.	Jacob Closer.
Peter Weaver.	Martin Holman.
Samuel Weaver.	Jacob Weaver (Miller).
Christian Snyder.	Michael Perkehous.
John Ronk.	Jacob Weaver.
Frederick Fouts.	Patt. McGlaughlin.
William Shaw.	

5th Class.

George Foults.	Jacob Snyder, Sen'r.
James Elderton.	Michael Sherk (Miller).
Robert Thomson.	Zacheus Peirsol.
Henry Weaver (Stiller).	Matthias Stofer.
John Amman.	Peter Springer.
Jacob Weaver.	George Davies.
Henry Waggoner.	

6th Class.

Jacob Conrod.	John Harbison.
Jacob Ronk.	Christian Carpenter (Jun'r).
Abraham Aycart.	Henry Root.
Daniel Aycart.	Jacob Cray.
John Shirk.	Joshua Evans.
Valentine Ronk, Jr.	William Smith.
Henry Weaver (Stiller).	

7th Class.

Boughman Weaver.
Jacob Hoover.
Alexander Martin.
Evan Evans.
Francis Slay.
Thomas Edwards.
Peter Carpenter.
David Apler.
Mattheis Springer.
Philip Ronk.
Jacob Morter.

8th Class.

Michael Shirk.
John Huston.
Christian Weaver.
John Folts.
Samuel Stofer.
John Mire.
Joseph Regh.
Adam Stocks.
James Keimon, Jun'r.
Henry Martin.
Christian Carpenter.
Henry Carpenter.
Ledowick Reel.

SEVENTH COMPANY.

Captain.

Emanuel Carpenter.

Lieutenants.

1st, Rudy Statfor.
2d, John Rudy.

Ensign.

James Harber.

Court Martial Men.

Andrew Rudy.
Henry Bastin.

1st Class.

Joel Carpenter.
Christian Forny.
Conrod Holtzinger.
Henry Peck.
Peter Brown.
John McConichey.
Adam Diller.
Jacob Carpenter.
John Fesler.
John Myre.

2nd Class.

Christian Myre.
Abraham Huntsberger.
Christian Garver.
Abraham Forny, Jun'r.
John Carpenter.
Lodowick Wolford.
John Mair.
Joseph Rup.
Conrod Rudy.
Jacob Sensenick, Ju'r.

3rd Class.

Abraham Woolf.
Adam Alts.
Christian Weyner.
John Penter.
Bernard Lutz.
Michael Weyner.
George Diderick.
Henry Carpenter.
Valentine Britch.
Jacob Waggoner.

4th Class.

Christian Mair.
John Smith.
Henry Good.
Martin Wolford.
Adam Brown.
Christopher Ryer.
Peter Myre.
Jacob Carpenter (son of Christ.)
John Grim.

5th Class.

Frederick Hiss.
Palser Acerman.
Jacob Capler.
Christian Swarts.
John Bast.
Jonathan Duple.
Lodowick Leckman.
Abraham Carpenter.
Abraham Forny.
Michael Tanner.

6th Class.

Philip Hogg.
Jacob Griner.
Palser Hipner.
Joseph Rowland.
Peter Stall.
Peter Tanner.
John Shalleberger.
Solomon Harman.
John Greybill.
Christian Harman.
Ulrick Wesler.

7th Class.

Henry Garver.
Solomon Sygrist.
Samuel Sheny.
Michael Grossman.
Christian Carpenter.
Peter Forny.
Matthias Engel.
Andrew Rudy.
Martin Myre.

8th Class.

John Myre.
Abraham Greybill.
Michael Olts.
John Myre, Jun.
Valentine Frunck.
David Rowland.
John Myre, Sen'r.
Elias Myre.
John Rup.

EIGHTH COMPANY.

Captain.

William Crawford.

Lieutenants.

1st, John Davies.
2nd, James Wallace.

Ensign.

James Vogan.

Court Martial Men.

Alexander Wilson.
Adam Overly.

1st Class.

Philip Road.
Christian Grove.
John Sheaver (Stiller).
Conrod Fosanought.
Joseph Horts (Senr.).
George Rine, Jun'r.
Adam Overly.
Leonard Stone.
Rudolf Shefer.
David Grove, Jun'r.

2nd Class.

John Wolf.
Henry Arter.
Andrew Fesler.
Michael Cover.
Bernard Woolf.
Jacob Grove, Jun'r.
George Minser, Ju'r.
Peter Diller.
James Irwin.
Abraham Brewbaker.
Jacob Brenizer.

3rd Class.

William Zill.
Christian Grove, Jun'r.
Abraham Rife.
Henry Summy.
Jacob Summy.
Henry Bowman.
Richard Davies.
David Martin.

4th Class.

Alexander Wilson.
Martin Grove.
Peter Summy (Davids Son).
John Sheaver (Farmer).
Henry Messener.
Joseph Horst, Sen'r.
Jacob Hole.
Marks Grove.
John Grove.
John Hoover.
Jacob Stofer.
John Widower.

5th Class.

Joseph Hole.
Martin Sheaver.
Leonard Gost.
John Bouchman.
William Randels.
Jacob Stone.
Casper Sherk.
John Divedaver.
John Irwin.
Andrew Luther.
Peter Creps.

6th Class.

Christopher Sower.
Alexander McCleery.
Henry Rorer.
Jonathan Irwin.
George Gest.
Abraham Grove.
Peter Burkholder.
John Mair.
Peter Miller.
George Higg.
Jacob Sensenich.
John Ronnick.
Abraham Grofe (Joseph Son).

7th Class.

Samuel Bowman.
David Gundy.
David Martin.
Philip Sheaver.
George Rine, Sen'r.
Philip Sprecher.
John Hearly.
Jacob Smith.
Henry Grim.
Jacob Shoewalter.

8th Class.

Frederick Rodaker.
Michael Brewbaker.
Abram Rife.
Samuel Sheaver.
Christian Hole.
Marks Martin.
Vendle Myre, Hang'd.
Jacob Acor.
Jacob Dile.
George Minser, Sen'r.
Jacob Becher.

DAVID JENKINS, Col.

A TRUE AND EXACT LIST OF ALL AND EVERY WHITE MALE PERSONS, BETWEEN THE AGES OF EIGHTEEN AND FIFTY THREE, BELONGING TO MY DISTRICT. GEORGE REESE CAPTAIN. 1777. (c.)

Captain.

George Reese.

Lieutenants.

1st, Valentine Kinzer.
2nd, John Difenderffer.

Ensign.

John Shibely.

Jo'n Hoober, jun'r.
Martin Hoober, Jo'n's Son.
Nath'l Zevecker.
Jo'n Brewbaker.
Valentine Bower.
Robert Filtson.
Geo. Lehner.
Felix Snyder.
Elias Peters.
Henry Peters, jun'r.
Anthony Hinkle.
Henry Reichwine.
Jacob Ludd.
Tho's Morgan.
Emigh Snyder.
Christopher Frederick.
Peter Baker.
Nicholas Yunt.
Reynard Sheebler.
Christian Brimmer.
Mich'l Brewbaker.
Peter Shaver.
Jo'n Shaver.
Ge'o Ealy.
Henry Road.
Henry Sherk.
Joseph Road, jun'r.
Adam Road.
Philip Road.
Jacob Road.
Jacob Breser.
Jonathan Roland.
John Kintzer.
Joseph Eby.
Bernard Coshet.
Alex'dr Martin.
James Martin.
James Thompson.
Gabriel Davis.
Michael Martin.
Christian Musselman.
Christian Musselman, jun'r.
Martin Hoober.
Christian Hoober, son of Martin.
Godlieb Poff.
Ge'o Rine, gone off to the English.
Mich'l Rine (George's Son).
George Rines (Carter).
Mich'l Rine, jun'r.
Jn'o Rine.

Mich'l Bear.
Peter Smith.
Dietrich Coshet.
Mathias Coshet.
Isaac Coshet.
Martin Bear.
Ge'o Bear.
Ge'o Bear, jun'r.
Anthony Ellmaker.
Nath'l Ellmaker.
Jacob Ellmaker.
Christian Smoker, jun'r.
Martin Kitch.
Christopher Wike.
Samuel Bear.
Jn'o Ritter.
Christian Eckert.
Mich'l Eicher.
Jn'o Grise.
Christian Getz.
Jacob Bear.
Jno. Lippert.
Ge'o Hildenbrand.
Henry Kinzer.
Mich'l Kinzer.
Jn'o Berkenhouser.
Adam Diller, jun'r.
Leonard Diller.
Jn'o Bolich.
Mich'l Greybiel.
Samuel Greybiel.
Andrew Morter.
Ge'o Lehner, jun'r.
Henry Stinebrink.
Mich'l Hildenbrand.
Mich'l Hildenbrand, jun'r.
Henry Hildenbrand.
Leonard Earigh.
Jacob Earigh.
Jn'o McMullen.
Valentine Petery.
Sebastian Bower.
Jn'o Kuntz.
Philip Stikleman.
David Herman.
Peter Kurtz.
Ge'o Steaver.
Ge'o Steaver, jun'r.
William Marshal.
Moses Mc Ilvain.
George Burkert.

MUSTER ROLL OF CAPTAIN JAMES WOTSONS COMPANY OF MILITIA OF LANCASTER COUNTY, COMMANDED BY CO'L DAVID JENKINS, 1778. (c.)

Captain.

James Wotson.

Lieutenants.

1st, John Kirkpatrick.
2nd, Alex'dr McIlvain.

Ensign.

Hugh Harbison.

1st Class.

Andrew Glasser.
Casper Shirk.
Christian Sneder.
Nathan Evans.
Jacob Sneder, pun.
John Weaver (fat).
Henry Stover.
John Porril.
George Fissecote.
Jacob Grim.

2nd Class.

Daniel Powil.
Ludwick Ranck.
Jo'n Weaver (Jacobs Son).
Peter Stover.
Daniel Stover.
James Karr.
Samuel Ranck.
George Stayle.

3rd Class.

Martin Martin.
Phillip Sneder.
Christian Root.
Balzer Petzar.
Jo'n Weaver, juner.
Jacob Widler.
Michel Sneder.
Wellis Davis.
William Karr.
Michael Rank.
Henrey Weaver.

4th Class.

Jacob Stover.
Henrey Weaver (torner).
Peter Weaver.
Samuel Weaver.
Christian Sneder.
Jo'n Ranck.
Fredrick Pouts.
William Shaw.
Martin Holman..
Jacob Weaver.
Michael Perkelizer.
Jacob Weaver (Mill).

5th Class.

George Fults.
Robert Thompson.
Henrey Weaver (Stiller).
Jacob Weaver (old).
Jo'n Amma.
Henrey Wagner.
Jacob Sneder (old).
Michael Shirk (Miller).
Zaccheuas Persil.
Matthias Stover.
Peter Springer.
George Davice.
Andrew Lutter, jun.
William Muddle, jun'r.

6th Class.

Jacob Keinerd.
Jacob Ranck.
Abraham Eicard.
Daniel Eicard.
Jo'n Shaw.
Vallentin Ranck, jun'r.
Henrey Weaver (Hill).
Jo'n Harbison.
Christian Carpentor.
Henrey Root.
Joshua Evans.

7th Class.

Evan Evans.
Alex Martin.
Frances Slay.
Tho's Edwards.
Peter Carpenter.
David Epler.
Matthias Springer.
Phillip Ranck.
Jacob Morther.
Jacob Huber.

8th Class.

Michael Sherk (Peters Son).
Christian Weaver.
Jo'n Foults.
Samuel Slover.
Jo'n Myre.
Adam Stock.
James Keimor.
Henrey Martin.
Christian Carpenter.
Henrey Carpenter.

MUSTER ROLL OF CAPT. W'M CRAWFORD'S OF THE EAIGHT COMPANI, TENTH BATTALON, LANCASTER COUNTY, 1779. (c.)

Captain.

W'm Crawford.

Lieutenants.

1st, John Davis.
2nd, Ja's Wallace.

Ensign.

Ja's Vogan.

1st Class.

Philip Roade.
Christian Grove.
John Shaffer, Stiller.
Conrade Fasanaught.
George Climer.
Edward Good.
George Rine, dead.
David Grove.
Adam oberly.
Leanard Stone.
John Gaist.
Rudolph Shaffer.

2nd Class.

John Woolfe.
Andrew Fesler.
Michael Cover.
Bernat Wolfe.
Jacob Grove, Jun'r.
George Mainsor, Ju'r. a lunatic.
Petter Dieler.
James Erwin.
Jacob Sencenick, Jr.

3rd Class.

William Zell.
Philip Sprecher.
David Martin.
Christian Grove, Ju'r.
Abraham Rife, Ju'r.
Jacob Summey.
Jacob Brenise.
Conrad mainsor.
W. Henrey Bowman.
Richard Davis.
Abraham Grove, Jo's son.

4th Class.

Alex. Willson.
Martin Grove, David's Son.
Peter Summey.
John Shaffer.
Henry Masoner.
Christian Horst.
Jacob Hole.
Marks Grove.
John Howsor.
Jacob Stowfer.
John Witmor.

5th Class.

Joseph Hole.
Martin Shaffer.
Lenart Goshet.
John Boughman.
William Randels.
Jacob Stone.
Casper Sherk.
John Divedaver.
John Erwin.
Andrew Luter.
Petter Craps.

6th Class.

Christopher Sower.
Alex: McClearey.
Henrey Rorer.
Johnathen Erwin.
George Gaist.
Abraham Grove.
Petter Burkholter.
Petter Miller.
George Higge.
Jacob Sencineck, Sn.
John Romack.

7th Class.

Samuel Bowman.
David Gundey.
David Martin.
Philip Sprecher.
George Rine.
Philip Sheaffer.
Jacob Grove, S'r.
John Hainley.
Jacob Smith.
Henry Crim.
Jacob Showalter.

8th Class.

Fredreck Rodacker.
Mikel Brubacher.
Abraham Rifé.
Samul Shaffer.
Christian Hole.
Marks Martin.
Jacob Acor.
Jacob Diel.
George Mainsor, Sn'r.
Christian Sencenick.
Jacob Becher.

GENERAL RETURN OF THE OFFICERS OF THE LANCASTER COUNTY MILITIA, 1780. (c.)

TENTH BATTALION.

Lieu't Col.
Rob't Elder.

Maj'r.
Jn'o Gilchrist.

Captains.

1. James Murray.
2. Geo: McMillen.
3. William Johnston.
4. Hugh Robinson.
5. Andrew Stewart.
6. Sam'l Cochran.
7. Martin Weaver.
8. Jon'a McClure.

Lieutenants.

1. John Ryan.
2. Matthew Gilcrist.
3. George Clerk.
4. William Montgomery.
5. John Mathews.
6. Joseph Smith.
7. John Chelsley.
8. John Hollebaugh.

Ensigns.

1. James Reed.
2. William McMillen.
3. George Taylor.
4. William Lochrey.
5. George Turbaugh.
6. William McClure.
7. Jon'a Woodsides.
8. Daniel Hoofman.

SAM. J'O ATLEE, L't L'r Co'y.

Com's made out agreeable to the foregoing return and dated the 10th May 1780.

OFFICERS OF TENTH BATTALION. (a.)

Returned August 26, 1780.

Lieutenant Colonel.

Robert Elder.

Major.

John Gilchrist.

First company.

Captain—James Murray.
Lieutenant—John Ryan.
Ensign—James Reed.

Second company.

Captain—George McMillan.
Lieutenant—Matthew Gilchrist.
Ensign—William McMillen.

Third company.

Captain—William Johnston.
Lieutenant—George Clark.
Ensign—George Taylor.

Fourth company.

Captain—Hugh Robinson.
Lieutenant—William Montgomery.
Ensign—William Lochrey.

Fifth company.

Captain—Andrew Stewart.
Lieutenant—John Matthews.
Ensign—George Turbaugh.

Sixth company.

Captain—Samuel Cochran.
Lieutenant—Joseph Smith.
Ensign—William McClure.

Seventh company.

Captain—Martin Weaver.
Lieutenant—John Sheesley.
Ensign—Jonathan Woodside.

Eighth company.

Captain—Jonathan McClure.
Lieutenant—John Hollenbaugh.
Ensign—Daniel Hoffman.

COL. ROBERT ELDER'S BATTALION. (a.)

CAPTAIN JAMES MURRAY'S COMPANY.

Upper Paxtang, April 12th, 1781.

A List of the Male White Inhabitants Between the ages of Eighteen and fifty-three Residing within the District of Capt. James Murray's Company of Militia, the first Class of the tenth Battalion of Lancaster County Militia, commanded by Col. Robert Elder.

Captain.

James Murray.

Lieutenant.

John Ryan.

Ensign.

James Reed.

First class.

John McCord.
William Bell, Jr.
James Watts.
Arthur Bell.
Robert Goudey.
George Johnston.
Christian Hattocks.
William Mountgomery.

Second class.

John Ayres.
John Bell, Jr.
Anthony Hoone.
Henry Hoone.
George Cochran.
David Davis.
George Straw.
Richard Wade.
Stephen Forster.

Third class.

Michael Stiver.
Samuel Plough.
Philip Tinturff.
William Forster.
Peter Kinter.
Thomas Boone.
George Bell.
John Stevenson.
Leonard Sheetz.

Fourth class.

John Bell, Sergeant.
John Boland.
William Foulks.
Peter Sturgeon.
John Duncan.
Elisha Lockard.
John Hattfield.
Thomas Nicholson.
Samuel Camble.

Fifth class.

James Forster.
John Richmond.
John Kinter.
John Bundle.
John Gartner.
James McNamara.
James McLanachan.
Alexander Douglas.
Joseph Keller.
Philip Newpecker.

Sixth class.

John Simpson.
Henry McCloskey.
John Collagan.
Joseph Collagan.
John Thomas.
John Cochran, Jr.
Alexander Givins.
James Birney.
William Murray.
Robert Armstrong.
Philip Stage.
Josiah Winn.
William Clark.

Seventh class.

Thomas Sturgeon.
James Bell.
Thomas Galachor.
Robert Smith.
Moses Lockard.
John Dice.
Frederick Yaneletz.
James Peacock.
Samuel Cochran.
William Hempson.
Jesse Weeks.
Charles McClanachan.

Eighth class.

John Brown.
Abraham Money.
John Bell, Sr.
John Gartner.
John Sloane.
Lud'k Minchker.
Thomas Beard.
Anthony Furnace.

April 12, 1781.

A return by me,
JAMES MURRAY, Captain.

CAPTAIN GEORGE McMILLAN'S COMPANY. (a.)

A Class Roll of the Second Company of the Tenth Battalion, Lancaster County Militia, April 12th, 1781.

Captain.
George McMillan.

Lieutenant.
Matthew Gilchrist.

Ensign.
William McMillan.

Sergeant.
Samuel Berryhill.

Major.
John Gilchrist.

Quarter Master.

William Swan.

Quarter Master Sergeant.

Richard Swan.

Rank and File.

First class.

John McIlhenny.
Jacob Miller.
John Meador.
Thomas Hardon.
David White.
Daniel Covenhoven.

Second class.

Andrew Smith.
George Shoap.
David Patton.
John Kinsley.
John Pattimore.
Henry Achia.
Michael Felty.
John Fleming.
George Mears.

Third class.

James Cochran.
Andrew Cochran.
William Hogan.
Anthony Withroe.

Fourth class.

James Boggs.
James Caldwell.
James McMillan.
John Willson.
William Jamison.

Fifth class.

Zachariah Stephen.
William Wilson.
William McRoberts.
William Calhoon.
Philip John Burres.
Samuel White.
John McCaughan.
Michael Miller.
John Allen.
John Gilchrist.

Sixth class.

Hugh Whray.
John Cochran.
John Hilton.
Abraham Wilson.
Thomas Gilchrist.
Samuel Martin.
Samuel Thompson.
John Whitehill.
Adam Harbison.
James Wiggens.
Adam Baruff.

Seventh class.

William Cochran.
Robert Gilchrist.
Andrew Stephen.
James Byers.
Robert Douglas.
Thomas Bell.
John Caldwell.
William Patterson.
Charles Mulroy.
Richard McGuire.
Michael Phillippee.
John Wiggens.

Eighth class.

Robert Heil.
John Millar.
Hugh Stephen.
John Cavett.
Alexander Johnston.
Joseph Huffman.
John Gilchrist.
Henry Pitner.
Andrew Barnett.
Robert Covenhoven.
John Hogan.
Alexander Wilson.

Certified by
GEORGE McMILLAN, Captain.

CAPTAIN WILLIAM JOHNSTON'S COMPANY. (a.)

Class Roll of Third Company, Tenth Battalion, Lancaster County Militia.

First class.

Isaac Joans.
Lodwick Shelman.
Joseph McElrath.
James Black.
John Brown.

Second class.

Michael Harman.
Joseph Litle.
James Walker.
John Butler.
Esiah Joans.
George Williams.

Third class.

Andrew Ritchison.
John Chambers.
Richard Allison.
William Thomson.
William Thompson.

Fourth class.

James McCall.
Robert Boyd.
Malachal Powel.
Jacob Strickler.
Gebirial Brodigal.

Fifth class.

Henry Dougherty.

Sixth class.

James Buckhannon.
Peter Swagert.
John Gilson.
George McElyar.

Seventh class.

Henry Vanderbeck.
George Simmons.
Daniel Black.
Henry Leeck.
Daniel Kisler.
Samuel Taylor.
Elisha Chambers.
Robert Kenedy.
Richard Gilmore.
Adam Swagert.
Felty Prough.

WILLIAM JOHNSTON, Captain.

CAPTAIN HUGH ROBINSON'S COMPANY. (a.)

A List of all Male white Persons Residing in the Bounds of Captain Hugh Robinson's Company, Between the Age of Eighteen and Fifty-three years, Being the Fourth Company of the Tenth Battalion of Lancaster County Militia.

Captain.

Hugh Robinson.

Lieutenant.

William Montgomery.

Ensign.

William Lochary.

Sergeants.

Samuel Brown.
Michael Limes.
William Stuart.
John Willson, clerk.

First class.

John Castle.
William Duncan.
Jacob Poorman.
John Buck.
John Millar, Sr.
John Boughman.
Adam Lafler.

Second class.

Matthew Calhoon.
Abraham Eagly.
Peter Smith.
William McClure.
Robert Gray.
James Spence.
John Page.
John Millar.
Samuel Dale.
Isack Hanna.
Philip Firebaugh.

Third class.

Peter Pancake.
George Sheets.
George Sample.
Jacob Snyder.
George Carson.
John Rutherford.
George Smith.
Robert McClure.

Fourth class.

Frederick Castle.
Barny Shoap.
George Pile.
Michael Castle.
Henry Pile.
Jacob Limes.
Andrew Wiley.
Michael Page.
George Bircly.
Thomas McCarter.
Benjamin Duncan.
Jacob All.

Fifth class.

Vendle Facklar.
Jacob Millar.
Leonard Sheets.
Elijah Stuart.
Michael Mark.

Sixth class.

Daniel Cooper.
John Gray.
Adam Kitchmillar.
Joseph Wilson.
Jacob Houser.
Martin Fritz.

Seventh class.

Jacob Beck.
Jacob Soop.
Conrad Pop.
David Ricky.
Stophel Soop.
Jacob Smith, Jr.
John Donal.
Valentine Pancake.
John Syder.
Robert Fleming.
William Walker.

Eighth class.

Joseph Shaw.
Michael Sheaver.
David Shaw.
Alexander Willson.
John Martin.
Joseph Mark.
John Willson.
Peter Pancake, Jr.
John Elder.
Shoap, on Beck's Place.
Thomas Alexander.
Francis Burly.
Samuel Cochran.
Samuel Shearer.
John Shearer.
Joseph Gray.
Martain Houser, Jr.

Certified by
HUGH ROBINSON, Captain.

CAPTAIN ANDREW STEWART'S COMPANY. (a.)

A return of the Fifth Company of the Tenth Battalion, the Militia of Lancaster County, Commanded by Colonel Robert Elder, April 13th, 1781.

Captain.

Andrew Stewart.

Lieutenant.

John Matthews.

Ensign.

George Devibaugh.

Almoner.

Jeremiah Sturgeon.

First class.

Felty Spangler.
Jacob Nass.
John Porter.
Nathaniel Randolph.
Michael Whitley.
John Wyley.
John Stoner.

Second class.

William Bell.
James Cogley.
Paul Randolph.
George Fridley.
Fredrick Switzer.

Third class.

Arthur Brisben.
Thomas Miller.
Conrad Yontz.
Alexander Porter.
Michael Smith.
Anthony Reel.
Joshua Elder.
John Dimpsey.

Fourth class.

Peter Bobb.
John Partner.
Icabod Randolph.
Mathias Whitmore.
Nathaniel Simpson.

Fifth class.

John Hersha.
Francis Yontz.
Robert Keas.
John Cogley.
John Bates.
Stophel Smith.
Andrew Berryhill.
Hugh Montgomery.
Samuel Clemans.
Conrod Leck.
Michael Gross.
Mongo Lindsay.

Sixth class.

Robert Elder.
John Elder.
William Kelso.
Samuel Simpson.
James Floid.
John Fochler.
John Vance.
Alexander Beryhill.

Seventh class.

Samuel Simpson.
George Sheets.
Cornelius Cox.
John Cline.
Robert Clark.
Thomas Baynon.
James Johnston.
Hugh White.
William Carson.
Thomas Galahur.
Paul Long.
Abraham Morrow.
Andrew Johnston.
William Vance.

Eighth class.

David Montgomery.
George Raniker.
Andrew Bell.
Patrick Henry.
Charles Stewart.
John Garber.
James McKee.
Thomas Moore.
John Miller.
William Morrison.
Joseph Simpson.
William Gibbons.
Samuel Morison.
Barnet Fridley.
Thomas Strahon.
John Montgomery.
George Bell.
John Smith.
Jacob Haldiman.
Thomas Forster.
Christian Swink.
John Murray.
James Rutherford.
John Harris, Jr.

Returned by
ANDREW STEWART, Captain.

CAPTAIN SAMUEL COCHRAN'S COMPANY. (a.)

A True Return of Captain Samuel Cochran's Company of the Tenth Battalion of Lancaster County Militia, Commanded by Colonel Robert Elder.

Captain.

Samuel Cochran.

Lieutenant.

Thomas Smith.

Ensign.

William McClure.

First class.

Henry Alleman.
Alexander McClure.
Nicholas Alleman.
George Leru.
Stophel Alleman.
Jacob Brand.
John Roop.
Elias Neagley.
John Roop.
Philip Brown.

John Armstrong.
Michael Huber.
Malshar Miller.
Robert Marshal.
John Chambers.
Jacob Lider.
Mathias Huber.
Martain Fritz.

Second class.

James Collier.
John Winderly.
Jacob Roop.
Chrisly Roop.
John Mumma.
William Murry.
William Smith.
Gustaves Graham.
Ludwick Dagen.
Richard Fultain.
Fredrick Winagel.
Thomas Brunson.
John Riblet.

Third class.

Stophel Earnest.
James McCoard.
John Little.
John Brand.
Conrad Alleman.
Mathias Winagel
Abraham Brunson.
William Steel.
Chrisly Fleakner.
Jacob Huber.
Samuel Shearer.

Fourth class.

Jacob Keer.
Abraham Nidy.
Stephen Poorman.
Jacob Fisher.
John Shewmaker.
Andrew McClure.
Hantater Winderly.
John Renick.
John Postlewait.
John Clindining.
Samuel Hutchison.
Jacob Noop.
Alexander McComey.
Thomas Daugherty.
Chrisly Page.
Richard Steel

Fifth class.

John Bowman.
John Concer.
William Right.
Chrisly Alleman.
Henry Alleman.
John Flickiner.
Samuel Wily.
George Neavland.
John McKeny.
Aurthar Chambers.
Samuel Smith.
Chrisly Turnor.
John Rowan.
William Postlewait.

Sixth class.

John Shearer.
Adam Means.
George Gray.
John Alleman.

Nicolas Nigh.
Peter Braner.
John Boyd.
Francis Lerue.
Philip Griner.
John Lider.
Philip Shewmaker.
Daniel Brunson.
Malshar Poorman.

Seventh class.

William Keer.
Richard McClure.
Michael Wolf.
Hugh Cuningham.
Hugh Crockert.
John Steel.
Joseph Hutchison.
John Fritz.
John Bowl.
Charles McCoy.
Peter Roop.
Jacob Dagon.
Jonathan Brunson.
John Morowson.
Henry Beader.
John Means.

Eighth class.

Robert Chambers.
Rowan McClure.
Joseph Gray.
Michael Bowl.
James Mahon.
James McKenny.
Rowland Chambers.
John Maxwell.
Thomas Murry.
John McChesny.
Jacob Rudebarger.

Return of the Male Whites of the Sixth Company of the Tenth Battalion, Lancaster County.

By SAMUEL COCHRAN, Captain.

April 16, 1781.

CAPTAIN MARTIN WEAVER'S COMPANY. (a.)

Return of Capt. Martin Weaver's Company of Upper Paxtang, April 23, 1781.

Captain.

Martin Weaver.

Lieutenant.

John Sheesley.

Ensign.

Daniel Steever.

Sergeants.

Matthias Deibler.
Ludwig Bretz.
John Harman.

Corporals.

John Motter.
George Ragel.
Christian Lark.

Drummer.

William Cline.

Privates.

First class.

Edward Wheelock.
Jacob Sheesly.
Frederick Paul.
William Ingram.
George Paul.
George Ream.
James Miley.
John Moyer.

Second class.

John Motter.
Abraham Jury.
John Miller.
Lawrence Kortz.
Henry Warfel.
John Ditty.
John Richter.
George Klinger.

Third class.

Michael Sallade.
Leonard Snyder.
Andrew Yeager.
Henry Ults.
Michael Shadel.
Frederick Bender.
Abraham Neighbour.
Andrew Spangler.

Fourth class.

John Hoffman.
Deidrick Stonebreaker.
George Deibler.
Jere Berger.
Zaccheus Spanaberger.
Peter Metz.
Adam Cooper.
George Shoop.
Christopher Yeager.

Fifth class.

Francis Conway.
Sebastian Metz.
Henry Umholtz.
Michael Melcher.
Leonard Steever.
Henry Henn.
Ludwig Shott.
Leonard Kauffman.

CAPTAIN JONATHAN McCLURE'S COMPANY. (a.)

A Return of the White Males from the age of Eighteen to Fifty-three in the Eighth Company of the Tenth Battalion of Lancaster County Militia, Commanded by Colonel Robert Elder.

Captain.
Jonathan McClure.

Lieutenant.
John Hollenback.

Ensign.
Daniel Huffman.

First class.

Henry Harris.
Frederick Oberlander.
Martain Hemberly.
Christian Shartz.
Adam Miller.
Mark Snider.
Henry Stoner.
Daniel Conn.
Christian Cridnor.
Stophel Consor.

Second class.

Valentine Walker.
John Kissinger.
Jacob Snider.
Conrad Toot.
Robert McWhorter.
James Harris.
Jacob Bargley.

Third class.

Adam Ritter.
Christian King.
George Snagance.
Simon Rardon.
Robert Kennedy.
David McClure.
Henry Moore.
Joseph Gregg.
John Wolfly.
Robert Plunket.

Fourth class.

Abraham Darr.
George Frey.
Christian Seabaugh.
Samuel Parks.
George Lowman.
William Walls.
Joseph Florey.
John Bowman.
Patrick Flanigan.
John Metzger.
Christian Spade.

Fifth class.

George Gross.
Samuel Searatzey.
Reter Reckeart.
Jacob King.
John Miller.
James Currey.
Michael Presinger.
Thomas Moore.
John McCann.

Sixth class.

Nicklous Castle.
Abraham Gross.
Henry McCann.
John Backerstoz.
Phillip Shockin.
Phillip Atley.
Henry Miller.
Peter Shuster.
Henry Davis.
William Widnor.
Jacob Strikler.
Daniel Dowdle.
George Consor.
Felty Walker.
Anthony Lipsey.

Seventh class.

Phillip Graft.
Thomas Crabb.
Peter Miller.
Christian Hepech.
John Parks.
John Lenning.
Abner Wickersham.
Hugh McLoy.
Conrod Atley.
Jacob Wolfly.
Conrod Bumbaugh.

Eighth class.

Lodwick Hemberly.
Conrod Toot.
Frederick Zebernick.
Michael Gross.
Christian Grass.
Patrick Scoot.
John Snider.
David Toot, Jr.
Emanwell Bullinger.
Alexander Jameson.
William Crabb.
George Toot.
John Barnett.
William Roland.
Frederick Hubley.

Returned the 11th April, 1781.

By JONATHAN McCLURE, Captain.

TENTH BATTALION, LANCASTER COUNTY MILITIA. (a.)

Called out by classes for actual service, June, 1781.

SECOND CLASS.

First Company.

John Ayres.
Alexander Givens.
George Straw.
John Bell, Jr.
David Davis.
George Cochran.

Second Company.

David Paton.
John Fleming.

Third Company.

Joseph Little.
John Butler.
James Walker.

Fourth Company.

James Spence.

Fifth Company.

James Cogley.
George Fridley.

Sixth Company.

William Smith.
Thomas Brunson.
Richard Fulton.

Seventh Company.

Did not march, being the fronteer.

Eighth Company.

Jacob Snider.
Robert Plunket (marched in Third class).

THIRD CLASS.

First Company.

Michael Stiver.
William Forster.
Leonard Shots.
Samuel Polick.
Peter Kinter.
George Bell.

Second Company.

James Cochran.
William Hogan.
Andrew Cochran.
Anthony Witbrel.

Third Company.

John Chambers.
William Kenedey.
William Thompson.
Richard Allison.

Fourth Company.

George Carson.
Robert McClure.
Michael Lines.

FOURTH CLASS.

First Company.

Elisha Lockert.
Samuel Campbell.
Thomas Nicleson.

Second Company.

James Boggs.
James McMillin.
Robert Huston.
Jacob Larison.
James Caldwell.
John Wilson.
William Jamison.
Thomas Askin.

Fourth Company.

Barney Shoop.
Andrew Wiley.
Benjamin Duncan.
Michael Castle.
George Byerley.

Fifth Company.

John Parker.
Ichabod Randolph.

Sixth Company.

Samuel Hutchison.
Handeater Winderley.
Thomas Dougherty.
John Postlethwait.
Richard Steel.

Eighth Company.

George Frye.
Christian Spayd.
George Lowman.
John Metzger.

FIFTH CLASS.

First Company.

John Kinter.
Joseph Keller.
Jacob Cobler.
John Gartner.
Philip Newpecker.
William Nickleson.

Second Company.

Zachariah Stephen.
William Caldhoon.
John Allen.
William McRoberts.
John McCahan.

Fourth Company.

Leonard Sheetz.
Francis Burley.
Elisha Stewart.

Fifth Company.

Robert Keays.
Andrew Berryhill.

Sixth Company.

John McKinney.
Arthur Chambers.

Eighth Company.

Jacob King.
John McCan.
John Miller.

SIXTH CLASS.

First Company.

John Simpson.
John Cochran.
William Murray.
John Colgin.
James Burney.
Isaiah Winn.

Second Company.

John Cochran.
Samuel Martin.
James Stewart.
John Hilton.
Samuel Thompson.

Third Company.

James Buchanan.

Fourth Company.

John Gray.
Adam Ketchmiler.

Fifth Company.

Robert Elder.
John Fockler.
Alexander Berryhill.
Samuel Simpson.
Adam Vantz.

Sixth Company.

Peter Brenner.
Philip Griner.
Francis Lerue.

Eighth Company.

John Bakestoe.
Philip Etlee.
William Widner.
Philip Shocken.
Peter Shuster.
Daniel Double.

SEVENTH CLASS.

First Company.

James Bell.
James Paycoe.
Jesse Weeks.
Moses Lockert.
Samuel Cochran.
James Burruff.

Second Company.

William Cochran.
Richard McGuire.
Michael Phillips.
Henry Humbarger.
William Patterson.
Charles Mulray.
John Wiggins.

Third Company.

Andrew Ritchison.

Fourth Company.

Conrad Bobb.
Jacob Smith.
Matthew Shaw.
Stophel Shoop.
William Walker.

Fifth Company.

Samuel Simpson.
Cornelius Cox.
William Vance.
Thomas Forster.
George Sheets.
Thomas Galliher.
William Buck.
Daniel Roberts.

Sixth Company.

Michael Wolf.
Joseph Hutchison.
Charles McCoy.
Jacob Dagan.
Hugh Crocket.
John Boll.
Peter Roop.
John Morrison.

Seventh Company.

Adam Vertz.
Anthony Freiich.
George Merrick.
Christian Vertz.
George Seale.
Henry Myers.

Eighth Company.

Peter Miller.
Abner Wickersham.
Conrad Bumbaugh.
John Fritz.
John Parks.
Hugh McLoy.
Henry Davis.

MUSTER ROLL OF 2D CLASS 10TH BATALL. LANC'R COUNTY MILITIA ON A TOUR OF DUTY AT LANCASTER. (c.)

Names of Persons who Served.	Names of Persons who Furnished Substitutes	Time when duty comm'd.	Time when duty ended.
Drum.		1781	1781
John Shinole,	James Collier,	June 27,	Aug. 24.
Privates.			
George Cochran,			July 29.
James Spencer,			July 29.
John Bell.			
David Davis,		July 2,	
Jno. Buttler.			
James Walker.			
Jacob Snyder.			
Thos. Brunson,		June 27,	
Robt. Richmond,	Wm. Smith,	July 4,	Aug. 14.
Jno. Swann,	Richd. Fulton,	June 27,	Aug. 24.
Jno. Curry,	Geo. Friedly,		Aug. 24.
Jno. Parker,	Jno. Ayres.		
Wm. Murrow,	George Straw.		
Michl. Gross,	David Patten.		
Thos. Cosgrove,	Jno. Fleming.		
George Mears.			
Jno. Ayres.			
George Williams.			
John Riblet.			

Lanc'r July 2d, 81. Then mustered the above company as above specified.

AD'M HUBLEY, S. L. L'r C'y.

MUSTER ROLL OF 3D CLASS, 10TH BATALL LANC'R COUNTY MIL'A ON A TOUR OF DUTY AT NORTHUMBERLAND. (c.)

Names of Persons who Serv'd a Tour of Duty.	Names of Persons who Furnished Substitutes	Time when duty comm'd.	Time when duty ended.
Capt.		1781	1781
Wm. Johnson,		July 7,	Aug. 25.
Lt.			
Wm. Montgomery.			
Ens.			
Wm. McMillan.			
Alex'r Taylor.			
Michl. Lewis.			
Jacob Huber.			
Henry Taylor,	Joseph Little.		
Barnabas Nave,	Robt. McLure.		
And'w Cochran.			
Wm. Forster.			
Michl. Stiver.			
Anth'y Witherill.			
Abr'm Brunson.			
Wm. Hogan.			
Elisha Chambers,	Jno. Chambers.		
Wm. Thompson.			
Geo. Bell.			
Jams. Black,	Hugh Stephen.		
Jon. Hanna,	Chris'n King.		
George Hempleman,	George Snagance.		
Michl. Drury,	Saml. Polick.		
Wm. Kennady,	Rich'd Allison,	July 20,	
Robert Plunkit,		July 7,	
Darius Mead,	Leonard Shirtz,	July 12,	
Barnabas Farren,	James Cochran,	July 7,	
Wm. Steel,		14,	
David McCord,	Jas. McCord.		
Jno. Kinter,	Peter Kinter,	7,	
Robt. Kennady.			
Jno. Armstrong.			
Jno. Ryan,	George Carson,	July 15,	

This company mustered in the 21 Aug. by

COL. HUNTER.

MUSTER ROLL OF THE 4TH, 5TH & 6TH CLASS OF THE 10TH BATTALION LANCASTER COUNTY MILITIA ON A TOUER OF DUTY TO BUCK'S COUNTY. (c.)

Names of Persons who perform a touer of Duty.	What Class.	Names of Persons who furnished Substitutes.	Time when Duty Commenced.	Time when Duty ended.
Capt.				
Hugh Robertson,	4th,			
Leiut.				
John Mathis,	4th,			
Ensgn.				
James Reed,	4th,			
Serjts.				
John Parker,	4th,			
Robert Ritchmon,	4th,	Philip Griner.		
Frederick Herman,	4th,	Frank Lerue.		
Corpl.				
John Bell,	4th,			
Nathaniel Landin,	4th,	Robert Boyd.		
Jacob Hewer,	4th,			

MUSTER ROLL OF THE 4TH, 5TH & 6TH CLASS OF THE 10TH BATTALION LANCASTER COUNTY MILITIA—Continued.

Names of Persons who perform a touer of Duty.	What Class.	Names of Persons who furnished Substitutes.	Time when Duty Commenced.	Time when Duty ended.
Drum.				
Alexr. Cumings,	4th,			
Privates.				
George Bierly,	4th,			
Jacob Shoap,	4th,	Barney Shoap.		
Michael Castle,	4th,			
Benjamin Duncan,	4th,			
Andrew Wily,	4th,			
Michael Limes,	4th,	Jacob Limes.		
Francis Burly,	4th,			
John McChegney,	4th,	George Lowman.		
Richard Johnston,	4th,	James McMolen.		
Thomas Askin,	4th,			
Thomas Nicleson,	4th,			
John Butler,	4th,	Malachi Pouel.		
Robert Huston,	4th,			
Jacob Larenson,	4th,			
John Wilson,	4th,			

James Bogs,	4th,	
Jacob Bearstead,	4th,	John Focklar.
Adam Miller,	4th,	George Fry.
George Joans,	4th,	John Jamison.
Richard Steel,	4th,	
James Calwell,	4th,	
Henry Hoon,	4th,	John Wenderley.
Thomas Dotherty,	4th,	
Peter Munto,	4th,	
John Gray,	4th,	
John Kayes,	4th,	
James Boughamon,	4th,	
William Whitner,	4th,	
John Hilton,	4th,	
Jonathan Brinson,	4th,	
John Hogon,	4th,	Samuel Marton.
Adam Cechwiler,	4th,	
Samuel Thompson,	4th,	
Samuel Camel,	4th,	
John Cochran,	4th,	

MUSTER ROLL OF THE 4TH, 5TH & 6TH CLASS OF THE 10TH BATTALION LANCASTER COUNTY MILITIA—Continued.

Names of Persons who perform a touer of Duty.	What Class.	Names of Persons who furnished Substitutes.	Time when Duty Commenced.	Time when Duty ended.
Capt.				
Andrew Stuart,	5th,		1781.	1781.
Leiut.				
John Smith,	5th,			
Ensgn.				
John Huffhan,	5th,			
Serjts.				
Arther [illegible],	5th,			
John Colegan,	5th,			
Privates.				
John Cocheran,	5th,			
William Murry,	5th,			
John Meads,	5th,			
Alexr. Gibons,	5th,	Alexr. Berryhill.		
Ichabod Randolph,	5th,			
John McCann,	5th,			

Andrew Berryhill,	5th,			
Robert Cals,	5th,			
Conrad Toot,	5th,	John Miller.		
Frederick Castle,	5th,	Jacob King.		
Samuel Nickim,	5th,	Lennard Sheats.		
Anthony Withrae,	5th,	William Gahan.		
[illegible]r. Tealer,	5th,	Alisha Stuart.		
Barny Neave,	5th,	John Postlewart.		
William Nicolas,	5th,			
John Abet,	5th,	Jacob Capler.		
Philip Lindof,	5th,	Zacheus Stevers.		
John Allan,	5th,			
Samuel Berryhill,	5th,			
John Winter,	5th,			
John Garner,	5th,			
James [illegible]ler,	5th,	say Joseph.		
John Bonnel,	5th,			
Philip Nubaker,	5th,			
William McRoberts,	5th,			
William Buck,	5th,	Samuel Simpson.		
Henrey McClusky,	5th,			
[illegible]ha Lokert,	5th,			
Daniel [illegible]r,	5th,	Peter Shuster.		
[illegible]an Cridler,	5th,	Philip Atley.		
William [illegible]ce,	5th,			
Josiah [illegible]n,	5th,			
Robert Elder,	5th,			
Peter Branard,	5th,			
William Johnston,	5th,			
George Johnston,	5th,			
Charles McCoy,	5th,			
John Baclstoe,	5th,			
Anthony Hamperly,	5th,			

(c.) These are to certify that Doct'r William Simonton was appointed Surgeon of the tenth Battalion L. C. Militia Commanded by Lieut. Con'l Robert Elder in the Beginning of the Year 1780 and Notwithstanding his removal with his Family to Conowago he was still continued and gave his Attendance in said Battalion until the latter end of the year 1784. Given under my hand at Paxton this 13th March A. D. 1786.

JNO. GILCHRIST, younger Maj'r.

To whom it may concern.

A LIST OF THE FOURTH CLASS OF THE 10TH BATTALION L. COUNTY M. 1782. (c.)

1 Comp'y.

John Boland.
William Fulks.
Peter Sturgeon.
John Duncan.
Elijah Lockert.
John Hatfield.
Thomas Nicleson.
Samuel Cambel.

2d Dito.

James Boggs.
James Caldwell.
James McMillin.
John Wilson.
Joseph Dougles.
Will'm Jamison.

3d Do.

James McCall.
Robert Boyd.
Mallchia Powel.
Jacob Stricker.
George Simming.

4th Do.

Fredrick Castle.
Barney Shoop.
George Pile.
Michael Castle, Junr.
Henry Pile.
Andrew Wiley.
Michael Page.
George Byerley.,
Thomas McArthur.
Benjamin Duncan.
Jacob all.

5th Do.

Nathaniel Simpson.
Peter Babb.
John Porter.
Icabod Randolph.

6th Do.

Samuel Hutchison.
Andrew McLure.
John Renich.
John Postle.
John Clindining.
Jacob Kirr.
Abraham Nidigh.
Stophel Poorman.
Jacob Fisher.

Hanteater Winderley.
John Shoamaker.
Jacob Noop.
Allex'r McCumprey.
Chrisley Page.
John McGeary.
Richard Steel.
Thomas Dougherty.

7th Do.

John Huffman.
Peter Meds.
Fredrick Stoanbreaker.
Adam Ruber.
George Divelar.

George Shoop.
Stophel Yeagor.
Eacheus Spaningbarger.
Charls. Barger.

8th Do.

Abraham Darr.
George Fry.
Christian Seabough.
Samuel Parks.

George Lowman.
Joseph Flora.
John Bowman.

A LIST OF THE 5 CLASS OF THE 10TH BATTALION L. COUNTY M. 1782. (c.)

1st Comp'y.

James Foster.
John Richmond.
John Kinter.
John Gartner.
James McNamara.
James McClanahan.

Allex'dr Dugles.
Joseph Keller.
Phillip Newpecker.
Archbed Murray.
Jacob Cobler.
Will'm Nicollisen.

2d Dito.

Zacheriah Stephen.
Will'm Wilson.
Will'm McRoberts.
Will'm Caldhoon.
Philip John Barris.

Samuel White.
John McCahan.
Michael Millar.
John Allen.
John Gilchrist, Ser.

3d Do.

Henry bender-Hack (?).
James Spear.
John Keays.

4th Do.

Vendel Focklar.
Michael Mark.
Jacob Millar, Jur.
John Lider.
Leonard Sheets.
Samuel Brawn.
Elijah Stewart.

5.

Robert Keays.
Stophel Smith.
Mongs Linsey.
Andrew Berryhill.
John Harsha.
Hugh Montgomery.
Frances Yontz.
Samuel Clemmons.
John Cogley.
Conrad Leek.

6.

Samuel Smith.
Henry Alleman.
Samuel Wiley.
Chrisley Turner.
John McKinney.
Will'm Right.
John Bowman.
John Rowan.
John Consor.
Chrisley Alleman.
John Fleckneer.
Arthur Chamber.
George Neveland.

7d.

Frances Conaway.
Henery Umholts.
Leonard Steaver.
Ludwick Shoots.
Sebastan Mades.
Michael Melgar.
Henery Heans.
Leonard Coffman.

8th.

George Goods.
James Cray.
Samuel Seratzy.
Michael Peatinger.
Peter Rikert.
Thomas Moor
Jacob King.
John McCann.
John Millar.
Larrey Smith.

A LIST OF SIXTH CLASS. LANC. CO. 10TH BATT. 1782. (c.)

1st Comp'y.

John Simpson.
Joseph Colgin.
Henery McCluskey.
John Thomas.
John Colgin.
John Cochran.

James Birney.
Will'm Murray.
Robert Armstrong.

Isiah Winn.
John Eakin.
Will'm Clark.

2d Dito.

Hugh Wray.
John Cochran.
John Hilton.
Abraham Wilson.
Thomas Gilchrist.

Samuel Martain.
Samuel Thomson.
John Whitehill.
Adam Harbison.
James Wiggons.

3d Do.

James Buchannon.
Allex'd George.
Petter Swaggert.

John Gilsey.
John Ringland.
George McElyear.

4th Do.

Daniel Cooper.
John Gray.
Adam Kitchmillar.

Joseph Wilson.
Jacob Houser.
Martain Fritz.

5th Do.

Robert Elder.
John Elder.
Samuel Simpson.
James Floyd.

John Fockler.
Adam Vantz.
Allex'd Berryhill.
Will'm Kelso.

6th Do.

John Sherer.
Adam Means.
George Gray.
John Boyd.
Will'm Postle.
Daniel Brunsor.
Peter Braner.

John Alleman.
Nicolis Nigh.
France Lerue.
Phillip Criner.
John Zider.
Philip Shoamaker.
Michael Foorman.

7th Do.

Peter Wellior.
Jacob Harmon.
Jonathan Woodsid.
Adam King.
John Ward.

Stophel Shisley.
John Woodside.
Will'm Armharst.
Philip Rouscaulp.

8th Do.

Nicolis Castle.
Abraham Groos.
Henery McCann.
John Bakestoss.
Philip Shockey.
Philip Atler.
Henery Millar.
Petter Luother.
Will'm Widnor.
Jacob Strickler.
George Consor.
Daniel Doudie.
Anthony Lipsey.

MUSTER ROLE OF THE 7TH CLASS 10TH BATTALION LANCASTER COUNTY MILITIA, 1782. (c)

Names of Persons who Serve a Tour.	Names of Persons who Furnished Substitutes.	Time of entry.
James McRoberts,	Wm. Paterson,	Sept. 27.
George Johnson,	Samuel Clemons.	
Jonathan Mathias,	Richard Meguire.	
Barney Murfey,	Cornilis Cox.	
Charls Mulroy.		
George Clark,	Samuel Cochran.	
John Butler,	Daniel Roberts.	
Adam Bitter,	Conroad Bumbough.	
Michael Limes,	Conroad Bobb.	
John Boob.		
John Williams,	Jacob Dagon.	
Thomas Dougherty,	Jacob Smith.	
John McGeary.		
Conroad Doot,	Joseph Florey.	
George Menick.		
Adam Wertz.		
George Reel.		
Mathew Shaw.		
James Burress.		
Henry Myer.		
John Morrison.		
George Seal.		
Michael Woolf.		
Georges Joahns,	Michael Philips.	
George Simmers,	Jacob Strickler.	
Wm. Steel,	Jacob Woolfley.	
Wm. Buck.		
Wm. Vance.		
Hugh McLoy.		
Andrew Ritchison.		
Frederick Harman,	Samuel Parks.	
Anthoney Freelick.		
Richard Hughes,	George Sheets.	
Robert Herren,	George Gross.	
James Connar,	Wm. Walker.	
James Burk,	Peter Roop.	

MUSTER ROLE OF THE 7TH CLASS 10TH BATTALION LANCASTER COUNTY MILITIA—Continued.

Names of Persons who Serve a Tour.	Names of Persons who Furnished Substitutes.	Time of entry.
John Nobel,	Abner Wikersham.	
James Bell.		
Philip Sellers,	John Parks.	
Thomas Corbet,	John Wiggins.	
Wm. Postlethrnot.		
Thomas Oram.		
Thomas Crafoard,	Joseph Hutchison.	
Archibald Taylor,	Henery Leek.	
Henery Davis.		
John Colgin,	Christopher Shoop.	
David Shaw,	Thomas Forster.	
John Richmond.		
John Bell,	Wm. Cochran.	
Christian Wertz.		
Henrey Venderbough,	Gallihar.	
Robert Paterson,	Robert Wiley.	
Moses Lokert.		
Wm. Johnson,	Henery Humbarger.	
John Gartner,	James Paycock.	
Larrey Smith.		
Henery Hoan,	James McCall.	
John Fillips,	John Fritz.	
Wm. Kilday,	John Duncan.	
John Brown,	Adam Means.	
John Wood,	Henery Moor.	
Jeremiah Morison,	Samuel Simpson.	
Petter Muller.		
Charls McCoy.		
Phelep Tenturp,	Jessa Week.	
Hugh Crocket.		

I do Swear the Within Muster Role is a True State of the Company Without fraud to the United States or any Indidual to the Best of my knoledge.

WM. McCLURE, Lt.

A TRUE AND EXACT LIST OF THE NAMES, OF EACH AND EVERY MALE WHITE PERSON, INHABITING OR RESIDING, WITHIN MY DISTRICT, IN THE FIRST COMPANY, OF THE TENTH BATTALION OF LANCASTER COUNTY, MILITIA, BETWEEN THE AGE OF EIGHTEEN AND FIFTY-THREE YEARS. TAKEN FOR THE YEAR 1782. (c.)

Capt.
James Murray.

Lieu.
John Ryan.

Ens.
James Mcnamara.

Almonar.
John Cochran.

First Class.

Robt. Goudy, Sergt.
John McCord.
James Watts.
Will'm Mountgomery.
Charls. Cain.
Will'm Bennit.
John forster.

Second Class.

John Ayers.
John Bell, jur.
Alex'r Gwins.
Henry Hoone.
Geo. Straw.
Stephen forster.
Geo. Cochran.
Patt. Lafferty.
Jas. Mcfadden.

Third Class.

Michal Stiver.
Sam'l Plouge
Philip Tintwiff.
Will'm forster.
thos. Bone.
Leonard Shots.
Geo. Bell.
John Stephenson.
John Cristey.

Fourth Class.

John Bolland.
Will'm foulks.
Peter Sturgeon.
John Duncan.

Elisha Lockard.
John Hattfeild.
Sam'l Camble.
Philip Meek.
thos. Kile.
thos. Nichoalson.
John Bell, Sergt.

Fifth Class.

John Richmond.
John Kinter.
John Gartner.
James McClanachan.
Alex'r Douglass.
Joseph Keller.
Philip Newbecker.
Arch'd Murray.
Jacob Cobler.
Wm. Nichoalson.
Wm. Killday.
John Bundle, Sergt.

Sixth Class

John Simpson.
Henry McCloskey.
John Collagan.
John Thomas.
John Cochran.
James Birney.
Will'm Armstrong.
Josiah Winn.
John Eakin.
Will'm Clark.
Cornelius Lafferty.
And'w Sponsler.
thos. Sturgeon.

Seventh Class.

James Bell.
thos Gallachor.
Robt. Smith.
Moses Lochard.
John Dice, Jr.
James Peacock.
Sam'l Cochran.
Will'm Hempson.
Jesse Weeks.
Peter Eyman.
James Burris.
Will'm Bundy.

Eighth Class.

John Brown.
Abraham Mooney.
John Sloane.
Loud'r Minchker.
thos. Beard.
Anthony furnace.
John Pursel.
Arch'd Finly.
Charis McClanachan.

I Do swear, on the Holy Evengilest of Almighty God: That the above list is a just and true state, of the Male White Inhabitants, residing in my District, agreeable to Law and without any fraud to the State, to the best of my knowledge.

JAMES MURRAY, Capt'n.

Sworn before me this
Tenth Day of May 1782.

MAX'LL CHAMBERS, S. Lt.

A TRUE AND EXACT LIST OF THE NAMES, OF EACH AND EVERY MALE WHITE PERSON, INHABITING OR RESIDING, WITHIN MY DISTRICT, IN THE SECOND COMPANY, OF THE TENTH BATTALION OF LANCASTER COUNTY, MILITIA, BETWEEN THE AGE OF EIGHTEEN AND FIFTY-THREE YEARS. TAKEN FOR THE YEAR 1782. (c.)

Capt.
George McMillan.

Lieu.
Matthew Gilcriest.

Ens.
William McMillan.

Almonar.
Robt. Whitehill.

Serjants.

Samuel Berryhill.
Robert Wylie.
Alexander Johnston.

First Class.

John McElheney.
Jacob Millar.
John Meador.
David White.
George Johnston.
John McKnaughlan.
David Pinkerton.

Second Class.

George Shoap.
David patton.
John Kinsley.
John pattimore.
Henry Achia.
John Fleming.
James McRoberts.
Ephraim Stephen.

Third Class.

James Cochran.
Joseph Barnett.
Andrew Cochran
William Hogan.
James Cowdon.
Peter Felty.

Fourth Class.

James Bogs.
James Caldwel.
James McMillen.
John Wilson.
Wm. Jamison.
Jacob Lawrison.
Robert Huston.

Fifth Class.

Zachariah Stephen.
William Caldhoon.
Philip Burras.
Samuel White.
John M'Caughan.
Samuel Swan.
Felty Rhodes.
John Gilcriest, Sen'r.
Robert Kees.

Sixth Class

John Cochran.
John Hilton.
James Wiggens.
Thomas Gilcriest.
Samuel Martin.
Samuel Thompson.
John Whitehill.
James Steuart.
Adam Burruff.
John McRoberts.
James Haynes.
John Gray.
Will'm Hayburn.
Mathew Blekly.
John Gordon.
Barney Ferren.
Wm. Dougan.

Seventh Class.

Robert Gilcriest.
William Cochran.
Andrew Stephen.
James Byers.
Thomas Bell.
John Caldwel.
William Patterson.
Richard McGuire.
Charles Mulroy.
Michael Philippee.
John Wiggens.
Henry Humbarger.
Thomas Cavit.

Eighth Class.

Robert Neel.
Hugh Stephen.
James Cavet.
John Gilcriest, Junior.
Henry petner.
Andrew Barnett.
Robert Covenhover.
John hogan.

I Do swear, on the Holy Evenglilest of Almighty God: That the above list is a just and true state, of the Male White Inhabitants, residing in my District, agreeable to Law and without any fraud to the State, to the best of my knowledge.

GEO. McMILLAN, Capt.

Sworn before me this
Thenth Day of May 1782.

MAX'LL CHAMBERS, S. Lt.

A TRUE AND EXACT LIST OF THE NAMES, OF EACH AND EVERY MALE WHITE PERSON, INHABITING OR RESIDING, WITHIN MY DISTRICT, IN THE THIRD COMPANY, OF THE TENTH BATTALION OF LANCASTER COUNTY, MILITIA, BETWEEN THE AGE OF EIGHTEEN AND FIFTY-THREE YEARS. TAKEN FOR THE YEAR 1782. (c.)

Capt.

Wm. Johnston.

Lieu.

Geo. Clark.

Ens.

Geo. Taylor.

Almonar.

Thomas Orom.

First Class.

Isaac Jones.
Ludwick Shelman.
Joseph Muckewrath.
James Black.
John Brown.

Second Class.

Micael Herman.
Joseph Lytle.
James Walker.
John Butler.
Isiah Jones.
Robert George.

Third Class.

John Eldor, Ser.
John Chambers.
William Thompson.
William Kennady.
Samuel Taylor, Sr.
Daniel Kitsler.

Fourth Class.

Robert Boyd.
Malachi Powell.
Jacob Striker.
George Simers, Ser.
Gabrail Brodigam.
Henry Dougherty.
William Baskins.
James Huling.
John Diven.
James Reed.
Marcus Huling.
John Woods.
James Hackert.

Fifth Class.

Henry Venderbeck.
John Keys.
James McCall.
Thomas Orom.
John Goldenberg.
Joseph Ashbridge.
Frances Conway.
Conrod Needler.
Thomas Rotten.

Sixth Class

James Buchanan.
Alexander George.
Peter Swagert.
John Gilsey.
George Mucklekeer.
Samuel Oacks.
Cutlip Cline.
Robart Boyd.
John Ashbridge.
Frances Kitsler.

Seventh Class.

George Simmons.
Daniel Black.
Henry Leeck.
Herman Leeck.
Daniel Kistaler.
Andrew Ritchardson.
Jacob Stowover.

Eighth Class.

Elijha Chambers.
Richard Gilmore.
Adam Swagert.
Samuel Taylor.
Nathaniel Landin.
John Kinch.

I Do swear, on the Holy Evengilest of Almighty God: That the above list is a just and true state, of the Male White Inhabitants, residing in my District, agreeable to Law and without any fraud to the State, to the best of my knowledge.

WILLIAM JOHNSTON, Capt.

Sworn before me this
Twenty fourth Day of June 1782.

A TRUE AND EXACT LIST OF THE NAMES, OF EACH AND EVERY MALE WHITE PERSON, INHABITING OR RESIDING WITHIN MY DISTRICT, IN THE FOURTH COMPANY, OF THE TENTH BATTALION OF LANCASTER COUNTY, MILITIA, BETWEEN THE AGE OF EIGHTEEN AND FIFTY-THREE YEARS. TAKEN FOR THE YEAR 1782. (c.)

Capt.
Hugh Robson.

Lieu.
William Muntgomerv.

Ens.

George Smith.

1 Serg't.

Michael Limes.

First Class.

John Castle.
William Duncan.
Jacob* Poorman.
John Buck.
John Millar, Jr.
John Boughman.
Adam Lafler.
William Stuart.
Philip Peter.

Second Class.

Abraham Eagly.
Peter Smith.
William McClure.
James Spence.
John Millar.
Samuel Dale.
Philip Firebough.
Martin Houser, Jur.
Robert Gray.

Third Class.

Jacob Limes.
George Sample.
Jacob Syder, Jur.
George Carson.
John Rutherford.
Robert McClure.
George Sheets.

Fourth Class.

George Dixon.
Fredrick Castle.
Barny Shoap.
Michael Castle.
Andrew Wiley.
Michael Page.
George Bierly.
Thomas McCarter.
Benjamin Duncan.
John Parker.
Robert Clark.
John Willson, Clark.
Jacob Lawrison.

Fifth Class.

Vindle Focklar.
Jacob Millar.
Leonard Sheets.
Elijah Stuart.
John Loider.
Samuel Brown.
John Megery.
John Hamilton.
Francis Burly.
Jacob Mook.
Allex'd Cummings.

Sixth Class

Daniel Cooper.
John Gray.
Jacob Mire.
Henry Chub.
James Cain.
Samuel Cochran, Capt. of 6th Company.

Seventh Class.

Jacob Beck.
Conrade Bob.
David Richy.
Stophel Soop.
Jacob Smith.
John Donley.
William Walker.
Mathew Shaw.

Eighth Class.

Joseph Shaw.
Michael Sheaver.
David Shaw.
Alexander Willson.
John Willson.
Jacob Shoap.
Thomas Alexander.
George Whitehill.
John Cummings.

I Do swear, on the Holy Evengilest of Almighty God: That the above list is a just and true state, of the Male White Inhabitants, residing in my District, agreeable to Law and without any fraud to the State, to the best of my knowledge

HUGH ROBINSON,
Capt.

Sworn before me this
Tenth Day of May 1782.

MAX'LL CHAMBERS, S. Lt.

A TRUE AND EXACT LIST OF THE NAMES, OF EACH AND EVERY MALE WHITE PERSON, INHABITING OR RESIDING, WITHIN MY DISTRICT, IN THE FIFTH COMPANY, OF THE TENTH BATTALION OF LANCASTER COUNTY, MILITIA, BETWEEN THE AGE OF EIGHTEEN AND FIFTY-THREE YEARS. TAKEN FOR THE YEAR 1782. (c.)

Capt.
Andrew Stewart.

Lieu.
John Matthows.

Ens.
George Devibaugh.

Almonar.
Jeremiah Sturgeon.

First Class.

Felty Spangler.
Jacob Nass.
Michal Whitley.
Henry Bosler.
John Misner.

Second Class.

William Bell.
James Cogley.
George Fridley.
Fredrick Switzer.
John Goudey.
Thomas Scott.
Daniel Roberts.
Jacob Nobb.

Third Class.

Conrod Yontz.
Alex'd Porter.
Michal Smith.
Anthony Reel.
Joshua Elder.
John Dimpsey.
Litle Jacob at Fockler's.
Gustavus Grimes.
James Fox.

Fourth Class.

Peter Bobb.
Thomas Erwin.
David Morrow.
Samuel Mann.

Fifth Class.

John Hersha.
Francis Yontz.
John Cogley.
John Bates.
Stophel Smith.
Hugh Montgomery.
Samuel Cleman.
Wm. Whitley.
David Davis.
Peter Bobb.
Richard Hughs.
Thomas Murray.
And'w Beryhill.

Sixth Class.

Robert Elder.
John Elder.
Samuel Simpson.
James Floyd.
John Fockler.
John Vance.
Alexander Beryhill.
John Boyd.
George Dindore.
David Scarlet.
Leonard Wallower.
Jacob Peters.
Christly Miller.
Jacob Cuntz.

Seventh Class.

Samuel Simpson.
George Sheets.
Cornelius Cox.
John Cline.
Robert Clark.
Thomas Brynon.
James Johnston.
Hugh White.

William Carson.
Thomas Galaher.
William Vance.
William Burk.
James Cunningham.
John Elder, Jun'r.
John Stoner.

Eighth Class.

David Montgomery.
George Ranlker.
Andrew Bell.
Patrick Heney.
Charles Stewart.
John Garber.
James McKee.
Thomas Moore.
William Morison.
Joseph Simpson.
Saml. Morison.
Barnet Fridley.
George Bell.
John Smith.
Jacob Haldiman.
Thomas Forster.
Christian Swink.
John Morrow.
James Rutherford.
John Harris, Jun'r.
John Bennet.
William Gefferey.
Richard Cavins.
Richard Cairns.
Anthony McGahaney.

I Do swear, on the Holy Evengilest of Almighty God: That the above list is a just and true state, of the Male White Inhabitants, residing in my District, agreeable to Law, and without fraud to the State, to the best of my knowledge.

AND'W STEWART, Capt.

Sworn before me this
Tenth Day of May 1782.

MAX'LL CHAMBERS, S. Lt.

A TRUE AND EXACT LIST OF THE NAMES, OF EACH AND EVERY MALE WHITE PERSON, INHABITING OR RESIDING, WITHIN MY DISTRICT, IN THE SIXTH COMPANY, OF THE TENTH BATTALION OF LANCASTER COUNTY, MILITIA, BETWEEN THE AGE OF EIGHTEEN AND FIFTY-THREE YEARS. TAKEN FOR THE YEAR 1782. (c.)

Capt.
Samuel Cochran.

Lieu.
Joseph Smith.

Ens.

William McClure.

First Class.

Allex'dr McClure.
Nicolis Alleman.
George Lerue.
Stophel Alleman.
Jacob Brand.
John Roop.
Eliab Negley.
Philip Brown.
John Armstrong.
Robert Marshal.
John Chambers.
Mathias Huber.
Jacob Early.

Second Class.

James Collar.
Jacob Roop.
Chrisley Roop.
John Mumma.
Will'm Murray.
Wm. Smith.
Ludwick Dagon.
Richard Fulton.
Fredrick Winagal.
Thomas Branson.
John France.

Third Class.

Stophel Earnist.
James McCoard.
John Brand.
Conrad Alleman.
Mathias Winagal.
Abraham Brunsor.
Will'm Steel.
Chrisley Fleckneer.
Jacob Huber.
Samuel Sherer.
Jos. Mark.

Fourth Class.

Jacob Kerr.
Abraham Nidigh.
Stophel Poorman.
Richard Steel.
Andrew McClure.
Hanteater Winderly.
John Renick.
John Clindining.
Jacob Noop.
Allex'dr McCumsey.
Thomas Dougherty.
Samuel Hutchison.
John Bumgarner.
Mathias Whitmor.
Allex'dr Clark.
Icabod Randolf.

Fifth Class.

John Bowman.
John Consor.
Henery Alleman.
John Fleckneer.
Samuel Wiley.
John McKeney.
Arthur Chambers.
Mehler Poorman.
Adam Lampart.
Fredrick Teits.

Sixth Class.

Max'll Chambers.
John Shearer.
Adam Means.
John Alleman.
Peter Brannor.
Frances Lerue.
Philip Griner.
Daniel Brunson.
Philip Shoamaker.
Henery Boll.

Seventh Class.

Will'm Kerr.
Richard McLure.
Michael Woolf.
Hugh Cunningham.
Hugh Crocket.
John Steel.
Joseph Hutchison.
John Bool.
Charls. McCoy.
Peter Roop.
Jacob Dagon.
John Morison.
John Means.
Robert Richmond.
Josep Fulton.
Fredrick Harmon.
Chrisley Consor.
Samuel.
John Montgomery.

Eighth Class.

Robert Chambers.
Rowan McClure.
Josep Gray.
Michael Bool.
James Mahan.
James Mckeney.
James Rutherfoare.
Rowland Chambers.
John Max'll.
Thomas Murray.
John McChesney.
Jacob Rudebarger.
Henery Teader.
Hugh Montgomery.
Barney Nave.

I Do swear, on the Holy Evengilest of Almighty God: That the above list is a just and true state, of the Male White Inhabitants, residing in my District, agreeable to Law, and without fraud to the State, to the best of my knowledge.

SAMUEL COCHRAN, Capt.

Sworn before me this
Tenth Day of May.
1782.

MAX'LL CHAMBERS, S. Lt.

A TRUE AND EXACT LIST OF THE NAMES, OF EACH AND EVERY MALE WHITE PERSON, INHABITING OR RESIDING WITHIN MY DISTRICT, IN THE SEVENTH COMPANY, OF THE TENTH BATTALION OF LANCASTER COUNTY, MILITIA, BETWEEN THE AGE OF EIGHTEEN AND FIFTY-THREE YEARS. TAKEN FOR THE YEAR 1782. (c.)

Capt.
Martain Weaver.

Lieu.
John Shisly.

Ens.
Daniel Steever.

First Class.

Evard Willcok.
Jacob Shisly.
freedrick poul.
Jeems Mecklin.
Willim Ingrams.
george poul.
george Ŕeem.
John mier.

Second Class.

John matter.
Henry Werfel.
Abraham Jury.
John Dedy.
george Klinger.
John meelier.
John Riter.
Jacob Cords.

Third Class.

Mikel Saladin.
Mikel Shedel.
Leonhard Shnider.
Abraham Nebour.
Andru yegor.
Henry uls.
freedrick Bend.

Fourth Class.

John hofman.
Peeter meds.
Deetrick Stonebreker.
Adam Kuber.
george Divlor.
george Shub.
garls Berger.
Stopel yegor.
John McElheney.

Fifth Class.

francis Canavy.
Leonhard Steever.
Sehastan Meds.
Henry hens.
Henry umhouls.
Ludwick Shods.
Mikel Melgor.
Peeter belnrd.
Leonhard garfeman.

Sixth Class.

John Harman.
John Matter.
feelb Rouskoll.
Peeter Willeor.
Jacob harman.
Jonathan Woodside.
Adam king.
John Werds.
Stopel Shisly.
John Woodside.

Seventh Class.

Mathais Divlor.
george Redel.
David Herman.
Andony frely.
george Seel.
Adam Werds.
Neeklos hofman.
george mink.
Christian Werds.
Henny mier.

Eighth Class.

Ludwick Breds.
Stopel Lerk.
Mikel Divlor.
Samuel Jury.
Christian hofman.
george Bofendon.
Henry Woolf.
Mikel Shods.
george Lerk.
Henry Norler.
George Wilt.

I Do swear, on the Holy Evengilest of Almighty God: That the above list is a just and true state, of the Male White Inhabitants, residing in my District, agreeable to Law, and without fraud to the State, to the best of my knowledge.

MARTAIN WEAVER, Capt.

Sworn before me this
Twenty second Day of May 1782.

A TRUE AND EXACT LIST OF THE NAMES, OF EACH AND EVERY MALE WHITE PERSON, INHABITING OR RESIDING, WITHIN MY DISTRICT, IN THE EIGHT COMPANY, OF THE TENTH BATTALION OF LANCASTER COUNTY, MILITIA, BETWEEN THE AGE OF EIGHTEEN AND FIFTY-THREE YEARS. TAKEN FOR THE YEAR 1782. (c.)

Capt.
Jonathon McClure.

Lieu.
Daniel Hoofman.

Ens.
Jacob Snider.

Almonar.
James Crouch.

First Class.

Henrey Harris.
Fredrick Oberlander.
Mairtan Hemberly.
Christian Shartz.
Adam Miller.
Mark Snider.
Henrey Stoner.
Christian Grednor.

Second Class.

Christian Spade.
John Kissinger.
Conrod Toot.
Robert McWhortor.
James Harris.
Jacob Barkley.
Abraham Mayers.
Felty Walkor.

Third Class.

Adam Riter.
John Mitsker.
Christan King.
George Snagance.
Simon Kardon.
Henrey Moore.
John Wolfly.
Joseph Gregg.

Fourth Class.

Abraham Tarr.
George Frey.
Christan Seabaugh.
Samuel Parks.

George Lowman.
Joseph Florey.
John Bowman.
Patrick Flanagan.
Samuel Laird.
Anthony Hemberly.

Fifth Class.

George Gross.
Samuel Seratzey.
Petter Reckert.
Jacob King.
John Miller.
James Currey.
Micheal pressinger.
Thomas Moore.
John McCann.
Larance Smith.
William Laird.
John Foster.

Sixth Class.

Abraham Gross.
Nicklous Castle.
John Backestoz.
Phillip Shokey.
phillip Atley.
Henrey Miller.
Petter Shuster.
William Widnor.
Jacob Stricklor.
Daniel Dowdle.
George Consor.
Jacob Jones.
John Williams.

Seventh Class.

Phillip Graft.
Thomas Crabb.
petter Miller.
Christan Hepeck.
John parks.
John Lenning.
Abner Wickersham.
Hugh Meloy.
Jacob Wolfly.
Conrod Bumbaugh.
Henry Davis.
John Fritz.

Eighth Class.

Lodwick Hemberly.
Fredrick Zebernick.
Michael Gross.
patrick Scoot.
John Snider.
Emanuell Bullinger.
William Crabb.
George Toot.
John Barnut.
William Roland.
Fredrick Hubley.
Albright Skeer.

I Do swear, on the Holy Evengiliest of Almighty God: That the above list is a just and true state, of the Male White Inhabitants, residing in my District, agreeable to Law, and without fraud to the State, to the best of my knowledge. Sworn before me this 8th Day of May, 1782.

JONAHTHAN McCLURE, Capt.
MAX'LL CHAMBERS, S. Lt.

A RETURN OF OFFICERS ELLECTED IN THE TENTH BATALLION OF LANCASTER COUNTY MILITIA, AGREEABLE TO ORDERS PUBLISHED FOR THAT PURPOSE ON THE 15TH DAY OF APRIL 1783. (c.)

Field Officers.

Lieut. Colonel.

Thomas Murray.

Major.

John Gillchrist.

Captains.

1. Jonathan McLure.
2. William McLure, Ju'r
3. William Murray.
4. Martin Weaver.
5. Andrew Stewart.
6. George McMillen.
7. Hugh Robertson.
8. William Johnson.

Lieutenants.

1. Daniel Huffman.
2. Joseph Smith.
3. Thomas Sturgeon.
4. Matthew—Deibler.
5. Andrew Berryhill, Ju'r.
6. William McMillen.
7. Michael Limes.
8. George Clark.

Ensigns.

Jacob Snider.
William Steel.
John Bown, Jur.
Daniel Stiver.
Thomas Forster.
Samuel Berryhill.
William Stewart.
George Taylor.

I do Certify that the above Gentlemen were chosen officers in the 10th Batallion Lancaster County Militia, after returns made to me.

ADM. HUBLEY, Ju. S. Lt. Lt. Cy.

ELEVENTH BATTALION
LANCASTER COUNTY MILITIA.

COL. TIMOTHY GREEN'S BATTALION. (a.)

Colonel.

Timothy Green.

Lieutenant-Colonel.

Peter Hedrick.

Majors.

1st. John Rogers. 2d. Abraham Latcha.

Standard Bearer.

Richard Crawford.

Surgeon.

Dr. John Leidig.

CAPTAIN JAMES ROGERS' COMPANY. (a.)

The return of Capt. James Rogers' company of militia of Col. Timothy Green's Hanover Rifle Battalion of Lancaster County Associators, destined for the camp in the Jerseys, 6th June, 1776.

Captain.

James Rogers.

First Lieutenant.

James Wilson.

Second Lieutenant.

Henry McCormick.

Third Lieutenant.

Andrew Rogers.

Fourth Lieutenant.

Robert Martin.

Non-Commissioned Officers and Privates.

1. Richard Johnson.
2. James Ripeth.
3. James Porter.
4. Thomas McCord.
5. Thomas McNair.
6. Samuel Stewart.
7. James Ripeth.
8. Charles Hamilton.
9. John Ripeth.
10. Hugh Wilson.
11. Joseph Wilson.
12. James Beard.
13. James Wallace.
14. John Hutchison.
15. Hugh Ripeth.
16. James Wallace.
17. Duncan Sinclair.
18. William Starret.
19. John Trousdel.
20. John Skiles.
21. James Johnson.
22. Joseph Hutchison.
23. David Hays.
24. William Mitchel.
25. John Kilpatrick.
27. Thomas Martain.
26. Thomas Walker.
28. William Hall.
29. John Murray.
30. John Morrison.
31. John Woods.
32. William Thompson.
33. William Moor.
34. Hugh Kenan.
35. Alex. Martain.
36. Jeremiah Rogers.
37. James Hambel.
38. William Snodey.
39. William Kithcart.
40. John Kithcart.
41. Jonas Robinson.
42. James Stewart.
43. John McClelan.
44. William Hagerty.
45. Joseph Wilson.
46. Neal McCoy.
47. Joseph Park.
48. James McCluar.
49. William Snodgrass.
50. Francis McCluar.
51. Charles Porter.
52. John Templeton.
54. John Snodey.
55. Edward Warnach.
56. Chris Bumberger.
57. Hugh Glan.
58. James Roney.
59. John Starrat.
60. John McCormick.
61. Patrick McKnight.
62. James Duncan.
63. James Thompson.
64. David Porter.
65. Thomas Strean.
66. Hugh Donely.
67. Andrew Woods.
68. John Morlan.
69. David Calhoun.
70. Alex. Gaston.
71. James Donely.

72. Samuel Swan.
73. Robert Hill.
74. John Darbey.
75. Archibald Carson.
76. David Strean.
77. Thomas Davis.
78. Andrew Wilson.
79. William Rogers.
80. James Wilson.
81. William McMeen.
82. George Chapman.
83. George Bradsha.
84. John Rahe.
85. John Dunlop.
86. Randel McDanel.

A MUSTER ROLL OF CAPTAIN WILLIAM BROWN'S COMPANY OF MILITIA OF COLONEL TIMOTHY GREEN'S BATTALION OF LANCASTER COUNTY, DESTINED FOR THE CAMP IN THE JERSEYS—AUGUST YE 31ST 1776. (d.)

Captain.

William Brown.

Lieutenants.

1st. James Willson.
2d. Henry McCormick.
3d. Andrew Rogers.

Serjeants.

William Barnet.
John Hutchison.
James Willson.
James Stuart.

Corporals.

Charles Barr.
Alexr. Gaston.
David Porter.

Privates.

1. William Wright.
2. James Thompson.
3. Joseph Willson.
4. Jeremiah Rogers.
5. Thomas Martin.
6. Samuel Starrit.
7. John Starrit.
8. William Rogers.
9. Barnard McNitt.
10. James Willson.
11. William Crean.
12. James Johnston.
13. Robert Sturgeon.
14. William Wallace.
15. John Patterson.
16. John Cooper.
17. Joseph Hutchison.
18. John Jamison.
19. John Templeton.
20. John Cathcart.
21. John Snodgrass.
22. Francis McClure.

23. James McClure.
24. James Johnston.
25. James Stewart.
26. Charles Porter.
27. Mathew Snoddy.
28. David Watson.
29. Thomas McAnare.
30. Robert Freckelton.
31. Neil McCoy.
32. Leonard Umberger.
33. James McMullen.
34. William Thompson.
35. Hugh Kennin.
36. John Carter.
37. John McClure.
38. Martin McClure.
39. James Wallace.
40. Duncan Sinclair.
41. David Calhoon.
42. Robert Hill.
43. David Vance.

43 Men at 50 shillings each	£107.10.0
4 Serjeants at 50 shillings each	10. 0.0
3. Corporals at 50 shillings each	7.10.0
	£125.0.0

Mustered and passed before the Committee of Observation & Inspection in Lancaster the 31st of August 1776. And the above One hundred & twenty five Pounds paid to Captain William Brown to enable him to pay to his Men the advance of fifty Shillings each.

Test. · WILLE A.LEE, Chairman of Com. &c.
WM. BROWN, Capt.

A MUSTER ROLL OF CAPTAIN RICHARD McCOWN'S COMPANY OF MILITIA OF COLONEL TIMOTHY GREEN'S BATTALION OF LANCASTER COUNTY, DESTINED FOR THE CAMP IN THE JERSEYS—AUGUST YE 31st, 1776. (d.)

Captain.

Richard McQuown.

Lieutenants.

1st. Ambrose Crain.
2d. James McCreight.
3d. David Ramsey.

Serjeants.

John Thompson.
William Clark.
James Norris.

Corporals.

Edwd. Taite.
Alexr. Martin.
Simon Toole.

Privates.

1. William Hill.
2. Robert Greenlee.
3. Hugh Watt.
4. Henry Graham.
5. William Strain.
6. John Todd.
7. Samuel Brown.
8. Robert Poe.
9. John Rammage.
10. William McFarland.
11. William Brown.
12. John Torrence.
13. James Fleck.
14. William Brandon.
15. Robert Hill.
16. Robert McCully.
17. Josiah Espy.
18. John Campbell.
19. William Brown.
20. Robert Strain.
21. Adam Mark.
22. Michael Philippy.
23. James Porterfield.
24. Samuel Espy.
25. John Cunningham.
26. Patrick Mealy.
27. John McBride.
28. Thomas Fredrick.
29. James Long.
30. John Ward.
31. Andrew Killinger.
32. Mathew Crosier.
33. John Tully.
34. Peter Fox.
35. John Harper.
36. John Hedrick.
37. John Strain.
38. Jacob Graeff.

41 Privates, 50 shillings each	£102.10.0
3 Serjeants, 50 shillings each	7.10.0
3 Corporals, 50 shillings each	7.10.0
47 Men's advance	£117.10.0

Mustered and passed before the Committee of Observation & Inspection in Lancaster the 31st of August 1776. And the above One Hundred & seventeen pounds ten Shillings to Captain Richard McCown's to enable him to pay to his Men the advance of fifty Shillings each.

Test. WILLE. ATLEE, Chairman of Committee.
RICHARD McQUOWN, Cap.

O A 39. Jacob Graff.
40. George Espy.
41. John McQuown.

A MUSTER ROLL OF CAPTAIN THOMAS KOPPENHEFFER'S COMPANY OF MILITIA OF COLONEL TIMOTHY GREEN'S BATTALION OF LANCASTER COUNTY ON THEIR MARCH FOR THE CAMP IN THE JERSEYS. (d.)

2d Major ....Abraham Latcha.
Surgeon ....John Lidig.

With the Company.

Capt. Thomas Coppenheffer.
1st Lieutent. Peter Bridebill.
2d. Lieutent. John Harchenrider.

Serjeants.

John Fierbend.
George Beasore.

Drummer.

John Dubbs.

Fifer.

William Hedrick.

Privates.

No.
1. Baltser Baumgartner.
2. Adam Baumgartner.
3. Christophe Frank.
4. Jacob Claman.
5. John Baumgartner.
6. Nicholas Snider.
7. Jacob Winder.
8. Adam Titler.
9. Jacob Musser.
10. George Frank.
11. Nicholas Bruner.
12. Nicholas Boob.
13. Nicholas Boor.
14. Christian Fox.
15. Henry Mark.
16. John McBride.
17. Peter Bridebill, junr.
18. Daniel Weaver.
19. John Weaver.
20. William Snider.
21. Henry Shell.
22. Christian Stuckey.
23. Martin Albright.
24. John Miller.
25. Mathias Baker.
26. Michael Feitiu.
27. Adam Henig.
28. Fredrick Henig.

29. John Fox.
30. Adam Weantling.
31. George Bombarger.
32. Michael Maurer.
33. John Huber.
34. Alexander Kidd.
35. Michael Brown.

35 privates, 50 shillings each	£87.10.0
2 Serjeants, 50 shillings each	5. 0.0
1 Drummer	2.10.0
1 Fifer	2.10.0
Advance money paid	£97.10.0

Mustered and passed before the Committee of Observation & Inspection in Lancaster the 12th of August 1776. And the £97.10.0 advance Money paid to Capt. Thomas Koppenheffer as p. this Receipt.

Test. WILLI ATLEE, Chairman of Committee
& their Treasurer & paymaster.
THOMAS KOPPENHEFFER.

Deserters from Capt. Koppenheffer's Co'y.

Baltzer Baumgartner.
Adam Baumgartner.
Adam Titler.
Jacob Musser.
John Dubbs.

they live in Hannover Township near Adam Harper's.

BATTALIONS NOT STATED.

LANCASTER COUNTY MILITIA.

CAPTAIN ROLAND'S COMPANY—1775. (a.)

The Associators of Leacock township, Lancaster county, belonging to Captain Roland's Company. Associated 5th day of July, 1775.

James Scott [in Leacock].
Henry Swope.
George Lyne.
Abraham Lyne.
Stofle Weaver.
Sicmont Shower.
Daniel Swope.
Joseph Biggart.
David Benter.
William Lyne.
Peter Eby.
Peter, Eby, Jr.
Jacob Hamer.
Emanuel Carpenter [of Earl township].
William McCormick [listed].
John Creake [in Lampeter township].
William Shellar [in Lampeter township].
John Eby.
Jacob Swope.
David Lyne.
Henry Foltz, Jr.
John Maxvel.
Bolsar Rombarger.
Marteen Maxvel, Jr.
James Hamilton.
Henry Wenger [Sener].
Peter Barngut.
John Roland.
John Moor.
Adam Swope.
Henry Foltz.
George Finfrock.
Martin Hillar.
Adam Rombarger.
Jacob Bear [listed].

John Botts.
Adam Hoofstetter.
Samuel Eby.
John Hiller.
Henry Eby.
Patrick Connel [of Leacock township].
John Scott [in Lampeter township].
David Crawford [in Lampeter township].
George Lambert.
John Snavely.
Jacob Barngut.
Aphraem Bear.
Philip Shower.
Hugh McDonel.
Jacob Maxvel.
George Bard.
James Kearns [listed].
John Foltz.

Endorsed. "Mr. JOHN FERREE, CORNEL."

CAPTAIN JACOB KLOTZ'S COMPANY. (a.)

Of Colonel Matthias Slough's Battalion of the Flying Camp, July 8, 1776.

Lieutenant.

Ludwig Meyer.

Privates.

Laurence Manning.
George Clay.
Nicholas Hutchison.
William Long.
Henry Illiger.
Jacob Hacketswiller.
Andrew Bower.
John Hysinger.
Anthony Ament.
Jacob Moss.
Jacob Baxler.
Jacob Hustater.
John Laub.
Matthias Keller.
Henry Miller.
John Burg.

Christopher Shertzer.
Hugh McGloughlin.
John Wygant.
Andrew Shrenk.
Jacob Brandt.
Philip Kutz.
John Mark.
George Wolfe.
John Bellough.
Stephen Rine.
John Philips.
Edward Kindry.
Christian Puttenstone.
David Dukart.
James Turner.
Christian Eberman.
Peter Galley.
Joseph McCurdy.
Philip Grupe.
Barnet Martin.
James Burk.
Adam Goodingberger.
Samuel Carson.
Michael Trislar.
Jacob Springer .
Philip Klime.
John Johnson.
John Parcifull.
Abraham Ribblet.
John Favourite.
George Wallace.
Henry Bose.
Jacob Ferree.
Jacob Lubly.
Adam Dambach.
John Weller.
Daniel Glazier.
Benjamin Fickle.
Christopher Bower.
Peter Dunkle.
William Keller.
John Shertzer.
Edward Madden.
John Funk.
Adam Lohrman.
Christopher Ling.
John Hoffman.
John Murray.
John Dougherty.
Alexander Hill.
Zacharias Hill.
Simon Yandes.
Sebastian McWart.
Thomas Williams.
Ludwick Miller.
Matthias Hoke.
Christian Sternman.
John Meyer.
John Rickle.
James Burace.
Casper Peter.
James Steward.
John Fisler.
Christian Grube.
John Rutzel.
Robert McCurdy.

A MUSTER ROLL OF CAPTAIN JOHN BOYD'S COMPANY OF MILITIA OF COLONEL THOMAS PORTER'S BATTALION OF LANCASTER COUNTY ON THEIR MARCH FOR THE CAMP IN THE JERSEYS. (d.)

Captain.

John Boyd.

Lieuts.

1st. David Reed. 2d. Benjamin Willson.

Ensign.

Peter Simpson.

Serjeants.

Samuel Willson.
Samuel Snodgrass.
James Savage.
James Moore.

Privates.

1. James Moore.
2. James Johnston.
3. John Cunningham.
4. John Reed.
5. William Moor.
6. Robert Snodgrass.
7. William Kennedy.
8. John Roggers.
9. James Snodgrass.
10. Joseph Willson.
11. James Steel.
12. William Steel.
13. Samuel Elliott.
14. William Brown.
15. Joseph Reed.
16. James Blair.
17. John Simpson.
18. Henry Wales.
19. Duncan Quigly.
20. Gabriel McKnight.
21. James McCall.
22. James Barns.
23. Moses Wilson.
24. Robert Snodgrass.
25. Robert McCurdy.
26. John Craig.
27. Gregory Farmer.
28. Fredrick Keble.
29. John Smith.
30. Andrew Douglass.

30 Privates, 50 shillings each £75.0.0
4 Serjeants, 50 shillings each 10.0.0

Advance money .... £85.0.0 paid.

Mustered and passed by & before the Committee of Observation & Inspection in Lancaster the 13th August 1776. And the £85.0.0 advance money paid to Capt. John Boyd to pay his Serjeants & Privates their advance p. Receipt.

WILL. J. ATLEE, Chairman of Committee.
JOHN BOYD, Capt.

A MUSTER ROLL OF CAPT. THOMAS WHITESIDE'S COMPANY OF MILITIA OF COLONEL THOMAS PORTERS BATTALION OF LANCASTER COUNTY, ON THEIR MARCH FOR THE CAMP IN THE JERSEYS. (d.)

Captain.

Thomas Whitesides.

Lieutenant.

2d. Robert Allison.

Ensign.

William McDowel.

Privates.

1. John Brooks.
2. William Patterson.
3. James Ramsey.
4. John McGahen.
5. Samuel Cooper.
6. David McCoomb.
7. Thomas Patterson.
8. James Patterson.
9. John Atchison.
10. Thomas Reed.
11. James McElvain.
12. Samuel Rheah.
13. William Mooney.
14. Fredrick Mcferson.
15. John Cooper.
16. James Cannon.
17. Thomas McDowel.
18. Abraham Whiteside.
19. Samuel Criswell.
20. Samuel White.
21. John Warnock.
22. Oliver Caldwell.
23. William McDawel.
24. John Pennel.
25. James Reed.
26. James McGraw.
27. James Watson.
28. John Miller.
29. Samuel McKenny.
30. Andrew Ritchey.
31. Edward Dugan.
32. James Stewart.

33. John Plunket.
34. James Black.
35. John Tannyhill.
36. Nathan Tannyhill.
37. James Marshall.
38. Robert Moore.
39. James Campbell.
40. John Mitchell.
41. John Neeper.
42. Thomas McDowell, junr.
43. Owen Murphy.
44. John Grimes.
45. Joseph McCrery.

45 privates, 50 shillings each £112.10.0

Mustered and passed by and before the Committee of Observation & Inspection in Lancaster the 13th of August 1776. And the £112.10.0 advance Money paid to Capt. Thomas Whitesides to pay his privates their advance—as p. Receipt.

Test. WILL J. ATLEE, Chairman of Committee.
THOMAS WHITESIDE, Capt.

A MUSTER ROLL OF A COMPANY LATELY COMMANDED BY CAPTAIN JAMES WATSON IN COLONEL THOMAS PORTER'S BATTALION OF LANCASTER COUNTY, NOW UNDER THE COMMAND OF LIEUTT. JOHN PATTON—ON THEIR MARCH FOR THE CAMP IN THE JERSEYS. (d.)

Lieutenant.

John Patton.

Drummer.

Robert Hamilton.

Privates.

1. Thomas Clark.
2. William McAdams.
3. John McCray.
4. John Reed.
5. Joseph Neel.
6. James McDermod.
7. Robert Snodgrass.
8. Robert Caldwell.
9. Patrick Campble.
10. Robert McEldowney.
11. John Stephenson.
12. John Caldwell.
13. Robert Brotherton.
14. William Brotherton.
15. Hugh Caldwell.
16. John Caldwell, Senr.
17. James Long.
18. Robert Long.
19. Jno. McMunigle.
20. Saml. McCullough.

21. John McCullough.
22. David McCullough.
23. James McWherry.
24. James Duncan.
25. James Johnston.
26. James Patterson.
27. William McMiller.
28. Thomas Culley.
29. Thomas Robertson.
30. John Robertson.
31. Alexander Orr.
32. John McMiller.
33. William Sheilds.

33 Privates at 50 shillings each £82.10.0
Drummer 2.10.0

£85. 0.0

No.
34. James Pagan.
35. Archibald Pagan.
36. Richard Pollock.
37. James McCants.
38. James Pagan, junr.

5 privates at 50 shillings each ....£12.10.0 advance paid.

Mustered and passed before the Committee of Observation & Inspection in Lancaster the 13th of August 1776—And the £85.0.0 advance Money paid to Lieutenant John Patton to pay above privates & Drummer their advance—as p. Rect.

Test. WILL. J. ATLEE, Chairman of Commitee &c.
JOHN PATTON, Lieut.

Mustered and passed before the Committee of Observation & Inspection in Lancaster the 15th of August 1776—And the above twelve Pound & ten Shillings paid to Lieutenant John Patton to enable him to advance to the privates above named fifty shillings p. man.

Test. WILLIAM ATLEE, Chairman of Committee &c.
JOHN PATTON, Lieut.

A MUSTER ROLL OF CAPTAIN JAMES MORRISON'S COMPANY OF MILITIA OF COLONEL THOMAS PORTER'S BATTALION OF ASSOCIATORS IN LANCASTER COUNTY —DESTINED FOR THE CAMP IN THE JERSEYS. (d.)

Captain.
James Morrison.

Lieutenants.
Robert King. Thomas Neal.

Privates.

No.

1. Hugh Rippey.
2. Samuel Morrison.
3. John Campbell.
4. Joshua Nelson.
5 John Robinson.
6. Joseph Ball.
7. James Neal.
8. William Long.
9. William Penny.
10. James Mulhollan.
11. Robert McCullough.
12. Hugh Penny.
13. Isaac Nelson.
14. Ephraim Hughey.
15. William McLoughlin.
16. Alexander McKnaught.
17. David Cooper.
18. Samuel Martin.
19. Robert Wallis.
20. David Mitchel.
21. Archibald Ankrim.
22. Sampson Smith.
23. James Mitchell.
24. James Marshall.
25. David Crawford.
26. Robert Steen.
27. Andrew Tegart.
28. Samuel Willey.
29. David Mahon.
30. John Mahon.
31. James Breckenridge.
32. James Long.
33. John Beggs.
34. Fredrick Shever.
35. James David.
36. James Buchannan.
37. Samuel Eager.
38. Samuel Gregg.
39. James Steel.
40. John Jones.
41. John Gordon.
42. Alexander Boyd.
43. Peter Flangan.
44. Hugh Holliday.
45. John Dennis.

45 privates, 50 shillings each £112.10.0

94.10.0 pd. G. McCullough Esq. for Capt. Morrison &c which he received.

18. 0.0 pd. Capt. Morrison & gave him up Mr. McCullough's Rect. as so much Cash.

£112.10.0

Mustered and passed before the Committee of Observation & Inspection in Lancaster the 15th of August 1776. And the above One Hundred and twelve pound & ten Shillings paid by Wm. Atlee to Capt. James Morrison to advance to his privates 50 shillings p. man.

Test. WILLM. ATLEE, Chairman of Committee &c.
JAS. MORRISON, Capt.

A MUSTER ROLL OF A DETACHMENT OF PART OF CAPTAIN WILLIAM STEEL'S COMPANY OF MILITIA OF COLONEL THOMAS PORTER'S BATTALION OF ASSOCIATORS IN LANCASTER COUNTY—UNDER THE COMMAND ENSIGN SAMUEL McENTIER—DESTINED FOR THE CAMP IN THE JERSEYS. (d.)

Ensign.
Samuel McEntier.

Privates.

1. John Long.
2. John Maxwell.
3. William Maxwell.
4. Aaron Black.
5. Casper Bowman.
6. James Porter.
7. William Porter.
8. Isaac Brubaker.
9. Jacob May.
10. James Carson.
11. Adam Nell.
12. John Simpson.

12 privates, 50 shillings p. man £30.0.0

Mustered and passed before the Committee of Observation & Inspection in Lancaster the 15th of August 1776—And the above Thirty Pounds paid to Ensign Samuel McEntier to enable him to advance to the privates above named fifty Shillings p. man.

Test. WILLI. ATLEE, Chairman of Com &c.
SAMUEL McONTIER, Ensign.

A MUSTER ROLL OF PART OF CAPTAIN DORRINGTON WILLSONS COMPANY OF MILITIA OF COLNEL THOMAS PORTERS BATTALION OF ASSOCIATORS IN LANCASTER COUNTY, UNDER THE COMMAND OF LIEUTENANT JOHN ECKMAN—DESTINED FOR THE CAMP IN YE JERSEYS. (d.)

Lieutenant.
John Eckman.

Ensign.
William Brown.

Serjeants.

John Moderwell. Stophel Byerley.

Privates.

1. John Leckey.
2. James Miller.
3. John Myer.
4. James Sheerer.
5. Martin Eckman.
6. Thomas Young.
7. James Duncan.
8. Robert Patterson.
9. John Ramsey.
10. Andrew Frank.
11. John Brown.
12. Joseph Work.
13. Martin Shope.

13 Privates at 50 shillings each	£32.10.0
2 Sergeants, 50 shillings each	5. 00.
	£37.10.0

Mustered and passed before the Committee of Observation & Inspection in Lancaster the 15th of August 1776—And the above £37.10.0 paid to Lieutenant John Eckman to enable him to advance 50 shillings p. man to the above Serjeants & Privates.

Test. WILLI. ATLEE, Chairman of Committee &c.
JOHN ECKMAN, Lieutenant.

A MUSTER ROLL OF PART OF CAPTAIN ROBERT CAMPBEL'S COMPANY OF MILITIA OF COLONEL THOMAS PORTER'S BATTALION OF LANCASTER COUNTY—DESTINED FOR THE CAMP IN THE JERSEYS. (d.)

Captain.
Robert Campbell.

Lieutenant.
2d. James Walker.

Privates.

1. James Jamison.
2. Andrew Walker.
3. John Walker.
4. Robert Ferguson.

5. Joseph Heslet.
6. Samuel Jamison.
7. Hugh McConkey.
8. Charles Harra.
9. Daniel Platteberger.
10. John Atchison.
11. William Atchison.
12. David Killough.
13. William Anderson.
14. Isaac Peters.
15. Daniel Peters.
16. John Creiton.
17. James Brice.
18. Hugh Patton.
19. Robert Willes.
20. Daniel Oharra.
21. Joseph Wilson.
22. Arthur McQuade.
23. John Perry.

22. Privates, 50 shillings each £57.10.0

Mustered and passed before the Committee of Observation & Inspection in Lancaster the 15th of August 1776—And the above Fifty seven Pounds and ten Shillings paid to Capt. Robert Campbell to enable him to advance to the privates above named Fifty Shillings p. man.

Test. WILL. ATLEE, Chairman of Com. &c.
ROBERT CAMPBELL, Capt.

A MUSTER ROLL OF THREE DETACHMENTS FROM THE COMPANY'S OF CAPTAINS ROSS, JOHNSTON AND PAXTON, BELONGING TO COLONEL THOMAS PORTER'S BATTALION OF LANCASTER COUNTY MILITIA—UNDER THE COMMAND OF LIEUTENANT JOHN TWEED, LIEUTENANT JOSHUA ANDERSON & LIEUTENANT JOHN RAMSEY—DESTINED FOR THE CAMP IN THE JERSEYS. (d.)

John Tweed, 1st Lieut. to Capt. Johnston.
Joshua Anderson, 1st Lieut. to Capt. Ross.
John Ramsey, 2d Lieut. to Capt. Paxton.
John Gahey, Ensign to Capt. Paxton.
Serjeant, Samuel Patterson.

Privates.

1. Thomas Anderson.
2. John McGrath.
3. William Kelley.
4. James McAtagart.
5. Robert Gregory.
6. Alexander Huston.
7. Robert Andrews.
8. John Kerr.
9. Robert Hendry.
10. Thomas Scott.

11. Andrew McCartney.
12. Mathew Park.
13. John Gaveley.
14. John Hanna.
15. John Latta.
16. Nathaniel Coulter.
17. John Scott.
18. William McConnel.
19. James Walker.
20. John Bard.
21. John Briggs.
22. William Longhead.
23. Jeremiah Cavin.
24. Stephen Heard, junr.
25. John Heard, junr.
26. Henry Pickle.
27. Joseph Benson.
28. William Henry.
29. John McWilliams.
30. Hugh Willson.
31. William Karr.
32. Henry Rockey.

32 Privates, 50 shillings each	£82. 0.0
1 Serjeant	2.10.0
	£82.10.0

Mustered and passed before the Committee of Observation & Inspection in Lancaster the 19th August 1776—And the above Eighty two Pounds & ten Shillings paid to Lieutenant Tweed, Anderson & Ramsey to advance to their men.

Test. WILLI. ATLEE, Chairman of Committee.
JOHN TWEED, JOSHUA ANDERSON, JNO. RAMSEY.

CAPTAIN HUGH PEDAN'S COMPANY. (a.)

A muster roll of Captain Hugh Pedan's company of militia of Colonel Bartrem Galbraith's battalion, Lancaster county, on the march for the camp in the Jerseys.

Captain.
Hugh Pedan.

First Lieutenant.
Joseph Work.

Second Lieutenant.
David Hays.

Ensign.

William Wilson.

Sergeants.

James Wilson. Benjamin Walker.

Corporal.

John McCauley.

Drummer.

Daniel Cowhick.

Fifer.

George Ratchel.

Privates.

John Conn.
William Lindsay.
Adam Ross.
Robert Moore.
James Cook.
Samuel Cook.
Samuel McClung.
James Scott.
John Parks.
Patrick Burns.
Jacob Hardy.
James MeLoney.
Robert Ballance.
Robert Carrey.
James Livingston.
William Ray.
James Clingman.
Samuel McCracken.
James Parks.
John Sculley.
Roger McFeley.
Patrick Hacket.
John Carrol.
James Cloon.
Hugh Spear.
Thomas Mentz.
Richard Allison.
Barnard Savage.
James Fligate.
Cornelius Bogle.
James Fulton.
Abraham Mitchel.
James Mitchel.
John Emmit.
John Mathews.
Timothy Minchan.

Mustered and passed before and by the Committee of Observation and Inspection, in Lancaster, the 12th of August, 1776, and the £102.10.0 advance money paid to Capt. Hugh Pedan, as per his receipt.

Test, WILL. ATLEE,
Chairman.
HUGH PEDAN,
Captain.

CAPTAIN ANDREW GRAFF'S COMPANY. (a.)

A report of Captain Andrew Graff's company, mustered at Philadelphia, July 16th, 1776.

Captain.

Andrew Graff.

First Lieutenant.

Sebastian Graff.

Second Lieutenant.

Mathew Graff.

Ensigns.

Edward Cowen. John Mitler.

Sergeants.

George Weiss, discharged. Henry Stauff.
Michael Layb. Andrew Geiss.

Corporals.

Geo. Luttman, sick at Trenton.
Henry Stoutter.
Michael Reinhart.
Henrich Yost.

Drummer.

John Singer.

Fifer.

Peter Shindel.

Rank and File.

George Ackerman.
John Bard.
William Flick.
Anthony Ginder.

George Hubetsmiller.
John Johnston.
Marcus Young, Jr.
Matthew Roub.
Jonas Metzgar, sick at camp.
Christian O'Donald.
Jacob Sands.
George Sands.
Henrich Scbaun.
Daniel Heidly.
Joseph Stumpt.
Elijah Hardy, to the Flying Camp.
John Patton, to the Flying Camp.
George Pintzel, to the Flying Camp.
Ernst Born.
Stoffel Doebler.
George Etter.
John Fisher.
John Getz.
Jacob Gross.
Philip Hardt.
Peter Hitzelberger.
Thomas Koutz.
Adam Pritzar.
John Stron.
George Shweitzer.
Henry Wagner.
Charles Hamilton.
Christopher Reigart.
Casper Brunner.
Abraham Braun.
Charles Jones, app. gunsmith.
Robert Jones, app. gunsmith.
George Bauer, app. gunsmith.
James Reed, app. gunsmith.
Jacob Reigart.
John Gander, app. gunsmith.
Philip Wolfheimer, app. gunsmith.
George O'Donnald.
William Ripper.
Jacob Martin.
Frederick Woeler.

CAPTAIN ANDREW GRAFF'S COMPANY. (a.)

[We have not the date of return of the following, but presume it was a year or two subsequent to the preceding.]

Capt. Graff's company, Lancaster county militia for boarding of said company by G. Graff.

No.	Name	£	
19,299.	Conard Carver,	1	
300.	Thomas Johnson,	1	
1.	William Gehoom,	1	
2.	Patrick Darby,	1	
3.	Charles Carver,	1	
4.	John Sherron,	1	
5.	Lawrence Dowling,	1	
6.	Robert Foster,	1	
7.	Alex. Foster,	1	
8.	James Wilson,	1	
9.	Peter Sefer,	1	
10.	Conard Blunkert,	1	
11.	Christian Blunkert,	1	
12.	John McMahon,	1	
13.	John Dougherty,	1	
14.	Levi Ehr,	1	
15.	Michael Bright,	1	
16.	Morris McGaghan	1	
17.	Christian Drumon,	1	
18.	Henry Guske,	1	
19.	John Wall,		10
20.	Frederick Charles,		10
21.	John McKinny,		10
22.	James Flory,		10
23.	John Flory,		10
19,324.	Thomas Danyhill,		10
5.	Benjamin Amwage,		10
6.	Samuel Blackburn,		10
7.	William McCrackan,		10
8.	Jacob Brown,		
9.	William English,		10
30.	Benjamin Pervile,		10
1.	William Boyer,		10

2. James Pratt,		10
3. William Weiss,	1	
4. Hugh Doyle,		10
5. Cornelius Diller,		10
6. John Ferguson,		10
7. Hugh Shannon,		10
8. David Brady,		10
9. Patrick Day,	1	
19,340. William Green,		10
	32	40

Amount settled, March 18, 1791.
Certificate opened, July 14, 1791.

Capt. Graff,	2 W...	2
22 men,	2	..22
20 men,	1	..10
		34

Certificate No. 19,299
19,341

A MUSTER ROLL OF A DETACHMENT OF CAPT. ROBERT McKEE'S COMPANY OF MILITIA OF COLONEL GALBREATH'S BATTALION OF LANCASTER COUNTY—ON THEIR MARCH FOR THE CAMP IN THE JERSEYS. (d.)

Capt.

Robert McKee.

Lieut.

2d. Hugh Hale.

No Serjeant—no Corporal—no Drum—no Fife.

Privates.

No.
1. Joseph Chambers.
2. John Riddle.
3. Patrick Lynch.
4. Alexander Dean.
5. John Gingery.
6. William McCoy.

7. Michael Kerr.
8. Charles Kean.
9. James McKee.
10. Fredrick Sellers.
11. James Caruthers.
12. James Fegan.
13. John Kerr.
14. James Brown.
15. John Dean.
16. John Hagan.
17. Thomas Ogle.
18. William Campble.
19. George Allen.
20. Peter Agnew.
21. John McGowan.
22. James Kennedy.
23. Robert Rea.
24. Barny Queen.
25. Samuel Clark.

25 privates, 50 shillings each £62.10.0

Mustered and passed before the Committee of Observation & Inspection in Lancaster the 13th of August 1776 and the £62.10.0 advance Money paid to Capt. Robert McKee to pay to the privates—as p. his Receipt.

Test. WILL. ATTLEE, Chairman of Committee
paymaster &c.

ROBT. McKEE, Capt.

A MUSTER ROLL OF CAPTAIN ROBERT McCALLEN'S COMPANY OF MILITIA OF COLONEL BARTREM GALBREATH'S BATTALION OF LANCASTER COUNTY—20TH AUG. 1776—DESTINED FOR THE CAMP IN THE JERSEYS. (d.)

Captain.

Robert McCallen.

Lieutenants.

1st. Mathew Hay.   2d. David McQueen.

Ensign.

Thomas McCallen.

Serjeants.

John Wear.   James Morrison.

Corporals.

James Kelley. Andrew Hunter.

Drumer.

John O'Neal.

Privates.

1. Joseph Falkner.
2. Samuel Johnston.
3. Andrew Duncan.
4. Robert Hay.
5. Robert Buck.
6. John McCallen.
7. Thomas Espy.
8. Samuel Campble.
9. James Willson.
10. John Campble.
11. James Willson, jur.
12. Robert Messer.
13. Alexander Fulton.
14. William Farmer.
15. David Forster.
16. William Harvey.
17. William Shaw.
18. Robert Allen.
19. John Farmer.
20. William Shearer.
21. David Hay.
22. Walter Clark.
23. David McDonald.
24. John Patton.
25. Anthony Buck.
26. James Walker.
27. Alexander Long.
28. Peter Sheilds.
29. George Bell.
30. John Donald.
31. John Rowan.
32. Hugh Hamilton.
33. James Kennedy.
34. John McClintock.
35. James Johnston.
36. James Wright.
37. James Queen.

37 Privates, 50 shillings each	£ 92.10.0
2 Serjeants, 50 shillings each	5. 0.0
2 Corporals, 50 shillings each	5. 0.0
1 Drummer	2.10.0
42 Men's advance	£105. 0.0

Mustered and passed before the Committee of Observation & Inspection in Lancaster the 20th of August 1776—And the above One Hundred & five pound paid to Capt. Robert McCallen to advance to his Men fifty Shillings each.

Test. WILLIM ATLEE, Chairman of Committee &c.
ROBERT McCALLEN, Capt.

A RETURN OF THE LOSSES SUSTAINED BY CAPT. JAMES WATSON'S COMPANY IN COL. JAMES CUNNINGHAM'S BATTALION, (FLYING CAMP,) COMMANDED BY MAJOR WILLIAM HAYS, ON LONG ISLAND, THE 27TH DAY OF AUGUST, 1776. (a.)

Men's Names.	Guns.	Blankets.	Knapsacks.	Cat-boxes.			
James Watson,	......	1	......	......	£1	2	6
William Steel,	......	1	......	......	1	2	6
John Steel,	1	1	......	......	5	8	
Alexander Scott,	......	1	1	......		15	
William Robb,	......	1	......	......		17	
William Walker,	......	1	......	......	1		
James Calhoon,	......	1	......	......	1		
John McKnight,	......	1	......	......	1	2	6
Andrew Cummings,	1	1	......	......	4	8	
John Polk,	......	1	......	......	1		
John Pegan,	......	1	......	......		10	
John Thompson,	......	1	......	......	1		
John Clark,	......	1	......	......		12	
Daniel Carmichael,	1	1	......	......	3	17	6
Hugh Caldwell,	1	1	......	......	4	3	
John Miller,	......	1	......	......	1		
Pettis Hanlin,	1	1	......	......	3	17	6
Robert Black,	1	1	......	......	4	17	6
John Post,	1	1	......	......	6	5	
Samuel Ankrim,	......	1	......	......		18	
William McGriger,	......	1	1	1	1	15	
					£47	1	

Lancaster County, ss:

Before me, the subscriber, one of the justices of the peace in and for said county, came William Steel, first lieutenant of Captain James Watson's company of the Flying Camp, who, on his solemn oath, deposeth and saith that the above amount of forty-seven pounds one shilling, as it stands above stated, is just and true, and that he the deponant has never received any satisfaction for the same nor any part thereof in any ways whatsoever.

Sworn and subscribed this 24th day of November, 1779.

WILLIAM STEEL.

Before JOSEPH MILLER.

(c.) This is to Certify that Alexander Mars has served as Millitia man, in my Comp'y in the Room of John Shenk, in the 2d Class of Lancaster Militia and is hereby Discharg'd by me.

JACOB KRUG, Capt.

November 1st, 1777.

(c.) This is to Certify that Jacob Blythe has Served as substitute in the Room of John Bassler of Manheim Township, in my Comp'y in the 2d Class of Lancaster County Militia, Commanded by Col'l James Watson, Esq'r, from the 24th day of Sept'r to the 24th Day of Oct'r, 1777.

Certify'd as above by

JACOB KRUG, Capt'n.

Lancas'r, Nov'r 10th, 1777.

(c.) This is to Certify Ulrick Tarr Having Honestly Serv'd in the Militia in the 3d Class as a Substitute for Mathias Graeff from the 24th Day of August till the 24th Day of Octo'r which being the full Dower of Two Months he is therefore Discharg'd from my Compa'y as wittess my hand this Date above Mentioned.

JOHN GRAEFF, Capt.

(c.) These Presents certify, that Christopher Crawford, Esquire, Sub-Lieutenant of the County of Lancaster, hath provided, hired and procured Jacob Blyth of the same County, Yeoman, to serve as a Substitute in the Second Class of Militia, of Lancaster County, in the Commonwealth of Pennsylvania, for and in the Place of John Bassler, in Manheim towsep, in the County aforesaid, for which Service the said Jacob Blyth is to have and receive the Sum of Forty Pounds lawful Money of Pennsylvania. And the said Jacob Blyth doth hereby acknowledge and declare, that he hath entered as a Substitute for the said John Bassler in the Second Class of the Militia aforesaid, and will well and faithfully serve and perform his duty as a Soldier therein, agreeable to the Laws of the said Commonwealth and subject to the rules and regulations of the said Commonwealth, in such Cases made and provided. And that he hath received, from the said Christopher Crawford, Esquire, Forty Pounds.

In Witness whereof as well the said Sub. Lieutenant, as the said Jacob Blyth have hereto set their Hands, the 24 Day of September, 1777.

(Signature mutilated.)

These Presents certify, that Christopher Crawford, Esquire, Sub. Lieutenant of the County of Lancaster, hath provided, hired and procured Phillip Gallaben of the same County, Yeoman, to serve as a Substitute in the First Class of Militia, of Lancaster County, in the Commonwealth of Pennsylvania, for and in the Place of John Knisle of Manheim town Sep, in the County aforesaid, for which Service the said Phillip Gallahen is to have and receive the Sum of Fourty Pounds lawful Money of Pennsylvania. And the said Phillip Gallaher doth hereby acknowledge and declare, that he hath entered as a Substitute for the said John Knisle in the First Class of the Militia aforesaid, and will well and faithfully serve and perform his duty as a Soldier therein, agreeable to the Laws of the said Commonwealth, and subject to the Rules and Regulations of the said Commonwealth, in such Cases made and provided. And that he hath received, from the said Christopher Crawford, Esquire, the Sum of Ten Pounds in Part of the said John Kuisle.

In Witness whereof as well the said Sub. Lieutenant, as the said Phillip Gallahen have hereto set their Hands, the 22 Day of September, 1777.

(Signature mutilated.)

CHRISTOPH MAYER'S Liut.
JOHN DEHUFF.

These Presents certify, that Christopher Crawford, Esquire, Sub. Lieutenant of the County of Lancaster, hath provided, hired and procured Georg Good of the same County, Yeoman, to serve as a Substitute in the First Class of Militia, of Lancaster County, in the Commonwealth of Pennsylvania, for and in the Place of John Maberts of the Borough of Lancaster, in the County aforesaid, for which Service the said George Good is to have and receive the Sum of Forty Fife pounds lawful Money of Pennsylvania. And thé said George Good doth hereby acknowledge and declare, that he hath entered as a Substitute for the said John Maberts in the first class of the Militia aforesaid, and will well and faithfully serve and perform his duty as a Soldier therein, agreeable to the Laws of the said Commonwealth, and subject to the Rules and Regulations of the said Commonwealth, in such Cases made and provided. And that he hath received, from the said Christopher Crawford, Esquire, the Sum of Ten pounds in Part of the said Forty Fife pound.

In Witness whereof as well the said Sub. Lieutenant, as the said George Good have hereto set their Hands, the Sixth Day of Septembr, 1777.

(Signature mutilated.)

Witness present.
MICHAEL APP, Captn.
CHRISTOPH MAYER'S.

These Presents certify, that Christopher Crawford, Esquire, Sub-Lieutenant of the County of Lancaster, hath provided, hired and procured Jacob Grob of the same county, Yeoman, to serve as a Substitute in the First Class of Militia, of Lancaster County, in the Commonwealth of Pennsylvania, for and in the Place of Jacob Hogstater of the Borough of Lancaster, in the County aforesaid, for which Service the said Jacob Grob is to have and receive the Sum of Fourty Pounds lawful Money of Pennsylvania. And the said Jacob Groh doth hereby acknowledge and declare that he hath entered as a Substitute for the said Jacob Hogstater in the First Class of the Militia aforesaid, and will well and faithfully serve and perform his duty as a Soldier therein, agreeable to the Laws of the said Commonwealth, and subject to the Rules and Regulations of the said Commonwealth, in such Cases made and provided. And that he hath received, from the sa'd Christopher Crawford, Esquire, the Sum of Then Pound in Part of the said Jacob Hogstater.

In Witness whereof as well the said Sub-Lieutenant, as the said Jacob Groh have hereto set their Hands, the 11 Day of September 1777.

Witness Present
MICHAEL APP, Capt. (Signature Mutilated.)

These Presents certify, that Christopher Crawford, Esquire, Sub. Lieutenant of the County of Lancaster, hath provided, hired and procured George Heckeswiller of the same County, Yeoman, to serve as a Substitute in the First Class of Militia, of Lancaster County, in the Commonwealth of Pennsylvania, for and in the Place of John Brubacher, Manhim towsip, in the County aforesaid, for which Service the said George Heckeswiller is to have and receive the Sum of Fourty Pounds lawful Money of Pennsylvania. And the said George Heckeswiller doth hereby acknowledge and declare, that he hath entered as a Substitute for the said John Brubacher in the First Class of the Militia aforesaid, and will well and faithfully serve and perform his duty as a Soldier therein, agreeable to the Laws of the said Commonwealth, and subject to the Rules and Regulations of the said Commonwealth, in such Cases made and provided. And that he hath received, from the said Christopher Crawford, Esquire, the Sum of Ten Pounds in Part of the said Forty Pounds.

In Witness whereof as well the said Sub. Lieutenant, as the said George Heckerwiller have hereto set their Hands, the 22 Day of Septembr, 1777.

(Signature mutilated.)

CHRISTOPH MAYER'S Lieut.
JOHN DEHUFF.

These Presents certify, that Christopher Crawford, Esquire, Sub. Lieutenant of the County of Lancaster, hath provided, hired and procured Jacob Kiechler of the same County, Yeoman, to serve as a Substitute in the Second Class of Militia, of Lancaster County, in the Commonwealth of Pennsylvania, for and in the Place of Henry Christy of the Borough of Lancaster, in the County aforesaid, for which Service the said Jacob Kiechler is to have and receive the Sum of Forty pounds lawful Money of Pennsylvania. And the said Jacob Kiechler doth hereby acknowledge and declare, that he hath entered as a Substitute for the said Henry Christy, in the Second Class of the Militia aforesaid, and will well and faithfully serve and perform his duty as a Soldier therein, agreeable to the Laws of the said Commonwealth, and subject to the Rules and Regulations of the said Commonwealth, in such Cases made and provided. And that he hath received, from the said Christopher Crawford, Esquire, the Sum of Ten Pounds in Part of the said Forty Pounds.

In Witness whereof as well the said Sub. Lieutenant, as the said Jacob Kiechler have hereto set their Hands, the Ninth Day of Septembr, 1777.

(Signature mutilated.)

Witness Prest.
LODWICK HECK.
JACOB KRUG, Captn.

These Presents certify, that Christopher Crawford, Esquire, Sub. Lieutenant of the County of Lancaster, hath provided, hired and procured George Lenhere of the same County, Yeoman, to serve as a Substitute in the 4 Class of Militia, of Lancaster County, in the Commonwealth of Pennsylvania, for and in the Place of Dahiel Whitelock of the Borough of Lancaster, in the County aforesaid, for which Service the said George Lenhere is to have and receive the Sum of Forty pounds lawful Money of Pennsylvania. And the said George Lenhere doth hereby acknowledge and declare, that he hath entered as a Substitute for the said Daniel Whitelock in the 4 Class of the Militia aforesaid, and will well and faithfully serve and perform his duty as a Soldier therein, agreeable to the Laws of the said Commonwealth, and subject to the Rules and Regulations of the said Commonwealth, in such Cases made and provided. And that he hath received, from the said Christopher Crawford, Esquire, the Sum of Seven pounds Ten Shillings in Part of the said Forty pounds.

In Witness whereof as well the said Sub. Lieutenant, as the said George Lenhere have hereto set their Hands, the Sixth Day of October, 1777.

(Signature mutilated.)

GEORGE FRANCISCUS, Capt.

These Presents certify, that Christopher Crawford, Esquire, Sub. Lieutenant of the County of Lancaster, hath provided, hired and procured Casper Lorentz of the same County, Yeoman, to serve as a Substitute in the Second Class of Militia, of Lancaster County, in the Commonwealth of Pennsylvania, for and in the place of Henry Hare of the Borough of Lancaster, in the County aforesaid, for which Service the said Casper Lorentz is to have and receive the sum of Forty Pounds lawful Money of Pennsylvania. And the said Casper Lorentz doth hereby acknowledge and declare that he hath entered as a Substitute for the said Henry Hare in the Second Class of the Militia aforesaid, and will well and faithfully serve and perform his duty as a Soldier therein, agreeable to the Laws of the said Commonwealth, and subject to the Rules and Regulations of the said Commonwealth, in such Cases made and provided. And that he hath received, from the said Christopher Crawford, Esquire, the Sum of Ten Pounds in Part of the said Forty Pounds.

In Witness whereof as well the said Sub. Lieutenant, as the said Casper Lorentz have hereto set their Hands, the Ninth Day of September, 1777.

(Signature mutilated.)

Witness Prest.
LODWICK HECK.
JACOB KRUG, Captn.

Received of Colnl. Galbreath Thurty Pounds the Remainder of the within obligation by the bands of W. Henry novem. 7th, 1777.

CASPER LORENTZ.

These Presents certify, that Christopher Crawford, Esquire, Sub. Lieutenant of the County of Lancaster, hath provided, hired and procured Jacob Long of the same County, Yeoman, to serve as a Substitute in the 4 Class of Militia, of Lancaster County, in the Commonwealth of Pennsylvania, for and in the Place of Henrey Musser of Lancaster town sep in the County aforesaid, for which Service the said Jacob Long is to have and receive the Sum of Forty Pounds lawful Money of Pennsylvania. And the said Jacob Long doth hereby acknowledge and declare, that he hath entered as a Substitute for the said Henrey Musser in the 4 Class of the Militia aforesaid, and will well and faithfully serve and perform his duty as a Soldier therein, agreeable to the Laws of the said Commonwealth, and subject to the Rules and Regulations of the said Commonwealth, in such Cases made and provided. And that he hath received, from the said Christopher Crawford, Esquire, the Sum of Seven Pounds Ten Shillings in Part of the said Forty Pounds.

In Witness whereof as well the said Sub. Lieutenant, as

the said Jacob Long have hereto set their Hands, the Fift Day of Octobr, 1777.

(Signature mutilated.)

GEORGE FRANCISCUS.
PETER DIFFENDERFER.

These Presents certify, that Christopher Crawford, Esquire, Sub. Lieutenant of the County of Lancaster, hath provided, hired and procured Alexander Mars of the same County, Yeoman, to serve as a Substitute in the Second Class of Militia, of Lancaster County, in the Commonwealth of Pennsylvania, for and in the Place of John Shank of the Borough of Lancaster, in the County aforesaid, for which Service the said Alexander Mars is to have and receive the Sum of Forty pounds lawful Money of Pennsylvania. And the said Alexander Mars doth hereby acknowledge and declare, that he hath entered as a Substitute for the said John Shank in the Second Class of the Militia aforesaid, and will well and faithfully serve and perform his duty as a Soldier therein, agreeable to the Laws of the said Commonwealth, and subject to the Rules and Regulations of the said Commonwealth, in such Cases made and provided. And that he hath received, from the said Christopher Crawford, Esquire, the Sum of Ten Pounds in Part of the said Forty Pounds.

In Witness whereof as well the said Sub. Lieutenant, as the said Alexander Mars have hereto set their Hands, the Ninth Day of Septemr, 1777.

(Signature mutilated.)

Witness Prest.
LODWICK HECK.
JACOB KRUG.

These Presents certify, that Christopher Crawford, Esquire, Sub. Lieutenant of the County of Lancaster, hath provided, hired and procured Jacob Miller of the same County, Yeoman, to serve as a Substitute in the First Class of Militia, of Lancaster County, in the Commonwealth of Pennsylvania, for and in the Place of Lewy Andrw Lewy of the Borough of Lancaster, in the County aforesaid, for which Service the said Jacob Miller is to have and receive the Sum of Fourty Pounds lawful Money of Pennsylvania. And the said Jacob Miller doth hereby acknowledge and declare, that he hath entered as a Substitute for the said Lewy Andrw Lewy in the Fierst Class of the Militia aforesaid, and will well and faithfully serve and perform his duty as a Soldier therein, agreeable to the Laws of the said Commonwealth, and subject to the Rules and Regulations of the said Commonwealth, in such Cases made and provided. And that he hath received, from the said Christopher Crawford, Esquire, the Sum of Ten Pounds in Part of the said Lewy Andrw Lewey.

In Witness whereof as well the said Sub. Lieutenant, as the said Jacob Miller have hereto set their Hands, the 22 Day of Septembr, 1777.

(Signature mutilated.)

CHRISTOPH MAYER'S Liut.
JOHN DEHUFF.

These Presents certify, that Christopher Crawford, Esquire, Sub. Lieutenant of the County of Lancaster, hath provided, hired and procured Mathias Sheib of the same County, Yeoman, to serve as a Substitute in the Second Class of Militia, of Lancaster County, in the Commonwealth of Pennsylvania, for and in the Place of John Long, Senr., of Manhime town Sip in the County aforesaid, for which Service the said Mathais Sheib is to have and receive the Sum of Forty Pounds lawful Money of Pennsylvania. And the said Mathais Sheih doth hereby acknowledge and declare, that he hath entered as a Substitute for the said John Long, Senr., in the Frist Class of the Militia aforesaid, and will well and faithfully serve and perform his duty as a Soldier therein, agreeable to the Laws of the said Commonwealth, and subject to the Rules and Regulations of the said Commonwealth, in such Cases made and provided. And that he hath received, from the said Christopher Crawford, Esquire, the Sum of Ten Pounds in Part of the said Forty Pounds.

In Witness whereof as well the said Sub. Lieutenant, as the said Mathais Sheib have hereto set their Hands, the 23 Day of Septembr, 1777.

MATHAIS SHEIB.

JOHN REICHMYSERT.

These Presents certify, that Christopher Crawford, Esquire, Sub. Lieutenant of the County of Lancaster, hath provided, hired and procured Casper Treble of the same County, Yeoman, to serve as a Substitute in the Second Class of Militia, of Lancaster County, in the Commonwealth of Pennsylvania, for and in the Place of Valentine Basler of town Sip, in the County aforesaid, for which Service the said Casper Treble is to have and receive the Sum of Forty Pounds lawful Money of Pennsylvania. And the said Casper Treble doth hereby acknowledge and declare, that he hath entered as a Substitute for the said Valentine Basler in the Second Class of the Militia aforesaid, and will well and faithfully serve and perform his duty as a Soldier therein, agreeable to the Laws of the said Commonwealth, and subject to the Rules and Regulations of the said Commonwealth, in such Cases made and provided. And that he hath received, from the said Christopher Crawford, Esquire, the Sum of Ten Pounds in Part of the said Forty Pounds.

In Witness whereof as well the said Sub. Lieutenant, as the said Casper Treble have hereto set their Hands, the Ninth Day of Septemr, 1777.

(Signature mutilated.)

Witness Prest.
LODWICK HECK.
JACOB KRUG, Captn.

These Presents certify, that Christopher Crawford, Esquire, Sub. Lieutenant of the County of Lancaster, hath provided, hired and procured Robert Wilson of the Same County, Yeoman, to Serve as a Substitute in the Frist Class of Militia of Lancaster County in the Commenwealth of Pennsylvania for and in the Place of John Meyers of the Town Sip of Manhim in the County aforesaid for wich Service the Said Robert Wilson is to have and Receive the Sum of Fourty Pounds Lawful Money of Pennsylvania and the Robert Wilson doth hereby acknowledge and declare that he hath entered as a Substitute for the Said John Meyers in the Frist Class of the Melitia aforesaid and will well and Faithfully Serve and Perform his duty as a Soldier therein agreeable to the Laws of the Said Commonwealth and subject to the rules and regulations of the said Commonwealth in Such Cases made and provided and that he hath Received, from the Said Christopher Crawford, Esqr., the Sum of Ten Pounds in part of the Said Forty Pounds.

In Witness whereof as well the as the Said Robert Wilson have hereto Set My Hand the 23 Day of Septembr, 1777.

ROBERT WILSON.

Witness Present.

CHRISTOPH MAYER'S.

(c.) The Berer Philip Galaher his Served in the first cles of Lanceiter Milisia and Beheved himself as a soldear I Do Discherg him to home it may Concern Both Sivel and Military.

MICHAEL APP, Capt.

Lancster October 29th 1777.

(c.) This is to Certify that Jacob Kleghler has served as substitute in the Room of Henry Christ in my Company in the 2d Class of Lancaster County Militia and is hereby Discharged by me.

JACOB KRUG, Capt.

Nov'r 4th, 1777.

(c.) This is to certify that Jacob Grub served in the first Class of the Lancaster Militia as a Substitute and he having faithfully served his Time I do hereby discharge him thereof.

Nov. 5, 1777.

MICHAEL APP, Capt.

Witness my Hand.

(c.) This is to certify that George Haggetswiller served in the first class of the Lancaster Meletia as a Substitute and he having faithfully served his Time I do hereby discharge him thereof. Nov. 5, 1777.

MICHAEL APP, Capt.

Witness my Hand.

(c.) This is to Certify that John Fisher Having Honestly Serv'd his full Tower of Two Months in the Militia of Lancaster County as a Substitute for Calep Cope in the 3d Class therefore is Discharg'd from my Company as Wittness My Hand.

JOHN GRAEFF, Capt.

Lancaster Nov'r 13th, 1777.

Lancaster December the 5th, 1777.

(c.) This is to Certify that Jacob Long has Served his tour of Duty as a Substitute honest and faithfully in my Comp'y Witness my hand.

GEORGE FRANCISCUS, Capt.

(c.) This is to Certify that George Lenhere has Served his Duty as a Soldier in my Comp'y honest and faithfully witness my hand this 5th Day of Decem'r, 1777.

GEORGE FRANCISCUS, Capt.

Lancaster the 5th of Decb'r, 1777.

A MUSTER ROLL OF CAPT. ISAAC ADAMS COMP'Y OF THE 4 AND 1 CLASS LANCASTER COUNTY MILITIA (NOW IN SERVICE OF THE UNITED STATES) COM'D BY COL. ELDER CAMP. (c.)

Commissioned Officers

Captain.

Isaac Adams, Entred Oct'r 9.

Lieutenant.

1. Adam Eholdes, Entred Sept'r 20th.
2. John Zegor, Entred Sept'r 20th.

Ensign.

Andrews Erman, Entred Oct'r 9th.

	Appointed.	Remarks.
Sargantes.		
1. Henry Hartman,	Oct'r 14th.	
2. Michel Young,	Oct'r 16th.	
3. David Berrengior,	Oct'r 22.	
4. Henry Eholds,	Oct'r 22,...	Discharged Nov. 20th.
Corporals.		
1. Conrad Mast,	Oct'r 14th.	
2. Henry Brandel,	Oct'r 22.	
3. David H. (mutilated) knell,..	Oct'r 14.	
4. Jacob Lead,	Oct'r 22,...	Diserted Oct'r 23rd.
Drummer & fiffer.		
1. Modis Holtre,	Oct'r 22,	Diserted Oct'r 26th.
	Entred.	**Remarks.**
Privites.		
1. John Krill,	Set'r 20th.	
2. George Pruner,	Set'r 20th.	
3. Andrews Ream,	Set'r 20th,	Sub'te.
4. Peter Snider,	Set'r 20th,	Sub'te.
5. William Snider,	Set'r 20th.	
6. Abraham Killeon,	Set'r 20th.	
7. Ludwich Ebright,	Set'r 20th.	
8. David Allspach,	Set'r 20th,	Diserted Oct. 27th.
9. Michael Silor,	Set'r 20th.	
10. Henry Louch,	Set'r 20th.	
11. Nicklass Luts,	Set'r 20th.	
12. Jacob Allspach,	Set'r 20th.	
13. George Urey,	Set'r 20th.	
14. Samuel Grove,	Oct'r 9th.	
15. Thomas Handley,	Oct'r 9th.	
16. Philip Shankel,	Oct'r 9th,	Diserted Nov'r 1th.
17. Peter Wiland,	Oct'r 9th.	

A MUSTER ROLL OF CAPT. ISAAC ADAMS COMP'Y OF THE 4 AND 1 CLASS LANCASTER COUNTY MILITIA —Continued.

	Entred.		Remarks.
18. Thomas Holmes,	Oct'r	13th.	
19. Ludwich Fredley,	Oct'r	9th.	
20. Philip Kreek,	Oct'r	10th.	
21. Andrews Hiddelor,	Oct'r	11th,	Sub'te.
22. Peter Grove,	Oct'r	12th.	
23. Jacob Snider,	Oct'r	14th.	
24. Casper Gipperd,	Oct'r	14th.	
25. John Kusswelor,	Oct'r	14th.	
26. Valintine Snider,	Oct'r	14th.	
27. Michael Winholds,	Oct'r	14th.	
28. John Penter,	Oct'r	15th,	Sub'te Diserted Nov'r 24th.
29. George Firestone,	Oct'r	15th.	Sub'te.
30 Christon Snider,	Oct'r	16th,	Diserted Nov'r 1th.
31. John Shulte,	Oct'r	20th,	Sub'te.
32. Michael Zardman,	Oct'r	20th.	
33. George Fox,	Oct'r	20th.	
34. Samuel Mether,	Oct'r	20th.	
35. Casper Sherriff,	Oct'r	20th,	Diserted Nov. 24th.
36. Jacob Andrews,	Oct'r	20th.	Subte.
37. Mathies Walk,	Oct'r	22nd,	Diserted Oct'r 28th.
38. Peter Smith,	Oct'r	22nd,	Subte.
39. Alexander Rathford,	Oct'r	22nd,	Subte.
40. Daniel Road,	Oct'r	22nd,	Subte.
41. Richard Adams,	Oct'r	22nd.	
42. Peter Fezor,	Oct'r	22nd.	
43. Christel Pricker,	Oct'r	22nd,	Diserted Oct'r 27th.
44. Adam Wiexel,	Oct'r	22nd,	Sub't sick on forlow Nov. 15th.
45. Robert Foster,	Oct'r	23d,	Sub't.
46. John Mclerey,	Oct'r	23d,	Sub't.
47. Hugh Shennon,	Oct'r	24th,	Sub't.
48. Joseph Hiddelor,	Oct'r	24th,	Sub't sick on furlow Nov'r 11th.
49. John Kiln,	Oct'r	23d,	
50. Jacob Duck,	Oct'r	23d,	Diserted Nov'r 3th.
51. Michel McCassgrove,	Oct'r	23d,	Sub't.
52. John Aarmstrong,	Nov'r	14th,	Sub't.
53. Frances Novland,	Oct'r	14th.	

Whitemarch Dec. 9, 1777. Mustred then Capt. Isaac Adams Company as Specified .n tne above Roll.

LODK. SPROGELL, M. M. G. OF P.

PROOF OF THE EFFECTIVES.

	Capt.	Lieut.	Ensign.	Sergant.	Drum'r.	Fife.	Privits.
Present,	1	2	1	3	......	......	46
Absent,	......	.....	......	......	......	......	2
Total,	1	2	1	3	......	......	48

I Do Swear that the Within Muster Roll is a true State of the Company Without Frade to these United States or to aney Individual According to the Best of my knowledge.

Sworn Before Me this 9th Day of Dec'r, 1777.

ISAAC ADAMS, Capt.

JNO. BULL,
A. gen'l, S. P.

(c.) This is to Certify that the bearer Valentine Sherland Searved Part of his time with Capt. Franciscus of the 4th Class of Lancaster County Militia Commanded by Co'l Robert Elder and the rest with Capt. John Slaymaker of the 5th Class. December 28th, 1777.

To whome it may Concern.

JOHN SLAYMAKER, Capt.

Rec'd Dec. 28, 1777, one gun and cartouch box with twenty three cartridges. Rec'd by me.

JOHN SLAYMAKER, Capt.

A RETURN OF CAPT. MARTIN BOWMAN'S COMPANIE FOR THE YEAR 1777. (c.)

Class 1.

Isack Gray.
John Ghere.
Peter Sensnick.
Joseph Zimmerman.
John Wenger, Senior.
Christian Schwartswelder.
Christopher Rodacker.
Jacob Crim.
Michael Hendly.
Conrath Holtzinger.
John Shuwalder.
Michial Bitzer.
Benjamin Shensman, Scolker.

2 Class.

Philip Wever.
George Otto.
Engelbart Holtz, gone to the English.
Andrew Harter.
Jacob Oberlin, Scolker.
Jacob Wisse.
Andrew Yount.
Henery Miller.
Jacob Werns.
Peter Resh.
Abraham Andrews, Scolker.
Peter Pence.
Henery Wever.
John Kittara.
David Hurman.

3 Class.

John McCleary.
George German.
Michial Hass.
George Ghere.
Christian Donner.
John Beck.
John Evanes.
George Werns, dead.
Jacob Hinckel.
Wm. Berry, Capt.
Michial Sower.
Adam German, Jr.
Philip Rinmood.

4 Class.

James Gault.
Peter Good.
Francis Hane.
Andrew Wisse.
Hennery Libert.
David Campher.
John Resler.
Sepastian Hower.
John German.
John Muman.
John Solenberger.
Jacob Rod.
George Wever.
Wm. Crow.

5th Class.

John Yount.
Martin Werns.
Josiah Kittara.
Abraham Low.
Fredrick Glaze.
David Morgan, Capt.
Joseph McCleary.
Conrath Brenisen.
John Swigert.
John Bitzer, Jr.
Tobias Mediger.
Philip Pence.
Ernst Miller.
Nicklas Trautwine.
Lodwick Seitz.

6th Class.

George Bowder.
Stofel Ely.
John Bowel.
John Fautsnaught.
George Pifer.
Benjamen Harlager.
John Sids.
Alexander Gault.
Balser Smith.
Philip Ronck.
Jacob Adam.
Wm. McClean.
Henery Norton.

7th Class.

George Schwickert.
Henery Nice.
James McCleary, Jr.
John Bitzer, Sener.
George Cloper.
Leonhart German.
George Hinckel.
Isack Davis.
Philip Faustnaught.
John Campfor.
Jacob Sherck.
Henery Snider.
Christian Wenger.
Wm. Wagen.

8th Class.

James McCleary.
Conrath Faustnaught.
Andrew Culp.
Joseph Melinger.
Christian Knisly.
Henery Shultz.
Andrew Swickert.
John Rod.
Adam German.
Conrath Pence.
Henery Otto.
John Gunty.
Wm. Olgiy.

(c.) Thiss is to certify that Jacob Gansler of Myrs Company Served his tower of Duty in the Borrow of Lancaster for the year 1777 in the 3d Class my Company.

HENERY KUSTER, Capt.
ALEXD'R NOBLE, Colctr.

May the 3d, 1781.

a true Coppy.

(c.) I Do certify that Abraham Fisher a privet in the 6 class of my Company musterd in the year 1777 and Likewise movd to Sheemoken in November 1777. pr me.

FRIEDRICH ZIEGLER.

May the 4th, 1781.

(c.) I Do hereby certify that John Shertz a privet in the 3 Class of my Company did one tower of Duty in Lancaster garrison in the year 1777.

Certifyed pr me,
FRIEDRICH ZIEGLER, Capt.

May the 10th, 1781.

CAPTAINS OF LANCASTER COUNTY MILITIA IN SERVICE IN 1777, 1778 AND 1779. (b.)

George Feather (Fedder).
Bernard Gardner.
George Foulke.
Christian Hollinger.
Joseph Gehr.
John Gingrich.
Isaac Addams.
John Smuller.
Bernard Geiger.
Jacob Metzgar.
—— Haverstick (Colonel).

Ensign and Surgeon's Mate.

John Dentzell.

(c.) I Do hereby certify that Johm and Barnot man and Casper and George Lutz did duly attened muster in the years 1777, 1778, 1779 priveets in my Company pr me.

CONRAD KARRER, Capitain.

May the 4th, 1781.

(c.) This is to Sertify that John Myer has Served his tower for the year 1778. on Guard in Lancaster.

SAMUEL McDAUL, 1st Lieut.

May the 21st, 1781.

This is to certefy that John Myar has done two towers of Duty in the garrison of Lancaster in the years 1777, 1778, 1779 under me and musterd in said years constantly unless prevented by sickness.

pr me.

SAMUEL McDAUL.

May the 21st, 1781.

(c.) I Do hereby Certefy that Criston Dominy a privet in my Company Class 8 Did Duly attend muster in the year 1777, 1778, 1779 and did one tower of Duty in Lancaster in the year 1777 pr. me.

CONRAD KARRER, Capitain.

May the 3d, 1781.

(c.) Thess is certify that Adam Martin has mustered and done his tower of Duty in the years 1777, 1778, 1779 in full.

pr. me.

FRIEDRICH ZIEGLER, Capt.

May the 10th, 1781.

(c.) I Do hereby certify that Fradrick Fenstrmaker has musterd and Done his Duty of 2 towers of Duty in the Garrisons of Lancaster in the years 1777, 1778, 1779. pr me.

FRIEDRICH ZIEGLER, Capt.

May the 10th, 1781.

(c.) I Do hereby certify that Cristopher Bryar has served his tower of Duty in the year 1777, 78, 1779. Certify'd p'r me.

JACOB METZGER, Capt.

May the 19th, 1781.

(c.) This is to certify that John Myar has done two towers of duty in the garrison of Lancaster in the years 1777, 1778, 1779 under me and musterd in said years constantly unless provented by seckness pr me.

SAMUEL McDOWEL.

May the 21st, 1781.

(c.) I Do hereby Certify that Jacob Miller has mustred and done 2 towers of Duty in Lancaster in the years 1777, 1778, 1779 as garrison Duty in Lancaster. pr me.

FRIEDRICH ZIEGLER, Capt.

May the 10th, 1781.

(c.) We do hereby certefy that Ulrick Kever was wagon mastr in the year 1778 one tower and wass townshep sessor for the year 1779. Certefed by us.

FRIEDRICH ZIEGLER, Capt.

ALEXD'R NOBLE, Adjton.

May the 10th, 1781.

(c.) I Do hereby certify that David Dacker a privet in my Company was constantly Driving a publick Waggon and Teem in Paul Housemans Bregaeds in the years 1778; 1779.

Certify p'r me.

FRIEDRICH ZIEGLER, Capt.

Millers Town, May the 11th, 1781.

(c.) I Do hereby certefy that Isaac Kuntz a privet in my Company Class the first did duly muster in my company unless prevented by sickness in the years 1778, 1779 pr me.

CONRAD KARRER, Capt.

May the 3d, 1781.

Lancaster January 2d, 1778.

(c.) This is to Certify that Simon Herman has served faithfully Two Months for Jacob Maurer of the Borough of Lancaster as a Substitute, part of which he served in the Sixth and thar Remainder in the Seventh Class of Lancaster County Militia under the comand of Capt. Samuel Davis, and he the join'd Simon Herman is hereby discharged of the Service for the presend tour of Duty. Witness our hands this date as above.

CHRISTIAN PETRIE, Capt.
JOHN BREONTIGAM, Lieutenant.
of Capt. Davis's Comp'y.

(To all whom it may concern.)

Lancaster January 2d, 1778.

(c.) This is to Certify that Michael Radmacher of the County of Lancaster has faithfully served the tour of Two Months as a Substitute for Jacob Kreider of Conostogo Township, County aforsaid, part of which time he served in the Sixth, and the Remainder in the Seventh Class under the comand of Capt. Samuel Davis, the said Michael Radmacher is hereby discharged of the present tour of Duty. Witness our hands this date as above.

CHRISTIAN PETRIE, Captn.
JOHN D. BROENTIGAM, Lieutenant.
of Capt. S. Davis's Comp'y.

(To all whom it may concern.)

Lancaster January 16th, 1778.

(c.) This may Certify that Marcus Unger has served his Two Months faithfully part of said time he served in Captain Samuel Davis's Company 7th Class and the Remainder in the Eight Class under Captain Adam Wilhelm, in test hereff we have here unto set our hands this place and date as above.

SAMUEL DAVIS, Capt.
ADAM WILHELM, Capt.

(c.) Febburary the 3d, 1778.

This is to Certyfy that Augusts Stoner Has Served his tour of Duty in my Company of Lancaster County Millity and now Discharged by me in Witness my band and Date above.

SAMUEL DAVIS, Capt.

(c.) I do hereby Certefy that John Stephy was out Driving a waggon and teem in the year 1778 when his Class was calld on to march the waggon was in publick service in Housemans Bregald.

May the 10th, 1781.

pr. me,
FRIEDRICH ZIEGLER, Capt.

Lancaster November the 5th, 1778.

(c.) This is to satisfy Casper Lutz That Christian Keller has Faith full Servet his Tow'r of Two month Tuty in Lancaster Garrison under mee.

HENRY KUSTER, Captain.

(c.) January 8th, 1778. Rec'd from Joseph Barnet three Pounds ten Shillings it Being for the Poor families of hanover Township who have Been in actual Service Belonging to Capt. W'm McCulloughs Comp'y of Militia of Lancaster County. Rec'd by

DAVID DAVIS.

January ye 2d, 1778. Received From Joseph Barnet four Pound it Being for the Use of the Poor of hanover Township Whose men are in actual Service Belonging to Capt. William McCoulloughs Company of Militia. Rec'd by me.

EASTER his X mark ROWLAND.

January 7th, 1778. Received from Joseph Barnet Four Pound it being for the Use of the Poor of hanover township Whose Men are in actual Service belonging to Capt. William McCoulloughs Company of Militia Rec'd by me.

JEAN his X mark CAMBELL.

January 8th, 1778. Received from Joseph Barnet three Pound Seven Shillings & Six pence it being for the Use of the Poor of hanover Township whose men have Been in actual Service Belonging to Capt. William McCoulloughs Company of Militia Rec'd by me.

DAVID HAYSE.

Aprile 6th, 1778. Received From Joseph Barnet three Pound it Being for the Use of the Poor families of hanover Township Belonging to Capt. Wm. McCoulloughs Company of Militia, who has Been in Actual Service.

Rec'd by me,

ELIZABETH his X mark WRIGHT.

January 7th, 1778. Received from Joseph Barnet three Pound it being for the Use of the Poor of hanover township Who have been in actual Service Belonging to Capt. William McCoulloughs Company of Militia. Rec'd by me.

LEONARD his X mark BRISBIN.

January 11th, 1778. Received from Joseph Barnet three Pound it being for the Use of the Poor of hanover Township whose men have Been in actual Service Belonging to Capt. William McCoulloughs Company of Militia. Rec'd by me.

DAVID McCRACKIN.

Hanover August 24th, 1778. Rec'd from Joseph Barnet Four pound it Being for the Poor of hanover Township whose men are in Actual Service Belonging to Capt. W'm McCoulloughs Company of Militia. Rec'd by me.

JEAN his X mark CAMMELL.

Recd. November 4th, 1778 of Joseph Barnet Three Pound Ten Shillings it Being for the use of the poor families of hanover Township who have Been in actual Service Belonging to Capt. Wm. McColloughs Company of Militia of Lancaster County. Recd By Me.

JOSHUA MAGUS.

I do Certify that it appears that I have paid to Mr. Joseph Barnet of Hanover Township the Sum of Thirty Six pounds for the Use of the Poor Militia Mens Familys of Capt. McCoulloughs Company, when Serving their tower of Militia duty on the Eighth day of December 1777 which he did not Account for, with me during my Continuance in the Lieutenants office.

23d Sept'r, 1782.

P. BARTREM GALBRAITH.

January ye 7th, 1778. Received From Joseph Barnet Four Pound it Being for the Use of the Poor of hanover Township whose men are in actual Service Belonging to Capt. William McCoulloughs Company of Militia. Recd. by Me.

NANCY his X mark HURVAY.

January ye 8th, 1778. Received from Joseph Barnet three Pound it being for the Use of the Poor of hanover Township whose Men Are in actual Service Belonging to Capt. William McCoulloughs Company of Militia. I Say Rec'd by Me.

CATHARINE his X mark McELHENY.

April ye 23, 1779. Received of Joseph Barnet four pound it being for the use of the poor of hanover township who have been in actual Service belonging to Capt. William McCulloughs Company of Melity.

Rec'd by me.

DAVID his X mark DAVIS.

February the 2d, 1778. Received from Joseph Barnet three Pound Seven Shilling & six pence it Being for the use of the Poor of hanover township whose men have Been in actual Belonging to Capt. William McCoulloughs Company of Militia. Rec'd by me.

GRIS'SY his X mark FEARLY.

(c.) Lancaster County ss.

These are to Certify that James Ramsey, D. C. G. H. hath taken and subscribed the oaths required by a resolve of the Honourable Continental Congress passed the third day of February last requiring all officers holding any office or turst under them to take the same under penalty of being casheird.

Given under my hand and seal the 4th day of March 1778.

THOMAS WHITESIDE. (Seal.)

Lancaster Octob'r 23th, 1778.

(c.) This is to Certify that Mathias Shib has Serve his Two Months In Camp A Substitute fore John Long Senj In the first class Millintoy In My Compay. I Say pr.

CAPT. APPE.

(c.) Lancaster November the 2d, 1778.

thiss is to Certefy that Felix Bugh has faithfully served the 2 months of Duty for Mechal Bender a privet in Captain Wrights company class in Lancaster Garrison. Give under my hand to all whome it may Concern.

HENERY CUSTER, Capt.

A true Coppy May the 3d, 1781.

ALEXDR NOBLE.

(c.) A RETORN OF THE SECOND COMPANY WITH THIR CLASSES—AND A RETORN OF THOSE WHO SERVED FOR THE YEAR—1778. (c.)

Class ye 1st.

First Lieut.—William Young, Served at Middleton.

Class ye 2d.

Capt.—Ambrose Crean, Northumberland.

Class ye 3d.

Ensign—John Armstrong, for want of command.

Class ye 4th.

Second Lieut.—James Stewart, Did not go for want of command.

Class ye 5th.

Serg't—Henry Graham, Lebanon.

Class ye 1st.

David Young, Middleton.
James Young.
Edward Eshoraft.
Adam Vance.
Archabald Sloan.

Class ye 2d.

John Cunningham, Northumberland.
Robert Young.
James Young.

Class ye 3d.

David Ramsey, Lebanon.
Daniel Brodley, Northumberland.
William Moor, in ye Continental Service.
Joseph Riddle, Northumberland.

Class ye 4th.

Josias Espy, Northumberland.
William McFarland, Northumberland.
Samuel Graham.

Class ye 5th.

Hugh Watt, Lebanon.
William Vance.
William Graham.
George Young.

Class ye 6th.

William Young, Northumberland.
John Young.

Class ye 7th.

Class ye 8th.

John Young, Junior, Servd.
John Graham, Served in ye second.

The Above Cartfied

By

CAPT. AMBROSE CREAIN.

(c.) This is to Certify that Daniel Wolf and George Wolf both of Jacob Ridlingers Company Served their Towers of Duty in the Borrow of Lancaster for the year 1778 in the 3d Glass my Company.

Certifyed by me.

HENRICH HUSTER (2), Capt.

May 3d, 1781.

A RETURN OF THE COMPANIES CALLED TO BEDFORD COUNTY APRIL 19TH, 1779. (c.)

Capt. Murray's Compy.

John Simpson.
Henry McCloskey.
Jno. Collogan.
Jno. Thomas.
Wm. Boyce.
Jas. Burney.
Robt. Armstrong.
Jno. Stephenson.

Capt. McKinney's Compy.

Max'l Chambers.
Jas. Finney.
Jno. Sheazer.
George Gray.
Adam Means.
Jno. Alliman.
Nicholas Neigh.
Peter Brand.
Francis Lerue.

Capt. Rutherford's Compy.

Daniel Cooper.
Jno. Gray.
Adam Kitsmiller.
Joseph Willson.
Jno. Davis.
Jacob Houser.
Peter Pancake, Junr.
Philip Firebaugh.

Capt. McClure's Compy.

Nicholas Castle.
Abraham Gross.
Henry McCann.
Jno. Backestoe.
Philip Shocking.
Philip Attley.
Philip Batemore.
Henry Miller.
Peter Shuster.
Henry Davis.
William Widner.
Robt. Nailor.
Jacob Strickler.
Jno. Hollaback.
Jas. Jackson.

Capt. Clark's Compy.

Jas. Buchanan.
Allex'r George.
Daniel Black.
Richard Gilmore.

Capt. Weaver's Compy.

Peter Willier.
Jacob Pickle.
Jacob Hermon.
Henry Normier.
Adam King.

Capt. Stewart's Compy.

Allex'r Berryhill.
Robt. Elder.
John Elder.
William Kelso, Jun.
Saml. Simpton.
Wm. McConnold.

Capt. Gillchrist's Compy.

Hugh Wray.
Jno. Cochran.
Jno. Hillton.
Abraham Willson.
James Wiggins.
Thos. Gillchrist.
Samuel Martin.
Jno. Whrite.
Samuel Thomson.

MEN WHO SERVED TWO MONTHS ON GUARD DUTY. (c.)

Lebenon the 29 Juni 1779. Rceved of Adam Orth the Sum of Fiften Pounds in Part of Fifty Pounds for Two monds Servis as gard by me.

JOHN his X mark CLERCK.

£15-0-0.

Receved July the 28th 1779 the Sum of Thorty five Pounds beleng the Remender Sum of Fifty Pounds in ful by me.

JOHN his X mark CLERCK.

£35-0-0.

Receved Juni the 30th 1779 of Adam Orth the Sum of Fifty Pounds in Pard for Two monds Servis as a militia man as guard. Receved by me.

PHILLIP DIBO.

£50-0-0.

Receved of Adam Orth Juni the 29, 1779 the Sum of Fifty Pounds in Pert for Serves as a militia man. I say Reced by me.

CONRAT JUNGST.

£50-0-0.

Reced June the 29th 1779 of Adam Orth the Sum of Fifty Pounds in Part of Two monds Serves as a militia man. I say Receved by me.

HENRICH JUNGST.

£50-0-0.

Recd Dec'r 23d, 1780 of Col. Atlee two Hundred Dollars in part pay for my Tour of Duty to Northumberland.

ADAM KELLER.

200 Dollars.

Lebanon Juni the 29 1779 Receved of Adam Orth the Sum of thorty Pounds in Pard of Fifty Pounds for Two monts Servis as gerd Receved by me.

JOHN PAUL KURTZ.

£30-0-0.

Receved July the 31 1779 of Adam Orth the Sum of Twenty Pounds bineng the Renombard of the above Fifty Pounds Receved by me.

JOHN PAUL KURTZ.

£20-0-0.

Receved of Adam Orth Juin 29th 1779 the Sum of Fifty Pounts in Part for Tow monts Servis as a militia man. I say Receved by me.

ADAM his X mark LEBOT.

£50-0-0.

Received Juni the 30th 1779 of Adam Orth the Sum of Fifty Pounds in Pard for Two monds Serves as a militiaman as a guard. Receved by me.

CASPER MIESS.

£50-0-0.

Recd Lebenon Juni the 29th 1779 of Adam Orth the Sum of Fifty Pounds in Pard for Two monds Serves as a card. Receved by me.

WOLTER his X mark NUMAN.

£50-0-0.

Recevd Lebenon Juni the 29, 1779 of Adam Orth the Sum of Fifty Pounds in Pord for Two monds Serves as a card. Receved by me.

JACOB his X mark NUMAN.

£50-0-0.

Receved Juni the 29th 1779 of Adam Orth the Sum of Fifty Pounds in Pard for Servis as a militia man. I Say Receved by me.

GEORGE STROW, Sergent.

£50-0-0.

Receved of Adam Orth the 29th Juni 1779 the Som of Fifty Pounds in Port for Two monts Servis as a militia man. Recevet by me.

JACOB SNEVELY.

£50-0-0.

Receved Augst the 20 1779 of Adam Orth the Rementer Ten Pounds for the above Sixty Pound in full by me.

JACOB SNEVELY.

£10-0-0.

Recevd Lebenon Juni the 29th 1779 of Adam Orth the Sum of Fifty Pounds in Pard for Two monds Serves as a card. Receved by me.

JOHANNES VALLENTIN.

£50-0-0.

Lancaster County ss.

These are to certify that James Ramsey D. C. G. H. hath taken and subscribed the oaths required by a resolve of the Honourable Continental Congress passed the third day of February last requiring all officiers holding any office or turst under them to take the same under penalty of being casheird. Given under my hand and seal the 4th day of March 1778.

THOMAS WHITESIDE. (Seal.)

Received July 20th 1779 of Adam Orth Sub. Lieut. for L. C. by the Hands of Philip Marsteller, the Sum of Fifty Pounds in full for my Service as a Substitute, in the Militia employed as Guard at Lebanon Town.

I say recd.

PM GOTTLOB YUNGMAN.

Lebenon the 29 Juni 1779 Rieved of Adam Orth the Sum of Fiften Pounds in Part of Fifty Pounds for Two Monds Servis as gard by me.

JOHN his X mark CLERCK.

Receved July the 28th 1779 the Sum of Thorty five Pounds hieng the Remender Sum of Fifty Pounds in ful by me.

JOHN his X mark CLERCK.

Receved Juni the 30th 1779 of Adam Orth the Sum of Fifty Pounds in Pard for Two Monds Servis as a militia man as guard. Receved by me.

PHILLIP DIBO.

Lebenon Juni the 29, 1779 Receved of Adam Orth the Sum of thorty Pounds in Pard of Fifty Pounds for Two monts Servis as gerd. Receved by me.

JOHN PAUL KUATZ.

Receved July the 31st 1779 of Adam Orth the Sum of Twenty Pounds bineng the Renembr bard of the above Fifty Pounds. Receved by me.

JOHN PAUL KURTZ.

Received Juni the 30th 1779 of Adam Orth the Sum of Fifty Pounds in Pard for Two monds Serves as a miliamen as a guard. Reçeved by me.

CASPER MIESS.

Recd. Lebenon Juni the 29th 1779 of Adam Orth the Sum of Fifty Pounds in Pard for two monds Serves as a card.
Receved by me.

WALTER his X mark NUMAN.

Receved. Lebenon Juni the 29 1779 of Adam Orth the Sum of Fifty Pounds in Pard for two monds Serves as a card.
Receved by me.

JACOB his X mark NUMAN.

Recevd. Lebenon Juni the 29th 1779 of Adam Orth the Sum of Fifty Pounds in Pard for two monds Serves as a card. Receved by me.

JOHANNES VALLENTIN.

RECEIPTS FOR SERVICES RENDERED IN THE WAR OF THE REVOLUTION. (c.)

Receved Juni the 29th 1779 of Adam Orth the Sum of Fifty Pounds in Part of Two monds Serves as a militia man I Say Receved by me.

HEINRICH JUNGST.

£50-0-0.

Receved of Adam Orth Juni the the 29th 1779 the Sum of Fifty Pounds in Part for Serves as a militia man I Say Receved by me.

CONRAT JUNGST.

£50-0-0.

Receved of Adam Orth the 29th Juni 1779 the Som of Fifty Pounds in Port for Two monts Servis as a militia man Recevet by me.

JACOB SNEVELY.

£50-0-0.

Receved Augst the 20 1779 of Adam Orth the Rementer Ten Pounds for the above Sixty Pound in full by me.

£10-0-0.

JACOB SNEVELY.

Receved Juni the 29th 1779 of Adam Orth the Sum of Fifty Pounds in Pard for Servis as a militia man I Say Receved by me.

GEORGE STROW, Sergent.

Receved of Adam Orth Jun 29th 1779 the Sum of Fifty Pounts in Part for Tow monts Servis as a militia man I Say Recevet by me.

ADAM his X mark LEBOT.

£50-0-0.

(c.) Received July 20th 1779, of Adam Orth Sub. Lieut. for L. C. by the Hands of Philip Marsteller, the Sum of Fifty Pounds in full for my Service as a Substitute, in the Militia employed as Guard at Lebanon Town.

I say recd.

p me GOTTLOB JUNGMANN.

[SEAL] By the Board of War and Ordinance of the United States of America to William Henry Esqr. of Lancaster in the State of Pennsylvania.

By Virtue of the Authority given us by Congress in their Act of the 23d. Instant herewith transmitted you are hereby appointed Commisary of hides for the States of Pennsylvania Delaware and Maryland—You will proceed immeditely in the faithful and diligent discharge of that duty, as pointed out in the following instructions & such others as the Board may from time to time think Proper to give you—You will correspond from time to time with this Board & the Clothier General informing us & him of all material transactions in Your Department.

From him you will receive Monies as the Exigencies of your business require them keeping an exact Account of your Expenditures & settling your accts. at least once a Year with the Commisioners of accounts—You will make regular Returns at least quarterly to the clothier General agreeably to the Directions of Congress—In all Cases of difficulty you will Consult the Board & on Common Occasions take the Advice & Instruction of the Clothier General—We would particularly recommend to you the strictest attention to Occonomy in your Expenditures, as in the present situation of our Affairs much depends on this.

You are to receive all raw hides as well of meat Cattle including Calves as of Sheep Killed for the Use of the troops & belonging to the United States within Your district & have them properly dried and Cured and Exchange the Same (under the following Exceptions as to Sheep Skins) either for Shoes or leather at the Customary rates of Exchange—So many of the Sheep Skins as are necessary are to be furnished the Commisary General or the Field Commisary of Meletary Stores or thier deputies for the Use of their Departments when you shall be by them required to deliver them, if you Can get the residue or any Part thereof made into Parchment for Drum heads let it be done & the Parchment delivered to the Commisary General or Field Commisary of Millitary Stores their deputies or their Order.

Such as are not disposed of in the manner above mentioned You are to Exchange with the wool for Leather of Shoes or make Sale thereof for the Benefit of the United States according to Circumstances We would Wheresoever it is practicable prefer the immediate Exchange for Shoes which in all Cases let be well made & substantial as much loss has heretofore accrued by the unsufficiency of many of the Shoes Supplied the Troops—The leather so obtain'd you will have work'd up into shoos & deliver them to the Clothier Genl. or his Order taking duplicate Receipts and whereof you will transmit to the treasury board—All Scraps or parts of leather proper for Mending the Soldiers Shoes or fit for Making Caps agreeable to a patron we will furnish, you will have Carefully preserved to be dispos'd of as Shall be hereafter derícted—When you shall be of Oppinion that Exchanges cannot be made on reasonable or convenient terms, you will contract with Persons to tan the Hides Coming into your Possession in the best terms Posible—but put no Hides out to tan except in Cases of Absolute Necessity, as not Only Great Delays in getting the leather but many Impositions are practised by Persons having Hides to Tan for the Publick—You are hereby Authorised to receive from all Persons either acting under the Old Departmt or by Any means having Possession of hides or leather belonging to the United States within Your District all such hides & Leather, transmitting Accots. of what You shall receive to the Clothier General and disposing thereof agreeable to the foregoing directions—

If you Can procure more Shoes to be made within Your District than can be produced out of the leather Blonging to the United States in Your hands, or if you Should have more of One species of Leather than Another You are hereby Authorised to Purchase Leather on the most Reasonable Terms for which Can be procured either for Supplying the deficiency or for delivering out to work-men to be worked up into Shoes, and as we fear withall our exertions that we shall be Able to procure but a bare Sufficiency of this Necessary Article you are hereby Authorised to purchase Good Substantial Shoes for the Use of the Army—In your Purchase of Leather or shoes you will confine Your Self to Your Own district as many Inconveniences will arise from extending Your Bussiness beyond the limits therof—You will Observe as to the Tallow offal &c. the directions of Congress contained in their Resolution of the 11th. Octob. 1777 in the Words following.

"Resolved

That the commissary General of Isues his deputies & Assistants, and all persons employ'd under him or them deliver over on demand to the Commissary of hides, all Hides Tallow fat and offal of all Cattle Killed for the Use of the Army, taking a Rect. for the same; any order or Direction of any Person or Persons to the Contrary notwithstanding."—

"That the Said Commissary of Hides shall receive and take care of the Tallow and all other Useful Offal of the Cattle belonging to the United States—and see that the said Tallow is properly Rendered & made fit to be Manufactured into Candles & Soap for the Use of the Army, and shall deliver the Said Tallow so rendered to the Commissary General of Purchases, or his Order taking Receipts for the same, reserving so much of the Said Tallow as may be necessary for the Manufactory of the leather and the use of his Own Departments.

In addition to this we Recommend to you to procure as much oil as possible from the feet of the Cattle for the purpose of Currying leather—When the Army is in Your neighborhood the Superintendent of Cattle will se that the Hides & Tallow are Seasonably delivered to you by the commisaries with the Army—You will Represent to the Board what assistants & Clerks will be necessary in Your District and on being informed we will transmit appointments for such as We deam necessary—As by the regulations of the Gloathing department it is recommended to the Governments of the respective States to purchase Cloathing for the Troops of their Several Quotas and as no doubt Shoes will be directed to be purchased in Consequence of this Recommendation we desire you will consult with the Executive Powers of the States of Pennsylvania Delaware & Maryland on this Subject & Cultivate all Posible harmony with them in this and every Other Part of your Business that no clashing may happen & the Prises of the Article be raised by a Compitition of Purchasers—

You will have the weight of the hide when green Cut on the But thereof. And when you are obliged to put Hides out to tan, you will Provide a Stamp or Brand with the letters U. S. for marking Such hides befor a delivery to the Tanners on the grain Side, so that the Same may be distinguish'd when tanned as Continental Property & Prevent Impositions in Substituting Inferior hides for those belongg. to the United States—You will Also have Express'd in the Rects. for Hides put to Tan their Weight as well as their Mark and the Number of them. There have been such Impositions in the Shoes Supplyed for the Army, we add this farther direction, that each individual Pair be Carefully Examined in every Part for the Purpose of discovering Frauds—These are generally in putting in bad leather, Cutting the quarters low the Vamps Short, almost Cutting through the Soal in hallowing the Heel bad Sewing Particularly the upper leather to the inner Soal which being Out of Sight few stitches are taken and they Presently come to Peices—We would have the Shoes made with a full Proportion of large ones, the quarters high and rather Short and fitting Close about the foot the Vamp coming up above the Buckel—You are also to Stamp Your Name on the Outside of the Soals of all Shoes procured by you—

You will in every hundred Pairs of Shoes either made or bought procure eight Pairs (& no more) fit for officers—As much Perplexity & Loss have arisen in the Business from the Variety of Persons heretofore employed in making Exchanges, and the Many Orders on the Commissarys for the delivery of hides, and as we deem you and your Assistants fully competent to Manage the Whole business within your district, you are hereby strictly forbidden to answer any Such Orders, given after your receipt of these Instructions unless they are Isued by the Authority of the Commander in Chief—

As there will be no Continental agents to interfere with you in Your district, & the Whole business is Committed to your Care, we Expect your utmost exertions will be used in procuring immidiate & Constant Supplies of Shoes for the Troops, who without great diligence in the Commissaries of Hides we fear will greatly Suffer.—

Given at the War Office the fifth Day of August Anno Domini 1779 & in the Fourth Year of our Indecendance.

(COPY) By order of the Board

RICHARD PETERS—

Endorsed on back "Commission to William Henry Esq. from the Board of War, Appointing him Commissary Genl. of Hides for Pennsylva., Delaware Maryland (COPY)

Original of above is in possession of Mr. Granville Henry, Belfast, Penna.

A RETURN OF THE SEVENTH & EIGHT CLASSES CALLED TO NORTHUMBERLAND COUNTY AUGUST 11TH 1779. (c.)

Capt. Murrays Compy ye 8th Class.

Thos Sturgon.
Martin Newbaker.
Jas. Bell.
Thos. Kearns.
Christie Eyeman.
Thos. Gallaher.
Robt. Smith.
Moses Lockert.
Jno. Dice.

8th Class.

Jno. Brown.
Abraham Mooney.
Jno. Bell, Junr.
Robt. Boyce.
Jno. Fisher.
George Adm. Gardner.
Jno. Sloan.
Lodwick Midzher.

Capt. McKinney, Do.

William McClure.
Michael Wolf.
Richard McClure.
Jacob Springer.
William Kerr.
Joseph Smith.
Hugh Cunningham.
John Steel.
Hugh Crocket.
Joseph Hucheson.
Jno. Fritz.
Felty Pancake.
Robt. Chambers.
Michael Boal.
John Means.
Rowan McClure.
Jas. Mahon.
Jas. McKinney.
John Maxwell.
Conrad Bumback.
Jas. Rutherford.

Capt. Rutherford, Do.

Milcham Miller.
George Page.
Jacob Beck.
Conrod Bobb.
David Richey.
Stophel Shupe.
Jacob Smith, Sr.
John Donnely.
Jos. Mark.

8th Class.

Joseph Shaw.
Michael Sheaver.
David Shaw.
Allexr. Willson .
John Toy.
John Saybourt.
Jacob Smith, Jr.

Capt. McClures, Do.

Philip Graft.
Valentine Wirrick.
Thos. Crabb.
Peter Miller.
Christian Hepach.
John Parks.
Jno. Lenning.
John King.
Abner Wickersham.
Robt. Watt.

8th Class.

George Mitzker.
Lodwick Hemberly.
John Myers.
Conrod Tarr.
Fredrick Zebernick.
Michel Gross.
Christian Gross.
Patrick Scott.
John Snider.
David Toot.
Emanuel Bullinger.
Allexr. Jamison.
William Crabb.

Capt. Clarks, Do.

Jno. Gillson.
Saml. Oram.
George Waggoner.
Peter Swaigert.
Jno. Gilmore.
Robt. Crawford.
John Butler.

8th Class.

John McElheny.
George McCandles.

Capt. Weaver, Do.

David Hermon.
Anthony Freeley.
George Seel.
Nicholas Hoofman.
George Menick.
Sebastian Mitz.
Henry Myer.

8th Class.

Michael Divler.
Henry Woolf.
Samuel Jura.
Christian Hoofman.
Joseph Philips.
George Buffington.
Christian Wertz.
Lodwick Bratz.
Stephen Bentz.

Capt. Stewarts, Do.

Samuel Simpson.
Cornelius Cox.
John Cline.
James Johnston.
William Carson.
Robert Clark.
Adam Eckart.
Joseph Cogley.

8th Class.

David Montgomery.
Robt. Cogley.
George Reniker.
Andrew Bell.
Patrick Heany.
Charles Stewart.
John Garber.
William Kelso, Sr.
James McKee.
Thos. Moore.
Robt. Fitzpatrick.
Barney Fridley.
Thos. Brynon.
Henry Irwin.

Capt. Gillchrists, Do.

William Cochran.
Robt. Gillchrist.
Andrew Stephen.
Jas. Buyers.
Thos. Bell.
David Caldwell.

8th Class.

Robt. Neil.
Jno. Miller.
John Murray.
Hugh Stephen.
Saml. Berryhill.
James Cavett.
William Downing.
Allexdr. Johnston.
Joseph Huffman.

(c.) This may certife that Capt'n Adam Wilhems Company of Lancaster County Militia Consisting of one Serjeant and twelve privats have faithfully performed their Tower of Duty at the Fronthieres in Northumberland County at Moors Fort, and are by these Presence therefrom discharged this 23th October 1779.

ADAM WILHELM, Capt.

(c.) This is to certify that Jesse Weeks did serve his tour of Duttey in the Seventh Class to which Class he belonged given finder my Hand October y'e 25, 1780.

THO'S MOORE, Lieut.

A GENERAL RETURN OF CAPT. JOHN SLETERS COMPANY OF THE FIRST CLASS OF LANCASTER COUNTY MILITIA DATED AT SUNBURY OCTOBER 31ST, 1780. (c.)

No. of Men out of the First Battalion.

Capt. Sleter's Comp.

Capt. John Sleter.
Baltzer Thumb.
Peter Busham.
Philip Bord.
Henry Peck.

Capt. Hasting's Comp.

James Douglass.
William Cammel.
Alexd. Wright.
Robert Grier for James Sterret.

Capt. White's Comp.

Thomas Buffington for Richd. Copland.
Neal Kenny for Henry Slaymaker.
Thomas White.
George Pursley.

Capt. Skiles Comp.

Dennis Kean.
William Mathers.

Capt. Henry's Comp.

James Regan.
Henry Norton.
Andrew Allison.

Capt. Smith Comp.

Peter Hole.
Simon Hinehole.
James Malston.

Capt. Hughey's Comp.

Abraham Myer.
Adam Winger.
John Rowland.
Ludwick Detrick.

Capt. Brisby's Comp.

Thomas McNeal.
Daniel Fleming.
Dennis Harkins.
James Cowen.
James Borlen for Archd. McCordy.

No. of Men out of the third Battalion.

Capt. Duck's Comp.

Jacob Duck, deserted.

Capt. Ream's Comp.

Lieut. Henry Ream.
Peter Grove.

Capt. Gear's Comp.

William Snyder.
Philip Hoffman.
Jacob Hoyle.

Capt. Lutz's Comp.

Jacob Hershey.
Christian Huber.
John Lesher.
John Lininger.
John Grill.

No. of Men out of the Fifth Battalion.

Capt. Crawford Comp.

Philip Rhoad.
Leonard Stone.
Edward Good.

Capt. Eliot Comp.

John Davis.

Capt. McIrain Comp.

Nathan Evans.
John Purrell.
Jacob Fox.

Capt. Jenkin's Comp.

Ensign Thomas Martin.
Amos Evans.
Joseph Isington.
Jacob Nothamer.
Ab'm Eshelman for G'o Weaver.

Capt. Bowman's Comp.

Christian Swartzwelder. James Keemer, Jun'r.

Capt. Lutz's Comp.

Fredrick Rhoad. Jacob Smith.

Capt. Holman Comp.

Philip Rhoad. Jacob Rhoad.

Capt. Statler's Comp.

Christian Ferrey, sick at Estherton & discharged.

(c.) Recd. Decr. 23d 1780 of Col. Atlee two Hundred Dollars in part pay for my Tour of Duty to Northumberland.

ADAM KELLER.

RETURN OF CAPTAIN BRANDS COMPANY OF THE LOWER PART OF THE TOWNSHIP OF MANOR, IN THE COUNTY OF LANCASTER, COMANDET BY COLONEL LODWIG MYER FOR THE YEAR 1780 WITH THEIR NAMES AND SIR-NAMES AS FOLLOWS, vizt.

November 1780. (c.)

Christian Stehman.
John Herr.
Daniel Lindner.
John Neave, Junr.
John Kauffman.
Jacob Choals.
Christian Burgholder.
Christian Herr.
John Grob.
Henry Neave.
Henry Shup.
John Neave.
Casper Halbruner.
Killian Boas.
John Newcomer.
Henry Histand.
John Hysinger.
John Wittmer.
Christian Hirshy.
Christian Kauffman.
Jacob Killheffer.
John Killheffer.
John Histand.
Rudolph Herr.
Henry Miller.
Benjn. Herr.
John Keller.
Michael Shank.

A True Return Given Pr. me,

JACOB BRAND, Capt.

A RETURN OF THE MALE WHITE FIT TO BEAR ARMS OF CAPT. M. BOWMANS COMP'Y: BETWEEN EIGHTEEN AND FIFTY YEARS OF AGE. (c.)

1 first Class.

John Ghere.
Joseph Zimmerman.
Christian Shwartzwelder.
John Shuwalder.
Michael Bitzer.
Conrad Holtzinger.
Jacob Sueeder.
Henery Zimerman.

2 Secand Class.

Jacob Wiese.
Andrew Yunt.
Jacob werns.
Abraham Andreas.
Peter Pence.
Jacob Swigert.
Martin Near.
Abraham Wolf.
Henery Sherk.

3 Third Class.

John McCleary.
George German.
Michael Hass.
George ghere.
John Evans.
Jacob Hinkle.
William Parry.
Adam German, Jr.
Philip Rinwood.
John Fistnawer.
Philip Wiese.

4 fourth Class.

James Goult.
Andrew Weise.
David Camphir.
John German.
John Muman.
John Solenberger.
George wever.
Henery Roth.
Samuel Saligley.

5 fifth Class.

John Yunt.
Martin Werns.
David Morgan.
John Betzer, Jr.
Jonathan Roland.
Abraham Solenberger.
Ernest Miller.
Henery Hempright.
John Lippert.

6 Sixt Class.

John Faustnaught.
John Sids.
Alexander Goult.
Philip Ronk.

William McClen.
Christopher Miller.
John Gordon.
Joseph McCleary, Jr.
Baltzer Hivener.
Zaubaus Davis, Jr.

7 Seventh Class.

Henery Nice.
James McCleary Jr.
George Clopper.
Isaac Davis.
John Campher.
Nicholaus Miller.
Daniel Hane.
John wenger, Jr.
Leonhart Spitznagel.
Jacob Sherk.

8 Eight Class.

John Roht.
John Gunty.
George Wiese.
Jacob Bratzer.
Valendin Britzge.
Michael Killian.
William Shaw.
Willias Davis.

The above Return is Certified by me this Tenth Day of May in the yeare Seventeen Hundred and Eighty one.

MARTIN BOWMAN, Capt.

A RETURN OF ALL THE MALE WHITE INHABITANTS BETWEEN THE AGES OF 18 & 53 YEARS CAPABLE OF BEARING ARMS IN MY DISTRICT IN CASSICAL ORDER THIS 29TH DAY OF JUNE ANNO DOMINI 1781. (c.)

1 Class.

George Weaver.
Jacob Nuthanler.
Amos Evans.
Joseph Essington.
Jacob Yoder, Junr.
Danl. Stofer.
George Wilson.

2 Class.

James Patterson.
Joshua Evans.
John Jenkins.
Thomas Rattew.
Will'm Morgan.
Thos. Caseburn.
George Wiseman

3 Class.

Will'm Eckerman.
John Evans, Junr.
Lot Evans.
Nahtl. Davis.
James Davis.
John Wilson.
John Bolen.

4 Class.

Jacob Cashner.
John Piler.
David Evans.
Henry Weaver.
Will'm Bell.
James Morgan.
Francis Wellman.
Thomas Fogerty.
Thomas Maxfield.
John Huston.

5 Class.

John Zill.
Henry Zill.
Thomas Morgan.
John Rees.
Thomas Douglass.
Michael Bamer.
William Fleman.

6 Class.

John Yoder.
Abr'm Dolby.
Will'm Evans.
Morris Hudson.
Emanuel Neyssanger.
John Morgan.
Thomas Jenkins.
Adam Nuthamer.
David Jenkins.
David Montgomery.

7 Class.

Theophilus Thomas.
James Withrow.
Saml. Stofer.
Elijah Hudson.
James Parks.
Isaac Jenkins, Jur.
Isaac Jenkins.
John Jenkins, Junr.
Will'm Hudson.
Joseph Norman.
Maths. Stofer.
Thomas Douglass.

8 Class.

Valentine Rank.
Theodore Willtmor.
Chris'n Curts.
John Nuthumer.
John Yoder, Ser.
Chris'n Yoder.
Will'm Meredith.

Nathan Evans.
John Cleland.
Jacob Stofer.
Samuel Iddings.
Hugh McLaughlin.

I Do hereby Certify the above to be True.

JOSEPH JENKINS,
Capt'n.

(c.) This is to Certify that Hendry McClusky Served his Tower in my Company in the Year 1781 Sept. 25 at Newtown Till Ragelerly Discharged.

Certified By

JOS. SMITH, Lieut.
of Capt. Wm. CLURES Comp'y.

To home it May Concern
Paxton, March 21, 1786.

A PROVISION RETURN OF THE 4TH DRAUGHT OF LANCR. COUNTY MILITIA COMMD. BY LIEUT. COL. JAMES ROSS FOR ONE DAY COMMG. & ENDING THE 3RD OF OCTOR. 1781. (c.)

Companies.	Lt. Col.	Major.	Capt.	Subaltern.	Adjutant.	Qr. Mr.	Serjt. Major.	Qr. Mr. Sergt.	Clerks.	Serjants	Drums & Fifes.	Rank & File.	Total of Rations.
Field & Staff Offrs.,	1	1	......	......	1	1	......	......	......	......	......	......	8
Capt. Wirtz's,	......	......	1	2	......	......	......	1	1	3	3	36	50
Capt. Boyd's,	......	......	1	......	......	......	1	......	1	3	2	31	40
Capt. Scott's,	......	......	1	2	......	......	......	......	1	2	2	54	65
Capt. Clark's,	......	......	1	2	......	......	......	......	1	3	......	35	45
Capt. Willsom,	......	......	1	2	......	......	......	......	1	3	..	53	63
Capt. Walker's,	......	......	1	2	......	......	......	......	......	3	......	36	45
Capt. Allin,	......	......	1	2	......	......	......	......	......	2	......	47	55
Capt. Bradley's,	......	......	1	1	......	......	......	......	1	3	......	39	47
	1	1	8	13	1	1	1	1	6	22	7	331	418

By order of the General:
JAS. BAYARD, B. M.
COL. CRUPIN, C. M.

ANDREW GRAFF, Qr. M'r.
HENRY MARCKLEY, Major.
Com't 4 D't L. C. M.

LANCASTER COUNTY MILITIA.

A Provision Return for the 4th Draught of Lanc'r County Militia (Commanded by Lieut. Col. James Ross), for Three Days Comm'g the 6th & Ending the 8th day of Octo'r, 1781, Inclusive. (b.)

Companies.	Lieut. Col.	Major.	Captain.	Subalterns.	Adj't.	Qr. Master.	Sergt. Major.	Qr. Mr. Sergt.	Sergeants.	Clerks.	Drum'r & Fifers.	Waggoners.	Rank & file.	Total of rations per day.	No. of days drawn for.	Total of rations.
Field & staff officers,	1	1	......	......	1	1	......	......	......	......	......	......	......	8	3	24
Capt. Wirtz's,	......	......	1	2	......	......	......	1	3	1	3	1	36	51	3	153
Capt. Boyd's,	......	......	1	......	......	......	1	......	3	1	2	1	31	41	3	123
Capt. Scott's,	......	......	1	2	......	......	......	......	3	1	2	1	56	69	3	207
Capt. Clark's,	......	......	1	2	......	......	......	......	3	1	......	1	35	46	3	138
Capt. Willson's,	......	......	1	2	......	......	......	......	3	......	......	......	45	54	3	162
Capt. Allen's,	......	......	1	2	......	......	......	......	2	......	......	......	46	54	3	162
Capt. Bradley's,	......	......	1	2	......	......	......	......	3	..	......	1	40	50	3	150
Capt. Walker's,	......	......	1	2	......	......	......	......	3	......	......	......	36	45	3	135
Total,	1	1	8	14	1	1	1	1	23	4	7	5	225	418	3	1,254

JAMES ROSS, Lieut. Col. 4th Draught Lanc'r Militia.

(c.) This to certify that John Kingry sent John Pifer as a substitute in his place on a tower of duty to New Town in Bucks County, November 22nd in the year 1781. Certifyd pr. me.

WM. KELLY.

N. B. Noah Ceasey Capt. at that time. May 23rd, 1786.

RECEIPTS FOR SERVICES RENDERED IN THE WAR OF THE REVOLUTION. (c.)

Paxtang November 29th 1781.

Rec'd of Max'll Chambers S. Lt. the several sums annexed to our names in part pay for serving a tour of Militia Duty in the 2d Class of Lancaster County Militia as Witness our hand.

Wil'm Morrow ....£8 17s 6d.
James Walker ....£1 2s 6d.

Paxtang November 29th 1781.

Rec'd of Max'll Chambers S. Lt. the several sums annexed to our names in part pay for serving a tour of Militia Duty in the third Class of Lancaster County Militia. Witness our hand.

John Annybrary (?) ....£8.11s.6d.
John Chambers ....£1. 8s.0d.

Paxtang December 3d 1781.

Rec'd of Max'll Chambers S. Lt. the several sums enexed to our Respective Names Being in full for serving a tour of Militia Duty in the 4th Class of Lancaster County Militia agreeable to a pay Role for that purpose

Witness our hands.

Adam Muller ....£3.10s.0d.

his
Thomas X Dougherty .... 3.10s.
mark

Michael Wein .... 3.10s.
Georg Beibe .... 3.10s.
Michael Gassel .... 3.10s.
John Parker ....£3.10s.
Fredrick Harmon ....£3.10s.
John Chasney ....£3.10s.

Paxtang December 3d 1781.

Rec'd of Max'll Chambers S. Lt. the several sums anexed to our Respective Names Being in full for serving a tour of Militia Duty in the 6th Class of Lancaster County Militia agreeable to a pay Role for that purpose.

Witness our hands.

William Whitner ....£3.10s.
Daniel Walter ....£3.10s.
Adam Kitzmillor ....£3.10s.
John Mathiws, Lieut. ....£6.13s.4d.
Jacob Hovere ....£3.10s.0d.

A RETURN FOR ADAMSTOWN DISTRICT COM'D BY CAPT. NICH. LUTZ IN THE FORE PART OF THE YEAR 1781. (c.)

Captain.

Nicholas Lutz.

Lieutenant.

John Beehtoll.

Ensign.

Henry Geiger.

Sergents.

David Bahrringer. Joseph Brendel.
John Lutz.

Corprals.

Henry Laush.
Philip Brendel.
Michael Winehold.

First Glase.

George Westhaffer.
Adam Grill.
Nicholas Lesher.
John Lininger.
Jacob Hershy.
Christian Hoober.
Philip Lutz.
Jacob Hyl.
Philip fernsler.
Friderick Steffy.

Second Glase.

Jacob Weeber.
Peter Steffy.
Philip Grell.

Third Glas.

Christian Weeber.
John Lesher.
Michael Harding.
Adam Leed.
George Coppes.
Ruty Miller.
George Keller.
Henry Zimmerman.
John Geetz.

Firth Glas.

Henry Bastian.
Henry Brendel.
Richard Adams.
John Miller.
Isaac Adams.
Philip Broadstone.
Peeter Wise.
Martin fernshler.
John Eigenberger.

Five Glass.

George Ury.
Joseph Wenger.
John Greell.
John Ruch.
Henry Leed.
Henry Shnider.
John Shwigerd.
Peter Shmith.
Peter Fry.
Henrey Laush.

Six Glas.

Nicholas Shower.
Michael Youg, young.
Jacob gemberling.
Friderick Gerner.
Rudy Bear.
Casper Bossert.
Henry Walter.
Henry Lutz.
Christian Shlaugh.
Marx Benckly.
John Gerber.

Sevend -Glas.

Henry Eicholtz.	Michael Kegrich.
David Tidlo.	Nicholas Rup.
Mathias Walck.	John Colman.
Jacob Voneeda.	Casper Shimpf.
John Hoober.	Jacob Zinn.
Jost Spengler.	Peter Ulrich.
Adam Kissinger.	Peter Benckly.

Eight Glas.

Christian Harding.	John Miller juner.
Christ Zimmerman.	John Wengert.
Charls Tritsh.	Peter Zimmerman.
George Rimmel.	Henry Keiper.
Isaac Betecoffer.	John Rahrer.
John Betecoffer.	Adam Martin.

I do hereby certifie theese to be a true Return to the best of my Knowledge.

NICHOLAS LUTZ, Captain.

A RETURN OF CAPT. ROBT. CAMPBLE'S COMPANY OF MILITIA IN LITTLE BRITAIN TOWNSHIP LANC. CO. 1781. (c.)

Capt.

Robt. Campble.

Lieut.

Isaac Walker.

Ens'n.

David McComb.

1st Class.

John Walker.	Wm. Johnson.
John Camron.	Thos. Loid.
Will'm Dunlap.	John patton.

2d.

Gilbt. Buchanan.	John Brobston.
John Brooks.	Dan'l Copple.
And'w Walker.	Peetter Hill.
James Petterson, Junr.	John Buchanan.
Alex'r Snodgress.	Will'm Vint.

3d.

John Atchison.	Joseph Walker.
Sam'l Reynolds.	Hugh Weir.
Joseph Haines.	Wm. Pennol Jur.
John Powel, Jn.	John Patton.
John Brown.	

4th.

James Black.	Joshua Haines.
Wm. Henery.	Alex'r Ferguson.
Hugh Glover.	David Beard.
Jacob Reynolds.	Thos. Badger.

5th.

David Alexander.	Daniel Burkard.
Alex'r Scott.	James Beaty.
Sam'l Gillcreist.	Hugh Johnson.
James Petterson.	James Buchanan.

6th.

Abram Whiteside.	Thos. Grist.
John Petterson.	Thos. Petterson.
Francis Henery.	Joseph Alison.
Wm. Brown.	John Grist.
Wm. Irwen.	George Nelson.
John Hill.	Wm. Ewing.
Robt. Alexander.	Robt. Moore.
Robt. Allison.	

7th.

Thos. Hill.	Mar'm Eickman.
John Gibson.	Jacob Moates.
Robt. Johnson.	John Alexander.
James Walker.	Wm. Brice.
Sam'l Reynolds.	Benj'm Zooe.
John Nesbet.	Collon Kerrol.
Abso'm Camron.	David Powel.
Wm. Leetch.	

8th.

Sam'l Mitchel.	Wm. Grist.
Hen'y Reynolds.	David Mitchell.
Thos. Campble.	James Jamison.
Isaac Reynolds.	John Campble.
Sam'l Logan.	James Osburn.

N. B. Sundry Men added to the Class's in this Role, who joined since class Role to 7th Con't Line was made.

ROBERT CAMPBELL, Capt.

1781.

A RETURN OF CAPTN. ROBT. CAMPBLE'S COMPANY OF MILITIA IN LITTLE BRITTAIN TOWNSHIP IN AUG. 1782. (c.)

Capt.

Robt. Campbell.

Lieut.

Isaac Walker.

Ens.

David McComb.

Clk.

Joseph Allison.

1st Class.

John Walker.	Thos. Finley.
John Camron.	George Kimer.
Robt. McPeack.	John Evans.

2d Class.

Gilbert Buchannan.	Peeter Hill.
John Brooks.	Thos. Loid.
Andrew Walker.	Robt. Ferguson.
James Petterson Junr.	Will'm Vint.
Alex'd Snodgress.	

3d Class.

John Atchison.
Joseph Keans.
John Powel Junr.
John Brown.
Joseph Walker.
Will'm Pennol Junr.
John Anderson.
Sam'l McGinnis.

4th Class.

Will'm Henery.
Alex'd Ferguerson.
Hugh Halladay.
Ruben Reynolds.
Isaac Grist.

5th Class.

David Alexander.
Alex'd Scott.
James Petterson.
James Beaty.
John Browgon.
Will'm Carter.

6th Class.

John Petterson.
Francis Henery.
Will'm Irwin.
John Hill.
Robt. Alexander.
Robt. Alison.
Thos. Petterson.
Will'm Ewing.
Robt. Moore.
Joseph Robison.
Patt'k Brown.
Hugh Steel.

7th Class.

James Walker.
Robt. Johnson.
John Nesbit.
John Gibson.
Thos. Hill.
Martin Ickman.
John Allexander.
Sam'l Reynolds.
John Buchannan.
Callon Kerrol.
David Powel.
James McPeack.
George McPeack.
Randell Lees.

8th Class.

Sam'l Mitchell.
Thos. Campbell.
Sam'l Logan.
David Mitchell.
John Campbell.
James Jamison.
Jno. McClanahen.
Robt. Bell.
Isaac Reynolds.
Henery Reynold.

A True Copy.

JOSEPH ALISON, Clk
Aug. 1782.

ROBERT CAMPBELL, Capt.

A TRUE AND EXACT LIST OF THE NAMES, OF EACH AND EVERY MALE WHITE PERSON, INHABITING OR RESIDING, WITHIN MY DISTRICT, IN THE COMPANY, OF THE BATTALION OF LANCASTER COUNTY, MILITIA, BETWEEN THE AGE OF EIGHTEEN AND FIFTY-THREE YEARS. TAKEN FOR THE YEAR 1782. (c.)

Capt.

Conrod Karrer.

Lieu.

Adam Fisher.

Ens.

John Kinkel.

Almonar.

William Wright.

First Class.

John Bender.
William Pratt.
George Brenor.
Joseph Musser.
Peter Schnider.
Michael Boughman.
Abraham Kaufman.
Andrew Hershey.

Second Class.

Benjamin Hershey.
Benjamin Muser.
Christain Martain.
Christain Steiner.
Frederick Hofman.
Frederick Weiser.
Mathias Miller.
James Pratt.

Third Class.

George Wagenor.
Christain Hershey.
John Sowder.
Henry Paules.
John Eshleman.
George Beck.
Rhudolph Funk.
Adam Bitner.
Christain Barrack.
Michael Shoeman.

Fourth Class.

John Funk.
John Butt.
Daniel Kindig.
Jacob Steiner.
John Kindig.
Edward Kelley.
Abraham Herr.
John Kremer.
John Behm.

Fifth Class.

Samuel McDanold.
Abraham Steiner.
Jacob Monning.
Christain Martain.
Christain Bowman.
John Monning.
Frederick Myer.
John Bortsfeild.
Frederick Zimmerman.
Joseph Hinkle.

Sixth Class.

Abraham Correll.
George Kindig.
Gotleib Yelder.
Christain Stopher.
Jacob Whistler.
Micheal Ritter.
Simeon Venger.
Ulrick Rever.
Joseph Kaufman.

Seventh Class.

Phillip Sower.
Peter Witmor.
Phillip Brenner.
Jacob Eshleman.
Christain Herr.
William McManuel.
Isaac Martain.
James Wrigh.
Isaac Kaufman.

Eighth Class.

Joseph Winger.
John Musser.
Henry Breneman.
Henry Eshleman.
John Cremer.
Thomas Wright.
Garhart Stake.
David Kaufman.
John Logan.
Adam Stake.

Serjants.

1st. Peter Dunkle.
2d. Peter Rummel.
3d. Peter Klien.

I Do swear, on the Holy Evengilest of Almighty God: That the above list is a just and true state of the Male White Inhabitants, residing in my District, agreeable to Law, and without any fraud to the State, to the best of my knowledge.

CONRAD KARVER, Capitain.

Sworn before me this 8th Day of June 1782,

JAMES BARBER, S. Lt. L. C.

A RETURN FOR ADAMEOTOWN DISTRICT COM'D BY CAPT. NICK. LUTZ IN THE LASTE PERT OF THE YEAR 1782. (c.)

Lieutenant.

John Bechtold.

Ensign.

Henry Geyer.

Dramer and phifer.

Jacob Zinn.

Sergents.

David Baringer.
John Lutz.
Joseph brendel.

Corprel.

Henry Laush.
Michail Winehold.

The 1st Clase.

George Westhafer.
Nicholas Lesher.
Jacob Hershey.
Christian Hooher.
Philip Lutz.
Jacob Hyl.
Friderick Steffy.
Andrew Shimph.
George Gensener.

The 2d Clase.

Philip Grell.
George Zinn.
Henry Sheffer.
Henry Branckmyer.
John Weber.
John Reller.
Abraham Maurer.

The 3rd Clase.

John Lesher.
Michal Hording.
Adam Lead.
George Coppes.
Rudy Miller.
George Keller.
Henry Zimerman.

The 4th Clase.

Henry Bastean.
Henry Brendel.
Richard Adams.
John Miller.
Isaac Adams.
Philip Broadstone.
Peter Wise.
Martin fernsler.
John Eigenberger.
Mathias Holdery.
Henry Brendel.

The 5th Clase.

John Grell.
John Ruch.
Henry Lead.
John Shweigert.
Peter Smith.
Peter Fry.
Henry Good.

The 6th Clase.

Nicholas Shower.
Michal Young.
Friderick Gerner.
Rudy Bear.
Casper Bosert.
Christian Shlang.
Marx Benckly.
John Shoub.
Hector Payne.

The 7th Clase.

Henry Eigholds.
David Didio.
Jacob Vanida.
John Hoober.
Jost Spengeler.
Adam Risinger.
Michal Regerish.
Nicholas Rup.
John Colman.
Henry Shnider.
George Sydebender.
George Mengel.
John Westheffer.
Philip Buch.

The 8th Clase.

Christian Harding.
Charls Tritsh.
George Rimel.
Isaac Beticoffer.
John Miller, Jr.
John Wengert.
Peter Zimerman.
Peter Ulrich.
Henry Walter.
Christian Eiseman.

I do hereby Certify these to be a true Return to the best of my Knowledge.

NICHOLAS LUTZ, Capt.

MUSTER ROLL FOR ADAMSTOWN DISTRICT COM'D BY CAPT. NICHOLAS LUTZ, IN THE FORE PART OF THE YEAR 1782. (c.)

Capt.

Nicholas Lutz.

Lieut.

John Bechtold.

Ensign.

Henry Gyger.

Clarck.

Philip Lutz.

Drumer & phifer.

Jacob Zinn.

Sergents.

David Baringer.
John Lutz.
Joseph Prendel.

Corprels.

Henry Lauch.
Michal Winehold.

the 1st Class.

George Westhaffer.
Nicholas Lesser.
Jacob Hershey.
Christian Hoober.
Jacob Hyle.
Frederick Steffy.
Baltzer Stone.
Andrew Shimps.
george gensemer.

the 2th Clase.

Jacob Weeber.
Philip Grell.
George Zinn.
John Weeber.
Henry Sheffer.
Henry brauehmyer.

the 3th Clase.

John Leesher.
Michal Harding.
Adam Leed.
George Copper.
Ruty miller.
George Keller.
Henry Zimmerman.

Clas the 4th.

Henry Bastian.
Henry Brendel.
Richard Adams.
John Miller.
Isaac Adams.
Philip Breadstone.
Peter Wise.
Martin Dernsler.
John Eigenberger.
Matias W. Holdy.
Henry Brendel, Sen.

the 5th Clase.

John Greell.
John Ruch.
Henry Lead.
John Shweigert.
Peter Smith.
Peter Fry.]

the 6th Clase.

Nicholas Shower.
Michal Young.
Friderick gerner.
Ruty Bear.
Casper Bussert.
Christian Shlaugh.
Marx Banckly.
John Shoup.

the 7th Clase.

Henry Eighholds.
David Ditlo.
Jacob Vaneeda.
John Hoober.
Jost Spengeler.
Adam Rissinger.
Michal Kegerise.
Nicholas Rup.
John Colman.
Peter Banckly.
Henry Sidebander.
george Mengel.
John Westhefer.

the 8th Clase.

Christian Harding.
Charls Tritsh.
George Rimel.
Isaac bettecoffer.
John Beticoffer.
John Miller, jun.
John Wengert.
Peter Zimmarman.
John Jost.
Henry Waltel.
george Miller.
Christ. Eiseman.
Mathias Sheffer.
Peter ulrick.

I do hereby Certify this to be a true Return to the best of my knowledge.

NICHO. LUTZ, Cap.

A TRUE AND EXACT LIST OF THE NAMES, OF EACH AND EVERY MALE WHITE PERSON, INHABITING OR RESIDING, WITHIN MY DISTRICT, IN THE COMPANY, OF THE BATTALION OF LANCASTER COUNTY, MILITIA, BETWEEN THE AGE OF EIGHTEEN AND FIFTY-THREE YEARS. TAKEN FOR THE YEAR 1782. (c.)

Capt.

Philip Baker.

Lieu.

Henry Detrick.

Ens.

John Row.

Almonar.

Micheal Haverstick.

Privates.

1st Class.

John Hess.
Christain Forry.
Christain Hoober.
Abraham Stetler.
John Bowman.
Frederick Rathoon.
george Albright.
Andrew Myer.

2nd Class.

John Boughman.
Chris'n Koughnour.
Christian Breneman.
Samuel Hess.
Jacob Barrack.
Benedict Mellenger.
Robert Reed.

Third Class.

Micheal Ritter.
Henry Lyne.
Christain Hess.
Daniel Kebortz.
Melchoir Breneman.
John Miller.
Samuel Kesberger.

Fourth Class.

Abraham Hess.
Henry Koughnour.
Chris'n Stayman.
Jacob Byar.
Jacob Smith.
Jacob Lyne.
John Gable.
John Breneman.

Fifth Class.

Henry Hoober.
Peter Hoober.
Jacob Krder.
Jacob Breneman.
Henry Miller.
Micheal Hess.
Jacob Kegler.

Sixth Class.

Rudolph Miller.
adam Koughnour.
Peter Good.
John Hoober.
Jacob Koughnour.
Chris'n Newcomer.
John Keler.
Abraham Werfel.
Isreal Beard.

7th Class.

Abraham Hoober.
John Behm.
Abraham Lyne.
John Kendig.
Jacob Behm.
Barnet Fagon.
Micheal Ragon.
Chris'n Correll.

8th Class.

Joseph Keller.
Chris'n Keagy.
George Rathvon.
Jacob Lutman.
Jacob Albright.
John Yelder.

Serjeants.

Henry Derr.
James Bryan.

I do swear, on the Holy Evengilest of Almighty God: That the above is a just and true state of the male white inhabitants, residing in my District, agreeable to Law & without any fraud to the state to the best of my knowledge.

PHILIP BAKER, Capt.

Sworn before me this
tenth day of December 1782.
JAMES BARBER, Sub. Lt. L. C.

(c.) I do certify that the Barer, Casper Deemer served a tower of two months in my company in the fourth class at Lancaster the said was his own tower.

DAVID KRAUSE, Capt.
Lebanon March 29, 1783.

JOHN GLONINGER, Sub. Lt.

Said Deemer, Demands the armirer money being £5.5.0 agreeable to Law.

FOURTH COMPANY (Lancaster County.) (a.)

Captain.

James Collier.

First Lieutenant.

William Young.

Second Lieutenant.

William Kelso.

LOSS OF BLANKETS AND ARMS. (a.)

As will be seen by the following lists, many of the citizens, including women, at the outset of the Revolution, loaned the troops such blankets and arms as they were in possession of. Most of those mentioned were lost at the surrender of Fort Washington and Battle of Long Island.

A List of Names who gave Blankets to the Use of the Continent at Amboy in Cap. Cowden's Company, & were paid for the same by Col. Cornelius Cox.

Elijah Buck.
John Hilton.
John McMachan.
John Boys.
Michael Spaid.
Anthony Frelock.
Jacob Kisner.
Henry Lerue.
George Lore.
David Ritchy.
David Caldwell, Taylor.
Richard Swan.
Jacob Heruff.
George Taylor.

John Maxwell.
Philip Fishburn.
Robert Neel.
Peter Grossclose.
William McClure.
David Caldwell.
William Calhoon.
John Steel, Sr.
Godfrey Crutchman.
James Mahan.
George McMullan.

A List of money to be paid for Loss of Guns &c., for men of Capt. Murray's Company.

Adam West in Right of Michael Saladen.
Sebastian Stonebracker.
Albright Divler.
James Woodside.
Lodwick Bretz.
Jacob Neveling.
William Ritter.
Joseph Stiver.
Jacob Shotts.
Christian Snoak.
Adam Wertz.
Widow Divler, Repair of George Cooper's Gun.

N.B. The Above Company went out in the Flying Camp.

Sir: The above sum of Forty Nine pounds & Twelve Shillings is the amount of the Loss of Guns, &c. Sustained by Capt. Murray's Compa.

The bearer Mr. Lodwick Bretz informs us that it will not be inconvenient for you to pay him the same out of the Batt. Stock. (If so) Mr. Joshua Elder goes to Lancaster on Monday to Receive the whole Loss of the Batt. and upon his Return will Replace the above sum.

I am, your most humble Servt.,

To Mr. JOHN GILCHRIST. JAMES BURD.

GRAIN AND FORAGE FOR THE ARMY.

The following is an assessment made and collected of grain and forage for the army in 1778:

	Bushels wheat.	Bushels forage.
John Alleman,	1	3
Stophel Alleman,	4	4
Conrad Alleman,	4	4
Christly Alleman,	4	4
John Achla,	4	4
Jacob Awl,	5	5
Jacob Brand,	3	3
George Bennet,	1	1
John Bowman, Sen'r.,	1	2
William Brown,	....	10
John Barnet, Jr.,	1	2
John Barnet, Sen'r.,	2	2
Andrew Berrihill,	2	....
Alexander Berrihill,,	1	1
William Boyd,	1	2
Thomas Bell,	2	4
Peter Bobb,	3	3
William Bell,	2	24
Henry Bool,	3	2
Peter Brenor,	2	1
James Burd,	4	4
Barefoot Brunson,	2	3
Jacob Barkley,	2	2
Casper Bierly,	2	2
Felty Baker,	3	3
Philip Brown,	2	1
Conrad Bobb,	4	3
John Borris,	1	2
Widow Booggs,	1	2
John Buck,	3	3
John Bachman,	2	2
James Biers,	3	3
John Brand,	3	2
Robert, Maxwell, & Rowland Chambers,	4	4
George Consert,	2	2
John Cavit,	1	2
William Caldhoon,	1	3
John Chambers,	....	2
William Cochran,	2	2
James Cochran,	2	2
Widow Cadwell,	3	3
Hugh Cunningham,	3	1

GRAIN AND FORAGE FOR THE ARMY—Continued.

	Bushels wheat.	Bushels forage.
John Clendening,	1	2
William Carson,	3	1
Cornelius Cox,	5	5
John Cline,	1	1
James Cogley,	1	1
John Cogley,	1	1
James Croutch,	3	3
Michael Cassall,	2	2
James Colliar,	2	1
John Clark,	1	....
Frederick Cassal,	2	2
George Carson,	2	[illegible]
Daniel Cooper,	2	1
John Cassal,	2	1
Matthew Calhoon,	2	2
Richard Carson,	....	2
Samuel Cochran,	2	2
James Cowden,	4	3
John Campbell,	1	1
Philip Criner,	1	1
James Duncan,	4	2
Robert Douglass,	1	1
Peter Duffey,	1	....
Christian Denney,	....	2
Rev. John Elder,	1	1
John Elder,	1	1
Joshua Elder,	7	7
Adam Ecker,	10	10
Stophel Earnest,	2	2
Abraham Eagly,	1	1
Joseph Flora, Jr.,	1	1
George Fockler,	2	2
John Foster,	3	3
John Fritz,	4	4
Philip Fisher,	2	1
John Flackiner,	2	2
Joseph Fulton,	2	6
Barnabas Fridley,	1	1
George Fridley,	1	1
Joseph Flora, Sr.,	4	4
Wendle Fockler,	1	1
Frederick Foster,	2	1
John Garver,	8	4
James Finney,	1	1
John Gilcrist, Esq.,	2	2
John Gallacher,	4	4
George & Joseph Gray,	4	4
William Gibbons,	3	3
Major John Gilchrist,	3	3
John Gray,	3	3

GRAIN AND FORAGE FOR THE ARMY—Continued.

	Bushels wheat.	Bushels forage.
Joseph Greg,	1	1
Robert Gilcrist,	4	4
Joseph Hutchison,	3	3
Samuel Hutchison,	3	3
Andrew Huston,	1	1
Joseph Hoofman,	2	1
Patrick Heaney,	2	2
Henry Humberger,	1	1
John Helton,	1	1
John Hershey,	3	3
John Harris,	8	8
James Harris,	3	3
Martin Hauser,	3	3
——— Huber,	3	2
Patrick Hogan,	....	1
John Hershey,	1	2
Alexander Johnston,	3	3
John Jameson,	3	3
Peter Issenhauer,	2	2
Joseph Irwin,	1	1
James Johnston,	1	1
William Karr,	4	4
Thomas King,	3	2
William Kays,	1	1
John Kinshley,	2	2
William Kelso,	2	2
Jacob Karr,	3	2
William Kirkpatrick's Land,	4	4
Edward King,	2	2
Patrick Lusk,	2	2
Adam Lambert,	1	2
Michael Limes,	2	....
Francis & George Lerue,	4	3
Jacob Limes,	2	2
George McMullen,	3	3
John Maxwell,	1	....
John Means,	2	2
Alexander McHargue,	1	1
William McMullen,	2	2
William McRoberts,	1	2
John McHeaney,	2	2
Robert Montgomery,	1	1
Jacob Miller,	4	4
Hugh Montgomery,	4	4
David Montgomery,	3	3
James McKee,	3	3
John Moor,	....	1
James McCord,	2	2
Jonathan McClure,	3	2
Rowen McClure,	2	2

GRAIN AND FORAGE FOR THE ARMY—Continued.

	Bushels wheat.	Bushels forage.
Alexander & Richard McClure,	4	6
John Mumma,	4	4
William McClure,	3	3
Jacob Miller,	3	3
Rev. Joseph Montgomery,	2	2
William McClanachan,	1	1
John Meadore,	2	1
John & James McKinney,	3	3
Robert McWirters,	1	....
Thomas McCarthur,	2	2
Andrew McClure,	2	2
Robert Neal,	4	3
Frances Nikkel,	3	3
Elias Nigley,	1	1
George Neveland,	3	3
John Noop,	8	6
Abraham Neideg,	5	5
David Patton,	3	2
Michael Pitner,	2	3
John Partimore,	2	2
Alexander Porter,	2	2
Stephen Poorman,	3	3
John Postlewalt,	1	2
Jacob Poorman,	2	1
Jacob Peck,	1	2
George Page,	3	3
Peter Pancake,	2	2
George Pile,	3	3
Hugh Robertson,	2	2
Paul Randolph,	1	1
James Rutherford,	2	2
George Renicor,	2	2
Jacob Roop, Sr.,	1	1
Widow Renick,	2	2
John Rutherford,	3	3
David Ritchey,	5	4
Jacob Roop, Jr.,	1	1
Michael Smith,	2	1
Jacob Strickler,	2	1
Henry Stoner,	6	4
John Steel,	3	3
William Swan,	1	1
Richard Swan,	4	3
Frederick Switzer,	2	3
George Soop,	2	1
Stophel Soop,	3	3
Jeremiah Sturgeon,	3	3
George Sheets,	2	....
Andrew & Charles Stewart,	4	4
Samuel Simpson, Sr.,	2	2

GRAIN AND FORAGE FOR THE ARMY—Continued.

	Bushels wheat.	Bushels forage.
Joseph Simpson,	2	2
William Smith,	3	3
Stophel Smith,	2	2
Andrew & Zacharia Stephens,	4	2
Hugh Stephens,	2	2
Jacob Smith,	2	1
Jacob Siders,	2	1
Michael Smith on Ecker's place,	1	....
Samuel Smith, Jr.,	2	....
Samuel Sherer,	2	2
Joseph Shaw,	4	4
Bernard Soop,	2	1
Elijah Stewart,	3	2
George Sheets,	3	2
Hugh Stewart,	4	5
Leonard Sheets,	2	2
John Shoemaker,	2	1
Peter Sherer,	2	2
Andrew Smith,	2	2
James & Mary Smith,	2	2
Samuel Simpson,	3	3
David Toot,	3	3
George Tivebach,	3	3
Christian Temy,	....	1
George Williams,	2	3
Hugh Wray,	1	1
John Wiggins,	3	3
Josiah White,	3	3
Leonard Wallier,	2	1
Thomas Wiley,	1	1
Joseph Wilson, Jr.,	2	2
Robert Whitehill,	3	3
Matthew Winogel,	2	2
James Wallace,	3	3
John Windurley,	2	2
Samuel Wiley,	1	2
John Wilson, Sr.,	4	4
John Wilson, Jr.,	2	2
John Wilson, Jr.,	2	1
Alexander Willson,	2	2
Joseph Wilson, Sr.,	1	2
Abner Wickersham,	4	4
Hugh White,	1	1
Widow Wiley,	1	1
Michael Woolf,	....	1
Moses Vance,	2	2
Conrad Yonce,	1	1
Middletown.		
Mark Sneider,	....	3
Christian King,	1	1

GRAIN AND FORAGE FOR THE ARMY—Continued.

	Bushels wheat.	Bushels forage.
Daniel Cann,	....	2
Peter Seister,	1	1
John Sneider,	1	1
George Simon,	....	2
Felty Welchor,	....	3
Abraham Tarr,	3	3
Henry Davies,	....	1
John Lenning,	1	1
Peter Eckerd,	....	1
John Miers,	3	2
Henry Shaffner,	....	1
Henry Harris,	....	2
Martin Hemberly,	....	2
Nicholas Cassel,	1	2
Philip Kraft,	1	1
George Frey,	5	5
Christian Spade,	1	....
Ludwick Hemberly,	....	2
Abraham Grose,	1	1
Daniel Hoofman,	....	2
Robert Kenedy,	1	1
Freemen.		
William Condon,	1	....
James Spence,	2	....
Anthony Witheral	1	....
John Miller,	1	....
John Cochran,	1	....
Henry Pitner,	1	....
John Darbey,	1	....
John Boy,	1	....
Thomas Trachan,	1	....
James Currey,	....	2
John Beard,	1	....
Barnard Fridley,	1	....
John Lachery,	1	....
Frederick Overlender,	1	....
William Whitnor,	1	....
John Miller, Stone Cutter,	1	....
Emanuel Bolinger,	1	....
Michael Gross,	1	....
Melchoir Miller,	1	....
Ludwick Dugan,	1	....
Henry Alleman,	3	....
John Page,	1	....
Philip Fisher,	1	....
Winagle, Saddler,	1	....
Robert Clark,	1	....
William Murray,	1	....
Jacob Sider,	1	....

GRAIN AND FORAGE FOR THE ARMY—Continued.

	Bushels wheat.	Bushels forage.
John Parks,	1	....
Thomas Murray,	1	....
John McNighton,	1	....
John Sherer,	1	....
John McCachan,	1	....
Andrew Berryhill,	1	....
Nicholas Nigh,	1	....
Middletown.		
Jacob Sneider,	....	2
Henry Miller,	1	....
Frederick Lebernich,	3	3
John Metsger,	2	....
John Beckestose,	2	1
John Hallabach,	....	1
John Defiance,	1	1
Michael Gross,	1	1
Conrad Wolfley,	3	3
William Walls,	1	....
Jacob King,	1	1
Thomas & William Crab,	2	3
Alexander Jamison,	....	1
Philip Strahey,	1	1
Chris. Shirtz,	1	2
Adam Mingo,	1	....
George Grose,	2	2
Patrick Ross,	....	1
Samuel Park,	1	....
Thomas Winthrop,	1	1
David McClure,	1	....
Daniel Dough,	3	3
Thomas & Henry Moore,	3	3
Peter Miller,	....	2
Adam Miller,	....	2
George Amon,	1	....
David Atlee,	1	....
Philip Pattemore,	1	....
Chris. Heppich,	1	1
Paul Hemberley,	....	1
Christopher Sebach,	1	....
Henry Myer,	1	....
Samuel Strahey,	1	....
Philip Atlee,	1	....
Frederick Hubley,	2	1

(c.) Henry Walter 6th Class of my Company belongs to the Eight Class. Henry Lutz of the 6th Class Likewise belongs to Eight Class.

Peter Ulrich of the Seventh Class belongs to the Eight Class.

Jacob Zinn of the 7th Class is the my Company fifer.

I do hereby Certifye that the above is a Just and true State of my Company.

Wittness my hand.

NICHOLUS LUTZ, Capt.

(c.) This is to Certify that Michael Hoak Sarved his towr of Duty at Lancaster in the Seventh Class.

SAM'L DAVIS, Capt.

Lightning Source UK Ltd.
Milton Keynes UK
UKHW050025081218
333419UK00006BA/76/P